The Early Quakers
and the 'Kingdom of God'

Peace, Testimony and Revolution

Gerard Guiton

Inner Light Books
San Francisco, California

The Early Quakers
and the 'Kingdom of God'

Peace, Testimony and Revolution

© 2012 Gerard Guiton
All Rights Reserved

Except for brief quotations, no part of this publication may be reproduced, stored in a retrieval system, or transmitted, in any form or by any means, electronic, mechanical, photocopy, recorded, or otherwise, without prior written permission.

Published by Inner Light Books,
San Francisco, California
www.innerlightbooks.com
editor@innerlightbooks.com

Library of Congress Control Number: 2011943258

ISBN 978-0-9834980-2-5, (hardcover)
ISBN 978-0-9834980-3-2, (paperback)
ISBN 978-0-9834980-4-9, (e-book)

The images on the cover are from the covers of the pamphlets:

A Declaration From the Harmles & Innocent People of God, Called Quakers, Against All Plotters, and Fighters in the World.
by George Fox, Richard Hubberthorne et al, dated (21/11th Mo., 1660 = 21st January, 1661)

A Declaration and an Information From us the People of God Called Quakers, to the present Governors, the King and Both Houses of Parliament, and all whom it may Concern.
by Margaret Fell et al, dated (5/4th Mo., 1660 = 5th June, 1660)

A Declaration From the People called Quakers, To the Present Distracted Nation of England.
by Edward Burrough et al, dated (20/10th Mo., 1659 = 20th December, 1659)

Courtesy of the Friends Historical Library of Swarthmore College.

Contents

		Page
	Abbreviations	viii
	Chronology of Events, 1599-1663 (Gregorian calendar)	x
	OVERVIEW: Seeking a Common Language	1

PART ONE: **The Puritans' Kingdom**

1	*Chariots & Horsemen of Israel*: The Kingdom of the Puritans	31
2	*Ruins, Miseries and Calamities*: A Divided Church	61
3	*War the Sickness of a Kingdom is*: The Good Old Cause and Military Britain	95

PART TWO: **The Quakers' Kingdom and Testimony**

4	*Pure Love to the Soul*: Early Quaker Language	111
5	*Since the Days of the Apostles*: The Kingdom of the Quakers	129
6	*Now Religion in itself is this*: The Bible, Three Declarations and the Lamb's War	181
7	*Open Shop for Soul-poisons*: Reaction to the Quakers' Kingdom	203
8	*Of the Nature of Christ Jesus*: Christology, Unity and Silence	226
9	*Demonstration of the Spirit*: Early Quaker Testimony	256
10	*Walk in the Narrow Way*: Witness and Prophecy	290
11	*Because of your much Earth*: Equity, Truth and Justice	306
12	*Dwell in that which Leads into Peace*: The Sword and Quaker 'Violence'	334
13	*Arise, Shine for Light is come:* Testimony, Pentecost and the Kingdom	369

	EPILOGUE: *Finding the Common Language*: Kingdom and Testimony and its Universality	391
	Glossary and Appendices	411
	Bibliography	459
	Index	494

Preface

The Early Quakers and the 'Kingdom of God' is born of my previous book, *The Growth and Development of Quaker Testimony* (2005). Its focus is the central feature of early Quaker faith and practice, the 'Kingdom of God'. Often called the 'Covenant of Peace' by leading early Friends, the Kingdom implied a mutual and loving rather than a purely contractual relationship.

Given the Kingdom's prominence *in practically every Quaker tract* published between 1652 (the year of the movement's first acknowledged written work) and 1663, the period I cover, I was astonished to find during the course of my research that the early Friends' understanding of the Kingdom had been largely neglected by Quaker scholars. This was particularly puzzling because nearly 90 percent of their works in the above period frequently and determinedly referred to the Kingdom and the plentiful alternative expressions they ascribed to it. Clearly, without Jesus' concept of the Kingdom—it was *the* focus of *his* life's work—a Quaker movement would not have arisen.

A principal aim of the book, therefore, is to examine the early Quaker emphasis of living in the Kingdom and its implications for us today. With this in mind, I first place the Friends in their ecclesio-political, social and military contexts, and then help to describe their understanding of the Kingdom and how, in their efforts to enact it, Quaker Testimony was born. I say 'help' because the book allows the Quakers to speak for themselves. In outlining the way in which Kingdom and Testimony characterised their 1650s experience, I emphasise the need to see *this* experience as *the* Friends' peace testimony rather than the famous Fox-Hubberthorne declaration presented to Charles II in 1661.

My investigation into the early Quakers' Kingdom faith and practice also emphasises the multi-generational nature of the Covenant of Peace and its capacity in any age to engender love, compassion, peace, justice, and, consequently, unity and wholeness (i.e. 'salvation') in God. Additionally, I describe how the Kingdom/Covenant underpins the cherished Testimonies of today's Religious Society of Friends and indeed any endeavour, Quaker or otherwise, in furthering God's justice for all humanity and our planet home.

For several reasons today 'Kingdom of God' carries negative connotations; some of the more significant are detailed in my Overview. Despite this, and remembering that a number of well-known theologians such as Elizabeth Schüssler Fiorenza employ the term, I use 'Kingdom' for four reasons while interchanging it periodically with 'Presence of Love',

'Rule of Love', 'Covenant of Love' or with George Fox's terms, 'Covenant of Peace' and 'Ocean of Light and Love'. My four reasons are:

1. Its early Quaker use helps us understand how they used the term and in what contexts.
2. It contains all the historical resonances and works theologically in all contexts.
3. It is recognised by many even if they object to it.
4. Its many alternatives (see pp.194-5) do not theologically fit all contexts. For example, while 'Peaceable Kingdom' is a useful expression, emphasising peace and modifying the modern impact of 'Kingdom', it, too, is theologically incomplete.

Jesus spoke of the Kingdom to mean the Kingdom or Rule *of Love*. He created a sharp distinction between it and the earthly, transient kingdoms of his day; the Roman Empire, too, was known as a 'kingdom'. He was saying how much better life would be for all people if God were 'king', that is, if they were to live in an intimate relationship with the God who loves and cares for us unconditionally. With this in mind I sometimes substitute 'king' with 'love' or 'over all', another well-used Fox expression.

The book's footnotes are intended mainly for those wishing to conduct further scholarship. Unless otherwise stated I refer to the Nickalls' edition of Fox's *Journal* (1986) and to the King James Bible (1611), the version most used by seventeenth century Quakers. I also capitalise the Quakers' 'New Israel' (i.e. the Kingdom, the New Covenant, the Covenant of Peace etc) to distinguish it from the Puritans' 'new Israel'.

I take special delight in thanking the following who read versions or sections of the manuscript and volunteered valuable insights—Ray Brindle, Derek Guiton, Douglas Gwyn, Bruce Henry, Sheila Keane, John McMahon, John Punshon, Arthur O. Roberts, Janet Scott and Ruth Watson. As ever, I wish to thank Bill and Donna Jaggs for their support in ways too numerous to mention, and to Barbara Mays who proofread the text. Francis Guiton and Miriam Hamel-Green assisted in the acquisition of source materials. The Cadbury Committee of Pendle Hill Quaker Study Centre in Philadelphia graciously awarded me the Henry J. Cadbury Scholarship for 2004-5. Many of the fruits of that research year have found their way into the following pages, particularly those concerned with sixteenth and seventeenth-century English Roman Catholicism. Charles Martin and Inner Light Books kindly offered sound advice. As no manuscript is perfect, any errors are mine alone.

My lasting gratitude as ever goes to my son and daughter, Joseph and Verity. I hope this work will be as meaningful to their own and subsequent generations as I trust it will be to mine. It is to them and to my partner, Anne Price, I dedicate this book.

Gerard Guiton
Alstonville (NSW)
Australia, 2012

Abbreviations

AOTW	*Apocalypse of the Word* (D. Gwyn, 1984)
Bds.	Broadside
BQ	*The Beginnings of Quakerism* (W. Braithwaite, 1955)
Cambridge	*The Journal of George Fox* (ed. N. Penney, 1911), 2 vols.
Clarendon	*State Papers Collected by Edward, Earl of Clarendon . . . 1621* (E. Hyde, 1786)
Collection	*A Collection of Many Select and Christian Epistles . . . George Fox* (1698)
DCFB	*A Descriptive Catalogue of Friends' Books* (J. Smith, 1867), 2 vols.
Doctrinals	*Gospel-Truth Demonstrated in a Collection of Doctrinal Books* (G. Fox, 1706}
ECCO	*Eighteenth Century Collection Online* (see Bibliography)
ECMC	*Eighteenth Century Microfilm Collection* (see Bibliography)
EEBO	*Early English Book Online* (see Bibliography and *Wing*)
EHR	*The English Historical Review*
Ellwood	*A Journal or Historical Account . . . George Fox* (1694)
Ep.; Eps.	Epistle; Epistles
EQL	*Early Quaker Letters from the Swarthmore MSS. To 1660* (G. Nuttall, 1952)
EQW	*Early Quaker Writings 1650-1700* (eds. H. Barbour and A. Roberts [1973] 2004)
FF	*First Among Friends* (H. L. Ingle, 1995)
Fell	Reference to Margaret Fell only
FFQ	*The Faith of the First Quakers* (R. Moore, 1994)
GADOT	*The Growth and Development of Quaker Testimony* (G. Guiton, 2005)
HJ	*The Cambridge Historical Journal*
J.	*Journal of. . .*
JBS	*Journal of British Studies*
Journal	*Journal of George Fox* (ed. J. Nickalls [1952] 1986}
KMOLW	*Knowing the Mystery of Life Within* (eds. R. M. Keiser and R. Moore, 2005)
LOGF	*No More But My Love: Letters of George Fox, Quaker* (ed. C. Sharman, 1980)
LRSF	Library, Religious Society of Friends (Friends House, Euston Rd., London)
MOP	*Ministrations of Peace* (G. Guiton, 1999)

Abbreviations

PP	*Past and Present*
QER	*The Quakers and the English Revolution* (B. Reay, 1985)
QFP	*Quaker Faith and Practice* (Britain Yearly Meeting, 1995)
QRT	*Quaker Religious Thought*
rev. art:	review article
RSF	Religious Society of Friends (Quakers)
Second	*The Second Period of Quakerism* (W. Braithwaite [1921] 1961)
STC	Short Title Catalogue
Sufferings	*A Collection of the Sufferings of the ... Quakers* (ed. J. Besse, 1753), 2 vols.
*SW/*ii/**123**	e.g. *Swarthmore MSS.*, vol. ii, letter 123
Thurloe	*A Collection of the State Papers of John Thurloe, Esq.* (ed. T. Birch, 1742), 7 vols.
TLITC	*The Light in their Consciences* (R. Moore, 2000)
TWTUD	*The World Turned Upside Down* (C. Hill, 1975)
Wing	*Short Title Catalogue of Books Printed in England, Scotland, Ireland, Wales, and British America, 1641-1700* (D. Wing. NY: Columbia Uni. Press, 1972-94), 3 vols.
WMC	*Wing Microfilm Collection* (see Bibliography and *EEBO*)

Chronology, 1599-1663 (Gregorian Calendar)

The (old style) Julian calendar began in March; the Quakers ordered the months by number (e.g. 1ˢᵗ Mo. = March).

1599
Birth of Oliver Cromwell
1600
Birth of Charles Stuart
1603
Accession of James 1 (VI of Scotland) on the death of Elizabeth 1
Plague kills 22 percent of London's population
1604
Death of John Whitgift, Archbishop of Canterbury
Richard Bancroft consecrated as Archbishop
1605
Gunpowder Plot
1607
Midlands rising against enclosures
First permanent British colony at Jamestown, Virginia
1610
Death of Richard Bancroft, Archbishop of Canterbury
1611
George Abbot appointed Archbishop of Canterbury
Publication of the King James Bible
1612
The heir to the throne, the future Henry IX, dies
1616
George Villiers made Viscount and master of the royal horse
1617
Villiers created Earl of Buckingham
1618
Sir Francis Bacon created Lord Chancellor
James VI/1's *Declaration of Sports* published

Beginning of the Thirty Years' War
1619
Synod of Dort (Dordrecht in Holland)
1620
Puritan Separatists (the 'Pilgrims') set sail in the *Mayflower* for North America
1621
William Laud consecrated Bishop of St. David's
1623
Prince Charles and Buckingham journey to Madrid to negotiate ill-fated Spanish match
1624
Birth of George Fox in Fenny Drayton (Leic.)
War with Spain
Commons' complaint against Bishop Richard Montagu's *A New Gag*
1625
Accession of Charles Stuart on the death of James VI/I
Charles marries (Catholic) Henrietta-Maria of France
Publication of R. Montagu's *Appello Caesarium*. Montagu attacked for Arminian views
Montagu created a royal chaplain
Feoffees of Impropriators established to buy impropriated tithes and use them to employ Puritan lecturers
1626
Buckingham upholds anti-Calvinists
William Laud nominated as Bishop of Bath and Wells
Charles orders collection of forced loans (for war with Spain)
York House talks on Arminianism fail
1627

x

Chronology, 1599-1663 (Gregorian Calendar)

Charles declares war on France
Buckingham repulsed off La Rochelle
1628
Petition of Right condemns forced loans: first concessions by monarchy to parliamentary claims
William Laud appointed Bishop of London
R. Montagu consecrated Bishop of Chichester
Buckingham assassinated at Portsmouth
1629
Dissolution of Charles's third parliament; personal government from April
End of war with France
Food riots in W. and E. Anglia—continue till 1631
Bad harvest
1630
Birth of future Charles II
End of war with Spain
Bad harvest
1631
Soaring food prices and food riots
1632
New colony founded in Maryland by Lord Baltimore
1633
Laud abolishes Feoffees of Impropriations because of their Puritan sympathies
Death of George Abbot, Archbishop of Canterbury
William Laud consecrated Archbishop of Canterbury
Charles and Laud visit Scotland
Birth of future James II
Charles re-issues 1618 Book of Sports
1634
Gregorio Panzani admitted to Court as first papal agent since 1558
Ship money levied on coastal towns and counties (extended 1635-39)
1635
Judges declare ship money illegal

1636
George Con replaces Gregorio Panzani at Court as papal agent
1637-40
Introduction of new Scottish Prayer Book (1637) produces Edinburgh riots
Petitioning movement in Scotland against Prayer Book
Trials of Puritans Prynne, Burton, Bastwick and Lilburne for their anti-Laud stance
Ship Money case: trial of John Hampden
Breakdown of Charles's government of Scotland and two attempts to impose his will by force
1638
Trial of 'Freeborn' John Lilburne for circulating Puritan literature
Scottish (Presbyterian) National Assembly draws up National Covenant abolishing Prayer Book
Charles withdraws Scottish Prayer Book
Scottish National Assembly abolishes episcopacy (which provokes war with Charles)
1639
Charles assembles army for Scottish campaign
First Anglo-Scottish Bishop's War ends with Treaty of Berwick
Growing resistance to ship money
1640
Short Parliament meets
Second Bishop's War. Scottish rout English at Newburn and control NE England; war ends with Treaty of Ripon
Long Parliament assembles; attacks on ship money judges and monopolists
'Root and Branch' Petition to abolish episcopacy
Laud impeached
1641
Seizure of power by parliament

Acts against dissolution without consent, against unparliamentary taxation, abolition of Star Chamber and High Commission
Imprisonment of Laud
Control of armed forces; first army plot
Charles reaches settlement with Scots who withdraw from England
Rebellion in Ireland; second army plot
Commons drafts (and publishes!) the Grand Remonstrance listing all faults of Charles's ministers
Charles rejects Grand Remonstrance
Ship money abolished.
Reprint of Foxe's *Book of Martyrs*: influential on George Fox

1642
Charles attempts arrest of five MPs. Cromwell advocates committee 'to put the kingdom in a posture of defence'
Bishops excluded from House of Lords
Skirmish at Manchester (July) between royalists and parliamentarian sympathisers
First civil war of the three kingdoms: Charles raises the standard at Nottingham (August)
Battle (indecisive) of Edgehill (Warwickshire); Charles advances on London

1643
Prince Rupert takes Bristol
Parliament accepts Scottish Solemn League and Covenant
Fox begins his spiritual search. First battle of Newbury
Death of John Pym, Speaker
Westminster Assembly begins

1644
Scottish army crosses into England
Battle of Marston Moor near York
Second (indecisive) battle of Newbury

1645
Execution of Archbishop Laud
Formation of New Model Army
Battles of Naseby and Langport effectively destroy Charles' armies
Parliament takes Bristol and West Country

1646
Abolition of feudal tenures
Charles shelters at Southall (Notts.) with Scots who hand him to Parliament
Oxford and Wallingford Castle surrender to Parliament: end of first civil war
Long Parliament abolishes episcopacy; sale of Bishops' lands approved
Book of Common Prayer dispensed with
Presbyterian Church established

1647
Westminster Confession (Humble Advises of the Assembly of Divines) accepted
Fox's spiritual experience of the indwelling Light, his unmediated revelation of God
Charles seized and taken to army HQ at Newmarket
Army intervenes directly in politics, occupies London
General Council of Army set up (June)
Charles imprisoned at Hampton Court
October: army debates at St. Mary's church at Putney; Levellers' 'Agreement of the People' offered as draft constitution
General Council of Army suppressed (Nov.)
Charles escapes and signs agreement with Scots
Fox at Dukinfield near Manchester

1648
Second civil war of the three kingdoms to bring 'that man of blood' to account
Scots enter England on side of Charles
Battle of Preston (Cromwell defeats Scots and ends second civil war)
Provincial uprisings suppressed

Chronology, 1599-1663 (Gregorian Calendar)

September: Levellers present Parliament with 40,000-signature petition

Army re-enters London: Col. Pride's Purge of the Commons

1649

Rump orders trial and execution of Charles

Rump abolishes House of Lords: England proclaimed a commonwealth

Charles II proclaimed king of Great Britain at Edinburgh

First Digger community at St. George's Hill est. and forcibly removed (Aug.)

Start of sale of crown, dean and chapter and cavaliers' lands (to 1651)

Army suppresses Levellers at Burford (Oxon.): 3 leaders shot

Massacre by Cromwell at Drogheda (Ireland)

Massacre by Cromwell (inc. 300 women) at Wexford (Ireland)

Those in official positions required to take Engagement Oath to demonstrate allegiance to the government

Westminster Assembly ends

1650

Sale of crown, dean and chapter and cavaliers' lands (1649-51)

Blasphemy Act: Suppression of the Ranters and Diggers

Charles II established in Scotland as king

Battle of Dunbar (Scots defeated) after which James Nayler leaves army

Compulsory attendance at parish church abolished by Toleration Act

Fox arrested at Derby

Engagement Oath extended to all men over 18 years

1651-3

Military occupation of the North

1651

Fox refuses army commission at Derby and sent to prison

Battle of Worcester; Charles II defeated and escapes to France

Fox at Lichfield

Rump declares Scotland incorporated into Commonwealth with England

1652

First Anglo-Dutch war

Publication 'first' Quaker tract from York Castle (gaol) by Thomas Aldam *et al*

Fox's vision on Pendle Hill (Lancs.) of a 'great people to be gathered'

Fox at Firbank Fell and meets Fell family at Ulverston (present-day Cumbria)

Richard Farnworth declares Lamb's War: 'We have pitched our tents . . . it is begun'

Fox before the quarter sessions at Lancaster

1653

January: James Nayler and Francis Howgill before Justice Pearson at Appleby

Cromwell expels Rump of the Long Parliament

Barebone's (or Nominated) Parliament

Instrument of Government (army-drafted Constitutional document)

Cromwell declared Lord Protector

Formal union of England and Scotland

Fox publishes *To All that would Know the Way to the Kingdom*

1653-5

Quakers descend on the South of England from the North

1654

Peace with Dutch

Fox and Aldam sign assurance of Quaker nonviolence against 'any man'

First Protectorate Parliament

Union of England and Scotland

1655

Cromwell dissolves first Protectorate Parliament

The Early Quakers and the 'Kingdom of God'

General Meeting of Friends at Swannington (Leic.)
War with Spain: Admiral Blake sweeps the Mediterranean: Jamaica (1655) and Dunkirk (1658) annexed
Fifth Monarchist rebellion
Penruddock's (royalist) rebellion crushed
Men Friends in London set up fortnightly Business Meetings
Henry Cromwell, Major-General of the army in Ireland
Rule of the Major-Generals
1656
Second Protectorate Parliament
Second chamber established
Nayler and others ride into Bristol — national scandal ensues
Nayler trial at Westminster: he is tortured and imprisoned
Quaker General Meeting at Balby (nr. Doncaster, Yorks.)
First Quaker missionaries land in American colonies
1657
Anglo-French treaty to attack Spanish Netherlands
Instrument of Government replaced by parliamentary paper Constitution, the Humble Petition and Advice
Offer of crown to Cromwell
Cromwell refuses crown and nominates his own House of Lords
Cromwell installed as Lord Protector
Fox sets up Quarterly Meetings
1658
Cromwell dissolves Second Protectorate Parliament
Battle of the Dunes: Anglo-French forces defeat Spaniards and English Royalists; acquisition of Dunkirk
Death of Cromwell from malaria; Richard Cromwell declared Protector
Quaker 'General Yearly Meeting' in Beckerings Park (Beds.)
1659
Third Protectorate Parliament
Military coup
Forced resignation of Richard Cromwell; Rump restored
Fox retreats into the Curtis' home at Reading (Berks.)
August: Booth's rebellion (Presbyterian-Royalist) defeated
Nayler released by Rump
Army expels Rump; General Monck demands its return
Committee of Safety with Sir Henry Vane Jr. established
Fox leaves Reading and tours 20 southern counties (between October, 1659 and December 1660)
The Quaker Pentecost-Paracletal 'moment' begins (to *c*.Jan. 1661)
Monck marches south
Committee of Safety disperses and three regiments reinstate Rump
Edward Burrough *et al* publish *A Declaration from the People of God called Quakers*
1660
General Monck enters London in February after marching from Scotland
Charles II's Declaration of Breda
Long Parliament dissolved. Convention Parliament elected
House of Lords restored
Monarchy restored
Quaker General Yearly Meeting at Skipton (Yorks.)
End of war with Spain
Margaret Fell presents *A Declaration and Information* to Charles II
September: death of Nayler
1661
Venner (Fifth Monarchist) rebellion defeated
Fox, Hubberthorne *et al* send *A Declaration from the Harmless People* to Charles II (Jan. 1661)
1663
Kaber Rigg (or Northern) Plot discovered and put down

The eternal Word, which was in the beginning before all languages were, breaks in pieces all languages and . . . brings all into one language, for that which keeps in many languages keeps in confusion.

- James Nayler, 1653 -

The clouds of the night fly, for the Kingdom of God is revealing which . . . consists in righteousness and in peace and joy . . . And this is the salutation of Life in the Love that is endless.

- Dorothy White, 1660, 1661 –

And our Holy City, the New Jerusalem, is coming down from Heaven and her Light will shine through the whole earth, even as a jasper stone clear as crystal, which brings freedom and liberty and perfect redemption to her whole Seed.

- Margaret Fell, 1666 -

To revive the visible ways of primitive Quakerism would be impossible and inappropriate. But to revive that which was at the heart of the original awakening and the original witness is to meet a need as old as humanity, yet still fresh, essential and new.

- Howard Brinton, 1953 -

Overview: Seeking a Common Language

The Quakers of the seventeenth century claimed to have made a powerful rediscovery, a pearl 'hid in the field' where it had 'layen under the earth'. The field was 'the world' and it was found in people's hearts. There they had to dig deep to find the pearl. And once it was found they had to 'sell all to purchase and redeem the field.'[1] The pearl was nothing less than Jesus' central and 'pure' 'doctrine', the Kingdom of God, which the Church had neglected for 1,600 years 'since the apostles' days'.[2]

Their figurative use of Matthew 13 came with an assurance that the Kingdom was both within and among all people. It stood not in mere words, the 'letter', but in the 'power of God'.[3] Their confidence in God, in the

---

[1] George Fox (1624-91), *The Pearl Found in England* (hereafter *Pearl*. 1658), Sig. A2. This important work outlines 1650s Quaker theology. For 'pearl' see Mt. 13: 45-46.

[2] Their accusation against the Church is found in *Pearl*, p. 1 but see also 4: 'the pearl is within you'; *A Reply to the Pretended Vindication* (1658), 18; *An Answer to the Papists ... Lately Out of Holland* (1658), *passim* but see esp. p. 1; *The Lambs Officer is Gone Forth* (1659), 4, 8, 12, 14, 16 and also *Journal*, 109 (for Fox on Firbank Fell.), 196, 294, 418-19. Early Quaker references to the Church's apostasy were common; see, for instance, Edward Burrough (1632?-63), 'To the Reader' (1658) in Fox, *The Great Mystery* (1659), unnumbered p.7. See also Viviano, *The Kingdom of God in History*, 61.

For 'pearl' see *Pearl, ibid.* and Dorothy White (*c*.1630-*c*.85), *A Trumpet of the Lord* (1662), 4.

The term 'Christ's doctrine' was used frequently by the Friends to mean the whole of Jesus' teaching and witness as encapsulated in the Kingdom; see James Nayler (1618?-60), *A Public Discovery of the Open Blindness* (1656), 11-12; Richard Hubberthorne (1628-62), *A True Separation* (1654), 3; Gervase Benson (d. 1679), *The True Trial of Ministers* (1655), 5.

[3] For the 'letter' see *Pearl*, 18-19 and Fox's *To All that would Know the Way to the Kingdom* (1653), 4. For 'Power [= Wisdom, Kingdom] of God' see, for instance, Fox, Ep. 131 (1656) in *Works*, 7: 126-7 and also Eps. 104 (1655), 130 (1656), 169 (1658), 189 (1659), 216 (1662) in *ibid.*, pp. 105-7, 122-6, 157-8, 178-9, 216-19 respectively. This is essentially Pauline theology; see 1 Cor. 1:24 but also Jm. 3:17.

Either 'within you' or 'among you' continues to be a source of controversy among theologians, something inherited from their late 19th and 20th century counterparts; see Lk. 17:21 (*cf*. Zeph. 3:15 and Gospel of Thomas, logions 2-3 at: <http://users.misericordia.edu//davies/thomas/Trans.htm.>). The controversy also raged in the seventeenth century. The Quakers, as indeed the later Richard Baxter, well-known Presbyterian divine and minister at Kidderminster (Warwickshire), were clear that Lk. 17:21 meant both but preferred 'within' (as the pearl was 'within'). See also Baxter, *The Glorious Kingdom of Christ* (1691), 14. In *Rusticus ad Academicos* (1660), the early Quaker Samuel Fisher (1605-65), a Greek scholar, entered this debate with John Owen, Vice-Chancellor of Oxford University, and Thomas Danson, minister at Sandwich (Kent) and former Fellow of Magdalen College (Oxford); see 'The First Apologetical', chp. 4, 140-1. Fisher would have known the extended meanings of the preposition ἐν ('en' = in) to include 'within', 'among', 'by means of' and 'with'. Fox in *The Great Mystery*, 373 highlights 14 times the ambiguities involved in the use of ἐν or its possible misuse. For the Kingdom of God as 'among' see also

majesty of divine Love, also allowed them to accept Matthew 5-7 completely and without deviation. Thus they adopted the Sermon on the Mount—which mentions the Kingdom of God nine times—as the absolute rule for their internal and external conduct.[4]

Knowing the Kingdom passionately 'in their bowels'[5], the first Friends saw themselves as heralds of a spiritual revolution, a 'revolution' typical in its seventeenth century meaning of rediscovering and restoring an old order. In their case it meant restoring the Way, the Kingdom path taken by Jesus of Nazareth and his followers in the years before the Roman destruction of the Jerusalem temple in 70 CE. Just as Jesus' revolution sought spiritual renewal for Judaism, the Friends pursued a similar path in respect to the British nations and, internationally, 'all people'.[6]

George Bishop (d. 1668), *Jesus Christ, the Same Today* (1655), 21. In this respect, Fisher, Fox, Bishop and other Quakers anticipated modern mainstream biblical exegesis by nearly 250 years. They also understood what later evidence from papyri and elsewhere confirmed, i.e. 'within you' (ἐντός ὑμῶν) also meant 'in your hands' and 'within your power/control', emphasising personal responsibility for one's spiritual welfare but also the 'now' factor of the Kingdom of God by its unveiling within. See also C. Roberts, 'The Kingdom of Heaven', 5-7; Dodd, *The Parables of the Kingdom*, *passim* but esp. 63; Ladd, *A Theology of the New Testament*, 61-5.

[4] See Matthew 5-7 for the full Sermon. The Friends clearly noticed how the Sermon constituted the biggest section in the Christian Testament and how it was placed at the beginning of Matthew, receiving more space in that Gospel than any other discourse. Other chapters in Matthew, and still others in Luke, contain various statements of its teachings and extend them. See also Nesti, 'Early Quaker Ecclesiology', 22. For 'not in word but in power' see Richard Farnworth (d. 1666), *A Voice of the First Trumpet* (1653), 15 and also 1 Cor. 4: 19-20.

My use of 'Sermon in the Mount' is both (i) *specific* (i.e. direct reference to Mt. 5-7 and the Beatitudes) including its influence upon the Epistle of James which was also vital to the early Quakers, and (ii) *generic* as it appears to represent the whole of Jesus' teaching or 'Doctrine' to use an early Quaker reference. Evidence for the latter rests on Luke 6: 17-49 in which the Sermon in the Plain reflects similar themes, but also when the following are compared: Mt. 5:13 and Mk. 9:50; Mt. 6: 9-13 and Lk. 11:2-4; Mt. 5:31-32 and Mt. 19:3-9; Mt. 6:13 and Jn. 17:15. For the relationship of the Sermon to James' Epistle see V. Porter, *The Use of the Sermon ... in ... James*, 1-2 and Shepherd, 'The Epistle of James', *passim*. And for Quaker references to the Beatitudes see, for instance, Fox's Eps. 133 (1656) and 158 (1658) in *Collection*, 106, 122.

[5] 'Bowels' as meaning 'the most feeling compassions of the heart' &c. was in common use during the seventeenth century. They were the seat of love, mercy and pity (see Mt. 9:36, 14:14, 15:32; Mk. 9:22; Lk. 1:78, 7:18; Col. 3:12). The first Friends use of 'bowels' was often strongly emotional and corresponded, whether knowingly or not, to the Greek *splagchnizomai* ('splonk-needs-oh-my'). See, for example, Isaac Penington (1616-79), *The Consideration of a Position* (1660), title pg. and *passim*; also *Letters of Isaac Penington* (1859), 7-8 of the Preface and Letters 19 and 29. For a seventeenth century definition of 'bowels' see Thomas Wilson, *A Complete Christian Dictionary* (1655), 273.

[6] Fox, *An Epistle to all People on the Earth* (1657), *passim*. For 'the Way' see Fox, Ep. 220 (1662) in *Collection*, 182; 'Christ's Way, Judas' Way' (1657) in *Doctrinals*, 123-5; *Some Principles of the Elect People of God* (1661), 14; *Christ's Light the only Antidote* (1662), 4

Their rediscovery was so urgent that it propelled George Fox, the movement's principal founder, to entreat the 'scattered ones over the world' to gather with haste into the peace, justice and compassion of the Way. They would do so for their own salvation, that is to say, their wholeness and unity in God. Only then could they 'continue' afresh in a true covenant (i.e. mutual relationship) with God but outside an apostate Church 'built by the will of men':

> Come all you wearied souls [Fox assured, echoing Mt. 11:28] who have been long travelling these many years since the days of apostasy from the true apostles and disciples, where darkness and mists have gone over the earth and blinded and darkened the minds and eyes of the people. The true ministry being lost since the days of the apostasy [means] people have run into heads and parties and sects, and truth among them held in unrighteousness, the sin and the enmity in everyone's mind, men slaying one another about religion and for religion, and about worship which was not the work of the true Christians, true ministers and true apostles [who] brought people into unity and wrestled against principalities and powers.[7]

Living the Kingdom, the Presence

By their example, the Friends would witness to the unity demanded of them as a loving, prophetic and covenanting people. They were to be a community of reconciliation and healing, a *Kingdom* community striving for justice and mercy for all, including enemies but also for the materially poor, the powerless ones. Like Jesus, the Friends were prepared to suffer and die for that ineffable Love they believed was manifest in their individual and collective 'flesh and bone'. Only *this* Love and its liberating Kingdom—what may also be called the Rule, Covenant or Presence of

---

(rpt. of *The Ground of Desperation*, 1655?); Nayler, *How Sin is Strengthened* (1657), 4 and *Milk for the Babes* (1661 and written in prison between 1656-9), 10; William Bayly (d. 1675), *A Short Discovery of the State of Man* (1659), 4-5.

[7] *Pearl*, 1, 3-6, 9-10; *An Epistle to all People on the Earth, passim*. For churches or temples built by 'the will of men' see *Pearl*, 8-10, and also *Journal*, 8, 40, 76 for 'built by hands' (a reference to Ac. 17:24). For references to 'principalities and powers' see Fox, Ep. 73 (1654) in *Collection*, 66 and John Crook (1617?-99), 'Truth's Principles' in Burrough *et al*, *The Principles of Truth* (1660), 11.

For the importance of mercy to the Friends see esp. Chp. 8 and Fox, *Justice and Judgment is to Rule* (1656), 7; Francis Howgill (1618-68/69), *An Epistle to the Friends in London* (1658) in *Works*, 141.

Love, or Fox's term, the 'Covenant of Peace'—could heal the deep wounds of the single heart and that of the world.[8]

Through their letters and epistles we can glimpse a little of what it was like to have lived the Kingdom in each moment at the most intense level of spiritual awareness, to have had the 'forces of their souls' gathered into the unity of the Spirit which the Kingdom represented, and to have rejoiced when they found each other 'as in [its] net'. In doing so, the Friends believed they were witnessing to resurrection and hope for all humanity.[9] Leading Quaker Francis Howgill, who, along with a number of Friends, went to some length to explain the Kingdom, experienced it initially as returning 'home to within', to what fellow Friend Humphrey Smith called 'the stillness of God's life and peace'. Another Friend, John Perrot, expressed a strong sense of continual blessing in knowing the Kingdom/Rule of Love had 'come down' and 'was coming down upon' him. From these and other Quaker writings it is clear that their every sinew, as with the Hebrew prophets, went into declaring and demonstrating to the world the wonder of this divine Love, its sanctuary but also its demands and challenges.[10]

Like many of their contemporaries, the early Friends had a comprehensive and penetrating knowledge of the Bible through which they forged an intimate relationship with the Hebrew prophets, with Jesus and the apostles—messengers all of the Light's (God's) sovereignty, the Light being their final authority.[11] At times the relationship was *so* intimate it was as if *they* were the prophets, *they* were Jesus and the apostles.[12] As such, the Quakers saw themselves as living the Kingdom experience of the primitive Jesus Way and at a portentous moment in history when the 'Day of the Lord'—that moment of conviction, the Kingdom of God itself—was ushering in the End-time.[13]

---

[8] 'Covenant of Peace' is found in Ezk. 34:25: 'And I will make with them a covenant of peace, and will cause the evil beasts to cease out of the land: and they shall dwell safely in the wilderness, and sleep in the woods. For 'Covenant of Peace' in Fox see his Eps. 63 (1654), 67 (1654), 106 (1655), 115 (1656) and 145 (1657), *Works*, 7: 60, 62, 86, 92 and 112 respectively.
[9] For 'forces of their souls' see medieval mystic Jan van Ruusbroec (1293-1381) in Underhill, *Practical Mysticism*, 72. See also Howgill, *A Testimony Concerning . . . Edward Burroughs* (1662: actually Feb. 1663), 5-6.
[10] Howgill, *Some of the Mysteries of God's Kingdom* (1658 [completed June, 1657]), 38-43; *A Lamentation for the Scattered Tribes* (1656), 6; Humphrey Smith (c. 1624-63), *A Sad and Mournful Lamentation* (1660), 2; John Perrot (d. 1671?), *To the Prince of Venice* (1661), 17.
[11] *Pearl*, 4, 12 and see R. Jones, *Spiritual Reformers*, 345.
[12] See Nayler, *Milk for the Babes*, 16.
[13] *Pearl*, Sig. A2. See also Janet Scott, 'The Meaning of Hope', 356.

End-time and Regeneration

But *how* had the Kingdom 'come down'? And what was their understanding of the End-time? We are told that if people chose the Light of the Jesus Way, then the End had come for the Beast within.[14] In other words, the time had arrived in which sin, 'death's kingdom' or separation from Love in the form of disobedience, deceit, violence, exploitation and ignorance, was convicted and eradicated.[15] The result, initially on the inner level, was the restoration of the peace and purity of Eden, indeed a Christic purity and thus God's reign. Such separation from God—not an irrevocable break since God always sought a healing unity with everybody—led to inner and outer violence.[16] This cleansing process was given the generic term 'convincement'. It was the first stage of a transformative and perfecting conversion (*metanoia*) in which the old self, or the old covenant within, was stripped away so that the new person could willingly submit to divine Love (God). And yet, to be caught up in what Thomas à Kempis called the 'stormy, generous and unfathomable love of God' often proved a long and harrowing Gethsemane-Golgotha-Easter experience.[17] The Day of the Lord, now dawning through convincement, anticipated the victory of God's love over 'Satan's kingdom'—the empire of evil—both within and in the 'carnal' world.[18] With the dénouement for evil came the end of history as it was known up to their own times, giving rise to a new messianic era, and a spiritual dispensation for themselves and humanity.

In dying to their old selves, people would be atoned or convinced into the Kingdom of God, into the 'immortal Seed' or the 'Foundation'.[19] Both were equated with the Christ or Light, the giver of true knowledge. Being 'born again' as pure 'babes' they would stand in solidarity with those other 'babes', those victims of injustices of which they were well aware—forced tithes and oaths, for instance, as well as the oppressive power of the State

---

[14] See Heb. 9: 26-28.
[15] Fox, *A Declaration Concerning Fasting and Prayer* (1656), *passim*; see esp. 4. For sin as 'death's kingdom' see James Sicklemore, *To all the Inhabitants of Youghal* (1657), 7 and as separation see Nayler (with Hubberthorne), *An Account from the Children* (1660), 52; Fox, *An Epistle General to them who are of the Royal Priesthood* (1660), 9. Youghal ('Yorhl') is in Co. Cork, Ireland. For 'convict' see Tt. 1:9; Jm. 2:9 (KJV).
[16] *Pearl*, 5; *Journal*, 27, 135; Ep. 115 (1656) in *Collection*, 92.
[17] Underhill, *Practical Mysticism*, 137. For 'old covenant' see Gal. 5: 1-6; Heb. 9: 10-15.
[18] *Pearl*, Sig. A2, 8, 9.
[19] Fox talks about being born again of the 'incorruptible Seed' and see his 'A Word from the Lord' in *News Coming up out of the North* (1654), 17. For 'immortal Seed' see 1 Pet. 1:23 and *Pearl*, 4, 18; Ep. 61 (1654) in *Collection*, 58-9. In second-Temple Judaism 'seed' was associated with 'remnant', the 'true Israel' returned from exile with the 'secret', that is, the 'Word'. We shall see how the early Quakers used these metaphors in their rediscovery of the Kingdom of God, their suffering place within it and their outer witness to the cross and Word. For 'remnant' see William Smith (d. 1672), *The Morning-Watch* (1660), 59.

such as these 'evils' represented.[20] The transformation they urged was initially expressed, then, on an individual level and, if true, led to a restructuring of the tangible relationships between people and a wholehearted welcoming of the Kingdom. This in turn led to authentic liberation and salvation at every level of human existence.[21]

Salvation, the atoning death of Jesus and other Christological concerns are examined in Chapter 5, but it will help to emphasise that 'born again' was not understood as in its modern Christian evangelical sense. Instead, in the words of early Quaker Edward Burrough, it involved 'regenerating and making like unto God, *being his image of justice, truth and righteousness... in which [we] may be saved everlastingly.*'[22] It meant being reborn into God's love and justice but also practising them. Howgill, too, underlined what all Friends believed: those 'not born of the Light' were not 'born of God' and knew 'not the virgin's womb' or the 'day of Christ' but looked instead for 'signs in the outward'.[23] In other words, rather than discount those not 'born of God', people's separation from Love was to be lamented. Importantly, Howgill's use of 'Christ' did not necessarily mean the physical Jesus. And being 'saved', redeeming the 'field', meant being whole in living the Rule of Love (Kingdom) individually *and* communally as if already in peace and unity with God and each other. Their Meetings, too, were to be reborn in their corporate discipleship and continually so as to ensure the permanency of a revolution that would be subordinate in all its aspects to the Light.[24]

But the Friends were not exclusivist. They went beyond the Church by opening the doors of salvation to everyone whether they had heard of Jesus or not. 'It was possible', Wilmer Cooper has observed, 'to be saved by Christ [the Spirit] through the inward work of grace.'[25] Their call of universal redemption, a characteristic of the Kingdom of God, invited 'all people' to experience the transformation into the Light of Christ which they had undergone themselves. Here was a resounding *metanoia* that was to roar like a great wind throughout the length and breadth of Britain and hopefully the whole world.

---

[20] Fox, 'To Call the Minds out of the Creatures' in T. C. Jones, *'The Power of the Lord Is Over All'*, 49-50; Farnworth. 'Preface' in Fox and Nayler *et al*, *Several Petitions Answered* (1653), Sigs. A4, A7. For 'babes' see *Pearl*, 4; Nayler, *Milk for the Babes*, title pg. and Martha Simmonds *et al*, *O England! Thy Time is Come* (1656), 16. See esp. Jn. 3:3; Mk. 10:14 and for the equivalent of being 'born again' see 2 Cor. 5:17.
[21] See Sobrino, *Christology at the Crossroads*, 44.
[22] Burrough, *The Everlasting Gospel* (1660), 18; my emphasis.
[23] Howgill, *A Lamentation for the Scattered Tribes*, 8-9; a probable allusion to Rom. 8:9. See also Tucker, 'Revolutionary Faithfulness', 24.
[24] Barbour, *The Early Quaker Outlook*, 154.
[25] Cooper, *A Living Faith*, 14; Brinton, *The Society of Friends*, 5.

A New Covenant of Promise and Peace

In 1653, among the first to encounter this Quaker *ruach* was a group of Westmorland clerics.[26] According to *Several Petitions Answered*, published in late June of that year by leading Quaker theologians including George Fox and James Nayler, the 'priests' had issued an order 'given forth . . . at Appleby sessions' to investigate a recent incursion of troublesome strangers into their county.[27] In the previous October some of these clerics had failed in their attempt to convict Fox at the Lancaster sessions, the proceedings of which, together with the replies of the Quakers, were published by the Friends in March 1653 as *Saul's Errand to Damascus*.[28] Agreeing to lodge an official complaint, the clerics hoped the local Justices of the Peace (JPs) would expel or (if any were Westmorlanders) silence the upstarts and confine them to a restricted area. The invaders, they cried, had caused

> sad divisions and distractions, stirred up much hatred . . . even between the nearest relations, and powerfully seduced multitudes of people away from the truth and true worship of God.[29]

They also practised 'pernicious ways' and preached 'horrid blasphemies', 'corrupt doctrines', 'damnable heresies' and 'dangerous errors'. They even had the nerve to call themselves 'apostles of Christ'! These Puritan clerics were in no doubt that the strangers were violent disturbers of the peace, a danger to the commonwealth and to holy government, and to themselves as the 'godly' or 'gospellers' as they preferred to be called. Like all Puritans,

---

[26] *Ruach* (Hebrew) = 'breath', 'creator Spirit', 'Spirit of God' (Gen. 1:2) with a strong sense of a mighty wind or rushing torrent (Isa. 30:28), yet also of love.

[27] *Several Petitions Answered* was published on the 29th June 1653 but much of it was written in late 1652 after the investigation of Fox for blasphemy at Lancaster during mid October of that year.

Prisons in the seventeenth century were usually private, overcrowded and invariably disease-ridden, factors which sometimes necessitated the sequestering of alternative accommodation such as taverns and private houses. At times it was possible for prisoners to hire rooms with a fireplace, fuel and bedding, and occasionally be granted restricted liberty within the local neighbourhood, besides being accompanied by their families. See de Groot, 'Prison Writing', *passim*.

[28] *Saul's Errand* was begun in late 1652 and published the following March (12th) possibly to pre-empt Francis Higginson's virulently anti-Quaker *A Brief Relation of the Irreligion* (1653) and his *A Brief Reply* (1653), specifically a counter to *Saul's Errand* and in particular Nayler whom he believed to be the chief Quaker. Higginson was among those opposing Fox, Nayler and others at Lancaster and was joined in his campaign by George Fothergill of All Saints, Orton (Cumbria) whom we meet again in Chp. 7.

[29] Fox and Nayler *et al*, *Several Petitions Answered*, 1.

they derived their beliefs from the stringent theologies of Jean Calvin and his son-in-law and successor in Geneva, Theodore Beza.[30]

In their reply Fox and Nayler denied any violence, declaring that the Way of Jesus could never be 'maintained by any weapon of this world'.[31] They condemned the 'priests' as 'Cain's children', as representatives of a class with blood on its hands. The priests, they said, were completely wrong in their assumptions of Quaker thought and practice, and mischievous in suggesting Quaker intention to destroy the 'commonwealth of Israel'.[32] In Fox's and Nayler's own description of the English polity as the 'commonwealth of Israel' lay a comparison with the true commonwealth of God's Dominion, the rediscovered Kingdom, and of the Quakers as its spiritual warriors, the Lamb's army of justice, peace and compassion. Another appellation for 'Kingdom' was the 'new covenant'. Rather than a contractual arrangement, the early Quakers' saw their 'covenant', based as it was on the *shema* of Jesus, as reflecting their own love for God and humanity but also their vision for a salvific, loving and guilt-free relationship between God and 'all people'.[33]

The two Quaker leaders insisted that a true Christian commonwealth would bring 'all into purity, justice and righteousness' away from religious formalism and 'the kingdoms of the world'. It was Mammon by which the Church and magistracy wielded 'corrupt' power. The aim of justice, they maintained, was to keep the peace rather than create strife. Quoting Romans 13: 4, as they would in 1661 to Charles II, they insisted that no magistrate

---

[30] See <http://en.wikipedia.org/wiki/History_of_the_Puritans> for a general insight into Puritanism. Reformed theology of the Calvinist variety was not monolithical; see J. D. Moore, 'Calvin Versus the Calvinists?', *passim*.

Generally, 'Calvinist' and 'Calvinism' are used throughout this book to identify the reformed theology of Jean Calvin (1509-64) and Theodore Beza (1519-1605), and of English Calvinists such as William Perkins (1558-1602) and William Ames (1576-1633). See Perkins, *The Golden Chain* in *Works* (1603 edn.), chp. 15 and Ames, *The Marrow of Sacred Divinity* (1642), 121. While Kendall's controversial *Calvin and English Calvinism to 1649* does not specifically address Calvin's doctrine of the atonement, his view is that (i) Calvin believed in universal rather than limited atonement, (ii) that it was *Beza* who believed Jesus died for a predetermined Elect only, and that (iii) Calvin believed Jesus died for all but did not pray for all. Perkins and Ames, he says, erroneously assumed Beza's thought as pure Calvin and that Perkins' deductions in particular gave rise to English Calvinism. Hence the attribution of Perkins as the 'founder of English Puritanism'. However, I agree with Nicole and Bruhn that limited atonement is indeed found in Calvin. See Nicole, 'John Calvin's View of the Extent of the Atonement', *passim* and Bruhn, ''Sinne Unfolded'', *passim; also* Kendall, 13-18 and esp. 13-14. See below 59*n* for Calvin's view of predestination.

[31] Fox and Nayler *et al, Several Petitions Answered*, 15, 28.

[32] *ibid.,* 26 and *Pearl*, Sig. A2, 20.

[33] The *shema* is the focus of Jewish early morning and evening prayer services. For Jesus' use of the *shema* see Mk. 12:30-31 and Mt. 22: 36-40, and for its Hebraic origin see Dt. 6:4. Nb. 15; 37-41; see Fox, Ep. 155 (1657) in *Collection*, 119; W. Smith, *The New Creation* (1661), 46-50. Also Fox, *An Epistle to all People on the Earth, passim*.

should bear the sword (i.e. their jurisdiction) in vain.[34] If their judgments were partial it proved they had 'an evil eye' and ruled with their own 'will and with tyranny'. Such behaviour meant the destruction even of the carnal commonwealth for want of justice. 'Let every soul', they wrote, 'be subject to the higher power for all power is of God.'[35]

The Westmorland episode, and others like it, anticipated the yawning gap between the Quakers and their godly detractors. Furthermore, it presaged the battle for the right understanding of the Kingdom of God and the struggle between what the Friends identified as the first and second priesthoods.[36] The first priesthood was characterised by outward ordinances and included such punitive measures as forced tithes and oath taking.[37] Puritan clerics in particular, they said, typified this Levitical form of priesthood which was obsessed with sin, fomented guilt among its followers and was violent; Christ had come to end it, maintained Fox.[38] The second or royal priesthood on the other hand was the possession of those who had come to know the Light of Christ. It was group-mystical, prophetic and compassionate; good works, involving outer justice and the welfare of all people, were natural to it.

In its prophetic form, this Light spoke of equity, truth, simplicity, peace and justice for everybody, including the spiritual rights of women as we shall see in Chapter 10. In the second priesthood, freedom from the ecclesiology of the 'hireling priests', such as those they encountered in Westmorland, liberated people for 'true worship'. True worship was practicable anywhere since it was based solely on silence and discipleship, what today is sometimes called 'holy obedience' or 'revolutionary faithfulness'.[39] According to the Quakers, the Kingdom of God was to be freely available to everybody.[40] '*You* may return to Moses if you will', they might have said if reiterating the words of the French spiritual reformer, Sebastian Castellio, 'but for us others Christ has come.'[41]

---

[34] Fox, Hubberthorne et al, *A Declaration from the Harmless* (1661), 5.
[35] Fox and Nayler *et al, Several Petitions Answered,* 11-12. See Cooper, *A Living Faith,* 26 and Jn. 4:24. See also Rom. 13:1-4.
[36] See H. Smith, *The First and Second Priesthood* (1657?), *passim*; Fox, *The Second Covenant* (1657), *passim.*
[37] For objection to ordinances see Fox and Nayler *et al, Several Petitions Answered,* 24-5.
[38] Fox, Ep. 45 (1653) in *Collection,* 41; H. Smith, *The First and Second Priesthood,* 6. For 'Levitical priesthood' see Fox, *An Answer to Dr. Burgess his Book* (1659), 8.
[39] For 'hireling' see Jn. 10:12 and Isa. 61:1. See Tucker, 'Revolutionary Faithfulness', *passim.*
[40] Fox and Nayler *et al, Several Petitions Answered,* 25 and see Burrough, *A Faithful Testimony Concerning . . . True Worship* (1659), 1 and in *Works,* 474.
[41] Emphasis belongs to Castellio (1515-63); see R. Jones, *Spiritual Reformers,* chp. 6 and esp. pp. 96, 103 (1*n*), 256. As 'John Theophilus', Castellio was the translator into Latin of the *Theologia Germanica* which was influential in England when, in turn, it was translated into English probably by Roger Brierly (1586-1637), the Grindletonian, rather than John

Declaring Apostasy

The Westmorland justices, however, were to stand their ground. They duly charged Fox and Nayler with blasphemy, indeed with rejecting the Scriptures.[42] The Quakers retorted that the priests had condemned themselves to a dead existence in the old, now outmoded, covenant or Mosaic Law like those who had refused Jesus' central message of the Kingdom.[43] Strategically quoting Ephesians 2:12, Fox and Nayler proclaimed a New Israel or new covenant of the rediscovered Jesus Way.[44] It was a Way that could be experienced as a relationship with God on the inner level and thence, hopefully, enacted and broadcast to the world.[45] Here in microcosm was the age-old battle between:

- the magisterial Church *AND* its radical, mystical and prophetic wing,

- the Church's 'apostolic' priesthood and ecclesiology *AND* the true 'apostolic' priesthood of all believers in the everlasting order of Melchizedek,[46]

- the worldview of the oft-punitive political establishment *AND* the compassion, justice, peace and equity of the Sermon on the Mount and its literal enactment,

- the imminence of King Jesus' physical Second Coming *AND* the Light's continuing presence in the consciences of individuals everywhere, the Second Coming being a present and inner reality,

---

Everard (c.1575–c.1650) as once thought. Everard was an English preacher, author, Familist (perhaps), Independent and mystic. Castellio is mentioned seven times by leading early Quaker William Caton (1636-65) in his *The Testimony of the Cloud of Witnesses* (1662), 5, 15-16, 41-2. For Brierly see N. Smith, 'Elegy for a Grindletonian', 339 and Darling, *The Grindletonians, passim*.

[42] Probably under the *Ordinance for the Punishing of Blasphemies and Heresies* (Long Parliament, 2/May/1648)—see Firth and Rait, *Acts and Ordinances of the Interregnum* i., 1133-6—and perhaps the Blasphemy Act of 9th August 1650 which was aimed principally at the Ranters and Diggers. Very few Quakers were convicted under either.

[43] *Pearl*, 11.

[44] Ephesians 2:12 reads: 'That at that time you were without Christ, being aliens from the commonwealth of Israel, and strangers from the covenants of promise, having no hope, and without God in the world'

[45] For the inner level they were much influenced by Jer. 31: 31-4; see, for instance, Richard Davies (1635-1708), *Works*, 13-14.

[46] There are ample references in the works of the Friends to 'Order of Melchizedek'; see, for example, Fox, Ep. 151 (1657) in *Collection*, 117.

- the need for rigid social and theocratic order *AND* continual revelation and a spiritual revolution with social and political consequences,

- and, despite exceptions, a general indifference to the needs of the poor *AND* social justice for all.

To the Friends, the outer Church had failed Jesus' sacred commission to spread the Light (Kingdom) for the world's healing, to seek after 'the good and welfare and doing that which tend[ed] to the peace of all.'[47] It had not only watered down his two great commandments (Mt. 22:38-40) and the Sermon on the Mount, but was guilty of casuistry in no longer acknowledging the need for their radical and literal implementation as Jesus had expected.[48] Fox and Friends strongly believed, for instance, that the Sermon was not about impossible, idealistic standards but that it contained transformative initiatives for reconciliation and participation in the Kingdom of God. They understood that the Sermon's major purposes were to illustrate how reconciliation and healing were possible only with the grace of the loving God and how to proceed through the 'narrow gate', the 'daily cross', into eternal life.[49]

The Church, therefore, was in drastic need of regeneration for the reasons already mentioned, besides being in error in preaching the Scriptures as the Word of God. Hence on two major accounts it was disobedient to God's Law as this was found in Jesus. In short, the Church had abandoned 'the doctrine of Christ'—the whole of Jesus' true teaching and witness as encapsulated in the Kingdom/Presence of Love.[50]

Another early Friend, John Whitehead, directly linking the Kingdom and 'doctrine', testified to the *primary function* of the Quakers' movement by emphasising how 'the ministers of Christ walk[ed] in the power of godliness and [went] from city to city and from village to village *preaching the Kingdom of God.*'[51] As itinerant preachers or 'Publishers of the Truth', the Kingdom was their prevailing travelling companion. And as partakers of

---

[47] For Jesus' 'great commission' see Mt. 28:19-20.
[48] Burrough, 'To the Reader' in Fox, *The Great Mystery*, 12-13. For 'the good and welfare' etc. see Fox, Hubberthorne *et al*, *A Declaration from the Harmless*, 1. Also Schnackenburg, *God's Rule and Kingdom*, 105.
[49] See Fox, Ep. 16 (1652) in *Works*, 7:24 and *Collection*, 14; Penington *et al*, *The Way of Life and Death* (1658), 52-3. For 'daily cross' see 2 Cor. 15:31. The phrase 'transformative initiatives' is found in Stassen, 'Recovering the Way of Jesus', *passim*. See also his *Just Peacemaking: Transforming Initiatives for Justice and Peace*, *passim*.
[50] Howgill, *The Mouth of the Pit Stopped* (1659), 17; *The Rock of Ages* (1662), 108; Fox and Nayler *et al*, *Several Petitions Answered*, 34.
[51] John Whitehead (1630-96), *The Enmity between the Two Seeds* (1655), 19; my emphases. He was quoting Lk. 8:1.

the Jesus Way, they were fortified by its 'Wisdom', 'Power' and 'Life' which would eventually overcome all oppression and violence, even the apparent invincibility of evil.[52]

A Righteous Remnant

Several Petitions Answered mentions justice and its correlate in this case, righteousness, eighteen times. Analysed further in Chapter 6, righteousness, which the Friends encountered four times each in the Sermon and the Epistle of James, was central to their Kingdom-inspired community, a community opposed to inequality including the widespread poverty and exploitation they observed among the general population. A distinctive feature of a righteous community, they believed, was its prophetic advocacy of truth, justice, reconciliation, redemption, peace and compassion as proof of God's love for humanity.[53] Besides its association with morality, righteousness bespoke wholeness (salvation) where only good would be returned for evil. For the Quakers, righteousness was a constant reminder of their divinely-appointed vocation.

Meanwhile, the titles given to Jesus—Messiah, Son of God, the (suffering) servant and Son of Man—were seen to herald a wider community of the Kingdom spearheaded by their own.[54] The Messiah was that Light to all nations, the ever-immanent anointed one of a great people (a Kingdom) to be gathered—the New Israel, that is, the collective son and daughter of God.[55] Like the Messiah, the real servants of God were neither rich nor powerful. Humble and 'meek', they accepted insult and privation without violent retaliation. Consequently, the path of righteousness meant living on the brink of death, often as a faithful few or lowly 'remnant' witnessing to the Kingdom in the world for its redemption.[56] Suffering of this kind, they believed, rose above despair. It absorbed and nullified hatred, and brought patience, perseverance, hope and eventually peace, justice and unity. The remnant as 'a people in scorn' constituted a true leadership and comprised the sons and daughters of Man who would do battle with the unbelievers around them. In doing so, the new and universal messianic age of the Light and its Rule or Covenant of Love, now instituted, would

---

[52] *Pearl*, 6.
[53] Fox, *Justice and Judgment is to Rule*, 7.
[54] 'Son of Man' references in Quaker writing are infrequent but see William Dewsbury (1621-88), *The Discovery of Man's Return* (1653), 8 and *Doctrinals*, 464. For 'suffering servanthood' see Margaret Fell (1614-1702) *et al, A Declaration and an Information* (1660), 7. As an aside, there is much scholarly agreement that Jesus' titles of 'Messiah' and 'Son of God' were the creation of the early Church.
[55] See *Pearl*, Sig. A2, 7.
[56] W. Smith, *The Morning-Watch*, 59.

transcend political and ecclesiastical limitations since it was unrestricted by time and space, or, as Fox said, 'made manifest . . . up to God, out of time, through time'.[57]

Three Expressions of the Kingdom

During the seventeenth century the Kingdom of God was expressed in three principal ways—within the Church by the Puritans and Arminians (higher Church or 'State Protestants') and outside it chiefly by the Quakers.[58] An examination of the wider ecclesio-political and theological contexts of early Quakerism will sharpen our appreciation of its worldview. This is found in Chapter 2, which also outlines Puritan and Arminian self-definition *vis-à-vis* Roman Catholicism.

Arminians—no English divine in the early seventeenth century actually identified as such—were named after Jacobus Arminius, a professor of theology at Leiden University in Holland. Like Luther, he believed that since Jesus died for all, salvation was potentially possible for every believer.[59] Unlike in stricter forms of Calvinism (such as we find in William Perkins and William Ames), the atonement was open to all people because Jesus' death had satisfied God's justice for all: Jesus had truly died for our sins. While every person was totally depraved at birth, s/he could be saved (justified) by accepting God's grace. Grace was God's initiative only, an invitation to salvation by means of faith in the Gospel of Jesus as it was conveyed by the Church, itself an indispensable means of salvation. In other words, humans could not initiate salvation: it was expressive of God's sovereignty alone. This saving grace, however, was not irresistible as in classical Calvinism. Since people possessed free will it could be rejected and in denying themselves salvation they would be eternally lost. Alternatively, as people were saved only in so far as they welcomed the Gospel completely and remained within it, they would enjoy membership of the Elect and predestination to son/daughtership of God through adoption, glorification and eternal life. Arminians, then, are said to have held to 'universal atonement'.

All Puritans, Arminians and Quakers sought to defeat Satan but they took different paths. The Puritans (who were never a single party or

---

[57] Fox, *To All that would Know*, 4. For the 'universal Light' see *Journal*, 14-16, 33, 143. For scriptural references to the Light's universality influencing the Friends see Isa. 49: 6; Ac. 2:17; Col. 1:23; Tt. 2:11.
[58] Arminianism is outlined well at: <http://en.wikipedia.org/wiki/Arminianism>. See also Kendall, chp. 10 for a helpful account of Arminius' theology.
[59] For 'Jesus or Christ died for all' see Rom. 4:5; 2 Cor. 5:15; 1 Pet. 1:10. See Farnworth, *The Brazen Serpent* (1655), 4: this tract condemns predestination as also Howgill's, *Some of the Mysteries of God's Kingdom*, 30-2.

homogeneous group) worked towards an earthly commonwealth. For them the Church was the Kingdom of God in this life and the only means of salvation and victory over the devil's kingdom. Starkly, salvation meant freedom from sin. This was a temporary affair, however, since the true Kingdom would be enjoyed after death by the Elect whom God had chosen before creation (predestination).[60] Other Calvinists, though equally Manichaean, held that the sinful, too, were determined by God before creation as the reprobated ('double' predestination).[61] Like the Puritans, Arminians held fast to many Calvinist beliefs but viewed predestination differently; it was a pre-decision on God's part to save those who repented and believed. They thus rejected double predestination.[62]

The Quakers leaned towards Arminianism in respect to predestination and likewise condemned double predestination. Going further, they declared any ecclesiastical *magisterium* redundant and denounced not only the Church's belief that it alone was the Kingdom of God on earth but also that the Bible was *the* Word of God.

The Ever-Pure Light

Though they held the Scriptures in great esteem, the Friends deduced from the Prologue to John's Gospel that, while the Bible contained God's words, only God was the Word, the pre-existent Christ, the Light or Jesus as a cosmological reality, the eternal emanation from God. This Light abided in *all* people as the *same* Light. It was the source of true knowledge of God alone and called everyone to perfection by challenging them to live up to its

---

[60] See Calvin, *The Institution of Christian Religion* (1634, hereafter *Institutes*), iii., chp. 21, 448-9 and esp. 451 in which he writes,

> Predestination we call the eternal decree of God whereby he had it determined with himself what he willed to become of every man. For all are not created to like estate: but to some eternal life and to some eternal damnation is fore-appointed. Therefore, as every man is created to the one or other end, so we say that he is predestined to either life or death.

For a scathing Quaker view of Calvinist predestination, election and reprobation see Nayler, *Love to the Lost* (1656), 32-4; Bishop, *A Treatise Concerning Election* (1664 [but dated 20th Aug., 1663]), 1 and *passim*.

[61] For Calvin double predestination was, as Foster tells us, neither fundamental nor necessary; see Foster, 'Liberal Calvinism', 5. I use 'Manichaean' in its modern non-theological sense of dualistic, presenting or viewing things in a 'black and white' fashion.

[62] For a Roman Catholic view of predestination see Coffey, *Grace: the Gift of the Holy Spirit*, 214-5. The view that the Church is the Kingdom of God on earth is largely Augustinian.

measure as given to each of them.[63] The Light was also prophetic in the way it taught and urged people to discover and enact the Kingdom.[64] As grace, the Light was the only means of unity with the living, loving God and the salvation this implied.[65] It could not be 'comprehended' by the darkness; that is, it could not be overcome because its power was from 'everlasting to everlasting.'[66] Chapter 8 outlines how the Friends identified the Light with the pre-existent yet *present* Christ, the actual Word—and all these with the historical Jesus. The Light was the Blood of Life, the Blood of Christ, the 'leaven' of the Kingdom of God, that which brought order out of inner and outer chaos.[67] The Friends were probably inspired in this respect by Ephesians, Colossians, Thessalonians, and clearly by John's Prologue which also provided the basis for their Light theology and Christology.[68]

Their opponents often confused the Light with natural light and thought it bizarre that it was everybody's final authority.[69] We will investigate differences such as these in Chapter 1 when reviewing Puritan faith and practice, particularly between the late Elizabethan period and the restoration of the monarchy in 1660. Part One, then, helps us understand why Puritans reacted so strongly to the Quakers, not only physically but also during their mutually acrimonious debates over Scripture, the nature of Church and State, worship and ministry, preaching, the sacraments, the moral perfectibility of the individual and the Church by the power of the Spirit/Christ, as well as Christology and the meaning of the cross. The Friends, for instance, held that the atonement and cross were inner realities, symbolic of the power of God's love. This love overcame the evil in human

---

[63] The same idea is found in the Benedictine Augustine Baker (1575-1641), *Sancta Sophia* (1657), 10; see Fox, 'A Word from the Lord' in *News Coming up out of the North*, 17.

[64] For 'measure of Light' see Rom. 12: 2, 3; Eph. 4: 7-13. See also Cooper, *A Living Faith*, 2, 13; T.C. Jones, *George Fox's Teaching*, 4; L. Benson, *What did George Fox Teach about Christ?*, 5; and Bien, *The Mystery of Quaker Light*, 15-21.

[65] Unity with God was mystically understood but it was a 'practical' awareness largely devoid of the mystical rapture experienced predominantly by medieval and Renaissance Roman Catholics. Quaker mysticism is discussed in Chps. 8 and 9.

[66] Barbour, *The Early Quaker Outlook*, 154. See Fox, Ep. 184 (1659) in *Works*, 7, 173; Burrough, *A Declaration to all the World* (1657), 2. Their understanding of the Christ within derived from such scriptural references as Jn. 1: 1-9, 5: 33; Rom. 10: 8; Col. 1:27; 2 Cor. 13:5; Jm. 1:21; 1 Jn. 2:14 and their term 'from everlasting to everlasting' probably derived from Dn. 4:3, 34; 7: 14, 27.

[67] See, for instance, Fox's *To All that would Know, passim* and *Pearl*, 15 both of which address the chaos of living outside the Kingdom of God and of the Light as remedy. For the Light as the Kingdom of God's leaven see *ibid.*, Sig. A2^2 and Crook, *A Defence of the True Church* (1659), 26. For Light (i.e. the Christ) as blood see Fox, Ep. 155 (1657) in *Works*, 7; 147-8.

[68] See Jn. 1:9, 8:12; Eph. 5:8; Col. 1: 15-22; 1 Thess. 5:5. For a concise explanation of the Light see Brinton, *Friends for 300 Years*, chp. 3 and esp. 38.

[69] See Fox, *To All that would Know*, 6.

nature thus liberating its Light-filled creativity. The more this happened, the greater the capacity for people to love themselves and their neighbour, and thus God.[70] By declaring that 'Christ had come to teach his people himself', they announced the Kingdom of God as already present although awaiting its freedom and eventual consummation in the fullness of time when God and humanity would be united as one. For the Quakers, their relationship with God was best sought in silence without clergy, bell, book and candle. God was personal but not a person. Like Jesus, they enjoyed a meaningful, intimate and loving relationship with an objectively existing God/Spirit/Light. The Quaker God, the Presence, differed markedly from the Puritan God as we shall see in Chapter 2.

Millenarianism and Fear of Popery

The Puritans and indeed much of the wider Church in Britain generally understood 'church' and the Bible in literal terms. To appreciate why, it will be necessary to grasp the appeal of millenarian thinking to the Protestant conscience particularly between 1630 and 1660; this is attempted in Chapter 1. It is enough to mention here, however, that theirs was a *pre*millennialism (or chiliasm) which anticipated the imminent, physical arrival of Jesus who would then rule with his Saints (Elect) for a thousand years. Evil would then be defeated and the Kingdom of God on earth finally established.

The Quakers loudly and persistently refuted this view and the violence, oppression and militarism they claimed it upheld.[71] Their experience of the Second Coming as a Kingdom of God event—inward and among people as a present reality—demands an analysis of their Christology which I undertake in Chapter 8.[72] Was Jesus God *and* human? Was he a human being only with an unusual gift for religious awareness and wisdom? Questions such as these help us recognise three aspects of the Quakers' skilful use of the Bible, *viz*: how it was their guide rather than their master, how they put into practice certain critical aspects of the Christian Testament such as the Sermon on the Mount, and how they radically empathised with Jesus and the Kingdom of God he inaugurated.[73] In elucidating their relationship to the initial Jesus Way, such questions also inform us about their view of, and interaction with, the wider Church of their time. And yet it is enough to say here that, as with Protestantism in respect to Rome, their differences *vis-à-vis* the Church and other groupings helped the Friends

---

[70] Cooper, *A Living Faith*, 43, 47, 55-9.
[71] See, for instance, Penington, *The Axe Laid to the Root* (1659), 12-13.
[72] Fell, *For Manasseth ben Israel* (1656/7), 5; *A Call unto the Seed of Israel* (1668), 24: 1650s theology.
[73] See Vail Palmer, 'Did William Penn Diverge Significantly from George Fox?', 62.

self-define as 'a peculiar people' charged with spreading the Covenant of Peace.

From the early days of the reign of James VI/I, long-drawn out disputes over Arminianism, Catholicism and Puritanism, including the thorny issue of predestination, were key factors in the lead-up to the three civil wars of the three kingdoms and the carnage and devastation they visited upon the British nations during the 1640s.[74] Fear and hatred of Catholicism in particular was fuelled by a number of factors such as the memory of the attempted Spanish invasion of 1588. The Armada may have been successfully repulsed but the national trauma it generated served to stoke nationwide abhorrence of Rome, a hatred that carried into the seventeenth century and arguably beyond. Other factors included the presence of the hated Jesuits continually smuggled into England from Europe, failed Catholic attacks on the Crown such as the infamous Gunpowder Plot (1605) and the Irish rebellion-cum-civil war of 1641. Utter repugnance of the Irish was a national obsession and it would result in lethal outcomes particularly under Cromwell.

By the time the Quakers made their appearance in the late 1640s, deep-rooted detestation of popery and all things Roman had long existed at every level of society. This was due in no small measure to the presence in every parish of John Foxe's popular anti-Catholic work, *Acts and Monuments*, first published in 1563. Commonly known as the *Book of Martyrs*, it described in lurid detail the torture and burnings of some 273 Protestants in the later years of Mary I (1553-8). By becoming a highly effective means of anti-Catholic propaganda, *Martyrs* provided a strong sense of national Protestant identity.[75]

The presence, too, of Catholics at the Court of Charles I, personified by his consort, Queen Henrietta-Maria, compounded antipathy towards the 'papists'. The Queen, a native of Catholic France and passionately devoted to her religion, was instantly despised upon her landing in England in 1625. As Charles' reign continued, Puritans became increasingly suspicious of the Queen but also of Charles' overtures towards Rome and those, too, of the Arminian hierarchy to which he showed favour.

---

[74] And it may be argued until mid 1653, by which time English forces under Cromwell's son-in-law, Henry Ireton, were completing their campaign against royalist and Catholic forces in Ireland. The government also kept the unruly 'papist' north under military rule until the end of the same year. See *Journal*, 315, 323 and A. Woolwich, 'The Cromwellian Protectorate', 208.

[75] Mary Tudor (1516-58). John Foxe (1516/17-87), one time Fellow of Magdalen College (Oxford) and exile in Strasbourg (France). We meet Foxe again in Chp. 2.

Kingdom, Testimony and Pentecost

The countdown to civil war and its annual progress makes for grim reading. And yet, while recalling how warfare tore the country apart, how 'destruction and misery' were so often the despairing lot of the ordinary civilian or soldier, it is important to acknowledge the inspiration people found in the Good Old Cause. It was a Cause for which many a parliamentary supporter fought, including some who later become Quakers. Discussed in Chapter 3, it was a grand amalgam of hopes, in some respects utopian and primitivist but also practical and visionary, particularly in respect to liberty of conscience and constitutional reform. Arguably, it remains one of the foundations of modern democracy, its spirit surviving as a moral counterweight to the erosion of hard-won freedoms. The Quakers endorsed many of its central provisions but claimed to enrich them with their own spiritual depth. In this way they saw the Cause potentially as an outward expression of 'true religion'. Thus synthesised, both provided the backdrop against which the Quaker 1650s expression of Kingdom and Testimony, *the* peace testimony as we shall see, emerged with its sometimes military, theophanous, theopoetic and anagogical language, its apocalyptic dynamic and spiritual urgency, its anxiety and anger, along with its heartfelt plea for God's peace, justice and reconciliation.[76] The importance of this synthesis of Kingdom, Cause and 'true religion' to Quaker faith and practice, to their *Weltanschauung*, is revisited in Chapter 4 when Quaker language itself is analysed and in Chapter 12 where it is explored at a deeper level.

I hope to demonstrate how Kingdom and Testimony came to be expressed in many of their tracts, epistles and letters but most crucially in three declarations issued between 1659 and 1661, each of which embodied the movement's theologically coherent spiritual campaign, the 'Lamb's War', and Jesus' ethical values found more programmatically in the Sermon on the Mount.[77] Published under the names of Edward Burrough

---

[76] For the seventeenth century meaning of 'apocalyptic' see Thomas Blount, *Glossographia* (1656), Sig. D3; Edward Philips, *The New World of English Words* (1658), Sig. C3. S. Fisher has 'veiled' and 'revealed' in ἈπόκρηπτΆ ἈπόκΆάγπτΆ (*Apokryta Apokalypta*). *Velata Quædam Revelata* (1661), title pg., 5. For apocalyptic and theophanous language see, for example, *Pearl*, 12 and Nayler, *The Power of the Lord* (1653), 11, 14-15: both quote Dn. 2:34-35 (*cf*: Mk.5:5): 'and now shall the stone cut out of the mountain without hands, break thee and thy image in pieces' (p. 11).

[77] For spiritual warfare see 2 Cor. 10: 3-4; Eph. 6: 10-17. The term 'Lamb's War' was probably invented by Nayler. I agree with Arthur Roberts and Hugh Barbour that the 1650s was a Pentecostal experience but which I have concentrated into the corporate 'moment' of 1659-61. See Roberts, 'Comments' (a discussion of Nesti's 'Early Quaker Ecclesiology' in *QRT* (1978), 40; and Barbour, 'The 'Lamb's War' and the Origins of the Quaker Peace Testimony' in Dyck (ed.), 150.

(December, 1659), Margaret Fell (June, 1660) and George Fox and Richard Hubberthorne (January, 1661), they were a tapestry of the previous eleven years of Kingdom and Testimony. Respectively they are: *A Declaration... to the Present Distracted and Broken Nation of England, A Declaration and Information* and, the most well-known of the three, *A Declaration from the Harmless and Innocent People of God* (see Appendix 2). As a consequence, I reconsider the hegemony accorded to the Fox-Hubberthorne declaration so often précised in creedal fashion on Quaker Meeting House notice boards worldwide as the Society's 'peace testimony'.

Their 1650s experience, itself Pentecostal, culminated in a highly concentrated Pentecost-type 'moment' between October 1659 (the year of political chaos) and January 1661, during which time Thomas Venner and some fellow Fifth Monarchists occupied London for three days in a crazed attempt to usher in a new millennium with the physical Jesus as its head.[78] The 'moment' is discussed in depth in Chapter 13. Suffice to say, it differed from its predominantly individual variant initially experienced by many in 1652 when Fox gathered Separatists into his fold. It was consciously a *corporate* and Paracletal phenomenon as in Acts for two reasons.[79] First, their theology and mature understanding of the Kingdom of God, including its orthopraxis as the Lamb's War for salvation, sought to put the Kingdom and its Sermon into practice, something openly demonstrated as early as 1653 on the title page of *Saul's Errand to Damascus*.[80] The War, discussed in Chapter 6, was designed to turn the world upside down by placing the Jesus Way, Jesus' *halakhah* (and now their very own) at the very heart of life.[81] Second, the large numbers of Meetings, settled by the movement's itinerant ministry, were akin to cellular structures. These enabled efficient communication among Friends in what was a spiritual guerrilla war.

---

[78] The Venner occupancy was from 1st-4th January.
[79] Throughout this work 'Paracletal' combines three meanings, *viz*: 'advocate', 'the comforter who is called in to help' and the 'Holy Spirit'.
[80] Orthopraxis = religious practice (in the sense of right walking/conduct), sometimes assertive and revolutionary in nature.
[81] *Halakhah* (Hebrew: 'huh-<u>luhkh</u>-khuh') derives from the Torah. It describes the Jewish Law and its way of life. It is akin to orthopraxis and can be literally translated as 'the path one follows'.

Brierly also put much stress on Mt. 5 and the Sermon; see his posthumously published *A Bundle of Soul-Convincing*, 112 and esp. 206-17 (chp. 22). For Grindletonian literary style see N. Smith, 'Elegy for a Grindletonian', *passim*. Specific early Quaker references to Mt.5: 1-7 are uncommon but selections from the Sermon are often embedded in many a key tract. See, for example, Fox-Hubberthorne *et al*, *A Declaration from the Harmless*, 1 ('follow after righteousness' – Mt. 5: 6).

Meetings were autonomous to a large degree but within the Kingdom they were all linked as 'one of another'.[82]

The Venner uprising itself was the last desperate effort of a small premillennial group whose messianic expectation had been a normative feature of the British political and ecclesiastical landscape, particularly since the 1630s. However, like Jesus, some of whose fellow Jews were equally gripped by eschatological expectancy, the first Quakers consistently presented an alternative vision. It was a vision that defined them as harbingers of a different politics—that of the Eternal and its compassion. Despite their disappointment over the fate of the republic and the Good Old Cause, they carried this politics of compassion beyond the Restoration.[83] Rather than a cowardly retreat into a suddenly discovered quietism, as a Marxist school and other historians have intimated, their response to Venner and the government's massive over-reaction, while pragmatic, was underscored by their Pentecost-type moment and their nonviolent 1650s experience of Kingdom and Testimony. Through it they 'arose' *united as never before* into a new level of spiritual insight, enabling them to possess a more powerfully collective awareness of a Kingdom with a cosmological dimension. What emerged was a mature, gathered and reinvigorated 'nation' that could speak to subsequent generations of the Kingdom's inevitable victory over evil.[84]

Neglect of the Kingdom

Just as theologians Glen Stassen and Benedict Viviano today echo the early Quakers by asserting that for two thousand years the Church has largely neglected Sermon ethics and politics, while its theology and liturgy have ignored or distorted the Kingdom beyond recognition, I will show how twentieth century Marxist, Quaker and other historians and theologians have also missed or hugely understated the Kingdom focus of the *Friends*.[85] It

---

[82] Horle, *The Quakers and the English Legal System*, 6; R. Moore, 'The Inevitability of Quaker Success?' in Dandelion (ed., 2004), 54.

[83] See Perrot, *Discoveries of the Day-dawning* (1661), 6.

[84] In Col. 2:15 they would have noted Paul's description of Jesus' cosmic battle with evil and the significance of the cross in his victory.

[85] See Stassen, 'Recovering the Way of Jesus in the Sermon', unnumbered pp 1-3, 12. It became 'obvious' to Viviano early in his Dominican formation and subsequent theology lecturing in Rome (since 1975) that the central theme of the preaching of the historical Jesus of Nazareth was the near approach of the Kingdom:

> Yet, to my astonishment, this theme played hardly any role in the systematic theology I had been taught in the seminary. Upon further investigation I realised that this theme had in many ways been *largely ignored in the past two thousand years, and when not ignored, often distorted beyond recognition*. How could this be?

needs saying that such an oversight is astonishing as Appendix 1 and the following figures show. Between 1652 (the year of the first known published work) and 1663, the period this book covers, approximately 1,000 of their works were published. Of over 800 of these in my possession, 735 are by authors with more than 20 works to their name. Of these, 88% refer (and often more than once) to 'Kingdom' or its equivalent expressions such as 'Dominion of God', 'Sovereignty of God', 'New Israel' or 'Law of God'. Of the 152 works Fox composed in the same period, the terms 'Kingdom of God/Heaven/Christ/of the Messiah' occurred 519 times in 72 works (i.e. 46% of 152), a figure that rises impressively to 144 (i.e. 93% of 152) when alternative expressions are included.[86] He also used the terms 95 times in 49 of the 225 epistles issued under his name, again in the same period, or 614 times in all from a total of 377 writings.[87]

There are seven basic explanations for the oversight which also derive from the difficulty of adequately translating the Greek *Basileia tou Theou* (or its Matthean equivalent, *Basileia tōn Ouranōn*—'Kingdom of Heaven'):

1. Jesus never succinctly defined the Kingdom. For him the Kingdom *was* God, an indefinable entity. The term was meant to puzzle, to challenge and evoke questions. Thus the Gospels have him proclaiming the Kingdom through stories, miracles and in the conduct of his life. During his day, the generality of people understood the Kingdom in political, apocalyptic or quietist ways. Certainly in some quarters it was a watchword for the Jewish national hope of self-determination, even a complete and universal revolution in human affairs through God's power which would result in the punishment of nations that had oppressed Israel. Thus an era of peace and righteousness that was law-abiding, law-loving, prosperous, faithful and of

---

My emphases; see his *The Kingdom of God in History*, preface. For confirmation of Viviano's position see Figueroa-Villarreal, *Gustavo Gutiérrez's Understanding of the Kingdom of God*, 20-43. See also G. Harkness, *Understanding the Kingdom of God*, chp. 4 (online).

[86] The works to which I refer number 776 (authors with 20+ works) and 171 (by Fox). The percentages remain unaltered even when the 235 entries from Fox's *An Answer to the Arguments of the Jews* (1661) are removed from the total. The alternatives are equally numerous. I did not include antonyms (e.g. kingdom of Satan) though they would have resulted in higher percentages. See Chp. 6 for similar alternatives and contradictions in the Fell (1660) and Fox-Hubberthorne (1661) declarations. And see Appendix 1.

[87] Caution is needed here in regard to the epistles and letters. Barbour and Roberts inform us that some epistles were copied by hand into Meeting minute books and remained there until they were included in individual authors' *Works* where these were published posthumously. See *EQW*, 258.

all blessing both material and spiritual, would be ushered in.[88] These ideas prevented people from comprehending the Kingdom as espoused by Jesus and what would be expected of them in terms of personal transformation and even perhaps physical danger to their person. That the Kingdom was already known in the Hebrew tradition and in Apocalyptic up to his times may have led subsequent generations to perceive it not so much as a reality but as a 'mystery', something that was puzzling. This divorced 'mystery' from one of its important theological meanings—that which is 'revealed'. This may help explain why, rather than being a single and identifiable entity, the Kingdom came to evoke a host of associations within the early Church. Fox's accusation that the institution was 'in apostasy since the apostles' days' meant that the Church at large had not only neglected this entity, the Kingdom, but was still living contrary to it.[89] Nowadays, technically seen as a tensive symbol—as a multifaceted phenomenon with present and future aspects—it possesses different meanings in a variety of places and settings. Often its interpretation remains largely the prerogative of the individual.[90]

2. For over a century an unfortunate link was made between the Kingdom of God and Jesus' apparent belief in an imminent and physical End-time. Now challenged, the theory that Jesus was an eschatological prophet achieved prominence in the late nineteenth century through the work of Weiss who himself sought a future Kingdom. In the early twentieth, Schweitzer developed Weiss' arguments. Their ideas found subsequent expression in the scholarship of Ritschl and Bultmann and then in the 1970s with such prominent theologians as Pannenberg, Moltmann, Perrin and E. P. Sanders by which time it had developed into a highly persuasive and influential theory.[91] However, their intimation of an interim

---

[88] For a helpful insight into the political, apocalyptic and quietist understandings of the Kingdom during first-century Palestine see Grant, 'The Gospel of the Kingdom', *passim* and esp. 129-30.

[89] Fox's accusation is found, *inter alia*, in *A Reply to the Pretended Vindication* (1658), 18; *An Answer to the Papists... Lately Out of Holland* (1658), *passim*; see p. 1; *The Lambs Officer*, 4, 8, 12, 14, 16; see also *Journal*, 109 (for Fox on Firbank Fell.), 196, 294, 418-19 and Viviano, *The Kingdom of God in History*, 61. One is reminded of Fr. Pierre Battifol's (1861-1929) famous quip: 'Jesus promised the Kingdom of God, what came was the Church'.

[90] See Donahue's useful article, 'Jesus and the Kingdom of God', 14-15 and for 'tensive symbol' see N. Perrin, 'Eschatology and Hermeneutics', 13.

[91] Weiss, *Jesus' Proclamation of the Kingdom of God, passim*; Schweitzer, *The Quest for the Historical Jesus, passim*; Ritschl, *Three Essays*; Pannenberg, *Theology and the Kingdom of God*; Moltmann, *Theology of Hope*; Perrin, *The Kingdom of God in the Teaching of Jesus* and Sanders, *The Historical Figure of Jesus*. For an excellent literature and historical survey of Kingdom concerns see Figueroa-Villarreal, *Gustavo Gutiérrez's Understanding of the Kingdom of God*, 17-19; 20-71.

ethics and mysticism is not true to the firmer portrait of Jesus drawn in the Gospels.[92]

3. Interest in the Kingdom among theologians was limited to academic circles. This remains the case, its fruits not yet reaching the generality of people. However, the work of the Jesus Seminar theologians, some of whom are allied to the 'Emergent (or Emerging) Church' movement, reflects recent and promising interest with better opportunities for wider dissemination through the internet.[93]

4. 'Kingdom' is regarded in various quarters as masculine and hierarchical, especially in its understanding of God, and has been associated with authoritarian régimes. As a consequence some link it to war, murder and various forms of injustice. For many it is a reminder of a difficult religious upbringing. Its dramatic language—such as we find in modern versions of Luke 16:16 (ERV): 'The law and the prophets were until John: from that time . . . the Kingdom of God is preached and every man enters violently into it'—can give offence and lead to misunderstanding: 'entereth violently' (here from the English Revised Version) can be contrasted to 'everyone is eager to get in' (New Living Translation). The verse suggests the eagerness and urgency of people to enter the Kingdom on hearing Jesus' explanations: it was 'urgent' in order to break the domination of forces which held people in thrall.[94] Many are unaware of such explanations. And while the Greek for 'kingdom', *Basileia*, is gender neutral, for many 'Kingdom' is associated with the so-called 'Christian Right' and traditional Christianity (what may be called 'churchianity') which many, including Quakers, have abandoned—and sometimes with bad memories of sexism, homophobia, and physical and psychological abuse of varying kinds. Guthrie is correct to say that 'Kingdom' can provide 'theological

---

[92] For an old yet still fresh discussion about the mysticism of Jesus and Paul see Buckham, 'The Mysticism of Jesus and Paul', *passim* and esp. 311.

[93] The Jesus Seminar of predominantly US theologians such as Funk, Crossan, Borg and Horsley have long quested after the 'historical Jesus'. Interestingly, the Seminar has ignored the advice of German theologian Martin Kähler (1835-1912) that any such quest is a 'blind alley'. Kähler's *The So-Called Historical Jesus and the Historic, Biblical Christ* (1892) anticipated the work of Schweitzer and Bultmann.

The Emergent Church is a young and growing phenomenon. Too recent for historical analysis, it has many different expressions around the world claiming new forms of mission and innovation appropriate for a 'post-Christian' context. It understands that mission needs holistically to include mercy. Consequently, it advocates for justice and does not merely evangelise. See Daniels, 'Convergent Friends', *passim* and for the Emergent Church's Quaker expression see Mohr at:
<http://robinmsf.blogspot.com/2006/01/robinopedia-convergent-friends.html>.

[94] See also Mt. 11:12 and Gray, *The Biblical Doctrine of the Reign of God*, 319.

justification for the misuse of human power in familial, social, and political relationships to oppress other people and to rape our natural environment.'[95]

5. The Sermon on the Mount, the *magna carta* of the Kingdom, has been domesticated by various denominations, something addressed by, among others, theologians Stassen, Viviano and Georgia Harkness as we will see in Chapter 5.[96] Thus rendered somewhat impotent, it is often understood individualistically, and as non-radical and non-transformative. Further, the Sermon has often been represented solely in ethical rather than political terms since politics is invariably associated by many with statecraft.

6. Seventeenth century understandings of the Kingdom were normally invested in Puritan perceptions of 'commonwealth' and 'church', both of which were often divorced from the spiritual imperatives of the Sermon.

7. Without a familiarity with early Quaker language and the Gospels, it is easy for modern Friends to miss the many embedded references in their works to 'Kingdom' and its equally numerous alternative expressions.

Conflict, Mutuality and Mysticism

The Burrough, Fell and Fox-Hubberthorne declarations reveal the spiritual power that underlies the early Quakers' perseverance in enacting Matthew 5-7, a perseverance experienced in conflict on three levels. The first, as we have seen, empowered an individual to convict sin so that the Light could prevent idolatry and separation from the Kingdom—in other words, salvation *from* sin as opposed to Calvinist salvation *in* sin.[97] The second was found among themselves at such times when they lost the common language and practice inherent in the Kingdom of God. The third form of conflict came their way from opponents, including the various authorities up and down the country such as those in Westmorland. The reaction to the Quakers' Kingdom and the sufferings they incurred, sometimes from extraordinarily violent responses, are the subject of Chapter 7.

---

[95] Guthrie, 'Human Suffering, Human Liberation', 22.
[96] For 'magna carta' see Tholuck, *Commentary on the Sermon on the Mount* in Brown (trans.), 167. See also Stassen, 'Recovering the Way'; Viviano, *The Kingdom of God in History, passim*; G. Harkness, *Understanding the Kingdom of God*, chp. 4
[97] L. Benson, *What did George Fox teach about Christ?* (1984), 6-7. Benson's emphases: He continues to say that Calvin failed to see that if everybody could be brought to the status of justified sinners, the sin they committed would have similar tragic and historical consequences as that of unjustified sinners. For 'convict' see Tt. 1:9; Jm. 2:9 (KJV).

In the meantime, their practice of the Kingdom; their interpretation of the Jesus event and what he meant to them in the present; their strong theology of unity and mutual support; their understanding of the Second Coming as a dynamic *now* event but also as the ultimate future experience; their subversive practice of silent worship and advocacy of perfection and holism—all these were elements of a prophetic witness to the power of 'the Life' and to their movement's group mysticism. They were a type of 'sword' that would spiritually cut through the political and ecclesiastical *status quo*.

The subject of a deeper examination in Chapters 8 and 9, Quaker mysticism reflected their intense unity with the loving God through an inner and outer transformation whereby the 'secret', life in its essentially divine form, was now revealed. However, theirs was not the mysticism we find among medieval and Renaissance religious. As Howard Brinton and Rufus Jones continue to remind us, such mysticism was too subjective to provide a bond of corporate union. Instead, they were Christ- or Kingdom-mystics *together*, and, through their work in and for the world, their ultimate aim was to 'present' the Kingdom to God. From the Kingdom within would come the Kingdom 'outer' involving others to enrich the Kingdom inner and so on.[98]

Chapter 8 shows how the new dispensation of the indwelling Light, the pearl now unveiled, was best celebrated in silence.[99] Here in the presence of God, in the wisdom and power of Love which they had 'waited for and sought after from [their] childhood'[100], they strove in holy obedience to conform to the purity of the Christ/Kingdom within, and to the righteousness, death and resurrection exemplified by Jesus. Public Friends such as Edward Burrough testified to the power of 'pure silence' as 'they met together often . . . for many hours together . . . being stayed with the Light of Christ within us.'[101] Their practice of silence reflected a Christ-mystical oneness with Truth, the divine consciousness that was at work for the Kingdom within each of them and for the world. John Burnyeat, too, revealed how their 'hearts melted as wax and [their] souls poured out as water before the Lord . . . when not a word was outwardly . . . uttered.'

---

[98] J. Whitehead, *A Word of Reproof from the Lord* (1656), 6. See Brinton, *Friends for 300 Years*, p. xiii and R. Jones' 'Introduction' in *BQ*, p. xlii.
[99] *Pearl*, 4. He most likely used Mt. 13:31; Mk. 4:31.
[100] Keiser, 'From Dark Christian', 44; see Burrough's similar statement in *A Discovery of Divine Mysteries* (1661), 15; Dewsbury, *The Discovery of the Great Enmity* (1655), 22; Penington *et al*, *The Way of Life and Death*, 89.
[101] Burrough, 'To the Reader' in Fox, *The Great Mystery*, unnumbered p. 10.

These were the waters of purity and the Life.[102] Silence strengthened unity among themselves and with 'all people'.

Nonviolence and the Military

Despite a witness shaped by physical and psychological suffering and the corrosive ever-presence of rumour, innuendo and mistaken identity, the Quakers made nonviolence their watchword. It was a remarkable stance because the British nations, like ancient Israel, could boast little precedence of such. Violence being contrary to both the Jesus Way and the second priesthood resulted in repeated denunciations of 'carnal' weaponry and warfare from the inception of their movement (see Appendix 5).[103]

After acknowledging the possibility that Fox's (?)[104] and Burrough's calls upon the government and army in 1659 to wage war upon Spain, Rome and 'the Turk' were momentary lapses in their long-standing nonviolent stance, I argue in Chapter 12 why it is better to appreciate these injunctions as theophanous exhortations with apocalyptic and anagogical characteristics whose task was to underline the desperate need for 'all people' to undergo convincement into the Kingdom of God. After all, 'Babylon' (chaos) had 'covered' their 'distracted nation' which was in political freefall with no effective government. Fox may have feared another round of civil war while both he and Burrough gloomily anticipated the return of popery in the guise of a re-established Church of England and its episcopacy—in short, the collapse of the Good Old Cause and with it the synthesis of Kingdom, Cause and 'true religion' which we have already mentioned. The same chapter analyses the complexities surrounding Quaker nonviolence within the contexts of the 'sword', their varied language-use and what Marxist historians in particular have identified as Quaker 'violence'. Some early Friends had indeed fought in the civil wars prior to their convincement while others, a tiny percentage of their total number, remained in the army until 1659/60 only to be a constant thorn in the side of their superiors. Irrespectively, a great deal of written evidence conclusively supports Quaker corporate *nonviolence* throughout the 1650s; some of this is presented in Chapter 12 and Appendix 5.

The Friends were pragmatic in respect to the authorities and the army. As Douglas Gwyn has observed, they 'expanded eagerly into the political

---

[102] John Burnyeat (1631-90), 'An Account of [JB's] Convincement' in *Works*, 9. See also George Whitehead, (c.1636-1732), *Works*, 10-11 and Luke Howard (1621-99), *Works*, 29. This Whitehaead came from Sunbiggen, nr. Orton (Cumbria). For 'water of life' see Rev. 22:1.

[103] See Cadbury, 'The Basis of Early Christian Antimilitarism', 66.

[104] Fox's authorship has been doubted; see Chp. 12 and Fox, *To the Council of Officers of the Army* (1659) and Burrough (and S. Fisher), *A Visitation and Warning Proclaimed* (1659).

space the army afforded them' providing 'more opportunity for advancement than any elected parliament was likely to allow.'[105] Coleby's research confirms the army's widespread *civil* role in society, a role that bore similarity to that of the Roman army in Jesus' time.[106] The army was thus an important arm of central and local government. Communication and a degree of co-operation with the soldiery was often a daily necessity for everybody; it could not be avoided. Sometimes the Quakers supported the military's civil authority and at other times condemned it, especially when they believed the army had reneged on the Good Old Cause. At no time were they in alliance with the military, although they upheld the honour of magistracy when that office was performed by either civilians or soldiers. And they were particularly supportive of any authority when it undertook its responsibilities with equity and truth.[107] Consequently, the Friends repeatedly urged the authorities, including the army, to use the sword with righteousness/justice, the 'sword' being the magistrate's legal jurisdiction which included the power and means of physical restraint. In other words, while they endorsed police-type action, they never countenanced physical damage to any person or estate.[108]

The Kingdom/Presence of Love Today

The early Quakers are little understood among present-day Friends, although there are encouraging signs this may be changing due perhaps to greater interest in the history of the movement's formative years. I use 'history' reluctantly because theirs is not merely a story, a thing from long ago. Stories, after all, can be set aside. As discussed in the Epilogue, the Friends continue to be a living and pulsating voice since they were born into a turbulent period in many ways not unlike our own and because their collective Pentecost-Paracletal moment was unrestricted by time and space. Rather than a 'history', then, the first Friends initiated a *continuing theology* which, among its many attributes, identified the Kingdom/Rule of Love as a discrete entity. Its disregard for time and space opens up the tantalising

---

[105] Gwyn, 'James Nayler and the Lamb's War', 179.
[106] Stambaugh and Balsh, *The Social World of the First Christians*, 34-5, 77-8. For an informative account of Roman army administration see A. Jones, 'The Roman Civil Service', *passim* and esp. 44-7. Also M. Hirst, *The Quakers in Peace and War*, 58-9.
[107] See Coleby's important investigation into the army's role in civil administration, 'Military-Civilian Relations on the Solent', esp. 952-7, a paper deriving from his 1985 doctorate, *Hampshire and the Isle of Wight, 1649-1689* published as *Central Government and the Localities*; see esp. 22-4. Also Hirst, *The Quakers in Peace and War*, chp.14 and esp. 113. The idea of an 'alliance' between the Friends and the military has been raised but we await conclusive evidence; see Boulton, 'The Quaker Military Alliance', *passim*.
[108] Fox-Hubberthorne *et al*, *A Declaration from the Harmless*, 5 and Barbour, 'The 'Lamb's War'', 154-5.

possibility of singular pre-eminence for the Covenant of Peace, that lost radiance of the Quaker way, in our Society's teaching and preaching ministries. Hence, these pages contain the hope of a deeper awareness among Friends worldwide of their Society's beginnings but more explicitly of the Kingdom roots of the Quaker way. I agree with Gwyn, therefore, that

> The apocalyptic impulse of the early Friends still rattles the cages of modern Friends and [others] who read their amazing writings. Something of the earthquake that jolted them still jars us. Even when we do not understand their message, something in its deep structures resonates with us. It is a disturbing word, a subversive memory. We hear and remember it with pain and chagrin at our present captivity. But we forget it at our peril.[109]

However, I would add that the 'apocalyptic impulse' was indelibly linked to their *Kingdom* witness, the 'earthquake' that is always within us, it being intrinsically something of who we actually are, and which screams to be released onto the world.

In sum, from its genesis within an ecclesiastical, political and military maelstrom, the 1650s experience of Kingdom and Testimony, *the* peace testimony, maintains an ability to unite the past, present and future. As I hope to demonstrate, it is an ability strengthened by their inclusive and still fresh Christian universalist message *in the Quaker image* that does justice to all who care to follow it. As such, theirs is still an eternal *kerygma* of a joyous, emancipatory and prophetic witness that as yet confronts those for whom the physical Church is the embodiment of the Kingdom on earth, the same Church that continues to prepare its 'faithful' for a heavenly Kingdom after death.[110] Such a Church, as in the seventeenth century, continues to be ecclesiocentric and triumphalist, but also Christocentric rather than Kingdom-centric. As Jesuit theologian John Haughey asserts, 'By their heavy concentration on Jesus' own identity, Christians have allowed the Kingdom which he preached to fall through the cracks.'[111] This leads to the suggestion that the Church remains in need of reform commensurate with the Sermon on the Mount in which Jesus explicitly taught the Way of faith, that is, the Way of discipleship.[112] We know that many within the mainstream denominations are of like mind.

---

[109] Gwyn in Dandelion *et al*, *Heaven on Earth*, 137-8.

[110] *Kerygma* = related to the Greek verb κηρύσσω (*kērússō*) meaning to cry or proclaim a message as a herald of the king. It also means 'announcement' and 'preaching'.

[111] Haughey, 'Schillebeeckx's Theology', 202.

[112] See Stassen, 'Recovering the Way of Jesus in the Sermon', unnumbered p. 1.

Always for the Quakers, the true Church, existing *from* the Kingdom of God *for* the world, was and remains an intersection *with the world* by which a new covenant or New Israel can emerge. Those who implement the new covenant in any age, the children of Light, will always be its 'first fruits' as mediators of God's caring activity of love, justice, truth, peace and compassion.[113] For these reasons, the early Quakers' message of the Jesus Way does not speak the language of 'churchianity'. Rather, its voice is that of an eschatological continuum, a voice of liberation and hope. It is a voice of redemption and wholeness for all, of love and unity in God, but unity also with our religious forebears, albeit with all their flaws, since the Kingdom/Presence of Love transcends time and space. Their coherent Kingdom message, the theological basis of the present-day Society's testimonies, can provide the Friends today with the common language needed for mature communication among themselves and 'spiritual space' for their dealings with the world's principalities and powers.

Seventeenth century versions of 'churchianity' incorporated a *status quo* political ethic which reduced the poor to a lowly and invariably hopeless station in the Great Chain of Being. It was a calamity witnessed by many Quaker itinerant preachers as they travelled the length and breadth of Britain. In confronting the principalities and powers of their own time, an important outcome of their Lamb's War was, therefore, a Concern for the materially poor.[114] The 'cry of the poor' amid a nationwide culture of despair and fear will be our starting point for an understanding of the Puritan phenomenon that would impact so mightily on the Quaker consciousness.

---

[113] For 'children of Light' see Jn. 12:36; Eph. 5: 8; 1 Thess. 5:5.
[114] See Fox, *To All the Magistrates in London* (1657), *passim* and in *Doctrinals*, 105-6. Throughout this book I capitalise Quaker Leadings and Concerns.

Part One

The Puritans' Kingdom

Chapter 1: *'Chariots and Horsemen of Israel'*

– The Kingdom of the Puritans –

While seventeenth century England enjoyed a greater degree of social and economic progress compared to its European neighbours, urban and rural poverty was rife. Indeed, poverty and vagrancy were deeply embedded features of national life.[1] In Cumberland alone in 1649, an estimated thirty thousand impoverished farmers were constantly threatened by starvation and rising taxes.[2] Poverty's high visibility led John Moore, a cleric from George Fox's home county of Leicestershire, to label it the nation's 'crying sin'. For Moore, poverty was unacceptable in what was a relatively wealthy country. In a sermon delivered in 1635 in Lutterworth, a market town with a radical history, he illustrated his point with a heart-rending account of local farmers, displaced and desperate like their northern counterparts, pleading piteously at fairs and markets for any kind of employment to sustain themselves and their families. He was speaking in the spirit of the famous 1552 Christmas sermon also given in Lutterworth by Bishop Hugh Latimer who pointedly linked God's purpose with the ordinary folk, the shepherds and servants.[3] Tellingly, Lutterworth was the first place Fox visited when he left the security of his home in 1643 as a nineteen-year-old.

Many factors contributed to the poverty, particularly after the civil wars. Various parts of Britain, for instance, suffered a flood of refugees and

---

[1] See Brigden, *New Worlds, Lost Worlds*, 295-300.
[2] Horle, *The Quakers and the English Legal System*, 2.
[3] John Moore, *The Crying Sin of England* (1653), 8; see also 3-4. Moore purposefully replicated Latimer's sermon. Lutterworth is twelve miles from Fox's birthplace, Fenny Drayton. The village and environs were established venues for rallying dissenting opinion. Lutterworth boasted the Lollard leader and Yorkshireman, John Wycliffe (*c.*1324-84), as its rector in his final years. The authorities distrusted Leicestershire, considering it 'efficiently indoctrinated with the Elizabethan religious settlement in its most radical form'. See Cross, *The Free Grammar School of Leicester*, 21 quoted in Jewell, 33; Whiteman, 'The Restoration of the Church of England' in Nuttall and Chadwick, 27 and *Journal*, xxv and 3.

a rapid increase in the numbers of war widows, orphans and invalids. These unfortunate people had been traumatised by the atrocities, carnage and the disruption to their own or their neighbours' families. They and many others were also forced to endure the widespread destruction to buildings and farms that the conflicts brought in their wake.

By 1650, the civil wars and the continuing enclosure movement had created a pool of landless paupers so large that they comprised a staggering one-third of England's population. Homelessness, increased levels of crime, unemployment and underemployment, illiteracy, landlordism and other forms of exploitation became commonplace. Swelling ranks of the 'vulgar' or 'meaner' sort, as they were called, were often driven by despair into appalling squatter hovels in wooded areas or on the edges of towns as in many parts of Africa, Asia and South America today. Imagine poverty in any one of today's 'third world' countries in the aftermath of war and a harrowing picture of seventeenth century England emerges.

Two more factors contributed to a culture of despair and fear. Although it was largely free of the subsistence economy typical of many European nations, England retained a domestic market. However, limited in scope and dominated by agriculture, it barely kept pace with an increasing demand for food since the proliferation of small farms sustained low output.[4] In addition, the devastating harvest failures of the 1620s, 1630s and 1640s were etched in the collective memory. According to Bowden, they were the worst years through which England had passed despite determined, but ineffective, efforts by the various authorities to eradicate poverty.[5] Further, as in today's developing economies, the ever-present spectre of disease greatly compounded the situation. Bubonic plague and other horrific 'visitations' were regular occurrences along with periodic starvation and malnutrition. All in all, luckier folk emigrated to Ireland or North America, but even they could not escape the high mortality rate and an average life-expectancy of thirty-four years. Both were constant reminders of life's fragility.

God Above

This brutal, fear-infested environment was subject to a hovering, wrathful, judgmental God. For the great mass of the people He—and He was most

---

[4] Coward, *The Stuart Age*, 33-4.
[5] For Bowden see Coward, *ibid.*, 66. The first major attempt at a national poor relief scheme was instituted in 1572 making it compulsory for parish authorities to provide relief. However, not all parishes complied with the Act and it wasn't until 1620 that the poor relief scheme was established in most parishes. An Act of 1598 provided relief for the old, sick and 'deserving poor'. Houses of Correction were set up in 1610 for 'sturdy beggars', i. e. those thought capable of work.

definitely male—was an absolute fact, a person who lived above the firmament in His physical home, heaven. God's actual son, Jesus, lived with Him and was alive as any human being since He had risen from the dead. He shared with His Father the power of divine judge and redeemer. From heaven, God (and Jesus as Christ transcendent) continually directed human affairs.[6] Omnipotent in His authority and power, this tyrannical Deity knew everybody's most secret thoughts. Nothing happened without divine fiat for God always had a plan. Consequently, people were certain their misfortunes and successes were dictated by Providence.

Such beliefs came with theological gravitas. Richard Hooker, Master of the Temple Church in London, affirmed in his magisterial tome, *Of the Laws of Ecclesiastical Polity* (1593-7), that the 'Providence of God is both general over the kinds of thing, and such also as extends to all particulars in each kind.'[7] Calvin, too, had accepted unquestioningly that 'there falls not a drop of rain but by the certain commandment of God'.[8] And he might have added such things as earthquakes, floods, good and bad crops, coincidences and misadventures. Providence was said to be 'general' in that God created the natural world and yet 'particular' in the way He could suspend the laws of nature to His own end—for instance, by working miracles and fulfilling prophecies. The immutable God was sovereign, then, in the sense of having almighty power over heaven and earth. His power upheld all things while determining the ends which they were destined to serve.[9] It is easy to see how ideas of 'Providence' influenced the varieties of predestination which were accepted in varying degrees by all parties at the time. Meanwhile, the Bible was clear proof of all such divine powers.

Proclamations, sermons, speeches and personal diaries gave testimony to this interventionist God. So, too, did prayer manuals like those by prominent Arminian clerics, Bishop Lancelot Andrewes (*Institutiones Piae*, 1630) and Daniel Featley (*Ancilla Pietatis*, 1626), chaplain to Archbishop of Canterbury George Abbot.[10] Andrewes and Featley, typical of all English churchmen, saw God as a far-off, abstract, unknowable, holy Other who was necessary for a highly ordered society. At the same time, He was also accessible through private, fervent prayer or even an effervescence of emotion.

---

[6] For the Elizabethan and Jacobean Puritan view of Jesus as Christ transcendent, divine judge and redeemer see Hudson, 'English Protestants and the *Imitatio Christi*', 557-8.
[7] Richard Hooker (1553/4-1600), *Of the Laws of Ecclesiastical Polity*, Bk. i., pp. 8, 11; Bk. iii., p. 9. The 'master' was the priest in charge. In the 1580s, the church was the centre of theological conflict among Church of England adherents some more Calvinist than others.
[8] Calvin, *Institutes*, i., chp. 16, p. 85.
[9] Kyle, 'John Knox's Concept of Divine Providence', 396.
[10] George Abbot (1562-1633), Archbishop of Canterbury (1611-33).

The reality of a God hovering beyond the sky, then, was held as axiomatic by most people even after the 1670s and 1680s by which time science and rationalist philosophy invited curious minds to question His existence. And yet, as early as 1653 the providential image of God was challenged by those who denied a literal interpretation of the Scriptures. So it was that Benjamin Nicholson, a Quaker, could deride Puritans for confining God to a physical space. The godly, he wrote, were liars and hypocrites for

> telling the people that God, and the Kingdom of God is without them, or in a place in heaven a great many miles above their heads, making the ignorant people think that God is as some great man sitting in a throne in the natural heavens: and thus they either know not, or else are willingly ignorant of, that God fills heaven and earth and all things, and that the heaven of heavens cannot contain him, and that he is omnipresent in all places, and that he lives in himself, and of him all things consists, and in him have their life and being.[11]

His co-religionists would go further. God, they maintained, could not be restricted to a specific space and time as, say, in a church with timed services. And did not the Book of Revelation demonstrate dramatically how God was no longer 'a great many miles above [people's] heads' but a hidden Presence among them?[12]

To the literal mind, the earth took a secondary position to God in the cosmos and it was ripe for taming and exploitation. The world was Satan's kingdom, and the underlying question for most people was how he would be defeated. Almost everyone knew his power at first hand. After all, he delighted in infecting the world with his demons, imps, goblins and giants like those inhabiting the caves in the Peak District, a region of the Pennine Hills in the witch-ridden North. All such creatures lurked everywhere to ensnare souls into hell, an easy thing to believe since humanity was considered inherently evil and thus already fallen. Every single person had inherited Adam's sin thus proving human nature to be a permanently fixed state. There could be no question about this dualism for the Bible supplied the evidence and King Jesus was about to affirm it. He was expected to appear at any moment from heaven, judge humanity and rule with his Elect, the saints, for one thousand years. And a growing number of saints, as the

---

[11] Benjamin Nicholson (d. 1660), *A Blast from the Lord*, 5.
[12] After completing this chapter I was intrigued to find an influential British Anglican theologian, Keith Ward, saying the same thing. For me, there is no doubt that the leading first Friends were sophisticated theologians who were far in advance of their times; see Ward, *Holding Fast to God*, 11. Ward's book is a withering criticism of the philosphical views of fellow Anglican priest Don Cupitt and his Sea of Faith organisation.

poor especially knew, had the land, money, social status, weapons and the power that went with them.

Accidents were also part of God's mysterious design. More pertinently, they were proof of God's affection in enforcing self-examination, something especially accepted among Puritans. Good luck and fortune were also signs of divine favour: 'and the Lord was with Joseph', so William Tyndale wrote into his 1530s translation of the Hebrew Testament, 'and he was a lucky fellow'.[13] The Rev. Ralph Josselin, too, as he went about his parish in Earls Colne (Essex) in the mid 1600s, could see the work of Providence in preserving his family during an outburst of plague or ensuring a profit from his sale of hops. If, on the other hand, things went badly it was because God had a hidden purpose.

Prolonged poverty and other misfortunes, as with our hapless Leicestershire farmers, were the consequences of sin. Greater calamities, such as the civil wars, were God's iron rod, His punishment of whole peoples for their rampant whoredom, drunkenness, adultery and blasphemy. And contingency, too, was questioned: 'there is no such thing as chance, no mistakes in Providence', cried Oliver Cromwell to his troops. George Fox also championed Providence. While he placed far greater emphasis than the Puritans on God's forgiveness, we read in his *Journal* how both good and evil 'visitations' and 'judgments' befell him and others.[14] There is no doubting, then, the wide influence of Providentialism which was at its height between 1620 and 1660. In fact, denying it was tantamount to denying God and ridiculing religion.

This all-pervasive and claustrophobic Providentialism, and the stifling hierarchy of relationships and status it spawned, was enshrined in the *Book of Common Prayer* and the King James Bible (1611). The 'Prayer Book' was, by law, the standard text to be used in all places of worship in England. Its ordered liturgy was calendared on a weekly basis and its 1559 edition was still in use in the mid seventeenth century. Both it and the King James Bible justified a precise ordering of the godly society, both Church and State, in which 'Christian subjection' was assumed and everyone's place in the Great Chain of Being (*scala naturae*) confirmed.[15] The assumption that every relationship in society was founded on hierarchy had already been underlined by the Geneva Bible, the King James' popular predecessor, and by a prevalence of other sources such as advice books with their solid religious basis. These appeared in abundance during King James' reign.

---

[13] William Tyndale (*c*.1494-1536), creator of the English language version of the Bible.

[14] *Journal*, 148, 177, 493; B. Worden, 'Providence and Politics in Cromwellian England', 55, 60.

[15] The other appellation for the King James Version, the 'Authorised', is misnamed. It was certainly commissioned though no evidence exists for its official designation as 'authorised'; and see Katz, *God's Last Words*, 38-9.

A vital component of the Great Chain of Being was the household. For Puritans it came to represent the all-encompassing presence of God. Indeed, as they took over the reins of central and local government after the civil wars, zealous efforts were made by Puritan authorities to ensure everyone was attached to a household. The well-being of the commonwealth depended on the good management of families so that the world would have proof that the British were a people of one Book. Many were influenced by two important works, John Dod's *Exposition of the Ten Commandments* (1603) and Thomas Fosset's *The Servant's Duty* (1613).[16] Typically, Dod and Fossett hoped that British social hierarchy and its accompanying societal order would be based squarely on the fifth commandment. They urged householders, therefore, to oversee the religious education and practice of their wives, children and servants by summoning them to (usually) twice-daily prayer sessions, Bible reading and Sunday worship. Regular catechising would safeguard their morals and was thus a paramount requirement. It was the householder's responsibility to ensure, in the words of Puritan Robert Cleaver, that all under his care 'may be obedient to such good order'. According to Schochet, the duty of the servant was regarded as 'an ordinance of God or as a consequence of the benefits received from the master, such as food, lodging, clothes, minimal Christian education and learning a trade in the case of apprentices.'[17]

Particularly during the 1570s and 1580s, Puritan devotion to the godly life was expressed in the names given to their off-spring. Though by no means a universal practice, children were given names such as The Lord-is-near, More-trial, Joy-again, Sufficient, Deliverance, Joy-in-sorrow, Repent, Fly-fornication, Thankful, From-above, More-fruit, Flee-sin, Arise, Sin-deny, Increased, Preserved and Good-gift. Worst of all, perhaps, was Dust. But the most exotic was the name bequeathed by Mr. and Mistress Barebone to one of their sons: If-Christ-Had-Not-Died-For-Thee-Thou-Hadst-Been-Damned grew up to be Dr. Damned Barebone. His bother, Fear-God, rebelled against his upbringing, ditched Jehovah, adopted the goddess Fortuna and wrote bawdy verse. Another brother, Praise-God, was a Separatist and Fifth Monarchist. He became famous for lending his name to the Nominated or 'Barebone's' Parliament of 1653.[18]

On Sundays, the Puritan routine of prayer, meditation and worship was particularly rigorous since their God was a tough judge. As their writings abundantly show, they were more concerned with thorough-going

---

[16] John Dod contributed to a later edition of Robert Cleaver's *A Godly Form of Household Government* (1598).

[17] Cleaver, *ibid.*, 383, Sig. I^2; Schochet, 'Patriarchalism, Politics and Mass Attitudes in Stuart England', 417.

[18] Tyacke, *Aspects of English Protestantism*, 90-101 and 'Popular Puritan Mentality' in P. Clark *et al*, 77-92; esp. 82.

conversion than their Arminian counterparts within the Church.[19] The conscientious among them prayed twice daily in addition to Bible reading. They were content to know that their dialogue with God was based on an immediacy of communication with heaven. Puritan prayer found its source in the Bible of course, but also in sermons and instruction manuals. Like the people with whom the young Mary Penington lodged, many attended two or three sermons on Sundays, took notes as the preacher spoke, consulted his proof-texts in their Bibles and discussed these after dinner with other godly parishioners.[20] By the early years of James' reign, people began demanding sermons that were down-to-earth. They shunned the 'witty' Episcopalian sermons with their 'puffed up' intellectualism (their harmony of Plato and Jesus, for example), what the Quaker Stephen Crisp would later call 'great swelling words of vanity', a commonly held feeling even among non-Puritans.[21] So it was that Lancelot Andrewes chastised those who saw his own sermons as a source of intellectual pleasure, for 'tend[ing] to curiosity of knowledge rather than conscience of practice.' Invoking James 1: 22, he concluded that 'the point indeed [is] to be doers.'[22]

The Bible

Katz maintains that the Jacobean, Caroline and Republican periods saw the high-water mark of bibliolatry in the Protestant world before the emergence, in our own time, of Christian fundamentalism.[23] So *popular* was the Bible that between 1557 and 1644, three hundred thousand copies of its various versions were printed in England. So *influential* was the 'holy book' among Puritans in particular that its very words expressed their joys, sorrows, compliments and curses. During our period it was *the general code of ethical conduct*.[24] So *important* was the Bible that it was regarded as the very proclamation of God's salvation, the inerrant record as the Word besides being the record of the deeds of Jesus. For most, therefore, the Bible *per se* was *infallible*. And it was influential in another important way. Despite its rigid social stratification, England enjoyed 'a common cultural base' with a complexity of images and metaphors due largely to the Bible itself: it was the text that was most read, heard and discussed by people, its

---

[19] McGee, 'Conversion and the Imitation of Christ', 22-4.
[20] Mary Penington (c.1625-82), *Account... of Mary Penington* (1821), 2-3, 10; future wife of Isaac Jr.
[21] Stephen Crisp (1628-92), *A Word of Reproof* (1658), 1; Crisp finished this work in 1657.
[22] Jm. 1:22 (KJV) reads: 'But be ye doers of the word, and not hearers only, deceiving own selves.' For Andrewes see Dorman (transcr.), 'Certain Sermons Preached (Sermon 9, 1607)' in *Works*, v., 193-4 at: <http://anglicanhistory.org/lact/andrewes/v5/misc9.html>.
[23] Katz, *God Last Words*, 40-1.
[24] Fogelklou, *James Nayler: Rebel Saint*, 16; Katz, *ibid.*, 58.

language being that of public and private discourse. In Chapter 4 we shall see how the Quakers made particular use of the Bible and the 'scriptural politics' it invited.[25]

The Bible empowered Puritans to be 'chariots and horsemen of Israel' for they were convinced that through the power of God's Holy Spirit this primary Word to humanity would lead to regeneration at all levels of society. The Bible was fundamental, then, to this process and regarded as a mysterious gift, the surest of guides for worship but also for the whole of life. This in turn was basic to their world-view which rested, as indeed for all Protestants in general, on Luther's understanding of Paul—that is, as a result of the crucifixion of Jesus, humanity could be justified (made holy) only by the grace of God without merit of its own. Grace was the power granted by the inscrutable 'Other' and good works were of little consequence for salvation since they were merely a sign of one's Election or divine favour. These beliefs were their focal point. In fact, as these were located in the Bible, they regarded them as the focal point of religion in general.

Puritans emphasised preaching over 'altar worship' and liturgy, and they came armed with the radical Geneva Bible. It was first published in 1559, the year following Elizabeth's accession to the throne. It superseded the Great Bible (1539) and the Bishop's Bible (1568) relatively quickly, becoming the principal family Bible and the most widely read book of Elizabeth's reign. Although never officially endorsed by the Tudor and Stuart governments, the Geneva became the text most quoted by Shakespeare, Spenser, Raleigh and many others. In all editions it displayed an impressive Calvinist exegesis. It also invited everyone to be their own apocalypticist in the rewriting of history as a premillennial polemic and to anticipate the imminent arrival of King Jesus. A literal interpretation of Revelation would play a significant role in the minds and hearts of many. For these reasons, including its high accessibility, the Geneva enabled the 'simple reader' more than ever to examine their inner lives as advised by Paul, Augustine of Hippo and Calvin, and by home-grown, sixteenth century exegetes such as John Knox, Laurence Tomson, Miles Coverdale, William Whittingham and Anthony Gilby.[26]

Each edition, with its roman and italic rather than gothic lettering, was thoughtfully annotated and easier to read than previous Bibles. Essentially a study Bible, it was verse-divided, readily acquired, relatively cheap, quarto-sized and easy to carry. The Geneva was read in shops, taverns and barber-

---

[25] For 'common cultural base' and 'scriptural politics' see Katz, *ibid.* 40-1.
[26] Laurence Tomson, Calvinist and lecturer in Hebrew at the University of Geneva; Miles Coverdale produced the first complete printed English translation of the Bible; Anthony Gilby translated and annotated the 1560 version of the Geneva Bible. See Danner, *The Theology of the Geneva Bible of 1560*, 118-28 and esp. 121, 129-34.

shops. Its prefaces and annotations proved popular but it was the provocative margin notes that would become its principal feature. Their three hundred thousand words comprised one-third of the complete text. Originally inspired by Calvin, particularly those relating to predestination, they reflected the Geneva's apocalyptic worldview.[27] Tomson's notes, which appeared in his version of 1576, were especially influential and brought the Geneva's anti-Catholicism to a more virulent level.[28] But by challenging 'tyrannical' rule, and carrying ideas of a conditional monarchy, they were also seen as opposing monarchy and favouring the 'lower sorts'—artisans, tillers, yeomen of varying degree and the lesser gentry. They may have contributed, wrote Richard Greaves, 'to the class orientation of Puritanism as well as the tension between traditional values and potentially revolutionary ideals.'[29]

King James, who banned controversial issues from the pulpit, was in no doubt that the Geneva was 'partial, untrue, seditious', that it held 'dangerous and traitorous conceits' and was used by 'brain sick and heady preachers'. With some justification, he pointed to Tomson's notes for Romans 13: 5 where Paul bid Christians to be subject to authority for conscience sake. The Bishop's Bible commentary for the same passage reads, 'We are bound in conscience by the word of God to obey the higher powers, and in disobeying we should hurt the consciences of others through our evil example.'[30] Tomson's more primitivist stance was interpreted by the Jacobean Court as nakedly republican: 'So far as lawfully we may: for if lawful things be commanded us, we must answer as Peter teaches us, it is better to obey God than men.'[31] James, like Elizabeth—both had Erastian inclinations—came to fear radical Puritan clerics whom he coupled with the hated papists.[32] These 'brainsick', 'rash-headie' 'fanatics', he fumed in

---

[27] Gribben, 'Deconstructing the Geneva Bible', 2; W. Worden, 'Text and Revelation', 17. For Calvin's view on predestination see McNeill and Battles (eds.), iii, 21, 5. Predestination and especially double predestination were not central to Calvin's theology; see Foster, 'Liberal Calvinism', 5. See also D. Wilson, 'The King's Good Book', 38.

[28] Danner, *The Theology of the Geneva Bible*, 112-14. The margin note for Rev. 17 reads, 'This woman is the Antichrist, that is, the pope with the whole body of his filthy creatures as is expounded'.

[29] Greaves, 'Traditionalism and the Seeds of Revolution', 109.

[30] Betteridge, 'The Bitter Notes: The Geneva Bible and its Annotations', 55; Fincham and Lake, 'The Ecclesiastical Policy of James I', 171-2. For 'seditious' etc. see Pollard, *Records of the English Bible*, lxii-lxiii, 37-64 and in (Bishop) William Barlow, *The Some and Substance of the* Conference (1605), 47.

[31] For this commonly held Puritan view see also George Gifford, *A Brief Discourse of Certain Points* (1581), 22.

[32] Erastianism is the practice by which the monarch claims supreme jurisdiction over the Church with the direct right to appoint bishops. The Primate, in Britain's case it is the Archbishop of Canterbury, sits 'at his/her right hand' as spiritual advisor. For James'

Basilikon Doron (1599), who 'breath[ed] nothing but sedition and calumnies' challenged his authority as supreme governor by attempting to subject him to the spiritual jurisdiction of an independent and doctrinaire Presbyterianism, a theocracy in all but name.[33] His fear was such that he sincerely believed, as Elizabeth had warned him in 1590, that the 'obstinate hypocrites full of spiritual pride' 'would have no king but a presbytery!'[34]

His apprehension was legitimate enough but only to an extent. Presbyterianism was not politically powerful until the late 1630s and Puritans had no wish at this stage to create disruptions between Church and State.[35] Any idea of their separation was contrary to the Puritans' embrace of unity and order for civil society. They were unwilling, therefore, to work for reform outside existing ecclesiastical structures. But such assurance only served to fuel suspicion at Westminster. And so, with the evidence of the marginalia before him, the prudent king ordered the process that eventually resulted in the 1611 Bible that bears his name, but which also owed much to Tyndale's translation of the Christian and Hebrew Testaments.[36]

The Geneva's popularity among the ordinary parish godly, however, including those who had voluntarily separated from the Church, remained unchallenged until long after publication formally ceased in England in 1616. One hundred and forty editions were thereafter imported largely from Holland. Between 1560 and 1644, the Geneva went into 200 printings despite William Laud's attempts (as Archbishop of Canterbury) to ban it in England in 1637.[37] George Fox owned a 1560 edition in addition to his King James and Great Bible.[38] For the soldiers of both the New Model and Northern Armies, a specially edited military version known as the 'soldiers pocket Bible' was also popular. It prepared troopers 'to fight the Lord's battles, both before the fight, in the fight and after the fight.'[39]

---

attitudes towards Catholic and Puritans see also Bishop James Montagu's edited version of James' *Works* (1616), 73-88.

[33] *Basilikon Doron*, Sig A3, 12, 41-2, 44. *Doron* was James' advice to his eldest son, Henry (d.1610).

[34] Elizabeth 1, letter (6th July 1590) to James (when King James VI of Scotland only) at: <www.anistor.gr/english/enback/s022.htm>. And see the bitter poem attributed to James entitled *A Puritan Set Forth* (1642), 4-5.

[35] See Coward, *The Stuart Age*, 82.

[36] The King James' Christian Testament is 83.7% Tyndale; its Hebrew Testament is 75.7% Tyndale. See Barlow, *The Sum and Substance*, 45 for James' immediate attraction to the suggestion of a new Bible by Dr. John Reynolds (1549-1607), a moderate Puritan and president of Corpus Christi College, Oxford.

[37] William Laud (1573-1645), Archbishop of Canterbury (1633-41).

[38] His Great Bible was the Coverdale-Cramer version now in Swarthmoor Hall, the former home of Judge and Margaret Fell and family.

[39] Edmund Calamy (as imprimatur), *Soldiers Pocket Bible* (1643), 1. And see Robert Ram, *The Souldiers Catechism* (1644), *passim*.

Chapter 1: 'Chariots & Horsemen of Israel'

Literalism and Millennialism

Most scholars agree that the generality of Puritans, whether conformist, nonconformist or Presbyterian, were premillennial and, like many in the established Church, double predestinarian. Predestination's link to millennial thought and practice invites a discussion of the three sub-genres of millennialism—pre, post and amillennialism—that were operative during the mid seventeenth century in particular.

Premillennialists or chiliasts believed King Jesus' physical return to earth was imminent—the Second Coming—and that he would inaugurate a one thousand-year rule with his Saints. Evil would then be defeated and the Kingdom of God on earth established. Lamont posits the view that Foxe's *Martyrs*, enormously influential among Puritans of all ages, 'encouraged men in the belief that they were living in the fifth age of history, the last age, when Christ and the Antichrist [would resolve] their struggle.' Through Foxe, he continues, 'chiliasm was absorbed painlessly into the English bloodstream.'[40]

Postmillennialism acknowledged a millennium *preceding* the Second Coming, that is, no literal return of Jesus until the end of the symbolic one thousand-year reign of his Saints. Though not a well-developed belief during our period, postmillennialism enjoyed some popularity during the 1640s and 1650s. Conceived in spiritual terms, it anticipated a time when God's rule over the earth would be progressively established through human missionary activity and the saving work of the Holy Spirit. In other words, according to Thomas Brightman the millennialist, the servants of Jesus were to prepare a 'holy utopia', to 'advance his Church unto the highest honour that [could] be'.[41]

Amillennialism took no account of a literal, future and earthly rule of Jesus prior to a last judgment. It referred instead to a spiritual environment in which good and evil developed continuously until the Second Coming—the moment, that is, when all humanity would turn to Jesus. Another characteristic of amillennialism was the belief that the Kingdom was already present since the victorious Jesus currently ruled the Church through the Holy Spirit. Amillennialists never saw the Bible as a source for predicting a physical End-time.

Central to millennialists, then, was their interpretation of the Kingdom of God and the role of the returned Jesus in its establishment. Besides Jesus' imminence, other key questions were raised. Would he remain for one

---

[40] Lamont, 'Puritanism as History and Historiography', 137. Lamont provides 'some further thoughts' on Professor C. George's paper of the same title.
[41] Brightman, *A Revelation of the Revelation* (1615), 852; Foxe, *Acts and Monuments* (1641). See Ball, *A Great Expectation*, 166-8.

thousand years on earth to rule with his Saints, the Elect (premillennialism)? After his one thousand-year rule would he *then* battle the Antichrist at Armageddon (premillennialism)? Alternatively, did the millennium end in 1300 as some thought and, if so, were people now living in a postmillennial era? Was not the Advent of Jesus (the Second Coming) a spiritual reality only (amillennialism)?

Puritans were obsessed with their personal salvation, discerning (some torturously) whether they were among the Elect or bound for damnation. They often suffered doubt and despair on their deathbeds as they realised their lives had not yielded perfect evidence of their Election.[42] For Gwyn, the signs of their salvation were a loathing of, and a desire to be without, sin, and esteem for those who were counted among the righteous as well as a love of sermons. These went hand in hand with hard work, social and business success, and good citizenship. For the most part this body of teaching and behaviour kept many on the straight and narrow. A minority of Puritans, however, developed rigid moral scruples and deep anxieties. Of these highly conscientious people, a number would break with the Church to join the ranks of Seekers, Separatists and, later, the Radicals (sectaries) including the Quakers.

With the rise of the Puritans a growing individualism crept into English Protestantism. In striving to forge a personal relationship with Jesus the God-man, Puritans understood the first duty of their preachers as bringing individuals to the fullness (and eternal glory) encompassed within their exclusive relationship with the Almighty. So, in the early 1630s, Robert Bolton urged his Broughton congregation in Northamptonshire to submit to a 'soul-exalting humiliation' in order to know the power of Jesus. The holy life was the principal aim of each person and Puritans grew ever more anxious if they failed to achieve the justification (holiness) that would eventually lead to sanctification and glorification, and thus a confirmation of their Elected state. Earthly life, after all, was granted as a preparation for the life to come.[43] But as physical life always teetered on the edge—they had all-too-visible evidence of this in their daily lives—it was hardly a surprise that their rise accompanied a growing fascination with the Endtimes. In fact, in the first sixty years of the seventeenth century in Britain, the study of apocalyptic prophecy occupied a solid position within orthodox Christian thought. The Books of Daniel and Revelation were its powerful ingredients.[44] So pervasive did millennialism become that the Quakers, too, adopted an apocalyptic worldview albeit of a different order, combining a

---

[42] See Endy, 'Puritanism, Spiritualism and Quakerism' in Dunn and Dunn (eds.), 295.

[43] Robert Bolton, *A Three-fold Treatise* (1634), 129-30. See also Gwyn in Dandelion *et al*, *Heaven on Earth*, 95.

[44] Ball, *A Great Expectation*, 193.

form of amillennialism with something akin to what today is called 'historicist premillennialism'. In other words, Jesus' Kingdom was spiritual only and was put into practice through the Saints on earth with the help of the Spirit/Christ.[45]

It is also true that millennialism struck a deep resonance in British theological circles many years *before* 1600. More accurately, the idea that the physical End was at hand had circulated for a century prior to the 1630s. Little had changed by 1650 when Joseph Hall, Bishop of Durham, could say that 'many have I heard joyfully professing their hopes of an imminent share in that happy Kingdom.'[46] Premillennialism took a number of forms, some of them theologically sophisticated. However, divines like Nathaniel Stephens, minister at Fenny Drayton in Leicestershire, cautioned against a too-literal interpretation of Daniel and Revelation. He proposed that the dreams of Daniel did 'not meet in the same juncture of time'. In other words, though apocalyptic meaning went beyond time and space, people could nevertheless encounter it from time to time. From Stephens' critical insight we can deduce that a minority Puritan argument existed for a metaphorical, allegorical and figurative interpretation of apocalyptic literature. It was an interpretation that distinguished between a crudely 'present truth' and a more visionary 'knowledge of truths' yet to be unveiled by future generations.[47] Here was an argument for continual revelation, a belief long-previously advanced by more learned divines such as Richard Bernard. Reflecting on Revelation in 1617, he wrote:

> we must take heed that we look further then into the letter and naked relation of things . . . otherwise the book should be full of absurdities, impossibilities, falsities, and flat contradictions unto the truths of Scripture . . . Therefore we must not . . . take the words typically, and not literally.[48]

To the majority of Puritans, however, there was something evil about metaphors. They were cunning and misleading, the devil's tools, the discordant trick of the sectaries and the too-clever-by-half who challenged the all-important unity that was the essential hope of the Puritan holy

---

[45] See I. Penington, *A Voice Out of the Thick Darkness* (1650), 3, 12, 26: a pre-Quaker work. For 'the victorious Jesus currently ruled the Church through the Holy Spirit': 1 Cor. 15:24-28.

[46] Walia, *Radical Religion in England and its Critics*, 48.

[47] Nathaniel Stephens, *A Plain and Easy Calculation* (1656), 114; see also 13. This Stephens is found in the *Journal*, 5-8, 48, 50, 71, 184-92.

[48] Richard Bernard, *A Key of Knowledge* (1617), 4, 130-1. 'Literal', therefore, was not an invention of the period 1630-50 as one scholar suggests; see Burke in Lamont, *Puritanism and Historical Controversy*, 134.

commonwealth, the Kingdom of God on earth. The battle between the literal and the figurative confronted many Puritans as they engaged their detractors in the numerous public philosophical and theological debates and pamphlet wars of the time.

As with some extreme religious sects today, many people were certain that Jesus' arrival could be timed. Necessary to this Second Coming were the Jews, their conversion leaving the way open for Jesus to return at long last. So it was that in the Nominated Parliament of 1653, Cromwell prophesied the rule of the godly and encouraged Jews to enter England in the hope that the conversion would take place. The Quakers agreed with the idea though for different reasons as we shall see in Chapter 5.[49]

Along with 'physik' (medicine) and natural philosophy in general, premillennialism had connections with superstition and magic. It was also a feature of panic in a fear-ridden environment. If highly educated men like John Evelyn the diarist could see terrifying and portentous meaning in the passage of a comet, it is hardly surprising that a meteorite could scare the wits out of the ordinary people of Aldeburgh (Suffolk) for whom it was an omen of the End. The Aldeburgh event of 1641 was enough for William Lilly the astrologer, with shrewd insight into the coming political and military cataclysm, to foretell an 'insurrection of the community against the nobility and gentry, horrible wars, many slain, counties depopulated, plagues, famine &c.'[50] Signs and symbols of the End were everywhere in the war-soaked 1640s.

Although by the 1630s, the vast majority of millennialists were premillennial, the years prior to the outbreak of the civil wars saw the emergence of what has been called a 'historicist premillennialist' school. It was represented by clerics such as Nathaniel Holmes, John Cotton, Joseph Mede, Thomas Goodwin and Richard Bernard. Like the early Quakers later, they interpreted Jesus' reign as spiritual only, a reign enacted through his Saints on earth. Holmes was alarmed at the idea of a physical millennium. In it he saw the potential for tyranny and corruption. Cotton took the cosmological view that scriptural prophecy, especially in Daniel and Revelation, rendered the entire history of the Church in symbolic form. Intellectuals such as these analysed the Church's past and present for prophetic fulfilments so they could locate themselves in God's timetable.

---

[49] The Whitehall Conference (1655-6) discussed the question of Jewish readmission, and yet small numbers of Jews from Rouen (France) had already settled in London in 1632. According to Healey, Oliver Cromwell (1599-1658) granted permission in 1656 for Jews to obtain a house for a synagogue and land for a cemetery. Unlike the Quakers, Jews were never physically harmed by the Commonwealth on account of their religion although anti-Semitism was alive and well. See Healey, 'The Jew in Seventeenth-Century Protestant Thought', 65.

[50] William Lilly, *A Collection of Ancient and Modern Prophecies* (1645), 19-20, 29.

The spiritual millennium was always available for anyone with the ability to perceive it.[51]

During and after the civil wars, the most extreme chiliasts emerged among the Fifth Monarchists. A marginal yet highly vocal group within this movement achieved notoriety in relation to their occupation of London in January, 1661. For *these* Fifth Monarchists, such as the fanatical Mary Cary, the execution of Charles I in 1649 was a sign that the true monarchy, God's reign, was imminent. Fifth Monarchists in general were also Independents and Baptists who believed that the four Beasts of the seventh chapter of Daniel were analogous to the four empires of modern and classical times. The fifth was yet to come.[52] For this state of purity, they demanded a theocracy with a rigid application of the Mosaic Law. Thus the worldwide reign of King Jesus would be quickly advanced, his Kingdom established. Like the Quakers, they saw no need for a legal profession or for the universities, Oxford and Cambridge.

Not all chiliasts, however, advocated violence as a means for establishing godly rule. In fact, by 1656 many were content to join the peaceable Baptists. Even by 1659, the year of political chaos, the leading and formerly fanatical Fifth Monarchist, John Rogers, came to believe in the spiritual coming of Jesus. Like the later Rogers, these more cautious Fifth Monarchists took solace from John Tillinghast's *Generation-work* (1653), their movement's written equivalent of the Quaker Lamb's War of salvation.[53] Despite a numerically small presence, and with a less distinguished school of preachers, some of the Tillinghast persuasion ran parishes such as in Wrexham in Wales where the moderate Vavasor Powell was visited by the Quaker Richard Hubberthorne in 1653. Their encounter gave rise to a lively debate.[54] Though many considered Fifth Monarchists to be wild, the *idea* as opposed to the practice of a Fifth Monarchy, a longing for the universal reign of King Jesus, enjoyed wide scholarly acceptance during the 1650s as indeed it had among Jacobean intellectuals such as the

---

[51] Ball, *A Great Expectation*, 170-1; Solt, *Saints in Arms*, 72-6. For Quaker references to the 'End' and related expressions and ideas see, for instance, Fox and Nayler *et al*, *Saul's Errand*, 17.

[52] The four beasts of Daniel are the lion, bear, leopard and the 'fourth' beast. They are usually associated with the Babylonian, Medo-Persian, Greek and Roman empires respectively.

[53] Mary Cary, *The Little Horn* (1651) 35-6, 122; John Tillinghast, *Generation-work* (1653); John Rogers, *The Plain Case of the Common-weal* (1658), 75-7. For Rogers' cruder chiliasm see *Sagir, Sagir, or Doomsday Drawing Nigh* (1653). See Hill, 'Millenarianism and Fifth-Monarchism' in Bray *et al*, 31 and Capp, *The Fifth Monarchy*, 19 in which Capp, like Hill, describes a violent premillennialism among Fifth-Monarchists.

[54] Hubberthorne, *Truth Cleared* (1654) and see a letter to parliament from a John Griffiths of Oswelstree (Oswestry, N. Wales) in *Several Proceedings of the Parliament* (22-29th Nov, 1653), 249-55 for disturbances by Quakers 'from the North'.

playwright, Ben Jonson, and the poet and former Catholic-turned-Church of England cleric, John Donne.[55]

Some Characteristics of Puritanism

Emilia Fogelklou described Puritanism as 'a renaissance on English soil of the religion of the ancient prophets of Israel'.[56] By 1603, the year of King James's accession, Puritan preachers were an embattled minority in the Church of England comprising about 570 men without an agreed dogma, discipline or political program. However, they possessed a fervent desire for a completed Reformation, a desire more rabid in some like 'hyper-Calvinists' William Perkins and William Ames. The Archbishop of Canterbury at this time, Richard Bancroft, referring to the Geneva Bible and the Swiss 'Babylon' that inspired it, labelled them contemptuously as 'false prophets' or 'Genevaters'.[57] Bancroft was in good company. Queen Elizabeth had already warned James of this 'sect of perilous consequence'. During her reign, 'Puritan' quickly became a derisory label, a weapon of an élite keen to stigmatise the 'deviant', if not subversive, thought that was gradually infiltrating both kingdoms.

And yet, for the most part, Puritans were less strident than Perkins and Ames. They were content at this early stage of their development to work within the Church which they perceived as potentially the most complete and comprehensive political society.[58] Besides regularly attending their local parishes, they even participated (annually at least) in the communion, a practice more widely accepted by the 1620s and 1630s than in the middle years of Elizabeth's reign. During the early Jacobean years, therefore, the desire for 'reform' was not yet synonymous with 'revolution'. Only after 1640 and during the 1650s would this be the case.

Nevertheless, the Elizabethan Church, with its enormous variety of liturgies and considerable latitude of dogma, continued to be guided by a hierarchy that was nervously enjoined to conformity. It banned local religious initiatives such as Puritan lectures and 'prophesyings' both of which were seen as troublesome. These initiatives were meetings of clergy

---

[55] See Jonson's *The Alchemist* (1612), Act 4, Sc. 5, Sig. K2 and Donne's 'Elergie XI: Death' in *Poetical Works*, 21.

[56] Fogelklou, *James Nayler: Rebel Saint*, 16. For a good account of Puritanism see *AOTW*, 3-12.

[57] Richard Bancroft (1544-1610), Archbishop of Canterbury (1604-10); see Haller, *The Elect Nation*, 73-4.

[58] See Williams, *Anglican Identities*, 46-7.

in the localities for prayer and sermons which were then followed by mutual criticism and discussions about the state of the Church.[59]

Puritanism, however, was never as monolithic as Archbishop Bancroft supposed for there was no Puritan 'party'. In fact, Puritanism was spread across the several quasi-denominations that made up the established Church. It was adaptable, responding to the world around it as 'a cluster of ideas, attitudes and habits, all built upon the experience of justification, election and regeneration [which] in turn differentiate[d] Puritans from other groups such as Arminians or the Quakers.'[60]

As far as the Quakers were concerned, historians Hugh Barbour and Geoffrey Nuttall saw them as a radical offspring of Puritanism. There is truth in this assertion, but did Barbour and Nuttall exaggerate? Lewis Benson, Douglas Gwyn and the New Foundation Fellowship within the present-day Religious Society of Friends suspect they did while assuring us that the Quakers militantly *attacked* Puritanism. The Quakers and Puritans, they maintain, held radically different views about Scripture, the nature of Church, Christian worship and ministry, the sacraments, the moral perfectibility of both the individual and the Church by the power of the Light of Christ, the Christian's relationship to the State, and the meaning of the cross. While agreeing in part with this view, I believe the Friends were, more pertinently, protagonists in a deeper struggle between two opposing concepts—that of the hierarchical and violent Kingdom of the Church and their own vision of the peaceable, inclusive and primitivist Rule of Love or Covenant of Peace. Puritans, for example, saw the early Christians as members of the Elect but not as a 'people' in the cultural or political sense. That accolade was reserved for the covenanting Israelites and was one reason why Puritans looked to the Hebrew Testament as their own. Alternatively, the first Friends saw the early Christians, and indeed themselves, as a 'peculiar people' devoted to enacting the Kingdom, which they saw as being central to the Gospel message. The Kingdom was also within, a present reality that awaited unveiling.[61]

Marxist historians such as Christopher Hill have described Puritanism as 'the revolutionary ideology of the bourgeoisie in their struggle against Church and State.'[62] As a consequence, they confined Puritans to an 'industrious sort' busily laying the groundwork for a capitalised and

---

[59] George, 'Puritanism as History and Historiography', 79; Brigden, *New Worlds*, 328. See also Collinson, *Godly People*, 473.

[60] Spurr, *English Puritanism 1603-1689*, 7-8; Tyacke, 'Puritanism, Arminianism and Counter Revolution' in Owens, (ed.), 132. Fox used the Geneva Bible in Worcester prison in 1674-5 when dictating part of his *Journal* to Thomas Lower, his secretary at the time.

[61] L. Benson, *Catholic Quakerism*, 10. For 'peculiar people' see 1 Pet. 2: 9. See also Endy, 'Puritanism, Spiritualism and Quakerism', *passim* in Dunn and Dunn (eds.).

[62] Hill, *TWTUD*, 162-5; Hill and Dell (eds.), 22.

industrialised society. It was natural for them to rebel against the monarchical order embodied in the stubborn and foolish Charles I, largely because of the oppression which the king's aggressive interpretation of monarchical power came to represent.[63] A contrary opinion has Puritanism better suited to a 'poor gentry' working to make ends meet in rural, independently-minded communities seeking religious autonomy. As such, they were well distributed across much of the social spectrum. Haller, on the other hand, believes the Puritans were a fifth column within the Church of England; 'with the collapse of the central government and its repressive system of church courts, the Puritans were able to take over the religious sphere.'[64]

Most varieties of Puritan could be identified with relative ease by their dress, speech and demeanour. Puritanism was a lifestyle as well as a frame of mind and it was stronger in urban areas, notably London where it flourished among the wealthy. It achieved prominence during the two generations prior to the civil wars, a time when concern over order in society was at a premium.[65] It was after the wars, of course, that Puritanism became England's dominant force. Sir Henry Parker, secretary to the House of Commons in 1645, was full of praise for Puritans who, he wrote, had a 'remarkable and singular zeal to God and the Truth'. They were of 'good quality', he continued, and they compared favourably with their adversaries. He noted that a Puritan's conscientiousness to matters religious meant s/he was willing to die for what was right, and to overthrow a wrong whether in the form of a tax, a law or a monarch.[66]

Their visibility elicited many a personal recollection such as *The Character of an old English Protestant Formerly Called a Puritan* (1646) probably by John Geree, himself a Puritan cleric. He imagined someone without pretence or superfluity, one 'who made conscience of all God's ordinances' nor 'lament[ed] liturgy but only its corruption'. A Puritan, he mused, also held preaching in the highest esteem and, in an era of widespread illiteracy, s/he knew the power of a well-delivered sermon. Sermons possessed greater efficacy than readings from the Bible and were

---

[63] Hill, *ibid.*; Hill and Dell, *ibid.*; Ashton, 'The Civil War and the Class Struggle' in Parry (ed.), 104.
[64] See Haller, *Foxe's Book of Martyrs and the Elect Nation*, 224 and Tyacke, 'Puritanism, Arminianism and Counter Revolution', 130.
[65] Collingson, 'Religion, Society, and the Historian', 158; Endy, 'Puritanism, Spiritualism, and Quakerism' in Dunn and Dunn (eds.) 286-9; Kishlansky, *The Monarchy Restored*, 31-3.
[66] Henry Parker (1604-52), *A Discourse Concerning Puritans* (1641), 58-9. For Parker see Zaller, 'Henry Parker and the Regiment of True Government', *passim*. Also Fogelklou, *James Nayler*, 16.

as necessary to one's own era as they were in the primitive Church.[67] Prayer was important, too, but usually in the context of the sermon. Music was best reserved for the psalms since sensual delight was an abomination. Further, music was a relic of popery and barred the way to 'spiritual enlargements'. Our Puritan's sense of 'church' necessarily included elders, a hallmark indeed of a true Church. Outward churches were only a means to the divine end. They were to be plain and free of pomp whether ecclesiastical or personal. Sunday was always special, the previous week being its 'most exact preparation' in which a 'variety of holy duties' to family, neighbourhood and parish were performed in accordance with conscience and the oncoming sabbath. Religion, then, was an 'engagement to duty' in which Puritans were to be the best of husbands, wives, parents, children and so on. Indeed the family was a mini-church, a 'little commonwealth', with children raised in the 'nurture and administration of the Lord'. There is much similarity here to the Quakers. For William Perkins, a husband's 'power [was] over all matters domestic'. Like the monarch, he was, as we have seen, the representative of the Lord's purpose in both family and estate in the Great Chain of Being as it descended from God through the earthly monarch and thence to the lowest in the land.[68]

Puritans, our commentator further mused, were to be good neighbours, merciful, honest and sober. Personal talents were for the good of all and always to be used with gravity. Perfection—in the seventeenth century it meant striving for purity but also the 'full growth or development of a thing'—was attainable only in the next life. Fasting, for instance, while it might help work towards such perfection, was never to replicate 'popish mock fasts'. Nor were Puritans opposed to amusements so long as 'refreshings' were not abused. In this as in everything else, self-examination was a significant duty and would help maintain frugality. Our commentator noted that even wealthy Puritan landowners tended to abandon the ostentatious funeral gravestones and monuments of their social peers. Uncompromising in their beliefs, Puritans knew Jesus as their captain just as the cross was their banner in the war against Mammon and sin. So it was

---

[67] For the spiritual underpinnings to Puritan preaching/sermonising see John Traske (1585-1636), *The Power of Preaching* (1623), *passim* and esp. 18-61. The motivation undergirding Quaker preaching bore much similarity to Traske's. He was also a major supporter of sabbatarianism.

[68] Anon (John Geree?), *The Character of an Old English Protestant* (1670), Bds.; Geree was much loved at parish level. His work is listed in Benjamin Brook's *The Lives of the Puritans* (hereafter *Lives*) as *The Character of an Old English Puritan Nonconformist* published in 1646; see Brook (1776-1848), *Lives*, iii., 101-3. Also William Perkins, *Christian Oeconomie* (1609), 164.

that in daily life, Caesar was to be honoured and obeyed except where the laws of the State contravened those of God.[69]

The Artisan Esteemed

At the same time, as we have seen, there were Puritans whose beliefs ran contrary to the Great Chain of Being, something about which Elizabeth and James were well aware. Adams provides us with helpful insights into the world of such Puritans whose esteem for the artisan anticipated the practical, no-nonsense frame of mind of the Quaker. Examining the work of rhetorician Alexander Richardson, for instance, Adams (quoted here at length) suggests that 'the ideal Puritan was

> a knowledgeable, good, and useful member of society who followed a calling and performed actions and produced things of value to others. His status in society was determined by his productivity and service and not by his inherited or accidental wealth, bloodline, appointed office, clerical rank or storehouse of knowledge. In [this] Puritan view, a self-centred life (whether sacred or secular), or the authoritarian intercession in others' lives, failed to fulfil or blocked man's stewardly obligation to be useful to others and to produce and act by the light of knowledge, like Adam before his fall from grace, like God commanded in Genesis, like God Himself [whom Richardson considered *the* artisan]. Knowing, doing and making were joined by Richardson as three parts of the whole man reflecting God's artistic character and thereby making it possible for individual men to live wholly in the image of God without the intercession of a priestly or royal class. In this view, each man is equipped to live as God intended him to. Any permanent institution requiring his dependence upon others, or unquestioning obedience that is based upon any sense of a permanent defect in some men, was a form of bondage that kept him from becoming fully human, as God intended him to be. Instead of bridging the gulf between God and man, the Church and the monarchy created a gulf that was supported by [papist] Scholastic metaphysics and the gulf between contemplation [*theorin*] and productive activity [*poesis*]. By joining *theorin*, *praxis* [practical activity] and *poesis*, and basing knowledge in God's idea, Richardson proved that the common artisan was inspired by God, had a proper understanding of God and was as close to God as any man could be.[70]

---

[69] Geree, col. 2. For an example of the 'uncompromising nature' described see Gifford, *A Brief Discourse of Certain Points*, 22.

[70] According to Adams, Richardson (c.1565-1621) had once been influential but fell into obscurity after his death; not mentioned in *Lives*. See his *The Logicians School-Master*

Thus, by rejecting Scholastic philosophy, the Puritan quest for knowledge was turned outward towards things and their utility. Contemplation, now no longer superior as in Scholasticism, became a form of action. As a result, and with the artisan skills of God and humanity now harmonised, Scholastic hierarchical distinctions were eliminated. This in turn countered the need for social distinctions between royalty, the clergy and the common artisan. Therefore, in a universe existing for humanity's use, Puritans of Richardson's ilk were free to elevate utility above human authority.[71]

Introspection, Public Morality and Egalitarianism

All Puritans brought something of this down-to-earth practicality into their private lives. One way mentioned by Geree was their compulsion to explore their consciences with the help of regular Bible reading and journaling. This 'self-writing', often scrupulously followed, could result in much intensity of feeling, unhappiness and depression. But always they searched the Bible for solace and internal order. Their journals reveal great spiritual labour combined with a pietistic personal discipline long-developed since the late sixteenth century. They often record agonised doubts and yet temporary moments of confidence in their Election. It is also possible to see something of the future Quaker in this activity which demanded

> a life of grinding warfare against the self. It began with lengthy preparations for conversion, involving prolonged self-analysis as the heart was cleansed in preparation for [Jesus'] entry. It continued in a lifelong watch of the heart in pursuit of an elusive and fleeting assurance of salvation, structured around regular routines and methods, informed by manuals of rules, directions and long lists of potential sins to identify, confess and root out.[72]

Geree neglected to say that Puritans were varied in their political allegiance, religious observance, in their vision of the new godly order and as administrators. It cannot be assumed, for instance, that Puritan faith led to parliamentary sympathies—Geree himself was an anti-war royalist—or that, once in power, they were authoritarian and punitive in prosecuting

---

(1657), *passim* but esp. 19-26 and also Adams' 'Alexander Richardson's Puritan Theory of Discourse', 263-4.

Scholasticism has been defined as 'the dominant western Christian theological and philosophical school of the Middle Ages, based on the authority of the Latin Fathers and of Aristotle and his commentators.' It was associated by many a Puritan with popery.

[71] Adams, *ibid.*, 274.

[72] T. Cooper, 'Reassessing the Radicals', 242.

crimes, particularly at the local level, or that they were rigid enforcers of church attendance and thundering prophets against immorality. Nevertheless, murder, adultery, incest, fornication, uncleanness, sodomy, drunkenness, filthy and lascivious speaking—all outlawed by the Blasphemy Act of 1650—constituted a typical, but by no means complete, list of evils the godly hoped to abolish for ever.

He also failed to mention how egalitarian, enlightened and charitable Puritans could be, as in Dorchester (Dorset) where the Puritan magistrates built a hospital for the children of the poor. Many Puritans considered good works an outward result of their Election and austere life, and proof therefore that they had been saved. In the spirit of Hugh Latimer, many were also outspoken about usury, economic greed and social injustice. Noticing how keen they were on education and the sciences, Dickens makes us privy to a claim made around 1635 that 'more money ha[s] been put into English hospitals, charities, colleges and schools during the past sixty years than in any previous century.'[73]

Puritanism, however, was never divorced from contradiction. Also in Dorchester, the minister, John White, who hoped to turn the town into another Geneva,

> was a whirlwind of activity, conducting services, lecturing, and overseeing the hospital, Bridewell [House of Correction] and free school. His successes could be measured in increasing church attendance and decreasing premarital sexual activity. His failures could be measured by the divisiveness his activities engendered. Zealous constables and beadles waged an unrelenting war with the town's miscreant population, somewhat swelled by a successful brewery from whose profits the reformers paid for their ambitious programs.[74]

Attempts, then, to define Puritanism continually fall prey to the bewildering complexity of the political-religious turbulence of the times.

The Puritans' Kingdom

Armed with premillennialism, Puritans saw themselves as prophets of heaven, proclaiming God/Jesus as king to the latter day Babylon they experienced in the chaos and unrighteousness surrounding them.

---

[73] Dickens, *The English Reformation*, 371-2 in which the claim is attributed to Arthur Hildersham, Puritan minister at Ashby-de-la-Zouche (Leic.); Ashley, *Life in Stuart England*, 107.

[74] Kishlansky, *The Monarchy Restored*, 32. See also Underdown's *Fire from Heaven*, p. x quoted in Lamont, *Puritanism and Historical Controversy*, 10.

Chapter 1: 'Chariots & Horsemen of Israel'

Unrighteousness was interpreted almost exclusively in moral terms and they observed it easily enough in apostasy as well as in popery, the empire of evil, that very Antichrist which began 'creeping up' (as Archbishop of Canterbury, George Abbot, believed) as soon as the power of the Roman emperors declined. Their predominantly Hebrew Testament worldview gave rise to a crudely dualist struggle against the powers of evil and disorder, and the triumph of God's cosmos over the chaos. The Puritan/Calvinist Kingdom, inspired by references and allusions to kingship in the Hebrew Testament, conformed to the Judaic understanding of a God who intervened in human affairs to restore the nation of Israel. In preparation for this likelihood it was necessary to defeat the powers of evil within as well as sin in every day life. For this momentous task, Puritans were prepared to use the military as an arm of the Almighty. Social, political, ecclesiastical and international movements were often bitterly condemned. Arminianism, for instance, was seen as a form of popery. And just as the Israelites had loathed Egypt and Assyria, Catholic Spain and France were equally hated by Puritans. All non-Calvinists were the new gentiles. They were ripe for conversion to the true religion, by force if necessary, so that the desired unity of the coming new Israel would be achieved.

The Puritan's Israel, like its Hebrew equivalent, was to be a great 'nation' subduing all others. They saw England in this triumphalist light, the medium through which God's design would be enacted. Since the English were the Elect nation, they, like Israel, would eventually rule over the modern equivalent of the gentiles and lead the cause of international Calvinism against the forces of the Antichrist—Rome and popery in general. Just as the Canaanites were conquered by Old Israel, this manifest destiny would lead the righteous to conquer new lands and indigenous peoples, such as those in the Americas, and to do so for their own good and salvation. Like the Hebrew rabbis who elevated the Law above love and mercy/compassion, Puritans came to see their 'law' in the form of a commonwealth with kingly or magisterial rule, a polity free of oppression and whose temple, or national Church (if Presbyterian), would satisfy all free-born Englishmen.[75]

To further this quest, they were forced to seek allies. Alliances were made with French Huguenots, Dutch Calvinist rebels in Holland (in the later sixteenth century) or with forces fighting the Catholic Habsburgs during the Thirty Years' War (1618-48). Much to their annoyance, popish customs (like bowing the head at the name of Jesus during church services) had persisted far too long, further proof that the 'true' Reformation in England had not yet begun.

---

[75] That Cromwell's plan for a national church was quasi-Erastian is powerfully argued by Jeffrey Collins, 'The Church Settlement of Oliver Cromwell', *passim*; see esp. 22-3.

They believed the Kingdom of God had been expressly promised to them as a people of the Covenant as it had been to the patriarch and prophet, David, who was a man 'after God's own heart'.[76] The Elect regarded itself as a royal priesthood, King David's descendants. Their task was to set up the 'meantime' Kingdom on earth—as opposed to an inner 'end-time' Kingdom—in preparation for David's pre-eminent descendent, King Jesus, so that he may rule for eternity. In this way they were the harbingers of a new history in the same way Deutero-Isaiah depicted God as king, creator and controller of history, as an Almighty Being who would physically come to the aid of the remnant. History would only be fulfilled through the commonwealth of the saints.

Hence, in England in particular, among all of the nations of Europe, there existed a determination to develop the 'commonwealth' as a national entity with the manifest destiny of the sort already noted. The Puritan Kingdom was predominantly a physical place, therefore, with a new Jewish nation or chosen people through whom God was encountered. 'Commonwealth' implied unity and was vital since it mirrored one's personal relationship with God, something which translated itself into the outward polity of household, private estate and the national State. Typically, Puritan divine Robert Abbott looked to the Mosaic Law as the principal, practical and strongest guide for the godly to 'build according to [divine] pattern ... lay[ing] the ground of all saving and wholesome truth according to the Scriptures.'[77]

For Puritans, God was the great Judge of judges, the Chief of Magistrates. The 'Day of the Lord' was God's catastrophic judgment and His manifestation as king. Since He was king of all the earth, His order extended over the inferior natural world which needed conquering for the benefit of humanity. Puritans gave no thought to alternative thinking in this respect. It was simply God's declared will, the work of Providence, which was at the centre of everything. Nothing was possible without God. The purpose of Church and State was to reinforce the earthly Kingdom of the commonwealth. Both had legal jurisdiction over the lives of people. Magistracy was born of God, created to maintain order, the 'civil sword'. In this way, godliness would prosper. Their goal in purifying the Reformation was the wholesale renewal of Jerusalem (Zion) politically and ecclesiastically (which amounted to the same thing) through 'a reformation of manners'.

Order in society through a literal application of the Hebrew Testament's moral injunctions was one way the Elect saw their privileged and divinely-ordained purpose in clearer sight. Their lifestyles and attitudes, too, needed

---

[76] See 1 Sam. 13:14.
[77] Robert Abbott, *The Danger of Popery* (1625), 3, 5.

to reflect the Kingdom that was about to come. Thus they were eager to be models of minimalism. The less clutter the greater the space for holy thoughts and practice; cleanliness was next to godliness. Puritan simplicity went in tandem with a practical view of the world, with their opinions about governance at all levels of society and in the way, for the most part, they opposed mysticism.

There *was* a mystical aspect to Puritanism but it was invariably embraced in relation to Scripture, the Church, the legal system, social conformity and personal discipline. Outside these confines, mysticism was considered vague and anarchic, dangerously corrosive to the religious cement that bound all aspects of society together.[78] They were clearly sensitive to mysticism's capacity to lead a revolt against dogma and the authority it implied.[79] Generally, then, mysticism, was regarded as devilish and thus divisive.

In theory at least, Puritans believed that all congregations of true believers were ecclesiastically equal, that they deserved the same privileges, prerogatives, orders, administrations and forms of worship. The physical Church was the Kingdom of Grace or Kingdom of Heaven on earth and the vehicle by which the Word (the Bible) was taught. The keys of heaven were the ordinances of Jesus, which He instituted so that they might be administered by His Church.[80] The Church at large was immutable, its 'journey from the Fall to redemption [being] the very point and purpose of human history.' While all sides laid claim to its history, we shall see how the Friends attacked that history and the bibliolatry that upheld it.[81]

'Live thus idlely and naughtily': Bans on Pastimes

Not surprisingly, traditions and practices considered suspect came under the Puritan spotlight. While not all such disapproval should be levelled at Puritans—non-Puritans, too, wished to put down 'disorder' and enforce Sunday observance—they were more obsessive about it. Sunday sports and other pastimes were perceived as devilish intrusions into the godly routine. The Quakers, who may be likened to 'social' Puritans with little patience for the aesthetic, also joined the assassins of fun and popular culture. Fox's *To the Parliament of the Common-wealth of England* (1659), usually known as *59 Particulars*, and his *The Fashions of the World made Manifest* (1657) as well as Humphrey Smith's *To the Musicioners . . . the Singers, the Dancers* (1658) together with Thomas Taylor's *To the People of England*

---

[78] William Ames, *English Puritanism, passim* and esp. 4-5.
[79] Jordan, 'Sectarian Thought', 199.
[80] Daniel Cawdrey, *Vindiciae Clavium* (1645), 1-2, 4.
[81] Spurr, 'A Special Kindness for Dead Bishops', 313-15.

(1660) and *A Testimony against Sporting and Playing* (1666), are good examples of Quaker pamphlets putting a damper on traditional leisure activities that represented the 'miserable and woeful' condition of the people.[82] Allies in this regard, Puritans and Quakers nevertheless misread the mood of the people during the 1650s as we shall now see.

In addition to the political-ecclesiastical contradictions within Puritanism, discussed in the next chapter, it was perhaps inevitable that a social backlash to the Puritan reformation of manners would take shape.[83] It expressed itself in many forms, especially in 'miscellanies' such as John Phillips' *Wit and Drollery* (1661). Conspicuously popular in the mid seventeenth century, they were full of short poems from diverse sources such as verse collections, stage play texts, theatrical or musical performances, song books and ballads.[84] Usually royalist and framed to appeal to the appetites of readers, they became an essential vehicle for self-education and proved difficult to ban for this reason. By far the most common subject was love, particularly the torturous sufferings of the snubbed male woo-er. But poems praising or criticising women (particularly extreme beauty or ugliness) or lauding friendship, drink, sex and death, were also eagerly sought after. Overt political or religious commentary within their pages were rare, another reason for their survival.

With a general tone of playful recklessness, the poems jostled with letters, dictionaries of difficult words, notes of mythology, brief histories, riddles and jokes. They were also full of bawdy, jesting fun which the moralists condemned as 'coarse' (i.e. anarchic), 'lascivious' and 'obscene'. The bawdy poems and songs are an important genre of the period. Often funny and titillating, they reveal much about the relations between men and women as well as social, political and economic attitudes and practices. Over time, these and other forms of popular literature had the effect of promoting a defiant challenge to the intrusive and generally disliked Puritanism of the 1650s. After 1660 they continued to present bawdy scenarios. However, within the changed political context of that decade,

---

[82] Fox, *To the Parliament of the Comon-wealth of England, passim* (hereafter *59 Particulars*) and *The Fashions of the World made Manifest, passim* in *Doctrinals*, 109-12 and in *The Priests Fruits made Manifest*; H. Smith, *To the Musicioners*: 'from one who loved dancing and music as his life'; Thomas Taylor (1617/8-82), *To the People of England* and *A Testimony against Sporting and Playing* in *Works*, 160-1. Also William Bradshaw, *English Puritanism* (1641), title page, *passim* and Bauman, 'Observations of the Place of Festival in the Worldview of Seventeenth-Century Quakers', esp. 136-7.

[83] For Puritan attacks on popular culture see Collinson, 'From Iconoclasm to Iconophobia' in Marshall (ed.), 279. The Puritans recalled early Church Fathers such as Justin Martyr who, differentiating between Christian and pagan worship, taught that music deflected from worship and was used by infidels. Another Patristic figure, St. Cyprian, thought melody tempted the ears and relaxed Christian vigour; see Finney, 'Ecstasy and Music', 166-7.

[84] See John Phillips, *Wit and Drollery* (1661), 260-63 for an anti-Cromwell poem.

Chapter 1: 'Chariots & Horsemen of Israel'

their emphases quickly altered. Puritans were still mocked but the anti-government strain fell away.[85]

Other protests took a physical form. In the 1640s but especially in the 1650s, townspeople began publicly to register their distaste for Puritan restrictions. In Canterbury (Kent) in the late 1640s, a large crowd, playing football in the streets in flagrant contravention of the rules, prevented the Puritan mayor from opening the market. In fact, frustration at the parish level was frequently aired in public. It was usually directed at Puritan, particularly Presbyterian, ministers who were always in the minority and unpopular among those who took their Sunday observance seriously but who also loved the Prayer Book and traditional forms of Episcopalian ceremony, worship and celebration.

But it was satire's sword, and more specifically the long tradition of English poetry and stage drama, that subjected Puritan religious and social mores to microscopic scrutiny and exaggeration. They played a significant role in generating negative attitudes towards Puritans who were increasingly portrayed as greedy or sexually licentious hypocrites given to fanatical and rambling sermonising, or too eager to condemn fun and leisure as living 'idlely and naughtily'.[86] The poet, John Cleveland, described Puritanism as 'religion put [in] black', displaying his disdain for its moral austerity.[87] Samuel Butler's character, Sir Hudibras, was an acquisitive and dishonest Cromwellian Presbyterian officer with 'a Babylonish [i.e. confused] dialect which learned pedants much affect.'[88] Long before Cleveland and Butler, however, Ben Jonson's *The Alchemist* (1612) had Tribulation Wholesome and Ananias cunningly engaging Subtle's skills for minting money in order to finance the establishment of Puritanism in England. At first, Ananias reported Subtle as heathenish but is chided by Wholesome: 'we must bend unto all means that may give furtherance to the holy cause'.[89]

Puritans were sometimes depicted as holding hysterical and irrational fears of Rome or being slaves to scruples. Sir Thomas Overbury's *Characters* (1614) cast them as ignorant and 'bound to the Bible'. Corrupting the 'whole text', he chided, the Puritan's 'life [is] but a borrowed blast of wind.'[90] Though Overbury and Jonson were early in the piece, they and Shakespeare possessed enough insight to warn of the threat

---

[85] Smyth, 'Printed Miscellanies'.
[86] John Northbrooke, *Spiritus est Vicarius Christi in Terra* (1577), 'To the Reader', 3. See Gucer, "Not Heretofore Extant in Print': Where the Mad Ranters Are', 85.
[87] For John Cleveland, royalist/satirist, see Craik, *Sketches of the History of Literature*, iv., 41.
[88] Samuel Butler, *Hudibras* (1663), Canto 1, p. 5.
[89] *The Alchemist*, Act 3.
[90] Overbury, *A Wife, Now the Widow* (1614), Sig. F-F2.

from this as yet small group of zealots. In *Twelfth Night* (1600/1), Malvolio declares ominously: 'I'll be revenged on the whole pack of you.'

And so it was. With the cumulative effects of attacks dutifully suffered and their patience rewarded, the Puritan Long Parliament banned the theatre in 1642. Puritans (and Quakers) had also regarded plays as lies since actors assumed roles other than themselves. William Prynne, lawyer and MP, was certain that plays were the devil's doing—'sinful, heathenish, lewd, ungodly spectacles, and most pernicious corruptions'. He was countered by Sir Richard Baker in a magnificently cultured vindication of theatre in which stage plays were extolled as 'epitomes of the world's behaviour'. Baker was a thoroughly contemporary man in the mould of Sir Francis Bacon whose own Jacobean optimism cast a long and powerful shadow over the gloomy prognostications of the Puritans and sectaries.[91]

And yet not all Puritans supported the bans. Bulstrode Whitelocke, the senior government advisor, loved dancing, music and the stage. Even Prynne admitted plays could be 'tolerable, if not lawful' provided they were not obscene. The Protector, too, enjoyed secular music, dancing and the company of artists and writers. Perhaps he saw the first English opera, *The Siege of Rhodes*, which was allowed a performance in 1656. He had a taste, too, for the arts, something that might have come to the attention of the well-informed and disapproving among the Quakers like Richard Hubberthorne.[92]

However, Puritan efforts for a full ban on leisure activities continued unabatedly. Another attempt in 1647 aimed to fill loopholes in the 1642 Act. JPs were ordered to break up stage galleries and seats, and to denounce stage players as rogues and vagabonds. Anyone caught acting was whipped and those intent on watching shows, even prominent figures such as General Thomas Fairfax, army commander-in-chief before Cromwell, could be fined a considerable five shillings. The aristocracy and higher gentry, however, turned a blind eye to Puritan strictures by underwriting their favourite playwrights and actors by staging performances in their homes. With covert support such as this, the bans proved futile as the 1646 ballad, *The World Turned Upside Down,* prophesied. The song, foreseeing the eventual ruination of the bans, lamented the official eradication of Christmas 'killed at Naseby fight.'[93] Its lyrics might have had some effect. A slight thaw in government policy occurred in 1656 but did nothing to appease the growing resentment of the general public.

---

[91] William Prynne (1600-69), *Histrio-mastix* (1633, 1649), title page. For Prynne, see Lamont, *Puritanism and Historical Controversy, passim* and esp. 15-25; Sir Richard Baker, *Theatrum Redivivum* (1662), 141; Sir Francis Bacon (1561-1626).

[92] Hubberthorne, *The Good Old Cause Briefly Demonstrated* (1659), 2.

[93] 'Blackletter Ballads' at: <www.lukehistory.com/ballads/worldup.html>.

Christmas in fact became a focal point of discontent. Around the turn of the century, it had developed into a holiday of celebration. It gradually assumed a special significance, especially in the wake of the many personal and societal problems and tragedies generated by the civil wars. But Cromwell was appalled at the spectacle of people 'making a God of their bellies'. Consequently, traditional Christmas decorations were forbidden and in London soldiers were dispatched to invade homes and confiscate cooked food, with force if necessary. However, the celebration was precious enough for people to take to the streets in protest. Riots occurred in Ipswich, Oxford and Ealing in 1647 and, in the 1650s, ten thousand Kentish men resolved to restore the king if the government continued to omit the holy day from the calendar.

The banning of Christmas and Easter focussed bitter attention onto other restrictions. The gentry, for instance, 'never forgot the interruption to their accustomed authority, the imprisonment of family and friends, the disruption of rural sports and freedom of movement.'[94] Among the public at large, enforced constraints symbolised official denial of the people's need to express deep-seated fears, hates, resentments, grief and pain over four significant factors—the dire living conditions suffered by many, their often heart-breaking struggles to earn a decent living and the physical strain of working twelve-hour days, their continually devalued opinions, and anger at the betrayal of liberties promised during the late wars. For the majority of people, then, but particularly the wealthy, the restrictions were the final twist of 'oppression' and 'humiliation'. Clearly, over-zealous enforcements did more harm to the governments of the Commonwealth and Protectorate than anyone could have anticipated.

Satirical and literary reaction together with outbreaks of open defiance, were also representative of a deep-seated disgust. Besides the perceived failures of parliaments and governments, its principal target was the execution of King Charles whose shadow hung over England like Banquo's ghost. The violent dissolution of the Caroline government and the fate of its leader were increasingly seen during the 1650s as the worst disasters to befall England.[95] For this reason alone, the new king's entry into London in May 1660 was seen by most as cathartic. The monarchy took on a new meaning as a catalyst for much needed change and the sight of cheering throngs greeting Charles II as he rode from Dover to London to reclaim the throne seemed to say it all.

The arrival of the 'merry monarch' resulted in a sudden reappearance of maypoles, communal expressions of joy and relief at the disappearance of

---

[94] Underdown quoted in Christianson, 'The Causes of the English Revolution: A Reappraisal', 74.
[95] Pocock and Schochet, 'Interregnum and Restoration' in Pocock and Schochet (eds.), 155.

Puritan harshness and hopes for happier times. Hardly able to contain himself and quoting Psalm 126, John Douch, the minister at Stalbridge (Dorset), expressed his joy for the king's safety; 'Our mouths must be filled with laughter, and our tongues singing, for the great things the Lord has done for England.' John Evelyn 'stood in the Strand [in London] and beheld it, and blessed God.' And the author of *An Anti-Brekekekex-Coax-Coax* (1660) gloated that the return of the Prayer Book, the Episcopalian liturgy and the bishops would see the end to those 'croaking toads and frogs', the Puritans, the idiotic Radicals and the evil Quakers among them.[96]

Conclusion

During an era when life was precarious at the best of times, Calvinism gave God's selected men and women certitude for their worldly affairs. It was hierarchical, deterministic and a doctrine of discipline and obedience rather than a means of reconciliation with God, something the Quakers would claim exclusively for their embryonic movement. In England, the vast majority of educated laity was probably Calvinist in varying degrees, and it was natural that the prosperous classes, searching for a political role in the affairs of State in tune with their growing financial status and power, should look to Zürich or Calvin's Geneva as an example of biblical order and good sense.

The yearning among Puritans for a godly commonwealth became a reality in the 1640s and 1650s, the time of the rise of the Quakers. But the Kingdom to which they gave birth, a Kingdom on earth (of commonwealth and Church) and preceding the true Kingdom of Glory in heaven for the Elect, was too demanding an experience for the mass of people. The Puritan revolution fell victim to its own contradictions and satire's cruel sword but, more essentially, to the lingering charism of monarchy—the regicide was deeply unpopular—as well as the ever-strong local communities with their ancient traditions. These were too embedded in the English psyche for Puritanism to succeed in the long term. When it fell apart it did so quickly. Its powerful moral legacy, however, lingered on. Indeed, strains of Puritanism are still with us.

To understand more of Puritanism and the Quakers' reaction to it, we now turn to the main disputes within the Church in England and their reverberation upon the fledgling Quaker movement.

---

[96] See John Douch, *England's Jubilee*, 30; Evelyn, *Diary* (edn. 1908), 204; Anon, *An Anti-Brekekekex-Coax-Coax* (1660), Sig. B1 and 4, 7, 11; the title is the author's simulation of a frog's call.

Chapter 2: *'Ruins, Miseries and Calamities'*

- A Divided Church -

Two principal images emerge of the English Church between *c.*1580, roughly twenty years after the accession of Elizabeth I, and 1611, the year when the King James Bible was published. Our first image shows large segments of the English population as recusants ignoring a legal obligation to attend church services on Sundays. In this image, a fifth of the population of Kent, for example, absented itself on a regular basis.[1] A closer look reveals that, nationwide, many remained ignorant of important Christian beliefs throughout the course of their lives. As we move closer, Puritan divine George Gifford is heard to complain in 1581 that the religion of the 'common sort' was riddled with superstition and vice

> which overflows everywhere, that drunkards meet together and sit quaffing and [their] minister which should reprove them, to be one of the chief, when he should be at his study, to be upon the ale bench at cards or dice.[2]

These 'loose Protestants', as they were called, were constantly alarmed the authorities who, for the large part, considered them potentially rebellious. Despite their concern, however, the problem of church attendance in England proved resilient to remediation. In Ipswich, for instance, constables were periodically discharged to alehouses in failed attempts to round up absentees. Alehouses, usually frequented by the 'lower sort', were focal points for community interaction but considered dangerous since they were often patronised by dissenters particularly in East Anglia. Other authorities in towns like Blackburn (Lancs.) experienced the same futile exercise.

This image of the ecclesiastical landscape is enriched by colourful accounts of Sunday observance. In 1607, John Norden, a surveyor-topographer and social commentator, found to his horror that the poor who lived 'far from any church or chapel' were 'as ignorant of God or of any civil course of life as the very savages amongst the infidels'. Of those attending church some frequently 'nudged their neighbours, hawked and spat, knitted, made coarse remarks, told jokes, fell asleep, and even let off

---

[1] Spufford, 'The Importance of Religion', 3.
[2] K. Thomas, *Religion and the Decline of Magic*, 159; Gifford, *A Brief Discourse of Certain Points* (1612 edn.), 4.

guns.'[3] He complained that people usually arrived late, left early, failed to take part in psalm singing, whispered, stood and gazed around or stretched out to sleep. Sometimes they would loudly chide the minister hoping he would quickly finish the service so they could attend 'ungodly entertainments' such as church-ales and fairs where they could enjoy something better—bear-baiting, athletic competition, May games, dancing, drumming, gambling and occasional brawling. The latter caused considerable concern to local officers. Church-ales were usually held in church yards: it was generally thought they led to drunkenness, disorder, crime and illegitimacy.[4] Many parish clergy, too, registered consternation at the disorder among their congregations with noted preacher John Angier of Denton (Lancs.), for instance, complaining of parishioners who snored; he was sure 'hell was made for sermon-sleepers'.[5]

Motives for attendance varied, but towards the end of Elizabeth's reign and during the early Jacobean years it was not uncommon for the conscientiously religious to find themselves in the minority within congregations. For many of their neighbours, church attendance was a mere social gathering rather than a spiritual experience.[6] Many like Norden, though, ignored the fact that in isolated places people often found it difficult to attend church, particularly during the winter months. Observers such as him, and especially the Puritans among them, had high, even impossibly high, standards. And as an added ingredient we might fold in their sense of class and religious superiority.

Yet their opinions came to nought since the people's quest for fun and relief from drudgery proved unrelenting. The fact that entertainments were more enthusiastically preferred over worship is hardly surprising considering that English workers, labouring usually twelve hours or more each day for six days a week, saw Sunday as their day of relaxation. They could even lawfully claim compliance with King James' *Declaration of Sports* of 1617-18—re-issued by Charles in 1633—which sanctioned traditional Sunday games (especially those with military value) as well as Morris dancing. These opportunities were granted provided people attended church service first. James was concerned lest 'the meaner sort who labour

---

[3] For Norden see Coward, *The Stuart Age*, 78-9; also Thomas, *ibid.*, 161.
[4] The church or parish ale was a festival at which ale was made and donated for the event. Ecclesiastically and socially important, their chief purpose was the collection of parish dues and a profit for the church from the sale of ale by the church wardens. Profits kept the parish church in repair or were distributed as alms to the poor.
[5] See Haigh, 'Puritan Evangelism', 47-50 and esp 47-8 for John Angier. Haigh's paper is an excellent overview of the often chaotic state of the Church in Lancashire in the late Elizabethan era.
[6] Maltby, 'Parishioners, the Prayer Book and the Established Church' in Marshall (ed.), 258.

hard all the week should have no recreation at all to refresh their spirits.'⁷ The king was more charitable and accepting of peoples' foibles than the likes of Angier and Norden.

On the whole, parishioners begrudgingly made their way to church because they could ill-afford the fine, the 'Sunday shilling', or because they feared the excommunication that might follow with its loss of civil rights. Forced attendance, then, came with much resentment from the majority of people who were simply content to lead quiet and decent lives by being good neighbours, not harming anyone in word or deed, following Jesus' golden rule and saying their night prayers.[8]

Puritanism cannot be blamed for forced attendance but once in power it would pursue it with vigour. And as Puritanism spread in its various forms so too did the anger of the ordinary parishioner. We have already observed the bitter reaction to Puritan bans on entertainments and age-old rituals that gave mutual assurance and divine protection in a hostile social and natural environment. Unlike the typical Puritan, ordinary and usually illiterate church-goers had no interest in theology. They were more concerned with their *earthly* sojourn and, if religion incorporated 'pagan' elements such as divining and astrology, so much the better. Both were immensely popular and people would travel ten miles to consult a wise woman or wizard at a time when two or three miles of bad road was enough excuse to dodge church.

What of the ministers themselves? Despite a long and sometimes angry anti-clerical tradition in England up to the start of the civil wars, there were plenty of clerics, many of them Puritan, who loved their parishioners and were loved by them in return. The poor of John Angier's Denton parish were beneficiaries of his quiet and persistent ministry.[9] Ministers such as these were probably responsible for attracting the very poor to church, who normally would have opted for recusancy. Take Thomas Furnace, the minister of Castleton in Derbyshire who relished 'good drink very well'. At the beginning of our period he was famous locally for conducting marriages while drunk. On one occasion he 'nearly married one village lad to another (the would-be bride was in drag), and had . . . changed his surplice for a woman's petticoat.' While Furnace-type eccentricities and pranks were hardly the norm among the clergy, priestly misdemeanour was loudly

---

[7] Katz, *God's Last Words*, 65. The point has been made elsewhere that the *Declaration* was also aimed at popish recusants accused of enticing people from Sunday services, and the Judaising extreme of Puritan sabbatarianism of which the King strongly disapproved; see Fincham and Lake, 'The Ecclesiastical Policy of James I', 140.
[8] This is what Wallace describes as 'commonsense religion', paradoxically well advocated by Gifford's ungodly character, Atheos, in *A Brief Discourse of Certain Points* (1581), 72 (1612 edn., p. 211); see Wallace, 'George Gifford, Puritan Propaganda', 37.
[9] See Oliver Heywood, *A Narrative of the Life . . . of John Angier* (1683), 56.

censured and often exaggerated by the 'hotter' Protestant persuasion. As for Furnace, his popularity remained unscathed; even the 'best sort' supported him when he was 'excommunicated after running foul of a clique of richer husbandmen who had bought the lease of the parochial tithes.'[10]

Let us now turn to our second image. It is a different picture. Here we find the English *steeped* in Christian doctrine, convinced of its truth and well versed in its basic theology. Although during the seventeenth century the majority of people could not write, there was widespread *reading* literacy. People were able to read the Bible in its still popular Geneva form or its counterpart, the King James. A huge market for cheap religious literature was also symptomatic of the times. Godly chapbooks ('penny godlies') and advice books encouraged Bible study, family prayer and religious instruction at home. Many of these twopenny and threepenny godlies included manuals with lists of scriptural questions and proof texts, *and* a small catechism.[11] According to booksellers' inventories and trade lists, even by the 1680s penny godlies accounted for approximately one third of all printed material.[12]

As we examine the second image closer it becomes clear, as Spufford found of Cambridgeshire villagers, that even the humblest of folk during the late Elizabethan and early Jacobean eras thought deeply about religious matters and were often profoundly influenced by them.[13] Later in 1650, Oliver Heywood as newly appointed preacher at isolated Coley Chapel in the parish of Halifax (Yorks.) could report a 'multitude . . . flock[ing] to show their free consent and call of me'.[14]

So infused was religion into the consciousness of people that even entertainment could transmit Puritan ideas. In 1624, the year of George Fox's birth, one third of ballads were religious. They extolled the virtues of anti-popery, social reform, the need for a saving faith and scriptural stories. The fear of death and the last judgment were popular themes in both song and godlies alike. Illustrations also played an important role in the formation of religious opinion. In addition to the dramatic depictions of the Marion martyrs in Foxe's *Acts and Monuments,* the walls of alehouses, for instance, were often adorned with religious images and those in many a private home displayed scriptural passages for memorisation, recitation, reflection and personal guidance.

---

[10] Wood, *The Politics of Social Conflict,* 193-4.

[11] A catechism is a small, cheap, easy to carry handbook of questions and answers for teaching the principles of a religion.

[12] Walia, *Radical Religion in England and its Critics,* 4-5.

[13] Spufford, *Contrasting Communities,* 350.

[14] S. Thomas, 'Religious Community in Revolutionary Halifax', 94.

Chapter 2: 'Ruins, Miseries and Calamities'

According to Green, 280 different catechisms were published in England between 1549 and 1646, 'not counting a number of larger works on how to catechise or integrate the catechism with sermons'.[15] By the early seventeenth century, 750,000 official catechisms were in use along with perhaps 500,000 unofficial publications, remarkable for a country with a population of about five million people. Catechisms were also an educational tool, being pivotal in many grammar schools for the teaching of reading. The combination of increasing literacy especially in urban centres, and catechising and godly publications 'probably induced a considerable number to a study of Scripture, attendance at sermons, more advanced reading material, and quite possibly a deep faith'.[16]

An important feature of the century, and perhaps something at the heart of the Furnace story, was the popularity of local clergy and the Prayer Book whose rituals 'for such rites of passage as baptism, matrimony, burying the dead and the churching of women were widely accepted'. These activities helped to create a sense of family and communal identity. During the republic when JPs were permitted to conduct marriages, the practice alarmed many and was passively resisted chiefly because it was thought to secularise one of life's major rites of passage. Also, the publication of the banns in the market place was seen, like enclosures, to undermine family and community cohesion.[17] It seems that by the outbreak of the civil wars in 1642, the attachment to the traditional Church had increased; attendance was often correspondingly high. One study conducted of Southwark parish in London discovered that 98.5% of those eligible to receive Easter communion did so. At St. Saviour's in the same area, the enormous traffic of communicants forced the ecclesiastical authorities to stagger attendance. Even after its disestablishment in 1646, the Church in general maintained its strong emotional appeal: the majority of churchgoers were strongly conformist and thus could not be dismissed as mere 'parish Anglicans' or 'church papists' who blindly attended services.[18]

Concluding this short survey of religious observance in England, we can say with some confidence that its practice covered the wide spectrum between regular attendance and recusancy. It appears that, despite anti-clericalism and indifference, and even scepticism in some parts of the country (and at certain levels of society), the vast majority of people held firmly to their own beliefs and practices despite the theological controversies raging above them. All this suggests a degree of immutability accorded to the Church, recognition that it was more a 'civilisation' as

---

[15] Green in Walia, *Radical Religion*, 10.
[16] Walia, 12.
[17] Wrightson, *English Society*, 200-5.
[18] Walia, 14-15.

Tawney put it, something as normal as the pastures and the passing seasons.[19]

'In Gilded Lies': the 'Romish Sort'

Although the developing Protestant tradition was varied, it was generally united in its hostility to the old Catholic faith and particularly from among the 'hotter sort' within it. Nevertheless, during our period it was by no means clear what precise form any replacement for Catholicism might take. This uncertainty was compounded by the failure of the Calvinists to capture popular attention. To proselytise their message they relied largely on sermons, lectures, catechisms and Bible readings, but these were no match for the instant appeal of 'popish superstitions'—paintings, statues, woodcut illustrations, crucifixes, pageants, processions and mystery plays—all of which were readily available. Another reason accounts for the fact that the 'old religion' should not be seen in terms of the 'doctrinal affirmation or drams of conscience' of counter-Reformation Catholicism but as a 'set of ingrained observances which defined and gave meaning to the cycle of the week and the seasons of the year, to birth, marriage and death.'[20]

When James ascended the throne, anyone who was not Protestant was 'papist', 'popery' generally being a much hated and feared system especially among Calvinists. Indeed, long before the turn of the century, 'popery' and 'papist' were already well-worn terms of abuse, and it was common to hear songs depicting Catholics as traitors and rebels. The Roman Church, particularly in its counter-Reformation guise, was thought to possess the mark of Cain. There was good cause for such fear. During the hundred years to 1690, the geographical reach of Protestantism shrank from one-half to one-fifth of Europe's landmass in favour of Rome, a significant temporal Power during the period. Catholicism had a looming, and to many, a menacing presence.

Meanwhile gossip, innuendo and rumour continued throughout the century to poison public opinion against Catholics. Wild calculations of Catholic numbers, for instance, were plentiful and probably led Puritans like Thomas Wood in 1577 to claim that papists were 'marvellously increased'. Beliefs such as his lingered well into the future and assumed greater significance with a supposedly larger presence of Catholics in London and among the peerage.[21] Also, the proliferation of Catholic publications added

---

[19] Tawney, 'Religious Thought', 472.
[20] Bossy, 'The Character of Elizabethan Catholicism', 39.
[21] Clancy, 'Papist-Protestant-Puritan', 228. One-fifth of peers in 1641 were Catholic (121 peers); by 1700, 10% were peers and gentry. See an anti-Catholic sheet by a parliamentary enquiry into the burning of London, *London Flames Discovered* (1667), 12-13, a work which inflated the number of Catholics in London in 1665 to 7,000.

Chapter 2: 'Ruins, Miseries and Calamities'

to the fear of Rome. They were plentiful in the years prior to the civil wars. Even in the later Stuart period (when both the quality and quantity seem to have declined), the corpus of Catholic writings far outweighed those of the Baptists and Quakers and was second only to the established church.[22]

For many, popery was a running sore despite the fact that, even as the Jacobean period dawned, its hold on ordinary people had weakened considerably. It was long in retreat from the high-water mark of its political engagement during the Elizabethan period.[23] Even as the storm over the gunpowder plot of 1605 raged—it had also shocked most Catholics—the new king, eager to calm parliament's anger, was confident enough to assure MPs that not all adherents of the 'Romish religion' were disloyal. Indeed, he was adamant that loyal Catholics could still attain the highest preferments of State; in this he was as good as his word. And yet his mercurial nature, or perhaps his well-honed sense of diplomacy, compelled him to go beyond his own assurances to his Puritan subjects by drawing up a new Oath of Allegiance in 1606. It was designed to outlaw rebellion and preserve his concept of the divine right of kings, but it was more specifically directed at Catholic resistance theories, especially those of Cardinal Roberto Bellarmine and Francisco Suarez. Both Jesuit intellectuals had affirmed a subject's right to depose heretical or tyrannical rulers in the wake of Pope Pius V's Bull, *Regnans in Excelsis* (1570). The Bull condemned Elizabeth I as a 'servant of crime' and as a heretic. It released Catholics from allegiance to her but excommunicated those who obeyed her.[24] Many English people saw the shadow of the pope everywhere in a seventeenth century variant of 'reds under the bed', and their vicious language left nobody in doubt about their concern. To Puritans such as Thomas Wilson, the pope was the Antichrist, neither man nor woman, but a monster who revelled in a devilish and brutish nature.[25] This definition from a 1655 edition of his *Complete Christian Dictionary* mirrored popular sentiment among his co-religionists. It was an attitude that would turn lethal during and after the reign of Charles I when the governments and parliaments of the Commonwealth and Protectorate railed against the devil in the Vatican.

One reason for Catholicism's survival in England was its stubborn refusal to see itself other than the one, true Church. Haigh tells us that

---

[22] Hibbard, 'Early Stuart Catholicism', 13.
[23] See Bossy, *The English Catholic Community, passim*; esp. 31.
[24] Walia, *Radical Religion*, 43. Roberto Bellarmine (Bellarmino, 1542-1621) was a member of the Holy Office (he was its principal censor) and other Vatican congregations besides being chief theological advisor to the Holy See. A later Bull by Pope Gregory XIII in 1580 allowed Catholics to obey Elizabeth in all civil matters until the opportunity arose to overthrow her.
[25] T. Wilson, *A Complete Christian Dictionary* (1655), 491.

during the sixteenth century 'there was a substantial survival of Catholicism in the parishes served by ex-priests.' Many of these ministers, now of the established Church, had remained loyal to Rome, ministers such as the vicar of Whalley (Lancs.). Dismissing the English Church as defiled, he encouraged his parishioners to pray 'according to the doctrine of the pope in Rome'. But such defiance gradually dwindled as the century drew to its close.[26]

England's adjustment from Catholicism was a slow and painful affair. It accelerated in the later years of Elizabeth's reign as unreformed Catholicism gave way to periodic waves of virulent Calvinism and also to counter-Reformation Catholicism itself characterised by an introverted, quasi-monastic life-style.[27] The effect was the emergence of small but more cohesively theological and disciplined groups of Catholics whose outlook and approach were more aggressive. This form of Catholicism was largely composed of labouring people though it was dominated by a seigneurial minority in the southern, wealthier counties where it enjoyed the protection of great county magnates. Some, like those in Norfolk and Essex, were powerful enough to evade the authority of the local Protestant magistrates.[28]

While Catholicism certainly grew during the sixteenth century, overall the total number of its adherents remained small. In Yorkshire in 1604, Catholics comprised a mere 1.5% of the population and they probably accounted for only 35,000 in England at the time of James' entry into London in 1603. Nearly forty years later their number had grown to perhaps 60,000 or 1.13% of the English population. Most Catholics lived in the North where the majority, as elsewhere in England, were agricultural labourers ('diggers') or workers in other rural occupations—according to diaries, commonplace books and court, tax, census and parish records.[29] In Lancashire (pop.150, 000) where 'widespread popular Catholicism' was supposedly practised, the towns of Preston, Wigan and Liverpool, in the period 1603-41, were home to 4,000 'papists' many of whom were plebeian. Some villages in Lancashire like Clifton and Blundell were entirely Catholic.[30] The denomination survived relatively well due to the county's far-flung setting, its geographical spread and poor communications—many of its roads were fit only for packhorses—and the incapacity of central government to successfully enforce anti-recusancy laws north of the Mersey. Indeed, so isolated were 'those Northern counties', both as a concept and as an actual region, they were frequently

---

[26] Haigh, 'The Church of England, Catholics and the People' in Marshall (ed.), 239.
[27] Coward, *The Stuart Age*, 80-1.
[28] Blackwood, 'Plebeian Catholics', 44-7.
[29] Terrar, 'Gentry Royalists or Independent Diggers?', 315; this work contains a good depiction of class differentiation among the Catholic population.
[30] *ibid.*, 320.

linked in the popular imagination to witches, feuds, lawlessness and Catholic rebellion.[31] The region was considered one of the 'dark corners of the land'.

That Lancashire had long been the heartland of post-Reformation English recusancy probably led some like the Bristol Presbyterian and Quaker-hater, Ralph Farmer, and a host of others such as the Independent Samuel Eaton, to presume a constant hatching of plots in the dreaded North.[32] Rumours nurtured the belief that Catholics were barbarians and they continued well into the century. After the so-called Popish Plot of 1678, for instance—it was actually a hoax by Episcopalian minister Titus Oates[33]—Thomas Shadwell's *The Lancashire-witches and Tegue ODivelly, the Irish Priest* (1682) could typically promote Lancashire's famous ancient link with popery and witches, particularly on those wicked 'Pendle-Hills'. His main popish characters, Tegue O'Divelly and Smerk the servant, were 'fools, knaves . . . and arrogant'.[34]

Memory of the Marian martyrs and the Armada (1588), horror over the Inquisition in Europe, plots against the Crown, deep suspicion of Charles I's Catholic wife, Henrietta-Maria, and growing fear among parliamentarians in the 1620s of Catholic-sympathising bishops, all served to produce much paranoia. During the 1600s, hearsay about Catholics was a powerful social and political tool in stoking fear in Whitehall and elsewhere about 'Romish' intentions. One such incident involved a young Dominican friar and scion of the Arundel family, Thomas Howard. The exiled Charles II had sent him to England in May 1659 to raise troops against the new Protector, Richard Cromwell. The result was the shambles during August of that year in Cheshire known as Booth's rebellion. Such was the national execration of Catholics that it prevented Ralph Farmer and others of like mind from admitting that it was an English Carthusian friar who had leaked Howard's plans.[35] Conspiracy theories were also alive and well in 1660 when Puritans were only too eager to believe the existence of a Vatican plot whereby the civil wars and the conflicts with the Dutch in the 1650s were clever concoctions to steer English attention from the ambitions of Rome and

---

[31] Bossy calculates that during the mid seventeenth century more than 20% of households in Lancashire and Durham, and between 11-20% in Northumberland and Yorkshire, were Catholic recusant; see Bossy, *The English Catholic Community*, 404-5.

[32] Ralph Farmer, *The Great Mysteries of Godlinesse and Ungodlinesse* (1655), 77; Samuel Eaton, *The Quakers Confuted* (1654), Sig.A4^v; also Mullett, *Catholics in Britain and Ireland*, 4.

[33] Titus Oates (1649-1705) with his friend, Dr. Israel Tonge (also a passionate anti-Catholic cleric), invented a Jesuit plot to assassinate Charles II, massacre Protestants and then place the King's Catholic brother, James (Duke of York), on the throne.

[34] Dolan, *Whores of Babylon*, 16. Thomas Shadwell, playwright and Poet Laureate in 1689.

[35] Jarrett, *The English Dominicans*, 182.

Spain for world conquest. Supposedly masterminded by another Dominican, the late philosopher and astrologer Tommaso Campanella, the conspiracy proved baseless.[36]

Numerous rumours were inspired by the many complicated intrigues that surrounded the royal Court. Worried gossipers pointed to the apparently close link between King James' favourite, the Duke of Buckingham, and Catholicism. Concern, too, arose over a secret clause in the proposed royal marriage settlement, negotiated by Buckingham, between Prince Charles and the Spanish infanta (before his marriage to Henrietta Maria); the settlement guaranteed freedom of worship for Catholics in England. And yet these particular fears may have been justified. Rushworth's *Historical Collections* ([1659] 1682) informs us that James, keen to curry favour with Spain in the early 1620s, released many Catholic recusants from prison and began favouring Rome-leaning prelates.[37]

Rumours later intensified when Henrietta-Maria granted a prestigious presence to Catholics at Court and assisted Catholic religious groups to re-establish themselves, including groups like the feared Dominicans of Inquisition infamy. Early in her husband's reign, she aggravated government suspicion by encouraging the Spanish embassy to open its chapel for public offerings of the mass while making her chapels in Somerset House and St. James' Palace available for the same purpose.[38] Large crowds eagerly attended the services and the government could do little to prevent them. Tensions created by incidents such as these developed greater potency thanks to the hugely successful counter-Reformation.

During the Commonwealth and Protectorate, Puritan fear and hatred of Rome were much stronger forces than their dislike of Episcopalians. John Thurloe, Cromwell's influential Secretary of State and spy master, constantly received letters such as the one dated 9th August, 1653, from 'NN', lately of Spain, who was convinced that London swarmed with 'numerous monks, friars and jesuits' who were an 'abomination' and 'dangerous guests' with a tendency to 'haunt bordellos', and who were 'returned to the old vomit despite parliament's decrees'. As Thurloe's correspondence shows, Catholics were normally seen as 'bastards', 'covert', 'crafty', 'clannish', 'disloyal' and 'distrustful'. They were 'filthy Jesuits', 'Franciscans', 'masters of disguise', 'occultists', 'sexually promiscuous', 'murderers' and they dealt 'in gilded lies'. The phobia generated by

---

[36] Tomasso Campanella, *Thomas Campanella an Italian Friar and Second Machiavel* (1660), *passim*. See 'Preface' by the rumour-monger William Prynne.
[37] Rushworth, *Historical Collections* (1682 [1659]), 62.
[38] Loomie, 'London's Spanish Chapel', 402-3.

Chapter 2: 'Ruins, Miseries and Calamities'

Catholicism and Spain probably spurred Cromwell's government into compiling lists of people considered to be of dubious loyalty.[39]

Protestant, and particularly Puritan, anti-Catholicism achieved a greater acuity in regard to Spain and Ireland. 'The Papists in England', declared Cromwell, 'have been accounted Spaniolised ever since I was born [in 1599]'.[40] By the 1640s, with popish scares commonplace, plans by Archbishop William Laud and Charles I to introduce Roman style liturgies into the Church only made matters worse for Catholics and exacerbated fear of foreign threats, real or imagined. Of course, foreign interference could never be discounted. The memory of the Armada hung in the nations' psyche as a relatively recent event. And during Charles' reign, the threat of invasion from Holland or Spain hovered over the English like the sword of Damocles.[41] The 'Turk', too, symbolised the eastern Antichrist. 'Mahometans' were the ultimate strangers. Regarded as heathens, they were seen as an ever-present danger to Christian Europe.[42] Also, regular raids by pirates-cum-kidnappers from the Barbary Coast, against whom governments were helpless, only reinforced the idea that anything foreign was evil. It was understandable in such a climate that assaults were made on Catholicism particularly by Calvinist lecturers ('town preachers'). Though Catholics under republican rule were less persecuted than previously despite their royalist or loyalist proclivities, smear campaigns against them were unrelenting.[43] When the Friends appeared, they too attacked Roman Catholicism and popery in all its manifestations.

English and Scottish hatred of Rome was coupled with the reduction of the Catholic Irish to animal status. They were devourers of raw flesh and cows' blood, 'degenerate,', 'brutish,', 'alien,'. 'violent' and 'anthropophagi' (cannibals). They were 'offal,' the very 'dregs of humanity' and 'bots that crawl on the Beast's tail.' Every English man and woman knew that the Irish were inveterately 'corrupt,' their minds idolatrous and closed to the Word of God, that they were prone to pillaging and tyranny. Poet Edmund Spenser, author of the famous *Faerie Queene*, proposed a policy of mass starvation, widespread confiscation of land, ruthless relocation of peoples

---

[39] See *Thurloe* (1742), i. 403. For 'in guilded lies' see Robert Abbott, *The Danger of Popery* (1625), 3.

[40] Clancy, 'Papist-Protestant-Puritan', 228.

[41] Holland, a republic, practised Calvinist austerity but was tolerant in religious matters.

[42] The seventeenth century meaning of 'Turk' meant followers of Islam, a cruel tyrannical person, ferocious, wild, unmanageable, and a human to shoot. An English version of the Qu'ran appeared in 1649.

[43] 'Royalists' were devoted to the King's person, 'Loyalists' to the office and authority of the position. See D. Smith, *Constitutional Royalism*, 319.

and the establishment of military rule over the whole island.[44] Even English Catholics joined the chorus of hatred. Though not entirely disparaging, in the early 1570s the Jesuit Edmund Campion had labelled the 'mere Irish' as 'loose to lechery above measure'.[45]

So far as the Puritans were concerned, the Irish were no better than the Midianites and thus ripe, as the Book of Judges told them, for civilising through forcible deliverance into the new Israel of the Puritan Kingdom.[46] English troops at Cashel in 1647 observed how dead Irish soldiers and civilians grew tails like the devil. Puritan hope of taming the 'wilde Irish' lay with their New Model Army. As an avenging angel it would sack the country with the aim of exterminating Catholicism to prepare the way for more English plantations. In anticipation, and anxious the army should ensure protection for its investments and profits, the largely Presbyterian London authority eagerly bought up vast portions of land. The land grab in Ireland had the dual purpose of ridding the city of undesirables and surplus population.

The burghers of London, in fact, were only continuing a long tradition. Between 1610 and 1640, many English and Scottish Protestants had already settled in the north of Ireland, thus beginning the Presbyterian domination of Ulster. More followed in the wake of Cromwell's savage ethnic cleansing campaigns of 1649 in whose grisly shadow Hugh Peter, Cromwell's warrior chaplain and fellow regicide, declared a new promised land.[47] Although there were exceptions like William Walwyn the Leveller and Vincent Gookin, the Surveyor-General of Ireland, English attitudes and behaviour towards the Irish resembled those of the Nazis towards the Jews.[48]

---

[44] Brady, 'Spenser's Irish Crisis', 3. See also Spenser, *A View of the Present State of Ireland* (1596) in *Works*, 201-58.

[45] Edmund Campion (1540-81), *The History of Ireland* (1633), 13-15. He was also complimentary calling the Irish at times kind-hearted, sharp-witted and lovers of children and learning.

[46] S. Barber, 'Nothing but the First Chaos', 26, 33-4. In Jg. 6-8 and Nb. 25:32 the Midianites (or Madianites) are the irreconcilable enemies of Israel who murder Gideon's brothers. The vengeance taken, in conformity with the law of the times, meant Gideon exterminated the tribes (Jg. 8) which henceforth disappeared almost entirely from the history of Israel. The Catholic Irish were to be similarly exterminated.

[47] Barber, *ibid.*; Hugh Peter (1598-1660), mentioned in *Cambridge*, i., 229. In a letter (17/Sept/1649) to William Lenthal (Speaker of the Commons), Cromwell maintained his campaign would, 'tend to prevent the effusion of blood for the future' regardless of the 'remorse and regret' such massacres produced. See Cromwell, *Letters from Ireland* (1649), 9.

[48] For Gookin see Coughlin, 'Counter-currents in Colonial Discourse' in Ohlmeyer (ed.), 70-73. See also Gookin's letter (22/11/1656) to Oliver Cromwell in *Thurloe*, v., 646-9. And Perrot, *Battering Rams against Rome* (1661), 123-4. Perrot calls his fellow Irish a 'bleeding people' (p. 123).

Chapter 2: 'Ruins, Miseries and Calamities'

English animosity towards, and compulsion to subjugate, the Irish underlines the seriousness with which Protestants considered the threat from Ireland to their very existence. The country's 1641 rebellion-cum-civil war was the tipping point, for instance, for influential author and politician, William Prynne, in rendering his complete allegiance to parliament. More generally, the rebellion confirmed the evil nature of the popish Beast, its culpability in genocide no less.[49] Hysterical estimates of two hundred thousand Protestant dead in Ulster stuck fast in the English folk memory. It convinced Sir John Temple, Master of the Rolls and himself born in Ireland, to press the government to deny all rights to the Irish, something to which the poet John Milton gave enthusiastic assent. In Temple's *The Irish Rebellion* (1646), which set the tone for English distrust of the Irish on both a national and local level until well into the nineteenth century, the author also advocated a scorched earth policy towards Ireland's 'cruel, enraged and barbarous' people.[50] Col. Richard Lawrence, Governor of Waterford, eagerly endorsed Temple in urging a form of *apartheid* so that the ethnically distinct Irish would not contaminate the English.[51]

The true figure of Ulster dead was dramatically lower of course— perhaps between three and four thousand out of a population of 30-40,000. This was surely appalling, but even if the true figure were then known, the horror of the nearly 1,300 Protestants slaughtered in County Armagh would have alone been enough to have raised Cromwell's ire to volcanic levels and justify his blood-soaked revenge in 1649. In a genocidal campaign, Cromwell ferociously sacked Drogheda and Wexford. Ethnic cleansing saw the forced removal of Catholics to poverty-stricken areas west of the Shannon.

While anti-Catholicism and its corollary, hatred of the Irish, were national unifiers for the English, they intensified during a century in which, ironically, there were relatively few Catholic clergy in England. In 1603, only 230 secular priests and about 255 religious from the great orders (mainly Dominicans, Jesuits, Benedictines and Carmelites) served the 'faithful'. By 1630 the figure had risen to about 700. Most of these men were sons of the gentry. Though dedicated, they tended to serve their own class more than their poorer co-religionists.[52] Their secret entry into the

---

[49] Lamont, *Puritanism and Historical Controversy*, 56-7, 68.
[50] Noonan, 'The Cruell Pressure', 151 where she quotes Temple's letter (Dec., 1641) to King Charles, State Papers (Ireland), 63/50.
[51] Temple's 'ethnic' suggestions—the Irish were a mongrel race descended from Scythians, Gauls, Africans and Goths—are found in *The Irish Rebellion* (1646), 2; for scorched earth policies see Sig. A5. See also Ohlmeyer, 'Introduction' in Ohlmeyer (ed.), 4-5. For Lawrence see Coughlin, *ibid*.
[52] Hibbard, 'Early Stuart Catholicism', 11 (29*n*); Terrar, 'Gentry Royalist or Independent Diggers?', 318-21.

country was organised from the English College at Douai in the Spanish Netherlands (now in France) where they were trained for missionary work. However, while it is true Jesuit numbers rose four-fold up to the outbreak of civil war in 1642, Catholic popular activism remained a myth, although the belief surfaced from time and time that the faith was dangerously dependent on foreign Catholic princes. In fact, despite the fanaticism and notoriety of the gunpowder plotters, scholars agree that English Catholics were generally loyal to the Crown, and especially so during times of national crises from the Armada onwards.

This was certainly true of richer Catholics but, as the century progressed, it would be a mistake to assume political cohesion among the Catholic community as a whole. Poorer Catholics, for instance, were not averse to supporting parliament and the 'Levelling sort' against the royalist order. On a social level, the situation was equally complicated. It was not unusual for Catholic and Protestant gentry to share a degree of class collegiality in respect to their life-style, social intercourse and intermarriage. When the son of the fervently anti-Catholic Quaker, Isaac Penington, turned papist he was tolerated by his family. During the 1630s the former Anglican priest turned Jesuit, Humphery Leech, and fellow Jesuit, John Fisher, were allowed to live out their days in peace, Leech in Cheshire and Fisher in London. This was a more common feature of English life than we may otherwise imagine. Even Cromwell could show leniency towards papists. Over a period of two years, Sir Kenelm Digby was allowed access to the Protector and argued tolerance for his fellow Catholics. In the 1670s, the Earl of Anglesey was happy to dine with his Catholic neighbours while at the same time writing a book attacking Jesuits.[53] Like the gentry he encountered elsewhere, Lord Anglesey would have socialised with people equally valuing their long links to land and ancestry. His attitude reflected a greater degree of give and take at all levels of English society than formally supposed by scholars.[54]

At the same time, while some continued in the faith largely for cultural reasons, all Catholics looked upon the fractiousness of their Protestant countrymen with disdain as they observed a multiplicity of non-Catholic Bibles. To them it signified the lack of authority among their apostate neighbours and rulers. And while many prominent Catholics were accepted locally as we have seen, they wisely cultivated the protection of highly-placed friends at Court and elsewhere. All in all, they never lost hope for their country of its return to the old faith and perhaps in their own lifetime.[55]

---

[53] Arthur Annesley, 1st Earl, 1614-86; urged tolerance post-Restoration, esp. towards Catholics.
[54] For the practices of social and political toleration in England see Cressy, 'Conflict, Consensus and the Willingness to Wink', 132-3.
[55] Questier, *Catholicism and Community in Early Modern England*, 289.

Chapter 2: 'Ruins, Miseries and Calamities'

John Foxe's 'Acts and Monuments': the 'Book of Martyrs'

Hatred can harbour long memories, and that towards Catholicism was fuelled by popular publications, the most important being the Geneva Bible and Foxe's *Martyrs*, the latter to which we now turn in more detail. Both were superb sources of propaganda for the Protestant cause. *Martyrs'* three detailed volumes portrayed the burnings of some 273 Protestants mostly at Smithfield in London between 1555 and 1558 during the reign of Mary Tudor whose consort was the Spanish king, Philip II.[56] According to Loades, the Queen's policy constituted 'one of the most ferocious and concentrated persecutions of the whole Reformation period'. He continues:

> More people died at the stake and in prison in England [1555-8] than suffered at the hands of the Spanish Inquisition and the French *chamber ardente* (the French King Henry II's attempt to hunt out 'heresy') together over the same period.[57]

Among the martyrs were the prominent churchmen, Thomas Cranmer, Hugh Latimer and Nicholas Ridley who all died at Oxford. The martyrs were never far from people's daily lives. As a boy, George Fox may have listened with keen attention to eyewitness accounts of the execution in 1612 of Edward Wightman in nearby Lichfield, the last person to be burned for heresy in England. And it is possible his mother, Mary, told stories of relatives who may have likewise perished. Fox was very quick to affirm his mother's 'martyr stock' in his *Journal*.

Martyrs' wide acceptance owed much to an Elizabethan directive ordering a copy to be held in every cathedral upon publication in 1563. Many parishes willingly followed suit. Elizabeth was keen to see its wide dissemination for two reasons—Foxe was an ardent defender of the Elizabethan Settlement, the name given to the 1559 Acts of Supremacy and Uniformity that set out the basis for Protestant England, and his work helped to destroy her sister's reputation.[58] *Martyrs* was hugely successful on both counts. In fact, so revered did the work become that copies were chained to walls to prevent theft.[59] With its gruesome woodcuts and

---

[56] Mary Tudor (1516-58; Queen, 1553-8); 'Royal supremacy' refers to the 1559 Act of Supremacy and Uniformity that outlined the basis for a Protestant England.
[57] Loades, 'The 'Bloody' Queen', 43.
[58] *ibid.*, 45.
[59] See Haller, *Foxe's Book of Martyrs and the Elect Nation*, 224. Also Loades, *ibid.*, 41 and see *Martyrs* online at: < http://www.hrionline.ac.uk/johnfoxe/edition.html>. Chained copies of *Martyrs* can still be seen in various English churches as in the twelfth century
St. Lawrence's in Appleby-in-Westmorland (Cumbria); its three-volume copy dates from 1631. See also Houlahan, *Writing the Apocalypse*, 41-9.

unalloyed anti-popery, the book went into ten editions in the century after Foxe's death in 1587. Even by James' accession, *Martyrs* enjoyed a secure reputation as a collective historical narrative that saw the English identifying as a people set apart with a manifest destiny. In recounting the epic struggle between true Christianity and the Antichrist represented by the Vatican, *Martyrs* kept alive the memory of the Protestant victims in the popular imagination. From its pages emerged an *apologia* for a national consensus against Rome. In fact, so powerful was the work's resonance with the perennial Roman threat, it featured in many later publications such as *Tithes No Property* (1659) by Quaker John Crook and more prominently in *The Arraignment of Popery* (1667) by George Fox and Ellis Hookes. Thus, along with their fervid anti-popery, it helped the English define a national identity, to look beyond Augustine of Canterbury's arrival in Kent in 597—for instance, to the Celtic fringe—for sources of their Church's foundation, autonomy and authority.[60]

John Foxe's powerful use of Revelation gave *Martyrs* a strident apocalyptic potency, and for this reason it was spiritual milk to the Puritans but also to the Radicals. George Fox was familiar with its 1641 edition. Its woodcuts and language particularly influenced him and he would not have missed some of the work's other major characteristics—its prophetic tone and anti-violence.[61] Consider, for instance, how it recalled the courage and sufferings of yesteryear in language usually associated with the young Quaker movement:

> If it be his Truth and Gospel that we possess, let us walk in the light of his Truth, and keep our selves within the compass of his Gospel . . . that who cannot see our excessive outrage in pompous apparel, our carnal desires and unchaste demeanours without fear of God . . . avarice insatiable . . . little or no mercy to the poor, racking of rents and fines, bribing and taking unmeasurable? What should I speak of the contentions and unbrotherly divisions amongst us, most lamentable to see . . . Such were the times once of the Church before the horrible persecution of Diocletian; for so we read, such hatred and disdain through much peace and prosperity of the Church to creep in amongst the Church-men . . . Let us therefore, having light given us, walk like the children of light.[62]

---

[60] Spurr, 'A Special Kindness for Dead Bishops', 324.

[61] For Foxe's nonviolence see Dickens, *The English Reformation*, 379.

[62] Foxe, *Act and Monuments* (ed. 1641), i., 36-7. George Fox might have read this edition prior to his entry into Lichfield where he had a vision of a massacre 'in Diocletion's time'. There is, however, no evidence of such a massacre. See *Journal*, 71-2. Foxe's work might have inspired Friends to record their sufferings and the eighteenth century appearance of Besse's *Sufferings*.

Radicals such as the Friends, but also those like Independents John Everard, Giles Randall and John Saltmarsh, looked to *Martyrs* as a manifesto for their political, social and economic revolution. They were not content with merely interpreting sacred texts, using them instead to challenge authority where this was deemed necessary. In *Martyrs* they found an important tool for their critique.[63]

Puritans, Arminians and Predestination

The Elizabethan Settlement preserved and codified many Catholic traditions which were subsequently included in the Prayer Book. According to Kishlansky, the Settlement was Calvinist in belief, Roman Catholic in structure and liturgically promiscuous. It retained elements of the old sacramentalism while the Thirty-Nine Articles of Faith were Calvinist in word and spirit.[64] The Settlement may well have been a fudged compromise between fundamentally irreconcilable forces, but it left room for divergent opinions. This was of advantage to the pragmatic Elizabeth, who understood the need for wariness of the Catholic gentry and the increasing number of Puritan merchants and financiers in London and East Anglia. England, in fact, was the one European country where the government tried hard to accommodate Catholicism and traditionalists on the one hand and reformers within the English Church on the other.

Since Puritans held that Church and State were co-extensive, they believed that responsibility for every sphere of life, including public order, consequently fell within the jurisdiction of the Church. For this reason, they were staunch upholders of the existing social and political apparatus, and remained so throughout the Jacobean period and well into Charles' reign. Tragically, as the Settlement began to unravel under the weight of Charles' intransigence but also because of the divisions already existing within the Church, the English would re-learn the bitter lesson that ecclesiastical schism inevitably led to political collapse.[65]

Despite the small number of Puritan divines—by 1603 the 570 preachers comprised High Churchmen, Presbyterian and Congregationalists (Independents)—Puritanism itself had long been a significant feature of English religious life, especially since Elizabeth's reign during which its influence grew steadily. Many divines began acquiring well-paid lectureships as well as support from the gentry and merchants, particularly

---

[63] See Chakravarty, *Like Parchment in the Fire*, 260.
[64] Kishlansky, *A Monarchy Transformed*, 72-5, esp. 74; Brayshaw, *The Quakers*, 16.
[65] Nuttall and Chadwick, *From Uniformity to Unity*, 4, 8.

in London. By the end of her reign, Puritans had progressed to the point where they enjoyed a majority in the House of Commons.[66]

By 1603 many Puritan MPs were confident enough to petition King James into modifying church services along Presbyterian lines. Chief among their targets were the abolition of the sign of the cross in baptism, the use of the ring in the marriage ceremony, freedom for ministers to dispense with church vestments, the abolition of non-residency and reform of Church discipline and the ecclesiastical courts. The courts were an illustration of Church (and therefore royal) power and possessed extensive jurisdiction over marriage and divorce, defamation, the probate of wills and every conceivable aspect of private morality. They had enormous influence over the type of punishments given to individuals (and the degree of humiliation incurred) as well as the resulting social ostracism and excommunication which, we remember, denied rights and access.[67]

An educated and preaching clergy was also of great importance to reformed Protestantism, and it would prove effective in countering critics during the 1630s and 1640s such as Thomas Edwards, whose *Gangraena* was not only hyper-critical of Radicals but also of the clergy itself. By 1640, a few years before the first civil war, clerics comprised between 12-13,000 individuals of whom 4,000 were High Church, 1,000 were strict Puritans and the remainder middle-of-the-road with less definable sympathies. An unknown but sizeable number lacked a true vocation, some clearly being time-servers and/or social climbers. Many clerics were habitual drunks or guilty of incontinent behaviour or extortion towards their neighbours, something that resulted in a number of inactive parishes or those with skeletal parish administrations. Many illegitimate children owed paternity to ministers. An albeit heavily biased report from the Long Parliaments' Committee for Scandalous Ministers (est. 1640) entitled *First Century of Scandalous, Malignant Priests* (1643) went into two editions. Accusations levelled at named clerics included 'buggery with parishioners and horses, baptising bastards, refusing the sacraments to individuals, excessive drinking, foul language, fornication, adultery and loving the pope'. For the committee's chairman, John White, episcopacy and conventional church government were 'evil and justly offensive and burdensome to the kingdom'.[68] Such behaviour was indeed the cause of scandal among the godly as it was among many Radicals like the Friends.

---

[66] Dickens, *The English Reformation*, 369-70.
[67] K. Thomas, *Religion and the Decline of Magic*, 181.
[68] Bridenbaugh, *Vexed and Troubled Englishmen*, 286 and see John White, *passim*. There were Puritans who were prepared to accept bishops (if strictly supervised by parliament) rather than accept Scottish Presbyterianism.

Chapter 2: 'Ruins, Miseries and Calamities'

With an uneducated clergy came a generally poor knowledge of Scripture. Their pre-1620s training, being almost entirely liturgical, resulted in a shortage of ministers with adequate preaching skills. By the 1630s this shortfall had become a normal feature of the Church's life, with many clergymen either not bothering to preach or lacking the capacity to do so.[69] However, by the end of the 1630s a marked improvement in the quality of clergy had taken place, largely due to William Laud, with about thirty to fifty percent of ordinands trained to some satisfaction. The Puritans among them would prove to be keen ministers and preachers, publishing sermons while encouraging lay prayers, Bible study and the keeping of spiritual journals. Where they could, they omitted or simplified liturgies, decorations and vestments. And yet, while most clerics were graduates by the 1630s, a degree was still no guarantee of a sound education or training since it could be granted without examination.[70]

In the meantime, King James, while shrewdly making few changes to the Settlement, was concerned to reassure his subjects as to his Calvinism, though we cannot be certain how fully he gave it his assent. It is well to keep in mind that, besides important matters of religion, his principal focus was the survival of his kingdom, which he considered to be his by divine right.

Calvinism was typified by five points:

- Human beings were totally depraved and incapable of generating any spiritual good.
- From the beginning of time God elected some to be saved, not for their intrinsic goodness but for His own praise and glory ('election').
- Jesus died for the sins of the Elect. All those for whom He died were guaranteed salvation ('limited atonement').
- At an appointed time the Elect would be drawn irresistibly to the Saviour.
- The Elect were granted grace on a daily basis to persevere in faith and holiness to the end. None of the Elect could fall completely from the state of grace.[71]

God divided humanity, then, into the chosen (the Elect) and the damned (the reprobate); human beings were permanently estranged from God, irredeemably fallen. This state was ineluctable since no one could break the bonds of divine *diktat*. If salvation was impossible, it was a duty of the

---

[69] Ashley, *Life in Stuart England*, 4.
[70] A. Milton, *Catholic and Reformed*, 534.
[71] This summary of Calvinism is merely a convenient description of a complex theology.

damned individual to glorify God through good works (this-worldly endeavours) using the Scriptures as their only permitted guide. But advocating good works as a means of salvation, as the Friends did, was considered open defiance of that overwhelming reality, the almighty divine will. Culprits who proposed such were 'filthy' and doomed to an eternity of hell-fire.[72]

Even though James appeared to lend it his royal approval, this form of predestination was considered extreme by a number of leading English prelates such as Lancelot Andrewes. Along with his mentor, Richard Hooker, he believed it was both cruel and contrary to the sacraments which, he maintained, were a means of accessing grace and salvation. Consequently, Andrewes and his followers refused to favour the 'godly' above other members of their congregations since everybody in their view was equal in worship. It was Hooker's writings (especially his *Laws*) together with the influence of Andrews and the Frenchman Peter Baro and *his* pupil, William Barrett, that helped check growing Calvinist power in the English Church. Peter Baro, Lady Margaret Professor of Divinity at Cambridge, taught that Jesus died for everybody ('unlimited atonement') and that human free will was important for salvation. The tussle between Barrett and the more traditionalist and Calvinist Heads of Cambridge University, a Calvinist stronghold, came to a head during a controversy over the nine Lambeth Articles of the mid 1590s, a proposed addition to the Prayer Book that reinforced predestination.[73]

During a sermon in April 1595, Barrett claimed that no-one 'by certainty of faith' could be sure of their own salvation. Even despite his recantations in May and then in January 1596, the failure of the Calvinists' nine propositions exposed the vulnerability of their position within the

---

[72] The map of predestination was intricate for two reasons. First, it had European dimensions—England was doctrinally a part of Calvinist Europe—and yet it was equally as divisive an issue among Europe's Protestants, particularly in Switzerland and the United Provinces (Holland), as it was among Roman Catholic theologians. Within Catholicism, the Dominicans gave it some support but the Jesuits opposed it in keeping with the Council of Trent's upholding of free will and its famous denial that predestination to salvation could be known with certainty. The Council regarded predestination, therefore, as presumptive knowledge of God's purposes. Second, because of the controversy surrounding predestination, people lost sight of the fact that Calvin's *Institutes* had subordinated it to God's absolute sovereignty and the successful establishment of a theocracy, the Kingdom of God on earth. For Calvin, double predestination was, as Foster tells us, neither fundamental nor necessary; see Foster, 'Liberal Calvinism', 5.

[73] See the debate between historians White, Lake, Lamont and Tyacke in White's 'The Rise of Arminianism Reconsidered' and 'The Rise of Arminianism Reconsidered: a Rejoinder', *passim*; for references see esp. the latter, 217 (1*n*, 3*n*). For a useful overview of the 'Nine Articles' controversy, see: <http://en.wikipedia.org/wiki/Lambeth_Articles> and also Gilliam and Tighe, "To Run with the Time", *passim*.

Chapter 2: 'Ruins, Miseries and Calamities'

Church.[74] Andrewes' compatriots, including noted bishops Richard Neile, John Buckeridge and John Overall, were strengthened in their refusal to countenance a doctrine they believed not only threatened their episcopal status but undercut the official Church's soteriological mission of assisting people to achieve salvation. But by 1604, the king had grounds to fear something worse—a wholesale takeover of the Church by the presbytery, which prompted his famous retort, 'no bishop, no king'.[75] He had merely to glance at Europe to see the worrisome effects of Calvinism on the *Vatican*'s monarchical authority—its attacks on the Roman *magisterium* and councils, on its dogmas, traditional roles and civil authority, on the power of the Roman clergy over the laity and on its canon law and the mass.

Dismissed as papists and free-willers by many Puritans, the Hooker-Andrewes school found itself saddled with the derisory sobriquet 'Arminian' after Jacobus Arminius, a member of the Reformed Presbyterian Dutch Church and Professor of Theology at Leiden University. As with many in the English Church, Arminius had questioned Calvin's doctrine of predestination although he never fully abandoned it.[76] However, he had particularly opposed 'supralapsarianism', upheld by Calvin's son-in-law and Arminius' former teacher, Theodore Beza. Supralapsarianism is the belief that God, in decreeing the saving or damning of each person before creation, permitted the Fall so that the decree could be carried out.[77] Arminius and his English supporters understood Jesus to have died for everybody. Furthermore, they maintained that each person possessed grace prior to requesting it and were morally responsible for their own actions and spiritual destiny. Arminius believed that people possessed free will and could therefore extinguish their innate capacity for salvation; because of this, good works and prayer were essential.[78]

Ecclesiastically, English Arminians went further than their European colleagues. They took advantage of the Settlement by balancing some

---

[74] Barrett revoked his first recantation in July.

[75] James made this remark at the Hampton Court conference (1604) he assembled for the principle factions within the Church of England. See Barlow's account of the proceedings, *The Sum and Substance* (1605), 36.

[76] See *Institutes* (1634), iii., chp. 21, p. 451.

[77] Supralapsarianism (*supra lapsum*) is the alternative to *infra lapsum* in which God permitted the Fall and *then* decreed election as a means of saving an Elect. See Collinson, *Godly People*, 10.

[78] Jacobus Harmenszoon (Arminius, 1560-1609) of Oudewater nr. Utrecht in Holland, professor of theology at Leiden from 1603 until his death. For a fine outline of the 1620s Arminian controversy see H. Schwartz, 'Arminianism and the English Parliament 1624-1629', *passim* and esp. 41-5. John Buckeridge of Wiltshire, great friend of Andrewes and chaplain to King James, tutor to William Laud. He was Bishop of Rochester (1611) and Ely (1628); John Overall of Hedleigh (Essex), Bishop of Coventry and Lichfield (1614-18), and Norwich (1618-19).

Catholic ceremony with Protestant belief. While they were suspicious as any educated Briton of the Roman Church and its 'corruption'—they believed corruption did not exist in the English Church—they took heart from King James' comment that Rome was indeed the mother Church though 'clogged with many infirmities'.[79] At the same time, they cautioned against rabid anti-Catholicism believing that it encouraged aberrant beliefs of the type embodied in strident forms of Puritanism. In this sense, noted Arminians were primitive ecumenists though never closet Catholics.[80]

Almost inevitably Arminians found themselves positioned between two irreconcilable forces. On one side lay virile Calvinism and on the other a generally perceived suspicion that Arminians planned a return to Rome, the Antichrist. Arminians had seen in the Settlement a better way of acclimatising Calvinist belief to conditions in England. In affirming the break with Rome, but affirming the Reformation had gone far enough, they agreed with Calvin over Christology, salvation, ecclesiology, sacraments and justification by faith alone. Their stance was similar to that of Arminius and the Zürich and Strasbourg Marian exiles (as opposed to the more disciplinarian and doctrinaire Geneva exiles). And yet, while Arminians and Puritans were loath to split the Church, their bitter disputes over predestination, free will, church tradition, the importance of beautiful church architecture and liturgy, episcopacy and the royal leadership of the Church continued to divide them up to the 1640s. Similar arguments raged elsewhere. The Baptists, for instance, suffered a painful split into two persuasions, General Baptist (Arminian inclined) and the hard-line Calvinist or Particular Baptists. In the 1650s, well-known divines such as Richard Baxter, the Radical John Goodwin and the Quakers were also influenced by Arminianism.[81]

Back in 1611, however, and keen to broadcast his Calvinist credentials, the king appointed the Calvinist George Abbot as Archbishop of Canterbury over Arminian Lancelot Andrewes. Though doubts were expressed about Abbot's suitability—he had no pastoral experience for instance—it was a largely uncontroversial appointment since the English Church, as we have seen, had accommodated forms of Calvinism for over fifty years.[82] Later, during the 1618-19 Synod of Dordrecht (Dort) in Holland, convened to settle a controversy in the Dutch churches following the rise of

---

[79] James took the Vincentian canon, the fifth century *Commonitorium* of Vincent of Lérins. He saw himself as a 'Catholic Christian' adhering to Scripture, the three creeds (Apostolic, Nicene and Athanasian), the first four general councils of the Church, and the Fathers of the first five hundred years. See Spurr, 'A Special Kindness for Dead Bishops', 314.

[80] Richard Montagu (1577-1641).

[81] A reminder: for example, Arminian attitudes to predestination compared to Calvinist views of the same.

[82] Holland, 'George Abbot, 'The Wanted Archbishop'', 172.

Arminianism, James was quick to support the Synod's condemnation of Arminianism's principal doctrines embodied in the *Five Articles of the Remonstrants* (1610).[83] Instead, he strongly endorsed Dort's five elements of Calvinism outlined above with the same vigour as he had opposed the appointment in 1610 of the suspected Arminian, Conrad Vorstius, to Arminius' vacant chair at Leiden.[84]

To English Arminians, Dort was nothing less than closet Presbyterianism but the underlying concern of both parties at the convocation was the right to express different opinions—*libertas prophetandi* it was called—in what was a highly restrictive and increasingly confusing theological and ecclesiastical environment. Despite much acrimony, the delegates were able to generate sufficient compromises and qualifications to produce an agreed set of doctrinal formulations against Arminianism.[85] James' underlying preference, probably influenced by Bishop Overall, was to arbitrate between Puritans and Arminians in England in the hope that a third way or 'broad Church' might be acceptable to all. His shrewd ecclesiastical preference was for an effective bishops' bench rather than a single pre-eminent theology. As a result, towards the end of his reign he began to favour a number of Arminian clerics in the hope of achieving a better balance between the two factions.

Rise of the Arminians

Between 1619 and 1621, the Arminian bishops, including Andrewes, Neile, Buckeridge, Overall and Richard Montagu (with Laud in the background at this stage), had succeeded in gaining the ear of the ageing king and his heir, Charles. Laud worked quietly on the king's favourite, the Duke of Buckingham (Sir Charles Villiers). Together, they grew adept at excluding Calvinist influence at Court and from ecclesiastical preferment. Arminian success meant that in 1624, not long before he died, James could exclaim, 'I think it all one to lay down my crown to the pope as to a popular party of puritans'. As already mentioned, he may also have been reacting to the virulently negative Puritan attitude to the ill-fated Spanish match (1620-1)

---

[83] For the five articles see Glossary and: <www.cresourcei.org/creedremonstrants.html>. See also Kendall, *Calvin and English Calvinism*, 142, 149-50.

[84] James had Vorstius' book, *Tractatus Theologicus* (1610), burnt in public in London, Oxford and Cambridge. Vorstius (1569-1622) was dismissed by the States-General in 1612 and exiled to Gouda, eventually dying in Tönning (Schleswig-Holstein, Germany) possibly as a Socinian as James had originally suspected. See James' *Declaration Concerning Vorstius* (1610).

[85] See A. Milton, 'Authority and Reason' in Hastings *et al* (eds.), 110. The dispute between the Remonstrants and the Dortists is called the Quinquarticular Controversy since both parties challenged the five doctrinaire points of the other.

between Charles and the Infanta, but also to the support Arminian bishops were giving him in foreign policy matters, especially with regard to his conciliatory approaches to the Catholic powers. So it was that the Arminians were on the way to their 1630s ascendancy. However, they would not gain absolute control of the Church for not all Charles' bishops would be Arminian.

The 1620s saw both Stuart kings contending with a still hard-line, overwhelmingly Puritan House of Commons now angry at the growing influence of Arminians in the Church and at Court. Members were particularly incensed by Laud's provocative claim in February 1626 that Puritans were fermenting revolution in both Church and State. They became further enraged in 1628, three years after James' death, when Laud was appointed Bishop of London and the equally hated Montagu translated to Chichester. Laud's new position was highly influential but it was also strategic since it gave him control of the London printing press. The two appointments hardened Puritan attitudes towards the new king, Charles, who was by now proving less amenable towards Puritans than his father.

The relationship between King and Commons deteriorated further in 1628 when the MPs' Petition of Rights condemned Charles' forced loans from the gentry as well as his arbitrary government and martial law. These were indeed unhappy times symbolised by the pinning of the Speaker of the House to his chair in 1629, while a resolution was passed identifying religious innovators like Laud, Montagu and the king himself as enemies of England. In the same year Charles suspended parliament and so began his eleven-year 'personal rule'. Further, in 1630 the death of the third Earl of Pembroke meant the loss of the most influential Calvinist Privy Councillor. It only served to clear the way for Laud's accession to the Chancellorship of Oxford University.[86] The Commons continued to oppose Arminians up to the bitter end of Charles' reign in 1649, ever suspecting them of manoeuvring the nation into the arms of Rome. There *was* substance to their fears: some Arminian theologians appeared to have indeed incorporated Catholic thinking into Church of England orthodoxy. Richard Montagu, appointed in 1625 as Charles I's personal chaplain and Canon of Windsor, was a special Puritan target in this regard along with Laud.

By the mid decade, both men and Arminians in general had positioned themselves well enough politically to press home their advantage by putting their case to the test. Relying heavily on the work of the late Benjamin Carier, a Jacobean royal chaplain and a former Canon of Canterbury, Montagu produced two highly controversial tracts, *A New Gag for an Old Goose* (1624)—a response to a pro-Catholic pamphlet distributed in his parish called *The Gag for the New Gospel*—and *Appello Caesarem* (1625),

---

[86] Marvin, *The Conversion Experience of Two Radicals*, 27.

an intensification of views expressed in *A New Gag*. Richard Neile was instrumental in negotiating the progress of both works through the censor. According to Tyacke, the tracts 'radically reduced the points of difference separating the English and Roman Churches and redefined Puritanism in terms of schismatic Calvinism'. The king asked the Dean of Carlisle, Francis White, to declare on *Appello Caesarem*. White concluded that it contained nothing controversial and authorised its publication.

The controversy around Montagu continued to simmer throughout the decade. We find the strictly Puritan William Prynne, for instance, issuing blistering attacks on Montagu in *The Perpetuity of a Regenerate Man's Estate* (1626) and *The Church of England's Old Antithesis* (1629), the latter reformulated into *Anti-Arminianism* in 1630. Though magisterial in their detail, *The Church of England's Old Antithesis* and its successors were bitter works in which Prynne hurled the entire Thirty-Nine Articles, the nine Lambeth Articles and Barrett's recantation of 1595, the Prayer Book and *Book of Homilies*, the complete history of the English Church, an accusation of Pelegianism and a huge and impressive list of theological opinion, all conveyed with great skill, at the 'heretical and grace-destroying novelties' of Arminianism.[87]

Pressurised by a hostile parliament and countering ongoing criticism that both his works championed Arminius at the expense of the Thirty-Nine Articles, Montagu made a tactical recantation in late 1628, repeatedly protesting his allegiance to the established Church, even to a form of predestination.[88] Although ably supported by Buckeridge, in the eyes of Calvinists he committed a treasonable act by constantly refusing to identify the pope as the Antichrist. Parliament's attempt to impeach Montagu failed, however, and the Arminians were handed a notable victory. As Tyacke comments, they had helped to redefine Puritanism

> in terms which included the very Calvinism that previously had linked nonconformists to the leaders of the established Church, and the nonconformist element in the former Calvinist partnership was driven into an unprecedented radicalism. The Arminians and their patron King Charles were undoubtedly the religious revolutionaries in the first instance. Opposed to them were the Calvinists, initially conservative

---

[87] See Prynne, *The Church of England's Old Antithesis* (1629), 42-8 for Barrett's May 1595 recantation; also Prynne's dedicatory preface in *Anti-Arminianism*, esp. Sig.A2. I have used its 1630 edn. See Schwartz, 'Arminianism and the English Parliament', *passim*.

[88] White, 'The Rise of Arminianism Considered', 36 (and 9*n*). I agree with White's view of Montagu's predestinarianism. See Montagu, *A Gag for the New Gospel?* (1624), 178-9; and see Cust, 'Was there an Alternative to Personal Rule?', 341-2 for the protracted political manoeuvrings between Arminians and Calvinists in the late 1620s.

and counter-revolutionary, of whom a typical lay representative was John Pym.

No wonder Pym, a leading parliamentarian, and Prynne rejected 'that odious and fractious name of Puritans'.[89]

Other points of long-felt contention for Puritans included the defection of Caroline divines John Pocklington and John Normanton to Rome. They had followed Carier who had gone over to Rome in 1614.[90] The Dean of Ely, William Fuller, also startled them by pronouncing 'no difference between our Church of England and the Church of Rome in matter of substance but in circumstance only which might easily be reconciled'. Andrewes and Overall approved of Roman-type confession to a priest, and a future bishop, Brian Duppa, while preaching before an undeterred Charles on Good Friday, 1635, lamented Henry VIII's 'unhappy breach' with Rome. He urged the king 'to take into his consideration the reuniting of this kingdom with the Roman Church'. The sermon naturally fuelled mounting Puritan fears.[91] In addition, as Cross tells us,

> the movement of bishops from one see to another of more strategic importance in the early years of the reign left Calvinist Protestants in no doubt of the direction from which the wind was blowing, and the advancement of Laud in particular provided the clearest indication of the king's intentions.[92]

But more was to follow. Reasonably reliable rumours circulated about Charles' favourable disposition towards the Inquisition as a means of discipline.[93] Also in 1635, Montagu is said to have told the pope's agent, Gregorio Panzani, that he was ready to subscribe to all the pope's articles except transubstantiation, an admission that only served to deepen Puritan suspicions that Arminians aimed to increase the power of its 'Romish' clergy. It was an understandable concern considering Charles' assurance to Panzani that,

> there was much in the Roman Catholic religion with which he agreed, and that nothing would please him more than a healing of the breach between the Roman and the Anglican Church . . . saying [further] he would rather have parted with one of his hands than have had such a

---

[89] See Tyacke, 'Puritanism, Arminianism and Counter Revolution', 133.
[90] Benjamin Carier (1566-1614); see his 1613 letter to King James from Liège cleverly entitled, *A Carrier to a King* (1614), *passim*.
[91] Questier, 'Arminianism, Catholicism and Puritanism', 57-9.
[92] Cross, *Church and People*, 177.
[93] Questier, *Catholicism and Community in Early Modern England*, 489-90.

breach occur. [When] one of his courtiers ventur[ed] to say that such sentiments were dangerous Charles instantly averred: 'I say it again: I wish I had rather lost one of my hands!'

As Aylmer says, Charles' remarks were certainly impolitic in view of his oft-repeated claim to fully support,

> the Church of England as by law established ... for a Church in the legal and ecclesiastical sense Protestant, in the generic and theological sense Catholic (as in the wording of the creed and elsewhere in the liturgy).[94]

Arminians had long understood the significant advantage in regarding the pope, if not as spiritual leader of western Christendom, then as its leading patriarch. Early in the century they had canvassed Catholic opinion by entering into debate with the erudite though intolerant Cardinal Bellarmine and were probably encouraged in this respect by King James' albeit unrealistic diplomatic overtures to the Vatican between 1603 and 1605 in regard to Christian unity. The king had opined that the Roman Church was indeed the true one since it believed in the incarnation and the trinity, though he was quick to stress it was in need of redemption.

His own and Arminian attitudes towards Rome should be seen in the wider European context in which theologians could jump confessional boundaries by borrowing from different traditions. Nevertheless, William Gouge, strongly Puritan in the mould of William Perkins and William Ames, spluttered with indignation over the 'treacherous' refusal to acknowledge the 'immortal feud'. He correctly understood that Arminian inability to recognise the Roman Antichrist was a denial of Election. What, then, were English Protestants protesting against? Was not the spiritual existence of the new Israel now in question? For Gouge the very identity of Protestantism hung in the balance.[95]

Holding their ground against such attacks, Arminians and, later, their cousins, the Laudians, defended Hooker's by now famous *Laws*. Hooker had opposed the Calvinism of Archbishop of Canterbury John Whitgift, biblical literalism and the way Puritans 'by one trick or other always restrain[ed] [the Word] in the way they 'delivered [it] unto us in sermons'. From which Hooker drew the conclusion that some 'special property or

---

[94] References to Panzani and Charles are from Nuttall and Chadwick, *From Uniformity to Unity*, 7. Panzani was agent to Pope Urban VIII. See also Gregg, *King Charles 1*, 278 and Aylmer, 'Collective Mentalities: 2', 11.
[95] A. Milton, *Catholic and Reformed*, 530. William Gouge (1575-1653); among other works he authored was *Of Domestical Duties* (1622); see Fincham and Lake, 'The Ecclesiastical Policy of James 1', 182.

quality... [is] nowhere found but in sermons'. Quakers would criticise all churchmen for the same reason, displaying impatience with those who reconstructed Jesus' message from the words of a mere book.[96]

It should not be assumed, however, that Whitgift's staunch Calvinism suggested unwavering support for Puritans. On the contrary, he disciplined them over their disdain for established Church practices. And he increased the powers of the Court of High Commission, a move that enabled him to persecute Puritans with greater energy and sometimes cruelty.[97] Understandably pro-episcopate, Whitgift was satirised for such by the mysterious Puritan pamphleteer, 'Martin Marprelate', as 'your Canterburiness'. Marprelate accused him of favouring papists and recusants, a slander given that Whitgift's inaugural lecture as Lady Margaret Professor of Divinity at Cambridge focussed on the identity of the pope as the Antichrist.[98]

Richard Neile, Laud's patron and Bishop of Durham in 1614 (when parliament had attacked his laxity towards Catholics) also weighed into the controversy. He alerted the king to the institutional Church's claim to apostolic succession, an argument for episcopacy. The Church, he maintained, was also the expression of Christian society as a whole, rather than the preserve of an Elect, and that it grew and changed organically as circumstances developed. After all, the Arminians continued to insist— again, like the Quakers later—Jesus had died for *everybody*, not merely for a mysteriously chosen few.[99]

An Intricate Theological Environment

Neile's views reflected a very public intra-Protestant brawl over the question of the Roman Antichrist and the apocalyptic interpretations it spawned. These in turn were characteristic of the intricate theological environment in England whose pedigree ran strong from Elizabeth's reign. Good examples were the 1584 sermon by the openly anti-Calvinist and future bishop Samuel Harsnet, and the Lambeth Articles controversy.[100] H.

---

[96] See Freiday, 'The Early Quakers and the Doctrine of Authority', 14-15.
[97] Brayshaw, *The Quakers*, 18.
[98] Marprelate may have been the Independent (or 'Brownist') John Penry who was later martyred.
[99] D. Hirst, *England in Conflict,* 43. John Whitgift (1530-1604), Archbishop of Canterbury (1583-1604); Richard Neile as Bishop of Rochester (1608-10) appointed Laud as his chaplain. Neile was Bishop of Durham in 1617, a Privy Councillor in 1627 and Archbishop of York in 1631 following Samuel Harsnet. See Questier, 'Arminianism, Catholicism and Puritanism', 57.
[100] Samuel Harsnet (1561-1631), Archbishop of York from 1629. His 1584 sermon propelled him before the High Commission and a stern silencing from Whitgift which he obeyed. It remained unpublished until appendixed to Richard Stuart's *Three Sermons* (1657).

Chapter 2: 'Ruins, Miseries and Calamities'

C. Porter has commented that the story of the Elizabethan Church was one in which the veins of doctrine ran side by side, of debate rather than unchallenged Calvinist oration.[101] We have seen how this was an ever-present feature of James' reign as indeed the conversion to Rome of prominent divines Humphery Leech and Benjamin Carier testified; the two men were certain they were the tip of an iceberg of dissent.[102]

We have noted how Calvinist divines could disagree with Luther's and Calvin's doctrines and make tactically positive admissions in regard to Rome. At the same time, hotter Calvinists were unwilling to concede that Calvin approved of bishops for England and Hungary. Even Perkins could admit some common ground with Catholics.[103] And the situation grew more complicated as the years passed.[104] The Rev. John Williams of Peterborough (Cambridgeshire), a Calvinist, keenly supported Sunday sports. Also in Peterborough, Arminians publicly dissented from Laudian excesses during the 1630s by preaching against his judgments as chairman of the Star Chamber.[105] Examples such as these were by no means isolated and were born of the intense theological debates of the Jacobean and Caroline years including the 1630s.

At parish level, too, the situation presented a mixed image. Underdown suggests that there was an extensive 'grey area' between Arminians and Puritans; people at all points on the spectrum admitted to being Protestants with much in common.[106] That the climate of varied ecclesiastical opinion was bewildering and even frightening to many was reflected, among other things, in poetry. George Herbert, an influential cleric and MP, tried to steer a course through the growing polarisation of Laudian and Calvinist thinking. He rejected the Hooker-Laudian emphasis on the holiness of place and object but remained steadfastly committed to the priestly role and to the uniformity of the Elizabethan Settlement. His poem, *Priest to the Temple* (1633), was a Laudian attack on what he considered the cold-intellectualism of Puritan preaching. In *The Windows*, he contrasted wordy preaching styles with colour and light, the transcendence guaranteed by a mystical listening upon the Word. The God he knew was the God of everyone and, in valuing community, he depicted God as a generous Lord of the Manor. The windows of which he wrote also opened him to the 'brittle crazy glass' of

---

[101] Porter quoted in White, 'The Rise of Arminianism Reconsidered', 35.

[102] For Leech, see his *A Triumph of Truth* (1609) whose dedicatory preface was supplied by Carier.

[103] Such as considering Mary as the mother of God, the efficacy and use of saints' relics and that many Catholics were certainly saved. See Perkins, *A Reformed Catholic* (1598), 246 and White, 'The Rise of Arminianism Reconsidered', 35 (8*n*).

[104] A. Milton, *Catholic and Reformed*, 534.

[105] See Sharpe, *Remapping Early Modern England*, 352.

[106] Underdown, 'A Reply to John Morrill', 472.

human frailty but also to the atomisation of the spiritual in the guise of a privileged (i.e. Elect) inner experience. Should these two converge, he prophesied, they would bring further disputation and religious dysfunctionalism, which would result in societal and political disintegration.[107] Herbert was not alone in his concern. Thomas Collier, the Baptist, blamed England's woes on the 'episcopal and Presbyterian faction'. But such warnings went largely unheard until as late as 1650 when many Puritan clerics were forced to admit that a dangerous partisanship now typified the religious environment.[108]

Countdown to Civil War

In contrast to King James, who sought to erect a system of Church governance by combining elements of High Church belief and practice and Presbyterianism, the obdurate Charles forced into radical opposition those who were previously willing to accept the existence of a bishop's bench.[109] But it was not until after his visit to Scotland in 1633, during which he registered shock at the apparently chaotic and dilapidated condition of the Scottish Church, that the fatal decision was made to impose bishops and the Elizabethan Prayer Book on its people, what their Presbyterian ministers called the 'superstitious service-book'.[110] Charles' belief, like his father's, that Presbyterianism was 'anti-monarchical' was too ingrained and he wanted to teach its followers a lesson in authority. His arbitrary decision was taken with the enthusiastic support of Laud, newly appointed in 1633 as the first Archbishop of Canterbury who was not completely Calvinist. A deeply unpopular choice, particularly with Calvinist factions, he accompanied Charles on the trip.

Ill-feelings towards Laud had deepened since he had begun chairing the Star Chamber and appointing supporters as justices. Harsh punishments came the way of Puritans, particularly lecturers and prominent thorns-in-the-side like William Prynne. For his anti-theatre *Histrio-Mastix* (1633), interpreted as an attack on the royal couple, Prynne was deprived of a portion of his ears in 1634 and the rest three years later. With Laud's authoritarian and ambitious nature, his aloofness and single-minded determination, it was not long before he became the most passionately hated Archbishop of Canterbury in English history. Sir Harbottle Grimston spoke

---

[107] George Herbert (1593-1633), *The Windows* (1633) and Sharpe, *Remapping Early Modern England*, 360.

[108] Newcomb, 'The English Puritan Clergy's Acceptance of Political Parties', 56.

[109] Brayshaw informs us that even during the 1630s there were Puritans who were prepared to accommodate bishops so long as they were stripped of Laudian accretions and restored to the Edwardian and Elizabethan patterns. See his *The Quakers*, 26 (2n).

[110] Anon, *The Beast Wounded* (1638), 10 (see its margin notes).

Chapter 2: 'Ruins, Miseries and Calamities'

for many in the Puritan parliament by describing him as 'the sty of pestilential filth' and the cause of 'ruins, miseries and calamities'.[111]

The descent into civil war quickened when Charles and Laud finally imposed their plans for uniformity in worship and church organisation upon England and Scotland during 1637 and 1638. The measure, which flagrantly ignored the two nations' different religious traditions, gave birth to an organised petitioning movement and the Scottish National Covenant. Both paralleled moves to establish a provisional government in Edinburgh; such was the level of Scottish anger. The so-called Bishops' Wars resulted with a tenth of Scottish males taking up arms. Charles' attempts to overthrow the rebel government failed, the Scots forcing his capitulation in 1639 at Berwick on the English border. In the meantime, the Scottish dissidents had contacted their English counterparts such as John Pym, by now the Speaker of the Commons, to co-ordinate resistance to the king. The ploy succeeded and the Commons withheld funds from Charles for his war effort. The refusal was in tune with the scant enthusiasm among England's county militias for any further hostility with its northern neighbour with whom many had religious sympathies. Rather than march northwards, therefore, the undisciplined militias and others were content instead to raid churches in order to smash communion rails and stained glass windows, whitewash popish images and rip up vestments, all of which had been re-introduced by Charles and Laud. As in Essex they chased pro-Laudian ministers from parishes and, throughout other parts of the country, took advantage of the situation by also pulling down the hated enclosure fences.[112]

Charles was now increasingly unpopular at home, particularly among key members of the nobility. Though he and his Archbishop were hardly papist—Laud publicly debated against Roman Catholicism, deplored Vatican errors and solidly refused a cardinal's hat from Pope Urban VIII [113]—their support of Arminianism as an antidote to Puritan intolerance and liturgical minimalism, together with their political and diplomatic *naïveté* in respect to the Scots, put an end to any influence they might have exercised over moderate English Puritan opinion. Even without a campaign restricting Calvinist preachers or catechisms at local levels, or a deliberate policy to publish Arminian tracts in support of their own position, their continued anti-Puritan actions drastically curtailed possibilities for a lasting

---

[111] Sir Harbottle Grimston, *Mr. Grymston's Speech in Parliament* (1641), 2. Grimston was a lawyer, M.P., Speaker of the Commons and deputy-lieutenant of Essex after 1642. See Morrill, 'Religious Context of the English Civil War', 164.
[112] MacCulloch, *Reformation*, 519.
[113] See Laud's 1622 debate with Jesuit John Fisher, *A Relation of the Conference* (1639); see, for instance, 100. This Fisher, who was actually John Percy (1569-1641), is easily confused with the sixteenth century martyr of the same name.

settlement.[114] And when conformist clergy began turning against Laudism, largely because of the draconian measures of the Star Chamber and other ecclesiastical courts that had caused many to emigrate, the writing was on the wall. That said, Charles and Laud remained steadfast. They outlawed justification (holiness/salvation) by faith alone and sabbatarianism (strict Jewish-type sabbath observance), destined to be one of the more longer-lasting features of Puritanism. James Nayler, George Fox and the Friends would ridicule it much later, though from a different standpoint.[115]

The king's relatively speedy, efficient yet autocratic actions also infuriated many a Puritan in the all-important parishes, particularly after the publication of the Church's *Constitutions and Canons* in 1640. These reified Laudian reforms and the divine right of kings.[116] But when the Scots invaded the North again in August of the same year, the lack of enthusiasm for the king's cause in England meant they easily defeated an under-resourced Charles at Newburn. Their swift occupation of Newcastle-upon-Tyne gave them the strategic advantage of commanding London's coal supplies.

Scottish success on the battlefield emboldened up to a third of the English nobility to demand a new parliament and control over a Treaty of Union with Scotland, which was finally ratified in 1641. But in May the following year, fearing that the king wanted to make war again, this time against parliament, the Commons resolved to raise an army in its defence. Parliament was strongest in London, the south-east, East Anglia, the cloth manufacturing areas and in ports that traded with the capital. The king, after a slow start to his recruitment, received able support in the Midlands, the western counties, the south-west and Wales.[117] Although skirmishes took place, for example at Manchester during July, the first battle of the civil

---

[114] See Cust, 'Anti-Puritanism and Urban Politics', *passim* for long simmering local disputes such as in Great Yarmouth where, in the late 1620s, the then Bishop of Norwich, Samuel Harsnet, restricted Puritan stipendiary lecturers and favoured anti-Puritan aldermen.

[115] The Observation of the Lord's Day Act (Long Parliament, April 1650) enforced church attendance; see Firth and Rait, *Acts and Ordinances of the Interregnum*, ii., 383-7. For Quaker anti-sabbatarian tracts see, for instance, Nayler, *A Salutation to the Seed of God* (1655), *passim* (in which Nayler conflates Puritan practice with its emphasis on sin) and Fox, *An Epistle to all the Christian Magistrates* (1658), 2-12: this tract is under Fox's name but the passage was possibly written by Anne Gould and four others; Fox, *An Answer to Thomas Tillam's Book* (1659), *passim*. For a fine Quaker exposé of the dangers of formal prayer including litanies, creeds &c. see W. Smith, *A Manifestation of Prayer* (1663), Bds.

[116] *Constitutions and Canons Ecclesiastical* (1640), see esp. Sig. B5-C2, E2-F1.

[117] As Stone suggests, geography was unable to account for apparently solidly parliamentarian Kent and Suffolk being home to large numbers of closet royalists; geography was suggestive but not decisive in the distribution of allegiance. See Stone, 'The Bourgeois Revolution', 46-7.

wars at Edgehill, an inconclusive affair as it turned out, was only three months away.

So it was that the Puritan religious and political coalition, which had long yearned for a secure ordering of society based on a rightly informed individual conscience, came to wage bloody war. They did so primarily against the person of Charles rather than the monarchy itself. Parliament eventually executed Laud in 1645 and the king in 1649, abolished episcopacy in 1646 and the House of Lords also in 1649. A republic was established in the same year dominated by Cromwell and the military grandees (gentlemen soldiers) or 'junto' (i.e. autocrats) so-called by the Levelling rank and file.[118]

During the 1650s that followed, the Church of England became a vast federation of parishes practically without central control, although local commissioners of 'ejectors' were empowered to expel clergy considered unfit to hold office, or, more precisely, if they held political and theological views at variance with the Commonwealth or Protectorate. Parishes were permitted to go their own way with personal adaptations of the now nominally illegal Prayer Book (abolished in 1645) or with a selective use of its prosaically titled replacement, the *Directory of Public Worship*. The *Directory*, which brought ceremonies into line with Presbyterian practice, was a product of the Westminster Assembly of 1643-9. It proscribed major feasts of the liturgical calendar and introduced a strictly sabbatarian Sunday and regular days for fasting and self-humiliation. It was one way the government put on notice its most serious of desires for a comprehensive reformation of manners designed to bring public morality into line with their vision of the Kingdom of God. Some congregations went further by establishing Presbyterian systems with lay elders.[119]

Conclusion

The antipathy of English Protestantism towards Rome and the Catholic powers fuelled suspicion, hatred and paranoia. At the same time, 'popery' helped to define Protestantism and English identity. Catholics at Court and rebellions in Ireland, particularly in 1641, intensified the loathing towards Catholics, an attitude long-nurtured by the Geneva Bible, Foxe's *Martyrs*, threats of invasion and plots against the Crown. But while much rumour and propaganda painted Catholics as mindlessly Romish, the vast majority were loyal to the State, whether in its monarchical or republican form. Still,

---

[118] Woolrych, 'The English Revolution: an introduction' in Ives (ed.), 19; Hayduk, *Hopeful Politics*, 237.
[119] See Craven, 'Ministers of State', 52. According to Craven, Morrill estimates that less than a quarter of English parishes purchased the *Directory*.

popery within the Church in the guise of Arminianism and William Laud's later reforms was one of the fuses that led to civil war along with the rise of 'the middling sort' and Charles' harsh fiscal policy, demands upon parliament and his stubbornness. While Charles, Laud and his Arminian colleagues refuted predestination, a basic tenet of their Calvinist opponents and particularly of the 'hotter sort', the Arminian ascendancy in the 1630s was arrested by a devastating series of wars in the three kingdoms and the establishment of a Puritan republic that was to reflect the Kingdom of God on earth. The wars, to which I now turn, were devastating and ruinous to the nations in a host of horrific ways.

Chapter 3: 'War the Sickness of a Kingdom is'

- The Good Old Cause and Military Britain -

The crises and conflicts of the late 1630s and 1640s were much more than a culmination of long-running campaigns by parliament to wrest government from the Crown. Broadly, three principal causes for the wars can be identified and these were entwined in complicated ways.

First, from the later Elizabethan years, the merchants, manufacturers and other entrepreneurs, all of whose families gained enormously from land speculation following the dissolution of the monasteries during Henry VIII's reign, continued to grow in number and economic influence. During Elizabeth's reign this 'middling sort' began to demand a greater say in government, especially as they were required from time to time to pay increasing, though still modest, amounts of tax.

Conventionally, before 1640, participation in government was open only to chosen advisers working in (the Privy) Council with the monarch. Before that date the executive and legislative authorities in England—the King, Council and Parliament—had no formal accountability to the people. 'Democracy' was largely a pejorative term.[1] To the monarch, parliaments were mere rubber stamps or occasional gatherings summoned and dissolved by him or her at will. As King James observed, in words that could have been uttered by Elizabeth herself, it was not the task of parliaments to 'debate publicly of matters far above their reach and capacity'. His son would later consolidate the traditional royal view: 'kings are not bound to give an account of their actions but to God alone'. England had no separation of powers, the monarch being the pinnacle of the three connected elements of political authority—the monarchy itself, the Commons (whose principal duty it was to grant supply to the Crown) and the more significant Lords. Indeed, in the 1620s when heir to the throne, Charles, occasionally sat in the upper house. Such was the Stuarts' contempt for parliament that by 1628 they had summoned it a mere seven times. Not one parliament was called in twenty-four of the thirty-seven years before 1640. This attitude extended to the judiciary; judges were regarded as the monarch's personal officials to be manipulated if need be.[2]

As the new social ranks consolidated their economic power, particularly as they married into the landowning class, their demands grew ever louder. Towards the end of the sixteenth century, Elizabeth and her ministers could

---

[1] See Braddick, 'How the people made their views count' (inset) in *History* (BBC), 56.
[2] Kishlansky, *A Monarchy Transformed*, 55-6; Ashley, *Life in Stuart England*, 116.

no longer satisfy them even with offers of an acceptable share in government. Under James, the situation grew more problematic. In the year following his accession in 1603, during which the Commons expressed alarm at the 'daily growth' of royal power, he remained impervious to the House's concerns believing his kingly office to be enshrined by Scripture. To legitimise his position he turned to Hooker's *Laws* and his own *The True Law of Free Monarchies* (1598), the latter a strident declaration of monarchical hegemony. The book, which went into at least four reprints in London in 1603, extolled the virtues of the monarch's exalted station as 'the true pattern of divinity', the 'supremist thing upon earth', adding that 'kings were God's lieutenants upon God's throne', and that 'even by God himself they [were] called gods'. James tolerated no disputation over 'what a king may do in height of his power'.[3]

As the formal public assembly for the Crown's conduct of business, therefore, parliament was legally the monarch's creation. For King Charles, who simply extended his father's constitutional injunctions, parliament's duty was to deliberate at *his* bidding only. Since MPs derived their position from the monarch, their legal status was likened to that of a jury.[7] Persuasion and recommendation, therefore, were the only effective powers open to MPs. The king's authority was absolute, and for Charles that was end of the matter.

Members of the Commons, angered much more by Charles than James, came to see him as a greater impediment to wealth creation and the political power to which they aspired. They were increasingly frustrated by (i) his endless demands upon the exchequer, especially schemes to finance the Court and his wars, (ii) the impossibility of the taxation system to keep up with those demands, (iii) his desire to control foreign exchange and (iv) his prosecution of landowners who evicted tenants, and of employers who did not pay full wages as well as magistrates who refused relief to the poor. In short, they blamed him for the parlous state the economy had apparently suffered since the early 1620s. By the late 1630s, with their anger bubbling over into fury and convinced their wealth confirmed them as the Elect of the new Israel, they felt divinely charged to seize government from the 'tyrant'. Economic and fiscal concerns, therefore, were highly significant factors affecting the evolution of a fatally negative attitude towards the king among mercantilists and a number of influential and disgruntled members of the nobility.

By far the stronger drives behind the opposition to Charles, however, were religious and constitutional—our second cause of the civil wars.

---

[3] *The True Law of Free Monarchies*, 3. For an interesting discussion re: Stuart concepts of kingship see Peck, 'Kingship, Counsel and Law in Early Stuart Britain' in Pocock and Schochet (eds.); see esp. 84-5 and Lake, 'The King (The Queen) and the Jesuit', *passim*.

Chapter 3: 'War the Sickness of a Kingdom is'

Indeed, on the eve of his execution he suggested as much to his children. He was being put to death, he told them, for 'maintaining the true Protestant religion'.[4] Meanwhile, in the early 1640s and particularly between 1640 and 1642, many who had supported the king partly out of fear of parliamentary absolutism, religious radicalism or popular rebellion—luminaries like Sir Edward Hyde (later Lord Clarendon) and Lord Falkland (Lucius Cary)—were driven more by a confidence in constitutional royalism. Their wish was to protect the so-called balanced constitution of King, Lords and Commons, and 'the privilege, dignity and security of parliament' that they believed was endangered by the rising tide of parliamentary radicalism. It was an odd position given that, in practice, no such balance existed.[5] Constitutional royalists believed Charles could be trusted to rule legally, to abide by safeguards erected in 1640-1 against non-parliamentary government, and that he should be free to choose his own advisers and military commanders. They were also determined to protect the Church against 'root and branch' reform by retaining bishops, clerical vestments, the Prayer Book and traditional Christian festivals. The more moderate royalists and loyalists like Hyde and Falkland persistently urged compromise upon the king right up to 1642.

It is well to remind ourselves at this point that the political map was complicated. Royalists often differed in their religious beliefs and constitutional principles. Not all adopted royalism in the same way or at the same time. Sir Henry Slingsby of Scriven (near York), for instance, who was to die for the royalist cause, admitted a distrust of episcopacy but believed its eradication would do more harm than good. Many Episcopalian royalists, like John Evelyn the diarist, did not fight for the king.[6] As for parliament, even by 1640 its principal supporters had offered little criticism of the monarchy.

But by the time constitutional arrangements began to unravel during 1640 and 1641, leading Puritans such as William Prynne, for whom even the Queen's Catholicism could be tolerated, began to change their minds. Charles' troublesome personality, our third principal cause of the wars, was by now a major factor in the growing tragedy. He often failed to follow his father's wise counsel to avoid contention whenever possible but 'to learn

---

[4] Clancy, 'Papist-Protestant-Puritan', 235. Charles' death coincided approximately with the publication of *Eikon Basilike* (1649), his testimony, which may have been written by Charles or as a pro-royalist work by John Gauden (1605-62), post-Restoration Bishop of Exeter and thence of Worcester; historical opinion supports the latter.
[5] Russell, *Unrevolutionary England*, 4-5. Lucius Cary, 2nd Viscount Falkland.
[6] D. Smith, *Constitutional Royalism*, 6-7; Morrill, 'Religious Context of the English Civil War', 160. For royalist heterogeneity see Aylmer, 'Collective Mentalities: 2', 1-5.

wisely to discern betwixt points of salvation and indifferent things'.[7] Whereas James was shrewd and manipulative, playing factions off against each other—he had long experience of negotiating his way through the Scottish clan system—Charles sought to drive home an uncompromising absolutism. He sought resolution to conflicts on his terms only, terms that underlined his administrative inabilities for ruling the three kingdoms. The suspicion this generated was a key concern for his parliamentary opponents but so, too, was his alleged support for Irish rebels. He denied seeking their aid, but the capture of his private papers after the battle of Naseby (1645) confirmed the worst suspicions of his opponents.[8]

At local levels, a belief grew that Charles misused agreements in inappropriate circumstances. Chief among the complaints were his 'emergency taxation in non-emergency situations, the way in which he allowed private individuals to profit from the use of powers reserved to the king himself, and the corrupting of justice'.[9] Something else that created anger and suspicion at local levels was the restricted access to the Court to a favoured few. Perceived limitations such as these placed the relationship between Court and the counties under increasing strain. Unfortunately, by constantly demanding unquestioned obedience, Charles failed to understand that absolutism was no answer to the newly unfolding political and economic realities.

The Good Old Cause

Charles' 'forced loans' on the gentry, his 'ship money' (taxes levied on towns with or without a port), and his demands for financial support to pay for unpopular and failed military ventures, were considered dubious forms of taxation from which the incensed merchants and other entrepreneurs sought freedom. Add the damage done to Anglo-Scottish relations, his suspected support of Irish papists, the rabid hatred that came his way from anti-Laudian Puritans and an increasing alienation of the localities from the Court and we have a lethal recipe for a war that few wanted. As Charles became ever more stubborn, the fear of tyrannical royal government gathered apace particularly towards the end of the 1630s. Despite fears of parliamentary absolutism, Members of the Commons, having lost control of the political and constitutional situation, eventually yet reluctantly took to the battlefield to safeguard parliament itself, along with their own financial

---

[7] See *Basilikon Doron*, 23. In *Doron* James was keen to challenge those opposing his claim to the English throne and was an ideological rebuttal of *De Jure Regni Apud Scotos* (1579) by his former tutor, George Buchanan (1506-82), a work that opposed James' succeeding Elizabeth.

[8] For Charles' apparent denial of culpability in the rebellion see *Eikon Basilike*, 83.

[9] Morrill, 'Religious Context of the English Civil War', 160.

liberties and the cause of true religion—'the reform of the Reformation' to recall Edward Calamy—which fell under the banner of the 'Good Old Cause'. The Cause was sloganised by the parliamentary leadership as the outward symbol of 'Truth', the grand means of salvation. However, it had more practical relevance for ordinary people as the Quakers and other Radicals would come to appreciate. Nor was the Good Old Cause a static political manifesto since, like royalism, it displayed a number of competing interpretations, particularly within the army and parliament.[10]

Its name is partially revealing. For its supporters, 'Good' implied the advantage of God's glory while 'Old' was designed to direct attention to a pre-Norman golden age when all power supposedly rested with the people. This was the better state, maintained Radicals like Sir Henry Vane, John Lilburne the Leveller and Gerrard Winstanley the True Leveller (or Digger), for the people deserved the return of their sovereignty.[11] 'Old' also affirmed governments in their proper role as acting for the good of all rather than for the fortunate few, that is, the 'Norman yoke' with its oppressive medievalism and wicked popery.

Despite such historical allusions, the Cause gave rise to concrete proposals in the wake of the political and military defeat of the royalists and the established Church. Wide-ranging demands from larger bodies such as the Independents and Presbyterians, but also later from Radicals such as the Quakers, included religious toleration and liberty of conscience except, however, for papists.[12] Radicals of every variety claimed to have taken up arms to save England forever from the tyranny of monarchy, nobility and

---

[10] Towards the end of 1659, for instance, Hugh Peter and William Prynne (both MPs) condemned their enemy, Sir Henry Vane Jr. (effectively government leader at the time), whom they suspected of establishing a coalition of commonweathsmen (largely Leveller), soldiers and sectaries, all of whom possessed utopian yearnings (the two MPs believed) for a lost 'golden' pre-Norman era. Around this time, while it reflected profound discontent among many like Vane, the Cause was seen by some Puritans 'to bind souls with secular chains', to use John Milton's expression. It contradicted their Calvinist interpretation of government based as it was on the theocratic rule of the Elect. See Morrill, 'Religious Context of the English Civil War', 166; Woolrych, 'The Good Old Cause and the Fall of the Protectorate', 133-5. And Edmund Calamy ('the elder'), *England's Looking Glass* (1642), 38, 45-6, 56.

[11] John Lilburne (*c.*1614-57) turned Quaker in the mid 1650s. For Gerrard Winstanley (1609 or 1614-*c.*1676) see *TWTUD*, 298; Mulligan *et al*, 'The Religion of Gerrard Winstanley', *passim* and esp. Bradstock, 'Sowing in Hope', *passim*. Although the evidence is thin, Winstanley may have turned Quaker in later life; the September 1676 burial register of the Westminster Monthly Meeting records a 'Winstanley' aged approx. 62 years.

[12] According to Woolrych, Cromwell's famous comment that 'religion was not the thing at first contested for', should not be seen as a denial that the wars were initially devoid of religious importance. 'Religion' in this sense, says Woolrych, signified 'liberty of religion'. Richard Baxter thought in similar terms; see Lamont, *Puritanism and Historical Controversy*, 96.

bishops, from the House of Lords and all forms of popery. Parliamentary officers such as Captains Richard Hubberthorne and George Bishop, both of whom would later join the nonviolent army of the Friends, together with a host of troopers of the 'meaner' sort, looked forward to establishing a 'free State' in which privilege would be abolished, where no taxation without fair representation would be the norm, and annual parliaments instituted with universal suffrage at eighteen years. The Cause anticipated parliament as the permanently supreme authority. A democratic constitution would guarantee basic 'spiritual and civil rights' for everybody and equal treatment of each person under the law. In the legal sphere parliament's supporters looked forward to a decentralised system of courts, and an end to the ecclesiastical courts as well as the unwieldy and inefficient central courts like Chancery. Justice was to be readily available at a local level and codified in English rather than Latin and French to ensure its free and intelligible availability for all.[13]

Advocates for the Good Old Cause demanded urgent reform of the universities as part of a greater restructuring of education, including the provision of schooling for both sexes up to the age of eighteen. Some, like the Quakers and Fifth Monarchists, went further and demanded the abolition of the universities and the privileges they were seen to uphold. Schools were to be stripped of their emphasis on the classics and divinity in favour of vocational and scientific subjects. Ecclesiastically, the Cause stood for the scrapping of the established Church and its bishops and tithes, and for some, including the Quakers, the clerical class itself. In fiscal matters, there was general agreement that excise duties, other forms of arbitrary taxation and feudal tenures should be outlawed. Common land enclosed by landowners was to be restored. The army was to be secured as the protector of people's rights with soldiers and sailors paid arrears, their security of tenure preserved as a matter of justice to individuals and their dependents. Provision was to be available for disabled soldiers, widows and orphans. The innovative Hugh Peter proposed a national legal service and bank, a single income tax, the abolition of Church patronage and the practice of purchasing army commissions, the replacement of imprisonment for debt with a reduction of earnings, and a nationwide program of canal building. Other Radicals like Winstanley proposed national health care.[14]

The Cause was given voice largely by men and women of the lower middling sort whose views were rarely heard on a national level in England before 1640 or after 1660. But it was also the rallying point for intellectuals like Richard Baxter, Samuel Hartlib who penned *Macaria* (1641), Samuel

---

[13] See Anon, *The Good Old Cause Explained* (1659), Bds.; Bishop, *Mene Tekel* (1659), 4-6; Fox, *An Instruction to Judges and Lawyers* (1657), 17.
[14] Adair, *Puritans*, 277.

Chapter 3: 'War the Sickness of a Kingdom is'

Rutherford who wrote *Lex Rex* (1644), James Harrington, the author of *The Commonwealth of Oceana* (1656) and Thomas Hobbes. *Literati* such as these lent their support to a radical critique of, and a constitutional program for, society at large. Winstanley's *The Law of Freedom* (1652) deserves an honourable mention in this respect. Harrington's and Hobbes' view that God should be left out of politics was daring indeed with Hobbes granting only a limited freedom to religion in his absolutist work, *Leviathan* (1651).[15] Both decried rebellion against the State and sought to improve the social and political conditions of the British republic, particularly in respect to the cataclysm suffered in the 1640s. The remedies of such writers, however, were utopian—arcadian in Hartlib's case—and reflected the breakdown of formal institutional politics.[16] Their writings also revealed an authoritarianism like the many other models for constitutional and political reform circulating at the time.[17]

The hopes that the Cause generally represented would be dashed by persecution, censorship and the ultimate failure of the Puritan republic.[18] But one thing is certain: it never included regicide, though many of the Radicals, the Quakers included, shed no tears for Charles and the monarchy. For a start, they agreed with Cromwell's depiction of the king as 'that man of blood' whose guilt extended to engineering the second civil war in 1648. However, the common people, never consulted over Charles' fate, considered it 'a devilish thing' that their nation should make war to *this* extent on its father the king. Tellingly, Charles' beheading was observed in respectful silence, a reminder perhaps of how the language, symbols and the very trappings of kingship were deeply embedded in the English psyche.

His execution, a sensational event, sent waves of sharp, searing panic through Europe's royal Courts. Monarchy, with its powerful and holy mystique, was one of *the* characteristic institutions of western Christendom. In England it embodied the political and legal system besides symbolising the nation's very identity. Suddenly, the severed head came to signify the broken body of the English polity, now a disintegrated and purposeless entity. The appeal of premillennialism, a common feature of the intellectual landscape, intensified as a result of the fear the regicide evoked. Nuttall contends that 'to be kingless surely heralded the end of all things [and]

---

[15] Thomas Hobbes (1588-1679), *Leviathan* (1651); see Part 1: 'Of Commonwealth', chps. 12 and 21; also Hayduk, *Hopeful Politics*, 306 (301*n*). Harrington believed that 'the Liberty of Man consists in the Empire of his Reason'; see *The Commonwealth of Oceana* (hereafter *Oceana*), 11 and *Works*, 45.

[16] For a useful introduction to Hartlib see Braddick, 'Small Steps Can Lead to Utopia', 54-7.

[17] Such as Sir Henry Vane Jr.'s *A Healing Question* (1656) and Marchmont Nedham's *The Excellency of a Free State* (1656).

[18] For an eloquent attack on censorship see John Milton, *Areopagitica* (1644), 1, 39-40 and *passim*.

many transferred the allegiance from King Charles to King Jesus.'[19] The effect of the king's demise on the constitution was so profound that questions about the nature of sovereignty, leadership, royal accountability and dissolution ran without resolution throughout the supposedly anti-monarchy period of the Commonwealth and Protectorate. More specifically, while it is true that a republican language developed during the 1650s, coupled with a de-mystifying of public authority by a host of intellectuals and groups such as the Quakers, questions about the constitutional nature of monarchy continued to be raised until well after the Restoration and up to at least the Glorious Revolution of 1688.[20]

'Destruction and Misery are in my Ways'

When Charles raised his standard at Nottingham in 1642—an ominously quiet, if melancholy, affair—he and others could not have foreseen the scale and extent of the calamity about to be unleashed on the lives of his people.[21] Massively changing the perspective in which physical conflicts were viewed, many were to witness the horrific impact of warfare at first hand. During the previous hundred years, wars had been fought largely by professional soldiers. England's battlefields were either far away on the European continent, on the northern borders of the country or in Ireland. The civil wars of the past, equally blood-soaked, were but a faint memory. Consequently, war was an abstraction and remote from people's minds, its barbarity largely unknown as in the United States in 1861.

This relative innocence would quickly change with Charles' fateful decision. From 1642 to the battle of Worcester in 1651, England suffered massive social, political and economic privation and only recently have we begun to appreciate the full extent of the casualties. The figures are chilling. Although large areas of southern and western England escaped military campaigns, the country as a whole lost between 3.7% and 4.2% of its 5.3 million inhabitants, approximately 190,000 to 220,000 people. This was a greater proportion than Britain's military losses in the 1914-18 world war. The civil wars also caused a greater decrease of 3.6% in the British population than the first and second world wars combined—2.6% and 0.6% respectively. The extent of the carnage becomes all the more explicit when one considers the fate of Ireland, probably deprived of a cataclysmic *41%* of its population or 618,000 victims. Scotland lost about 6% (60,000) of its

---

[19] Nuttall, *The Holy Spirit*, 121-2.
[20] See Pocock and Schochet, 'Interregnum and Restoration', 146-8; Jonathan Scott, *England's Troubles*, 47; Sharpe, 'An Image Doting Rabble', 54.
[21] For Charles' attempts to raise an army in 1642 see Malcolm, 'A King in Search of Soldiers', 246.

Chapter 3: 'War the Sickness of a Kingdom is'

population. In total, 13.5% of the population of the British Isles of 6.65 million perished in the battles and their aftermath.[22]

The number of men under arms was also immense. In 1642 alone, 60-70,000 troops lined up to fight. Between 1643 and 1645 the English armies comprised nearly 150,000 men or 11% of the 1.4 million males between the ages of sixteen and fifty, a higher proportion of the English adult male population than during the first world war. Again, the proportion for the Scots and Irish was much higher. Diseases such as plague, typhoid, smallpox, TB and diarrhea accounted for a large number of the war dead. For example, the wars brought plague to Bradford (Yorks.) in 1643, accounting for 493 deaths. Of the 11,817 people who perished in Devon, nearly a quarter were victims of disease contacted during the siege of Plymouth (1643).

Greater numbers still finished their days as invalids. There were so many wounded on the parliamentary side during the battle at Edgehill in Warwickshire (1642) that carts from the *king's* former train were used for the 'relief of maimed soldiers who were to the number of 3 or 4 hundred sent to Warwick from the Edgehill fight to be cared for and cured of their wounds'. George Bishop, the future Quaker, enthusing about the parliamentary victory at Naseby, reported 'about 400 slain in the place . . . [and] abundant wounded . . . and 200 carried that night wounded into Leicester; many women slain that were in their army, and many taken, which are every one wounded'.[23]

After battles, the sick and wounded could linger on for weeks. They were often left to their own devices in alien billets or became dependent upon the compassion of cottagers' wives. They were sometimes attacked by hostile villagers when seeking relief.[24] Besides the 'rapes and outrageous violence', tens of thousands of war widows were created. Refugees, many from the Irish and Scottish 'troubles', periodically thronged England's roads. The returnees, the disease-ridden wounded and the absence of those formerly alive added to the trauma, fear and economic hardship of families and whole villages. Widespread, too, was destruction to property and the human distress it wrought on huge numbers of innocent people. Many ancient monuments and buildings were destroyed, including churches and castles such as that in Scarborough, which suffered devastating bombardments during the twenty-two-week siege of the town in 1645.[25]

---

[22] Morrill, 'The Causes and Course of the English Civil Wars' in Keeble (ed.), 23-4.
[23] Bishop, *A More Particular* (1645), 2.
[24] Tennant, 'Parish and People: South Warwickshire in the Civil War', 148.
[25] M. Edwards, *Scarborough 966-1966*, 150. See 'a dyer', *Study to be Quiet* (1647), 2 and *passim* for a vivid first hand account of the first civil war.

Even in counties like Surrey, which remained free of invading armies, the atmosphere of fear was fuelled by rumours of possible troop incursions. In response, civilians protested at the war, their objections becoming a major feature of the military scene up to 1645. Some formed into non-aligned local trained bands or 'clubmen' who prepared for the worst. Originating in Dorset, clubmen were usually poorer yeomen disillusioned with the civil wars although they were not a unified political-military movement. Though easily routed by parliamentary and royalist forces, the clubmen movement nevertheless spread. In Hereford, some sixteen thousand of them appeared in the city in March 1645, reinforced by others from Worcestershire and Radnorshire (Wales). Many were well armed and horsed believing they were 'able to keep the forces of both parties from exacting contribution and quarter in their county'. However, at Ledbury in Herefordshire, most of the clubmen fled when Prince Rupert dispatched his horse and one thousand of his troop. As was typical for the soldiery of both sides, his forces plundered 'every parish and house poor as well as others leaving neither clothes nor provision'.

Nevertheless, despite such frequent setbacks there is strong evidence by 1645 of continued and widespread civilian resistance to the armies by the trained bands in the central-southern and south-western counties of England and in South Wales. In other places, individuals grouped together to make non-alignment pacts, agreeing not to support either side. While many county neutrality treaties were motivated by self-interest, there was also a genuine feeling that right and wrong existed on both sides.[26]

If Surrey remained free of fighting, then Warwickshire was a good example of a heavily conflicted area. The battle at Edgehill exemplified the extent of destruction to local life and the degree of personal loss for rich and poor alike due principally to quarter and theft. Understandably, one Thomas Calloway complained bitterly when robbed of books, two coats, ten cheeses, five yards of flannel to the value of ten shillings and seven sheep. Ralph Ellis of Butlers Marston lost '73 sheep at 10d per sheep' to parliamentary forces. Passing troops of whatever colour demanded taxes and unpaid labour—and all this in the context of a breakdown of poor relief at parish level which served to exacerbate the plight of the needy and the disruption to markets, harvests and trade in general.[27] After the battle of Naseby, George Bishop reported much 'plunder for the soldiers'.[28] Articles

---

[26] Bennett, *The Civil Wars Experienced*, 34, 126. See John Vicars, *A Sight of Ye Transactions* (1646), 23 and 21 for iconoclasts. Also Rollinson, 'The Civil War in Hereford' and Aylmer, 'Collective Mentalities: 3', 3.

[27] Tennant, 'Parish and People', 148. For local royalist night raiders see Gough, *Myddle* (ed. 1979), 5.

[28] Bishop, *A More Particular*, 2.

of war for both sides, and the few records of internal army discipline that have survived, confirm that the violence inflicted by soldiers on civilians, including theft, rape ('ravishing virgins') and murder was of considerable concern to the various authorities and a testimony to the poet's lament that 'war the sickness of a kingdom is'.[29] As the wars intensified, the armies made good use of reprisal, which brought the usual atrocities and duplicitous behaviour of which there is much evidence:

> During the siege of Colchester [1648], negotiations were conducted for the mutual release of prisoners. Lord Fairfax, the leader of the roundheads besieging the town, wanted certain parliamentary committee men released. He offered the royalist commander, the Earl of Norwich, a list of royalist captives and suggested a one-for-one release of prisoners. Norwich refused on the grounds that not one name was known to him—he was being asked to deliver important parliamentarians while receiving low-ranking men in return. On 19th June, Fairfax retaliated by issuing an order that, from the royalists his forces had captured in Essex, one in every fifteen unmarried men and one in every ten married men would be shot. In addition, one in every five men captured in Kent (where Fairfax had just put down a rebellion) would suffer the same fate. The captives drew lots and Fairfax's order was carried out. Following a later, unsuccessful, royalist break-out from Colchester, during which the king's men incurred severe losses, it was recorded that parliamentarians severed the hands and fingers of the dying and the dead to obtain rings, and that, having offered mercy, they proceeded to maim and kill prisoners.

> After the battle of Bolton in 1644, royalists entered the town 'killing all before them without any respect . . . pursuing the poor amazed people, killing, stripping and spoiling all they could meet with, nothing regarding the doleful cries of women and children, but some they slashed as they were calling for quarter . . . many hailed out of their houses to have their brains dashed out in the streets, those . . . not dead in the streets already, pistoled, slashed . . . or trodden under their horses feet . . . children crying for their fathers, of women crying out for their husbands, some of them brought on purpose to be slain before their wives faces . . . the dismembering, cutting of dying or dead bodies . . . boasting . . . how many Roundheads . . . killed that day.'[30]

---

[29] Coster, 'Fear and Friction in Urban Communities' in Naphy and Roberts, *Fear in Early Modern Society*, 101.
[30] Channel 4 (UK) history website; Anon, An *Exact Relation . . . at Bolton* (28th May, 1644), 2-3; Anon, *England's Division* (1642), 5.

Such was the misery caused by the conflicts that the soldiery, as in all wars, frequently expressed anguish to those at home. Writing to his wife from Farnham Castle (Surrey) on a cold November day in 1643, one 'A.W.', a parliamentary officer, confessed to his foolishness in placing trust in the leadership only to discover it had feet of clay. His disillusionment had clearly set in long before the end of the civil wars, a common experience. Plenty, mirth, peace, riches, liberty, order, loyalty and wisdom, he said, had turned respectively into scarcity, sorrow, war, poverty, bondage, confusion, rebellion and folly. As a Puritan he was in terror of God's judgment since he had 'wilfully hardened' his,

> Self against the truth, [and so was] now given over to a reprobate sense, that I should only believe a lie. My feet were swift to shed blood, therefore as it follows, *Rom.3.16.* destruction and misery are in my ways. For these and other sins is the wrath of God.

For our beleaguered soldier, war and its atrocities was the scourge of God whose wrath was upon the nations. The rotting crops, mud infested pastures and price hikes, all of which A.W. experienced, were further proof of divine anger.[31] Edward Calver, the poet, lamented how civil war was 'the most grievous' of actions in which the 'devouring sword' had plunged England into 'a deluge of its own blood'.[32] The anonymous female authors of *The Midwives Just Complaint* also lamented in 1646 how the 'great havoc' had been, and continued to be, a massive assault on marriage and family life and that their livelihoods were being ruined. But the tract was also an anti-war call demanding an immediate end to hostilities that they 'may not eat up and devour the youth of this kingdom'. At the same time they took 'notice of what devilish new engines for war are daily invented by the Cyclops and such like artists, to destroy one another'. Their revulsion of warfare and its weapons led them to declare that the only arms they wanted were 'such as will lovingly embrace women' and so, they pleaded,

> let not the drum wound the air no more with false strokes, not the pike be bathed in blood of guiltless men, let not the sword ravish from our bosoms the delight of our lives . . . [so they may] declare their undaunted valour in the soft and delightful field of love.

---

[31] A.W., *A Letter from one . . . in the Army* (1643), 3.
[32] Edward Calver (*c.*1598-post 1644), *England's Sad Posture* (1644), 'Preface'.

Their good sense went unheard and the 'great effusion of Christian blood' continued.[33]

The ferment and controversy so typical of the times extended into much of the 1640s and 1650s with the theological basis of government and the nation-State itself hotly debated. A major concern, for instance, centred on the purpose of the military in society. On occasions it approximated to a police force and in various areas it was keenly involved in local government.[34] At other times it acted as a repressive instrument of central and local administration, the sole guarantor of governments with minority support. Martial rule was always a possibility after the execution of Charles in 1649, and so it turned out. The North, militarised since 1638, experienced military governance until 1653. By October 1655, the stern, unpopular and semi-dictatorial rule of Cromwell's major-generals was 'well bedded' at central and local levels. Cromwell's hold on the reins of power would have been impossible without the military which in 1655 stood at 57,000 men eating up a monthly budget of £90,000.[35] Its power and influence was given ample and impressive demonstration when 40,000 troops accompanied Cromwell's body to its resting place in Westminster Abbey, an event witnessed by the Quaker, Edward Burrough.[36]

Among the Radical groups, including the Quakers, but also among a growing number of the educated, opinion increasingly focussed on the huge cost of the standing army to the exchequer. Such opinion was especially aired in the 1650s when the military was suspected of corrupting parliamentary processes and institutions. Throughout the decade a minority among the military and its supporters centralised power to itself. Though high-principled, it was clear to many that its rule owed much more to tough, top-down government than to consent. High personal stakes were also at issue as powerful forces jockeyed for hegemony, particularly after the death of Cromwell in 1658 and the political demise of his son and successor, Richard ('Tumbledown Dick') in 1659. The status and power of the New Model Army at this particular moment in England's history can be compared to the military powerbrokers of today's 'Third World'. Small wonder that in 1659, the year of political collapse or 'prodigious confusion', as the diarist and royalist John Evelyn described it, the Protectorate yielded

---

[33] See Anon, *The Midwives Just Complaint*, 5; *England's Division*, 3-6; *The Good Old Cause Explained*, Sig. A.
[34] For the army as a crude form of police force see Boswell, *Plotting Popular Politics*, 227-34.
[35] Woolrych, 'The Cromwellian Protectorate', 208; Durston, 'The Fall of Cromwell's Major-Generals', 18; *Journal*, 240-1; the £90,000 figure is from Royle, *The British Civil War*, 692.
[36] Burrough, *A Testimony against a Great Idolatry* (1658), 4.

for a short time to a junta of senior officers who inherited a government bankrupt of ideas but equally lacking a vision for the future.[37]

Inexperienced in governance, the army grandees with their internal dissensions were unable to offer the nations a viable alternative. General George Monck's long march from his Scottish base to London, where he arrived on February 3rd 1660, met with popular distrust of politicians and the army, simmering anger over social and religious constrictions and dissolution over the failure of the Good Old Cause. But when the social hierarchies—throughout the years they had remained secure and powerful in the tiers of London, county, and local communities—threw in their lot with 'Black Bob', as Monck was known, a return to monarchy and with it the rapid re-instatement of episcopacy and the peerage, became a foregone, and, as already noted, popular outcome.[38]

Conclusion

Economic, ecclesiastical and constitutional factors played significant roles in the tragic events that precipitated the civil wars of the three kingdoms. Charles, too, must take the lion's share of blame for the carnage, but he was also a man of his times and the product of a rigid and closed upbringing. Divine right theory, equally an obsession of his father, dominated his Court. Its effect was to reduce parliaments to mere gatherings at the service of the monarch. This was an affront to the sensibilities of the 'middling sort' who identified as the Elect. They, too, came to believe they had a divine right to rule. And when they did, despite their single-minded attempts at a wholesale 'reformation of manners', the demands of government proved overwhelming. Meanwhile, although the plunge into civil war was taken reluctantly, parliament propagated it with a determined ruthlessness, eventually reforming the army into the 'New Model'; the royalists had no answer to Cromwell's generalship and religious zealotry.

The wars took a terrible toll. The numbers of men under arms was immense while disease, death, injury, homelessness, the proliferation of widows, orphans and refugees—not to mention the trauma, fear and economic hardship that resulted—caused lasting pain and sorrow that Puritan rule could not cure. Widespread, too, was destruction to property, including ancient monuments, churches and other buildings, in addition to

---

[37] Evelyn, *Diary*, 202; Braithwaite, *Second*, 3.

[38] For the rapid restoration of the peerage (socially, economically and ideologically) see Hexter, 'The English Aristocracy', *passim* but esp. 74-8.

the human distress it wrought on huge numbers of people. Atrocities were committed on both sides but it was the regicide that left an indelibly negative imprint upon the nation.

The Good Old Cause largely became the preserve of the more radical leaning parliamentarians and sectaries, including the Quakers. The latter's synthesis of the Kingdom and the Cause, which was not merely political but an expression of the Quakers' understanding of 'true religion', would prove strange, if frightening, to the political and ecclesiastical authorities. Major reasons for the loathing that came the Friends' way were not only their theology and conduct but also their language, including its incisive and powerful application upon which I will now focus.

Part Two

The Quakers' Kingdom and Testimony

Chapter 4: *'Pure Love to the Soul'*

- Early Quaker Language -

Early Quaker language took mystical, apocalyptic, theophanous and military forms. With these four dramatic elements a linguistic style developed that was often turgid and repetitive and yet capable, too, of descriptive beauty, poetic fluidity and spiritual incisiveness. Like all religious language, it came with the power of metaphor, allegory and symbolism, and could be spontaneous and informal.[1] Qualities such as these sometimes rendered it difficult to interpret especially when addressing theological and political concerns. And yet, along with seventeenth-century literature in general, whether political, religious or social, Quaker written works reflected the importance of rhetoric and metaphor to intellectual and religious discourse. They did so at a time when controversy, fanaticism and open denunciation of one's opponents, often combined with bitter invective, were normal features of a polemical and highly verbal cultural milieu.

The skilled use of language was always the domain of the powerful—the aristocracy, bishops, other clerics and politicians, army commanders, lawyers and judges, and those in the two universities at Oxford and Cambridge. It was powerfully reinforced by the exclusive use of classical languages, which was an attempt to fix meaning, to render language stable and henceforth create a contrast with the vernacular whose fluidities were considered unstable, untrustworthy and 'mechanick'.

'Pure Language of the Spirit'

In challenging this monopoly the Quakers' 'plain' language, as with Leveller and Digger language before it, sought to command the heights of public speech. Their 'plaining', however, was never consistently 'plain'

---

[1] See Kolp, *Fresh Winds of the Spirit*, 42.

since at times it could be complicated or soar to mystical heights as in Fox's Pauline-type vision of a flaming sword early in his ministry.[2] Their language, even in its anagogical form, was certainly plain to *them*, although the Friends acknowledged, as the learned Thomas Lawson from Furness (Lancs.) did in 1680, that while it was of 'heavenly eloquence and rhetoric... though plain [and] simple', Quaker language was often regarded as 'rude, clownish and babbling by the worldly wise.'[3]

'Plaining', however, acted on a deeper level. For Richard Farnworth in 1653 it was evidence that a 'pure language of the Spirit' existed that could and should 'disquiet the birth born of the flesh', a belief confirmed by their scriptural reading such as Zephaniah 3:9: 'For then will I turn to the people a pure language that they may all call upon the name of the Lord, to serve him with one consent'.[4] This pure or Edenic language, according to Fox, was also that of the Kingdom and its truth.[5] It demonstrated the Quakers' 'innocency' as well as their pursuit of equality, love and friendship in the Spirit, all of which they gleaned from Matthew 5—including the Sermon— the Gospel of John and the Epistle of James.[6] It was much more than mere communication, therefore, and it confirmed that Truth (God) 'existed which was not relative to language and which transcended it.'[7] Like Paul, the Friends used language as a spiritual weapon, a sacred medium by which God was channelled. Words were to give authority and power to their Kingdom message. Spoken or penned with love, and yet often in the stern and robust tone common to the polemical style of the day, Quaker language invariably sought to change the structure of public discourse in the service of the Jesus Way.

But more: inspired by Zephaniah's loud declaration against falsehood in speech, their plaining and rhetoric, filtered through the vernacular, was meant to affect a measure of social and cultural destabilisation. Farnworth could therefore declare with relish, 'The people of this generation profess

---

[2] *Journal*, 27-8; see 2 Cor. 12:2-4 and Gen. 3.

[3] Thomas Lawson (1630-91), *A Mite into the Treasury* (1680), 17. I use anagogical throughout this book in the sense of having a mystical interpretation, that which is intended to reveal a hidden, spiritual meaning, or that which is allegorical. For anagogy see Woodman, *The Apocalyptic Vision*, 159-60, 177; Erskine, 'Margery Kempe and Her Models', 78-9.

[4] Farnworth, *A Call Out of Egypt and Babylon* (1653) in *An Easter-Reckoning* (extended version, 1653), 29; see also his *The Pure Language of the Spirit* (1655), *passim* and esp. 2, 5; John Audland, *The Innocent Delivered* (1655), 23; Fox, *News Coming up out of the North*, 4.

[5] Fox, *Concerning Good-morrow* (1657), 6 and esp. 7.

[6] See Jn. 11:2, 15; 16: 25-33.

[7] C. Spencer, 'Holiness: the Quaker Way of Perfection' in Dandelion (ed., 2004), 158.

themselves to be the people of God . . . and if any speak to them in plainness of speech . . . they . . . cannot bear it'.[8]

Their reading of the prophets such as Zephaniah and of Acts led the Friends to use speech in the manner of *parrhesia*, that is to say, plainness and boldness of speech in which a speaker expressed a personal relationship to Truth, and who bore the consequences as Jesus did. It involved what Thomas Wilson's *The Arte of Rhetorique* (1553), still influential in the seventeenth century, called 'freeness of speech'.[9] Truth telling for the Friends was an Edenic requirement for addressing 'that of God' within people, and for improving or helping others. As God was pure so, too, speech and conversation (behaviour) should be pure.[10] They saw the story of Babel with its confused voices enacted all around them while discovering the common language of the Kingdom and quoting Genesis 11:1 for the purpose: 'In the beginning God created heaven and earth, and all the earth was of one language'.[11] By appreciating their own use of rhetoric, then, we will come to know the Quakers' passionate, daily commitment to the Jesus Way as Truth and Peace, as the Life.

The 'Arte of Rhetorique'

Sixteenth and seventeenth century rhetoric was not merely a polemical or poetic tool. Its structure contained personal invective or artistic 'abuse' in the form of hyperbole which sent an audience a clear message—the user was a *literati* and therefore to be taken seriously. According to Thomas Wilson, rhetoric aimed to teach, delight and 'win the chief hearers good wills, and persuade them to our purpose'.[12] For Wilson, it helped people define questions and focus critically so that ambiguities were opened up and favourable slants and winning moves achieved.[13] Taking sides in order to vigorously win arguments and debates was considered normal and eagerly expected by audiences as in the days of Paul of Tarsus.

During the seventeenth century, and largely due to the influence of Sir Francis Bacon as Michael Graves informs us, rhetoric incorporated a form of plain style in discourse away from ingratiation and emotion in which

---

[8] Farnworth, *A Call Out of Egypt and Babylon, ibid.*; Warren, 'The Quakers as Parrhesiasts', 1.
[9] Thomas Wilson (*c.*1524-81), *The Arte of Rhetorique*, Bk. 3, Fo. 107. Wilson was a diplomat, judge and privy councillor in the Elizabethan government but best remembered as a rhetorician.
[10] Warren, 'The Quakers as Parrhesiasts', 21; see also Colclough, 'Parrhesia', 195-6.
[11] Farnworth, *A Call Out of Egypt and Babylon, ibid.*
[12] Wilson, *The Arte*, Bk. 1, Fol. 2.
[13] *Ibid.*, Bk. 2, Fo.55.

reason was applied to imagination.[14] Consequently, in promoting plain speech, Baconian rhetoric shunned abstraction: instead, discourse was 'managed' by addressing a specific 'faculty' in the hearer's mind.[15] Generally, though, rhetoric was regarded as being akin to a theatrical skill where actors, in forcing the 'soul ... to [their] whole conceit', underwent a transformation.[16] So, too, the impassioned speaker or writer whose presence would be felt through the creative and intimate use of words, something with which readers of Quaker pamphlets and other literature of the times will be familiar.

By the time the leading Friends were born, rhetoric had long been a familiar part of a student's academic equipment prior to university. As such, it occupied an important place in many school curricula as well as at Oxbridge. Charles Butler's 1598 abridgement in Latin of Omer Talons' *Rhetorica* (1548), for instance, was a popular textbook.[17] But rhetoric was not an easy discipline. 'We are today struck with amazement,' writes Ong,

> at the variety and rigidity of Tudor [and Stuart] training in rhetoric, the more remarkable because it was imposed in a second language, Latin, with a sprinkling of a third, Greek, upon schoolboys of ten to fourteen years of age.[18]

We can reasonably assume that a number of leading Quakers such as Edward Burrough, Samuel Fisher, James Nayler and Isaac Penington experienced such a régime in their youth, and it may have contributed to their more systematic approach to theology when compared to Fox's.

Rhetoric had a powerful effect on the English language giving it immediacy and urgency.[19] And let us not forget that the Bible, too, was a major influence in this respect. Many definitions in *A Complete Christian Dictionary* (1655) by Wilson's namesake had a scriptural basis and their use lent prestige to an argument. Rhetoric flourished in the energetic and passionately literary atmosphere of the seventeenth century during which the spoken and printed sermon of whatever tradition set spines a-tingling.

---

[14] Graves, *Preaching the Inward Light*, 55-4, 57-9.
[15] *Ibid.*, 50.
[16] Wilson, *ibid.*, Bk. 1, Fol. 3; for the above Wilson quotes see also Mair (ed.), 60, 158, 200. And see N. Sharp, 'Thomas Wilson: Introduction to 'The Art of Rhetoric' at: <http://www.people.vcu.edu/~nsharp/wilsint1.htm> (21/2/06); Scott-Warren, *Early Modern English Literature*, 25, 25, 90. Thomas Hobbes, *Leviathan*, chapters 4 ('Of Speech'), 7 ('Of the Ends of Discourse'). For a 1680 Quaker view of rhetoric see Lawson, *A Mite into the Treasury*, 17-21.
[17] Charles Butler (c.1560-1647), vicar, grammarian and musician. For rhetoric at Tudor Cambridge see Jardin, 'The Place of Dialectic Teaching', 50.
[18] Ong, 'Tudor Writings on Rhetoric', 46.
[19] Miner (ed.), p. x.

Chapter 4: 'Pure Love to the Soul'

Sermons, such as those by William Perkins, usually followed a systematic and logical form unlike their impromptu Quaker equivalents which were spoken only through God's immediate inspiration. It is possible that Perkins and others from the more esoteric Calvinist circles of the time were influenced in some degree by Peter Ramus (1515-72), a French philosopher and Protestant martyr. Other rhetoricians, however, such as Alexander Richardson, Leonard Cox, Fenner Dudley and Omer Talon himself were equally important.[20]

The seventeenth century was a time when, in the public imagination, the theatre of ideas often eclipsed the stage itself. Writers and polemicists took advantage of both a rapidly developing intellectualism enriched by linguistic experimentation and the 10-29,000 words which entered the language in the early modern period mainly from Europe. The century also saw both science and religion involved in new thinking about the natural and social world.[21] This favoured intellectuals such as Thomas Hobbes. Devoting two chapters of *Leviathan* (1652) to discourse, he was aware of rhetoric's profound effect on language and culture, particularly at a time when literary discourse was becoming increasingly grounded in religious, political and social life, and when literary experiences were 'expressed in terms of oral-aural engagements (and not merely written-read text) and as a mode of action rather than a countersign of thought'.[22] Thus the spoken word retained a greater potency than its written equivalent even by the mid century.

Seventeenth century works reveal an evolving style of English expression, therefore, often characterised by lexigraphical and grammatical spontaneity, which occasionally translated into street performance, the language of public metaphor as demonstrated, for instance, in Quaker 'signs'.

---

[20] Ramus (Pierre de la Ramée) was a humanist, logician and educational reformer. The extent of his influence in England is conjectural but his ideas seemed more at home in Scotland. Essentially Ramism was a reaction to Scholasticism. Sixteenth century works of interest are Leonard Cox, *The Art or Craft of Rhetoric* (1532) and Fenner Dudley's *The Arts of Logic and Rhetoric* (1584), an adaptation of Ramus' *Dialectique* (1555). Talon's (Tallaeus) *Rhetorica* was itself revised by Ramus after Talon's death in 1562. For Ramus see Conley, *Rhetoric in the European Tradition*, 128-44; McKim, 'The Functions of Ramism in William Perkins' Theology', *passim*; Graves, *Preaching the Inward Light*, 50-4. Also Adams, 'Alexander Richardson's Puritan Theory of Discourse', *passim*.

[21] Gwyn, 'Captivity Among the Idols', 7.

[22] Scott-Warren, *Early Modern English Literature*, 90. Also O'Brien, *Female Verbal Crime*, 83.

A Confrontational Milieu

It was a century in which functional discourse was paralleled by symbolic expression whether in mathematical form or through the growing fascination with science, music and art.[23] Pamphlets frequently featured strong visual images such as the devil defecating into the mouth of an anti-royalist pamphleteer, or the pope vomiting demons into the mouths of monopolists. They also portrayed bitter parodies—for example, of a 'gracious king' holding hands with Heresy but swearing commitment to Truth. The aim was to shock. Quaker language itself sought to enact something similar by bringing adversaries to the point where they could confront the Beast within, that is, their own sin/disobedience and separation from God/Love.[24] Confrontationist language such as this had a long tradition in England and Europe, and was understood as an essential means for delivering the vital message.

As with Matthew's Jesus, the act of opposing was an important means of advancing ideas and opinions. For this, people took their cue mainly from the Gospels, Revelation and the Pauline letters, the latter containing invective to win arguments. From an early age the educated were taught, by way of rhetoric, that invective and satire appealed to the emotions and that they should be exploited for this purpose. Both were considered punitive and curative. Their purpose was to praise or blame.[25] Consequently, 'railing' was often seen as appropriate behaviour and fair game if undertaken between equals. Though it is difficult to imagine nowadays, it was normal for opponents to be met in kind, their wit capped, their authorities seized and metaphors manipulated; any abuse was returned.[26]

According to Hughes, insults were 'deliberately provocative' and designed to 'egg' people into action. Although the language often contained exaggeration, he writes, there was at the same time a certain element of play involved. Skill in barbed insults and dexterity in the use of the wounding phrase were part of the linguistic armoury of the North, for instance, where verbal interchanges were like virtuoso sword play.[27] In other words, so-called 'rude' language was the *lingua franca* of public debates and, as O'Brien has observed, insults also acted as a safety-valve permitting some alleviation of unresolved tensions.[28] It provided, in all, a powerful imprinting for many and it greatly influenced the way the Friends'

---

[23] For a helpful overview of language in the seventeenth century see de Grazia, 'The Secularisation of Language', *passim*.
[24] For sin as separation see Nayler (with Hubberthorne), *An Account from the Children*, 52.
[25] Ong, *Rhetoric, Romance and Technology*, 180.
[26] Leslie, *'A Friendly Debate'*, 133, 224-6.
[27] G. Hughes, *Swearing: a Social History*, 469.
[28] O'Brien, *Female Verbal Crime*, 83.

conducted their verbal and written intercourse, particularly those from the northern reaches of England.

As one might expect, there was more to this outward form of communication. The Quakers and others, for instance, became skilled advocates of meaning-in-context, garnering their rhetorical energies into linking familiar Bible stories (with political, social, economic and military references) to similar experiences in their audiences. Hence, a greater visual and oral meaning-in-context may have been created as audiences saw or physically touched the Friends as they acted and spoke in the manner of the old prophets and the disciples of Jesus. By preaching and being 'patterns and examples' to others in this way, the Friends were acting as tropes of familiar meanings and contexts.[29]

Quaker public language and conduct could thus display a passion and tone that reflected a spiritual inscape in which their *mystical*, or, more specifically, *Christ-* or *Kingdom-mystical*, discourse never objectified God in the way ordinary language could describe objects. Objects, after all, could be separated from human understanding but God could not. Mindful of the limitations of language, they were careful about the words they used to describe their experience of God; this was especially pertinent for their Christology as we will see in Chapter 8.[30]

It is interesting to compare Quaker language with that of the Levellers and Diggers both of whom had similar social and political aims. Whereas the three groups in their opposition to forced tithing criticised clerics for commandeering the Spirit, Quaker campaigns against tithes and 'hireling priests'—'Babylon's merchants' as Fox called them, those who were paid for preaching—took a different path. Rather than pressing for the free availability of property like the Digger or a Leveller-type freedom of choice—for example, clerics being paid by the parish and enjoying freedom from patronage—it was in possessing an engaging and commanding language that the Quakers saw a greater means of achieving material and spiritual liberty. This was a more far-reaching, revolutionary position because it meant attacking the *commodification* of the Word. 'While the Levellers', writes Hazleton, 'sought to apply free market principles to the world of language and ideas', the Quakers sought 'a full democratising of cultural capital leading to freedom for the Word'.[31] The Word could be freed, therefore, from ecclesiological, soteriological and liturgical constraints, thus disempowering the clerical class through a radical attack

---

[29] Farnworth and Nayler, *A Discovery of Faith* (1653), 9.
[30] Howells, 'Mysticism and the Mystical', 1. See also Creasey, *Early Quaker Christology*, 352-7.
[31] Hazleton, 'Mony Choaks': The Quaker Critique of the Seventeenth-Century Public Sphere', 258.

on the economic (including property) and social bases upon which it survived.[32]

As with James 1:25, the Friends believed the Light or Word was the 'perfect law of liberty' and therefore available to everybody. Its moment-to-moment 'speaking' was the ultimate language of the Kingdom.[33] Those in a position to hear and experience the Light, they believed, but who ignored it demonstrated a dangerous lack of integrity thus putting their religious existence in jeopardy. As such they could be a corrupting influence upon society in general. In this they agreed wholeheartedly with the well-known Baptist, William Dell:

> a poor, plain countryman by the Spirit which he has received, is better able to judge of truth and error, touching the things of God, than the greatest philosopher, scholar or doctor in the world that is destitute of it.[34]

For the Quakerish and revolutionary Dell, the especial 'things of God', the inner Church and the Kingdom, were his chief concern. Naturally, such beliefs were unpopular with anyone with a vested interest in the *status quo*.

For the Friends, society would be judged by whether or not the free expression of the Word (i.e. the Gospel message in this case), and thence the Kingdom, was allowed to flourish. The Kingdom was, and would always remain, the true guide to the holy life of justice, peace and compassion—*the* only life worth living. No wonder their language was so offensive and terrifying to those who had the most to lose by the implementation of their vision of the Kingdom, and that it invited extraordinary levels of verbal and physical violence and other repressive measures.

Biblical Grooves of Thought

Though the English language was still structurally unstable during the seventeenth century, and experiencing enormous change, it was heavily influenced, as already acknowledged, by the increased use of the Bible, particularly the King James Version. People began moving in 'biblical

---

[32] Fully demonstated by Fox in his *Surely the Magistrates of Nottingham* (1659), Bds.
[33] For 'perfect law of liberty' see S. Fisher, *Rusticus ad Acedemicos*, 'The First Apologetical', chp. 4, 129; Penington, *The New Covenant of the Gospel* (1660), 31-2 and a later work by Fell, *A Call unto the Seed of Israel* (1665), 18.
[34] William Dell (1607-69), *The Way of True Peace and Unity* (1651), 217. Dell was formerly an Army chaplain and William Laud's secretary. See also *TWTUD*, 100 and Coward, *The Stuart Age*, 240.

grooves of thought'.[35] In concert with Melvin Keiser, it is important to stress that, 'theological language was the coin of the realm ... in which ... personal and social, psychological and political, economic and communal issues were discussed'.[36] Keiser's six categories, which today we tend to compartmentalise, were not mutually exclusive during the 1600s since they were indicative of a shared public discourse that was *all-embracingly* theological. This shared public discourse was born of the 'common cultural base' we have observed before. It arose from the Bible, which itself acted as a common denominator providing the vocabulary of a 'secret language', a language that needed only to be invoked to be understood. Even a partial biblical phrase, even a sanctified word or two, could be beneficial or dangerous. It could, for instance, serve the purpose of conveying a synecdochic message with the stamp of divine authority, provide the ability to circumvent the censor or land a speaker behind bars.[37] Friends like George Whitehead and Edward Burrough deftly engaged this kind of discourse which was also a subtle form of polemics or 'scriptural politics', a 'practical application of the English Bible in an era of common cultural assumptions'.[38]

The Quakers' public language conveyed their Kingdom experience in a highly repetitive style dubbed 'incantatory' by Jackson Cope. Repetition is a key element of all prophetic literature and verbal pronouncements, and the Friends were particularly influenced by the literary form of the Hebrew prophets, Matthew, the Books of Revelation, James and the Johannine writings. Paul was a particular influence. What Wills notes as Paul's 'Greek arguing style'—'epistolary, didactic, celebratory ('epideictic')', given to 'diatribe' and, as we find in their tracts, a 'staccato drumbeat of questions'—all greatly influenced the Friends.[39] Further, absorbing mystical and apocalyptic imagery from Revelation and re-interpreting it for their generation, the Quakers often resorted to a flowing yet agrammatical mode. It was as if their quills failed to keep up with the cascade of ideas, images and words tumbling from their brains.

Indeed, on paper their words sometimes look and, if read aloud, sound as if they bunch into each other, a device designed perhaps to overwhelm their readers with the 'Truth'. In many instances, they certainly display a

---

[35] Fogelklou, *James Nayler: the Rebel Saint*, 31.
[36] Keiser, 'Reading Penington Today' in *KMOLW*, 124 and see Hill, *Puritanism and Revolution*, 29.
[37] Synecdoche: a more inclusive term used for a less inclusive one and *vice-versa* (e.g. 'Whitehall' for 'the workings of the government'; 'sword' for 'legal jurisdiction; 'ranters' for people of unsound mind or immoral behaviour). For Fox's own attitude towards synecdoche see his *A Primer for the Scholars* (1659), 11 and esp. 13.
[38] Katz, *God's Last Words*, 40-1.
[39] Wills, *What Paul Meant*, 68-9. Wills' parenthesis.

passion and conviction at once unsettling and demanding. Their sermons sometimes take like forms. According to Cope, Margaret Fell's grammatical structure could progressively disintegrate into shorter and shorter sentence members that were linked by tenuous, sound-dictated conjunctions. Being loose with grammar in similar ways, there was a tendency for the Publishers of the Truth to concentrate on the words themselves, intensifying and projecting them outwards as a testimony to their passionate relationship with God. Here is a theophanous example from an early Friend, John Swinton:

> A lamentation, a lamentation, a lamentation, in the Life, over the Seed, the oppressed Seed. Oh, oh! how shall Jacob arise, for he is small? Oh! how shall Jacob arise, for he is small, and the mountains and hills are high and weighty and the rubbish, the rubbish, the rubbish is great.[40]

Cope explains that this 'incantatory' style was evident when the Spirit spoke through them. And yet at other times, when addressing the authorities for example, they could be down-to-earth and crystal clear.[41]

Fox, of course, also moved in 'biblical grooves of thought'. Though he was, in my estimation, one of the most innovative figures of English spiritual experience, he was not as literate as some other leading Quakers such as Edward Burrough, Samuel Fisher, Francis Howgill, James Nayler and Isaac Penington. To a degree, his style was undisciplined and he could blur or meld concepts to the detriment of understanding. His often unsystematic and prolix approach, perhaps due to a penchant for dictation and a lack of theological training, conformed to the language of those 'bred on parabolic readings of Scripture . . . more given to searching for truth in analogies . . . than to establishing facts.'[42] However, his lack of eloquence, and his direct and concrete, often spontaneous, communication proved more effective with a general audience than the erudition of writers such as John Milton. When revolutionary language becomes literary it loses its power. And yet his language *could* be beautifully theopoetic, often possessing, as

---

[40] See John Swinton, *A Testimony for the Lord* (1663?), 6-7. For 'in the Life' see Nayler, 'Concerning Light and Life' in *Love to the Lost*, 1-3; Fox, *The Second Covenant*, 5; Howgill, *Some of the Mysteries of God's Kingdom*, 13; Fox, *An Epistle General to them who are of the Royal Priesthood*, 5 and W. Smith, *The Morning-Watch*, 3.
[41] Cope, 'Seventeenth-Century Quaker Style' in Fish (ed.), 210, 213.
[42] Miner (ed.), p. x.; See also T.C. Jones, *George Fox's Teaching*, 6; Graves, 'Mapping the Metaphors in George Fox's Sermons' in Mullett (ed. 1991), 54; Hobby, 'Prophecy, Enthusiasm and Female Pamphleteers' in Keeble, 167.

Chapter 4: 'Pure Love to the Soul'

Arthur Roberts informs us, a rhetoric that was 'vibrant with life because it was full of sensory metaphor'.[43]

Consequently, his writings sometimes harbour a certain lyrical prose and his epistles are a case in point. They have a freer, anagogical quality than the majority of his tracts and through them, as with the letters of Augustine of Hippo, he was better able to express his delicacy of feeling, mysticism and non-violence at deeper levels. In 1653, for instance, he famously advised the Friends to 'bring your minds out of the earth . . . towards God, where the pure babe is born in the virgin mind'.[44] In another example from the same passage, metaphors of tree and fountain are combined: all those in the 'night' were 'corrupt trees which cannot bring forth good fruit' while 'the good Fountain [sent] forth sweet water, joy [by which] the living streams proceed out, where there is no guile, but the living streams of life'.[45] Like other Friends, Fox could also speak of the 'dew of heaven' that would fall on them as they kept to the Light or Truth. When the news of Burrough's death in 1663 sent ripples of panic through the movement, Fox rallied his spiritual troops in words that ring down the ages:

> Sing and rejoice, you children of the day and of the light; for the Lord is at work in this thick night of darkness that may be felt. And truth does flourish as the rose, and the lilies do grow among the thorns, and the plants atop of the hills, and upon them the lambs do skip and play. And never heed the tempests nor the storms, floods nor rains, for the seed Christ is over all, and does reign.[46]

Nayler, too, displayed mystical authority through the written word. God's love, he wrote in 1655, was 'known and seen in the Light, from whence is the spring of Love, which runs out to the whole of creation of God, and for the same end; for as the Love is One, so the End is but one'.[47] Other beautiful examples from early Quaker works abound, their literary skills often inspired by Scripture where they met the poetic and apocalyptic Book of Revelation with its similar profusion of dream-like images.

---

[43] A. Roberts, 'The Relevancy of George Fox', 405. See also Halvorsen, *The Quaker Understanding of Conversion and the Inner Light*, 113-14. The early Quakers never used 'inner light'.

[44] Fox, 'To Call the Minds Out of the Creatures' in T. C. Jones, *'The Power of the Lord Is Over All'*, 49-50. Also John Pain (Payne), *A Discovery of the Priests* (1655), 35-7. Fox's epistles may have been edited after his death to omit material embarrassing to the late seventeenth and early eighteenth century movement.

[45] Fox, *News Coming up out of the North*, 42-3.

[46] Fox, Ep. 227 (1663) in *Works*, 7: 241. See Jn. 1:14; 14: 6. Also Nayler, *Deceit Brought to Daylight* (1656), 28.

[47] Nayler, *Love to the Lost*, 17.

Military, 'Rude' and Tough Language

Let us now turn to military imagery since it was a normal feature of written and spoken communication at the time. Exercising enormous literary power, it enjoyed an ancient lineage being found in a myriad of works and in those of more recent times by such writers as John Knox, the Scottish Presbyterian leader and a composer of the Geneva Bible.[48]

As a consequence, it was natural that biblical military terminology found its way into early Quaker teaching and their verbal and written interchanges with opponents and various authorities. They and their Puritan detractors were well aware that Paul of Tarsus and his followers saw the Christian life not only as a 'walk' but as spiritual warfare in which God's power and love would 'destroy fortifications' (obstacles to the Kingdom), 'take captives' (turn people to the Christ) and 'punish resistance' (introduce right inner discipline for the successful spiritual life). It is in this light that early Quaker writings should be understood such as Stephen Crisp's *A Word of Reproof* (1658) with its own plentiful complement of military metaphors. Burrough and Howgill also used biblical military language abundantly. In one sentence alone in *A Visitation of the Rebellious Nation of Ireland* (1656) they recalled twenty-five such references from thirteen biblical books. This was not untypical of the early Quakers and is a good example of how their movement appropriated biblical language to an amazing degree as its own.[49]

Biblical phraseology, of course, can be extreme—Isaiah, Jeremiah, Jesus and Paul often used harsh and inflammatory language with those whose actions they despised. The Friends, too, declared that they employed 'the same language of the prophets, Christ and the apostles'.[50] Nuttall reminds us that similar phraseology during the seventeenth century was 'internalised passionately, used vehemently and in a style still consonant with contemporary use.'[51] Given that 'rude' or strident language was often a

---

[48] Dawson, 'The Apocalyptic Thinking of the Marian Exiles' in Wilks (ed.), 87-8. Dawson draws attention to the use of military imagery. See also Firth, *The Apocalyptic Tradition in Reformation Britain*, 123-5. For military imagery in Knox see his *The Copy of an Epistle* (1559), 5.

[49] Burrough and Howgill, *A Visitation of the Rebellious Nation of Ireland* (1656), 12-13. The passage reads: 'I made thy walls as iron (Dt. 3:5; 1 Sam. 23:7; 1 K. 4: 13; Jer. 1:18?), and thy gates as brass (Ps. 107: 16; Isa. 45:2) . . . and I gave their carcasses (Isa. 14:19; Jer. 16:4; Na. 3:3) to fall by the sword and for the fowls of the air to feed upon' (Gen. 6: 7; Dt. 28: 6; 1 K. 14:11, 16:4, 21:24; Jb. 12:7, 28:21; Isa. 17:44, 46; Mt. 6:26; Mk. 4:4, 32; Lk. 8:5, 13:19; Ac. 10:12, 11:16). Rosemary Moore uses this passage to illustrate early Quaker closeness to the military: see *TLITC*, 122-3, 67.

[50] Fox and Nayler *et al*, *Several Petitions Answered*, 57 (wrongly paginated as p.14).

[51] Nuttall, *The Holy Spirit in Puritan Faith and Experience*, 182; Hill, *The Experience of Defeat*, 35, 110 and 310-11.

Chapter 4: 'Pure Love to the Soul'

feature of public debates, Thomas Danson, minister at Sandwich (Kent), could accuse Samuel Fisher, for instance, of 'spitting venom'.[52] Other examples have been mentioned already and it must not be forgotten that people raised with the 'arte of rhetorique' were expected to go beyond accepted and mostly private language in what was a highly charged socio-ecclesial-political environment.

Today we can be over-sensitive to the 'harsh' or 'rude' expressions of those times. Used in the manner of Isaiah, Jeremiah, Jesus and Paul as a cleansing agent, such language was a means by which the Friends and others made points with vigour and urgency. In their highly combative times, the Friends were concerned to emulate Jesus' harsh judgment of those who were 'out of the Life'. This may help explain why their heightened religious sensibilities, combined with the rhetoric they were taught or heard when younger, could result in behaviour that was often verbally tough but loving at the same time. In fact, their message of divine wrath was one that was based primarily on restorative love as Nayler was to plead:

> So that this love of God consists of reproofs, judgment and condemnation against all that defies the creation, and against the creature who yields to that pollution. And this is pure love to the soul, that deals faithfully therewith in declaring its condition. And that was the great love Christ showed the Jews when he told them they were hypocrites, blind guides, liars.[53]

In this way, they hammered home their calling as sons and daughters of the Light, seeing themselves, therefore, as an extension of God in a similar way servants were regarded as an extension of their master and his family.[54] The movement, therefore, could act as if it were one personality with one language whose coherence was based entirely on the Kingdom, the Word being its epicentre. 'The eternal Word', wrote Nayler, 'which was in the beginning before all languages were, breaks in pieces all languages and . . .

---

[52] Danson, *The Quaker's Folly* (1659), 28.

[53] Nayler, 'Concerning Love' in *Love to the Lost*, 18. For the much used phrase 'out of the Life' or nearest approximation see, for instance, Nayler, 'Concerning Light and Life' in *Love to the Lost*, 1-3; Rebecca Travers (c.1609-88), *This is for Any of that Generation* (1659/6), Bds.; Penington, *The Way of Life and Death*, 16-17. For 'now' and 'not yet' see Burrough, *The True Faith of the Gospel of Peace* (1656), 22-3 and in *Works*, 147.

[54] For 'sons and daughters': Ac. 2:17, 18. Also Fox, Ep. 35 in *Collection*, 31; *A Woman Learning in Silence* (1656), 1-2; *An Epistle to all People on the Earth*, p. 1 in which Fox quotes Ac. 2: 17-18 (= Jl. 2: 28 which Fox also quotes from Joel's theophanous second chapter).

brings all into one language, for that which keeps in many languages keeps in confusion'.⁵⁵

As the truly convinced, both on an individual basis (a personal theophany so to speak) and as 'one of another', the Friends believed they were granted prophetic insights and sought to reach the essence (that of the Spirit/Christ) in people, situations and experiences.⁵⁶ Infusing everything with the Spirit, their language had the power to mock time itself, but it also gave them an authority to declare and admonish. Early Quaker warnings, declarations and so-called 'rude' behaviour were designed to crack the shell of complacency and ignorance of their opponents who would then, hopefully, learn what it was to be truly of the Light and thus be able to enact primitive Christianity for their times.

All sides in the great religious debates of the seventeenth century used a rhetoric rich in pejoratives. Terms such as 'Babylonian bawd', 'Egyptian darkness', 'Turk', 'Jew', 'Rome', 'papist' and other imagery were used to describe unsavoury influences within the Church in England.⁵⁷ On another level they represented the 'carnal' which, as with most people of the time, signified a sinful nature. Where appropriate 'carnal' also described 'wild', 'heady' and 'brutish' people or situations. In the carnal lay the danger of separation from God, of being plunged into 'darkness', an idea reminiscent of medieval thinking in which sin was understood as a rejection of God's Kingdom through self-will. As spiritual swords, these expressions had the potential to unleash inner fears and scruples especially in relation to sin or disobedience, an incomplete relationship with God. As Fox wrote,

> by forgetting God and doing wickedly [one goes] from the Life and Power . . . into the separation from [God] . . . and so the Power, Light and Life goes over them who go on in wickedness that leads out of God.⁵⁸

As in other Quaker writings, Margaret Fell's use of stark polarities was equally influenced by the Bible. By describing a local magistrate, John Sawrey, as 'a caterpillar', she evoked seven biblical images which painted him as a plague or as a general malaise at large intent upon devouring all

---

⁵⁵ Nayler, *A Lamentation (by one of England's Prophets,)* (1653), 17.
⁵⁶ Hubberthorne, *A True Testimony of Obedience* (1654), 2-5. Hubberthorne uses Jer. 23:29.
⁵⁷ For spiritual Egypt see, for instance, Fox, *Truths Triumph in the Eternal Power* (1661), 12 and Howgill's spiritual autobiography, *The Inheritance of Jacob Discovered* (1655), *passim*; also Jer. 42: 7-22.
⁵⁸ Fox, *Some Principles of the Elect People of God* (1661), 23; see Margaret Killam and Barbara Patison, *A Warning from the Lord* (1655), 3.

that was good and wholesome.[59] For Fox in 1649, the priest of St. Mary's in Nottingham was 'a great lump of earth', that is to say, one who was dishonourable and in desperate need of the Light of the New Israel, the covenant of love and peace.[60] Sometimes the Friends used 'dumb dogs', a commonly used term from Isaiah 56:10, when describing other clerics as representatives of corrupt earthly powers such as the Church and State.[61] Today we may regard such behaviour as distasteful but, as we see in Burrough's *An Answer to Giles Firmin* (1656), the Friends justified such invective on biblical grounds. Firmin, wrote Burrough, was a mere 'hireling' who made

> a prey through covetousness upon the people acting the horrible filthy thing which Jeremiah cried against. And to call you evil Beasts . . . which teach for filthy lucre, as Paul did. And much more such like may truly be spoken of you by the Spirit of the Lord which spoke the same language.[62]

Of course not all ministers were caterpillars, dumb dogs or great lumps of earth. Like the reverends Furnace and Josselin, many displayed deep concern and love for the people they served. Nor were they necessarily stooges of the *status quo*. Still, this did not deter some Friends from hurling abuse at clerics and opponents, even at 'steeplehouses'. And not all their name-calling was biblical. Their language could at times be contrary to the movement's call for tolerance, compassion and peace. Certainly, no Scriptural justification exists for lambasting individuals (if we are to believe the anti-Quakers Francis Bugg and Charles Leslie) as 'green-headed trumpeter', 'wheelbarrow', 'whirligig', 'moon-calf', 'gimcrack', 'devil-driven dungy God', 'threadbare tatterdemalion' or a 'grinning dog'.[63]

---

[59] Fell, *To the General Council of Officers of the English Army* (*DCFB/Wing* 1659), 7; Alexander Parker (1628-89), *A Call Out of Egypt* (1656), 1, 3 for 'Kingdom'. For 'caterpillar' see 1 K. 8:37; 2 Ch. 6:28; Ps. 78:46 and Jl. 1:4.

[60] See *Journal*, 39. The Quakers were not alone in attacking the clerics. And see also Ezk. 34:25, 37:26.

[61] See, for instance, Burrough, *A Warning of the Lord to . . . Underbarrow* (1654), 9, 22; Fox and Nayler *et al*, *Several Petitions Answered*, 48, 56. Also Mt. 5:1; 7:6. 'Dumb dogs' had a long history. Before 1603 and during his reformist period, the revolutionary Puritan, John Robinson (pastor to the *Mayflower* Puritans) also aimed the insult at parish clergy.

[62] Burrough, *Stablishing against Quaking* (1656), 23 and in his 'An Answer to Giles Firmin' in *Works*, 172-3. Burrough margined references from Isa. 56: 9-10; Mi. 3:5 (error: should have been 3:11), Ezk. 34 (see 19, 25, 28), Jer. 5 and Tt. 1.11.

[63] 'Steeplehouse' was probably first used in 1644 by Francis Quarles (1592-1644), lawyer and royalist. For 'hirelings' see also Winstanley, *The Mystery of God* (1649), 33. For late century, anti-Quaker reactions to Quaker language see Francis Bugg, *Some of the Quakers Principles* (1693), 8-10; Leslie, *The Snake in the Grass* (1696), 32. Leslie's complaints

Deeper Theological Issues

Colourful and tough language apart, profound theological issues were at issue. Expertly versed in the Bible, Fox and the public Friends opposed the accepted view, circulating among Protestants generally, that divine inspiration without intermediaries could be dismissed because revelation had ceased in 'the post-Apostolic age or that Scripture was sufficient for delivering God's message to humanity'.[64] Fox's language conveyed a God who was personal and thus relational. The Light was never exclusively an 'it' and God's presence, rule, leadership or governance (the Kingdom) was in the *now* and would continue for all time. Samuel Fisher wrote of this eternal *now* in *Apokryta Apokalypta* (1661) as 'the Light which God *now* is ... and dwells [within and forever]'.[65] Its revelation, he continued, required discernment so that its secret—that is, the Kingdom discerned only by those familiar with God's hope for humanity—may be recovered and shared with all people. For Isaac Penington, those out of the Light were 'outward Jews', the Jews having failed generally to recognise the Light in Jesus. The Friends considered those 'in the Life' as 'inward Jews' with true Jewishness demanding a circumcision of the heart—an opening-up of oneself to the Life, the true Israel, and its purity both Edenic and Christic.[66]

The Friends frequently applied metaphor to evoke an apocalyptic purpose. Apocalyptic writing is 'a special kind of literary work ... more closely akin to poetry than to prose' though to read it in a literal way is to distort its messages.[67] Reay, for instance, asserts that Fox's statement in *The Lambs Officer is Gone Forth* (1659), 'now shall the Lamb and saints have victory', indicated a non-pacifism.[68] But it was a commonly-used phrase by the Friends from Revelation 14:17. Rather than a rallying call to physical arms, the tract portrayed Fox as a spiritual general apocalyptically invoking spiritual weaponry to confront the mighty citadels of apostasy—popery

---

derived from Bugg and surfaced forty years later in Anon, *The True Picture of Quakerism* (1736), 48-56; see esp. 48.

[64] McDowell, *The Radical English Imagination*, 141.

[65] See *Journal*, 358 for unconditionality; Fisher, *Apokryta*, 8. Fisher's emphasis.

[66] Penington, *The Jew Outward* (1659), *passim*; *Some Considerations Propounded to the Jews* (*DCFB* 1660), 3, 1-8 and see his *Examination of the Grounds and Causes* (1660), esp. the section, 'Concerning the Person of Christ'. Thomason dates this work April 1660; it may have been in preparation, therefore, on the cusp of the new decade; see Rom. 2: 28-29 for 'inward Jew'. And see Fox, *A Voice of the Lord to the Heathen* (1656), 2, 5.

[67] Reddish (ed.), 35. See Fox, *The Lambs Officer*, 13 and his use of Revelation in *To the King of Spain* (1660) in *Doctrinals* in which he lets loose a torrent of metaphor as vitriol.

[68] According to Burrough, the Lamb had the victory as early as 1653. See his 'Epistle to the Reader' in Christopher Atkinson *et al*, *The Standard of the Lord* (1653), Sig. A2; Nayler, *Milk for the Babes*, 10.

within Christianity as well as the Roman Church itself.[69] Since apostasy in the Church had been exposed by Fox's understanding of God's Dominion, the task now was its exorcism. This would be achieved through a wholesale turning to the Light by which 'all people' would be sanctified so that iniquities and the separation from God they induced would be vanquished forever. In the same tract, Fox recalled Revelation 19:11-21—'there went a sharp sword with which to smite the nations'—the point of Revelation's Christology being the spiritual victory of the defenceless and weak (the Lamb) over the powerful (the empire) by means of the everlasting Kingdom. This theme was visited repeatedly in Fox's epistles and in such seminal works as *To All that would Know the Way to the Kingdom* (1653) and *News Coming up out of the North* (1654).[70] He and the Friends were reacting to that same separation that they, too, experienced in their lives thus demonstrating a craving for unity with God—a craving with a language that was both dramatic and urgent, a unity that could be enjoyed by every single person on earth.

Conclusion

Early Quaker language-use was upsetting if not frightening to audiences because it displayed an obvious and disturbing intimacy, even a potential and disconcerting oneness, with God. For the Friends, as with Jesus, God was intensely personal.[71] Such a mystical intimacy was outside the non-Quaker's normal code of social and religious hierarchy. As a result, it appeared dysfunctional if not psychologically unbalanced.

The Quakers pursued ascendancy in public discourse and sought to eradicate any commodification of the Word. They did so through a powerful application of the spoken and written word in an atmosphere in which controversies, fanaticism and open denunciation were normative. Another strong feature of their language was their use of Biblical military metaphor and allegory.

At a deeper level, Quaker language invited people to confront ultimate reality as never before amid a physical environment that was forever uncertain, another reason perhaps for the often gratuitous violence that

---

[69] Fox, *The Lambs* Officer, 13 and *To the Pope* (1661), 61-6; *Doctrinals*, 202; *QER*, 101-11, esp. 101; Hill, 'Quakers and the English Revolution', 170, 172. For 'spiritual weapons' see 2 Cor. 10:3; Eph. 6: 10-17.

[70] Reay, 'The Quakers and 1659: two newly discovered broadsides by Edward Burrough', 101-11. See 101 and *cf. The Lambs Officer*, 12-14; Fox, *News Coming up out of the North*, 27; *FF*, 114.

[71] See W. Smith, *A Manifestation of Prayer*, Bds., col. 2.

came their way.[72] By such means, the Quakers' faith and practice, and their prophetic and apocalyptic language, directly challenged conventional thinking into reclarifying the muddle of life in the light of God's revelation, something that the Gospel of John had done for the Christians of *its* time. But rather than a plea for individual salvation only, their language-use, and the 'conversation' (behaviour) that accompanied it, attempted to invert social and political priorities, as they understood the Beatitudes to have done, in favour of the poor (themselves and others) so they may be liberated from all manner of 'oppression'.[73] Thus they attempted to advance the cause of the ruled over the ruler.

Early Quaker military rhetoric, 'plaining' and confrontational language, then, were conduits for the deliberate creation among their many audiences of a critical awareness of the revolutionary Kingdom, the truest guide to the holy life of justice, peace and compassion in the Light. This indeed was *the* only life worth living. Its outward form became a Lamb's War for salvation (wholeness, unity in God) for all. Words, thoughts and even their 'conversation' were seen as sacred in conveying *the* Word, the Christ; otherwise, according to Nayler, 'the broken language is bought forth' in opposition to 'the pure language of Rest [God]'.[74] If they engaged in tough polemical interchanges it was because they took their cue from Jesus, Matthew, Paul, James and the Hebrew prophets and psalmists who boldly attacked spiritual complacency and ignorance. Of course, some Friends were indeed 'rude' in the modern sense.

And finally, rather than 'replacing' rhetoric with a new 'community' of speech, as Hazleton maintains, it is perhaps better to say they *redefined* the art of rhetoric in their egalitarian eagerness to spread the Kingdom of God.[75] In fact without the metaphor, early Quaker written and spoken language would have been rendered lifeless since it relied completely on 'key recurrent metaphor clusters drawn from Scripture and everyday life, which together [became] the conceptual analogical system through which they view[ed] spiritual truth'.[76]

We shall now see how Quaker personal, social, political, economic, ecclesiastical and communal Concerns were communicated through the language of the Kingdom.

---

[72] Gwyn in Dandelion *et al*, *Heaven on Earth*, 118; O'Day, 'Jesus as Friend in the Gospel of John', 155; Peterson, *Reversed Thunder*, 145-6; *FF*, 141.

[73] See J. Audland, *The Innocent Delivered*, title pg.; Edward Billynge, *A Word of Reproof* (1659), 64.

[74] Nayler, 'An Epistle to Several Friends about Wakefield' (1653) in *Works*, 26; written from Appleby gaol.

[75] Hazleton, 'Mony Choaks', 269.

[76] Graves, *Preaching the Inward Light*, 184.

Chapter 5: *'Since the Days of the Apostles'*

- The Kingdom of the Quakers -

As our survey of Quaker language shows, the Friends were incapable of neutrality in the great political and religious debates of their time. It is well known that some public Friends had fought with the parliamentary forces during the wars while a small number remained in the army after the battle of Worcester in 1651, continuing their careers until at least 1659 or 1660. People who enlisted to fight the king generally believed the army to be 'the most radical, political, religious, and social force in the land, a vessel for the aspirations of the 'new men' and the putative power for translating revolutionary ideas into action ... [which] threatened to upset the old order completely'.[1] While not every Quaker supported the parliamentary side, the overwhelming majority did. They continued to give it qualified support during the 1650s as they still endorsed the Good Old Cause, particularly its demand for religious liberty and more importantly when it (the Cause) was seen to conform to the Kingdom, the Jesus Way.[2]

The concerns of leading Friends such as ex-soldier George Fox the Younger were typical in this respect. In 1659 he acknowledged those non-Quaker soldiers and officers who 'truly desire[d] the good of God's people, and that mercy and justice might be established by righteous laws whereby equity and justice might be done to all'.[3] Richard Hubberthorne, another war veteran, insisted the Cause was one of 'true' religion, 'the work of God in the Light of Christ in the conscience, in the soul, a spiritual hearing the voice of the beloved Son of God'.[4] True religion, synthesised thus with the Cause and the Kingdom, led from inequality and persecution to righteousness, justice and mercy. Hubberthorne insisted in *The Good Old Cause Briefly Demonstrated*, completed in May 1659, that peace and nonviolence were also hallmarks of true religion.[5]

Early Quaker understanding of righteousness (analysed more in Chapter 6) was intrinsically linked to their knowledge of the Kingdom, something

---

[1] Booy, *Autobiographical Writings by Early Quaker Women*, 161.
[2] Burrough, *To the Whole English Army* (1659), Bds.; Christopher Fell *et al*, *A Few Words to the People of England* (1655), 3, 14. Christopher Fell concentrated on tithing.
[3] No relation to George Fox of Fenny Drayton, this Fox was 'younger' in the Quaker faith. See his *A Few Plain Words* (1659) in *Works*, 85 and Christianson, 'The Causes of the English Revolution', 72.
[4] Hubberthorne, *The Good Old Cause Briefly Demonstrated*, 1-3.
[5] *Ibid.*, 2, 10, 16.

they would have especially met in Matthew in such passages as 6:33: 'But seek ye first the Kingdom of God, and his righteousness; and all these things shall be added unto you'.[6] Wherever God's righteousness was found, either in the individual or generally in society, there, too, was the Kingdom. Their view of righteousness was akin to the Greek *dikaiosýnē* (Latin: *justitia*) as we find it in Paul and in the Sermon where it is mentioned five times, that is, to set things right (*dikaoiun*), the right conduct among, and social relations between, 'all people' before God. Here was an inclusive idea antithetical to the Calvinist premillennial rule of the Elect.[7] The movement took heart from the Pauline message that through Jesus God brought about a new humanity in order to break down all barriers between men and women, races and classes. Violence, therefore, had no place in this divine scheme.

For the Quakers, the Good Old Cause was both a metaphor for, and a manifestation of, this new world order—the new or second covenant or the New Israel—the covenant of love and peace. It promised a world where people could enjoy liberty of conscience and freedom from the Church's theology of sin, a bondage into which it was locked. If anyone dwelt in that which was pure, wrote Fox, by 'exercising the conscience towards God and [humanity]', the [Mosaic] Law could not take hold of them for 'it was not made for such the righteous, but for the sinners'.[8] Just as water was vital for life, there could be *no* freedom for the conscience without an inward and outward witness to the Light, which the Friends often referred to as 'Truth'. On an individual level, where the Light/Truth 'convinces [i.e. convicts] of sin', so then could the Light shine on the *world's* sin to invite a new and glorious sunrise. Thus by the Light they were guided and inspired.[9]

'The Grand Oppressor': the Tithe

Their interpretation of the Good Old Cause and understanding of righteousness allowed the Friends to adopt uncompromising positions over such issues as refusing to pay hat honour (doffing one's hat to someone of superior class) or, like the Baptists, not swearing oaths chiefly on the basis of Matthew 5:34 and James 5:12, or declining to pay forced tithes for

---

[6] See Hutchins, 'The Fundamental Thought and Purpose of Matthew', 199.
[7] Marcus, 'Entering into the Kingly Power of God', 670. Paul's epistle to the Romans concerns itself with the righteousness of God and its unveiling. See esp. Rom. 3: 21-26 and also the Sermon in Matthew.
[8] Fox, *A Warning to the Rulers of England* (1653) in Nayler, *A Lamentation*, 12.
[9] Burrough, *A Discovery of Divine Mysteries*, 19. For the necessity of Light for a free conscience see Brinton, *Friends for 300 Years*, 34-5. See also Tt. 1:9; Jm. 2:9 (KJV).

'hireling priests' and the upkeep of churches.[10] Their opposition to the tithe had a dual effect. It crystallised Quaker grievances in respect to the various authorities and the widespread poverty among the people, and deepened their insights into the Jesus Way. The Light/the Way, they believed, exposed the evils of the tithing system. Those who supported tithes were in 'deep slumber, error and blindness', in a state of 'strong delusion'. They dwelt still in the 'old covenant' and its 'first priesthood'.[11] Morrill suggests however that, until the rise of the Quakers, the number of tithe refusals based on the scruples of churchmen, or because 'the minister was not discharging his proper duties, were more numerous than instances of refusals based on a radical critique of hireling priests'.[12]

During the first half of the seventeenth century, tithing was indeed one of *the* controversial features of local and national life, and campaigns for their abolition were highly charged. The well-known Radical Independent, John Saltmarsh, resigned his preferment in Heslerton (Yorks.) because, like other opponents of tithing, he could see the poverty it caused at first hand. Its supporters were keen to underline the central position tithing had enjoyed over the course of many centuries in English religious, political and social life. By the time the Friends burst onto the public scene in the 1650s, abolition was still the subject of numerous court proceedings, debates, pamphlets and acrimonious debates in parliament. Such was the depth of the controversy that the Nominated or 'Barebone's Parliament' in 1653 came close to abolishing them—one reason for that parliament's demise.

Great tithes, so-called, were arbitrarily extracted from people for bulk products such as grain and livestock. Small tithes involved lesser items. In effect, the tithe was a tax on the 'fruit or lawful increase of the earth, beasts or men's labours' equalling about a tenth of the agricultural produce of a single parish, although the situation varied between parishes.[13] They were comprehensive in nature, as William Sheppard, a Westminster law reformer

---

[10] Refusal to pay hat honour and tithes, to swear oaths and use 'thou' instead of 'you' when addressing those of higher social degree had a long history in England stretching back to the anti-clerical 'free-willers' of Henry Harte (d. 1557?), a spiritual-political descendent of Wycliffe and the Lollards. Wycliffe is mentioned re: tithes by Burrough, Howgill and in Anthony Pearson's *The Great Case of Tithes Truly Stated* (1657), 24-5. See *Journal*, 244-5 and Admiral E. Mountagu's letter (16/Sept/1656) to John Thurloe in *Thurloe*, v., 422 describing a full ship's compliment of Quaker sailors in Lisbon refusing to pay hat honour to the Portuguese. Winstanley and William Everard refused hat honour in General Fairfax's presence in 1649; see Anon, *The Declaration and Standard* (1649), 3.

[11] Fox, *A Reply to the Pretended Vindication* (1658), 15; H. Smith, *The First and Second Priesthood, passim*.

[12] Morrill (ed.), *Revolution and Restoration*, 109.

[13] William Sheppard (d. 1674), *The Parson's Guide* (1654), 2.

and Cromwell's principal legal adviser, outlined in his *Parson's Guide* (1654), the law concerning them being highly complex.[14]

Originally, tithes were earmarked for vicars, parsons or other ordained ministers, the descendants of the church builder or the purchaser(s) of the monastic property on which the parish church was built. There is no doubt that tithes, if paid, helped many ministers (and even some bishops) augment their salaries of between £8 and £15 a year, although 600 of the 9,284 benefices in England and Wales guaranteed a better living.[15] In Lancashire in 1650, for instance, while seventeen of the county's rectors were due £100 or more per annum from tithes, the rector at Croston received £349, that of Wigan earned £417 and the vicar at Winwick could expect £660 annually. Generally, a payment of £50 per annum was considered a good stipend though many, as again in Lancashire, could earn £20 or less. Many of those in charge of chapels of ease were often reliant on parishioners for their maintenance.[16]

Even before John Selden's banned *The History of Tithes* (1618) questioned clerical claims to tithes as a divine right, they had been long regarded by many as oppressive, indeed *the* 'grand oppressor' as William Erbery the Ranter later called them in 1652. The Levellers and Diggers had taken up the fight against tithing with the Levellers' Second and Third Agreements of the People (1647, 1649) eagerly anticipating their abolition.[17] And according to Richard Hubberthorne who fought at Dunbar (1650), hopes were raised among the soldiery when, before the battle began, Cromwell solemnly promised the troops that parliament would indeed abolish tithing.

Tithes often went hand-in-hand with anti-clericalism. Tract after tract, not all Quaker, highlighted clerical covetousness, selfishness and outrageous demands. William Walwyn the Leveller railed against the clergy calling them 'swarms of locusts who made merchandise of the blessed Word of Truth'. They divided people, he wrote, 'into factions, sects and parties, and whereby the end of the Gospel, which directs [us] only to love,

---

[14] *Ibid.*; see esp. pp. 17-22.
[15] The figure of 600 is that of Archbishop Whitgift. See Green, 'Career Prospects', 71.
[16] Craven, 'Ministers of State', 55. Croston lies between Chorley and Southport; Winwick is north of Warrington; Wigan, northwest of Manchester, is now situated within the Greater Manchester conurbation. Though impossible to calculate precisely, £1 (1650) is roughly equivalent to £103 (using the retail price index) or £1,920 (using average earnings). This data is only available to 2009; see <MeasuringWorth.com>.
[17] William Erbery (1604-54), *The Grand Oppressor* (1652), 1-15. See Hubberthorne, *A Word of Wisdom and Counsel . . . to the Army* (1659), Bds., col.1; Anon, *An Agreement of the People of England* (1649), Bds. Also Nuttall, *The Holy Spirit*, 13; Solt, 'Anti-Intellectualism in the Puritan Revolution', 313; Kent, 'Relative Deprivation and Resource Mobilisation', 532.

is [lost].'[18] In 1656-7, Edward Burrough calculated that, as a social rank, 'hireling priests' collected a colossal £1.5 million each year in tithes mainly from the poor.[19] George Fox, when told that a priest near Fenny Drayton had died and that eight or nine men sought his benefice, echoed many of his Puritan and sectarian opponents: 'they are like a company of crows when a rotten sheep is dead'.[20] It would be a different matter, he said, if the revenue raised by tithes went to widows, the poor and strangers or to eradicate beggary rather than to the priests to 'go away with all'.[21]

Penalties for non-payment were often harsh. Robert Minter, a Quaker from Elmstone (Kent), who refused to pay tithes to a local cleric, 'priest Bradley', was deprived of a host of family goods including two feather beds and three feather bolsters, twelve other beds, two tables, fine linen, children's clothing, thirty hogs and pigs, three sheep, five calves, twenty-one lambs plus crops, all to the value of nearly £100.[22] Worse, Nicholas Homwood in 1675 was still urging Friends to obey their duty of refusal from the prison cell he had endured for ten years: 'Do not flee the Cross lest you miss of the Crown'.[23] John Lilburne the Leveller and future Quaker changed his mind about purchasing land when he realised he would have to confront 'lazy' 'anti-Christian' priests 'which tithes I should sooner be hanged than pay'. John Bunyan, also implacably opposed to tithes, cried out: 'will it not grieve you (oh you priests) . . . you were afraid to tell us of our sins, lest we should not put meat fast enough in thy mouth'.[24]

Before 1640, to offset a lack of tithe payment and to keep pace with the rise in prices, it was not unusual for the clergy to hold more than one benefice ('pluralism') or to keep cattle in their churchyard or on glebe land attached to the church. Such arrangements were regarded as normal because church buildings and land had secular functions that were not easily erased. Many clerics were schoolmasters or engaged in other professions. For instance, Thomas Speed of St. Philip's outside Bristol was a trader while

---

[18] William Walwyn (1600-81); Jonathan Scott, *England's Troubles*, 23 quotes Walwyn's *The Vanity of the Present Churches* (1649). See Miller, 'A Suffering People', 75.
[19] Burrough's calculation needs treating with very great caution; in respect to the above *purchasing power* ratio, his sum converts to £2,879 million in 2009 value.
[20] Maclear, 'Popular Anticlericalism in the Puritan Revolution', 449 and *Cambridge*, i., 195.
[21] Fox, *The Eternal, Substantial Truths of God's Kingdom* (1661), 21.
[22] For Minter see Thomas Robertson, *A Horrible Thing Committed* (1658), 7-8. This tract recommends readers to Hubberthorne's *The Record of Sufferings for Tythes* (1658).
[23] Homwood, *A Word of Counsel* (1675), 3.
[24] Burrough, *A Just and Lawful Trial of the Teachers* (1656/7), 18. Dennis Hollister, *The Harlots Vail Removed* (1658), 3, 7. See Bridenbaugh, *Vexed and Troubled Englishmen*, 286; Spaeth, *The Church in an Age of Danger*, 142-3. For Lilburne, Bunyan and Fox see Maclear, 'Popular Anticlericalism in the Puritan Revolution', 447-52.

Ralph Josselin in Essex bought and sold hops. These non-priestly functions gave a negative impression of the duties and reputation of the clerics.[25]

Even before the Reformation, many tithes and ecclesiastical property were owned by lay impropriators, a practice that continued with increasing regularity throughout the seventeenth century. Impropriators were sometimes absentee investors and they included the two universities, Oxford and Cambridge. Tithes from 3,849 livings in England were paid directly to laymen of whom the majority were gentry like John Evelyn or George Purefey of Fenny Drayton in Leicestershire, the parish of George Fox. Evelyn eventually sold his impropriation in South Malling (Sussex) for the considerable sum of £3,000. Impropriation could come with the church advowson, the right of patronage to nominate the clergyman to a parish. Purefey certainly maintained this privilege. Christopher Marshall, the Independent rector at Woodkirk in Yorkshire where James Nayler worshipped before his convincement, was nominated and subsequently paid £30 a year by the Earl of Sussex.

While Lord Sussex and George Purefey took an interest in their parishes many lay impropriators did not. Such neglect was keenly felt in the North where it could cause serious discontent. Feelings, for instance, ran high among the parishioners of Cartmel and Hawkeshead in Cumbria over excessive demands by two lay impropriators, parliamentarian Nathaniel Nicolson and royalist Thomas Preston.[26] Nationwide, such neglect invariably resulted in the impoverishment of churches as well as the employment of poorly educated clergy or 'reading ministers' who were prevented from delivering sermons but allowed to read from special books such as the *Book of Homilies*.[27] In general, tithe ownership varied from region to region. In Wiltshire, 57% of tithes were in the hands of clerics, a figure close to the national average.[28]

Many a parliamentary soldier was certain that freedom of conscience in Christian worship would be realised only when parishioners, rather than lay impropriators, supported approved preachers. However, while measures were taken to combat the growing power of the laity in this respect, at other times not-so-hidden agendas were at work. Sir Philip Warwick's *Memoirs* tell us how William Laud persuaded 'the king to shut down [in 1633] the London trust known as the Feoffees for Impropriators which sponsored a

---

[25] James, 'The Political Importance', 10-18; Harlow, 'Preaching for Hire' 39-40 tells us that St. Philip's supposedly commanded £50 p.a. in tithes and an extra £50 p.a. from ex-Cathedral revenues.
[26] Horle, *The Quakers and the English Legal System*, 2.
[27] Neelon, *James Nayler*, 70 gives a good account of this practice.
[28] See Spaeth, *The Church in an Age of Danger*, 142-3; Harlow, 'Preaching for Hire', 42 (6n) and Evelyn, *Diary*, 3, 146.

Chapter 5: 'Since the Days of the Apostles'

kind of Puritan preachers' bureau'. His hope was to thwart the introduction of nonconformists into too many churches, since [they]

> Had a design to buy in all the lay-impropriations, which the parish churches in Henry VIII's time were robbed of, and lodging the advisors [i. e. the right to appoint clergymen to livings] and presentations in their own feoffees, to have introduced men, who would have introduced doctrines suitable to their dependences.[29]

Behind Laud's thinking was the Church's financial independence of the Puritan nobility and 'middling sort'. Meanwhile, in regions outside London with their fierce local loyalties, intense feeling over the tithe continued unabatedly. As among Galileans at the time of Jesus, outside rulers or absentee landlords generated a great deal of resentment, particularly when they interfered in local affairs or extracted unfair taxes.

Tithing was such a powerful vested interest that even during the republic when widespread agitation against it continued, opposition to its eradication persisted within parliament. Besides the failure of the Nominated Parliament to abolish tithes, Article 35 of the Instrument of Government, which approximated to a written constitution, tolerated them pending 'a provision less subject to scruple and contention'. The result was a deepening of frustration, anger and disillusionment among anti-tithers towards politicians and the army. Instead, the fear of abolition among the 'better sorts' probably contributed to the restoration of the monarchy mainly because, from 1647 onwards, anti-tithe sentiment came to be associated with the scary Radicals—in particular the Levellers, Diggers and, a little later, the Quakers. Many people were drawn to the Friends because of their passionate hatred of tithes and contempt for the clerical class that largely enforced and benefited from them, often by charging unreasonable fees for ordinary church services. In 1655, Quaker Henry Clark objected to clerics, who, in the absence of a fee, denied the customary sermon to the memory of a recently deceased person. It was a financial burden, he said, which deeply offended the poor.[30]

A popular complaint of the Friends focussed on conflicts of interest. They maintained that, as magistrates, JPs (who were often clerics) had responsibility for imposing tithes and were thus judges in their own cases.[31] Giving voice to this and other related complaints, the few Quaker

---

[29] Kishlansky, *The Monarchy Restored*, 128-9. See Sir Philip Warwick's *Memoirs* (1701), 78-82, 89-93.
[30] Henry Clark, *A Description of the Prophets* (1655), 3.
[31] See Herrup, *The Common Peace*, 196 and 56-8 for the composition and conduct of Assizes; Amussen, 'Punishment, Discipline', 5; D. Hirst, 'Locating the 1650s', 370-1.

impropriators refused to collect their legal entitlement while, during the 1650s alone, more than a thousand Quakers like Minter and Homwood were prosecuted for tithe refusal. It was a witness that continued in the northern counties when cases were recorded during the 1730s.[32]

Along with other Radicals, the Friends gave their campaign a global character by portraying tithes as typifying Church and State 'tyranny' and a sign of general covetousness. Moreover, not only were they another proof of Church apostasy 'since the apostles' days', and therefore a popish relic, but they were also contrary to Kingdom values. As the well-researched histories of tithing by Anthony Pearson (1657) and Francis Howgill (1665) show, Quaker campaigns for abolition arose from a relentless commitment to the Jesus Way rather than from secular thinking. Pearson, himself a judge, argued that the 'unchangeable priesthood' of the new creation, those who were convinced of the truth of the Kingdom which stood 'not in figures and carnal ordinances', were 'clear [that] the primitive Church ... for some hundreds of years, and till the mystery of iniquity began to work, never called for the payment of tithes'. Fox in *The Pearl Found in England* (1658) extended Pearson's argument to include the worldwide Church:

> and all these crosses and images, pictures and worshipping of names and idols, and all these pulpits, priests, tithes, churches with crosses in the churchyards ... and all this making of ministers by the will of men, by their schools and colleges for covetous ends ... are of the Beast ... since the days of the apostles in the apostasy.[33]

The Church, they maintained, had forsaken the substance (the witness of Jesus) for 'types', 'figures' and 'shadows' (ecclesiological indulgence) besides adapting pagan customs for its own ends. The immediate work of Jesus and the Christ within him had been replaced by the *Church's* mediated work of the Christ.[34]

The Quakers' campaign against tithing was largely successful in the short term. Where tithe strikes occurred, either by Quakers or others, clergy were brought to their financial knees. The life of their parishes suffered

---

[32] See Ashley, *England in the Seventeenth Century*, 26; *QER*, 43; Booy, *Autobiographical Writings by Early Quaker Women*, 5; Horle, *The Quakers and the English Legal System*, 21 (35*n*). For 1730s Quaker tithe refusal see N. Morgan, *Lancashire Quakers*, 280-1.

[33] *Pearl*, 8; For Quaker conviction in the anti-Kingdom nature of tithes see Pearson, *The Great Case of Tithes Truly Stated*, 17, 19; Howgill, *The Great Case of Tithes and Forced Maintenance* (1665), 40, 53, 56, 59-60; S. Fisher, *To the Parliament of England* (1659), 2; Henry Clark, *A Description of the Prophets*, 1-2. For the same language re: tyranny and tithing see Winstanley, *New Law of Righteousness* (1649), 59, 112.

[34] My emphasis. *AOTW*, 107. See Fox, *The Great Mystery*, 76-7; *Journal*, 333 and Col. 2:17; Heb. 8:5, 10: 1, 34 and 11:1.

accordingly.³⁵ As a result, ministers who had supported toleration of religious observance now came to see it as a grave mistake that left the door open for heterodoxy, heresy, blasphemy, and 'atheism', a possible return to prelacy or, worse still, popery.³⁶ They envisaged the end of civilisation no less. But such fear was of little concern to dissenters who, as John Punshon informs us, saw only

> a disunity and a persecuting spirit, a clergy which often displayed worldly ambition rather than religious achievement, and a prevailing theology that confirmed and worsened the sense of sin and inadequacy from which they desperately sought relief.³⁷

For the sectaries, the Good Old Cause reinforced their primitivist conviction that it was *they* who were the chosen people charged with missionising the British nations out of 'apostasy'. Fox, never gentle with 'tithe-mongering' clerics, spoke for many:

> That which one spews out and vomits out in their books and pamphlets, that another priest he takes the same up, and eats the book and vomits it up again, till the whole nation is filled with their vomit. And this has been the state since the days of the apostles, in the apostasy. What a sickness has been because of vomits!³⁸

The Kingdom Revived

By the 1640s and 1650s many had become thoroughly demoralised over tithing, the failures of politicians and civil government, and the legal system. Some were disillusioned over the failure of the authorities and the army to implement the Good Old Cause. However, their chief concern lay with the English Church in general caught up as it was in internal disputation and a multiplicity of unsatisfying and conflicting theologies. According to Rufus Jones, these lost and seeking people came to believe not unreasonably that the Church could not be the true one. Consequently, with 'no valid sacraments, no person with apostolic unction', 'the sincere souls [could] only wait for a fuller revelation and a more efficacious ministry . . .

---

³⁵ Spaeth, *The Church in an Age of Danger*, 142; Hayduk, *Hopeful Politics*, 38; *Caton MSS.*, iii, 147.
³⁶ Aylmer, *Rebellion or Revolution?* 66. Seventeenth century 'atheism' did not necessarily signify a non-belief in God but instead any belief contrary to the prevailing view of Christianity held by the Church of England and leading groups such as the Presbyterians and Independents.
³⁷ Punshon, *Portrait in Grey*, 35.
³⁸ Fox, *Here is Declared the . . . Naming of Children* (1658), 7.

the letter of the Scripture [being] carnal and insufficient'. The Church looked to 'Christ after the flesh', Jones continued, while for the disaffected 'worldly preaching without spiritual experience was empty.'[39] William Penn made the observation that people 'left all visible churches and societies, and wandered up and down as sheep without a shepherd . . . seeking their beloved, but could not find Him'.[40] The complaint of Quaker-to-be Thomas Briggs was a common one: 'the ministers that were then called Puritans never could direct me to my teacher within'.

Eventually, many of these Seekers or 'Expecters' as Ephraim Pagitt's *Heresiography* (1645) labelled them, sought the fellowship of like-minded worshippers outside the Church.[41] Diverse in their theologies, they gathered like the recusants of old in clearings in woods, in isolated chapels, homes, barns or on mounts like Firbank Fell in present-day Cumbria where, in 1652, George Fox spoke to over one thousand Separatists about 'God's everlasting truth and word of Life'.[42] Some, believing in the imminent, literal fulfilment of the prophecies of Daniel and Revelation were certain they lived in a time of dereliction, the physical End-times, and that the only 'constructive religious posture' was to wait for the expected divine initiative.[43] But while some sought an outward Kingdom through a deep, personal relationship with Jesus—by now a dominant feature of religious practice—others 'opened' themselves to an unmediated relationship with God without the spiritually claustrophobic dominance of Bell and Book. In the King James Bible 'open' meant an unfolding, a revelation. It also carried connotations of an invitation to God's gift of the Kingdom.

The number of these dissenters grew rapidly, particularly after the demise of episcopal government during the civil wars and especially in regions beyond the reach of the ecclesiastical authorities and tithing ministers. Many of these 'gathered Churches', a 'widespread but amorphous conglomeration', strove for a life of purity and practised a simpler form of worship.[44] Since late in Elizabeth's reign, Separatist groups such as these, sometimes describing themselves as 'children of Light' and often relying substantially on women for their founding, maintenance and development,

---

[39] See also Brinton, *Friends for 300 Years*, 42.
[40] R. Jones, *Studies in Mystical Religion*, 452, 455.
[41] Pagitt, *Heresiography*, 128. The testimony of lesser known Friend Thomas Briggs (*c*.1610-85) is instructive; see *An Account of Some of the Travels* (1685), esp. 3. Also Howgill's spiritual autobiography, *The Inheritance of Jacob Discovered*, esp. 1-13.
[42] *Journal*, 109. Ambrose Rigge (*c*.1635-1705) visited Seekers in Staplehurst (Kent) in 1652; see *Cambridge*, i., 394. Catholic recusants, for instance, post-1559 met for worship in homes and isolated areas.
[43] Acheson, *Radical Puritans in England*, 61.
[44] For a contemporary description of Separatists see John Jackson, *A Sober Word to a Serious People* (1651), 3. Also Punshon, *Portrait in Grey*, 25; *TWTUD*, 184-97; *FF*, 56; Hoare, 'The Balby Seekers and Richard Farnworth', 194-207.

had been a peripheral but important part of the English religious environment.[45] As we have seen, something similar had occurred centuries before among the Lollards and other movements but during the late sixteenth and early seventeenth centuries their numbers expanded. By 1646 they were an influential force, only exceeded in importance by the Presbyterians, Independents and Baptists.[46]

By 1600, links had been established between groups such as the Scattered Flock, whose inspiration was John Hetherington (or Etherington), and the Familists who followed Hendrik Niclaes. Familists advocated a doctrine of the Light of Christ within was similar to that of the sixteenth century Anabaptists Hans Denck and Caspar von Schwenkfeld, and later, Digger Gerrard Winstanley and others.[47] There was considerable cross-fertilisation among such groups long before the advent of sectaries such as the Quakers. The Flock, who were mystics of varying kinds, met in small gatherings at convenient moments. They held that the true Church was in a 'wilderness estate' and that the outward Church could not improve until special emissaries or prophets of renewal were sent from God. For this special moment they were prepared to wait for many years if necessary. They came together in silence without ministers or leaders, eschewing the Church's ordinances of baptism and eucharist but, as far as it is known, without the experience of inner purging that the early Friends would practice. Their silences also anticipated the seventeenth century distrust of language in conveying God's designs.[48]

It is possible that groups flourishing around the Westmorland village of Preston Patrick formulated similar ideas to Hetherington, Niclaes and Roger Brierly, the Grindletonian. In Westmorland, they formed a more cohesive community, following a mild yet serious form of Seekerism.[49] John Saltmarsh noticed how they believed the primitive Church had been 'visibly and spiritually endowed with power from on high and with gifts of the Spirit':

> But now in this time of apostasy of the churches, they find no such gifts, and so dare not meddle with any outward administrations, dare not preach . . . They find in the churches nothing but the outward

---

[45] See Greaves, 'The Role of Women in Early English Nonconformity', *passim*.
[46] See G. Johnson, 'From Seeker to Finder', 300.
[47] For Winstanley's Light theology see *New Law of Righteousness*, 34, 73, 78, 109, 114, 120. For Hans Denck (c.1500-27) see Liechty (ed.), 124 and R. Jones, *Spiritual Reformers*, chp. 2. For Schwenkfeld (1489/90-1561) see Furcha, 'Key Concepts', 161, 165-6.
[48] Burrage, 'The Antecedents of Quakerism', *passim* and esp. 87-90. See de Grazia, 'Secularisation of Language', 329. And Etherington (?), *A Description of the Church of Christ* (1616), 2-7.
[49] R. Jones, *Studies in Mystical Religion*, 461.

ceremony ... Therefore they wait ... with power from on high finding no practice for worship ... in prayer ... pretending to no determination of things nor any infallible ... interpretations of Scriptures. They wait for a restoration of all things ... for an apostle or some[one] with a visible glory and power, able in the Spirit to give visible demonstration of their sending [i.e. being sent].[50]

Gatherings such as these were already predisposed to George Fox's ideas. Indeed, many of their adherents already held sophisticated understandings of the Kingdom like Sarah Jones, the author of a remarkably Quaker-like work, *This is Lights Appearance*. It was published in 1650, two years before the generally-agreed date of Quaker beginnings.[51] Her work can be condensed into an essential Kingdom message—inner peace which leads to outer peace leads to the way of God, a formula that would quickly become a central motif of the emergent Quaker movement. With a quiet confidence, Sarah Jones' work anticipated Quaker beliefs in describing a Kingdom that awaited rediscovery. She began by assuring her audience that God's testimony was 'eternal love' for all and that they should 'sink down into that eternal word, and rest' into that which was pure. This would guard against idolatry. She counselled against distractive 'manifestations': people were to focus on that which was originally manifest ('which eternal word was before manifestations were'). To receive 'the eternal life', another allusion to the Kingdom from John's Gospel, they were to 'dwell' in 'the eternal Word [i.e. God]'. It was better, she continued, to concentrate on God's love rather than on personal weaknesses. It was also self-defeating to be 'gadding and hunting' like Esau. It was much wiser to 'live at home' like Jacob and 'retire thy mind' and work towards 'perfection'. In the seventeenth century, perfection implied the acquisition of maturity by means of the Spirit, the 'full growth or development of a thing'. With a return to innocence, to the inner Eden, one could attain 'righteous judgment' by which she meant freedom from inner and outer oppression.

Jones advised people to trust completely in the loving God who would always pull down the mighty 'from their fear'.[52] If God was held firmly in the heart, any outward work for the Kingdom would be true and only then

---

[50] Saltmarsh, *Sparkles of Glory* (1647), 289-98, esp. 289-92; and see R. Jones, *ibid.*, 455-6. Also Ac. 3:21 for the restoration/restitution of all things.

[51] This is probably the same Sarah Jones from Yorkshire recorded as signatory to a petition to parliament in 1659 by 7,746 women; see Mary Forster *et al*, *These Several Papers* (1659), 27, col. 2. For a good account of Separatist/Seeker-Quaker encounters see *FF*, 72-89.

[52] For an excellent and informative account of Friends trusting in the Inward Guide, the Light of the Christ, see Grundy, 'Learning to be a Quaker', *passim*.

would it be advanced.[53] God offered security for all through 'salvation' (wholeness, freedom from sin/separation), which came through Jesus. Like the Word, this promise or Kingdom was unchangeable. And because it was 'from everlasting to everlasting' it could never be defeated. In effect, Jones informed her contemporaries that the work of the Kingdom, the work of inward and outward peace, could *never* be a secular endeavour:

> Therefore come down, come down to the Word of his patience, which is nigh in your hearts, which if you do, he will keep you in the hour of temptation, which shall come to try all upon what foundation they are built; for said Christ, which is the Word of God, 'my sheep hear my voice, and they follow me': and 'I the Word will give them eternal life' ... from whence this testimony of mine proceeds.[54]

Drawing on this religious vitality, one such Separatist church emerged in Sedbergh, a northern Yorkshire village nestling beneath the magnificent Howgill Fells. Gervase Benson was its most prominent member. A wealthy yeoman, he had held a number of senior positions—colonel in the New Model Army, mayor of nearby Kendal, JP for Cumberland and Westmorland, Proctor at Civil Law and Commissary of the Archdeaconry of Richmond before the wars.[55] Understandably, he would be a leading figure among the Friends as would fellow lay preachers Francis Howgill and John Audland, each of whom received a voluntary financial contribution. The church, which rejected the tithe system, was known enough to warrant a visit by George Fox. And so it was that on Whit Sunday in June, 1652, the Separatists in Sedbergh and environs were brought together by a mixture of anticipation and curiosity. They would soon succumb to Fox's charismatic presence and the powerful religious experience for which he stood.[56] Those who made their way up the steep tracks of the fell would have formed a huge crowd in any period but, more pertinently, their physical effort typified their hopes and intense religiosity.

---

[53] S. Jones, *This is Lights Appearance*, 3. For other examples of 'counsel of God' as an alternative for the Kingdom see, for instance, Fox's epistle to Oliver Cromwell (1655), *Journal*, 193-5: 'stand still, and in the counsel of God'; Nayler, *The Lambs War* (1658), 6-7; Penington, *To the Parliament, the Army, and all the Well-affected* (1659), Sig. A2. See Isa. 30:1; Ac. 20:27.

[54] S. Jones, *This is Lights Appearance*, 3. See Lk. 9:23; Mt. 16: 18; 'from everlasting to everlasting' probably derived from Dn. 4:3, 34; 7: 14, 27.

[55] For a useful description of the yeomanry see Brockbank, *Richard Hubberthorne of Yealand*, 22-7.

[56] See Gentiles *et al* (eds.), 196; E. Taylor, *The Valiant Sixty*, 50-1. Also John Lawson (1615 or 1616-89), letter (Nov. 1653) to Fell, *SW*/iv/69 describing Separatists in Malpas (Cheshire).

They were Fox's first significant audience and the critical mass he needed for an on-going and successful prophetic mission.

His sermon would be a solemn moment for them, a Torah moment and a revolutionary one. Like Jesus' opener at Capernaum, he centred tellingly on 'the Light of Christ Jesus leading to the Kingdom' but also on the Church's failure to bring people to it. Adopting the mantle of Moses and Jesus on other mounts, he had been 'sent', he said, so that all people might 'come to know Christ... to open the prophets... the parables of Christ... and the state of the apostasy [of the Church] since the apostles' days'.[57] This was a constant refrain of Fox and the Friends during the 1650s. In 1659 he was to respond to one 'Priest Bennet':

> As the pharisees got the words of the true prophets and Moses out of the life, so the papists and you have got the words of Christ and the apostles, and are out of the life, and persecuting them that are in the life, as the pharisees did... And you, with your dark eyes, have looked upon the Scriptures ever since the apostasy, and ravened from the spirit of God and the pure eye... you are apostatised from the apostles in life, and power, and doctrine, and so are in heaps about their words, out from that which is the ground of communion, the bond of peace.[58]

Like Moses he would shape the Separatists he encountered on the Fell into a 'nation' 'with a sense of its destiny and a moral consciousness of God's demands and with the sovereign, righteous rule of God' holding them together.[59] If it is true, as Lewis Benson, Douglas Gwyn and Rosemary Moore say, that Fox was predominantly concerned with the nature of the Church, it was because *his greater desire was for a prophetic community of saints to live the Jesus Way, a community in which love, forgiveness, reconciliation, healing and spiritual communication would reign.* The Way *was* the Church rather than that 'built by hands', a true Church that superseded the outer Church and its traditions and practices.[60] While in Hebrew prophecy 'the dialectic between the Kingdom of God and the kingdom of Israel seemed an open-ended process with no well-defined yet revealed end', for Fox and the Friends the End was now revealed in their times through the prophetic witness of Jesus, king and prophet, and through themselves as an example of the true Church, the body of Christ.[61] All this

---

[57] *Journal*, 65, 83. See Lk. 4:16-22 and Rom. 5:6; 2 Cor. 5:15 for 'that all might believe'. Also Mt. 5:2.
[58] Fox, *The Great Mystery*, 314 and quoted in *AOTW*, 121; see also 190 and Ep. 222 (1662) in *Works*, 7; 234-5.
[59] G. Harkness, *Understanding the Kingdom of God*, chp. 4 (online).
[60] *AOTW*, 28-30. For 'built by hands' see *Journal*, 8, 40, 76 and Ac. 17: 24.
[61] Gwyn, untitled reply to Durland, 'Was George Fox a Prophet?', 28-9.

was balm to an audience which fitted Saltmarsh's description. Some, maybe all, saw Fox as their long-anticipated messenger, perhaps an 'angel' as in Revelation 11:15 and 14:6, who lent legitimacy to their own vision of the Kingdom and who would lead them as children of Light in spiritual renewal.[62]

Neglect of the Kingdom

As a complement to their disillusionment with Church and State, then, came Fox's powerful articulation of their spiritual hunger and anxieties. They enthusiastically imbibed his proclamation of a direct, immediate relationship with God—'the Lord's true witness in the soul'—to which metaphors such as the 'Light' were applied. Claiming he stood in the apostolic line of succession as a messenger of the Jesus Way, Fox reinforced his startling assertion that the wider Church had been in apostasy 'since the apostles' days'.[63] It had failed in all that time, he said, to enact the Kingdom, and by implication the Sermon on the Mount, and was still living contrary to it. Other marginal thinkers had similar thoughts about the Kingdom. It was of paramount importance, for example, to Winstanley, Saltmarsh and the Baptist William Dell: their public admission of such was just as revolutionary.[64]

Fox's pronouncement brought to the fore a long tradition, stretching back to the early Church, in which the Sermon on the Mount was understood as a list of negatives—Jesus' 'commands' that we should have no anger, lust, divorce, oaths or that evil should never be resisted with evil. Therefore, knowing they could never avoid anger, people came to believe (or were taught) that the Sermon's demands were too difficult. It was praised for its idealism to be sure but was soon regarded in the early Church as impractical for the 'real world'. Consequently, ethical principles from other sources were often adopted and refined. And so, over the years, Sermon teachings were seen as a means of repentance rather than obedience, that is to say, listening to the Word and being open to personal transformation. They were also seen as illustrations of general principles

---

[62] For 'messengers' see John Burnyeat (1631-90), 'An Account of John Burnyeat's Convincement' in *Works*, 1 and for Friends as agents or messengers of Jesus Christ see Dewsbury, *The Discovery of the Great Enmity*, 3; Henry Clark, *A Cloud of Witnesses* (1656), 23, 26.

[63] For apostolic succession/preaching see Ac. 3:22; 7:37. For neglect of the Kingdom from 'end-time' into 'meantime theology' see also *AOTW*, xix-xx.

[64] See Dell, *Right Reformation* (1646), 1-2. William Penn (1644-1718) considered Dell a proto-Quaker; see *No Cross, No Crown* (1682), 513-17.

(such as 'love') but without the necessity of following them, or they were reserved for a future dispensation without sin.[65]

Fox, however, gave his audience a kerygmatic vision of a Kingdom that was immediate and potent. And he would put a precise date on the beginning of the apostasy, namely, forty years after the death of Jesus, a time coinciding with the destruction of the Jerusalem temple by the Romans. Fox conflated this event with his belief that the Old Jerusalem was about to be destroyed in his own time and that a New Israel, a temple within, would rise up 'without might of arm'.[66] The 'true foundation of God', he would always maintain, had been 'laid in the primitive Church'. Since the Reformation had failed to reform the outward Church, it continued to lack the secure underpinning of the primitive Jesus Way. As a result, it was 'violent' as the imposition of forced tithes and other forms of 'oppression' all too clearly proved. The Church needed awakening to its present condition so that it may

> obey Christ's command, love one another, love enemies; and love doth edify which has been wanting among both papists and protestants since the apostles days, having the form of godliness but denying the Power.[67]

Here was a major Quaker theme that would be repeated time and again in their works during the 1650s, not least in Fox's *To All that would Know the Way to the Kingdom* (1653) which was republished on a number of occasions throughout the decade. People, including the Church, could not live in the Kingdom promised by Jesus unless they allowed the Christ to reign or be 'exalted' within.[68] Not accepting this reign meant the Beast of Revelation would be 'unchained' and 'the kingdoms of this world' would be empowered to war yet again. In the wake of the Kingdom, Fox stated, 'all sects and opinions' would be overturned and judged as mere chaff.[69] Only the Kingdom led people to the true Church in God and away from the Church in the world. Fox's *The Pearl Found in England* is another powerful annunciation of this Quaker spiritual revolution.

Was Fox right to accuse the Church of apostasy? Despite his recognition of 'tender' Puritan clergy, was it not too harsh a judgment given

---

[65] Stassen, 'Recovering the Way of Jesus in the Sermon', unnumbered p. 4 at: <www.epcra.ch/papers/belgien/strassen.htm>.
[66] For the 'new Jerusalem' see *Cambridge*, i., 170-4 and for 'temples of the Spirit' see Nayler, *A Salutation to the Seed of God* (1655), 29.
[67] Fox, *Something in Answer to the Old Prayer Book* (1660), 10, 15-16. For the destruction of the Temple and its idolatrous replacement see Fox, *To all the Ignorant People* (1654), 1.
[68] Dewsbury, *Christ Exalted* (1656), 5, 8-9.
[69] Langford, *Quakers and Christianity*, 12-15.

some of the wonderful people known today to have emerged from it—Meister Eckhart, Francis of Assisi and Hildegard of Bingen just to mention a few? Fox, of course, may have known very little, if anything, about these mystical giants and his knowledge of, say, the sixteenth century Anabaptist devotion to the Kingdom would have been scant at best.[70] And yet he and the first Friends were certainly not without knowledge of church history as Howgill and Pearson were to prove with their discourses on tithes.[71] Fox, too, may have read *The Ancient Ecclesiastical Histories* by Eusebius, a work that was not unknown to the Friends. An abridged version of his history would be published in 1661 by the early Friend, William Caton.[72] It is reasonable to assume that the accusation presupposed some understanding that Patristic references to the Kingdom and the Sermon were few despite the fact that in the later writings of Irenaeus of Lyons both underwent a brief renaissance only then to flicker fitfully in the works of Justin Martyr, Origen, Chrysostom, Eusebius himself and Augustine of Hippo. Augustine's *Civitas Dei*, a highly significant text for medieval, Renaissance and post-Reformation Europe, failed to mention to the Kingdom in its Hebraic sense; in fact, in the first ten books of the work, the Kingdom proclaimed by Jesus hardly features. Augustine ignored the Synoptic tradition being content instead to describe a perfect state which he contrasted with the city of Rome, a metaphor for the evil polity of the world.

Today, we see with more clarity how the Patristic authorities like Augustine followed Paul who, though he never ignored the Kingdom, as I Corinthians 13: 1-13 clearly shows, and even offered a 'definition' of it in Romans 14:17 and 2 Corinthians 8:9—what Albert Schweitzer called a 'creed for our times'—nevertheless concentrated much more, like John's Gospel, on Jesus as Lord and Saviour. Foakes-Jackson has argued that Paul transferred 'the rule of Jesus from earth to the sublime abode of heavenly powers [so] agreeing with the Johannine teaching that his Kingdom [was] 'not of this world'.'[73] And while Paul certainly presented Jesus as already transforming the lives of his followers, Georgia Harkness was surely right to maintain that the Synoptic Gospels being 'compiled considerably later

---

[70] Much similarity exists between early Quakerism and early Anabaptist thought, i.e. Peter Walpot's (1521-78) views on Mt. 13 and Dirk Philips' (1504-68) 'born again' theology; their understanding of the Melchizedekan priesthood and how to locate the Kingdom in others are indistinguishable from the Friends. See Liechty (ed.), 149, 202, 216, 224-5.

[71] See Howgill's *The Glory of the True Church* (1661), *passim* and esp. 1-19 and Pearson, *The Great Case of Tithes Truly Stated*, *passim*.

[72] Howgill, *ibid*. Caton's *An Abridgement and Compendium . . . of Eusebius* (1661) was rpt. in 1698. See Spurr, 'A Special Kindness for Dead Bishops', 319. I refer to the possibility of Fox and Friends having access to an edition of Meredith Hanmer's original 1577 translation of Eusebius. John Foxe, well read by Friends, relied heavily on Eusebius for his *Martyrs*.

[73] Foakes-Jackson, 'The Kingdom of God in Acts and the 'City of God'', 194.

than any of Paul's letters, [were] evidence that the Kingdom teachings of Jesus had persisted in spite of, and perhaps because of, the centrality given to Jesus as the Christ'.[74] Perhaps from the very beginnings of the Church, then, a struggle began to protect the orthopraxis of Jesus from segueing into orthodoxy.

Come medieval times and the 'apostasy' had little changed. Though mendicant preachers, particularly Francis of Assisi and Bernardino of Siena, did indeed centre their lives and message on the Beatitudes, their appeal was localised and Bernardino's principal concern was with the lives of his confreres.[75] And while it is true Thomas Aquinas, following Augustine, believed the Beatitudes and the Sermon summed up 'the whole process of forming the life of the Christian', he failed, in the words of Viviano, 'to devote any significant portion of his principal theological enterprise, the *Summa Theologica*, to the Kingdom of God' despite the vast moral construction he built around justice.[76]

One would expect a concentration on the Kingdom during and after the Reformation with its return to scriptural exegesis. However, despite isolated efforts by such figures as Martin Bucer, the ex-Dominican reformer and Regius Professor of Divinity at Cambridge in 1551, it was not to be.[77] Paul's (and John's) emphasis of Jesus as Lord and Saviour over the Kingdom remained intact, as indeed it does today among the mainline Churches. Broadly speaking, the Reformation concerned itself chiefly with a radicalisation of the Pauline-Augustinian message of justification by faith without the works of the Law.[78] And like Aquinas, Jean Calvin never fully addressed the Kingdom in his *Institutes*. As we have seen, his followers were obsessed with such matters as predestination and the godly commonwealth of the new Israel. For them the Kingdom was an otherworldly entity, achieved by the Elect after death and that the physical Church (or their version of it) represented the Kingdom on earth.[79] Bender tells us that by abolishing the distinction between the believer's private and public morality, Calvin placed the public morality of the State under the authority of the Hebrew Testament. He writes that Calvin believed 'the Sermon on the Mount could not conflict with the politics of the pious kings of Israel and the Hebrew Testament code and that he defended war as a

---

[74] G. Harkness, *Understanding the Kingdom of God*, chp. 4 (online). For Pauline assertion of Jesus as already present see Rom. 8: 1, 10; 2 Cor. 5:17, 13:3, 5 and also *AOTW*, 162.
[75] Muessig, 'Preaching the Beatitudes in the late Middle Ages', 137, 150.
[76] Thomas Aquinas (1225-74), *Summa Theologica*, Commentary II-1, q.108, art.3, 4. See *Pearl*, 2; *To All that would Know*, 2-3. See also Viviano, *The Kingdom of God in History*, 9 and *passim*.
[77] See Martin Bucer (1491-1551), *A Treatise how by the Word of God* (1557?), *passim*.
[78] See Rom. 14:17; 2 Cor. 8:9.
[79] See Viviano, *The Kingdom of God in History*, 84-99 and esp. 84-5.

Chapter 5: 'Since the Days of the Apostles'

means of public vengeance against evil'. Theodore Beza, too, affirmed the rightness of religious warfare on historical, biblical and dogmatic grounds.[80] Calvin in fact had followed Luther in what has become known as a 'two Kingdoms' or 'two Realms' theology. The secular and the sacred were separate; the demands of the Sermon were to be obeyed in the spiritual realm only since it had no practical application in the physical world. Consequently, one was obliged to adhere to duties commensurate with the secular office.[81]

It is fair to say, then, that Fox and the Friends made a bold discovery for their times and were probably justified in believing that the Kingdom and the Sermon, the latter with its clear ethical and political commands—reconciliation, truth and integrity, righteousness, justice and peace, mercy and joy, trust in God and the importance of prayer—which Jesus expected to be carried out to the letter, may indeed have been little studied, discussed or acted upon. The result, according to Fox, was a tragic paucity of faith and unity within the Christian world, a paucity whose outcomes were sometimes lethal.

But now with the advent of the Quakers, Fox maintained, a new age was dawning, an age that would challenge the dragon of 'apostasy'.[82] His piercing questions to the parishioners of Ulverston (Cumbria) in 1652 illustrate this point well: 'What canst thou say? Art thou a child of Light and hast thou walked in the Light? And what thou speakest, is it inwardly from God?' The questions made such an impression on one member of the congregation, Margaret Fell, that her world was suddenly turned upside down. It was the moment when she awoke to the real meaning of the Kingdom. 'I saw clearly we were all wrong', she wrote years later; 'we [were] all thieves [having] taken the Scriptures in words and know[ing] nothing of them in ourselves'. So taken with the discovery she 'stood up in [her] pew' and wept. It is important to understand that Fox's questions were not merely about faith *per se* but about the *type* of faith his audience had been taught since their birth, a corrupted faith divorced from the very Kingdom that was their true Christian tradition and home.[83]

---

[80] Bender, 'The Pacifism of the Sixteenth Century Anabaptists', 121.

[81] For a useful discussion on the Sermon by patristic, medieval and Reformation theologians see Gallagher, *Citizens of Heaven*, 42-67. The Mennonites also had a two-Kingdom theology.

[82] Fox's accusation of the Church's apostasy 'since . . .' etc. is also found in *A Reply to the Pretended Vindication* (1658), 18 and in the following: *An Answer to the Papists . . . Lately Out of Holland* (1658), *passim*; see p. 1; *Here is Declared the Manner* (1658), 8; *The Lambs Officer*, 4, 8, 12, 14, 16; *A Few Plain Words* (1660), Bds., col. 2; see also *Journal*, 109 (for Fox on Firbank Fell.), 196, 294, 418-19. And see Viviano, *The Kingdom of God in History*, 61.

[83] Fell, 'The Testimony of Margaret Fell Concerning . . . George Fox' in *Ellwood*, pp. ii-iii. See also *QFP*, §19.07.

Fox's accusation, made in the manner of Matthew's combative Jesus, was no less applicable to the Church of England which he knew best. We have noted how only a tiny number of clerics like Nathaniel Holmes and Joseph Mede, or Radical Puritans such as Walter Cradock, William Dell, William Erbury and John Saltmarsh, saw Jesus' reign as spiritual, that Jesus would not return physically to enact a temporal Kingdom and that the Church comprised the people not buildings.[84] A New Englander, Roger Williams, also made passing reference to a spiritual Kingdom.[85] By 1652, the Independent and newly appointed Vice-Chancellor of Oxford University, John Owen, came to a similar conclusion but, like the vast majority of believers, he preached a Kingdom that was operative only through the 'laws, ordinances, institutions and appointments of the Gospel'—the Church. The idea, he said, that 'Jesus does not rule in these things and is not to be obeyed as a king in them is but a late darkness' and would pass like a cloud.[86] Other Puritans, such as Thomas Temple before the Commons in 1642 or John Cotton in New England, did devote time to the Kingdom but their numbers were miniscule. Like Owen and Calvin, they, too, identified the Kingdom with the physical Church from a literal interpretation of Matthew 16:9 in which Jesus is said to have offered Peter the keys to the Kingdom. Temple, again like most mainstream churchgoers, advocated its spread by force if necessary.[87] Whatever their circumstance or beliefs, they were merely accused by the Quakers of continuing the apostasy.

In short, the Calvinists of the main denominations and other religious groups never made the Kingdom the central subject of their writings and sermons. The reason is puzzling given that it was Jesus' principle concern. We can only surmise that Calvin, although he saw the Sermon as a guide, assumed that it was impractical for his times. Further, his followers may not have pursued the Sermon's demands because of its direct challenge to their 'notions' (as the Friends would say) of authority, social order and cohesion. Perhaps, too, it threatened their own spiritual and material security, all of

---

[84] Thomas Goodwin, Independent, chaplain to O. Cromwell and Master of Magdalene College (Camb.). Richard Sibbes, *The Bruised Reed* (1630), 214-17. Sibbes was preacher at Gray's Inn (Lond.), Master of St. Catherine's (Camb.). William Dell's theology was chiefly concerned with the Kingdom; see his *Several Sermons and Discourses* (1651), *passim*. Such believers were usually dubbed 'Spiritualists'.
[85] Williams, *The Bloody Tenent yet more Bloody* (1652), Sig. E2, 31, 60.
[86] Owen, *A Sermon Preached to the Parliament, Octob. 13th 1652* (1652), 12. This work illustrates a shift from his more chiliastic sermon of the previous year, *The Advantage of the Kingdom of Christ*.
[87] Temple, *Christ's Government in and over his People* (1642), esp. 4-7; J. Cotton, *The Keys of the Kingdom* (1644), 2.

which they had carefully sculptured for themselves. 'Notions' for the Friends were ideas there were 'out of the Life', alien to the Kingdom.[88]

The Kingdom: Specific Interpretations

On Firbank Fell, Fox challenged the northern Separatists into following the same adventurous and Church-less path into the Kingdom he had taken. The first step would be the judgment and crucifixion of one's sin. The inner cross and the resurrection that would follow would affirm the Spirit's saving grace and, on an inner and outer level, reveal those who were in possession of a true faith. In his spiritual autobiography Howgill described this same experience as standing 'in' the cross.[89] Fox, emphasising Jesus as a living teacher, counsellor, king and prophet, advocated the Jesus Way as an active rediscovery of the Kingdom. Its 'elect seed' would follow in the same line of apostolic succession as himself—'the [same] spirit and power the apostles were in'. The Quakers' 'royal priesthood' was to be the anointed means of the Word's desire for reconciliation, healing and wholeness. Being truthful to the Way of the 'everlasting gospel' meant achieving perfection—spiritual maturity involving oneness with God and thus an absence of sin or error—in one's 'own measure'. The outcome was knowing and doing the will of God truthfully in the best way possible. Perfection at any time was thus a possibility in this life bringing individuals into oneness with the Spirit—the 'Substance'—the same Spirit or Christ that was in Jesus.[90]

If his recent imprisonment in Derby (1651) was an indication, Fox advocated a ministry and missionising that would meet with physically dangerous responses. Nevertheless, the Way was one of hope because the Second Coming had already taken place for God's Light and Kingdom were already present in and among everybody awaiting revelation. This insight probably derived, as with much early Quaker theology, from Paul's letters, possibly 1 Corinthians 15: 24-28 and 2 Thessalonians, the latter warning against stressing an imminent and physical Second Coming. To John's reinterpretation of the physical End-times as the presence of the Holy Spirit in the community of the Church, Fox and the Friends would add Paul's understanding in Romans and 1 Corinthians of the Kingdom as the Spirit's present, cosmic rule.[91] In other words, the task *now* was to reveal 'that of

---

[88] For notions out of the Kingdom see Penington, *The Jew Outward*, 13.
[89] Howgill, *The Inheritance of Jacob Discovered*, 13.
[90] See Nayler, 'On Perfection' in *Love to the Lost*, 21-22 and *Sin Kept Out of the Kingdom* (1653), 3-4 in which he quotes Rom. 6:2, 22-23 and 1 Jn. 3:2; Rigge, *On Perfection* (*DCFB/Wing* 1657 or 58), 2; John Whitehouse, *The Doctrine of Perfection Vindicated* (1663), 7-8; Whitehouse quotes 1 Jn. 12-13. See *AOTW*, 77.
[91] See Rom. 14:17; 1 Cor. 4:20. Paul normally referred to the Kingdom in its future aspect.

God' in oneself and thereby recognise this Light in others and draw it out.[92] For Fox, the Light was not an intellectual facility. Nor could it be equated with rationalism or conscience; these were subject to change. It was pre-existent and thus preceded conscience.[93] As God's 'flame to sin', the Light acted as a deliverer from the hands of inward adversaries. It was the very 'Blood of Christ', the 'appearance of the Day' (the Kingdom) and offered an eternal morning, joy, cheer and spiritual comfort. Supernatural and universal to all people since creation, it would continue to be so until the eventual consummation of humanity in God.[94]

Calvinists understood the Kingdom in four principal ways. First, as a transcendent, heavenly dimension (*Regnum Caeleste*). Second, as God's providence over the world through the Holy Spirit and the Word (*Regnum Dei*). Third, as Jesus' redemptive rule or presence which they timed from his ascension to the last judgment (*Regnum Christi*). Fourth, as the life of sanctification in the individual believer. However, the Church took precedence over the individual since on earth it *was* the Kingdom and its vehicle as John Owen emphasised.

For the Quakers, much more was needed to demonstrate conclusively that the life of sanctification was neither a mere sign nor other-worldly. Instead, the Kingdom incorporated the dynamic strength of God's Life and Power translated into the daily routine of the individual as if they were as one with his or her consciousness. The Kingdom was their special way of speaking about, and enacting, God. Their intimacy with the Kingdom took shape through worship based on silence and holy obedience, on their suffering and works of justice, peace and mercy. In this way, their Kingdom lives were made tangible, and would automatically become patterns and examples to all people. Implied here was the hope that the Kingdom would be made even more real if they succeeded in deepening *humanity's* commitment to the 'now' of the divine Presence. The compassion, hope and wholeness that were of the Kingdom could never, therefore, be abstractions emanating from a remote Other. And in God's Love, hope and wholeness were eschatological. The 'now' factor differentiated the Quakers from the Calvinists and rationalists who were convinced their faith and practice would be enriched only with the physical Second Coming.

---

[92] Paul's letters are 1 Th., Gal., Ph., Phm., 1 and 2 Cor. and Rm and may have been made up of a dozen or more letters by him. Deutero-Paul, written during 70-100 CE, are 2 Th.(?), Col., Eph., 1 and 2 Tm. and Tt. Deutero-Paul is more universal in tone. See Wills, *What Paul Meant*, 15-17. Also Hubberthorne, *The Good Old Cause*, 1 and G. Whitehead, *The He-Goats Horn Broken* (1660), 39 in which the Second Coming is inward. For 'perfection in their own measure' see Burrough, *To all that are Moved to Go unto other Nations* (1658) in *Works*, 387.

[93] Fox, *The Great Mystery*, 10.

[94] *Cambridge*, i., 24 and see Hadley King, *George Fox and the Light Within*, 105.

So what *was* the early Friends' understanding of the Kingdom? Well versed in the Bible, people like Sarah Jones had (before meeting Fox) deduced the Kingdom's centrality to Jesus. They knew he began his ministry with it in a synagogue in Capernaum, that he preached and told stories about the Kingdom and finally died for it. For their part, the Friends would have seen in the Hebrew Bible how the Kingdom in the form of God's 'kingship' (or kingly rule and order) was given classical expression in such passages as Exodus 15:18 and Psalm 10:16, in the Enthronement Psalms (e.g. Ps. 103:17) and in other parts of the Psalter, particularly where the plaint of the suffering individual or community evoked a kingly response from God or an acknowledgment of God's kingship. Psalm 22, which evoked Jesus' cry of desolation from the cross, may not have escaped their notice in this respect.[95] They were familiar, too, with how the pre- and post-exilic prophets vociferously affirmed God's kingship through their eschatological and apocalyptic writings, and also with God's suzerainty in the covenant tradition.[96] And so also, therefore, with Isaiah's futuristic vision of the messianic and peaceable Kingdom in which the lion would sit down with the lamb, his message of hope and consolation and the final victory of the Day of the Lord. Thus they were alive to the way in which the prophets' oracles were socio-political *and* religious, alive to the way the ancient Jews often saw no distinction between the secular-political and the sacred.[97]

The Friends were also conscious of the frequency with which 'Kingdom' appeared in the Christian Testament (162 times) and more specifically as the 'Kingdom of God/of the heavens' in the Synoptic Gospels (104 times).[98] Matthew's Gospel mentions 'Kingdom of Heaven/s' 32 times in a variety of phrases and 'Kingdom of God' four times. In John's Gospel they would have twice encountered 'Kingdom' and may well have understood 'eternal life', mentioned nine times, as its alternative or close equivalent.[99] Indeed, we may be confident that early Quaker knowledge of

---

[95] The Enthronement Pss. are 47, 93, and 96-99. See, for instance, Pss. 24; 29; 48; 68; 74:12-17; 84; 68:2, 6-19; 149 and Ex.15:1-18. Also Gray, *The Biblical Doctrine of the Reign of God*, chps. 2, 3 and esp. 7.

[96] Gray, *ibid.*, esp. chp. 3.

[97] Gwyn, 'Was George Fox a Prophet?', 27.

[98] That 'heaven' was common in first century Hebrew as a reverential circumlocution (esp. in Matthew) for 'God' has been effectively challenged by J. Pennington. However, he confirms Matthew's oft-use of 'heaven' as an indirect reference to God in cases of metonymy for rhetorical, polemical and theological purposes. See his *Heaven and Earth in the Gospel of Matthew*, 7-8 and chp.1, esp. 23, 36.

[99] See Jn. 3:3, 5. 'Kingdom' or 'Reign of God' appear in Aramaic Targums. Chilton believes it is plausible that Jesus used eight Prophetic Targums containing the precise terms 'Kingdom of God' or 'Kingdom of the Lord'—Isa. 24:23; 31:4; 40:9; 52:7; Ezk. 7:7, 10; Ob. 21; Mic. 4:7, 8; Zech. 14:9. The key issue here is their portrayal of the Kingdom as God's

the Kingdom resulted from a painstaking analysis of each passage in the Gospels in which it appeared.

All in all, they read how God's Kingdom confronted every sphere of life—economic, social, political and religious—through Jesus' radical questioning and conduct, his Way or *halakhah*, an *halakhah* that continued in their own times to turn the world upside down.[100] It is no exaggeration to say that the Kingdom was the *alpha* and *omega* of their religious life: 'thus have I travelled through the world, even unto the end', reported Burrough to the inhabitants of his home village, Underbarrow (Cumbria), but yet had 'come to the beginning of that which shall never have end'.[101] It was enough for leading Friend William Bayly to declare in 1659 that in leaving the Baptists 'for when I being unsatisfied... a word was powerfully in me, seek first the Kingdom of God'.[102] John Whitehead was certain, no doubt from his own personal experience, that 'the ministers of Christ walk[ed] in the power of godliness and [went] from city to city and from village to village preaching the Kingdom of God'.[103] William Britten assured all Quakers that their primary duty was to seek first the Kingdom.[104]

From the moment of its initial appearance as 'the doctrine of Christ' in the first-known published Quaker tract in 1652, *False Prophets and False Teachers Described* by Thomas Aldam and others, the Friends also used many equivalent terms for the Kingdom.[105] These were usually capitalised and, in context, included Christ's Kingdom, the Dominion of God/of immortal life, the Kingdom of Heaven, the Garden of God, the Royal Law, the Hope of Glory, Eternal Life, the Life, Life and Power, Declaration of the Word of Life, Word of Faith, the Word, the Everlasting Covenant, the Pearl, Leaven, Piece of Silver, the Crown, the Right Way of God, the

---

healing activity or as the very manifestation of God at work in the world which, as we will see, is similar to the early Quaker orthopraxis of the Lamb's War. But, while Brian Waldon's *Biblia Sacra Polyglotta* (1657) is a good example of seventeenth century knowledge of Targumic literature, no evidence suggests early Quaker familiarity with that genre. That said, their interpretation of Isaiah is uncannily akin to Jesus' supposed understanding of, say, Isa. 24:23 (which in part reads (KJV): 'when the LORD of hosts shall reign in mount Zion') in its Targumic form ('because the Kingdom of the Lord of hosts will be revealed on Mount Zion'). See Chilton, 'Regnum Dei Deus Est' in Dunn and McKnight, 'The Historical Jesus in Recent Research', 115-22; esp. 118.

[100] See Jackson, *Essays on Halakhah*, passim and Nolan, *Jesus Before Christianity*, 119.
[101] Burrough, *A Warning of the Lord... to Underbarrow*, 35. Also *Journal*, 21 and Ep. 239 (1664) in *Works*, 7:263. And *AOTW*, 116-18.
[102] Bayly, *A Short Relation or Testimony* (1659), 10.
[103] J. Whitehead, *The Enmity between the Two Seeds*, 19.
[104] William Britten (d.1669/70), *The Power of God* (1660), 2. See Appendix 1 in which I tabulate the frequency with which the Friends mentioned the Kingdom and its equivalent expressions between 1652 and 1663.
[105] And subsequently throughout the decade (e.g. Fox, *An Instruction to Judges and Lawyers*, 7).

Chapter 5: 'Since the Days of the Apostles'

Way/Truth/Life, Government of Christ, the Voice of the Gospel, the New Covenant, the New Israel, the New Creation, the Spirit of Christ, the Sword/of the Spirit, the Ministry of Christ, the Law of God and the power of God, where the last listed did not specifically mean Christ or the Gospel. It is also present in such phrases as 'where Zion is known', 'in the Life of our king', in references to the mustard seed, and as an antonym of such terms as 'Satan's kingdom', 'the wisdom of the world' and many others.[106] Sometimes, 'Jesus' was synonymous with the Kingdom as 'in Jesus', 'the Word', 'the Life'.[107] Chapter 6 and Appendix 2 show how the three crucial declarations published between December 1659 and January 1661 highlighted the Kingdom 12 times and accounted for 40 equivalent expressions.

Two further references, however, need special mention because they have been long misunderstood. The Quakers' use of 'the Day' and/or 'the Day of the Lord', indeed their use of 'Kingdom', should not be confused with a physical End-time or with the traditional Christian interpretation of God's wrath or indeed with the last judgment. In Hebrew apocalyptic writings, the 'Day' is portrayed as a Sinai theophany, a divine intervention or the hope of deliverance and is usually linked to Exodus. The Friends seemed to have had a similar messianic understanding and expectation. They, too, were a people of hope who would bring deliverance from the wilderness of apostasy and other forms of darkness, but they also constituted the new 'promised land' carrying a rediscovery of the Kingdom. In Daniel 2, of great importance to Matthew, and in Mark 4 they would have read of the Kingdom's triumph over the kingdoms of the world.[108] The Friends maintained that as a 'people', as a living Kingdom, they had come with 'power and might' from their inner exile as in Zechariah 4:6, thus emphasising the spiritual immanence of the Kingdom and its universal redemptive power. This is certainly an underlying theme of Nayler's *A Lamentation* (1653) which includes the Day in his title.[109]

In addition to Fox, Nayler, Burrough, Bayly and John Whitehead, a number of other prominent figures between 1653 and 1663 provide us with insights into the Quakers' Kingdom—Thomas Aldam, George Bishop,

---

[106] See Mt. 13:31; Mk. 4: 31. For 'dominion of immortal life' see Burrough, *A General Epistle* (1660), 5. For 'sword' as the Law (Kingdom) see Dewsbury, *The Discovery of the Great Enmity*, 14 (Dewsbury quotes Gen. 3:24) and Dorothea Gotherson, *To all that are Unregenerated* (1661), 93.

[107] Thomas Aldam (c.1616-60) *et al, False Prophets and False Teachers Described* (1652), 2.

[108] There are 30 textual and conceptual allusions to Daniel in Matthew: see Mt. 13:10-15 (*cf*: Dn. 2: 27-28); Mt. 11: 25-27 (*cf*: Dn. 2: 21-23, 28-29) and the Gospel mentions Daniel in 24: 15. But see esp. Dn. 2: 44-45 in which the Kingdom of Heaven is contrasted with the world's religions.

[109] Nayler, *A Lamentation*, 9-10.

William Britten, Sarah Blackborow, William Dewsbury, Margaret Fell, Isaac Penington, Humphery Smith, Thomas Stubbs and the Friend who begins our survey, Francis Howgill.

Francis Howgill

Convinced by Fox in the churchyard at Sedbergh in 1652, Howgill described the Kingdom mystically and apocalyptically, not in the sense of a physical End-time but as the divine mystery now 'revealed'. For Howgill the Day had already come and it would remain an ever-revealing reality, a mystery initially gifted to a remnant.[110]

In a beautiful passage in *Some of the Mysteries of God's Kingdom Declared* (1658) in which he mentions 'reveal' in this sense ten times, Howgill presented the 'Kingdom' as an everlasting, spiritual rule of God (Love) replete with 'purity' which

> comes to be felt working in the heart, and as it is loved and obeyed, it leads and converts the heart, to the Lord, and draws towards itself, out of unholiness, and from under the dark power.'[111]

The Kingdom, he said, was home to those who were formerly exiled, home to those spiritual refugees who now knew the balm of God's righteousness/justice and peace of conscience together with joy, felicity, pleasantness, virtue, eternal life, assurance of God's love, comfort and consolation, eternal dignity, quietness, grace and hope.[112] It was, he continued,

> eternal brightness shed abroad through all things which pierces through and searches the [most] secret place, even that which is invisible, and makes manifest all things. And the nature of everything by the Day of the Lord comes to be seen, and it appears in the heart. [People are] to wait for the day to dawn . . . [for] that which makes evil manifest and brings it to light.[113]

---

[110] Fox was probably influenced in this sense by Col 1:26: 'Even the mystery which hath been hid from ages and from generations, but now is made manifest to his saints.' Nesti explains the 'Day' well but fails to connect it overtly to the Kingdom; see 'Early Quaker Ecclesiology', 14-15.

[111] Howgill, *Some of the Mysteries of God's Kingdom*, 39-40. For Winstanley, the Kingdom within was something 'moth and rust' could not corrupt since it was of God; see *The Fire in the Bush* (1649/50), 71.

[112] See Rom. 14:17-18 and Howgill, *The Invisible Things of God* (1659), 144.

[113] Howgill, *ibid.*, 147 and Hubberthorne, *A True Testimony of Obedience*, 1-2.

The Kingdom was the 'Day' itself. It was 'pure Light' and already present with its justice and the possibility of regeneration. It was free grace, 'God's appearance', and it satiated the hunger within, setting people on a path different to that of the world and thus nearer to God. Describing his own experience in finding the Kingdom at long last, Howgill was amazed at the depth of unity with others with whom he was 'caught up as in a net':

> And from that day forward our hearts were knit unto the Lord, and one unto another in true and fervent love, not by any external covenant or external form but we entered into the covenant of Life with God. And that was as a strong obligation or bond upon all our spirits which united us one unto another . . . in the unity of the Spirit and of the bond of peace.[114]

In this way the covenant of death was 'disannulled' by the 'power and arm' of God, and the new 'babe' was born 'from above'. The begotten of the Kingdom were 'heirs to the promise', the 'heirs of God's Kingdom', as they unveiled the new covenant that was within.[115] This same Light or grace was given to all but 'not in the same measure' for some were more prone to evil than others. 'It is a lamentation', cried Howgill, 'to see how people are gone out of the pure simplicity which is in Christ.'[116]

Acknowledging that words could never fully describe the indescribable, he affirmed them as mere sounds, veils that covered the true beauty and meaning of this spiritual 'habitation', the 'treasure house of wisdom'. All who believed of God—all who partook of 'the divine nature' as Britten wrote two years later—received this wisdom of Life, Power and Virtue and would be filled with divine love, the 'word of the Kingdom, the word of Power', the 'word of Life'.[117] To be of the Kingdom was to live in the Spirit as a prophet just as Jesus was a prophet. The Kingdom's 'fullness fills all things', Howgill continued, and in its many mansions there would be an eternal welcoming for the children of the resurrection, the poor in spirit who would experience 'birth immortal'.[118] Their self-description as children of Light, was, as Nuttall observed, a natural expression of their belief that in *them* primitive Christianity, the Kingdom, was being revived.[119] Thus as

---

[114] Howgill, *A Testimony Concerning . . . Edward Burroughs*, 6.
[115] See also John Anderdon (1624?-85), *God's Proclamation* (1659), 5 and esp. Gal. 3:29 for 'And if ye be Christ's, then are ye Abraham's seed, and heirs according to the promise'; also Jer. 49:2; Tt. 3:7; Jm. 2:5. Also Dewsbury, *Christ Exalted*, 5.
[116] Howgill, *Some of the Mysteries of God's Kingdom*, 34.
[117] Howgill, *The Glory of the True Church*, 3.
[118] For life immortal see 2 Tm. 1:10.
[119] Nuttall, *To the Refreshing of the Children of Light*, 4-5. See Lk. 16:8; Jn. 12: 36; Eph. 5:8; 1 Thess. 5: 5 and also Mt. 5: 9 and Lk. 20:30.

the 'children' they would be saved from death and quickened into the Life to be whole.

The Life (i.e. the Kingdom) was hidden, however, from those in the reprobate condition. For Howgill and Friends such as Rebecca Travers, Sarah Blackborow, Benjamin Nicholson and William Tomlinson, their generation and particularly its Calvinists and chilialists, resembled the pharisees in the way they perceived the Kingdom as an 'earthly and literal' place, but also in their pessimistic view of humanity, their remote God and legalistic observance. Despite their learned understanding of Scripture, they said, the Puritans 'gaz[ed] abroad in their earthly knowledge' and 'yet they knew it not' for only from the Light, the Christ, could true illuminating knowledge come. For this reason, they disagreed passionately with the Puritans' view of the Kingdom as the 'seed, conception, or bud' of grace planted in the individual through water baptism which in turn was linked to their desire for a God encountered only after death (the Kingdom of Glory, *Regnum Caeleste*).

According to the Quakers, Christ's doctrine was always a stranger to such people who continually used abstract formulations ('notions' out of the 'Life') to obfuscate, confuse and persecute. Howgill believed that, despite their constant self-examination and scruples, the 'pharisees' failed to see that the Kingdom, being within as the Friends understood Jesus to have said, meant that one needed to 'dig deep, sweep clean and search narrowly' to discover the pearl in the field, the mustard seed, the lost piece of silver. These, and especially the pearl, represented the advent of the Kingdom, the anticipation of the inner and outer worlds turned upside down. This demanded faithfulness, a patient waiting in the peace and righteousness of the Spirit. In this respect, Howgill quoted the Sermon on the Mount to assure his readers that anyone who cared to seek would find: 'so first every one must come to feel in [them] the Kingdom [and they] that believe [are] entered into the rest'—'blessed are the poor in Spirit' therefore. At this juncture he also emphasised Luke 6:20: 'blessed are the poor for theirs is the Kingdom of God'. And so, he continued, as the Kingdom was revealed through God's power, glory and grace to those who wait, it could be fully experienced on earth when a loving unity and justice existed among people and thus between humanity and God.

In this way, the Kingdom was the 'Crown immortal'. As the world's 'end' was experienced in people it was possible to give witness to a fresh 'beginning' in the Christ. In the *now* of this loving Spirit, time disappeared. In fact, there *was* no beginning and end. Here Howgill answered the dualism, the 'imaginings', of the Puritans. Their Kingdom of Glory and Kingdom of Grace (the Kingdom of the present) were to the Friends one and the same—that is, the Kingdom in the way Jesus taught and demonstrated, and continued to do so as the living Word.[120] The world was not about to come to a physical end; rather, it was the old dispensation, the old Israel, even the Beast within, that was about to meet its end. Thus the individual and Kingdom would give birth to the new beginning of peace, justice and compassion.[121]

George Fox

In Fox's *Journal*, 'Kingdom' first appears on page 13 where he refers to Jesus, the holder of the key to the door of the Kingdom. Previously, on pages 11 and 12, he describes his fellowship with Christ who, by means of the key, opened the door to Life and Light (the Kingdom). When, in the very early passages of the *Journal*, Fox talks of light, life and love, he draws our attention to the Kingdom and its contradiction—the world of Mammon, sin, the 'dark world' or the kingdom of Satan, the empire of evil.[122] From page 12 this contrast continues until the well-known passage on page 19 in which an ocean of Light and Love is compared to an ocean of darkness. This contrast is not merely between goodness and sin but the joy of being 'in the Life' as opposed to being outside it and therefore in separation from the Source (of Light), that is, Love or God. He tells us on page 27 in a Pauline manner that as he experienced the 'paradise of God', all 'things were new, and all the creation gave another smell unto [him] than before beyond what words can utter'.[123]

---

[120] Howgill, *Some of the Mysteries of God's Kingdom*, 2-5, 38-43.

[121] Howgill, *ibid.* and esp. 39-40; this is one of the few direct references by the early Quakers to Mt. 5: 1-7 and Luke's equivalent, the Sermon on the Plain. Also William Britten, *Concerning the Kingdoms of God and Men*, (1660), 1. See Bishop, *An Epistle of Love* (1661), 3. For other strong anti-literal stances see Britten *Silent Meetings, A Wonder to the World* (1660), 7; Travers, *For Those that Meet in Worship at the Steeplehouse* (1659), 16-18; Sarah Blackborow (or Blackbury, d. 1665), *A Visit to the Spirit in Prison* (1658), 9 and her 'Preface' to Nayler's *How Sin is Strengthened, and How it is Overcome*; Benjamin Nicholson, *A Blast from the Lord*, 5; Hubberthorne, *The Horn of the He-Goat Broken* (1656), *passim*.

[122] There are many references to 'dark', 'darkness' etc., but specific reference to 'dark world', can be found, for instance, in Nayler, *To All Dear Brethren and Friends in Holderness* (1653) in *Works*, 30; *A Public Discovery of the Open Blindness*, 6 and *The Power and Glory of the Lord* in *Works*, Sig. D2. Early Quaker references to its equivalent, to what I will call the 'spiritual void', can also be found in Nayler, *A Lamentation*, 4-6; James Parnel (1637?-56), *A Trial of Faith* (1654), 6. And see Fox, *A Testimony of the True Light*, esp. 9: 'The Light shines in darkness, though darkness does not comprehend it [Jn.1:5], and you are sometimes darkness.' 'Dark world' can also be found in the works of Jakob Boehme; see *Four Tables of Divine Revelation* (1654), 12 where it is described as the 'ground of the properties of self-desire and will' whereas the Light is the 'ground of the joyful divine revelation.' For 'Mammon' see, for instance, Fox, 'Moved of the Lord' in *News Coming up out of the North*, 25.

[123] Fox was inspired here by 2 Cor. 12:1-4.

He emerges restored, as he would again in 1659 from a time of sickness at Reading, into a new covenant. There is a hint in this passage of the exilic journey—from Egyptian slavery or the prodigal son returned to the bosom of the Lord. On page 34, God lets Fox 'see the depths of Satan . . . [which] open[ed] to me . . . the divine mysteries of his own everlasting Kingdom' and he expresses gratitude to God for preparing him for the service to which he was appointed—preaching the everlasting Gospel and Kingdom. Equivalent expressions, however, appear much earlier in the text. On page one, in a dedicatory to God and a statement of aim for the *Journal* itself, he is at pains to tell us that 'the work unto which he had appointed me' came to him as a child. On page two readers are again invited into his formative years when the 'covenant of life' came into focus when he was saddened by those who were 'strangers' to it.[124]

In *To All that would Know the Way to the Kingdom*, Fox describes the Kingdom as a guide, teacher and something that was always present, even in bed! It stood in contrast to the temporal world but was not divorced from it. The 'nearness' of the Kingdom is a constant theme running through his works. As in the words of Sarah Blackborow in 1659, his fondest wish is that everybody would know again

> the Kingdom of God in them, and that near them, and not afar from them, but hid in them, which leads into the Kingdom of God; and truly this I know to be the breathings of eternal love in man, which checks and reproves him.[125]

In *A Testimony of the True Light* (1656/7), the Kingdom is the Light which shows up sin, a theme developed in *A Distinction between the Phanatick Spirit* (1660) in which the 'rage, fury, madness and foolishness' of the 'fanatic spirit' is exposed and defeated by the 'love, joy, peace, gentleness, righteousness and true judgment' of the 'spirit of God', the Kingdom.[126] For Fox, the Kingdom also acted as a corrective by which people were kept from their 'wandering minds' so they would remain within the compass of God's love ('in the fear of God'). It was something that would lead from the false Church to the true Church in a world (the 'wilderness') that had forsaken the Kingdom. 'And never had you a prophecy', he scolded the Puritans, 'that you should be gathered again to an outward Jerusalem'.

---

[124] Pickvance, *A Reader's Companion to George Fox's Journal*, 66-7: a most helpful guide to the Nickalls *Journal* and its word-use.
[125] Blackborow, *Herein is Held Forth the Gift* (1659), 3; Fox, *Something in Answer to the Old Prayer Book*, 30.
[126] Fox, *A Testimony of the True Light*, 13; *A Distinction between the Phanatick Spirit*, Bds.

Chapter 5: 'Since the Days of the Apostles'

Fox understood the Jews as a living metaphor for unity, for being a united nation or people before God. Rather than advocating the conversion of the Jews as an essential ingredient for the imminent physical coming of Jesus, as others like Cromwell were doing, the object of the Kingdom was the coming together of the nations and peoples of the world and thus the restoration of the true Israel in the Spirit that was already present.[127] In this way, the world would be saved (i.e. the people would be secure in God) and the peaceable Kingdom established. The false Church had set up many rulers 'amongst them[selves] who had gone',

> from the seed of God in themselves, in the male and in the female, then they forsook their head Christ Jesus ... and then [came] to be covered in darkness ... and then come up the fightings about earthly things, and warrings with carnal weapons about earthly things, and self-interest, and man's honour and titles, and about their churches, and religions, and worships, and ministry.[128]

Salvation for such people was placed in the hereafter or at a future date, a convenience for those with no desire to change (at least just yet) and especially if they were wealthy or powerful. According to Fox, such people did not understand the full implications of the Kingdom. It was a failure that had inevitably led people to disregard the real teaching of Jesus as the Friends understood it from Matthew 5, an apostasy that resulted in division and violence among God's children.[129] Thus, very early in his ministry, Fox linked the Kingdom to the pursuit of inner and outer peace, a realisation that led, for instance, to his refusing an army commission in 1651. Violence was a flagrant contradiction of Jesus' great commission that the true Church, the Kingdom and its peoples, should be carried to 'all people' for their transformation into the Light. The Quakers' itinerancy was ideal for this purpose. Fox would have agreed wholeheartedly with William Britten's 1660 assertion that, like Jesus and the apostles, the Friends could meet anywhere with 'no one place being preferred before another'.[130]

In concert with all Friends, Fox counselled that no one could enter the Kingdom, that its restorative and redemptive potential would remain out of reach, without their transformation, without being 'born again' to an Eden-type 'innocency' as children. In the Overview we saw how 'born again' meant something far removed from its modern Christian Evangelical individualism. It meant being prepared to undergo an inner crucifixion and

---

[127] For 'coming together of the nations and peoples of the world' see Mt. 8: 11.
[128] Fox, Ep. 131 (1656) in *Works*, 7:127-8.
[129] See Langford, *Quakers and Christianity*, 2, 18.
[130] Britten, *Concerning the Kingdoms of God and Men*, 2.

resurrection so that a new person, a Pauline 'new order of being' (2 Cor. 5:17), would emerge who would then dwell daily in God's presence and eternal Life. Such a person would necessarily face down the darkness within. Automatically (following James 1:20; 3:18), they would be led to perform works of justice and peace, works that would instil compassion into the heart of the body politic. Everybody needed to convict that which separated them from God—that which was 'below', latent within them— before it showed up in external conduct. In other words, their task was to convict that capacity to deny one's relationship with God, that capacity to deny the Kingdom. Fox wrote:

> while there is enviousness in you, there lodges the man-slayer, and all the wisdom is from below, while that nature stands: there's sects, and there's opinions, and there's conceivings arisen out on this earthly part, where lodges this wisdom, and self-conceit, and pride, and by this wisdom the living God is not a known.[131]

In the spiritual house there was no room for 'outward pleasures, delights, lightness, wantonness, vain glory and profaneness', all of which would perish along with 'idle talk, unrighteousness, proud boasting, loftiness and haughtiness'. Those who occupied the house would hold the sceptre of righteousness, their inner victory bringing peace and justice to themselves and so to others.[132] This same theme is found in a letter by Fox to Cromwell in 1655 and six years later in his *The Line of Righteousness* (1661). Here the Kingdom is the Power, Wisdom, Strength and the Dominion of righteousness, peace, truth, holiness, justice and equity. Together, Fox saw these as acting as a great buffer against all manner of immorality, an example we might say today of *dikaiosýnē* in the sense of right conduct before God.[133]

Fox further expounded on the Kingdom in *An Answer to the Arguments of the Jews* (1661). Here he countered Jewish belief, and by implication that of the Church and other authorities, that the Messiah had not yet come. The tract outlines how Jesus' spiritual Kingdom, mentioned 235 times in its 52 pages, is the culmination of all history. Judah's own story, it continues, is that of the evolving understanding of God's sovereignty or kingship and its inevitable fulfillment in the person of Jesus as the Kingdom. The long pre-

---

[131] Fox, *To All that would Know*, 1-3; *A Declaration to the Jews* (1661), 4, 7, 11. Jm. 3:18: 'And the fruit of righteousness is sown in peace of them that make peace.' See also Nayler, *A Discovery of the First Wisdom* (1653), 4-17 and Sobrino, *Christology at the Crossroads*, 51.
[132] Fox, 'Concerning the Kingdom of God' in *Doctrinals*, 1089-90. See Isa. 32:1.
[133] See *Journal*, 194-5 and *The Line of Righteousness* (1661), *passim* and esp. 6-7. Also A. Roberts, *Through Flaming Sword*, 93 and Mt. 3:15, 5:6, 5:10, 6:1, 6:33; Lk.1:75; Ac. 13:10, 24:23; Heb. 7:2; 1 Jn. 2:29, 3:10; Jm. 1:20, 3:18.

incarnational shadow disappears as the Light of Christ shines freely, its promise of Love embodied in Jesus' teaching, healing, suffering, death and resurrection, all of which enable humanity to fulfill its own destiny of wholeness and unity in God. If, as Fox preached elsewhere, Christ had come to teach his people himself then it was the Kingdom that was present. God was present *now* to all people, the 'Day' was *now*, the Word incarnate *now* among those who lived in Truth.

Before the Kingdom's advent, humanity was in captivity and yet, when the Light did periodically shine (for instance, through the prophets), the reign of darkness was already threatened. The spiritual Kingdom was and is freedom, the freedom of the Messiah who 'dashes what is contrary to it'. It is the freedom from internal captivity so that liberty in the outer, we repeat, can be manifest in the work of healing, peace, justice and mercy, in nonviolence. Outward kingdoms, the Friends maintained, were drenched in blood and would continue to be so without the Light. For these reasons, the Kingdom was 'distinct', that is to say, an everlasting reality. It rose above time and space, reaching in any era into the hearts and minds of all for their transformation into the Life and its child-like, Edenic purity. This gave the Kingdom its unique power: whoever was in this power was truly Christian in deed rather than in words.[134]

For the Friends, 'children' and 'Kingdom' were inseparable. As in Jesus' era, seventeenth century children often came last in the pecking order but in the Kingdom the least would be first. Fox insisted that the Friends should stand as an example to others as children of the Kingdom and of the Light by virtue of their own spiritual awakening and right walking. They were to prove to a hostile world that the Kingdom was one of peace (he quotes Mi. 4:3), of righteousness and justice (Jer. 23: 6), forgiveness (Jer. 31: 34) and meekness, and that violence was a stranger to it. In the Kingdom everyone was a neighbour. It was the 'place' where the poor and despised found justice and sanctuary.[135] Dwelling in the Light was the sure way of experiencing God, of being in the divine Presence, a belief he hammered home in works devoted solely to the Kingdom such as *A Testimony of the True Light*, *The Pearl Found in England* and *To All that would Know the Way to the Kingdom*.

---

[134] Fox, *An Answer to an Argument by the Jews*, *passim*; see esp. 10, 20, 44.

[135] For 'righteousness and justice': Jer. 23: 6; 'forgiveness': Jer. 31: 34 and *ibid.* for 'meekness, and that violence was a stranger to it. The Kingdom was where everyone was a neighbour.'

Margaret Fell, James Parnel, William Bayly, Humphery Smith and George Bishop

Margaret Fell drew the same conclusions as Fox in *For Manasseth ben Israel* (1656/7): the Light of the new covenant, the new Law of love and mercy, would be upon all those wishing to experience it. The Kingdom had been freed from the darkness by Jesus, so everybody could truly see their destiny as the real Elect, as a people liberated from inner prisons so they may sing the song of joy, freedom, justice and righteousness:

> The figures and the types and the shadows are ceased. The Lord God is departed out of them, and the substance of them is come, the holy seed is risen the substance thereof. The Lord has sent the strength of his rod out of Zion, who is the covenant of light to open the blind eyes, and bring out the prisoners out of prison, and them that sit in darkness out of the prison-house, that they may sing a new song unto the Lord, and his praise from the end of the earth. And the Day of the Lord's power is come, in which he makes his people willing, and as many as receives him, to them he gives power.[136]

For Fell, like Fox, the 'Day of the Lord' offered the chance to overcome and eradicate sin while signalling the Kingdom as a present and living reality in 'all people'. It awaited disclosure to enact redemption, that is, forgiveness and wholeness through the power of Love. Just as James Parnel saw the 'perfect Day' as the moment in which 'sorrow and sighing flies away', William Bayly's Kingdom meant rejoicing, comforting and eternal well-being.[137] It was a life-giving experience of prayer as well as the promise of God in which the Antichrist was destroyed by the Light. To be in the Kingdom was to be 'in' the 'true God' or 'eternal life', unified to all who were 'in' God. It was the spiritual place where 'they might be one' 'in Christ', when each could say authentically 'thou in me and I in them'.[138]

Humphery Smith's *The Lamb and his Day Proclaimed* (1660) was a declaration of the 'now' factor of God's presence, of salvation and eternal Life, and an invitation to all people to enjoy the Kingdom through which God's loving kindness was being revealed. The long wait was over because the Light had conquered the darkness, the Christ within showing up the inner darkness. The great task, continued Smith, was to proclaim its victory

---

[136] Fell, *For Manasseth ben Israel* (1656/7), 21. For 'shadow' see Heb. 10:1.
[137] Parnel, *To Friends in Essex* (1655) in *Works*, 439. For 'perfect day' see Prov. 4:18.
[138] Bayly, *Deep Calleth unto Deep* (1663), 29-31. See Jn. 1:4; 17:11, 23. C. Spencer informs us that the phrase 'in Christ' occurs 164 times in Paul; see Gal. 3:27; 19-20; Ph. 1:21 and Dandelion (ed., 2004), 126, 151.

so that the 'prudent of the world' may have their eyes opened to the 'beauty' of the 'fountain of living mercies'. He issued a characteristically Quaker challenge: were people prepared to follow the Light in obedience, patience and long suffering if needs be, and were they prepared for regeneration so that Truth may reign in their hearts in order that justice would reign in the world?[139] His *First and Second Priesthood* (1657) provides an insight into the spiritual and psychological régime of the Kingdom. In the new covenant there would be no need for oaths and tithes. Here in the world of the Spirit, worship would reveal the eternal beyond the need for outward ordinances, the 'handwriting' of which all Friends believed Christ had 'blotted out'.[140] It would be a place of blessing, tenderness and forgiveness rather than guilt, punishment and 'hardness of heart'. It would be a place of freedom and life as opposed to the tyranny of the letter, of perfection and mercy instead of war and destruction.

Also in 1660 and in a way typical of Quaker language, George Bishop, like Burrough three years earlier, blended the Kingdom with the Christ within, the Light and the Comforter which 'shall reprove the world of sin'. The Lord and the Kingdom were one, being the 'power of God', the 'gospel of salvation', the 'everlasting gospel', the 'law' and 'rule', and the measure of all things' that was 'over all' (i.e. was reigning). He was sure that the Kingdom was 'the principle of seeing and knowing the things of God'.[141]

Edward Burrough

Burrough's *A Measure of the Times* (1657) repeated Fox's warning about waiting for a physical Kingdom. It was not sought 'without you [nor] to obtain it with your carnal weapons, but . . . spiritual'. It was necessary to defeat that within which opposed the Kingdom before its enemies in the outer could be likewise defeated. All this inevitably entailed suffering. Only this way would the Kingdom of Christ be spread rather than by 'secret policy and turbulent risings'.[142] Nevertheless, as with Benjamin Nicholson in 1653, the Kingdom for Burrough had a physical aspect, a Presence in the world which would inevitably defeat evil including all carnal kingdoms. Justice and righteousness would then reign on earth because their 'laws shall be changed and the poor shall no more be oppressed'.[143] The Kingdom had a political character, therefore, with its proclamation of liberty to the captives and calls for a radical restructuring of the Church's 'worships and

---

[139] H. Smith's work is a broadside.
[140] For 'blotted out' see Fox, *The Second Covenant*, 4-5.
[141] Bishop, *A Tender Visitation of Love* (1660), 18. See Burrough, *Truth (the Strongest)* (1657), 24.
[142] Burrough, *A Measure of the Times*, 34-5.
[143] *Ibid.*, 38; Nicholson, *A Blast from the Lord*, 5

ordinances', but also of outward government with its lies, 'imitations, superstitions, hypocrisy'.

So far, we have seen how the Quakers' understanding of the Kingdom overlaid their interpretation of the Good Old Cause giving the latter their own spiritual stamp. The old Law had been fulfilled long ago by Jesus whose determination was being repeated again: 'there shall be no law but the Law of God'.[144] In *A Standard Lifted Up* (1657), Burrough went further by stating that the Kingdom stood in truth, mercy, peace and justice. Its government was love, unity and perfect liberty to the just. It bound and chained the unjust and yet, as with all Friends, he reflected on the increasing success of the Antichrist at the same time as separation from the Kingdom increased. His 'strength and power' is

> put forth in defence of his kingdom by persecution, injustice, false imprisonments, beatings and whippings, and spoilings of goods and persons, and railings, accusations, slander and reproach.[145]

Emphasising the importance of a total, personal commitment to *the* peace testimony that was the inward and outward expression of the Kingdom or the Law of God, it was vital that each person—and particularly the Friends as exemplars to all—was an ambassador of the Lamb whose weapons also included 'long suffering' and 'downright sincerity of heart and tongue'. It was in worship where God's 'counsel' could be 'stood in' and the new 'covenant felt . . . without respect to times or things'.[146] 'Love', Burrough continued in 1659, 'shall overcome hatred, meekness shall overcome wrath, truth shall overcome deceit and falsehood, and God shall overcome the devil'.[147] He assured his readers that the Kingdom was to be spread among all nations for the final victory (consummation) of good over evil.

From their inception the Quakers were alive to tensions between the 'now' and the 'not yet' aspect of the Kingdom as in Burrough's *The True Faith of the Gospel of Peace* (1656). In this tract the Kingdom was, as with Fox, the 'pearl' within, something inherent in the soul, in the heart. As with breathing, it was the very make-up of human beings and naturally worthy of everyone's allegiance. As such, the Kingdom would create a 'new nature' within, a 'second person' in the same way that Jesus was the second Adam. It was God's Life-giving testimony unto people's hearts. The truly

---

[144] Burrough, *ibid.*
[145] *Ibid.*, 35, 38; *A Standard Lifted Up* (1657 [*DCFB* 1658]), 12; *A Discovery of Some Part* (1659), 3. See also Fox, *A Declaration Concerning Fasting and Prayer*, 4.
[146] Burrough, *A Faithful Testimony Concerning . . . True Worship*, 1 and in *Works*, 474.
[147] Burrough, *A Discovery of Some Part*, 4. For 'deceit', that which is contrary to the Kingdom, see also Fox, Eps. 87 (1655), 96 (1655) and 111 (1656) in *Works*, 7: 96-7, 161-2, 110-12 respectively.

Chapter 5: 'Since the Days of the Apostles'

convinced, the Saints, would carry the Kingdom within, among and for themselves, and for the whole world. The climactic or theophanous inner event was the struggle to overcome disobedience and separation from God/Love so that the new person would arise and be revealed along with the inner Kingdom to and for the world.[148] The great commission, both inner and outer, was not to 'limit' God but to grow God.[149]

Let us allow Burrough himself to speak of the Kingdom. In a lyrical and uplifting passage from *A General Epistle to all the Saints* (1660) we see how the intimacy of his mystical Kingdom experience radiates outwards to the movement and beyond:

> And so Friends, live in the seed of God, for in that is your victory and heavenly dominion, and also your election and your assurance for ever. . . therein does man inherit eternal life, rest and peace to his soul . . . and life inwardly and outwardly, and all fullness is enjoyed . . . And [God] is become to us the all in all . . . the end of all, and all the contrary put under, even the lion and the lamb laid down together and man lives in peace according to the Promise. And the mountain of the Lord's house is established on the top of all in which nothing can destroy or hurt the pure Life; but Life is in dominion over all and death is swallowed up in it.
>
> Oh Friends! This is the mark that is before you, press on towards it, that you may obtain the final end of all your travel and waiting, of your obedience and suffering, and the end of your hope and patience, and the very end of the message sent of God and delivered to you by us. The end of all is this: That you may dwell in God and he in you, and be gathered up to him to be ever with him . . . and you may be to him an honour and praise throughout the world in your generation.[150]

Thomas Stubbs, Rebekah Travers, William Dewsbury and Thomas Aldam

With equal assurance Thomas Stubbs in *A Call into the Way to the Kingdom* (1655) equated the Kingdom with the Light of Christ, 'the alone way to the Kingdom'. Along with Burrough, he put similar weight on eradicating sin and on the danger of limiting God. Stubbs warned his movement against

---

[148] Burrough, *The True Faith of the Gospel of Peace*, esp. 10; also *A Measure of the Times*, 22. See *AOTW*, 160 in which *apokalupsis* is addressed as the revelation of God's righteousness in Christ to those who believe. For the Kingdom as 'among' see Bishop, *Jesus Christ, the Same Today*, 21.

[149] Burrough *et al* (?), *A Declaration of the Present Sufferings of above 140 Persons* (1659), 33.

[150] Burrough, *A General Epistle* (1660), 6.

those 'in Egypt' who would 'shut the way of the Kingdom of God against [them] and draw [them] from [their] guide and strength, and resting place'. Like Stubbs, the Friends as a whole did not trust human nature as a reading of Rebekah Travers' broadside makes clear. In *This is for any . . . Looking for the Kingdom* (1659) only the pure and righteous, she emphasised, could enter the Kingdom.

In their imitation of the prophets, Quaker advice about the Kingdom could be ostensibly negative and judgmental. However, like Jesus, they were careful to stress that *love* was the basis of their condemnations. As we will soon see with Nayler, love was the first motion in establishing the Kingdom anew and propagating its outward manifestation as the Lamb's War. There was a desperate need, then, to avoid 'the vanities of the world' for 'what [would] it profit any to gain the whole world and lose [their] soul'? Stubbs' remedy was self-denial and the 'daily cross' so that 'through the regeneration' Jesus may be followed and 'the pure Law of God will be set up in you, and judgment will pass upon the vain, earthly, carnal part in you'.[151]

William Dewsbury was equally apocalyptic and strident in *A True Prophecy of the Mighty Day of the Lord* (1654). People needed to repent—change their thoughts and habits which prevented them from entering the Kingdom—and to prize their time, to turn immediately to the Lord, to love and obey the pure Light of Christ which would lead out of all unrighteousness to eternal life. Time was short for 'the Lord's anger . . . is coming upon the children of disobedience in this nation and elsewhere'. Only a loving God would act in this way. As with Fell, Dewsbury's reference in his title page to the 'Day of the Lord' expressed the Kingdom and its power of redemption.[152] Burrough, too, demonstrated in his *The Fourth General Epistle* (1660) how the 'Day' was synonymous with the Kingdom. Along with other Friends, he was to use the expression immediately in 1661, after the Restoration, when premillennial expectation began to subside, thus underlying our assertion that the Quakers never used 'Day' as an anticipation of the imminent and physical End-time. Instead, it was used in relation to the restoration of *God's* rule through the resolution of *the* historical crisis (the separation of God and humanity) and thus the deliverance of 'all people'.[153]

---

[151] Thomas Stubbs (d. 1673), *A Call into the Way to the Kingdom* (1655), 7-8.

[152] Dewsbury, *A True Prophecy of the Mighty Day of the Lord* (1654), 10.

[153] Burrough, *The Fourth General Epistle to all the Saints* in *Works*, 659, 662, 665 and 'The 'Preface' in *A Discovery of Divine Mysteries*, 5 in which he writes, 'the light of the Day of God almighty is arisen upon us in our day.' See also Caton, *The Testimony of a Cloud of Witnesses*, Sig. A2 which Caton opens with a reference to the 'latter-days'. Such sentiments can be found in 1664; see Howgill, *A Visitation of Love* (1664), 5. And see Barbour, 'The 'Lamb's War'', 150.

Joining Dewsbury on his tortuous spiritual journey we see how his discovery of the Kingdom within was in fact the story of his convincement. We can observe the signposts that led him to lend an ear to those who 'said they spoke from the mouth of the Lord, so [I] was deceived and caused to err by their lies that did draw me to seek the Kingdom of God in observations without' and in their deadening formalities. In this state he experienced physical illness. He recalls how the true knowledge he sought to heal his 'ignorance' of, and separation from, God, caused him to quit the army for he could no longer reconcile the material sword with his discovery of the Kingdom. Being within, the Kingdom's compass meant knowing God's solace which opened up his desire for innocence and the joy of David, the singer of the psalms. Now naked, 'the righteous justice of God' was upon him and he knew at last where the Light of Christ was to be found.[154]

Thomas Aldam and others in *A Brief Discovery of the Kingdom of the Antichrist* (1653) looked to the first of Jesus' two commandments, to love one's neighbour as oneself, as a gateway into the Kingdom.[155] Aspirants for the Kingdom should 'feed the hungry, clothe the naked, and let the oppressed go free'. They were to deny their own wisdom (their destructive ego) and be meek and lowly in heart. In this way, true rest for the soul would be found. The Kingdom beckoned for those who followed the straight way of obedience and self-denial.[156]

James Nayler

James Nayler's theology of the Kingdom is found in three tracts in particular—*A Discovery of the First Wisdom* (1653), written from Appleby prison, *Love to the Lost* (1656), a more systematic statement of Quaker belief, and *What the Possession of the Living Faith Is* (1659) which he addressed to 'the rulers and people'. *First Wisdom* contrasts the earthly and spiritual person. This 'second' person is a citizen of the Kingdom when s/he is 'meek', 'peaceable', 'gentle', 'patient', 'humble', 'full of love to all', and is 'content to suffer wrongs'. S/he is also a Kingdom person in having no favourites, when actively seeking 'purity' and 'unity' with God and all people, and when s/he 'stands in the will of God in all things' desiring to grow in 'the knowledge of God' for perfection—to be 'changed into the

---

[154] Dewsbury, *The Discovery of the Great Enmity*, 13-17 and in *Works*, 44-50.
[155] See Mk. 12:30-31; Mt. 22: 36-40 outlines Jesus' two great commandments: 'Love God with all your heart and with all your soul and with all your mind. This is the first and great commandment. And the second is like unto it, You shall love your neighbour as yourself. On these two commandments hang all the Law and the prophets'. Also Nayler, *Milk for the Babes*, 6.
[156] Aldam, *A Brief Discovery of the Kingdom of the Antichrist* (1653), 11.

image of the Lord'.[157] A Kingdom citizen worships God 'at hand' not at a distance. As a prophet s/he is a son/daughter of God who breaks the customs and traditions of old Israel so that the world turns upside down, the new citizen bringing 'a flaming sword to the earthly wisdom'.

For Nayler, being in the Light equates to being in the Kingdom, that state in which the 'serpent's wisdom has no jurisdiction, where one is brought to discern 'that which leads to obedience and disobedience' and witnesses the 'ministry of Christ to the 'spirit in prison'. In the Kingdom one encounters a unity with the 'pure Light within', the Light of Christ, which opens the meaning of 'all parables and Scriptures' as well as the Law of the new covenant which is written in the heart. This hidden treasure is eternal and is seen only with the pure, spiritual eye, a theme he emphasised in *Sin Kept out of the Kingdom* (1653) also written from Appleby gaol.[158] So, as the worldly wisdom is exposed by the Light one comes to 'righteousness, peace and joy in the holy ghost', another description of the Kingdom.[159]

The title page of *Love to the Lost* directs the work's central message to all who would come to the 'living way of Truth as it is in Christ Jesus' so they 'may come to the Life and Power', the Gospel and its Kingdom. Many of the tract's ideas had been aired in *First Wisdom* and in *The Power and Glory of the Lord* (1653), another description of Quaker theology in which he throws open his mystical frustrations to the world in the manner of the Hebrew prophets:

> O you people of England! How long will it be before you are obedient to the Kingdom of Jesus Christ! How long will you profess him in words and forms, and yet will not own him in power! You can be content to let him the name of a king, so that you yourselves may reign, and under the name of Christ's Kingdom act your own wills; and though you cannot bear it to be judged by the Spirit of Christ where it is in his people, which judges all the world, and all things; yet you cannot escape.[160]

In *What the Possession of the Living Faith Is*, Nayler again reiterates much of the above but emphasises rebirthing into the Spirit. By renting the veil, the Kingdom comes into view as spiritual sight is restored; 'all violence' as a consequence 'shall cease' and the Prince of peace 'shall reign in

---

[157] Nayler, *A Discovery of the First Wisdom*, 6, 10-16. Fox also inter-changed 'purity' and 'unity' in God; see Eps.10 (1652) and 13 (1653) in *Works*, 7: 20-2.
[158] Nayler, *Sin Kept out of the Kingdom*, 2.
[159] Nayler, *A Discovery of the First Wisdom*, 4-15.
[160] Nayler, *The Power and Glory of the Lord* (1653), 4.

Chapter 5: 'Since the Days of the Apostles'

righteousness'.[161] For Nayler and the Friends, Jesus and the Spirit were inter-generational and had the power and authority to revolutionise relationships between people. But also to change worldly structures so that the poor, needy, oppressed and the stranger were automatically care for, and where the Kingdom would be the 'sword of justice':

> Was not [Jesus'] work ever to change shadows and forms and religious traditions set up in men's minds above the life of Truth and leadings of the Spirit ... [and] do you think he is changed ... become proud and lofty' [and violent]?[162]

Like many Friends, Nayler chose to *live* the Kingdom so that it would be continually incarnated. His recounting of his missionary beginnings in court at Appleby, also in 1653—'I was at the plough, meditating on the things of God, and suddenly I heard a voice, saying to me, get you out from your kindred, and from your Father's house'—was a Kingdom saying employing a figurative use of Luke 9:62: 'And Jesus said unto him, 'No man, having put his hand to the plough, and looking back, is fit for the Kingdom of God.'' Quotations such as these are vintage early Nayler who knew nobody could escape the hound of heaven, that self-deception prevented anyone from entering the Kingdom.[163]

The Light, then, *had* to reign with its authority manifest in daily life. Everybody at heart knew this because potentially they were convinced children of the Light who secretly craved to return home to the Presence. Thus inward sin had to be confronted. So, too, the outward sin of injustice and oppression, themes rammed home in *The Lambs War* (1657, 1658), a highly significant work since it presents the 'weapons and colours' of the Kingdom for healing a distracted nation. Though its tone is softer than his previous works, the message of *The Lambs War* is actually a tough one—God leads those who wish to respond to the Light 'by the gentle movings of his Spirit out of all their own ways and wills ... into the will of the Father, by which they become more clean and holy.' If everybody kept to God's 'counsel' they would be safe; 'the kisses of his lips is life eternal ... and he makes all his subjects wise ... [and] ... a meek spirit does he beget in them'.[164]

---

[161] See also Blackborow, *A Visit to the Spirit in Prison*, 7.
[162] Nayler, *What the Possession of the Living Faith Is* (1659), 36; see 29-44.
[163] Nayler, 'Concerning Love' in *Love to the Lost*, 18.
[164] Nayler, *The Lambs War*, 6-7 in the sub-section 'What the Kingdom is'. The extended second edition is used throughout this book; it allowed Nayler to elaborate on the Kingdom. The original edition might have been written in 1656; see Barbour, 'The 'Lamb's War'', 157-8 (37*n*).

Underlying Nayler's concern were four important issues. First, he was eager for his opponents to fully understand that the Light, the Kingdom within each person, was unchangeable and everlasting. This was a ringing endorsement of the importance of every individual, that all were beloved of, and potentially whole in, God. Any violence done to them was contrary to the Kingdom, the 'Garden of God', where they were fed. Second, the Friends were not content to promote a mere reformation of outward manners. The Lamb's War was a spiritual campaign against the 'world's pleasures' that distracted people from the true worship of God and knowledge of the Kingdom. 'Returning to within' required nothing less than a total commitment to the revolutionary Jesus Way, even 'to give up their lives unto death' as the Friends were to remind the nations again in their all-important three declarations of 1659-61. In the six works mentioned above, Nayler calls upon 'all people' to face their own consciences which he identifies as the 'throne of Christ', to examine their lives, to ask themselves if they had peace within and to be utterly honest in their answer. Third, he expressed scepticism about the intentions of those previously convinced of the Quaker way but now only half committed to the Kingdom's demands, content to make compromises with the world. Echoing Margaret Fell in Ulverston church, he declared that they who 'preach the Kingdom of Christ in words, without victory, is a thief that goes before Christ'.[165] Fourth, it was vital to work towards the end of injustice for the realisation of the Kingdom. Together these four issues constituted a clear statement of early Quaker nonviolent, social and political transformation.[166]

The four issues and more can be found in Nayler's beautifully written and nuanced understanding of the Kingdom, 'Not to Strive, but Overcome by Suffering'; it makes for highly recommended reading (see Appendix 3). In a partially paraphrased selection it is easy to see evidence of a deep spirituality:

> The Kingdom is a tree that grows high, hard and strong, yet is full of fruit and power and knows the poor, the innocent, the sufferer and [person] of sorrows. And the end of this growth is the pure rest, soft, tender and the true fold for lambs, where the lions must lie down in the end if they come to rest. In the Kingdom there is no strife in the mind, no secret smitings which defile the rest and lead to division and separation. The little child leads into the rest, and that which is lowly gives the entrance.[167]

---

[165] Nayler, *The Lambs War*, 15.
[166] *Ibid.*, 6-7 For Nayler's voice of God episode see 'The Examination of James Nayler' in *Works*, 12-13. Also Gwyn, 'James Nayler and the Lamb's War', 184.
[167] Nayler, Ep. 11 in *Works*, 727-30. The work, probably written from prison, may have been titled by George Whitehead, editor of the *Works*.

Chapter 5: 'Since the Days of the Apostles'

Isaac Penington

In *The Flesh and Blood of Christ* published in 1675, Isaac Penington reminisced about how the Quakers 'wanted the presence and power of [the] Spirit to be inwardly manifested in our spirits', how they 'wanted the power from on high', 'life', 'the presence and fellowship of our beloved', and 'the knowledge of the heavenly Seed and Kingdom and an entrance into it' besides needing 'the holy dominion and reign of the lord of life over the flesh, over sin and death in us'. The section continues by outlining in trinitarian terms how the Quakers' saw beyond the 'letter' to 'see and feel the light and brightness of the inward day' which gave them freedom from the 'darkness of the inward night'. In this new 'day-spring' they would dwell in 'the Son, their 'Lord and savour', hear 'his voice' and be 'gathered home by him to the Father's house'. While they read of the pearl in the field, now they *experienced* finding it. The pearl was real and glorious, the 'Morning Star', the 'Truth' beyond time and space, a truth to be shared with all people, a truth that would rescue them from 'head-notions' so they may come to know 'heart-knowledge' and 'heart-experience', that 'sense of the living power of God inwardly' which 'puts an end to disputes'.[168]

In his earlier years, Penington devoted the first part of his large pre-Quaker work, *Expositions with Observations* (1656)—an eighty-three page meditation on the Sermon on the Mount, the path to the Kingdom—to what he, too, called 'Christ's doctrine'. Here and elsewhere Penington described the doctrine in terms of the Gospel, itself the doctrine of the Kingdom, the governance of Christ or the 'new covenant with all the laws of it in the heart of every Christian' who comes to the Substance. The Substance had been hidden by the old Law but had always lived within it.[169] Respecting the poor in spirit who would inherit the Kingdom, he says apocalyptically that

> Herein lies their blessedness . . . wherein all the glories of God are unveiled and . . . are intended for these perfectly poor ones . . . The right to this large rich inheritance is written in their nature, in their state and condition, in their very poverty; therefore they without doubt are blessed. He is not blessed who appears great in a vain show, but he who is great in truth: Not he who hath a present shadow of life, but he who hath an external seed of life is blessed. He is not rich who abounds with

---

[168] Penington, 'A Brief Account' in *The Flesh and Blood of Christ* (1675), 23-28 and *Works* (1784), iii, 419-22.
[169] See also Penington's *Some of the Mysteries of God's Kingdom Glanced At* (1663), *passim*.

trash, but he who hath the true substance hid within his meanness, lowness and poverty.[170]

The scandal of poverty, material and spiritual, angered God who demanded the healing of the broken Christ. Ignoring Jesus' Beatitudes invited divine judgment in the same way, as he wrote in *The Jew Outward* (1659), that propagating false teaching and 'expounding the Scriptures out of the Life' shut out the Kingdom,

> for the Life is the Kingdom and words from the Life yield the favour of the Kingdom. But words out of it . . . only build up a knowledge in the contrary wisdom.[171]

Penington's *Some Considerations Propounded to the Jews* (1659/60) expanded Margaret Fell's understanding of the Kingdom, of the Light, as the new Law, the new covenant of love, mercy and redemption. Of its nature it was cleansing. *The Jew Outward* and *Some of the Mysteries of God's Kingdom Glanced At* (1663) also help us grasp the fundamental place of Love at the heart of the 1650s experience, their Kingdom-as-peace testimony message. Like Britten who, by quoting John 13:35 emphasised how the Kingdom's disciples were 'known by the cognisance of Love', Penington wrote that

> (Love) is the sweetness of life. It is the sweet, tender, melting nature of God, flowing up through his seed of life into the creature, and of all things making the creature most like unto himself, both in nature and operation. It fulfils the Law, it fulfils the Gospel; it wraps up all in one, and brings forth all in the oneness. It excludes all evil out of the heart, it perfects all good in the heart. A touch of Love does this in measure, perfect Love does this in fullness. But how can I proceed to speak of it! O that the souls of all, that fear and wait on the Lord, might feel its nature fully; and then would they not fail of its sweet overcoming operations, both towards one another and towards enemies. The great healing, the great conquest, the great salvation is reserved for the full manifestation of the love of God. His judgments, his cuttings, his hewings by the word of his mouth are but to prepare for . . . And this my soul waits, cries after, even the full springing up of eternal love in my heart, and the swallowing of me wholly into it, and the bringing of

---

[170] Penington, *Expositions with Observations, sometimes on Several Scriptures* (1656), 52.
[171] Penington, *The Jew Outward*, 13.

my soul wholly forth in it, that the life of God in its own perfect sweetness may freely run for through this vessel.[172]

In *The Way of Life and Death* (1658) he repeated Fox's 'apostasy' claim and devoted the first 73 pages to outlining the implications for Christians of losing the benefits of the Kingdom—true faith, worship, ministry, love, joy and liberty, hope, peace and everlasting rest, prayer, obedience, repentance, conversion, regeneration, wisdom, righteousness, justification, sanctification, reconciliation and redemption. Lost, too, was the true Church because the 'pharisees' looked only to Scripture as their authority. The work strongly supports Fox's belief that the Kingdom is neither 'literal, traditional nor fleshly', that it could not be 'received by natural understanding', that it was spiritual.[173] Penington asserted boldly that the Quakers were not a re-hash of the old religious formulae but emissaries of a new branch of the family of Jesse. Here he taught the Kingdom as a present and future reality. The realised and realising Second Coming was shaking, destroying and eradicating the old and ushering in the new:

> Now mark, we are not persons . . . shot up out of the old root into another appearance, as one sect has done out of another till many are come up one after another, the ground still remaining the same out of which they all grew: but that ground has been shaken and shaking, destroyed and destroying, removed and removing in us, and the old root of Jesse has been made manifest in us, and we have been transplanted by the everlasting power of life, and a real change brought forth in us out of that spirit wherein the world lives and worships, into another spirit into which nothing which is of the old can enter.[174]

His *The Scattered Sheep Sought After* (1659) extolled an inner apocalypse, the means by which the Light was revealed out of a nature inherently dead to the Spirit, a nature that usually preferred it that way. With the rediscovered new Law of the Kingdom, the old spirit of darkness was now subject to the 'fundamental principle of the gospel' which was that 'God is Light and in him is no darkness at all'.[175] Only by entering the Kingdom could people call out to the Light within them as a way of crucifixion and death to the old covenant so they may experience resurrection and Life in

---

[172] Penington, *Some of the Mysteries*, 9-10; *Some Considerations Propounded to the Jews*, 5-7; *The Jew Outward*, 13. See Britten, *Concerning the Kingdoms of God and Men*, 4. Jn. 13:35 reads, 'By this shall all [people] know that you are my disciples, if you have love one to another'.

[173] Penington, *The Way of Life and Death*, 46.

[174] *Ibid.*, 89 (Sig. N).

[175] For 'God is Light' etc. see 1 Jn. 1: 5.

the new. This was the true wisdom in which one waited in humility and love in the service of God.[176] The themes of Light and Life are revisited in *The Consideration of a Position* (1660). Adopting Fox's 'pearl' theme, he wrote,

> Yet in this earth, in this field of the world, God has hid somewhat, even the everlasting pearl which when [people are] awakened to seek and find in the living Breath, in the eternal Light of Life, it is able to redeem [them].[177]

The Light could not deceive, he continued, and if people were true to it they would be formed by its movings, stirrings and leadings. These were the 'steps of the Lamb' which would, in turn, bring those who aspired to be disciples of the Kingdom out of their 'spiritual wilderness' into the 'land of Rest' or the inner promised land. It was well to know that God brought forth the 'weak' and 'foolish' who were offensive to the powers of their present age; the Kingdom appeared where the eye of humanity least looked for them.[178] *The Consideration of a Position* is an essential work because it outlines the way in which the exercise of a pure conscience is related to suffering and the purity, patience and obedience that suffering demands if the 'Kingdom in the heart' is to grow and bear 'spiritual fruit':

> The knowledge of Christ is life eternal, and in his cross is the spiritual virtue which cuts off the uncircumcision of the heart, whereby it is enabled to love the Lord. Now Christ is the Lord from heaven, the quickening spirit, who sows the Seed of the Kingdom in the heart, and causes it to spring up, out of which Seed the faith, the love, the hope, the meekness, the patience, and every spiritual fruit springs and grows. And he that is thus born of this Seed and receives the knowledge of life which springs from this Seed, he cannot but love him which begat him, and he reaps the fruit of all that Christ did and suffered in that prepared body: and God is both just and the justifier of him who is thus united to Jesus.[179]

In a fine passage in *The Axe Laid at the Root* (1659), Penington similarly portrayed the Kingdom in Edenic terms—of purity, freedom, unity, discernment, truth and light. Looking back to the time of the post-Pentecost apostles, he compared their experience to his own and that of the

---

[176] Penington, *The Scattered Sheep Sought After* (1659), 13-14 and *Where is the Wise?* (1660), 8.
[177] Penington, *The Consideration of a Position*, 26.
[178] *Ibid.*, 28-9.
[179] *Ibid.*, 17.

Chapter 5: 'Since the Days of the Apostles'

Friends. But this was no wistful reflection, no utopian dream. Like the apostles, all followers of the Jesus Way were the true Church ('living stones') who would have the Spirit in their midst and the existential Jesus as their comforter and companion. Jesus' Love would be *the* guide, *the* very means of life itself, *the* standard that would be over all.[180] The tract presented a scenario in which the Kingdom (Zion, Jerusalem) was an ever-present event with a constant promise for the future. What was real for the apostles, in other words, could be real for the present and the future. The new covenant, the Kingdom, could never be limited by time and space.

But Penington also warned that the Kingdom was highly vulnerable to corruption. While it could cut through the sin of church-centricity like a two-edged sword, there was an especial need to be aware of the false Church. The wolves within it led people into the 'thick night of darkness' that 'overspread the beauty' of the Kingdom, and they promoted the letter of Scripture rather than its Spirit. More importantly, he attacked the Calvinist belief that the outward Church was the Kingdom of God on earth but also how the Roman Catholics and Calvinists, following Augustine of Hippo and Luther, had separated the Kingdom and the Earth. He and the Friends maintained from their own experience that there was no relation between the Kingdom and the true Church that did not intersect with the world, that there was no way of serving God without serving the world:[181]

> There was a glorious day and bright appearance of truth in the times of the apostles. They had the true Comforter who led them into all truth and kept them alive in truth, and truth alive in them. By this Spirit they, as living stones, were built up a spiritual house founded on Zion the holy mount, into Jerusalem the holy city, the church of the living God, the pillar and ground of truth. And here they had their conversation in heaven, with God the Judge of all, with Christ the mediator, and with the Spirits of just men and the holy angels which always behold the face of God. They lived in the Spirit, they walked in the Spirit, they prayed in the Spirit, they sung in the Spirit, they worshipped in the Spirit, and in that understanding which the truth had made free, and had God dwelling in them, and Christ walking in the midst of them, and by the presence and power of his life in them, were truly dead unto sin and alive unto God, they being not strivers against sin with man's legal spirit, but by the power of grace, which made them more than conquerors through him that loved them. This was part of the glory of that state, in that day of the sunshine of the gospels.[182]

---

[180] For 'living stones' see for instance Dn. 2:34.
[181] See Braaten, *The Future of God*, 115.
[182] Penington, *The Axe Laid to the Root*, 'Preface', Sig. A2.

The Kingdom: a Commentary

The Kingdom occupied *the* central position in early Quaker thinking and witness. It linked God and the children of Light in a profoundly intimate relationship. As such, it governed their daily lives, transforming them into new creations and thus, as they believed, into true Christians. For the Friends the Kingdom was a unifying, loving and healing reality—an inclusive reality—which placed the now and future in relation to the saving activity of the Spirit together with the birth, ministry, death, resurrection, ascension and glorification of Jesus, all of which they understood spiritually. But while the Kingdom was their intrinsic dynamic, and they its messengers, it was not in their power to control. It was *God's* Kingdom. As followers of Jesus, the world that included spouses, children, personal friends, property and even life itself, was secondary to the Kingdom. However, in renouncing the world as Paul advised, they were not to be ascetic. Possessions and relationships were not wrong if they did not deflect from the Kingdom, and they were certainly opposed to the monastic life.[183]

The Kingdom was unconditional, that is, independent of time and space—'it stands not upon condition but upon free love and mercy', wrote Burrough to the Independent, Samuel Eaton.[184] By definition it could not end. But it could be lost in which case the Day of the Lord would come again to remind people of the Kingdom as the manifestation of Love 'being over all'. 'Over all', which we have met before, was a much used expression of Fox. It signified the Kingship or kinship of Love, God, Light and their power within. The 'Day' was a messenger, a corrective, a mediator and it was revelatory. As we also find in the non-Quakers William Erbery and William Dell, its realisation within would be realised by God's 'sword' or 'wrath'—the desire for purity came with a great price since the Way was 'narrow', difficult to follow and many would fall on stony ground.[185] But if the heart were true, sin would be washed away in the Fountain of Life. Being open to the Day meant it could be experienced as pure Light, a pure shining forth of God, of Eternity, of the Life 'putting itself forward', of holiness shedding itself. Only those born of the Light could see it with the spiritual eye since the spiritual person was the image of God. Put another way, only those blind to the carnal could see the Day and receive its warning and peace. The Day—and here again the term merges with the Kingdom—was the birth from above; it was the Light which discerned all things contrary to it. But as there was always an element of

---

[183] See Mt. 7:13, 25:14; Lk. 14:26, 16:10.
[184] Burrough, *Some False Principles and Errors* (1659), 12.
[185] See Erbery, *The Bishop of London* (1652), 20; Dell, *The Building and Glory* (1647), Sig. A^{4v}. Also Saltmarsh, *Sparkles of Glory*, 11.

crisis in birthing, the Friends saw the 'Day' in prophetic and apocalyptic terms, as a crisis that would painfully usher in the new era of the Kingdom.

Fox understood Jesus—he who never fell like Adam—as both the advent and the fulfilment or embodiment of the new messianic age, of the Kingdom that was (and would always be) present in the *now*.[186] This eternal now, so to speak, was the spiritual 'place' where Jesus continually passed on his mantle to a new people, a holy 'nation' or Kingdom, a dimension with no new outer religion or personality cult.[187] Consequently, the Friends would come to objectify themselves as 'they who are called Quakers' or 'a people in scorn called Quakers', internalising the Hebrew idea that a kingdom was impossible until a 'nation' was formed. That is to say, while the world knew them as 'Quakers', what concerned Fox and the movement was their readiness as a chosen people or 'nation' to be at the command of God in ever walking the Way of peace until the fullness of time.[188] The Kingdom, then, could never be a short-term event or experience because God alone was its eternal and ever-immanent inspiration. This devotion also implied, as it might have done for Jesus, a desire for an immersion (not necessarily annihilation) into the personal God who was totally loving and forgiving, and that everything, even death, was in the gracious gift of God.[189] In other words, God could be incarnated at any point in time, or, more precisely, at a point always in the present with the future at its heart. By cutting across time, Fox believed Jesus had liberated God's love from 'history', symbolically bound so far within the strictures of the Mosaic Law, so proving the Kingdom independent of time and space, universal in application and the means by which unity and wholeness in God may be achieved.

Their obedience to the Word would ensure that God's sovereignty would 'cover' the earth. Walking the Way of peace, equality and truth was to be their sole vocation just as the Kingdom was Jesus', and they were to bring it to all people.[190] Matthew 5-7 and the Epistle of James—into which the Sermon on the Mount was partially incorporated (as they may have noticed)—provided the ethical basis of their Lamb's War which led to that

---

[186] Of the four evangelists, Matthew uses 'Kingdom' terminology the most freely. See *Journal*, 23. For Fox's knowledge of the Bible see Croese, *The General History*, 14.

[187] For 'holy nation' see Rev. 14: 4, 5.

[188] Henry Clark, *A Cloud of Witnesses*, 23, 26. I doubt Fox distinguished between 'history' and 'religious history' as Cadbury hints in *Quakerism and Early Christianity*, 35: the Quaker purview had all history, i.e. time etc., as cosmological. For a Foxian disavowal of Puritanism see *Cambridge*, i., 333. For 'wholeness' and 'universality' of the Kingdom see George Keith (c.1639-1716), *The Benefit, Advantage and Glory of Silent Meetings* (1670) written in 1669 but with a 1650s theology.

[189] See W. Smith, *A Manifestation of Prayer*, Bds. and Farnworth, *The Spiritual Man* (1654), 18.

[190] See Ac. 2:17-18; 2 Cor. 5:17.

The Early Quakers and the 'Kingdom of God'

same unity and wholeness, unity with each other and with all humanity and creation thus fulfilling God's intention.[191] The Kingdom bespoke a worshipping community discerning the will of God. It was perfect since perfection, only possible through the Light, was attainable in this life. The Kingdom that had no beginning was present, then, but it was also future; through the fulfilment it would be presented to God.

Although for the Friends the Light of Christ was the 'universal saving necessity', they did not believe all people would enjoy salvation, that none would be eternally lost.[192] God's universal saving activity intended that everybody could respond to divine grace by virtue of the universal nature of the spiritual atonement. People could choose between the Light and darkness (unrighteousness, separation); the responsibility was theirs alone. They did not agree with the Protestant-Catholic position that the atonement was fixed in a particular time, 33 CE. It was a continuing phenomenon and they internalised it through their convincement. Therefore, as mentioned in the above survey of the Kingdom, individuals could crucify the old self and resurrect something that was always potentially present, 'that of God within'. They could give birth to the Light for liberating their power to love themselves and their neighbour.[193]

Living beyond himself like his Saviour, Jesus, Fox the mystic found from the earliest moments of his public life that he, too, could rise atop time to see 'into that which was without end, and things which cannot be uttered, and of the greatness and infiniteness of the love of God, which cannot be expressed by words'.[194] By claiming to abolish the old history and in creating a new one, Fox and Friends yearned to restore the spiritual revolution of Jesus by bringing the future to the present so that hope could be manifest in Love and liberation, and in both for a life in the Spirit.[195] Their understanding of Isaiah led them to internalise the prophet's post-exilic hope for the restoration of a New Israel within. The image of the outer, physical End could now be replaced by the reality of the inner End-time that would free individuals from the old dispensation which still lingered in the world's corruption and 'struck at [Fox's] heart'. In this way, like the writer(s) of Revelation, they wished to redeem time. Here was the most potent of brews for turning the world upside down. From the start, therefore, and unlike the Church after the first Council of Nicea (325 CE), it was the *Kingdom aspect* of Jesus' public and private teaching that was the

---

[191] For the relationship of the Sermon to James' Epistle see V. Porter, *The Use of the Sermon . . . in . . . James*, 1-2.

[192] For 'universal saving necessity' see Crook, *A Defence of the True Church*, 26.

[193] Penny, *Freewill or Predestination*, 161 (110*n*).

[194] *Journal*, 21; see also 11. Quaker mysticism is discussed in Chp. 9.

[195] See *AOTW*, 206.

central focus and motivation for the first Friends.[196] We cannot fully understand them without knowing *their* understanding of the Kingdom.

In sum, the Friends made a linguistic distinction between, on the one hand, the Kingdom and, on the other, God or Christ. And yet they existentially recognised both could not be separated. The Kingdom was not only the expression of God or a way of speaking about God, 'seeing and knowing the things of God', but was God in actual fact who sought the necessary co-operation with his children of Light. Here the Quakers long anticipated progressive, mature modern theology.[197] Importantly, their enormous concentration on the Kingdom effectively isolated it as a theological entity worthy of study in itself.

Conclusion

The Quakers were not neutral in the political debates of the time. But while they fully endorsed the Good Old Cause, their Kingdom and its nonviolent politics of righteousness/justice, peace and compassion which incorporated many of the principles of the Cause itself, was more important. The Cause became a metaphor for a new world order free of the first covenant into which the Puritans were locked. The tithe represented the old covenant, the tyranny of Church and State. It was a sign of covetousness, a relic of hated popery. The Friends believed passionately that they were the Jesus Way revived in which the unchanging Kingdom was central. As Canby Jones has written, they 'felt they were witnesses of full salvation and redemption through Christ and that his Kingdom had fully come in their midst'.[198] It was something for which they were prepared to die like Jesus himself. Highly condemnatory of the Church, they were convinced it had neglected the Kingdom 'since the apostles' days' and was thus in a state of apostasy. The Church in England itself was no exception and, again, the tithe was a sign of the apostasy. To combat this evil the Friends preached a redemptive process of Love in which the individual was required to play his or her part in the Lamb's War for salvation, a war for righteousness/justice, a war for wholeness through unity with God.

Through various early Quaker understandings of the Kingdom we saw how it was a 'sword' and the 'main war' against the kingdom of Satan, that is, the corrupted world which had its genesis in the hearts of people. The Kingdom, however, would never be defeated for it was from everlasting to

---

[196] McGrath, *Modern Christian Thought*, 301. See Howgill, *Some of the Mysteries of God's Kingdom*, 38: 'his Kingdom rules over all'.
[197] See, for instance, Goergen, *The Mission and Ministry of Jesus*, 225-6, 229-30.
[198] T.C. Jones, *George Fox's Teaching*, 27.

everlasting.[199] It was both of the earth—the earth being part of Eternity—and of heaven. It was a living corrective, an 'everlasting trial for apostates', the ultimate standard by which all could expect God's wrath *which was based on Love*. Its outcome and holy banner involved suffering which was its 'pure Life and conversation', just as Jesus' sufferings were 'free for love's sake'.[200]

Finally, the Kingdom was a vocation, the 'narrow way' of the 'daily cross' to which few were called. It was a faith and practice that needed grounding in each day. Since it was never violent and eschewed outward rebellion, it necessarily had love of one's enemies as a pillar. The Kingdom reflected the immanence and transcendence of God, as well as God's almightiness 'in his creation' because the Lord was 'over all'. Without an understanding of the Kingdom as the Friends came to appreciate it, we cannot hope to fully understand them or their 1650s experience and its Testimony.

---

[199] Fox, Ep. 74 (1654) in *Works*, 7: 84-5.
[200] Fox, Ep. 129 (1656) in *Works*, 7: 121-2.

Chapter 6: *'Now Religion in itself is this'*

- The Bible, Three Declarations and the Lamb's War -

In his introduction to Fox's *The Great Mystery* (1659), Edward Burrough recalled the movement's progress from its acknowledged inception in 1652. Like William Penn many years later, he made it clear that it was the *Kingdom* he and his fellow Quakers 'saw in the beginning', a 'discovery' (a revelation, an unveiling) that led them to take 'up the cross to all earthly glories, crowns and ways'.[1] From that moment on, the restoration of the Kingdom 'established in righteousness' was to be *the* Quaker task in announcing the saving effect of the Light of the Christ. Burrough's friend, Francis Howgill, also looked back with wonder to those joyful days when 'the Kingdom of Heaven did gather us and catch us all as in a net'. Their joy signified an unexpected treasure, the great blessing of salvation. For the Friends, it also meant 'the Life', the wedding feast and fullness, and a new understanding of 'church' as an inner experience to be shared and demonstrated with all people.[2]

The Kingdom filled their every moment. Indeed, we have seen that under the guise of its many titles, it was the central focus of almost all of their one thousand written works from 1650 to 1663. Furthermore, its message was the matrix out of which the first Friends fashioned their assault on the world's 'apostasy' by means of a nonviolent Lamb's War for salvation, for the sake of righteousness/justice. This was a spiritual war that would result in three highly significant declarations already mentioned—*A Declaration . . . to the Present Distracted and Broken Nation of England* (December, 1659), *A Declaration and Information* (June, 1660) and *A Declaration from the Harmless and Innocent People of God* (January, 1661). Each work was solidly based on skilfully selected biblical references.[3] Before they and the Lamb's War are discussed, however, I wish

---

[1] Burrough, 'Epistle to the Reader', *The Great Mystery*, unnumbered p. 10. See Penington, *The Way of Life and Death*, 69-70; Fox, *A Warning from the Lord to the Pope* (1656), 8-9. Penn wrote of Fox 'setting up the Kingdom'—'the Way' as Fox's 'work'. The Kingdom, the initiation of a new 'Gospel time', was thus the focal point of Fox's 'testimony' as it was also of the whole movement. See Penn, *A Brief Account of the . . . Quakers* (1694), 28-9, 32, 35, 83, 88.

[2] For Howgill's reaction see *BQ*, 95; *Journal*, 109. Also Mt. 13:47 for the 'Kingdom's net'.

[3] See *Journal*, 13-18, 35 and *To All that would Know* (Thomason, 25/March/1654); for 23 more references (among the very many extant) see *GADOT*, 329 (59*n*). The Kingdom also appears in 1652 as 'the doctrine of Christ' in the first known published tract written from a York Castle dungeon by Aldam *et al*, *False Prophets*, 2.

to look briefly at the Friends' use of the Bible and what they understood as 'righteousness', both of which are important for an understanding of the declarations themselves and Testimony in general.

The Bible as Guide to the Kingdom

Through the prism of Fox's critical analysis of the ecclesiastical environment as well as his mystical intimacy with God, the Separatists whom he initially encountered realised that, at last, the divine Word could be experienced immediately without clerical go-betweens and that their sin and guilt could be taken away. They heard him launch his belief that, though the Bible contained the inspired words of God, it was not *the* Word of God as the Church had long taught. Nor was Scripture, as Nayler advised later, a 'private interpretation' for it was 'given forth to be read and fulfilled in the saints', this is to say, it was potentially the preserve of everyone and should be used to further the Kingdom.[4] Instead, the Inward Light of Christian experience was *the* paramount authority. It superseded Scripture and ecclesiastical jurisdiction each with *their* own self-proclaimed political and teaching authority.[5]

What would soon be fuel for its Puritan gainsayers, the young movement loudly declared its confidence in the Bible as an experience of God's Kingdom, but that it was only a book, a template, a medium, a guide of 'pen and ink' according to leading Quaker, Martin Mason. He was reiterating Ralph Cudworth, the Cambridge Platonist, whom he might have read.[6] Reliance on 'ink and paper', Cudworth had preached in 1647, denied the living principle within and a new nature ever arising: 'words and syllables, which are but dead things, cannot possibly convey the living notions of heavenly truths to us'.[7] This was the Quaker sentiment exactly. Though valuable, loved and used as a matter of course by the Friends—they had, after all, been steeped in it since childhood—and undoubtedly a source of validity and *gravitas* to their spiritual experience, the Bible had been composed by flawed human beings and could not of itself offer salvation.[8] It was not the only fount of Truth. 'What if a man could repeat all the Bible', cried Mason, 'yet . . . the spirit of Christ live not in him, all will avail him nothing'. Richard Hubberthorne, too, declared a preference for

---

[4] Nayler, *Truth Cleared from Scandals* (1654), 1-2.
[5] See Dobbs, *Authority and the Early Quakers*, esp. 336. For 'Name' see Howgill, *A Lamentation for the Scattered Tribes*, 8. For the Bible as a medium see G. Whitehead, *The He-goats Horn Broken*, 13 and for 'Name' as Word of God see Fox's *A Catechism for Children* (1657), 31; also *TWTUD*, 267.
[6] For Cambridge Platonists see below, Chp. 9.
[7] Cudworth (1617-88), *A Sermon Preached* (31/May/1647), 5.
[8] For 'steeped in the Bible' see *EQW*, 27.

that 'faith [which is] the ground of the Scriptures, and not the Scriptures the ground of faith.'[9]

No friends to bibliolatry, therefore, the Quakers, and Samuel Fisher in particular, denied that the Bible portrayed 'a notional and literal knowledge' of God or that all biblical truths were applicable to every situation. Having gone through many translations, the Bible had to be read on an 'inner' and 'outer' level. Levine says that for Fisher, as his giant work *Rusticus ad Academicos* (1660) testifies, the Bible was 'essentially a human composition, humanly transcribed and transmitted and thus far from being the direct and unmediated word of God.' 'To have the gospel preached in men is one thing', said Fisher, 'and for men to learn the mystery of it is another'.[10] Like all Friends, he looked upon its text 'in the light of the same inspiration as that which had caused it to be written'. Fisher's view, indeed the view of all the Friends, accorded with that of Luther and the Reformed Confessions of Faith.[11] In other words, for the Friends, the Spirit, the Word, was the touchstone for testing and verifying the Bible, the same touchstone that the Hebrew holy men and women possessed before the Scriptures were written. It was the Spirit that gave forth the Scriptures which were, in turn, a confirmation of, rather than *the*, source of truth.[12] Nor had the Bible, stated Fisher, been homogeneously composed by scribes,

> that wrote either out of other copies, or from the mouths of men more immediately inspired, or from what was commonly reported, and generally believed . . . and what they retained in their memories, and some way or other comprehended beforehand.[13]

Although the Friends admitted the Bible was a secondary guide to the reality of the Inward Light, it nevertheless contained their doctrines. It was,

---

[9] Martin Mason (*fl.*1655-76), *The Proud Pharisee Reproved* (1655), 10; Hubberthorne, *Truth and Innocency Clearing Itself* (1657) in *Works*, 44 (beware pagination); Fox, *The Great Mystery*, 111. See Christopher Feake, Joseph Kellet *et al*, *A Faithful Discovery of a Treacherous Design* (1653), 33-5; John Stalham, *Contradictions of the Quakers* (1655), 25 (answered by Hubberthorne in *The Rebukes of the Reviler* [1657]); see p. 5 where Stalham is described as having a 'wicked, old lying heart' with 'devilish wisdom'.

[10] Fisher quoted by Angell, 'Universalising', 38.

[11] The Reformed Confessions of Faith comprise the Heidelberg Catechism (1563) and were adopted by the Canons of Dort (1618-19), the Scottish Confession (1560) and the (Presbyterian) Westminster Confession (1646), a modification of which was the (Congregational) Savoy Declaration (1658).

[12] Langford, *Quakers and Christianity*, 1; Underwood, *Primitivism*, 22-3; Fox, *The Great Mystery*, 369-75. See *Cambridge*, i., 34 and Cadbury, *A Quaker Approach to the Bible* at: <www.universalistfriends.org/Cadbury-1.html>.

[13] Levine, 'Matter of Fact in the English Revolution', 320; Fisher, *Rusticus ad Academicos*, 'The Third Apologetical' chp. 2 in *Works*, 421 and see 436.

said Thomas Salthouse, 'a witness with us of what we teach and of what we believe'.[14]

Christopher Hill maintained *Rusticus* effectively ended 'the epoch of Protestant bibliolatry' enhancing the 'end of the authority of the Book'. While Hill was exaggerating, Quaker writings certainly reveal a dogged refusal to follow the Bible slavishly. They disagreed, for instance, with Paul's theology of justification from faith alone rather than from faith *and* good works as found in the Letter of James. As Stephen Angell notes, the Friends saw in Colossians 1:24 (unlike the Puritans) that 'the process of salvation, while open to everybody, required an active participation [in good works], not a passive reception of grace'.[15]

But to Puritans, Episcopalians and others such a position was dangerously radical: the Bible offered visible proof that God was recorded faithfully. 'The holy Scriptures were denied to my face to be the word of Truth', complained the Puritan divine John Stalham of the Quaker Richard Farnworth. They *were* the Word of God, he insisted as if Farnworth were mad, and they who denied such a truth would be judged 'by the Scriptures' at the last day.[16] However, drawing attention to the multiplicity of biblical texts, Samuel Fisher protested to John Owen that they were varied and variable. It was indisputable, he wrote, that 'the naked letter of the Bible was fallible and corrupt, if only through [the Bible's] mistranslations'.[17] Equally, Isaac Penington in 1658 maintained that the 'Kingdom of Christ is not literal, traditional or fleshly; nor can it be received by the natural understanding: but it is spiritual'. At the same time, while they regarded the theology of the times as 'soaring, airy head knowledge', the Friends never endorsed theological illiteracy nor were they adverse to doctrine so long as it did not separate people from the Truth, the Word. According to Penington,

> Any teaching or expounding of Scriptures out of the Life shuts up the Kingdom, for the Life is the Kingdom. And words from the Life yield the favour of the Kingdom, but words out of it (though never so good and true) reach not to the Life in another but only build up knowledge in the contrary wisdom, and teach to hold the Truth in the

---

[14] Thomas Salthouse (1630-91), *The Line of True Judgment* (1658), 12.

[15] See Jm. 2:14-24 and Angell, 'Universalising ', 53 and 37. My insertion.

[16] Stalham, *The Reviler Rebuked* (1657), part 1, p. 1; also his *Contradictions of the Quakers*, *passim*. In 1675 clerics were still warning of Quakerish beliefs. Herbert Croft (1603-91), Bishop of Hereford (1661-91, in words that might have been spoken 20 years earlier warned gravely that, 'Once we leave Scripture and hearken to the doctrine of men, ever so holy, ever so learned, ever so primitive, we shall soon be wheedled into the papists' religion'. See *The Naked Truth* (1675), 55 and Spurr, 'A Special Kindness for Dead Bishops', 315.

[17] See *TWTUD*, 266-8 for Fisher and the Bible.

unrighteousness ... And so this kind of teaching and knowledge shuts up the door and way of Life and must be lost before the Kingdom can be found'.[18]

For us today, the early Quakers' prose can be off-putting, giving the impression they were 'Bible bashers', 'fundamentalists' or 'literalists' proclaiming the physical end of the world as 'nigh'. They could indeed be literal in their interpretation but, for the most part, their literalism was confined to their outer witness—fasting, attempts at healing, quaking, refusal to pay tithes or hat honour, their conscientious objection to oath taking and nonviolence, walking naked 'as a sign' of their purity and openness to the Christ in all things, and their forthright (and sometimes offensive) language.[19] Invariably, they went beyond the accepted interpretation of the Gospels, James' Epistle and the other Pastoral Letters, including the Pauline epistles, to escape literalism and the sin-soaked Puritan determinism that went with it. Rosemary Moore tells us that they used the Bible as proof of how people including their enemies should act, as a vindication of their own beliefs and as a guide or source of remonstration to their own communities.[20] But they also used Scripture to parallel themselves with the Gospel story so that as latter day disciples they were seen and understood as the living narrative of the rediscovered Kingdom. The margins of their tracts often brim with apposite biblical references bearing testimony to this desire.[21]

The Bible, then, was the teaching tool of the Friends, a key polemical weapon of the Lamb's War and a means of guiding people to the Kingdom message of Jesus, to its inclusiveness and righteousness. And their ability to quote it accurately and at length, and in some cases in a manner that demonstrated their proficiency in Greek and Latin, may have had an

---

[18] Penington, *The Jew Outward*, 13; *The Way of Life and Death*, 46; Fox and Nayler *et al*, *Saul's Errand*, 7, 16; Keith, *The Benefit, Advantage*, 1; Henry Clark, *A Cloud of Witnesses*, Sig. A2, 4, 6-7, 9; Thomas Greene (*c*.1634-99), *An Alarm to the False Shepherds* (1660), 10-11. Also *GADOT*, 12; P. Anderson, 'Continuing Revelation-Gospel or Heresy?' in Scully and Dandelion (eds.), 15-18, 25. For Barclay's commentary on theology see his *Apology* (1678), Prop. II, 'Of Immediate Revelation'), §1, p. 4 also quoted in Frost, 'The Dry Bones of Quaker Theology', 507.

[19] For 'naked' in this context see Heb. 4:13: 'naked' in the seventeenth century could denote any stage of undress.

[20] *TLITC*, ch. 4; see esp. 53.

[21] A good example is Nayler's contribution to *Saul's Errand*, 16-19. In four pages he margined 93 references plus three textually from 23 biblical books. This calculation excludes uncited references embedded within the text. Particularly on pp.18-19 he parallels Kingdom values and his thinking on ministry and right behaviour, especially in relation to 'hireling priests'; for this purpose he quotes Isa. 56:10, 11 and 2 Pet. 2: 3, 14, 15.

additional benefit, that of enhancing their public image as *literati* when debating those who would otherwise dismiss them as 'mechanicks'.

The Quakers and Righteousness

Since 'righteousness' has been mentioned several times already, let us now examine its early Quaker interpretation more closely. To our modern sensibilities, the word smacks of the stern patriarch of the Hebrew Testament, God in the sky wagging a wrathful and punitive finger and declaring forth with a booming voice of thunder. This was certainly the capricious God of the Puritans. But the Friends painted a different picture, linking God's righteousness to justice, redemption, liberation and, importantly, to love, tenderness, compassion and holiness. Much of their understanding came from Matthew 5-7, the Sermon. With these connotations 'righteousness' occurs with noticeable frequency in all three declarations—nineteen times in *A Declaration . . . to the Present Distracted and Broken Nation of* England, and on nine occasions in *A Declaration and Information* and *A Declaration from the Harmless and Innocent People of God* combined.[22]

From their diligent reading of the Bible they would have first encountered the term in Job 27:6 where it is linked to integrity (as in upright living), the desire to be clear in conscience about a particular stance. An individual's integrity, probably associated in various stages of the Israelite story with tribalistic honour, was to be open, as clear as the Light (Ps. 4:5). Happiness (inner peace) was the reward for such righteousness. Psalm 112 first links it to justice, the right relationships between 'all people' on earth, as well as virtue and integrity. In the Wisdom tradition, familiar to the Friends, virtue is also akin to 'justice' and 'righteousness', a perfect accord of mind and thus a sense of wholeness and holiness. Here, virtue is also undying and, if true, cannot be threatened by pagan surroundings (Ws.1: 8-9); any injustice observed and/or experienced is likened to death.[23]

In Daniel, the arrogance of Babylon is humbled and only when the true God is recognised does King Nebuchadnezzar recover his wits. He is saved when he overcomes the cruel dominance of his self-will. In any case, his use of force is rendered impotent by the helplessness and perseverance of

---

[22] See Burrough *et al*, *A Declaration . . . to the Present Distracted and Broken Nation of England* (14 pp.), 2, 4, 6, 8-14; Fell *et al*, *A Declaration and Information* (8 pp.), 3, 5 and Fox-Hubberthorne *et al*, *A Declaration from the Harmless* (8 pp.), 1, 3-5. See R. Moore's *Notes on Lists of Seventeenth Century Publications*, 6 (under 'Burrough, Roberts').

[23] For 'to be open, to be as clear as the light': Ps. 4:5; 'virtue is also undying' etc.: Ws. 1: 8-9. For early Quaker use of the Wisdom tradition see, for instance, Parnel's *Goliah's Head Cut Off* (1655), 63 in which he quotes Ws. 4: 8-9. The ancient Hebrew readers among the Friends may have been aware of the root קדש = holiness = akin to ethical completeness.

Chapter 6: 'Now Religion in itself is this'

the scorned. Here God is portrayed as promising to obliterate the oppressive powers and grant justice for all. Similarly in Malachi, Yahweh sometimes delivers the guilty by means of the humble or the clean hands of the righteous, a theme later taken up in Corinthians. In Isaiah it is suffering Israel that is the pointer to salvation. In other words, those in the true Israel, those who trust in God, are the descendants (seeds) of Abraham who himself trusted absolutely in God. As a consequence, they who also trust are blessed and receive the promise (or oracle) of salvation.[24] Clearly if Israel, the 'son', is restored to righteousness it will be secure. The chosen people learn that the worldly wealth of Jerusalem is of nought compared to the wealth of discipleship. Those who are taught by the Lord instead have the might of the spiritual Jerusalem (Zion) within, that centre of God's redemptive activity for the whole world.[25] In Revelation, Jerusalem signifies the unity and hope of all humanity but also a peaceful conversion in which everybody will be righteous. All nations will, therefore, come to adore God and the defilement of the inherently pure earth will be reversed; the early Quakers often spoke of the earth being 'dirtied' by sin and ignorance.[26] For Isaiah and Amos, integrity (or righteousness) is equivalent to judicial equity, whereas for Micah the 'rightness of the ways' of Yahweh approximates to the climacteric events of history by which Yahweh shows loyalty to the chosen people. Since the covenant itself was the issue of a divine initiative, this 'righteous justice' is freely given.[27]

In the Christian Testament, Jesus' last act preparatory to the messianic era was baptism, thereby expressing his wish to satisfy the saving righteousness of God (compassion/mercy and justice) that governs the whole plan of salvation. Through the Spirit, the new righteousness fulfils/perfects the old Law, something strongly maintained by Fox in *Justice and Judgment is to Rule* (1656): 'Is it not justice and the perfect Law of God ... that must rule men and rule courts?'[28] The close bond between righteousness and the Kingdom is peculiar to Matthew's Gospel rather than to Mark and Luke. Matthew's righteousness is diametrically opposed to its pharisaic version. Similarly, Quaker and Calvinist understanding of righteousness stood eyeball to eyeball. In Matthew 21:32, righteousness signifies humble conformity to the divine will, while in the Sermon on the Mount the proclamation of the righteous is linked to justice, the justice of

---

[24] See Grundy, 'Learning to be a Quaker', *passim*.
[25] See *Cambridge*, i., 170-4.
[26] See Massyngberde-Ford, *Revelation*, 213 and Isa. 2:1, 45:14; Jer. 3:17; Mic. 4:1-5.
[27] For 'Babylon is humbled': Dn. 4:27; 'Yahweh sometimes delivers the guilty' etc.: Isa. 54:13-14; 'receive the promise (or oracle) of salvation': 2 Thess. 1:5; 2 Tm. 2:12 and Rev. 1:9; 'equivalent to judicial equity': Isa. 1: 26; 'rightness of the ways': Mi. 6.5.
[28] Fox, (*Here all may see, that*) *Justice and Judgment is to Rule* (1656), 7.

the Kingdom that must be realised inwardly but also outwardly each day.[29] In Acts 6 and 7 the Friends encountered Stephen whom they saw as a model of righteousness, the suffering and forgiving servant, the ambassador of the remnant; his memory can be found in Fell's declaration.[30]

For Paul, faith that is operative in God's eyes is at one with righteousness and is perceived in Romans 4 and 10 as the act of believing with a living faith.[31] Again, the idea of *dikaiosýnē* (*justitia*) is present with its links to the Kingdom (*Basileia*), to right relationships between God's people where justice and righteousness allow a full sharing in the Life of the risen Christ. Echoing Deutero-Isaiah, Romans 9 discusses Israel as a people remaining as unbelievers despite God's promise of salvation. Though the old Israel played an important part in salvation history, the role is now carried forward by the righteous and united remnant into the new dispensation, that is, the new or second covenant of Christ Jesus. Paul sees a presentiment of the new Law in Deuteronomy in which the whole Law is summed up in the precept of love and the 'circumcision of the heart'. The 'word of faith' which is uttered and made effective by Christ is now deeper in the heart and sweeter in the mouth than the 'word of the Law' could ever be.[32]

With righteousness we put on a new nature or person (Eph. 4:24), the aim of which is to be saintly and religious, filled with faith and love, so that we become patient and gentle (Mt. 6:11); the disciples' vocation needs to conform to their inner disposition or Light (Mt. 5:21). As through the life, death and resurrection of Jesus, the early Friends sought to declare their own discipleship and priesthood to everybody as potential citizens in the Kingdom of reconciliation, redemption and mercy. In Hebrews 5:13, Jesus' priesthood of mediation is prefigured by Melchizedek, the king of righteousness. To follow the Melchizedekan tradition of royal priesthood is to be a peacemaker, actively working for the Kingdom of peace and thus sowing the seeds which bear fruit in holiness (Jm. 3:18).[33] What is

---

[29] For 'fulfils/perfects that of the old Law': Mt. 3:15, 5:17, 20.

[30] Fell *et al*, *A Declaration and Information*, 6 (see ref. to Ac 7: 60, Appendix 2); Farnworth, *The Spiritual Man*, 15-16.

[31] For 'faith . . . at one with righteousness': Rom. 4:5; as the act of believing with a living faith see Rom. 4:13, 10:6.

[32] 'Paul sees a presentiment of the new law in Deuteronomy': Dt. 30:6 and 16:20; 'word of faith': Rom. 8: 2, 14.

[33] Fox, Ep. 9 (1652) in *Works,* 7: 20. This very early epistle is a clear call for peace above outward war. For the synonymy of 'Life' and 'Power' to the first generation of Friends see, for instance, Ep. 18 (1652) in *Works*, 7: 23. For 'royal priesthood' see Farnworth, letter (8/June/1653) to Fell *et al*, SW/iii/46-7.

important here is the need to internalise Scripture to discover the true nature of one's vocation.[34]

The Friends also knew that the names given to Jesus such as 'Messiah', 'Son of God', 'the (suffering) servant' and 'Son of Man' were linked to righteousness and the Kingdom.[35] The Messiah brought forth a great people to be gathered—the people of God, the New Israel or the collective son and daughter of God—who, as sons and daughters of 'Man', would battle with the unbelievers around them and consequently suffer as 'a people in scorn' so that the Kingdom may be realised. Significantly, the Burrough, Fell and Fox-Hubberthorne declarations refer to this aspect of Quaker leadership and suffering on forty occasions.

The Three Declarations

Without the early Quakers' concept of the Kingdom as it was bound up with their interpretation of righteousness, the three declarations could never have been conceived.[36] And since their understanding and orthopraxis of both righteousness and justice was the very rock and foundation of the Lamb's War, their battle for the Kingdom, it ensured from the movement's inception a faith and politics that were revolutionary in demanding the complete reformation of Puritan political, ecclesiastical, social and economic relations. This is why the declarations are pivotal to our

---

[34] For specific early Quaker references to 'righteousness' see, for example, Aldam *et al*, *False Prophets*, 8; Fox, Ep. 19 (1652) in *LOGF*, 9. For biblical references for 'we put on a new nature or person': Eph. 4:24; 'we become patient and gentle': Mt. 6:11; 'inner disposition or Light': Mt. 5:21; 'sowing the seeds which bear fruit in holiness': Jm. 3:18.

[35] 'Son of Man' references are infrequent but see Dewsbury, *The Discovery of Man's Return*, 8; *Doctrinals*, 464. For 'suffering servanthood' see esp. Fell *et al*, *A Declaration and an Information*, 7.

[36] Fox-Hubberthorne *et al*, *A Declaration from the Harmless*, 8 quotes the second commandment directly and assumes the first. Hence, for 'Loving God with whole heart/soul/mind etc.', the following are extremely close approximations: Fox-Hubberthorne (F-H), title pg., 2, 3 and Fell, title pg., 2, 4, 5. As 'Kingdom' see F-H, 2, 3, 4, 7 and Fell, 6; as 'Life and Power': F-H, 7 and Fell, 2; as 'Life': F-H, 8 and Fell, 5, 7; as 'Way/Truth/Life': F-H, 8; as 'Everlasting Covenant': Fell, 5; as 'Spirit of Christ': F-H, 2ff and Fell, 5; as 'doctrine of Christ': Fell, 3.

For the Sermon on the Mount, the following are extremely close approximations: 'poor in spirit': Fell, 1; 'mourn': Fell, 2; 'meek': F-H, title pg., 4, 8; 'thirst after righteousness': F-H, 1; 'merciful/mercy': F-H, 6; 'pure in heart': F-H, 3 and Fell, 4, 8, 16; 'peace/makers': F-H, 1, 4 and Fell, 4, 5, 7; 'children of God': Fell, 5; 'persecuted/for righteousness sake': F-H, 4 and Fell, 2, 5; 'revile' (hate): Fell, 2; 'persecute you, and shall say all manner of evil against you falsely, for my sake': this is practically the same in F-H, 3.

See Nayler, *The Lambs War*; Burrough, *A Standard Lifted Up*, chps. 9, 11, 12 in *Works*, 246-7 and 249 respectively. See 'The Examination of James Nayler', *ibid.* and *A. R. Barclay MSS.*, 18. Also Thomas Taylor, letter (18/May/1653) to Fox, *SW*/iii/29 and *Journal*, 357; Fox, Ep. 183 (1659) in *Works*, 173.

understanding of 1650s Quakerism and why it is necessary to state from the outset that

their 1650s experience =
the Quaker expression of Kingdom and Testimony =
<u>the</u> peace testimony

We will see how this formula was *fully realised* among the whole body of Friends—collectively, in an intensely concentrated manner within a Pentecostal-Paracletal moment, a mass re-convincement, one might say, which covered the period between the illness Fox suffered at Reading during August-October 1659 and the issuing of Fox-Hubberthorne in January 1661. This same period saw the publication of the three declarations, each one of which, though connected in terms of content and purpose, stood on its own. The Friends did not plan a trilogy of publications by which to address the various authorities and yet the works represented the Quaker *zeitgeist* and the 'moment' already mentioned, a renewal among the whole movement, an 'upper room' moment, which developed at a deeper level of spiritual awareness as the cosmological nature of the Kingdom dawned on them. It was a profound deepening and comprehension of their faith and practice so far, and expressive of their ultimate meaning and purpose as a 'holy priesthood' and 'nation'. The Pentecost was experienced, therefore, on the cusp of a new cosmological era, an *eschaton* that was as real, forceful and penetrative of the future as it was materially uncertain and daunting.[37]

Rather than address the purpose of the declarations, which is discussed in Chapter 12, I wish at this point to highlight three aspects of their content and create a link to the 1650s experience:

1. In concert with Quaker works in general, the declarations are *apocalyptic* in the way they announce and reveal the Kingdom and what England (or the world, this age) must do to achieve peace, wholeness and holiness: 'that (by the Word of God's power, and its effectual operation in the hearts of men), the kingdoms of this world may become the kingdoms of the Lord' (Fox-Hubberthorne, p.3). As *prophetic* utterances, they brim with judgments about the state of the nation (or, again, the world, this age): 'ambition and vainglory, and for corrupted ends to themselves; whereby this our nation is brought into present confusion' (Burrough, p. 2).

2. The declarations are highly *critical* though helpful pronouncements about organisations such as the parliament, the army, the Church and the

---

[37] *eschaton* = here to mean the edge between the old physical and spiritual dispensation and the present and ever-pending new covenant, a reversal of ideas and events as in the Sermon on the Mount.

universities, and about groups of people including clerics, lawyers and politicians: 'for what is a King? and what is a Parliament? what is a Protector, and what is a Council? or any other sort of men, while the presence of the Lord is not with them' (Burrough, p. 11). They are *authoritative* in the way they warn, reproach, advise and recommend. They are stern, employ plain speaking and yet at times are meek, even placatory: 'neither do we desire to give any just occasion of offence to these present Governors, who yet have not done us much wrong, in making any law against us that we know of' (Fell, p. 3).

3. They are *intellectually and theologically challenging*: The Kingdom is presented to the principalities and powers in full force: 'We are a people that . . . desire that all may be saved, and come to the knowledge of the Truth, the Way and the Life, which is Christ Jesus, the everlasting covenant' (Fell, p. 5).

By being challenging in this way, they invited readers to study biblical sources. At the same time they forced people to contrast the Jesus Way with the parlous condition of their 'distracted' nation and its governmental institutions, the causes of its discontent and how these impacted upon individual conscience. This approach was as applicable to the inner life as it was to the outer.

The message of the declarations is cosmological, eschatological but, more importantly, loving. They attempt, in other words, to reach the Light in each person by pointing to the Kingdom within and among them, the Kingdom that is always challenging, independent of time and space ('unchanging') and a source of hope and happiness as these are found in the Spirit/Christ, the same loving God as portrayed in Jesus.

The declarations' nonviolent, Kingdom message was directly opposed to the violence of Church and State. In Nayler's *The Lamb's War*, for instance, we read tellingly that Jesus the Lamb had come 'to take the Government to himself', probably a reference to Isa. 6:9: 'and the government shall be upon his shoulder and his name shall be called . . . the Prince of Peace'. Whatever its origin, the phrase represented the inward authority of the prophet who, having chosen the peaceful path to salvation through the Christ, could adopt an outward authority (being thus spiritually ordained) to proclaim Truth and its Kingdom. Being a call *par excellence* to spiritual arms for Gospel transformation, Nayler's phrase and others like it cut deeply into traditional Church practice and profoundly challenged the earthly powers.[38] It still resonates with a critical authority because the faith that underlines it was never merely belief but instead demanded the *doing* of truth and justice, an orthopraxis of peace that still reaches beyond time and

---

[38] Nayler, *The Lambs War*, 3.

space. Fox's assurance to the Friends in a 1659 epistle that 'fighters are not of Christ's Kingdom . . . for his Kingdom stands in peace and righteousness' was no less true for the three declarations with their plea that the movement had never plotted or rebelled against any authority, that both Christ's Doctrine (the Kingdom) and the Apostle's doctrine (Paul) demanded that they *lived* the peaceful Kingdom,

> which is the same today, as was yesterday, Christ Jesus, the Power of God, and the seed of life, and the word that was in the beginning; so . . . that . . . in . . . [their] unity and communion . . . eternal unity with the eternal God [would be] seen.[39]

The Kingdom was to be experienced in their daily lives as a pattern and example to the world. Fox's advice to his fellow Quakers to be 'patterns and examples', however, was neither merely a suggestion that they should act as a guide nor a moral injunction only. It was, more importantly, an apocalyptic imperative. For those truly convinced, the Kingdom would automatically reveal their inner resurrection in which new life was brought forth, a sign that the separated (the sinner) could be whole again, and that such a revelation was entirely possible in a deadening climate of Church apostasy. It was a message that they repeated many times over the course of the 1650s.

Burrough's declaration, which he wrote with the authority of the London Men's Meeting, was published five days before the still banned Christmas holiday of 1659, as that politically and constitutionally chaotic year came to an end. The future was dangerously uncertain. The possibility of another civil war loomed. But when General George Monck approached London from Scotland also in December, it was clear the Puritan experiment was at an end. According to Burrough's tract, Britain was clearly a 'distracted nation'. The generality of people, including the Friends, had been long-disillusioned by events. Some tried desperately to shore up the ailing Good Old Cause. Fox's *To the Parliament of the Common-wealth (59 Particulars)*, which he published before August of that year, might have been a last ditch attempt by him to salvage the Cause in the Quaker image. In another indication of how the Kingdom demanded nonviolence, he strongly advocated such not only in the tract but also in his *Catechism for Children* (1660) which appeared some months *before* the Fox-Hubberthorne declaration.[40]

---

[39] *Journal*, 357; Ep. 183 (1659) in *Works*, 173.
[40] Fox, *A Catechism for Children*, 98-9 also quoted in Angell, 'The Catechisms of George Fox', p. 10 of 13. The precise date for Fox's catechism is not known; Fox, *59 Particulars*, 16: 'where the devil [murders and persecutes] . . . the true Magistrates never did with carnal weapons'.

Chapter 6: 'Now Religion in itself is this'

For its part, the Burrough declaration comprises nearly 6,500 words contained in fourteen pages. Like the Fell and Fox-Hubberthorne declarations, it was a joint effort, co-signed by fifteen Friends, though Burrough's signature is missing since the manuscript went to press while he was in Ireland. The tract expressed deep concern over the plight of the nation 'in this gloomy day'. It repeated the Quaker mantra that human greed ('lusts') ultimately led to injustice, bloodshed and further oppression. All governments needed the Kingdom as their basis otherwise governing would be meaningless, even delusional. For this, people (and especially those in authority) needed to undergo a transformation in their own lives, a turning to God (repentance) as expressed through Christ Jesus and the values of the Kingdom if they wished to be spiritually and materially free. Unity in the Spirit would only materialise if there was unity among all the children of God. Unlike Fell and Fox-Hubberthorne, Burrough had no margined biblical references. However, uncited single words, phrases and sometimes whole sentences from the King James Bible were directly planted into the text. In fact, about 102 such entries can be found in Burrough that are wholly consonant with the Quakers' view of the Kingdom. It is not difficult to locate the same or similar entries in their works of the 1650s.

Burrough's embedded approach is replicated in Fell and Fox-Hubberthorne. As Appendix 4A shows, 83 key words or phrases can be highlighted in the latter declarations; they have been located in 637 selections from 206 works by 46 authors during the period 1652-61 (see Appendix 4B). Thus the 83 words/phrases act as a direct and exemplary link between the two declarations and the Quaker works of that formative decade. Indeed, it is remarkable how the authors of the three works concentrated the words and phrases into their short formats. Two examples suffice. The term 'Life and Power', an alternative expression for the Kingdom (and sometimes for 'Gospel') and a common expression among the Friends, is found on page 14 of Burrough, pages five and seven of Fell, and page seven of Fox-Hubberthorne (see table below). It is not surprising it found its way into the declarations: its frequent use over the course of the decade is verified by reference even to a small selection of works, for instance by nine public Friends—Burrough, Dewsbury, Fox, Howgill, Nayler, Penington, William Smith and John Whitehead, all of whom wrote more than 30 significant works.[41]

---

[41] See Burrough, *Discovery of Divine Mysteries* in *Works*, 824; *General Epistle to the Saints* (1658) in *Works*, 389; Dewsbury, *Christ Exalted*, 10; Fox, Ep. 14 (1652), *LOGF*, 6; Howgill, *General Epistle to the Camp* (1655), 30; *This is Only to Go* (1656), 8; Nayler, *A Discovery of the First Wisdom* in *Works*, 79; Penington, *The Scattered Sheep Sought After* in *Works*, 111. W. Smith, *The New Creation*, 7; J. Whitehead, *A Word of Reproof from the Lord*, 7.

The Three *Declarations*: No. of references to 'Kingdom' and 40 equivalent expressions all highlighted in Appendix 2

[B = Burrough *et al*; F = Fell *et al*; F-H = Fox-Hubberthorne *et al*]

'KINGDOM' & EQUIVALENTS	B	Pages in B	F	Pages in F	F-H	Pages in F-H
Covenant of the Lord	1	7				
Counsel of the Lord	7	2, 3, 5. 10-12, 14				
Christ's/Apostle's/doctrine (and practice)			3	2, 3	1	5
Day					1	7
Day of Visitation	2	2, 5				
(Everlasting) Covenant	1	6	1	5		
Everlasting Kingdom and Government	1	13				
Faith and Doctrine			1	3		
Fruits of Holiness	1	12				
Glory of God			1	5		
God's Government					1	3
God's power					1	3
Government (as Kingdom)	5	10, 11, 12, 13				
Government of Peace and Truth	1	7				
Government of Righteousness	1	12				
Government of Truth and Righteousness	1	12				
King(dom) of Righteousness	3	7, 11, 13				
Kingdom	4	9, 13	3	7	1	3
Kingdom (of Christ, God etc.)					4	2, 3
Kingdoms of the Lord					1	3
Life and Power			2	5, 7	1	7
Mercy and Truth	2	3, 11				
Mercy, Justice, Judgment	3	3, 11, 12			1	6
Mercy, Truth and Justice	2	11				
Peace and True Freedom	1	11				
Peace and Truth	1	12				
Peace, Love and Unity	5	1, 2, 5, 11	1	7, 8		
Peace, the Way of Peace	3	3, 9				
Power and Presence	1	12				
Righteousness (+ sake; of faith; God's)	5	4, 9-11, 14	4	3, 5	3	1, 3, 4
Righteousness and Truth	6	2, 12, 14				
Spirit of Christ					3	2, 5

Chapter 6: 'Now Religion in itself is this'

'KINGDOM' & EQUIVALENTS	B	Pages in B	F	Pages in F	F-H	Pages in F-H
Spirit, Power and Life			1	2		
Sword of the Spirit						
The Fruit of Peace	2	5, 6				
The Perfect Way	2	5, 7				
The Right Way	1	14				
The Way, Truth and Life			1	5		
The Word (as Kingdom)	6	2, 5, 6, 10, 12	1	5	2	3
Voice	1	6				
TOTAL	69		19		20	

Another phrase, 'exalt according to His promise', appears on page three of Fox-Hubberthorne and was used in connection with their determination never to 'fight and war against [anybody] with outward weapons'. It reinforced their long-held belief that God's promise of the Kingdom had been kept alive throughout the ages by a remnant, among whom were Abraham, the prophets and, of course, Jesus, Paul and the early Church. It was now finding expression through the Quaker movement, as a form of Christ exalted itself, and was sure to grow and flourish despite oppression. No doubt through their familiarity with biblical passages such as Galatians 3:29, the Friends felt they were exalted according to God's promise of the Kingdom through convincement and its acceptance of the new covenant. Such an option was open to all.[42] This reasoning is swiftly and directly linked a few lines further on the same page to Zechariah 4:6—'not by might, nor by power (of outward sword), but by my spirit, said the Lord'—the Hebrew context of which critically underlines their nonviolent desire for the true temple to be rebuilt, a temple of peace, justice and compassion. All outward temples, steeplehouses and their hirelings would eventually disappear when 'all people' turned to the Light, the inward Government of God and enacted by them in the world.[43] Consequently, physical violence was rendered absurd because God/Love, enshrined in the Kingdom, would always defeat Satan if people were wholly responsive to God's desires for humanity. All else was useless and false.

It is also possible to locate 325 uncited biblical references in Burrough in addition to the Kingdom or to its equivalent expressions and very close approximations. Together, the embedded and margined references, and the highlighted 83 single words, phrases and sentences reveal a biblical knowledge of breathtaking depth and proportion. As we saw in the nearly 100 references in Fell and approximately 200 in Fox-Hubberthorne, this is a

---

[42] Dewsbury, *Christ Exalted*, 5.
[43] John Harwood, *A Description of the True Temple*, (1658), *passim*.

staggering number considering the declarations together constitute thirty pages. As we saw in Chapter 4, the declarations and the 1650s tracts in general are examples of how biblical language was a generic feature of their daily discourse and thinking, something demonstrated by the speed with which Fox and Hubberthorne composed their own declaration within a few days in January 1661. The declarations also display the Friends' skill in their use of the Bible. Again, two examples may suffice. 'Divisions and confusions' on page one of Burrough is mentioned in the context of the need for 'peace and unity', a synonym for the Kingdom of God whose enactment was desperately needed for the healing of their 'broken nation'. Burrough and Friends looked forward to an inward commonwealth to complement an outer one, a commonwealth from which peace and unity may be restored, a unity that would herald the victory of the Light. 'Divisions and confusions' derives from six biblical sources while the author(s) possibly gleaned the restoration of 'peace and unity' from four sources.[44]

The Fell declaration takes a similar approach but has much less of a Hebrew Testament 'feel'. It is warmer, possibly because the audience was different. Burrough addressed the dying Puritan parliament, Fell the new king. Her well-known 264-word passage on page seven beginning with 'We are a people that follow after those things that make for peace, love, and unity' and concluding with 'under whom we have undergone cruel sufferings' contains eight embedded references in addition to three margined references.[45] Fox-Hubberthorne, signed by twelve Friends, completes the pattern.

Clearly, the signatories were familiar enough with the above references to contextualise them *à propos* their thinking concerning the Kingdom. This approach is typical of the nearly one thousand Quaker works published in our period, almost all of which concentrated either directly or indirectly on the Kingdom as enunciated by Jesus. And if the number of works is extended to include those published before 1700—3,853 in all—the same pattern is found. Their core motivation in using the Bible, then, was the location and propagation of the Kingdom, further reinforcing the view that the *Kingdom*, primitive Christianity revived, was the very centre of the Quaker 1650s message just as it had been for Jesus. It was *this* that was the 'doctrine' that 'Christ had come to teach his people' again.

What was being 'revived' was the Christian Testament's centrality of the Kingdom, which the Church had neglected 'since the apostles days'. In other words, not only did they accuse the Church of apostasy but they spoke

---

[44] For 'divisions and confusions': Ps. 109:29; Isa. 41: 29; Jer.20: 11; Lk. 11:7; Rom. 16:17 and 1 Cor. 3:3. For 'peace and unity': Lk. 6:10; Heb.13:19; Rom. 2:9 and 1 Thess. 3:4.
[45] Her eight embedded references are: Eph. 4: 3; Gal. 5:16; 1 Jn. 1: 7; 1 Pet. 2: 11; Heb. 2:10, 5: 8; Jn. 13: 14; Lk. 6: 29. Her three margined references are: Jn. 18: 36; Lk. 9. 56 and 2 Cor. 10: 4.

up for the Church's true tradition, the Kingdom, the *Basileia*. This identification was their happy obsession as Kingdom extremists or purists. It was a factor that would play an important role during their Pentecost-Paracletal moment of 1659-61 in determining a cosmological perspective on the 'way of life and death', including the death of the Good Old Cause and the Restoration that followed it.

With nearly three thousand words, the Fell declaration effectively comprises seven pages. It was signed by fourteen Friends including George Fox and Fell herself and published on the 24th June 1660, just two days after her audience with the king. Her presentation to Charles consolidated the unfolding Quaker Pentecost already characterised by the Burrough work and currently being expressed in word and deed, particularly by Fox. By then he had extensively toured the south of England, including London. The Fell declaration re-expressed Burrough's concern with persecution and again reassured the authorities that Quaker intentions were peaceful, that any form of sedition was opposed to the injunctions of the Kingdom. The tract reiterated the Friends' 1650s testimony against oath taking and affirmed the morality of plain speaking and truthfulness in everyday life. It also expended much energy condemning hirelings and tithes. Finally, echoing provisions of the Good Old Cause, Fell petitioned for liberty of conscience, the establishment of civil rights and tolerance for other religions. By doing so it reflected similar beliefs running through the movement as a whole. It concluded with forgiveness.

Fox-Hubberthorne, which contains about 2,600 words, is, of course, generally regarded as the peace testimony of what is now the Religious Society of Friends and snippets of it appear on Quaker Meeting House notice boards throughout the world. However, rather than being regarded as such, the declaration is best understood as a significant component of the tapestry that is the Quakers' 1650s experience of Kingdom and Testimony. In its six and a half pages, two important features stand out. The first is its repetition of the Burrough and Fell nonviolence stance in affirming that war proceeds from lust (greed) and is antithetical to the unchangeable Kingdom, the Spirit of Christ, by which the Friends were guided. Building on a number of recent pronouncements to the same effect, and the many similar ones from the 1650s, they declared their opposition to fighting even for the 'Kingdom of Christ', quoting Zechariah 4: 6 for this purpose. They were prepared to offer their 'hair, backs and cheeks', even to die for 'righteousness sake', rather than disobey God. Their hope was for the worldly kingdoms to be brought into love, peace and unity with God.

The second feature is its argument for police action as a cautious extension of a scrupulously honest magistracy. Here they make use of Romans 13:1-7: 'neither turn your swords upon such as the law was not made for, i.e., the righteous, but for the sinners and transgressors to keep them down' (p.5). Our two features are not contradictory and, importantly, magistrates are exhorted to uphold civil rights and the values of the Kingdom. Practising mercy and justice was the way of finding favour with God. This particular section of the document is further discussed in Chapter 11. However, it is sufficient here to suggest that, though not its central content, the immediate aim of Fox-Hubberthorne was to exonerate the Quakers from accusations of insurrection in the wake of Venner's three-day occupation of London and to assure the authorities that they were innocent and truthful. As 'the heritage of God', it pleads, they should not be wronged just as their movement had never wronged people, damaged possessions, used violence, plotted against the authorities or sought revenge. Instead, they maintained, they had only sought peace and had followed after righteousness, 'caring for the good and welfare of all'. But while they complained about their persecution and being disregarded as transgressors like Jesus, the declaration's clear inference is that their sufferings were as yet a further fulfilment of Scripture. Anyone continuing Jesus' work must expect 'blood and persecution' [Col.1:24].[46] Finally, while declaring their support of the king's position, the tract also attacked the swearing of oaths in reference to the enforcement of the Oath of Allegiance by the Restoration government.

The Lamb's War

Let us now turn to the outer enactment of their 1650s Kingdom experience, what the early Friends called the 'Lamb's War'. The term was probably coined by James Nayler, and it appears in his *A Vindication of Truth* (1656), an answer to Thomas Higgenson's attack on his *Love to the Lost* (1656). It is also the title of another one of his better-known works, *The Lamb's War* (1656?-8), the extended second edition of which allows an elaboration on the Kingdom. In the following year, two other Friends used the term— Joseph Fuce on the title page of his *The Fall of a Great Visible Idol* and John Crook who linked it to salvation.[47] Nayler outlined its aim, which was to be enacted at first on the inner level:

---

[46] Fell *et al*, *A Declaration and an Information*, 4.
[47] Nayler, *A Vindication of Truth*, 21; Higgenson, *A Testimony to the True Jesus* (1656), *passim*. R. Moore mentions the Lamb's War on p. 260 (25*n*) of *TLITC*. Ingle does not dwell on it in *FF*, but both he and Moore approach the subject—Moore in chps. 5 and 6 and Ingle with theological references such as that on p. 168—from the standpoint of the widespread premillennial perception of the Kingdom at the time and the Quakers' reaction to it. See Joseph Fuce, *The Fall of a Great Visible Idol* (1659) and Crook, *A Defence of the True Church*, 54. Chiefly among historians, Gwyn elevates the Lamb's War to significance, initially in *AOTW*, but he, too, sees it primarily as a reaction to the Puritan covenant of grace. Also Underwood, *Primitivism, Radicalism, and the Lamb's War*.

Chapter 6: 'Now Religion in itself is this'

To judge [the] deceiver openly before all the creation showing that his ways, fashions, and customs are not what God ordered for man to live in, in the beginning, to bind him, and to redeem out of his captivity, all who will but believe in the Lamb and are weary of this service and bondage to his enemy, and who will but come forth and give their names and hearts to join with him, and bear his image and testimony openly before all men, and willingly follow him in such ways as wherein the Father hath given him victory over this power, for himself and all that follow him, to redeem them to God, and the rest who will not believe and follow him, and bear his image, them to condemn with the destroyer into everlasting destruction, and to restore all things and make all things new, as they were in the beginnings, that God alone may rule in his own work.[48]

This was a call to be a martyr for the Kingdom if necessary. Nayler's use of 'Father' in the context of quoting Revelation 21:5—'to restore all things and make all things new'—appears calculated considering that the Gospels' use of 'Father', whether he or his co-religionists were aware of it, may have denoted the Kingdom's sovereign opposition to the Roman empire just as the Quakers' own vision of the Kingdom stood against the 'empire' of their day. *The Lambs War* describes this 'empire' as apostasy, the 'deceiver', 'enemy', carnal 'power'.[49] The 'Lamb' was the active Word but also the proclamation that the Kingdom had been rediscovered and was within *and* among those who believed in the risen Christ. Fox, after all, laid great store by Luke 17:21 ('Neither shall they say, 'Lo here! or, lo there!' for, behold, the Kingdom of God is within you') and John's Gospel in which the Word or Logos was God's work of unity throughout history—the Kingdom and Christ exalted.[50] Initially, the Lamb's War was to be a conflict with the 'deceiver' within, that which promoted separation from the loving God who only wanted the best for humanity. If the Puritans desired a reformation of the Reformation, Nayler and the Friends demanded a transformation not only of 'all people' but in the way humanity itself was understood. The Lamb's War, in redeeming people from their 'captivity', afforded a politics as equally threatening to the authorities as Jesus' own proclamation of the Kingdom was to the powers in *his* day.

Here, then, was a spiritual war that owed much to their reading of Matthew 5, to which Fox as early as 1648 attached great importance:

---

[48] Nayler, *The Lambs War*, 2. For 'to restore all things and make all things new' see Rev. 21: 5.
[49] See D'Angelo, 'Abba and Father', 621, 628-9.
[50] See Fox, *A Testimony of the True Light*, 8.

> I met with a great company of professors in Warwickshire who were praying and expounding the Scriptures in the fields. And they gave the Bible to me and I opened it at the fifth of Matthew where Christ expounded the Law; and I opened the inward state to them and the outward state and they fell into a fierce contention.[51]

Fox tells us that the 'great company' had completely missed the point of preaching—the propagation of the 'Law' of Jesus, the new Law of the Kingdom whose Light would generate conflict within as well as conflict among people. The Friends also referred people to passages such as Matthew 22: 36-40, which outlined Jesus' two commandments to love one's neighbour as oneself and to love God. It was also to *these* two Laws, the life-blood of the Kingdom, that the first Friends would give witness as its prophets, as a city set upon a hill and as a people of God willing to suffer under the feet of humanity.[52] In doing so, they broadened the Puritan definition of 'neighbour' in the same way Jesus widened it to include enemies by putting the love of God and humanity on the same plane. Like Jesus, the Friends sought to bring 'these two principles [that lay] apart in the [Hebrew] Testament into vital, organic union, making love to humanity the test and proof of love to God.' What Borg says of the prophets is equally applicable to the early Quakers,

> Their relationship to the Spirit led them to see things from a perspective very different from the dominant [i.e. Puritan] consciousness. Moreover, they did not simply *see* differently; they also *felt* deeply. They not only knew God, but *felt* the *feelings* of God: the divine compassion for the victims of suffering, the anger of God at the oppressing classes, the divine grief about the suffering that would soon come upon victimiser and victim alike. What happened in history— war, oppression, injustice, the institutionalisation of greed—was one of the greatest sources of human suffering, and therefore one of the greatest sources of divine concern.[53]

Importantly, Burrough's *To the Rulers* (1659) affirms the two commandments of Matthew 22 as the basis of 'true religion', one that liberates death into life:

---

[51] *Journal*, 23.
[52] See Fox, *A Catechism for Children*, 36. For 'city set upon a hill': Mt. 5:14; 'under the feet of humanity': Mt. 5:13; Nayler, *Milk for the Babes*, 6.
[53] Borg, *Jesus: A New Vision*, 155-6. Borg's emphases; my insertion. See also Hugh Scott, 'The Teachings of Jesus' (1893), 417-8.

Chapter 6: 'Now Religion in itself is this'

> Now religion in itself is this: the fulfilling of the Law and the prophets, loving God with all their hearts and the neighbour as self, and doing to all men as they would have men to do to them, and not otherwise.[54]

The Lamb's War, therefore, was essentially a quest to enact daily the Sermon on the Mount and the two commandments. The Sermon was to be lived perfectly, a desire from which no deviation was envisaged. Nayler and other leading Friends observed how the Sermon definitively taught the way of discipleship and how it must be operative on the inner and outer levels among the people of God, that is, among 'all people on the earth'. In this way, Nayler vigorously proclaimed the War as a spiritual campaign against,

> spiritual wickedness in the hearts [i.e. the conscious soul] of men and women, against the whole work and device of the god of this world, laws, customs, fashions, inventions, this is all enmity against the Lamb and his followers who are entered into the covenant which was in the beginning.[55]

It was a call to bring forth the Day of the Lord, the Kingdom, before which people should stand in humility so they could admit their separation from the Light. In contrasting themselves to the Light they judged themselves but only with the strength given to them through the Spirit's grace, the Life and Power. Thus the trumpet could be sounded, Jerusalem conquered and a people gathered for the consummation of all things. Consequently, just as the Day of the Lord was pronounced in the Book of Joel (1:5), the Lamb's War was similarly described in apocalyptic and theophanous terms. The Friends' reading of the prophetic oracles helped them bring forth God's indictment and sentencing of kings and their officers, a judgment designed to alleviate if not eradicate the oppression and suffering of God's people.[56] And their identification with the Spirit in Jesus gave them an anchor, their

---

[54] Burrough, *To the Rulers* (1659), 2.
[55] Nayler, *The Lambs War*, 3. References to 'Lamb' occurred frequently in works prior to and including 1657. See for example Fox, *News Coming up out of the North*, 27: 'a day of slaughter is coming to you who have made war against the Lamb': Thomason, 21/Dec/1653 and *The Vials of the Wrath of God* (1654), 3-4; William Dewsbury, *The Discovery of the Great Enmity of the Serpent*, 13-14: '... my garment is washed, and made white in the blood of the Lamb' [Rev. 7:14]: Thomason, 29/Sept/1655; Crisp, *A Word of Reproof*, 1; Burrough, 'Epistle to the Reader', *The Great Mystery*, Sig. B2ʳ. See also *FF*, 89, 99, 166; *GADOT*, 14 and *Journal*, 23.
[56] Horsley, *Jesus and Empire*, 81. See Brinton, *Ethical Mysticism*, 28-9.

'foundation' or 'rock', without which they would have been formless to everybody including their opponents.[57]

Conclusion

The early Quaker experience of the 1650s was not only a witness of, and devotion to, the Kingdom, it *was* the peace testimony proper of which the Lamb's War was the outward, cross-filled manifestation. The three declarations should be seen as a tapestry of that experience. Our examination of the declarations revealed not only the wide range of alternative expressions for the Kingdom but also the depth and extent of the Friends' biblical knowledge and how they used it. We found how their Lamb's War and its Kingdom message were as dangerous to the ruling political, military and religious élites in their day as it was in Jesus' time. Following the example of Jesus, the Friends placed themselves in conflicted situations, a deliberate strategy that exposed them to a discontinuity with their carnal surroundings and which, they hoped, would give more power and authority to their message of salvation. We will now see how the reaction to the Quaker message was at once visceral, calculated and remarkably vicious.

---

[57] They were probably influenced here by Lk. 6:48: 'He is like a man which built an house, and digged deep, and laid the foundation on a rock.'

Chapter 7: *'Open Shop for Soul-Poisons'*

- Reaction to the Quakers' Kingdom -

The first Friends sought to convince 'all people on the earth' of the Jesus Way. They did so through personal example and a ministry undertaken in a variety of ways that included (particularly during the 1650s) interruption of church services, 'going naked as a sign', refusing hat honour, a conscientious objection to oath taking and tithe payment, and suffering for the consequences of such testimonies.[1] But it was the spoken word and skilfully distributed publications that had the greatest effect in projecting their coherent theology and politics of compassion despite some differences of opinion among them. Their solidarity was given considerable impetus by a willingness to submit their written works to the leadership prior to publication. Particularly during the first years of their movement, this process was encouraged by the use of Swarthmoor Hall near Ulverston and the home of the Fell family as a communications centre from where spiritual advice and material aid was given. Between 1652 and 1660, approximately seven hundred letters made their way mainly to Margaret Fell herself.[2]

By 1660 there were about 240 itinerant Quaker preachers claiming a Kingdom *kerygma* of hope and direction during times that were regarded by their contemporaries as confusing, fearful, violent and disappointing. The Friends set out to assure audiences that despite this ocean of darkness there was 'an infinite ocean of Light [and an] infinite love of God'.[3] As one of its fundamental aims, the Lamb's War looked forward to a radical and nonviolent restructuring of society with spiritual and material justice for the poor, whom the Friends regarded not as an inferior 'sort' but beloved of the Kingdom.[4] Inevitably, their determination, sense of urgency and their Gospel-inspired evangelism invited hostility from the political, military and

---

[1] Fox, *An Epistle to all People on the Earth*, 3-4, 6 and *Doctrinals*, 93.
[2] E. Taylor, *The Valiant Sixty*, 43; *EQL*, 11-22 and Fox, Eps. 65 (1654), 114 (1656) in *Works*, 7: 78-9, 113. Also *GADOT*, 76, 103, 108, 113, 224; *MOP*, 27, 143. Rex Ambler also maintains a coherence to Fox's writings; see *Truth of the Heart*, p. x.
[3] Fox in 1647; see *Journal*, 19. Also Barbour, *The Quakers in Puritan England*, 106-7. The *Journal* mentions 'dark' 25 times, 'darkness' 66 times. See Lake, 'Deeds against Nature' in Sharpe and Lake (eds.), 270; R. Porter, *Flesh in the Age of Reason*, 34.
[4] For 'beloved of the Kingdom of God': Mt. 5:3; Lk. 6:20; Jm. 2:5.

ecclesiastical authorities despite Cromwell's occasional tolerance towards the movement and a certain respect for Fox.[5]

At first, the fledgling republican authorities, themselves painfully coming to terms with the realities of government, were indifferent to the finer points of Quaker belief. But that quickly changed. The papers of Cromwell's Secretary of State and security chief, John Thurloe, albeit with few significant references to the Friends, recorded the anger, confusion and frustration of magistrates, army commanders and local gentry towards the Quaker unpredestinarian mission as it spread from its largely royalist northern and 'papist dark corner' where the writ of the Church and State had failed to dominate. In a letter to Sir Edward Hyde, while 'Lord Chancellor' under the exiled Charles II, a 'Mr. Broderick' mentions an address to parliament 'from an odd sort of people called Quakers, tending to liberty of conscience'. This was a time when 'freedom' and 'liberty' were code words for 'whoring'—unaccountability for one's actions.[6] Deductions such as these need contextualising in respect to government sensitivities *vis-à-vis* Catholic influence from France, Spain and Ireland and the continuing success of the counter-Reformation.

In time, the authorities were hearing more and more rumours of the Friends' determination to subvert the familiar order of society, to which, incidentally, even the 'vulgar sort' was firmly attached, that Quakers were undermining 'the authority of husbands over wives and children ... [and challenging] the comfortable even if inequitable local hierarchy [while splitting] parish communities'.[7] Not alone in their distaste for the 'fractious schismatic spirit' that was springing up in their midst, clerics such as those in the Oxfordshire villages of Adderbury and Over Worton were forced to cover their ears against the discordant sounds of Quaker trumpets blowing out of Zion. Others, like the gentle Ralph Josselin in far away Essex, complained of being personally confronted by Quakers. In October, 1655, he was 'set upon by one called a quaker' but gave thanks that 'the Lord was with my heart that I was not dismayed'. The Quakers, he concluded, were 'deluded, in error and evil' and worked

---

[5] *QER*, 43f. Even though Fox could apparently command huge crowds (3-4,000 in May 1658, according to Ingle), and was known to various high officials during the 1650s including Cromwell, it is easy to exaggerate the early Quaker influence upon the political life of the country, even during the turbulent year 1659. See also Mullett, "Men of Knowne Loyalty'; *FF*, 165.

[6] See Broderick's letter (3/June/1659) in *Clarendon* (edn. 1786), iii. 480. Also D. Hirst, 'Locating the 1650s', 366.

[7] Underdown, *Revel, Riot, and Rebellion*, 292; Caldwell, *The Puritan Conversion Narrative*, 16-17 for Puritan fear of those believed to have upheld the authority of the self over civil and ecclesiastical restraints.

Chapter 7: 'Open Shop for Soul-Poisons'

to revile the ministry, made a disturbance at [Coggeshall] and were sent to gaol; oh, many fear the Quakers to ruin Cromwell; it is not words that alter governments, and not armies; it must form itself into a military posture first, and when that appears, their enemies of the State, disturbing of the peace, seizes on them'.[8]

The Rev. Josselin's fear was understandable. After all, on another occasion a Quaker woman had interrupted one of his sermons, a deeply shocking occurrence for minister and congregation alike. He was afraid that his beloved home county was rapidly becoming fertile ground for the Quakers' targeting of local Independent parishes. Many others in Essex, like magistrate John Stephens MP, were afraid to sleep at night lest the 'fanaticks' slit their throats. In the hope, therefore, of preventing the 'damnable opinions' of the Quakers from seducing people away from proper Church allegiances, village constables were ordered to arrest wanderers and strangers.[9] During the seventeenth century, suspicion and fear of strangers were thoroughly embedded in the general culture. They were often seen as reprobates who associated with the criminal underworld. Since it was assumed they dodged church, strangers were automatically excluded from the accepted social order and, as a result, official reaction towards them could be severe depending on the magistrate. Without local support and family ties, strangers were often drilled about their 'outward means', a gross humiliation and one that in 1654 in Norfolk befell Quakers Christopher Atkinson, James Lancaster and Richard Hubberthorne, all of whom were incarcerated in Norwich Castle for vagrancy.[10]

It seemed the dark ruminations of Thomas Edwards were horribly prophetic. After all, his *Gangraena* 'proved' that links existed between the hated papists and the Radicals, an animosity reinforced in 1654 by the reappearance of Ephraim Pagitt's *Heresiography* (1645).[11] Like Edwards, the Presbyterian Pagitt had died in 1647 but this did not prevent the editors of the republished work from describing the Quakers as an 'upstart branch of the Anabaptists' (i.e. violent).[12] They were 'made up out of the dregs of

---

[8] 'Extracts relating to Quakers from the Diary of the Rev. Ralph Josselin (1616-83), Vicar of Earls Colne, Essex', 85-6. And see MacFarlane (ed.), 348-50, 362-3, 366-7, 384, 388, 450; S. Davies, *Unbridled Spirits*, chp. 9 and esp.181-92; *BQ*, 500.
[9] Warmington, *Civil War, Interregnum*, 120; Bennett, *The Civil Wars Experienced*, 202.
[10] For Atkinson and Lancaster (d.1699) see Hubberthorne, *The Testimony of the Everlasting Gospel* (1656), 4-7 and *BQ*, 162; Hill, 'Millenarianism and Fifth Monarchism', 31; Coward, *Oliver Cromwell*, 165-6.
[11] For Ephraim Pagitt (1574/5-1647) see *TLITC*, 74.
[12] Long memory existed of the Münster 'Kingdom' of the Anabaptists (1534-5). The city had been taken by a revolutionary group of the otherwise peaceful Melchiorite Anabaptists named after Melchior Hofmann (d. 1540), who taught a peaceful apocalypticism. A long

the common people' who 'poison[ed] the Scriptures called barely by them the letter.' They were 'selfish', 'giddy' and 'rude'. Richard Farnworth's *An Easter-Reckoning* (1653) was dismissed as a 'rambling piece of foppery'. *Gangraena* depicted Farnworth and the Quakers as an unpredictable rabble busily contaminating Britain with bellicose and often bizarre demonstrations such as spilling animal blood on church altars as a sign that the eucharist was idolatrous.[13] Dramatic outbursts such as these were never monopolised by the children of Light but their occurrence in a Quaker guise nevertheless led to the belief that the Friends and their ilk were as crazy as Mr. Josselin would suppose and good excuse for introducing strict uniformity of religious observance.[14]

The truth is that the Friends had come at a bad time for clerics. Since the effective abolition of the Church of England in 1646, the government had failed to support the parish system adequately. In many parts of the country the number of settled benefices fell drastically with one fifth disappearing by the mid 1650s. Many parishes were left priest-less and, although tithes remained a major political and ecclesiastical issue, many were not collected. Additionally, people under the Commonwealth were not obliged to attend their parish church so long as they worshipped elsewhere. Worse, the clergy were convinced that the new generation of gathered Churches, popping up everywhere it seemed and led by 'mechanick' thinkers with apparently no theological training, were leading people into confusion and heresy. Factors such as these had a detrimental effect on priestly morale. The result was that the disgruntled and disaffected projected their fears onto the Radicals, and particularly the Quakers whose sword cut savagely into the very political and religious heart of the Puritan commonwealth. More terrifyingly, they undermined premillennial assurances against the coming rule of King Jesus.[15]

---

siege forced their capitulation but not before considerable loss of life and cannibalism among themselves. To its English detractors, Münster *was* Anabaptism, a recipe for disunity, disaster and violence insurrection.

[13] Pagitt (1654), 136, Sig. U.

[14] Bauman, *Let Your Words Be Few*, esp. 32-42, 87-8 and chp. 6 in which Quaker metaphor is addressed in its physical manifestation; see Caton, letter (16/Nov/1660) to Fox, *SW*/iv/272, describing 'prophetess' Elizabeth Adams in Canterbury with 'a torch or such like thing . . . [riding] up and down the city with it burning in her hand'. Adams was imprisoned, her male partner freed. As we see in Ch.10, the self-description 'prophetess(es)' was commonly used by Quaker women during our timeframe and mentioned eight times in the King James Version: Ex. 15:20 (Miriam); Jg. 4:4 (Deborah); 2 K. 22:14 (Huldah); 2 Chr. 23:22 (Huldah); Neh. 6:14 (Noadiah); Isa. 8:3; Lk. 2:36 (Anna) and Rev. 2:20. See Barbour, 'Quaker Prophetesses and Mothers of Israel' in Frost and J. Moore (eds.), 46. Also Fox, *The Woman Learning* (1656), 4-6 and *Doctrinals*, 80-1.

[15] D. Hirst, 'Locating the 1650s', 303; Harlow, 'Preaching for Hire', 32.

Chapter 7: 'Open Shop for Soul-Poisons'

An avalanche of vituperation threatened to engulf the Friends. Leading Puritans such as Richard Blome pulverised them for their 'swollen pride', for being 'willingly ignorant' and 'misunderstanding Scripture', believing they could judge it by their own spirit.[16] The latter was a most serious accusation. Questioning Scripture, and apparently appropriating it as their own, brought the very function of the ministry, even the semi-theocratic Puritan State, into critical focus. Blome's conviction that the Quakers indulged in 'mad pranks' was echoed by Josselin and letters of complaint to parliament. One such letter from Oswestry (Wales) in 1653 described Quaker 'designs and practices' as dangerously focussed upon

> opposing of all ministers and public ministry, the breaking and dividing of congregations, the censuring of all saints that are not of their way for hypocrites, the total overthrowing of the work of faith, and holiness in saints: and the bringing of them again into bondage, (or as they say of Mount Sinai) and besides those common errors of universal redemption, free will, and falling from grace; they hold that all men have the pure seed of God in them and that they themselves are perfect, and without sin; boasting of a false gift, to discern upon the first sight any Christian or hypocrite, and speaking big and swelling words, void of sense and full of censure ... [T]heir manner of quaking or trembling (as was testified by several eye-witnesses to their faces) is thus; at their meetings, after long silence, sometimes one, and sometimes more (as at one time five together) fall into a great and dreadful shaking and trembling of their whole bodies, and all their joints, with such risings and swellings in their bellies and bowels, together with such screechings, yellings, howlings and roaring, which does not only amaze and frighten the spectators, but also cause the dogs to bark, the swine to cry, and the cattle to run.[17]

Contemporaries saw the Quaker form of worship as insane behaviour, and evil and dangerous since many of the Quaker preachers were women who posed a considerable threat to a highly conforming patriarchy. To Blome, the women Friends were 'immodest, shamefaced, brazen and disobedient', as they were surely 'prohibited by apostolic injunction to speak in the Church'.[18] To the godly in general, the seemingly ubiquitous presence of such 'scolds' highlighted the anarchic, if not satanic, nature of their Inward

---

[16] Horle, *The Quakers and the English Legal System*, 12.
[17] Griffiths, *Several Proceedings of the Parliament*, 249-55; esp. 249-50.
[18] See Richard Blome, *The Fanatic History* (1660), 68, 69-70; *Thurloe*, i. 591-2; ii. 94, 116-17; iv. 408, 508; v. 188; vi. 136, 145, 241, 708-10. And S. Roberts, 'The Quakers in Evesham', 63-85 for the conduct of, and travails caused by, the Friends and reactions from the local populace.

Light thinking.[19] The diarist and Episcopalian conformist, John Evelyn, writing in 1656 at a time when magistracy and the Church ministry were seen as the twin pillars of civil society, was certain the Quakers were a 'fanatic sect of dangerous principles who show no respect to any man, magistrate or other, and seem a melancholy, proud sort of people, and exceedingly ignorant'.[20]

In line with our Oswestry correspondent, Ralph Farmer of Bristol saw in the Friends' quaking evidence of physical illness and psychological disturbance.[21] To John Bunyan they were the 'abominable children of hell'. Indeed, one is tempted to see Mr. Ignorance in *The Pilgrim's Progress* as a parody of Quakerism. Like Bunyan's character, the Quakers did not know the true import of God's word or themselves.[22] Francis Higginson was certain James Nayler was 'Satan's nuncio'.[23] William Prynne, the lawyer and MP who strongly suspected that papist activity lay behind England's moral decline, believed the Quakers were the 'spawn of Romish frogs'.[24] In 1649 he had already aired his distrust of a Quaker-like emphasis on personal experience, declaring he had seen 'so much experience in the world, that I dare not trust none with my own or the kingdom's safety but God alone'. For Prynne, private conscience was virtually indistinguishable from fleshly will. Not surprisingly, the Quakers' 'Light in the conscience' sent shivers down his spine.[25] For people like Prynne, the entire corpus of Quaker theology stank of previously condemned heresies. Even late into the century, Quakerism could evoke outrage. Cotton Mather, the New England Puritan leader, cast the Quakers' mysticism and their apparent amillenarianism as another Romish disease, 'the vomit cast forth in the by-past ages . . . licked up again for a new digestion and once more exposed for the poisoning of mankind'. It was fit only for ignorant and 'feeble' souls.[26]

---

[19] This had a long tradition in England before Quakerism. See the Particular Baptist John Spilbery's *Heart-Bleedings for Professors Abominations* (1649), 2.
[20] Evelyn, *Diary*, 191. For a contemporary account of the pivotal role of magistracy in society see William Durham, *Maran-Atha, the Second Advent* (1656), 36.
[21] Farmer, *The Great Mysteries of Godliness and Ungodliness* (1655), 77.
[22] John Bunyan (1628-88) from *Works* (1692), 768 and quoted in Bitterman, 'The Early Quaker Literature of Defence', 205. For quaking as a symptom of illness see Bridenbaugh, *Vexed and Troubled Englishmen*, 4. Also Hardin, 'Bunyan, Mr. Ignorance and the Quakers', 500.
[23] Higginson, *A Brief Relation of the Irreligion* (1653), Sig. A, 3.
[24] Lamont, *Puritanism and Historical Controversy*, 16-17.
[25] Prynne, *The Quakers Unmasked and Clearly Detected* (1655), 2, a work of spitting vitriol; Lamont, *Puritanism and Historical Controversy*, 87. Also Baxter, *The Quaker's Catechism* (1655) answered by Nayler's *An Answer to a Book called The Quaker's Catechism* (1655); Donald Lupton, *The Quacking Mountebank* (1655) answered by Fox in *The Great Mystery*, 31.
[26] Cotton Mather, 'Preface' in *Principles of the Protestant Religion Maintained* (1690), unnumbered p. 3; Walia, *Radical Religion in England and its Critics*, 158.

Chapter 7: 'Open Shop for Soul-Poisons'

Although Cromwell was generally satisfied with the peaceable intentions of the Friends, the panic that popery perennially stirred up carried over to the movement. In the public mind, 'Quaker' often translated as 'Catholic priest'. William Dewsbury, for instance, was mistaken for a Jesuit when missionising Devon in 1657.[27] Activities such as his meant the Friends were often identified by the authorities as a Vatican fifth column, particularly since their uncompromising objection to oaths included the Oath of Abjuration (1643, 1655) which principally targeted Catholics. As with the Baptists, swearing implied dishonesty and thus a failure to be a pure witness to truth-telling.[28] By now, the otherwise sober and well-known Presbyterian, Richard Baxter, who in later life would take a more favourable view of the Friends, was also persuaded of Quaker jesuitical designs; they were intent on exploiting the godly by corrupting them with 'distracted raptures'. Baxter was in good company when warning that the Quakers were enemies of Scripture, of sobriety and (with all truth) the clergy.[29]

He was also clear that the Quakers' 'barking and bawling' would present no alternative to his own 'religion, ministry and church'. As for their organisation, they did not even possess 'a catechism or confession [of faith] to tell us what their own religion is.'[30] For Baxter, God was found in the despair people were currently experiencing, and, along with the poets Donne and Herbert, emphasised the crucified Jesus as the remedy. To show good will, said Baxter, he was willing to mix with and teach the poor, even attract their lice. To the Quakers, however, the Baxters of this world simply misread the signs. For the Friends, the despair was of a different, more fundamental nature and indicative of God's absence in the hearts of those who did not submit to the Light in their consciences.

For Baxter, the Quakers' spiritualising of Scripture was a dangerous return to that 'allegorical exegesis customary in the Middle Ages which, it was held, had often led to extremes that were superstitious or simply fanciful', or even to popery.[31] His advice to a student that the Quakers' allegories merely provided 'incoherent scraps' rather than an ordered and

---

[27] J. Davis, 'Religion and the Struggle for Freedom', 515-16. See *Thurloe*, iii, 119 for a letter (22/Jan/1654, i.e. 22/Jan/1655) to Thurloe from a George Cowlithay linking Quakers to Franciscans. For Dewsbury as Jesuit see Ann Dewsbury, letter (3/Nov/1657) to Fell, *SW*/iv/145 and Vivers, *The Saints Testimony* (1655), 9 for Quaker 'Jesuits' in Banbury (Oxon.).

[28] The first Baptist Confession of Faith of 1612 (Article 36) and that of 1614 (Article 86) forbad Baptists from oath taking. See John Sturgion's *A Plea for Toleration* (1661) presented to Charles II. For 'to the 'Truth' as Kingdom: Jn.18: 34.

[29] Lamont, *Richard Baxter*, 40, 47-8 and esp. 132.

[30] Baxter, *One Sheet Against the Quakers* (1657), 3.

[31] Nuttall, ''Nothing Else Would Do', 658.

coherent system of belief, underscored his own sincerely held fear.[32] Just as Thomas Hobbes saw a direct connection between language and culture—verbal chaos leading to cultural chaos—Baxter believed the Quakers were intent on breaking a treasured tradition, dating from the Reformation, of a careful linguistic study of original biblical texts whose principal goal was to arrive at their true meaning.[33] By the mid century much analysis of ancient languages had taken place in order to discover their etymological roots, the aim being to reconstruct an original Edenic language.[34]

Furthermore, as he and other theologians were expressing such fears, they were also mindful that the English language was absorbing new, unsettling scientific and religious concepts that forced painful reassessments and reconstructions of long-treasured models. Inevitably, anxiety over linguistic imprecision and irregularities resulted in a desire for a clear and logical expression of religious identity and purpose, both of which were being questioned by skilled polemicists like Hobbes and James Harrington, and now the Quakers.

The Friends were among the arch-disrupters, then, but the criticism that came their way was not confined to Protestants. It was clear to John Cannes, the Catholic Franciscan, who echoed Baxter, that Quaker writings were confusing. Their words were 'jumbled together' with little substance; 'dreaming conceits', he said, were interlaced with 'undeniable truths' but also 'endless tautologies' without connection. Their speeches added to the confusion by often resembling 'Mahamets Alcoran'.[35]

The Friends were also considered by many to be the Antichrist, which included the antinomian Ranters and other wayout mystics.[36] Even Baxter confused the Quakers' indwelling Light with the ideas of Jakob Boehme, the German Lutheran mystic. He was not alone in considering 'Behemism' vague if not nonsensical and that it had influenced such people as the Ranters.[37] Indeed, Ranters *could* be vague perhaps due to a pantheism that ran through their ideas or, according to Rufus Jones, because they 'had no fixed authority anywhere no criterion of morals, no test of spiritual guidance, no ground and basis for goodness'. Maybe for similar reasons Baxter envisioned the Quakers as 'but the Ranters turned from horrid

---

[32] See Stillman, 'Hobbes' Leviathan', 796; Hayduk, *Hopeful Politics*, 251.

[33] Baxter, *A Christian Directory*, 727; Lamont, *Richard Baxter*, 176.

[34] Poole, *Radical Religion*, 149.

[35] John Cannes, *Fiat Lux* (1661), 155-62 and esp. 156. An English version of the Qu'ran appeared in 1649.

[36] Ranters were mentioned by Thomas Fuller as active in 1604 along with Familists; see *The Church History of Britain* (1655), x., 33.

[37] Also Mosse, 'Puritan Radicalism and the Enlightenment', 434.

profaneness and blasphemy to a life of extreme austerity'.[38] Bunyan said much the same, the only difference being how Ranters frequented alehouses and smoked. Smoking was still a novel and 'naughty' activity at the time.[39] Pagitt's *Heresiography*, too, was sure the Quakers came 'from the same puddle as the Ranters'.[40]

For Friends, such a charge cut to the quick; they despised Ranters, believing their mixed bag of theologies was satanic or at best nihilist. Thomas Lawson, from the same Furness region as Margaret Fell, was certain they fed off 'nothing but the forbidden, abominable swine flesh'. Fell warned Ranters that, 'in the eternal light that never changes do we see you and know you . . . and race you out of the presence of the Lord'. Another leading Quaker, George Whitehead, protested that 'we do utterly deny the principles and practices of Ranters, who from the Light of Christ which is pure in the conscience are turned into the liberty of the flesh'. Fox, however, was never so harsh on the Ranters. While they irritated him, he believed they had merely lost their way through insufficiently waiting upon the Spirit.[41]

And yet there *were* similarities between the two as Baxter sensed, especially when both 'looked upon [Jesus] as a "figure" or "type" of the true dispensation of the Spirit'.[42] Ranters such as Abiezer Coppe also denounced the clerics' pride in their learning. He advocated personal

---

[38] Newcomb, 'The English Puritan Clergy's', 51-61 and esp. 53 for how leading Puritans could tag all Catholics as Jesuits.

[39] *TWTUD*, 201.

[40] Pagitt (1654), 143.

[41] R. Jones, *Studies in Mystical Religion*, 469. For an early Quaker reference to 'antinomian' see Thomas Barcroft, letter (26/May/1657) to Fell, *SW*/i/173. For Fox and Ranters see *Journal*, 79, 183. Nigel Smith's *Perfection Proclaimed* contains an informative account of Ranter and other radical sectarian language; McGregor, 'Ranterism and the Development of Early Quakerism', 351-60; McDowell, 'A Ranter Reconsidered: Abiezer Coppe and Civil War Stereotypes', 178; Davis, *Fear, Myth and History*, 124 in which Davis famously questions the Ranters as a corporate entity although Rufus Jones preceded him in this respect in *Studies in Mystical Religion* (1925), 452; Aylmer, 'Did the Ranters Exist?', 208-19, esp. 219. See also *BQ*, 22; Lamont, *Richard Baxter*, 40, 47-8 and esp. 132; Baxter, *A Christian Directory* (1673), 727; Gibbons, *Gender in Mystical and Occult Thought*, 126 for Baxter and Behemism.

Thomas Lawson, letter (July-Aug. 1655) to Fell, *SW*/i/242. See also Farnworth, letter (12/Nov/1653) to Fell *et al*, *SW*/iii/50-51 in which Farnworth converses with 'one partly of the ranting strain' and see his *Light Risen Out of Darkness* (1653), 57 and *The Ranters Principles and Deceits* (1655), 4-5; Fell, 'Some Ranters Principles Answered' in *A Testimony of the Touch-Stone for all Professions* (1656), 31-6 and esp. 36; Burrough, *The True Faith of the Gospel of Peace* in *Works*, 133; Richard Hickock, *A Testimony Against . . . Ranters*, passim. For G. Whitehead see Braithwaite, *Spiritual Guidance in Quaker Experience*, 42-3 and Whitehead's *Works*, 45.

[42] R. Jones, *Studies in Mystical Religion*, 469. For a useful exposé of Ranter theology see Nelson, *Play, Ritual Inversion and Folly among the Ranters*, 141-97.

perfection through unity with God and an internalised apocalypse. However, the Quakers' concept of a possible oneness with God never resembled Ranter-like infallibility. For the Friends the individual was not the sole authority.[43]

It was understandable that amid the swirling confusion of ideas and movements characterising the middle decades of the century, the Episcopalian, Presbyterian and Independent gentry expressed horror of the Radicals. They were certain society was being led into sexual permissiveness, gender equality and an end to property (including the payment of tithes)—in short, to the collapse of public order, even the end of civilisation itself. Such fear could be profound indeed; the chaos anticipated among some was no mere disorder but something akin to the cosmic anarchy before creation, an almost unimaginable horror.[44] The bewilderment of the traditionalists was genuine enough and Gwyn is correct in saying that the Friends, along with other Radical groups and especially those accused of popery, shook the dualism of Calvinist first covenant theology to its foundations by fusing 'spiritualist ecclesiologies ... with ... far-reaching [socio-] political and economic agendas'.[45]

And yet, as we saw in Chapters 4 and 5, the Quaker movement was no wilting flower. The power of their invective both written and spoken, their close corporate bonds and efficient itinerant ministry, and their theological confidence meant they withstood the onslaught of criticism, ridicule and persecution.

Publishers of the Truth

Another cause of anti-Quakerism was the movement's literary output, which was remarkable in its plenitude. From 'Satan's library' and flying 'as thick as moths up and down the country' came hundreds of tracts and other polemical writings, letters, essays, treaties, queries, catechisms and maxims. Many such works were written in quasi-theological language and covered concerns as diverse as doctrine and evangelism, religious organisation, politics, economics, social issues and history. They contained apocalyptic visions and biblical commentaries. With possibly 43 outlets for their books in England and Ireland, the Quakers indulged in well-organised evasions of the press laws to the extent that, of the 34,225 titles published in England between 1652 and 1684, they accounted for 3,030. Between 1659 and 1660,

---

[43] Abiezer Coppe, *Some Sweet Sips* (1649), 15.
[44] Daly, 'Cosmic Harmony', 7.
[45] Gwyn, *The Covenant Crucified*, 196-7.

the Friends contributed 10% of all known titles.[46] Corns suggests they 'professionalised and institutionalised the production of radical pamphlets to an unprecedented degree, matching the Protectorate's own attempt to dominate the work of the press.'[47]

Since the Commonwealth had never been entirely or efficiently censorious, it was commonplace by the mid decade for pamphlets and books to be sold openly by hawkers, and for posters and broadsides to be attached to market crosses and public buildings. Quaker works were read aloud in market places, in public houses, churchyards, during and after worship wherever it was held—in fields, private homes, on moors and hills or in rented halls. The Quakers also distributed books during their court appearances. It *did* seem as if their publications were everywhere, though in reality only small batches were distributed at any one time with runs averaging between 200-300 prints.[48]

Such was the fear evoked by their pamphlets, however, that when the Quakers emerged from their northern stronghold in 1654, Westminster quickly counterattacked by questioning their Christian credentials, in particular their apparent claim, similar to that of the Radicals Gerrard Winstanley, John Everard, William Dell and Abiezer Coppe, that the inward Christ or Light superseded the historical Jesus. As we shall see in the next chapter, the Friends responded by publicly affirming a continuity between the Jesus of history and the Christ of faith.[49]

There was little the authorities could do to stem the flow of these writings which, by 1656, had peaked at roughly 290 works. So pivotal was publishing to the Quaker enterprise that William Tomlinson, speaking for the movement in 1653 and only ten months after Fox's Firbank Fell sermon, enthusiastically endorsed publications as a highly effective way of countering Puritan preaching. It was not the letter but 'the pure offering of the Spirit' that was to be 'declared abroad'. In this way, he said, 'preaching [was] publishing'. Humphery Smith went further: 'Who can withhold the

---

[46] Greaves, *Enemies Under His Feet*, 169; *BQ*, 303-5; O'Malley, 'Defying the Power and Tempering the Spirit', 72-7. Farnworth, in a letter (2/Dec/1652) to Fell et al, *SW*/iii/45, mentions 300 hundred books for distribution to Friends to be read 'in the steeplehouse garths after [the priests had] done', and in market places on market days.

[47] Corns, 'Radical Pamphleteering' in Keeble, 72; Gill, 'Identities in Quaker Women's Writing 1652-60', 268-9.

[48] Peters, *Print Culture*, 67. See Farnworth, letter (2/Dec/1652) to Fell, *SW*/Tr2:15-16; 2:19. For Winstanley's Light theology see *New Law of Righteousness*, 34, 73, 78, 109, 114, 120.

[49] See Burrough, *Something in Answer to a Book called Choice Experiences* (1654), *passim* (a commentary on a book by J. Turner, *Choice Expriences* publ. in 1653). Cadbury, *Quakerism and Early Christianity*, 34-9 has interesting thoughts on the historical Jesus/spiritual Jesus issue. See Fox, Ep. 45 (1653) in *Works*, 7:54-7 for an early treatment of this question. Also *TWTUD*, 262.

pen from writing and the tongue from declaring . . . light to the gentiles?'[50] He, like most people, understood 'publish' to mean the act of declaring, proclaiming or disseminating information but pertinently in relation to the Word, the Dominion (Kingdom). Smith also referred to Isaiah 60:3 and 52:7 about which Fox may also have been thinking as he spoke of the Kingdom and the salvation it offered from the rock on Firbank Fell:

> How beautiful upon the mountains are the feet of him that brings good tidings, that publishes peace; that brings good tidings of good, that publishes salvation; that said unto Zion, 'Thy God reigns!'

Quaker works were normally published by Giles Calvert, Thomas Simmonds and Robert Wilson who was a Quaker.[51] In the aftermath of Thomas Venner's Fifth Monarchist uprising of January 1661, the government confiscated materials from Calvert's shop and burned the rest of his stock. The much raided Calvert was a well-known publisher of other radical literature such as that written by Winstanley and Dell. To Baxter, his office was an 'open shop . . . for . . . soul-poisons'. Calvert was also the brother of Martha Simmonds, a Quaker, whose husband (Thomas) worked out of the Quaker centre in London, the Bull and Mouth.[52] Similar harassment afflicted Quaker homes. Books were seized, for instance, from the personal library of leading Quaker Ambrose Rigge, 'a pernicious fellow', with Rigge himself arrested.

Of course, publications were used by all sides in the wider political and religious controversies. Some highlighted profound concern over issues such as religious toleration and the need for further ecclesiastical and constitutional reform. Others proved to be effective weapons when lobbying politicians. Many a tract worried over perceived threats against the Presbyterian design for a National Church while still others pondered the security of the commonwealth—in short, the need for tighter religious and political controls.[53]

---

[50] See William Tomlinson, *A Word of Reproof* (1653), 17-19; H. Smith, *The True and Everlasting Rule from God* (1658), 36; see also 29 for Dominion, 32-3 for 'light to the gentiles' and 37; Isa. 60:3.

[51] *MOP*, Appendix 1 (B), 269; Peters, *Print Culture*, 21, 56; *BQ*, chp. 12 (2nd edn.); *TLITC*, Table 3, pp. 241-2. See Baxter, *The Worcester-shire Petition* (1653) 35, 39, a reply to Aldam et al, *A Brief Discovery of the Kingdom of Antichrist* (1653). Also *TWTUD*, 251; *FF*, 141.

[52] Raids on dissident publishers took place under the Unlicensed and Scandalous Books and Pamphlets Act (Long Parliament) Sept., 1649; see Firth and Rait, *Acts and Ordinances of the Interregnum*, ii., 245-54. Also *TWTUD*, 373.

[53] Lesser known Friends also attacked the idea of a National Church; see Henry Clark, *A Rod Discovered* (1657), *passim*. For more about Ranters see Gucer, 'Not Heretofore Extant in Print', 76.

Public argumentation was popular in the mid seventeenth century, often attracting enormous crowds. In the clothing town of Coggeshall (Essex), for instance, two thousand people heard the sermons of Independent John Owen. Drawing in deep theological breath, gatherings such as these helped ventilate the public's enjoyment of polemics. The Quakers took full advantage of them to further the Lamb's War. Although debating was fraught with intellectual and physical danger, they deliberately sought it out, often using debates like publications to advance subtle agendas whose true audiences were not necessarily those present. In 1653, for instance, the Fifth Monarchists used public forums with the Quakers to attack politicians of the Rump over reform of the Church ministry and tithes. Public verbal and written assaults on Ranters were often a means of dissuading people from using their own reason when considering sectarian claims to authority.[54] The Quakers sometimes plunged into disputes, such as that between Samuel Fisher and Thomas Danson in 1659, to argue for a reformed magistracy and religious toleration. Reminiscent of the controversies surrounding Arminian intentions, Fisher argued the Quaker case for toleration by daringly evoking the memory of Cardinal Bellarmine (d.1621) whose ideas, he maintained, were more reasonable than hitherto supposed.[55]

Church Interruptions

Another means of publishing the truth, although it is questionable whether it assisted the movement's cause, was their colourful and at times illegal interruption of 'steeplehouse' services and verbal harassment of clerics. It could be startlingly dramatic as in Josselin's Earls Colne parish and it was meant to disturb. One Quaker tactic, for example, was to march up to the sanctuary and harangue both cleric and congregation. Some held a candle while performing this act or wore a white sheet, even a halter, as a sign of purity or, conversely, as a way of shaming people in their apostasy. Such behaviour, however, was not uncommon during the republican years before the Quakers appeared. Many non-Quakers like the Fifth Monarchists also disrupted services. The government finally clamped down on the activity in 1655 with its *Proclamation Prohibiting the Disturbing of Ministers*. It restricted those present at worship to speaking only when the preacher concluded his sermon, usually when sand ran out of an hour glass normally perched on the pulpit's ledge.[56]

---

[54] Peters, *Print Culture*, 177-9; McDowell, 'A Ranter Reconsidered', 149-52.
[55] See Luke Howard, *The Devils Bow Unstringed* (1659), *passim* for the circumstances surrounding the Fisher-Danson interaction. And Danson, *The Quakers Folly*, 57-8.
[56] *A Proclamation Prohibiting the Disturbing of Ministers*, Bds.; promulgated 15/Feb/1654.

In the first days of the movement, Fox and other Friends such as Farnworth and Thomas Aldam perfected the interruption but landed themselves in prison as a result. The rage that the interventions generated could be extraordinarily intense and have vicious outcomes. The *Journal* records incidents such as that in which Fox was struck repeatedly on the head by a furious Bible-wielding cleric. Other beatings he received are recalled throughout its pages and some were near fatal; his accounts bristle with indignation and dark judgments. James Parnel's interruption of Independent ministers in Coggeshall propelled him to a disastrous end in Colchester castle. Robert Widders' efforts demonstrated his total commitment to the Lamb's War to be sure, but no sooner had he endured a severe thrashing at Caldbeck (Cumbria), he immediately trudged the considerable distance of 'seven miles' to Aikton where the minister saw fit to call in the local JP, gleefully volunteering to be executioner. Widders ended up in Carlisle prison. On his release shortly afterwards he made his way to Lamplough only to be attacked again, this time his hair being ripped from his head.[57]

It is difficult to account for such violence, except that the Quakers, by severely criticising the Church's very history, may have upset people already ill at ease in fear-ridden, violent and uncertain times. And let us remember that Church liturgies, rituals and the Bible, particularly its literal interpretation, may have acted as secure buffers against terrifying realities both physical and ontological. The Friends, then, may have challenged people's highly-tuned sense of their own salvation and election by exacerbating anxieties that surrounded them daily. Is it possible, therefore, that individual identity and meaning, including age-old parish and community structures and loyalties, were exposed as open wounds by Quaker interference?

Sometimes interruptions could be humorous. When a Quaker stalked into All Saint's in Orton (Cumbria) as the minister was in mid sermon, the congregation witnessed the following exchange to their astonishment:

Quaker: Come down thou false Fothergill!
Cleric: Who told you my name is Fothergill?
Quaker: The Spirit.
Cleric: Then your Spirit is a lying Spirit, for it is well known that I am not Fothergill, but one-eyed Dalton of Shap![58]

---

[57] Robert Widders (or Withers, c.1618-86) in *Works*, 3-4. Widders of Over-Kellet (nr. Lancaster) was a preaching companion of Fox. The villages of Caldbeck ('Coldbeck') and Aikton ('Ackton') today are approx. 12 miles (approx. 16-17 km.) apart by road.

[58] Breay, *Light in the Dales*, 31. This was probably a trap by Fothergill and Dalton in the wake of (i) recent incursions of Quakers into Westmorland and (ii) the Lancaster investigations of Fox and Nayler in 1652. See Overview and *BQ*, 284; *Journal*, 18-19, 92

Chapter 7: 'Open Shop for Soul-Poisons'

The command 'come down!', often said in this context, may be likened to spiritual shorthand addressing those who should know better and come to judgment (rigorous self-examination) so they may 'come up into the Light', a call to the Kingdom as we saw in Sarah Jones in Chapter 5. Anne Gargill, a former Catholic, could write at the time: 'Come down unto the Lord and mind innocency. It will bring you to know an eternal Kingdom . . . which is endless'.[59]

Behind Dalton's teasing was the serious charge that the Quakers' Inward Light began with Satan, the lying Spirit. Undeterred, the Friends were uncompromising in their confrontations with mainline Church 'apostasy' and Puritanism in particular. In 1655, for instance, Thomas Goodaire aimed Quaker salvos at Richard Baxter in his Kidderminster parish.[60] Sometimes the targeting of certain clerics revealed a specific strategy. For a short time in 1656, Jane Higgs, that 'common disturber of ministers in public', proved a persistent nuisance to the well-known Thomas Hall of King's Norton in Warwickshire whose spiritual crimes, besides his support of the universities, were his campaign against 'unlawful', 'sinful' and 'dangerous' 'private persons' who 'take upon them[selves] public preaching'. Higgs might have appreciated her victim more had she known of his vehement opposition to chiliasm.[61] Indeed, women such as Higgs were prominent and persistent interrupters. Of the more than 300 Quakers arrested for the activity between 1654 and 1659, 34% were women.[62]

Despite the opportunities for public pronouncements which their court appearances gave them, the Quakers objected loudly to the punishments they received. But it was their prosecution under an Act from 'Bloody Mary's time' (Mary Tudor) that proved especially galling. It justified their complaint that a corrupted magistracy applied popery to an 'innocent people in scorn'.[63] Farnworth and, later, Burrough, protested the legality of the

---

(for Fox at Warmsworth, 1652), p. 111 (for Farnworth at Wakefield, 1652), p. 104 (for Fox at Wensleydale, 1652). Interruptions were not confined to the Quakers; see Tangye, *The Two Protectors: Oliver and Richard Cromwell*, 158. For a good account of interruptions particularly by Essex Friends see A. Davies, *The Quakers in English Society*, 20-30. And see Gough, *Myddle*, 99.

[59] Anne Gargill, *A Brief Discovery* (1656), 14; S. Jones, *This is Light's Appearance*, 3.

[60] *Journal*, 73, 100; Gilbert, 'The Puritan and the Quakers', 118-121; esp. 118. See Farnworth, letter to Fox (7/May/1655), SW/iii/57 for mention of Goodaire and Baxter.

[61] Thomas Hall, *Chiliastro-mastix Redivivus* (1657), *passim*; *The Pulpit Guarded* (1651; 3rd edn.). See Gilbert, 'The Puritan and the Quakers', 120. Also Mason, *A Check to the Lofty Linguist* (1655); McDowell, *The English Radical Imagination*, 39, 40-1 (44n), 87; And see Peters, *Print Culture*, 166-7 (61n) for 27 Quaker tracts condemning Puritanism.

[62] Bittle, *James Nayler*, 41. He quotes one John Taylor, pamphleteer: 'When women preach and cobblers pray, the friends in hell make holiday'; see *Lucifer's Lacky* (1641), 6.

[63] *Journal*, 345.

1655 *Proclamation* claiming that the Marian Act it incorporated had been repealed at Elizabeth I's accession in 1558. It was a fair point; there *were* wide discrepancies in the application of the laws as they were applied to the Quakers.[64]

Nevertheless, irrespective of the punishments that resulted from the *Proclamation*, the Friends persisted with church invasions throughout the 1650s as a provocation to the religious establishment. It did not stop there; they also targeted other Radicals. John Camm and John Audland, for instance, accepted an invitation in 1654 to hold a worship meeting at Filton, the scene of much proselytising by their rivals the Broadmead Baptists in nearby Bristol.[65] And yet, although some suffered for interrupting services, most Quaker itinerant preachers remained free of arrest and experienced easy passage through towns and villages. Indeed, they avoided confrontation with the authorities and parishioners as much as possible by setting up Meetings on county boundaries and in other locations already noted. On the whole, congregations were also prepared to listen patiently.

However, abhorring 'that filthy way the Quakers were in', there is no doubting the eagerness with which local magistrates' metered out punishments to the recalcitrant Quakers. For John Atherton of Warrington, Quaker blasphemy, civil disobedience, exhibitionism and irresponsible social and political ideas were sources of 'pestilence'.[66] Parliamentarians, too, considered the Friends as dangerous; they would later lump the Quakers with the violent wing of the Fifth Monarchists in whose 50-man suicidal uprising in 1661 the Friends would be accused of taking part.[67]

Bristol, 1656 and the Kingdom

During the mid decade, however, a scandal arose over another form of public demonstration, and it was to have far-reaching implications for the Quakers. In 1656, despite successes, unease began to stir among the Quaker leadership. While their movement was seen by detractors to be riddled with

---

[64] Peters, *Print Culture*, 197-9, 215: on p. 198 (21*n*) she lists 20 tracts that follow legal proceedings re: interruptions. See Aldam *et al*, *A Brief Discovery of the Kingdom of Antichrist*, esp. 2; Burrough, *A Measure for Instruction* (1658), 23.

[65] *BQ*, 167; Warmington, *Civil War, Interregnum*, 117.

[66] See A. Anderson, 'A Study in the Sociology of Religious Persecution: The First Quakers', 254 but esp. 252; Barbour, *The Quakers in Puritan England*, 207.

[67] See Hill, 'Millenarianism and Fifth-Monarchism', 31; Capp, *The Fifth Monarchy*, 19. Venner's manifesto denounced the 'the old, bloody, popish, wicked gentry of the nation'. Woolrych, *Commonwealth to Protectorate*, 393; Morrill, *Revolution and Restoration*, 109. W. Abbott (ed.), iv. 350 adopts the view that Cromwell was once sympathetic to the idea of the Inward Light but nevertheless humoured Quaker leaders such as Fox and Pearson (see iii., 640 and 373 respectively). *Cf.* W. Abbott's account of Fox's interview with Cromwell (6/March/1655) and Fox's own recollection in *Journal*, 198-200.

Chapter 7: 'Open Shop for Soul-Poisons'

contradiction and 'treasonous design', it was hard to deny that a 'Ranterish' presence within the Quaker fold had consolidated itself, particularly in London. Thomas Hamm tells us that Quaker Meetings which fell under the influence of the Ranters tended to cause strife, one reason perhaps why Fox, Burrough and Howgill foresaw trouble in the capital where the behaviour of the much loved James Nayler came under increasing concern. The so-called Nayler incident of 1656 caused the first major controversy among the children of Light, a controversy that had more to do with method than theology or politics.[68] Particularly poignant was the rift it caused between Fox and Nayler; unlike Paul and Peter, the two leading Friends never fully reconciled.

What happened in Bristol? Having trudged through Glastonbury and Wells, Nayler and seven others finally entered the rain-soaked city in October. Ostensibly, he and his small band of followers were enacting Jesus' entry into Jerusalem.[69] His companions, including the irrepressible and domineering Martha Simmonds and a number of Ranter sympathisers, chanted, 'Holy, holy, holy, Lord God of Saboath', sometimes adding 'Lord God of Israel' as they dripped their way through the muddy, narrow streets to the White Hart Inn in Broad Street, the home of two local Friends.[70] Like Fox at Reading in 1659, Nayler was emotionally vulnerable, due perhaps to a combination of over-work, poor diet, a recent incarceration in Exeter prison, a two-week long fast and a predisposition towards ill-health—he had suffered a 'tuberculosis-type illness' in 1654.[71] Utterly exhausted and in the absence of other public Friends, he had also felt the weight of the London mission on his shoulders. And, according to Braithwaite, he was probably 'smarting under the censures of Fox'.[72] Nayler may have carried some hope that his 'sign' would achieve a measure of success; at the same time, I suspect he knew the 'Pharisees' would have other designs. So, *did he anticipate martyrdom?*[73] We may never know but his Jesus-like demeanour

---

[68] With some irony we point to Nayler's own plea for unity in 1653 in *A Discovery of the First Wisdom*, 3. See Hamm, 'George Fox and the Politics of Late Nineteenth Century Quaker Historiography' in Mullett (ed., 1991), 17.
[69] For 'Jesus' entry into Jerusalem': Lk.19:41-44.
[70] The Geneva Bible explains the Hebrew and the ritual surrounding the use of 'Hosanna'; see notes 'e' and 'f' for Mt. 21: 9 in the 1607 version.
[71] Reference to *DCFB* reveals that in 1656, Nayler, astonishingly, wrote or contributed to 10 works of significance.
[72] *FF*, 143, 85, chp. 10; *BQ*, chp. 11, 241-78; see esp. 251; Bittle, *James Nayler*, chp. 4; Damrosch, *The Sorrows of the Quaker Jesus*, 140-6; Gwyn, *The Covenant Crucified*, 181.
[73] For 'sacrificial death of the Lamb in the manner of Revelation': Rev. 5:12; 17:14.

during his subsequent trial, torture and imprisonment does appear consistent with a desire for 'crucifixion'.[74]

So what were Nayler's motivations? Being profoundly driven in spiritual matters—and since Quakers were a public people—it is reasonable to assume that such a Friend would want to perform a sign as others had done before him. Prior to Bristol, he had repeatedly addressed the 'secret' nature of the Kingdom that was 'hid from that which feeds on earthly things', hidden still from the spiritually blind who, due to their ignorance or pride, 'gathered against Christ and his Kingdom'.[75] Perhaps he felt compelled to bring the Kingdom into the open so to speak, by doing something that would prefigure the immanency and potency of the Kingdom within and what it meant once it was truly among people.[76] How was this to be done? Nayler, it seems, turned to the image of Jesus, considered at that time the most dramatic of human beings, to highlight the need for all people to undergo convincement by confronting 'Satan's wiles and temptations'. In doing so they would liberate the 'imprisoned Seed' within them and counter that most dreadful of realities, separation from God.[77] The sign would urge onlookers to take their part in the Easter story by internalising the atonement—to suffer, die and arise from their former dead selves so they could be 'in' God. The support of the strong-willed Martha Simmonds and other adoring followers could have served, then, as a catalyst for enacting his concern which the 'brightness of the Lamb's appearance' would reveal.[78]

Our speculation also allows us to see Nayler's horse as a silent partner. It is an overlooked metaphor and one in the manner of Zechariah 9:9-19 in which a king of peace, riding on a colt, exorcises war and oppression from the hearts of men and women and thence reconciles them to God. For Nayler and the Friends this peace was already present as the Kingdom but was still to be known among all people. His horse may also have acted as a metaphor for Revelation 19—the final battle of Revelation in fact—in which Jesus, himself on a white horse, commences his rule by means of spiritual warfare (19:11-14), a Lamb's War of righteousness and salvation. The horse being important to the Book of Revelation meant Nayler may

---

[74] See *TWTUD*, 256, *Thurloe*, v., 694, 708-9, 726 and references to James and Anne Nayler in *Journal of the House of Commons* (1803), 465-8 for the period 15th August 1651-16th March, 1659.

[75] Nayler, *Churches Gathered against Christ and his Kingdom* (1654), 6-16; *A Public Discovery of the Open Blindness*, 10-11, 21, 24, 31, 39 and also 'Not to Strive, but Overcome by Suffering' (1658) in *Works*, 727-8.

[76] For 'immanency and the dramatic potency of Christ within': Col. 1:27; Rev. 11:3.

[77] See Nayler's *A Door Opened to the Imprisoned Seed* ([1659] 1667), title pg., sig. A2, 4-5 and his (and Hubberthorne's) *An Account from the Children*, 52.

[78] Nayler, 'To Friends in Lincoln' (8/May/1655) in *Works*, 704.

have understood its significance, particularly for himself on his pilgrimage-like journey. In other words, at Bristol it is possible he wished to represent the Christ as the 'faithful and true' (white horse) head of the Lamb's army (in white linen = pure) who wears a crown (of the Kingdom) and conquers Death (on a pale horse) with peace (red horse) and justice (black horse). For Nayler, the 'pale horse' could have symbolised the old, defunct covenant and, in contradiction, the ushering in of the life-giving Kingdom for which he was prepared to die like Jesus.[79] His own horse and sign, therefore, may have represented respectively the horses of Revelation (except, of course, its 'pale' opposite which it outshone) and the revelation of the new Church and, as we have seen, the covenant of the Lamb.

As street-theatre in the manner of a medieval mystery play, the Bristol episode might have been planned to highlight, if not embody, Zechariah 9:9-19 but also Revelation 19:7 in which, as the then accepted interpretation had it, Jesus would come to claim his bride (the Church) at the end of time. By means of the physical presence of the patient, faithful, peaceful and willing-to-be-martyred Nayler (Rev. 1:9; 14:12; 17:6), the marriage between the true Church of the Light (for which the Quakers were witnessing) and the Christ was given some visible form: the Friends had always accepted that both were, as Fox would say in 1659, 'as nigh together as husband and wife'.[80] This marriage was eschatological; it mirrored the era of the spiritual warrior of the peaceable Kingdom, 'the dawnings of the Gospel day and its Light and Glory discovered' and the new Messianic era of reconciliation and unity.[81]

Bristol: a Theological Interpretation

Before Bristol, much in Revelation 19 had in fact been worked into early Quaker writings, including those of Nayler himself, as an *inward* experience.[82] Once convinced, he and the Friends assumed that the last days had passed (the old Israel was dead), that judgment and wrath had poured forth, and that Christ had been freed at last from the contortions of human self-deception and apostasy. With the New Israel, the true church of the Inward Light, now in their midst, Bristol was to be a visible demonstration of continuing revelation, a testimony to incarnational Christianity that

---

[79] See Rev. 6:2, 4, 5, 8; 15:6; 19:11, 14, 19, 21. For Nayler's preparedness for possible martyrdom see Gwyn, 'James Nayler and the Lamb's War', 182.
[80] See Fox, *The Great Mystery*, 49 but esp. Ep. 147 (1657), *Collection*, 112.
[81] The very apt title of Howgill's *Works*.
[82] This is particularly true for Rev. 19:1-2; 6-11; 13-16; 19-21. For specific use of Rev. 19 see, for instance, Fox, *The Lambs Officer*, 16-17; Nayler, *A Discovery of the First Wisdom*, 22; Dewsbury, *The Discovery of Man's Return*, 14-15.

Puritan divines such as Nathaniel Holmes and Richard Bernard might have understood better than many of Nayler's fellow Quakers.[83]

To the mystical Nayler, everything in that 'now' in Bristol possessed divinity. His sign was a glorification and verification of his own oneness with God, and of the possibility that others may enjoy the same. It was a sign that said a great deal about perfection, a perfection that was attainable in this life when people were, without reserve, 'in' Christ.[84] Consequently, it openly questioned Calvinist predestination and was a deliberate assault on the prevailing premillennialism of those who, like Cromwell, deluded themselves into thinking that Jesus' physical return was imminent. In his own way, Nayler went 'naked' as Fox had done at Lichfield in 1651.

Whatever else is said about the incident—its timing, supposed *naïveté* or even whether the Friends were theologically too advanced compared to their contemporaries—'Bristol' was an urgent attempt to draw attention to the Quaker claim that the new messianic age had indeed arrived, that the Kingdom was here and now. Like the Jesus of the Gospels, Nayler was saying in active and dramatic language that the Quakers were initiating a new but *unwarlike* era, that the unchanging Kingdom was a present reality of peace and mercy. As with Fox's c.1647 experience of meeting 'Christ Jesus who spoke to his condition', Nayler's action may have been an attempt to change the perception of God from a holy and distant 'Other' to a real, loving Presence that was within and among all people rather than an Elect only.

Nayler, a former quartermaster under Maj.-Gen. John Lambert of the Northern Army, was no doubt familiar with the soldiers' pocket version of the Geneva Bible in whose preamble to Revelation he would have read, 'the Lamb Christ shall defend [the members of Christ], which bare witness to the truth' as Jesus had done before Pilate in Jerusalem.[85] Since Nayler never explained his motivations in Bristol, it can be assumed that, during that

---

[83] Bernard, *A Key of Knowledge*, 4, 130-1; Holmes, *The Resurrection-Revealed* (1661), 278-9; A. Y. Collins, 'Apocalyptic Themes in Biblical Literature', 117-28, esp. 117.

[84] See Nayler's *Weakness above Wickedness* (pub. 18/July/1656), esp. 13, a reply to Leveller Jeremiah Ives' *The Quakers Quaking* (1656); also Fox, *Some Principles of the Elect People of God* (1661), 23-4.

[85] Fox and some early Friends used the Geneva Bible, though not exclusively; some *Journal* passages reveal a use of its 1560 version *and* the King James Version. W. Worden, for instance, has noted (as an example among others) Fox's Geneva Bible use of Eph. 2:5-7 ('dead by sins') rather than the King James's 'dead in sins'. Here Worden cites *The Works of George Fox* (Philadelphia), vol. 2; see also his 'Text and Revelation: George Fox's Use of the Bible', 17 (25*n*) and Metzger, 'The Geneva Bible of 1560'. For "witness to the truth' as Jesus had done before Pilate' see Jn. 18:36-37.

Nayler was quartermaster in the Northern Army under Major Christopher Copley and thence Lambert; see Neelon, *James Nayler*, 45, 49-51 and Anon, *The Rider of the White Horse* (1643), 6 for Nayler (?) at a skirmish at Leeds, 23rd Jan., 1643.

fateful 'now', the everlasting Christ, that glimpse of Eternity, which he may have believed was in him in full measure at that point, stepped onto the 'world's' stage as a sign towards 'all people'. Adapting something from the poetry of Gerard Manley Hopkins, we may say Nayler was acting 'in God's eye' what in 'God's eye he felt he was'—that is, being of Christ Jesus and perhaps existentially of the very Spirit.[86]

His was a witness with enough revolutionary potential to create deep unease among the authorities whose callous response saw Nayler tortured, publicly humiliated and gaoled. Through such incidences it is possible to appreciate something of the power inherent in Quaker hopes for unity with God, from which 'certain, hidden, or veiled spiritual verities [were] revealed'.[87] And especially so when one remembers how, in January 1653, Nayler had declared boldly before Justice (and later Quaker) Anthony Pearson, that 'the Christ is not divided'.[88] Here, too, is another clue to the incredible national over-reaction to Bristol—the troublesome, often unspoken, distinction between the historical Jesus of the Synoptic Gospels and the spiritual or cosmological Jesus as revealed in John. It is a tension that persists within the Church to this day.

The Importance of Conflict for Testimony

Disputation among the Friends such as that arising from the Bristol event, particularly between Fox and Nayler and their respective supporters, was seen as 'an evil thing begot among' themselves. Disciplinary concerns—for instance, Christopher Atkinson's sexual behaviour or 'backsliding' on Quaker beliefs and practices—gave rise to conflicts as did the growing disquiet among men about the authority and influence of women within the movement, something we will address in Chapter 10.[89] And yet, the disputes were not destructive of the Quakers' essential theological unity. In fact, they may have helped crystallise and strengthen Quaker belief and practice since some arguments were subject to effective mediation by Friends such as Hubberthorne and Dewsbury or were resolved by travelling preachers like Farnworth. One might say disputes were intrinsic to the Quakers' quest for unity. This form of conflict ran parallel to that experienced on an inner level where the Beasts of separation and egotism

---

[86] Hopkins, 'Untitled', *Poems*, 95.
[87] See Fisher's *Apokryta*.
[88] Nayler, 'The Examination of James Nayler' in *Works*, 14 and 'Concerning Justification' in *Love to the Lost*, 50-2. See also Burrough, *A Seasonable Word of Advice* (*DCFB/Wing* 1658), Bds.; G. Whitehead, *The He-Goats Horn Broken*, 17. For seventeenth century literature see Sharpe and Zwicker (eds., 1987), esp. 15. And for 'the Christ is not divided': 1 Cor. 1:13.
[89] *TLITC*, 57-8.

were confronted, and externally from society at large. In short, conflict was a school through which Quaker Testimony developed.[90]

At the same time, if the letters to Swarthmoor Hall are believed, it would be inadvisable to exaggerate the tenor or number of disputes within the movement during its formative years, especially in view of the close bond the Friends clearly enjoyed. Their Kingdom orthopraxis had demanded unity in matters of faith and practice, which resulted in a significant degree of theological cohesion. This in turn allowed frequent collaboration of which *Saul's Errand to Damascus* (1563) between Fox, Nayler and others is just one example of the many extant joint efforts.[91] Rufus Jones observed that 'many of the early Quaker books show how remarkable was [their] corporate character and the group-spirit . . . at this period'.[92] The movement, therefore, often appeared as one spiritual personality with individual expressions of convincement being the common ground from which forgiveness and reconciliation within and outside the movement were pursued. Considering the rigorous demands of their convincement, their internal disputes and external pressures (often of an extreme nature), and the rapidly changing political and military circumstances during the 1650s, it is amazing that the movement experienced rapid numerical growth. By 1660 there were possibly 60,000 people admitting allegiance to the ideas of Fox and other public Friends.[93]

Conclusion

The itinerant Quaker preachers claimed to have brought hope and direction to 'all people' at a time of great uncertainty. Their determination was fuelled by a sense of urgency and a radical evangelism whose discourse often took the form of public 'signs'. As the Lamb's War pursued its radical socio-political and economic agenda, these 'signs' were deliberate means of

---

[90] See Richard Roper (d. 1658), letter (20/Oct/1656) to Fell, *SW*/iii/131 for 'an evil thing begot' etc. in London, the Friends 'Corinth'; John Lilburne, letter (27/June/1657) to Fell, *Thirnbeck MSS.* and in *JFHS* 9 (1912), 53-8; John Brown (or John Robinson?), letter (1/Nov/1659) to Fox, *SW*/iii/90.

[91] For collaborations among leading Friends see my *MOP*, Appendix 1 (Section B). Nigel Smith conjectures that by laying stress upon Scripture as 'an interior allegory' the Friends possessed little by way of a recognisable inherited framework (i.e. one based on dogma). But did Scripture and their hermeneutic of the Kingdom provide such a framework?; see Smith's 'Hidden Things Brought to Light' in Corns and Loewenstein, *The Emergence of Quaker Writing, passim* and esp. 65.

[92] *Ibid.*, and R. Jones, *Spiritual Reformers*, 338 (1n).

[93] These figures vary among historians. Braithwaite in *BQ*, 512 mentions 30-40,000 men, women and children by 1660 as a rough estimate. *QER*, 26-7 has 60,000 by 1660. See also Broderick's letter to Sir Edward Hyde which mentions 30,000 in 'extreme discontent', *Clarendon* (edn. 1786), iii. 480.

subverting the familiar social and religious order in a nonviolent way. Inevitably, the reaction from the political, military and ecclesiastical authorities as well as from ordinary people was one of hostility. As dissenters, the Friends were physically attacked, sometimes viciously, or dismissed as deluded and dangerous fanatics who were likely to slit the throats of innocent people. They were accused of popery, of being Jesuits, of being the Antichrist or mad Ranters. Not only did they undercut premillennial assurances against the coming physical rule of Jesus, but gave considerable freedom to women to preach, generally considered a horrific license. For the Episcopalian, Presbyterian and Independent gentry, who loudly and constantly expressed fear of an impending collapse of public order, the Quakers represented nothing less than the end of civilisation. The 'hotter sort' of Puritan was especially vitriolic.

The Friends saw themselves as 'Publishers of the Truth' and as prophets of the Kingdom. Their publications were many, about a thousand between 1652 and 1663, at a time when religious tracts and public debates were hugely popular. But publications and debates were obviously not enough. Church interruptions and public demonstrations, including the notorious entry of James Nayler into Bristol, were part of their public repertoire. The conflict that came their way proved important for the growth of Testimony. While disputation was experienced within the movement from time to time, it would be wrong to overstate it. Rather, they displayed a remarkable degree of social and theological cohesiveness. Of vastly more concern to many were their beliefs about Jesus, the Second Coming, the Light, the Trinity, the practice of silence, and their obvious unity among themselves and with God as an 'example and pattern' for the British nations and 'all people'. It is to these concerns we now turn.

Chapter 8: *'Of the Nature of Christ Jesus'*

- Christology, Unity and Silence -

1654 was highly significant for the Quaker movement. It was the year when the Friends, with their heady language and tenacious message of the Kingdom, descended upon southern England—from rural, northern and rebellious Galilee to Jerusalem, so to speak—to launch their regeneration of the British nations and, through them, 'all people on the earth'. Filled with apocalyptic power and a highly-tuned capacity for spiritual contemplation, the Quakers saw themselves as prophetic and priestly heralds of the New Israel, as primitive Christianity revived.[1] Burrough marvelled how the 'branch', 'spring' and 'star' of the Kingdom had emerged from 'the least of the nations'.[2]

Two years earlier Yorkshireman Richard Farnworth had proclaimed presciently, 'We have pitched our tents, drawn our swords, made ready for the battle: it is begun'. Convinced the movement was divinely charged with the mediation of the Spirit/Christ for 'all people', his was a rallying call to 'the valiant soldiery of the army of the Lamb' to reveal the Word so as to enact the Kingdom.[3] The Lamb—Jesus and/or the almighty power of Love—would ride at their head

> on a white horse conquering . . . and the Lamb and the bride his wife . . . will rule all nations with a rod of iron, he is come to make work with you, and the Lamb, and the saints shall have the victory over the Beast.[4]

For the Friends, this imagery from the Gospel of John and Revelation 19 portrayed the bride (the true Church 'built without hands') and the

---

[1] See Watkins, *Spiritual Autobiography*, 4 and his chp.3 for Quaker journaling. For Gill, 'Identities in Quaker Women's Writing 1652-60', 269, early Quaker journals are autobiographical ('life narratives'). However, with aspects of them being written for all times, they went beyond introspection and were not necessarily examples of Puritan individualism.

[2] Burrough in *To the Camp of the Lord* (1655), 6. Horle tells us that 160 out of the 250 most active Friends in the 1650s were northerners; see *The Quakers and the English Legal System*, 2.

[3] Llewellyn-Edwards, 'Richard Farnworth of Tickhill', 205. See Nb. 1:52; Dt. 1:33; 1 Chr. 15:1, 16:1.

[4] Fox, *The Lambs Officer*, 16-17. For 'the bride and bridegroom . . . inner and outer peace': Jn. 3:29, 2:9; Rev. 18: 23, 19: 2, 7, 11 and 21:2. For a further reference to the Quakers' southward thrust see Burrough, 'Epistle to the Reader', *The Great Mystery*, unnumbered p. 17.

Chapter 8: 'Of the Nature of Christ Jesus'

bridegroom (the Lamb) as representing the marriage of earthly and heavenly history, the marriage of inner and outer peace. It also envisaged the reign of the peaceful Lamb as a deep Presence in a Kingdom-dominated *now*. Unlike its carnal equivalent, *this* victory would be achieved with spiritual weapons only, the war being won with righteousness and mercy. Essentially, this was the message Nayler brought to Bristol with ill-fated effects.

As a 'sign' to a fallen, idolatrous world, their concern was that 'all people' would find salvation, that is to say, wholeness through unity with God by means of the special saving grace of the Spirit. The Lamb would work within people to bring transformation, forgiveness, reconciliation and healing.[5] As a consequence, their comm*unity* claimed to have rediscovered the compassionate God, hitherto a remote and holy Other and lost as in Jesus' day in an ecclesiastical labyrinth with narrow lines of dogma, liturgy and hierarchy. Their battles would bring liberation for the equally hidden Jesus and his central message of the Kingdom now spiritually invading the present age to conquer the Beast.

What did Jesus mean to Fox and his fellow Quakers? Maurice Creasey pointed out that the connection between the Jesus known by tradition (the 'historical Jesus') and that known by revelation (Jesus as cosmological, pre-existent Spirit) they left unexamined.[6] It seems the majority of Friends were content to hold both these understandings together existentially. In other words, while following the movement's leadership in emphasising the spiritual import of Jesus' virgin birth, miracles, suffering, resurrection and ascension, they also considered themselves in a relationship with Jesus the man, and his witness and teaching. Clearly for some Public Friends such as William Bayly, John Crook, Isaac Penington, George Whitehead, Humphry Wollrich, Margaret Fell and Fox, the spiritual or cosmological Jesus took precedent: 'We know no other Christ', wrote Penington, 'than that which died at Jerusalem, only we confess our chief knowledge of him is in Spirit'.[7] Probably inspired by Paul for whom the resurrection suggested exaltation in

---

[5] Farnworth and Nayler, *A Discovery of Faith*, 4. For wholeness and/or oneness see Fox, Eps. 25 (1653) and 73 (1654) in *LOGF*, 13, 33; Fox, *To All that would Know*, 3; Fell, *An Epistle to Friends by M.F.* (1654) in *Works*, 56-7 and *An Epistle of M. Fell to Friends ... Lancaster Castle* (1654) in *Works*, 59; see Nayler in *Saul's Errand*, 17; Fox and Nayler *et al*, *Several Papers*, 10.

[6] Creasey, *The Christ of History and of Experience*, unnumbered p. 9.

[7] Penington, *The Jew Outward*, 18. The Friends were not alone here: see the work of the Cambridge neo-Platonists Peter Sterry (1613-72), esp. his *The Appearance of God to Man* (1710), 15, 18, and Cudworth, *A Sermon Preached*, 15. Sterry was sympathetic to Quakerism. See Fell's *To the General Councel and Officers of the Army* (1659), 7: 'whosoever believes that Jesus is the Christ is born of God'. Here she writes of the *risen* Jesus, confirmation of which is found in the preceding sentences and in her letter to the 5th Monarchist, Maj.-Gen. Harrison, *This was given to Major-General Harrison and the Rest* (1660), 2-3.

heaven rather than bodily resuscitation, these Friends believed Jesus' body was the 'garment' of the Spirit. Bayly, for instance, emphasised a spiritual resurrection.[8]

That said, all seventeenth century Friends looked to Jesus as *the* example of a God-filled person who, by his love and witness, was humanity's true guide to God, an avenue to spiritual maturity and eternal life. The Light resided within Jesus in 'full measure' and he and the divine Light within him were best known in the silence. The silence gave space for a mystical relationship with the spiritual Jesus as the Word. The names they gave him, or by which they already knew him, tell us about their intimate relationship with this Jesus and the Kingdom, something we will examine in a few moments. Along with the Spirit, Jesus was understood as the Way of unity and truth between God and humanity, and similarly so among their community as they grew it, and as a shared path between it and 'all people'. Jesus the human being together with the Spirit (Christ) and the Kingdom were their 'rock' and 'foundation' which they would pass on to future generations. The Quakers understood 'rock' and 'foundation' from Matthew as being synonymous with 'Light' and 'Kingdom'.[9]

More profoundly, they linked Jesus to the memory and vitality of their own religious experiences and convincement. According to Keiser, the power of Jesus' revelation for Penington was 'to make [the Friends] aware of the indwelling presence of life in its potentiality within each of [them], and to draw it forth so as to pervade [their] lives'.[10] Jesus showed them the way to inner and outer peace, therefore, and how righteousness and justice were dynamically related. In giving humanity the path to the cross and reconciliation with God, they believed he '[took] away the sins of the world'.[11] Jesus and his Kingdom were the pillars of their Lamb's War, the outward result of their faith and hope in the Life and Power of Love. He inspired their understanding of 'church' and true (second) priesthood as well as prayer, obedience, humility, truth and gifts of prophecy.

---

[8] Bayly, *A Short Discovery*, 4 and *Deep Calleth unto Deep*, 26; Crook (and Penington), *Truth's Principles* (1662), 8-9; Penington, *An Echo from the Great Deep*, 32-3; *The Way of Life and Death*, 46; Humphry Wollrich (or Woollrych, *c.*1633-1707), *One Warning More* (1661), 6; G. Whitehead (and Burrough?), *Son of Perdition* (1661), 8. Also *FF*, 112-14 and see esp. Phil. 2: 5-11; Col. 1: 15-22; Rom. 1:3-4; 4:5; 6:4.

Creasey and Edward Grubb (Swarthmore Lecture, 1914) are agreed that these Friends were responsible, in part at least, for the uneasy 'split' among Quakers in the modern era crudely between those emphasising Jesus as God (and some regarding the Bible as the Word of God) and those preferring a Spirit or Light-orientated mysticism with Jesus as a prophet, guru or guide. See Creasey, *ibid.* and for Grubb's hostile stance *vis-à-vis* Penington's Christology see his Lecture, *The Historic and Inward Christ*, 32-9.

[9] For "Foundation' and 'Rock'": Mt. 7:20-25; 16:18-19.

[10] *KMOLW*, 250.

[11] Fox, Ep. 79 (1654) in *Works*, 7:89.

Chapter 8: 'Of the Nature of Christ Jesus'

Through Jesus, the marriage of human and divine history, the Second Coming and the Spirit's unconditionality to time and space became realities. They associated him with their own sonship and daughtership in God, with perfection and purity, good works, spiritual authority, freedom and freewill and, crucially, with the unity of their movement and its manner of worship.[12] There could be no question, therefore, of any dissociation from the human Jesus; but it was an accusation that came their way from many an enemy nevertheless[13]:

> And [wrote Penington] as Christ said in the days of his flesh, that the way to know his Father, was to know him; and that he that knew him, knew the Father also. So we now witness, that the way to know Christ is to know the Spirit; and that he that knows the Spirit, knows Christ also, with whom Christ is one, and from whom he cannot be separated.[14]

Because Jesus was pivotal to their community as guide and anchor, he and the Spirit in him were described as the 'king, prophet and high priest' of a nonviolent Way.[15] He was their Teacher, the Truth, the Seed, the Light, the Power, the Messiah, the Son of God, Son of Man, the Servant, the Way to God, the Voice, Witness, Gospel, the living Word (as opposed to the biblical word), the Life and Name.[16] 'Voice' underlined the intimacy and

---

[12] For 'sons and daughters of God' see for example Fox, *The Law of God the Rule for Lawmakers* (1658), 4.

[13] Such as that from Independent Thomas Weld and his Newcastle colleagues. See Weld *et al*, *The Perfect Pharisee* (1653), 8-9 ('position 5'), an attack on *Saul's Errand*. Weld was answered by Nayler in *A Discovery of the Man of Sin* (1654).

[14] Penington, *The Jew Outward*, 18; see esp. 'Answer 2'.

[15] Calvin said the same thing; see the 1936 edn. of the *Institutes*, i., Bk. 11 (chp. 15), 540-1 quoted in T. C. Jones, *George Fox's Teaching*, 40.

[16] Fox, Ep. 71 (1654) in *Works*, 7: 82. See *Cambridge* ii., 393. Other titles included Altar, Bishop, Brother, Captain, Commander, Counsellor, Ensign, Foundation, Friend, Gospel, Justifier, Law-giver, the Life, Living Path Out of Death, Orderer, Prophet, Redeemer, Rock, Sacrifice, Sanctifier, Shepherd. Pickvance isolated 60 titles from the *Journal*, which he says is 'an inadequate source for the study of this important element in Fox's teaching'. For many more names see Pickvance, *A Reader's Companion to George Fox's Journal*, 59-60. Kuenning has trawled the 8 vols. *Works* (1831) and maintains Fox used 'gospel' about 1,800 times. I agree with Kuenning that Fox equated 'gospel' with the 'power of God' (429 times according to Kuenning). Fundamentally for Fox, 'gospel' = Light = Life = Truth = Seed etc. = Christ within = Kingdom. See Kuenning, 'Fox's Message was not about a Message', 22. Barclay in *Apology*, 108 said that 'gospel' also meant the 'saving spiritual Light' and the 'inward power of life' (metaphors for the Kingdom). See also W. Smith, *The Morning Watch*, 11-12. For 'Messiah' see Bishop, *Jesus Christ, the Same Today*, 20; Fox, *A Visitation to the Jews* (1656), 21; Perrot, *A Visitation of Love* (1658), 19; Fox, *A Declaration to the Jews* (1661), title pg., 3. See also Cope, 'Seventeenth-Century Quaker Style' in Fish (ed.), 206.

immediacy of God, the Friends' vocation as prophets and how the Spirit 'could be known in the measure' in which Christians knew it in 'the time of the apostles'.[17] In the seventeenth century, 'Name' theologically signified an object of devotion but also, as in the Hebrew and Christian Testaments, something of the essential nature of a person. When Fox used phrases such as 'in the Name of Jesus' or 'but by the Name of Jesus is salvation brought', he and other Friends, probably with the Prologue of John's Gospel and Revelation 19 in mind, were steering people towards the possibility of spiritual completeness through the power of the Word. Happiness would follow only when one was in this Power, Light, Life and Truth—that is, in the glory or beauty of Love itself. Only then, for instance, would prayer have authenticity. The 'Name' (or Light, Christ, Life), which existed before Jesus, was seen to challenge Puritans and others to

> feed upon the milk of the Word, that was before tongues, . . . you must go before Babel and Babylon was (i.e. confusion) . . . up into the Word Christ, whose name is called the Word of God.[18]

We can see from their various names for Jesus how they attributed a cosmological dimension to him—the (eternal) Word, the (pre-existent) Light—which they also gleaned from John's Gospel. And like John it was to the eternal Christ the Friends ultimately turned and absorbed. In a 1654 epistle, Fox urged his fellow Quakers to accept this Christ into their 'flesh and bone', that is, to live 'in the Life (Christ)', the parenthesis being his.[19]

The Christ who was in Jesus could fulfil within *them* the symbols, leadings and prophecies of the Hebrew tradition. In other words, the fulfilment Jesus brought to the old Law could be known within each truly convinced Friend—that is, the spiritualisation of Hebraic theocratic ideas of kingship and what this meant for their transformation into a merciful Kingdom.[20] 'If I cannot witness Christ nearer than Jerusalem', Nayler said at his Appleby trial in 1653, 'I shall have no benefits by him; but I own no other Christ but that who witnessed a good confession before Pontius Pilate;

---

[17] See Pickvance, *George Fox on the Light of the Christ Within*, 17-21, and esp. 19.

[18] *Journal*, 11-12. See W. Smith, *The Morning Watch*, 11-12; Crook (and Penington), *Truth's Principles*, 8-9; Howard, *A Few Plain Words of Instruction* (1658), 18, all quoted in Cope, 'Seventeenth-Century Quaker Style' in Fish (ed.), 204-9; see esp. 206. For 'the Light before Jesus' see 1 Cor. 10:4 and Prologue to John.

[19] Fox, Ep. 71 (1654) in *Works*, 7: 82. For 'flesh and bone' in this context see Heb 2:11; Eph. 5:30.

[20] For Jesus' spiritualised fulfillment of the Law as the Kingdom and proclaimed at Capernaum see Meyer, 'The Relation of the New Testament to the Mosaic System', 143-4. Though not addressing Quaker ideas, Meyer unwittingly captured the spirit of early Quaker internalisation.

which Christ I witness in me now.'[21] There was an immediacy, an immanence, to this Jesus, but he was not exclusive to the Friends. Existentially, like his Kingdom, he was *in* everybody, though he awaited unveiling which came primarily through individual convincement. They also sought to emulate the existential bond between Jesus and the Kingdom, a bond that was a fulfilment of the Judaic idea of kingship and the gift from which the Quakers' Lamb's War emerged. Critical of first-century Jews for refusing salvation through Jesus, they saw themselves as Jews of the New Israel.[22] Thus, they were inextricably bound up with Jesus who was not merely historical but also spiritual and cosmological with saving (soteriological), hope-filled (eschatological) and revelatory (apocalyptic) powers.

Fox's own Christology derived from the intense certainty of his oneness with both the temporal and spiritual Jesus who had, Damascus style, spoken 'to his condition' in *c.* 1647.[23] Here Jesus was alive to him; the Light offered salvation from sin. Similar experiences of the 'Christ within' were recorded by many Friends and, like Fox, they found in Paul a significant influence for their respective ministries. According to Edward Grubb, Paul himself had owed much,

> to the inward teaching of his master's Spirit—of the pre-existence of Christ: that the historical life of Jesus on earth was the manifestation in a real human personality of an eternal Spirit, who was (to use a Pauline expression) the 'image' of God'.[24]

Grubb continued:

> Paul's main interest was neither speculative nor historical: he does not dwell on his theory of Christ, and has little to say about his life or teaching: what he is mainly concerned to do is to bring out the new life of sonship with God into which Christ raises the believer by leading him into a 'mystical union' with Himself. It is the inward or spiritual side that mainly interests Paul.[25]

Fox had a deep love for Jesus and his meaning for humanity, although I agree with Jerry Frost that, when echoing Christian orthodoxy, his preaching downplayed the historical Jesus and the trinity, stressing instead

---

[21] Nayler, 'The Examination of James Nayler' in *Saul's Errand*, 32. Also Lampen, *Wait in the Light*, 44.
[22] Penington, *The Jew Outward, passim* and Rom. 2:29.
[23] For immediate experience of Jesus and Christ see 1 Cor. 3:11; Col.1:27.
[24] For Fox's use of 'image of God' see *Journal*, 27-8, 39, 367-8. Also see Rom. 8:29.
[25] Grubb, *The Historic and Inward Christ*, 17.

the heavenly and inward Christ.[26] Fox normally avoided propositions about Jesus' nature since details about his life were of less concern to him than faith in the Christ *in* Jesus *and the Kingdom that Jesus had proclaimed*. For Fox, Jesus 'encompassed all aspects of human spiritual experience', writes Arthur Roberts, and he fulfilled 'all the covenants of God with Israel and all other people'. While religion may have been a worldwide phenomenon like the Roman Church, only the Christ possessed true universality with the power to link all people through his 'body'.[27]

The Friends craved to free this Christ from deadening outer forms of worship and Church organisation and governance so that people could experience the immediacy of the human-God relationship without impedimenta of any kind. Their hope was that the saving effects of Jesus' life would be incarnated in all.[28] We have seen in Chapter 5 why they felt compelled to confront the 'hireling priesthood' and the tithing system that upheld it. The Word, after all, was to be freely available to all and was not for hire.[29] They also registered dismay that Jesus, *the* reference for God, and his Kingdom, were trapped within the covers of a Bible whose many translations rendered it historically unreliable. It was a mere book, the Friends claimed, its words compiled by fallible, albeit inspired, human beings. We have observed how Fisher's *Rusticus ad Academicos* has been recognised as a devastating indictment of bibliolatry, the religious fashion of the times.[30]

Fox and such Friends as Burrough believed that the body in which Jesus died at Jerusalem not only 'filled all things' (including themselves as the saints) but that it had existed from all eternity.[31] It is important to note that in the seventeenth century the word 'body' could mean 'person' or

---

[26] Manning, in his 'Accusations of Blasphemy', 33, seems to suggest a full docetism: [For the Quakers] 'Christ [in this case Jesus] was wholly supernatural and provided a uniquely spiritual soteriology.' However, docetism maintains that Jesus was human in appearance only, having no real human nature but a wholly spiritual one. He suffered in appearance only, not in reality.

[27] Frost, 'Review of . . . Ingle, L., *First Among Friends*', 294. See *Journal*, 5-6; *AOTW*, 95; Roberts, 'The Universalism of Christ', 5. Also Josiah Coale (1633-69), *The Whore Unvailed* (1665), 8 in which Coale acknowledges the true Church as universal/catholic but denies the universality of the Roman Church as insufficient grounds for *its* claim to be the true Church.

[28] *AOTW*, 93.

[29] Farnworth and Nayler, *A Discovery of Faith*, esp. 10-12.

[30] For an acknowledgment of Fisher's skill see *TWTUD*, 266-8. In 'Christ's Light Springing' in *Rusticus ad Academicos*, Fisher comments that, 'dark minds diving into the Scripture divine lies enough out of it to set whole countries in fire' (*Works*, 781). On p. 294 he says Christians were not 'to stand fast in . . . the bare Bible itself' and on p. 45: 'none can walk in the letter till they walk in the Spirit . . . It is the Spirit of Christ, and the Light, that is both the creator and preserver, the author and finisher of the faith'. See also Fox and Nayler, *Saul's Errand*, 8.

[31] Kuenning, *The Bunyan-Burrough Debate*, 181.

Chapter 8: 'Of the Nature of Christ Jesus'

'individual', and the three could be theologically interchanged. When using 'body' and 'person'—as in the dispute, for instance, between Burrough and John Bunyan—the Friends referred to the *essence* of Jesus, that which was *one in substance and indivisible* that had come from 'heaven' (God) and had returned there.[32] An example is found in Fox's 1667 dispute with Lodowick Muggleton:

> If the being of Christ, or his essence, or nature, or power be not in you which is in the saints, and was revealed in the apostles, that spoke in the person of Christ [i.e. in the essence of Jesus], you have manifested yourself to be no minister of him.[33]

This 'body', therefore, was not corporeal but spiritual and glorious. In other words, the carnal body of Jesus died but the Christ, the divine essence in him, could not.[34] In a 1675 tract with a 1650s theology written from Worcester gaol, *A Testimony of what we Believe of Christ*, Fox wrote,

> For natural knows not the things of God, and carnal is sold under sin as the Apostle tells you. And is not human from the ground? But does not Christ say he is from above? The second man is the Lord from heaven, and his body is a *glorious body*, and he is the *heavenly spiritual man* [Fox's emphases].[35]

Fox's *Catechism for Children* (1657, 1660) and *A Testimony of the True Light* (1657) are typical of the later 1650s Quaker tracts in that they are straight-forward devotions to the universal Light of Christ rather than to the historical Jesus whose words (along with the apostles) 'were declared forth from the Light'.[36] Analysing tracts published in 1657 and 1658, Rosemary Moore noticed how only six focussed on the atoning death of Jesus while 35 continually interchanged 'Christ' and 'Light'. This is amply demonstrated in Fox's *The Pearl Found in England* where 'the drama of salvation, based on a real historical happening for most contemporaries, was internalised by

---

[32] For this dispute see Burrough, *The True Faith of the Gospel of Peace*, 12; *Truth (the Strongest of All)*, 20, 56 and Bunyan, *Some Gospel Truths Opened* (1656). Also Kuenning, *The Bunyan-Burrough Debate*, *passim*.
[33] Fox, *Something in Answer to Lodowick Muggleton's Book* (1667), 14.
[34] See Cooper, *A Living Faith*, 42-3.
[35] Fox, *A Testimony of what we Believe of Christ*, 86-7. The work was published in 1677. Fox's objection that 'human' (in describing Jesus) was unscriptural is correct. See also Bishop, *A Treatise Concerning the Resurrection* (1662), *passim* but esp. 9-12.
[36] See Appendix 6. Fox, *A Testimony of the True Light*, 42, 46. Burrough provided the preface in which his 'Christ Jesus' was spiritual which 'John bore witness of'; see Sig. A2. Also Fox, *The Unmasking and Discovery of Anti-Christ* (1653), 1.

[him] to the point that the historical Jesus was almost an irrelevance'.[37] For polemical reasons the Friends de-emphasised Jesus the man because they were forced to defend their understanding of the Light. Nevertheless, from the late 1650s their preference in any case was to speak of the Light of Christ.[38]

A concentration on the Christ or Light is evident among other leading Friends such as in George Whitehead's *The Path of the Just Cleared* (1655) and *Jacob Found in a Desert Land* (1656). The same emphasis continues in his *The Seed of Israel's Redemption* (1659) and *The Son of Perdition Revealed* (1661), the latter co-authored with Edward Burrough. Burrough's own *A Description of the State and Condition of all Mankind* (1656) and *A Standard Lifted Up* (1657) emphasise the eternal Christ over the man Jesus but infer that Jesus' incarnate deeds were a pointer to salvation in God.[39] In these tracts Christ is no less cosmological than in Nayler's *Love to the Lost* (1656) which typically stresses Christ as being 'without beginning of days... of whose dominion there is no end'.[40] Tellingly, such theology was not limited to the middle and later years of the decade. It had surfaced as early as 1653 in *Saul's Errand* as well as in Fox's seminal *To All that would*

---

[37] *FFQ*, 228, 262; *TLITC*, 107; R. Moore quotes *Pearl*, 4: 'Come hither... discovers as you walk in the light'. And see her chapter 8, 'Serious Theology' and Cooper, *A Living Faith*, 42. Rachel Hadley King found that Fox linked the Light to God twenty times but related it to Jesus 112 times. But, we may ask, to what 'Jesus' does she refer? She does not satisfactorily account for the fluidity of Fox's language or that of the Friends generally, or the ramifications this had for Quaker Christology (and continues to have). See her *George Fox and the Light Within*, *passim* and esp. 87. See Appendix 6.

[38] See T. C. Jones, *George Fox's Teaching*, 183.

[39] G. Whitehead (and Burrough?), *The Son of Perdition*, *passim*; *The Path of the Just Cleared* (1655), 4; *Jacob Found in a Desert Land* (1656), 14; *The Seed of Israel's Redemption* (1659), 33-4. However, Melvin Endy writes,

> When pressed by opponents about his failure to mention the historical Christ, Burrough admitted that the Christ he had been referring to was the same as the one who had died at Jerusalem and risen again, making it clear that he took the Gospels literally, but his admission did not imply that Christ's incarnate deeds were essential to salvation.

Endy refers to the two Burrough tracts I also mention. I cannot see how Burrough takes the Gospels literally; he merely says Jesus died at Jerusalem. The evidence Endy quotes from Burrough's *Works* (pp. 117-20, 243-53 and 440) also do not support his view that Burrough's 'admission did not imply that Christ's incarnate deeds were essential to salvation' which, as I understand it, implies a dissociation of the man Jesus and the spiritual Christ; see his 'Puritanism, Spiritualism and Quakerism', unnumbered p. 10 (online version).

[40] *Love to the Lost* devotes slightly over three pages to the eternal pre-existent Christ; see 56-9 and esp. 56. Also J. Whitehead (and Penington), *A Small Treatise* (1661), esp. 10: 'Christ, the eternal Life and Light... the Word that lives and abides for ever'. And *TLITC*, 291 (18*n*).

Chapter 8: 'Of the Nature of Christ Jesus'

Know the Way to the Kingdom and Nayler's *A Lamentation*. In both, the Kingdom, with the Christ at its helm, was spiritual only.[41]

This emphasis permeated the movement's leadership in its most formative days and in other individuals well before Firbank Fell. Sarah Jones' *This is Light's Appearance* (1650), for example, does not mention Jesus but understands the eternal Christ instead as 'the living Word of God'.[42] If the Friends, as some believe, were Light-mystics it was because they were, more accurately, Christ- or Kingdom-mystics where 'Christ' and 'Light' were predicated on the historical Jesus as a 'type'.

Their worship of Christ as the Light or Word, their equally intimate relationship between the Spirit and their vision of the Jesus Way, and the zeal with which they put into practice what they preached, all came together to form a revolutionary theology. To this may be added, as we shall see shortly, a deeper awareness of the spiritual Jesus as a cosmological reality full of eschatological hope. Hailing mostly from practical backgrounds like farming, weaving and shopkeeping[43], and reacting strongly to the otherworldliness of the Church, its corruption and lack of experiential knowledge of the Inward Light, this hope would be grounded in the everyday. Consequently, because they never divorced themselves from the *actuality* of Jesus and his fleshly life, they refuted any idea he was a mere example or guide in the figurative sense. This was a common criticism and it came from such clerics as the Independent Thomas Weld from Newcastle-upon-Tyne. Rather, Jesus was an example by virtue of his deeds and teaching, in the way he suffered and in the manner of his death for the Kingdom, for Love (God).[44]

To the early Quakers, this fleshly Jesus was united to the Spirit—they 'answered' each other. Underwood tells us that for the Friends, 'the outward, physical work of Christ [i.e. Jesus] in the past was of little consequence without an inward, spiritual experience of Christ [i.e. the spiritual Jesus] in the present'.[45] If one was deprived of the other, their belief and faith were radically diminished. It was the task of all people to 'enter' into this experience and, if need be, to suffer the consequences. Such a mutual identification would signal the eventual end of Babylon's empire (chaos, Mammon) and its oppression. It would also signal the end of the world—that is, the end of the old Law—and a welcoming of the new covenant of the Kingdom within and among the saints. Justice, peace and

---

[41] Fox and Nayler *et al*, *Saul's Errand*, 16; Fox, *To All that would Know, passim*; Nayler, *A Lamentation*, 3, 9. See also Fox, *The Unmasking and Discovery of Anti-Christ, passim*.
[42] S. Jones, *This is Light's Appearance*, 3.
[43] See Forde, *Derbyshire Quakers*, 228-9.
[44] Weld, *The Perfect Pharisee*, 8-9 ('position 5').
[45] Underwood, 'Early Quaker Eschatology' in Toon, *Puritans, The Millennium*, 96; *EQW*, 26.

compassion would then have their victory, a victory for which the Lamb's War demanded their own unity and theological cohesion.

In this way, the Friends replicated Pauline mysticism whose essential feature was the unity of all who shared the new life in Christ Jesus, that is, unity as a movement acting as one person *in* the *spiritual* Jesus who, as Fox said, 'was come and coming' 'to teach his people himself', he 'who is without beginning of time, or end of days'.[46] Anyone *in* this Jesus was 'in the Life', *in* a 'Jesus' distinct from the historical figure who himself was vital, as I have stressed before, as an ideal or 'type'. In being one with the Spirit they, too, would automatically be one with the earthly Jesus. The historical 'facts' of Jesus' life, then, were symbolic of an inner experience.[47] He was an element of, and conduit for, the Light, he who 'made manifest the true Light', which, according to John 1: 9, en-Lightened everybody that came into the world.[48] In this way, the spiritual Jesus (God) was their anchor, focus, power and source of hope and 'cheer' (i.e. courage).

Underlying Whitehead's argument, which mirrored Burrough's dispute with Bunyan, was the Friends' conviction that the Christ or Spirit in Jesus, in themselves and in all people was beyond time and space—as Howgill said, 'immortal', 'spiritual', 'eternal' but 'not carnal'.[49] Hence, there could be no distinction between the eternal Christ *per se* and the eternal Christ in Jesus or any other human being. And because it was 'above' temporal limitations, the Word-Spirit-Christ-Light-Kingdom was available to every single person now and in the future as it had been in the past. But more: it was intrinsic to their very humanity and had the potential to be manifest in their flesh.[50] In believing the Spirit had taken over Jesus' 'prepared' body, the wonderful result being the depth and quality of his compassion and the Kingdom, the Friends could never deny that the Christ had 'come' in the flesh or that it would cease to do so, *though it awaited incarnation or resurrection through convincement*. Here was the source of the Quakers' confidence in forging Testimony and conducting the Lamb's War for salvation. As Howgill knew, 'the Spirit of God [was] operative and work[ed] a change in the ground'.[51] Therefore, no physical Second Coming was needed except on an inner level for those who had not yet undergone convincement.

Their detractors' confusion over Quaker Christology may have resulted from what we have encountered before—'scriptural politics'. It will be

---

[46] *Journal*, 283.
[47] For 'being as one person in the spiritual Jesus': Gal. 3:28; Jn. 1: 4, 9.
[48] See Nayler, 'Concerning Christ Jesus' in *Love to the Lost*, 56. And Rom.1: 9-10, 3:24, 6:23; Ph. 2: 5; Kourie, 'Christ-mysticism in Paul', 73.
[49] See Howgill, *The Inheritance of Jacob Discovered*, 11.
[50] See Gal. 4:19.
[51] Howgill, *ibid*., 27.

remembered that (according to Katz) the Bible provided a 'secret language' that only needed invoking to be understood, and that partial biblical phrases and a sanctified word or two often conveyed hidden, coded or, more accurately, synecdochic messages with the stamp of divine authority. They were 'coded' to avoid as much as possible the government censor and/or imprisonment. The Quakers certainly engaged in 'scriptural politics' of this nature, though not deceitfully. It amounted to a subtle form of rhetoric and polemics with a generous dose of metaphor as we saw earlier in this chapter and in Chapter 4.[52] This was normal for their times and some examples from the Friends will help us.

George Whitehead in *The Path of the Just Cleared*, for example, reiterated the constant Quaker refrain that the eternal Word existed 'before Abraham was'. He stated that:

> Christ we own and witness . . . who was in the beginning which was the Word by which all things were made, which Word became flesh and dwelt among the disciples and suffered at Jerusalem . . . and [was] put to death concerning the flesh but is raised up by the Spirit and ascended into glory.[53]

'Concerning the flesh', though seemingly innocent in this context, makes room for Jesus' body to act as a conduit for the Word. Rosemary Moore noted that the 'resurrection' and 'ascension' in the quote appear to be spiritual.[54] I agree, and we meet the same elsewhere—for instance, in George Bishop's understanding of the resurrection which he penned in 1661/2. Confirming Quaker belief in the fate of the historical Jesus, Bishop wrote,

> But as for flesh, blood and bones; that is to say, that which being in the world is maintained or lives by that which is of the world, as meat, drink &c., that is not suitable to the estate of a spirit or of a spiritual body, nor a thing to be conceived as in the resurrection. For Paul, speaking of the resurrection said, 'It is sown a natural body, it is raised a spiritual: there is a natural body and there is a spiritual body', 1 Cor. 15:44.[55]

---

[52] Katz, *God's Last Words*, 40-1.
[53] G. Whitehead in *The Path of the Just Cleared*, Sig. A2.
[54] *TLITC*, 221-2.
[55] Bishop, *A Treatise Concerning the Resurrection*, 9-12 and esp. 9. See also Bayly, *Deep Calleth Deep*, 26.

As for Nayler, the Appleby trial was convened primarily to examine whether or not he denied the historical Jesus. The trial is crucial for Quaker theology and our understanding of the early movement's Christology. Arraigned before Anthony Pearson, he affirmed Quaker belief in Jesus as a man but laid emphasis on the unity between Jesus and the Spirit/God as *the* inspiration for unity between God and humanity. This unity could be enacted in the present with the help of the same Spirit that was in Jesus. For Nayler, too, Jesus' body had been 'taken over' by the Christ/Spirit:

Pearson: 'Christ was man or no?'
Nayler: Yes, he was, and took upon him the seed of Abraham, and was real flesh and bone; but [it] is a mystery not known to the carnal man; for he is begotten of the immortal seed, and those that know him know him to be spiritual; for it was the Word that became flesh and dwelt among us; and if he had not been spiritual he had not wrought my redemption.'
Pearson: Is Christ in you as man?
Nayler: Christ fills all places and is not divided; separate God and man and he is no more Christ [1 Cor: 1:13] . . . The ministers affirm Christ [Jesus] to be in heaven with a carnal body, but I with a spiritual.[56]

Just as in *The Boaster Bared* (1655) where he described a pre-incarnate spiritual body of which people were to partake, Nayler was not saying the physical Jesus was God but that Jesus was aware of the divinity he carried inside him and that *that* divinity was the Word.[57] Nayler was emphasising the spiritual Jesus because the time for the outward was past and the task now for men and women was to deepen their faith by relying on the inward testimony. As in John, therefore, the *Word* in Jesus was God, Jesus being the *way* to God, the Truth and the Life, in the manner in which he gave the Word its fullest and unifying expression so far. The key to love and unity among Friends and all God's creatures, Nayler was saying, was to dwell in the Light of Christ, the spiritual Jesus, the Word. Any separation among

---

[56] Nayler, 'The Examination of James Nayler' in *Saul's Errand*, 31 and *Works*, 13. It was as a result of Nayler's evidence that Pearson was soon convinced; see Also 'Concerning Justification' in *Love to the Lost*, 50-2. The importance of the Pearson-Nayler interchange has only been acknowledged, I believe, by Grubb in his *The Historic and Inward Christ*, 36-9. Levy in his *Blasphemy* mentions it in relation to his subject; see Levy, 180, but beware his mistaken assertion of 1650s Quaker antinomianism. Also my *GADOT*, 21, 46, 51, 64, 91 and *MOP*, Chp. 2, p. 26, Chp. 5, p. 101. For the 'Christ is not divided' see also Bishop, *The Throne of Truth* (1657), 66 and Francis Higginson's *A Brief Reply*, 48; see also Higginson's work for a fuller (more accurate?) account of the Appleby trial, pp. 53-7, 69-73.

[57] Dewsbury, *Christ Exalted, passim*; Burrough, *A Declaration To all the World of our Faith* (1657), 2-3; Bishop, *A Treatise Concerning the Resurrection*, 5-8. See Feullenbach, *The Kingdom of God*, 86.

Chapter 8: 'Of the Nature of Christ Jesus'

God's children or between God and humanity was an utter scandal, indeed blasphemy. Here he was at one with Paul: when authentically in the Word, division and imperfection were impossible.[58]

Correspondingly in 1652, Fox, when answering the claim that he professed unity with God and was thus divine, told the magistrates that while in such a state he spoke as George Fox but that 'the Father and the Son [Fox in this case] is one: I and my Father are one'. 'Outside' the Christ, the carnal George Fox was the same flawed individual as anybody else.[59] Nayler would say the same at his trial in Bristol in 1656. Both were expressing Pauline orthodoxy. For Paul, Jesus was the Son of God and they who shared his life shared his sonship.[60] Consequently, to the question, 'Are you the everlasting Son of God?', Nayler reportedly replied that any in whom Christ dwelt was the everlasting son, 'and I do witness God in the flesh; I am the Son of God and the Son of God is but one'.[61] Meaning, Jesus was the only Son of God and the Son was 'but one' dwelling in many. Because Jesus was subject to carnal flesh, his body died as every body does.

The Friends were aware that Jesus chose to demonstrate his authority by means of his understanding of the Hebrew prophetic tradition and fulfilling that tradition's partial success by transforming Hebrew kingship into Kingdom. Thus in Luke 4:18, in which he began his ministry by heralding the Kingdom as a present reality, the Quakers saw that Jesus, in quoting Isaiah 61:1, knew how,

> The Spirit of the Lord is upon me, because he has anointed me to preach the gospel to the poor; he has sent me to heal the broken-hearted, to preach deliverance to the captives, and recovering of sight to the blind, to set at liberty them that are bruised.[62]

---

[58] Nayler, *The Boaster Bared* (1655), 6 in which Nayler probably refers to Jn. 3:13 and Eph. 4:10. See also Underwood, *Primitive*, 43 and 140 (34*n*) in which he cites G. Whitehead (and Burrough?), *Son of Perdition*, 10; they quote Eph. 5:30 wrongly as 5:13.

[59] *Saul's Errand*, 5-6. We have seen how Fox was still saying the same in 1667 to Lodowick Muggleton.

[60] See Hincks, 'The Apostle Paul's Mysticism', 327.

[61] See Levy, *Blasphemy*, 186; Anon, *Memoirs of the Life . . . Nailor* (1719), 29; William Grigge, *The Quakers Jesus* (1658), 5; Ralph Farmer, *Satan Inthroned in his Chair* (1657), 14; John Deacon, *The Grand Impostor* (1656), 14-15; see also Deacon, *Nayler's Blasphemies Discovered* (1657), *passim*. Like Farmer, Deacon was a rabid anti-Quaker and one of the Bristol magistrates who cross-examined Nayler. The same 'Son of God' controversy arose earlier in Lancaster, 1652; see Nayler's reply to Thomas Weld in *The Discovery of the Man of Sin*, 14-15.

[62] For early Quaker awareness of Jesus' understanding of the Hebrew prophetic tradition see H. Smith's *The True and Everlasting Rule*, 6.

For the Friends, the task of fulfilling the Law—in this sense initiating the new covenant—required yielding to the Light so that they may unite with the Kingdom as Jesus united with the Word. Often speaking of the Light as the Law, the Quakers looked to the Kingdom to sustain their own authority as prophets of the New Israel, just as the proclamation of the Kingdom gave Jesus *his* authority, his sonship.[63] As with Jesus, this authority enabled them to be sons and daughters of God, a status underscored by their 'innocency'. Only in purity as a 'babe' could the Kingdom be authentically proclaimed within so that it could in turn empower others to share their (the Quakers') restored humanity which they achieved through convincement. Hence the importance of 'authentic' prayer as in William Smith's *A Manifestation of Prayer* (1663), a condemnation of the 'Church without' and its conventional prayer practices, worship and Prayer Book:

> and so the babe, begotten by the Spirit, prays in the Spirit, and receives from the Spirit, and is strengthened with the virtue of the Spirit; and this is true prayer, though never a word be spoken through utterance.[64]

Prayer was authentic only when uttered or experienced *in* the Spirit, only when it was *lived* in their minds, hearts and very 'flesh and bone', only when forgiveness was at its core thus ensuring inheritance of the Kingdom. And only in this way would integrity be guaranteed by opening oneself to God's grace.[65]

Cosmological Jesus

What has been described so far is a Christ (or Logos or Kingdom)-mysticism that allowed the first Quakers to hold the spiritual and physical Jesus in balance but with the fulcrum tilting decidedly towards the spiritual.[66] Writing apocalyptically and cosmologically to opponents in 1653, James Nayler declared:

---

[63] For the Light as the new Law (of the new covenant) see Fisher, *Rusticus ad Academicos*, 'The Fourth Apologetical', chp. 3, 94; Fox, *A Testimony of the True Light*, 15; Fox, 'Christ's Way and Judas' Way' in *The Second Covenant*, 20.
[64] See W. Smith, *A Manifestation of Prayer*, Bds., col. 2 for authentic prayer.
[65] *Journal*, 283. For the folly of inauthentic prayer, which Fox describes as hypocrisy and apostasy, see his *Something in Answer to the Old Common Prayer Book*, 5 and *A Declaration Concerning Fasting and Prayer*, 8.
[66] See *TLITC*, 109. Also Fox and Nayler, *A Word from the Lord, Unto all the Faithless Generation of the World* (1654), 3-5. And Ion, *The Theology of the Early Quakers*, 48 in which Ion quotes Penington's belief that 'Christ came as Jesus'. See Howgill in *Works*, 72 where he paraphrases Jn. 1: 8.

Chapter 8: 'Of the Nature of Christ Jesus'

where Christ is revealed and known, he is known to be spiritual, not carnal, not limited to one place, but fills heaven and earth, is all, and in all his, but not seen by the carnal man, though he be the light of the world; for the God of this world has blinded the eyes of the world, that they cannot see him, for he is a mystery to them.[67]

For the Friends, the cosmological Jesus of John—the Logos, the Truth, the Word, the Life, Light and Kingdom—could cut through ecclesiastical, liturgical and doctrinal barriers like a sword.[68] Being the Word or Wisdom, the interpretation of God to humanity, *this* Jesus gave eternal life with abounding generosity.[69] In *this* Jesus time was conquered; the Hebrew Testament and the Gospels were now understood as 'event' of which, again, *this* Jesus was its agent rather than its object. The Life, mentioned above, constituted the 'perfect Law of liberty', that is to say, a unity as understood in James 1:25: 'But who so looks into the perfect Law of liberty, and continues therein, he being not a forgetful hearer, but a doer of the work, this man shall be blessed in his deed'.[70] For the whole movement this unity was fundamental to the universal enactment of a Kingdom that was not an earthly, fixed state or an other-worldly phenomenon because the Light/Spirit they worshipped 'was activity [itself] in relation to the world'.[71]

But while their cosmological Jesus was never without reference to the earthly Jesus, it was the Light that had encompassed and transfigured him into the pre-existent Christ who was their ultimate authority. For Lydia

---

[67] Nayler, *A Discovery of the First Wisdom*, 20. For 'Christ is revealed and known' see Lk. 17:30; Rom. 1:17. See also Higginson, *A Brief Reply*, 48 for Nayler and the cosmological Jesus/the Christ.
[68] Fox, *An Epistle to all People on the Earth*, 2, 4, 6.
[69] For 'Being the Word': Jn. 1:14; 'Wisdom': Jm. 3:17; 'eternal life': Jn.5: 24; 'abounding generosity': Jn.10:10. For Seuse (Suso), the medieval mystic, Christ was also Eternal Wisdom; see his *Horologium Sapientiae* published in English by Caxton in 1491, and Newman, 'Henry Suso', 3. The early Friends were not to know that Jesus was mentioned twice as Sophia, i.e. as personified Wisdom, in *Q*; their instincts were correct in this respect however. Wells notes that 'it is interesting that the *Q* source material of Matthew and Luke, as a sayings source, resembles the Wisdom books. In what is thought to be some of the very earliest Christian testimony available to us, the *Q* source sees Jesus (together with John the Baptist) as child and emissary of Wisdom (Lk. 7: 35 = Mt. 11: 19). Especially in Matthew, we find Jesus identified as the pre-existent Hokmah/Sophia. See Wells, 'Trinitarian Feminism: Elizabeth Johnson's Wisdom Christology' (rev. art.), 335 and Freyne, 'The Galilean Jesus', 293-6.
[70] For 'perfect Law of liberty' see Fisher, *Rusticus ad Academicos*, 'The First Apologetical', chp. 4, 129; Penington, *The New Covenant of the Gospel*, 31-2 and a later work by Fell, *A Call unto the Seed of Israel* (1668), 18.
[71] Tim Peat in Dandelion *et al*, *Heaven on Earth*, 64. He cites, for instance, 2 Cor. 5:19; Gal. 3:26; 5:16. See also Creasey, 'The Quaker Interpretation of the Significance of Christ', 5.

Fairman in 1659 it was *this* Light that existed 'before Jesus' and 'before Adam' which led,

> from under the powers of darkness of this world into . . . a Kingdom which hath no end; And Christ the Light he becomes their guide and leader, and in all truth they are led, and great is their peace.[72]

By 'he' we should not assume maleness but that which will always be manifest in time and yet beyond time—that is, the androgynous Christic function in Jesus as it worked *now* in those who turned authentically to the Light. In this way, Fairman underlined the early Quaker desire for an immediate, experiential knowledge of Jesus as the eternal Word. The new covenant of the Word went beyond gender, nationality, social position and the like. It was a guarantee of divine peace and justice, and of a knowledge that carried an automatic response in practical works of compassion. These, in turn, were a working reflection of the Sermon on the Mount which demonstrated love of one's neighbour. The early Friends believed that the Word *and* the resulting charitable works freed people from the bondage of Mosaic, and by implication Calvinist, legalism with their logic of inner violence and external destructiveness.[73] Through the eternal Christ they were gifted with an immediate, experiential understanding of what was required of themselves and others in giving birth to the Kingdom in their own time and in their own measure.[74]

Of the immanence Quakers felt in their religious experiences, of their relationship with the eternal Christ, the spiritual Jesus, Francis Howgill wrote:

> He is now in the world and this is he that convinces the world of sin, and shows you your evil deeds by his Light in your conscience; and as you wait upon that Light that is given from God, it will open your understanding, and let you see all that ever you have done, and will bring trouble upon you, and a true sensibleness of your condition, and

---

[72] Lydia Fairman, *A Few Lines Given Forth* (1659), Bds. For 'before Jesus was' and 'before Adam was': Fox and Nayler *et al*, *Several Papers*, 6; *Journal*, 98, 104; Mason, *A Check to the Lofty Linguist*, 10.

[73] For a succinct rendition of early Quaker thought on justification, righteousness and good works see 'The Difference betwixt the Faith which is Feigned' in Howgill, *A Lamentation for the Scattered Tribes* in *Works*, 78. Also Nayler, 'Concerning Good Works' in *Love to the Lost*, 30-1 and 'Concerning Righteousness' in *ibid*. in *Works*, 265-7.

[74] For simplicity and the Christ see Fisher, *Apokrypta*, 2; J. Whitehead (and Penington), *A Small Treatise*, 18.

will bring wrath upon that nature in you which is corrupt and contrary to the Light; for the Light is of the nature of Christ Jesus.[75]

Christ Jesus was already 'come' (returned) as the Light in one's conscience for salvation and everyone should welcome 'him'. In their yielding to the Light lay their initial testimony to the Life, their voluntary act of obedience that would bring them away from sin (separation).[76] Unlike the Puritans, the Friends believed that obedience did not entail a mindless subservience to an autocratic deity but an acknowledgment that only by a courageous acceptance of Love and its inherent unifying power would true freedom be experienced.[77]

Unity in the Spirit

'Love and unity with God and one with another' was so utterly basic to the Friends that 'running out', as they accused Nayler in 1656, was considered not only a monumental disloyalty to a movement that conceived itself as ordained of God but also an act of cowardice and deceit.[78] It was a spiritual crime and they had no doubt that backsliders were destined for perdition. Hell was not a physical place but the 'dark world', a spiritual void, a terrifying state of self-separation from Love where people were 'dead to God and alive to all evil'. For Samuel Fisher, hell was 'within the consciences of every malefactor'.[79]

Collectively and as individuals, the Quakers could be tough on anyone committing such an offence. The clue to this uncompromising position lay in their total commitment to the Kingdom. As it found expression initially on the individual level, its outward working in the world demanded the help and approval of the collective in their oft-chaotic times. And it is clear from

---

[75] Howgill, *A Lamentation for the Scattered Tribes*, 34. 'Convinces the world of sin' is a reference to Jn. 16:8. See also Lilburne, *The Resurrection*, 2 and Freiday, 'The Early Quakers and the Doctrine of Authority', 19.

[76] See Underwood, *The Controversy between the Baptists and the Quakers*, 84-5 for reference to Howgill's pre-Baptist understanding of the Light as mediator; see Howgill, *The Inheritance of Jacob Discovered*, 8. Lilburne's account of his convincement is found in *The Resurrection*. Also Dewsbury, *The Discovery of the Great Enmity*, 12; Farnworth, *The Heart Opened by Christ* (1655), 12; Bayly, 'Epistle to Friends' (n.d.), *Crosse MS*.

[77] See W. Smith, *A Manifestation of Prayer*, Bds.

[78] For 'Love and unity with God and one with another': Fox-Hubberthorne *et al*, *A Declaration from the Harmless*, 3. See also Fox, Ep. 4 (1652), *LOGF*, 2: Fell, 'Epistle to Friends, 1654' in *Works*, 53; W. Smith, *The New Creation*, 7, 8.

[79] S. Fisher, *Apokryta*, 21-2. The Quakers in this respect were similar to many Ranters. William Erbery, for instance, admonished Baptists for believing that heaven and hell were physical places, and for 'their fleshly apprehensions of Christ, and him crucified, of his coming and Kingdom, which your carnal misunderstandings represent unto men'. See Erbery, *The Testimony of William Erbery*, 127 also quoted in Underwood, *Primitivism*, 65.

their tracts and letters that the individual voice had in fact become an intrinsic part of their *collective* life even in the early years in the movement, by 1652-3 in fact.[80] Every Friend was expected to grasp the central reality that only the Spirit could bind them together in loving communion. Therefore, any deviation from themselves as an obedient community, a *Kingdom* community, was quickly condemned with the individual reproved or, in a few cases, cast out.[81] The latter rarely happened but the reaction of the Friends to Nayler immediately after Bristol, their initial failure to reach out in love to support him through his ordeal of torture and imprisonment, was emblematic of how seriously they regarded themselves collectively as the voice of God.

Thus the view was reinforced that only through their spiritual and visible unity as a movement would the Light be shared effectively throughout the world so that the Kingdom might be fully established. The bond that united them was the result of their love of, and loyalty to, the Spirit and the Kingdom as these were manifest in Jesus. False unity, such as a National Church advocated by Cromwell could only entrench apostasy, injustices, inequalities and violence. That kind of 'Church' was a mere chimera, doomed to chaos as Babylon of old. The Friends aimed instead at forging not only a unity of souls equal in the Spirit against the travails of the world, but also a dwelling 'in the Word' and 'in the cross' that would bring humanity 'to the beginning before wars was, working out that nature that occasions war'.[82] Theirs was an appeal as a 'remnant' to the nations so that their peoples may recognise and accept Christ Jesus, the one whose presence could be incarnate only through human beings working towards the Kingdom as agents of forgiveness, reconciliation, healing and mercy.[83]

Mercy/compassion was all-important to Fox who closely associated it with justice. In 1650 he wrote to his then small band of followers:

> Now love begets love, its own nature and image; and when mercy and truth do meet, what joy there is! Mercy does triumph in judgment; and love and mercy do bear the judgment of the world in patience.[84]

---

[80] Angell, 'The Rise of Elderism' in Angell (ed.), 1.

[81] For 'individual reproved . . . cast out': Mt. 8:12.

[82] See Fox and Nayler *et al*, *Several Papers*, 7. In this tract they use six metaphors for the Word—fire, hammer, sword, mouth of the Lord, Light and Lamb. Also Stevens, 'The Teaching of Jesus', 435.

[83] See references to the saved remnant in Rev. 12:17, 19:21; Ezk. 6:8; 14:22 and to the saving remnant in Deutero-Isaiah (Isa. 40:55).

[84] For 'agents of mercy': Mt. 25:34 and *Journal*, 13 and esp. 59 for 'Now love begets love' etc. Generally, Fox closely associated justice with mercy; see, for example, Ep. 43 (1653) in *Works*, 7: 51-3, 97-8, 104-5. He also wrote of a 'door of mercy' in Ep. 118 (1656), 7: 115. See Punshon, *Testimony and Tradition*, 9-15, esp. 11.

Chapter 8: 'Of the Nature of Christ Jesus'

He was certain that the immanence of God's presence, the ability and desirability to dwell *in* it but also to *live it*, *was* the merciful Kingdom of which Jesus had spoken and which would ever lead to a more fruitful manifestation.[85] In this way, the early Quakers saw themselves as God's declared will and only through the filter of the Jesus Way would the Light be universalised. So it was that the early Quakers were Christian universalists. It was the Light/Christ and the witness of the earthly Jesus that brought people into a unity that was utterly essential if humanity were to fulfil its inherently divine purpose. Consequently, Fox and Nayler proclaimed in 1654 that all they who 'are in the Light are in unity; for the Light is but one ... all who know the Word, which is a mystery, are come to the beginning, are sanctified by the Word.'[86]

I conclude this sub-section with a few words about the unity between the Friends and Jesus, and the Second Coming. We have seen how unity for the movement meant forging a special relationship with both the corporeal and spiritual Jesus. This unity always implied eschatological expectation. Adapting Hebrews 8:11, Fox preached that 'the Lord is coming to teach his people by his Spirit'. In stating such, he, like Paul, conveyed a belief that the Kingdom was revealed to everybody, that there was no need for its mediation by priests, liturgies or Bibles. At the same time, it was not theoretical: it could be encountered directly, experientially. By quoting Hebrews 9:11 he celebrated how 'Christ has come, high priest of good things already in being', something reiterated alongside the familiar 'Christ is come'.[87] Was it not, after all, in the nature of the Messiah to be ever present and yet ever coming? In other words, was not love and its promise of wholeness in God always available to those who would 'come to know the Substance'? By such statements Fox melded the present and future tense to reflect a holistic view of life towards which he directed the young movement for the hope-filled purpose of bringing humanity closer to its ultimate destiny with God.[88] The Quaker hope envisaged the unity of human and divine history as the loving Fulfilment.[89]

---

[85] For 'the Kingdom of which Jesus had spoken': Lk. 9:55; 17:20-21.
[86] Fox and Nayler *et al, Several Papers*, 6.
[87] For 'Christ is come': Jn. 3:31-32, 34.
[88] Fox and Nayler *et al, Several Papers*, 6. *Cf.* Fox's use of the future and present tense here with Paul's as in Heb. 8: 13: 'By speaking of a new covenant, he [i.e. Jesus] has pronounced the first one old; and anything that is growing old and ageing will shortly disappear'.
[89] See Firth and Rait, i., 1133-6. Also Levy, *Blasphemy*, 120-1. For Quaker-Puritan controversies see *TLITC*, chps. 7, 8 and *AOTW*, chp. 4.

The Second Coming: 'without respect of time, places or things'

We can see how the Friends' confidence in the presence of the Christ-*now* differed markedly from the Puritan view that Jesus would imminently return. It also differed from the wider Church generally, which anticipated the Second Coming at a more future date. While they consistently assured opponents of their belief in Jesus' incarnation, ministry, death, atonement, resurrection, ascension and glory—he 'in Jerusalem' whom the apostles 'handled, tasted and felt of the Word of life in them'—they affirmed these as spiritual realities as we have seen.[90]

On first reading, however, a number of their prominent tracts appear to predict a physical Second Coming.[91] Burrough's *A Declaration to all the World of our Faith* (1657), addressed to non-Quakers, reads like an orthodox Christian work with more than a hint of trinitarianism. It also appears to confirm the blood atonement:

> [Jesus] that was dead is alive and lives for evermore; and that he comes, and shall come again, to judge the whole world with righteousness, and all people with equity, and shall give to every man according to his deeds, at the day of judgment when all shall arise to *condemnation* or *justification*; he that hath done good shall receive Life, and he that hath done evil everlasting condemnation.[92]

---

[90] Burrough, *The True State of Christianity* (1658), 10; Bishop *et al*, 'To the Reader' in *The Cry of Blood* (1656), 2. See Dodd, *The Parables of the Kingdom*, esp. 34 and for the resurrection, atonement and ascension etc. as spiritual realities, 'all *within*', see Underwood, *Primitivism*, 34. Underwood's emphasis.

[91] Endy, 'Puritanism, Spiritualism', 292. See Burrough, *A Description of the State and Condition of all Mankind* (1657), Sig. A2; Blackborow, *The Just and Equal Balance Discovered* (1660), 4. Also Greaves and Zaller, *Biographical Dictionary of British Radicals*, i. 68.

[92] Burrough, *A Declaration To all the World of our Faith*, 2-3, 8. Burrough's emphasis. See also his *A Standard Lifted Up*, 5 and T. C. Jones, *George Fox's Teaching*, 252-3. In his introduction to G. Whitehead's *The Divinity of Christ* (1669), Fox agreed with Whitehead that Scripture did not represent God as three separate entities. They were one and inseparable but manifest in three. While Whitehead's pamphlet was published outside our period, Fox endorsed its 1650s theology. Meanwhile, Penington's *Examination of the Grounds and Causes* sums up the Fox-Burrough-Whitehead view: the Father, the Word and the Holy Spirit are 'distinct' as three beings or persons . . . but one . . . their wisdom one, their power one'.

According to Keiser, Fox and Friends were trinitarian but not in the doctrinal sense (i.e. mainline Church sense). 'Father', 'Son' and 'Holy Spirit' were used metaphorically 'rather than restricting their meaning to certain set acceptable ideas'. The divine Light within was like a 'Father and Son, and [was] a Spirit'. See Keiser, 'Christ in the Mesh of Metaphor' in Fager (ed.), 99. Paul of Tarsus, who much influenced the Friends, was not trinitarian. Belief in the trinity was compulsory under the Blasphemy Act (Long Parliament) May 1648; see Firth and Rait, *ibid*.

Chapter 8: 'Of the Nature of Christ Jesus'

A study of Burrough's work generally reveals another story. His purpose is always to portray the never-ending joy of being with God in an eternal now, the same God who is forever prepared to be with the truly convinced as Love, Justice, Peace, Mercy and Truth. For Burrough, the 'day of judgment' was the Kingdom or Light within all people that confronted their sin/separation. For many today, 'day of judgment' conjures up negative associations. However, while Friends like Burrough used 'judgment' frequently in the context of God's wrath for sin, they also linked it necessarily to the realities and demands of the *loving and just* Kingdom. God's 'wrath', that is, God's justice, love and power (the Light), awakes us to our sin so that we can confront it, thus ensuring freedom to enjoy God's purpose for ourselves and humanity.[93] Since the Kingdom was of divine Love, those who foolishly denied 'the Life' did an injustice to themselves through self-condemnation; 'destruction is of a man's self', wrote Burrough. One's spiritual welfare was a matter of personal responsibility, therefore, a view more Arminian than Calvinist.[94]

A Declaration to all the World also needs reading with an amillennial and historicist premillennialist eye both of which, it will be remembered, interpreted Jesus' reign as spiritual. Seen in this way, Burrough's statement above would have it that, as 'all people on the earth' consciously came to the already-revealed Second Coming as an *inner* reality and, in unity, undertook the peaceful responsibilities accompanying that inward acceptance, then a complete and joyous turning to the Light would automatically signal Jesus' return as a collective, metaphysical and cosmological reality, the Fulfilment.[95] The first Friends did not deny the futurity of the Spirit since the Kingdom awaited consummation in its fullness among all the nations of the earth. There is certainly a strong sense of the 'now' and 'not yet' in the Gospels and Pauline texts; Burrough and the leading Friends were imbued to some degree with the same.[96]

---

[93] Nayler, 'The Examination of James Nayler' in *Works*, 12.
[94] For personal responsibility for salvation see, for instance, Burrough's *A Declaration To all the World of our Faith*, 3 and J. Whitehead (and Penington), *A Small Treatise*, 6.
[95] Peat in Dandelion *et al*, *Heaven on Earth*, 238 draws the same, essentially Pauline, conclusion. See also Punshon's thoughts on this matter in *Reasons for Hope*, 300-26, esp. 311-12.
[96] See Fox, *News Coming up out of the North*, 27, 36; this is 'realised eschatology', a term coined by British theologian C. H. Dodd in *The Parables of the Kingdom* (1935) and reinforced in *The Interpretation of the Fourth Gospel* (1953), though a genesis of the term is found in H. Scott's work, 'The Teachings of Jesus' (1893); see Dodd (1935), 45, 50-1; Scott, 415 and K. Clark's 1940 commentary on Dodd's 1935 work in 'Realised Eschatology', *passim*. Abundant examples of realised eschatology exist among the prominent Friends but see H. Smith, *The Time and Everlasting Rule from God*, 36 and 70 and also J.G. (John Gibson?), *The Ancient of Days is Come* (1657).

Finally, their Christology invites a yet further understanding of their Second Coming theology. Through their convincement, Jesus' atonement was internalised. In other words, in crucifying their old self they allowed the Seed to resurrect and give new life and direction for attaining inner purity, an inner Eden. In this way, they were 'cleansed and forgiven' of their sin (i.e. separation, ignorance, disobedience). Importantly, they were certain that this state could not be achieved without the grace of God. If Jesus' sacrifice freed people from the bondage of sin it was because, more vitally, in dying for God's rule, *he died for Love*. Only within Love were God and humanity united, only in this unity was sin no more. The greater the Light within, and the more unity with God as a result, then the less hold sin had on the individual. That is to say, the Second Coming would now be indelibly and existentially of their 'flesh and bone' and through them, in accordance with the Light, it would become the Kingdom-in-action. The Kingdom was the very umbilical cord to God, the means by which the terror of the 'darkness' or the 'bottomless pit' (the state of separation) would be avoided.[97] Their preference, therefore, was to emphasise Love, redemption and consolation rather than 'roar for sin', which they accused the Church and particularly its Puritans of doing, that is, of promoting sin's inescapability as well as over-emphasising moral evil.[98]

The Puritans, other Calvinists and Catholics were baffled by the Friends' Christology, including their concept of 'the Light within'.[99] Many regarded both as sheer nonsense along with the Quakers' specialised religious vocabulary with which the Calvinists in particular were confronted. The Light was the subject of many a pamphlet war or well-attended public debate such as that between Samuel Fisher and Thomas Danson in which competing vocabularies added to the confusion, thus entrenching opinions. Was the Light natural or supernatural? Was it reason or conscience? How could it be anybody's sovereign authority? How could the Light/Spirit be manifest in people as it was in Jesus?[100] 'How could there be a resurrection', Thomas Hall asked, if 'flesh and blood [could] not inherit the Kingdom of Heaven'? The movement's Christology was also far too optimistic for Bunyan, whose *Grace Abounding* (1666) would be a picture of Calvinist despair. For him the Quakers' inward Christ was at best a myth.[101] Calvinists were deeply suspicious of the Quakers' form of

---

[97] Nayler, 'What his Kingdom is' in *The Lambs War*, 5-8, esp. 5 and 6. Also Burrough, 'Concerning the True Ministry of Christ' in *A Standard Lifted Up*, 15-16.
[98] See the exchange between Nayler and Jeremiah Ives (*c*.1626-74) in Nayler's *Weakness above Wickedness* (1656) and Ives' *The Quakers Quaking*. Also *AOTW*, 78.
[99] Farnworth, *The General Good* (1653), 29-30 and quoted in *TLITC*, 80-3.
[100] For an example of how the Light was manifest as in Jesus see James Strutt (b. *c*. 1622), *A Declaration to the Whole World* (1659), 8-9.
[101] See Kuenning, *The Bunyan-Burrough Debate*, 65.

Arminianism and its passionate belief that everybody could be saved if only they liberated Christ or the Light within them, something that inevitably involved an overturning of daily behaviour and religious profession. For those of Bunyan's, Danson's and Hall's persuasion, it was incomprehensible how this could lead to true happiness in God.

When Burrough offered Bunyan assurances in *The True Faith of the Gospel of Peace* (1656) that 'we take the Scripture in plain words, without adding or diminishing', Bunyan must have thought at first that the Quakers really did take the Bible at face value. But Burrough, a more skilled polemicist and 'scriptural politician', chose his words carefully. With Katz we are reminded that during the seventeenth century 'plain' could imply a deeper reality 'behind' the narrative, something not visually noticed but nonetheless understood.[102] With the Word of God independent of space and time, it was to the Spirit, the inner meaning rather than the letter, to which Quakers appealed: 'God is worshipped only in Spirit and Truth', wrote Burrough confirming unconditionality, 'without respect of time, places or things [and] Christ . . . is the wisdom and power of the Father'.[103] It was the Spirit ('which was before the world was') that had moved the Jesus whom the Quakers 'prized', the same person who 'was slain in the streets of the great city'.[104]

Still, for all its many explanations, Quaker Christology continued to confound its Protestant and Catholic critics. They could never accommodate to the Friends' belief that it was Jesus' union with God through the *Spirit* that was *the* quintessential unity, a unity already present in the *now* as the Kingdom to be lived and pursued, a unity by which everybody could partake through accepting the Light as their final authority.

Silence: a Second Coming Medium

If God was to be worshipped in 'Spirit and Truth' as Burrough said, and if their individual and collective religious experiences could never be fully captured in words, then the Friends could do no other than to exercise holy obedience through worship in silence. Capitalising on a tradition already practised before the arrival of Fox by the gathered Churches in the North, as indeed among some Ranters, worship based on silence was given apocalyptic, saving and unifying functions by the children of Light. Their chief inspiration for this form of prayer would have been Jesus himself.

---

[102] Mullett, *John Bunyan in Context*, 132-7, esp. 135 in which Mullett refers to Burrough's *The True Faith of the Gospel of Peace*, 15—a reply to Bunyan's *Some Gospel Truths Opened* (1656). See Kuenning, *The Bunyan-Burrough Debate, passim*.
[103] Burrough, *A Declaration to all the World of our Faith*, 1-2. See also Nayler, 'Concerning Worship' in *Love to the Lost*, 8-11.
[104] Burrough, *The True Faith of the Gospel of Peace* in *Works*, 149.

They also knew how Moses and Isaiah also spent long hours in contemplative solitude.[105] Silence was not an end in itself. It was a gathering and unifying time that might give rise to vocal ministry from an inwardly deep place. Richard Davies, a Welsh Friend, has left us an account from 1657 of a Meeting for Worship:

> Though it was silent from words yet the Word of the Lord God was among us. It was as a hammer and a fire. It was sharper than any two-edged sword. It pierced through our inwards parts. It melted and brought us to tears that there was scarcely a dry eye among us. The Lord's blessed power overshadowed our Meeting and I could have said that God alone was master of that assembly.[106]

Without the hindrance of dogma, creed or liturgy—although at various times they acknowledged singing and music as a legitimate part of worship—the Friends enriched their new-found state of salvation through the spiritual space that silence granted.[107] There they contrasted themselves to 'apostate Christians, who inwardly ravened from the Spirit'.[108] And silence was especially liberating for Quaker women. Socially a sign of their suppression and inferiority, it 'gave access to that witness in themselves leading to outward public witness' as priests and prophets.[109]

In assuming the roles of priest and prophet, the Friends were to minister to each other and the world through the silence. Margaret Fell encouraged her fellow Quakers to 'let that love constrain you to love one another, and be serviceable to one another'. Such behaviour was expected to unite and deepen the Kingdom witness of the wider Quaker fellowship at local, regional and national levels as they created Meetings throughout the country.[110] Silence was the medium through which the Light would shine and be refracted throughout their work for the Kingdom. A constant attempt, therefore, was made in worship and prayer, as in convincement, to purge the self of the inner Beast and enact the crucifixion, resurrection and

---

[105] Fox, 'To all you that Stumble at the Silent Waiting' in *An Epistle to all People on the Earth*, 8.

[106] Richard Davies, *Works*, 40.

[107] As in the established Church, they objected to choirs and singing by the unconvinced. See Hamm, 'George Fox and Politics' in Dandelion (ed., 2004), 15-16. Also Farnworth, *Truth Cleared of Scandals* (1654), 3: 'hymns and spiritual songs with grace in the heart, that we own, as it is written and witnessed, Col.3: 25-26 . . .'.

[108] Fox, *Something Concerning Silent Meetings* (1657), Bds. William Erbery liked to worship in silence; see Gwyn, *Seekers Found*, 120.

[109] S. Davies, *Unbridled Spirits*, 222. See Ps. 6: 6.

[110] Fell, Ep. 45 (1653) to Friends in *Works*, 7: 57.

ascension of Jesus in order to confirm the body-with-Spirit as a holy sanctum for the Light within.

In 1669, George Keith, a leading Quaker from Aberdeen who would later leave the Friends in some bitterness, reflected on Quaker experiences during the movement's formative years, looking back to that time when all manner of people, disillusioned with the established denominations and their practices, 'came to be gathered out of all that

> bulk and heap of words into the waiting place, . . . so as to wait upon the Lord in his light in all possible stillness and quietness, and silence of mind, not only out of all outward performances and words, but even out of all thoughts and apprehensions of God, or Christ, and all inward motions and workings which had not the light, or word, or Spirit of God in their hearts; for the rise and spring, and this they were brought unto, through the ministration aforesaid, which pointed or directed them unto this place, even silence, both as to words, and thoughts, and that both apart; and together, by which ministration also they were called, to assemble or gather together in the Name of Christ, whose name is the Light, the Wisdom and Power of God, and the second Adam, the quickening Spirit, to wait together in this silence.[111]

This passage illustrates how the Meeting for Worship and its silence was Quakerism's great strength. Bunyan correctly observed that Quaker worship was the 'motionless centre of the revolving wheel'.[112] So powerful was the experience that the Friends were 'afraid to open the mouth till the Lord opened it'. As temples of the Spirit, they were 'new creatures' in the silence, representatives in thought, word and deed of the 'New Earth', 'New Heaven' and the 'New Jerusalem', metaphors for a complete spiritual transformation needed for unity with God in the new messianic age, the Kingdom.[113] Consequently, for William Britten, silence was the 'place' where they were to come,

> like Solomon unto self-experience, in seeing all our joys, pleasures, profits, or other things delightful to the flesh, to be but vanity and vexation, we become silent thereunto, not answering, to obey the lusts

---

[111] Keith, *The Benefit, Advantage*, 7.
[112] See Alexander Parker letter (Jan., 1660) to Friends in Loukes, *Friends Face Reality*, 69 and at: <http://www.hallworthington.com/Historical Letters/HLetters-8.html#Salthouse>.
[113] For 'unity with God in the new messianic age': Rev. 20:1-21, 21:1-2. For 'temples of the Spirit': 1 Cor. 6:19.

of the carnal mind, but as dead to the world, that we may live unto God.[114]

But also to pray. The centrality of prayer to Quaker worship stressed that 'any might pray vocally *out of the silence* (not as an inlay clumsily inserted in it) when moved by God's Spirit so to do and *only* so moved'.[115] From now on prayer was no longer the formulaic mantra of the church pew. Real prayer, to borrow the words of the fourteenth century mystic, Julian of Norwich, was seen to 'oneth the soul with God' and to set in motion their faith in hope and charity for the Kingdom.[116] In a 1655 letter from York Castle, the Friends were advised to observe a deep centring in the silence to encourage unity with God:

> wait for the increase in God [wrote Roger Hebden], being content of what is made known of him ... every motion that calls upon you to act or speak, do not lend an ear to it ... return in again ... and be not hasty ... but wait that you may know the mind of God that you may not be deceived ... such waiting is not disobedience but, on the contrary, when the mind of God is clearly seen in it, and nothing of self at all to be seen upon the examination ... then be faithful ... to put you into a search in your selves that you may know from whence all your obediences and performances do arise.[117]

These gatherings have been described by Norman Talbot as being *shaped* by the reverent silence. The impassioned, even

> quaking spoken ministry that arose from them was at its best ... organic, a new and powerful form of communication, no more fragmentary than a sermon: it was open-ended, needing no more frame than a vignette does, and shaped, when it was shapely, only by the energies of its own contents, by its inspiration ... No doubt some ministry was planned ahead, no doubt some was over-long, but most if it was genuinely impromptu, an unstudied improvisation that expressed the searching—or celebratory recognition—experienced by the

---

[114] Britten, *Silent Meetings*, 6. For fine writing on early Quaker silence within the apocalyptic genre see Farnworth, 'A Mite given forth' in *A Message from the Lord* (1653), 36-7. For 'New Earth and New Heaven': Rev. 20:1-2, 21:1-8.
[115] Nuttall, *The Holy Spirit*, 69. Nuttall's emphasis.
[116] Julian of Norwich (*c*.1342-*c*.1423).
[117] See Nayler, 'Concerning Hope' in *Love to the Lost*, 15-17. 'Hope' is not mentioned in the four Gospels but in the Wisdom tradition that so influenced early Quakerism. See Roger Hebden, letter (12/March/1655) to Friends at Swandale, Bishoprick (Co. Durham) from York Castle in *Works*, 29-30.

Chapter 8: 'Of the Nature of Christ Jesus'

individual spirit. By its nature it implied that many of its audience could understand and perhaps vicariously share the speaker's unique experience . . . the unique openness of [his or her] spirit to renewing inspiration.[118]

Hence Friends could walk cheerfully, that is, with joy and courage, over the earth as priests sanctified by God. The very immediacy of their individual and group mystical dialogue with the divine, their desire to be shaped by God and to transform the world meant Friends required themselves to inwardly retire or to 'wait upon', 'dwell in', 'stand still in', 'walk in', 'draw more and more into', and strive to be 'in the Life of' and 'in the Power of', God's presence. Since their contemplative and vocal prayer was an experience of the divine Presence and a foretaste of eternal union with God, they also saw it as a way of participating in and enhancing the Kingdom *now*. Through the silence, the Second Coming could be experienced repeatedly not in words but 'in the Power' as we saw in Davies and Keith.[119] Quaker worship was also a corrective to any domestication of the Spirit or co-option of the vision and language of the Kingdom for limited and transitory goals. Without authentic prayer-lives, the Friends and others were in danger of failing the Kingdom and handing it over to cynical and destructive worldly powers.

Silence also served other purposes. By insisting that the primary intention of speech was 'to bring into the life . . . to feel God's presence', Fox and Friends hammered home something of great importance: silence was to be a special sort of religious language and through it a different tonality was to be born which could teach the world a 'strong lesson', a lesson that would disrupt and re-order social hierarchies and the rules solidifying them.[120] As such, silence threatened to subvert the traditional role of the parish clergy who saw in its practice a theft of their authority, not to mention an assault on their regular income and social prestige. And all the more frightening since bishops had been abolished by the Long Parliament in 1646. Were they next? Meanwhile, the Friends' outward witness, their Testimony, meant they could do no other than to 'flow into [carnal] experiences' in order to transform them.[121] Silence was a key logistic in the Lamb's War, therefore, a portable testimony to the Spirit and

---

[118] Talbot, *Myths & Stories*, 38-9. The present tense has been converted into the past for quoting purposes.
[119] William Penn said the same of 1650s Friends in 1694; see *An Account of the . . . Quakers*, 35.
[120] Fox, *Something Concerning Silent Meetings*, Bds.; Britten, *Silent Meetings*, 4; Orlie, *Living Ethically, Acting Politically*, 102, 104.
[121] Britten, *Silent Meetings*, 11.

to their place in the world, one reason why Meetings authorised individuals to testify publicly to the Word beyond their own fellowships.

Conclusion

The Quakers invasion of the South in 1654 as priestly heralds of the New Israel was an apocalyptic, priestly and prophetic act for the Jesus Way. In the way that YHWH for Jesus was not only the One who Is, but *Immanû'el*, the One who is both with and within us as the inward Messiah and Ruler, the Friends' own intimate relationship with God and Jesus was *their* determining reality.[122] It bound them together as a redeemed community which, in turn, linked all to God. Jesus was their source of freedom and inspiration since he had died primarily for Love. In arguing that their Christology was scriptural, indeed what the primitive Church had upheld, they aimed to identify intimately with the experience of Jesus and the disciples. They did so in order to become an authentic people of the Kingdom, a royal priesthood, and, like Jesus and the disciples, the human interface with God.[123] But all Quakers insisted they were devoted to, and united with, the earthly Jesus as well. Many among the leadership would have agreed with Origen of Alexandria that Jesus was the Kingdom realised in a 'self'.[124] We have seen how there were public Friends, including Isaac Penington, who saw Jesus as the human 'garment' of the Spirit, the man who gave the world the Kingdom. Clearly, however, the movement as a whole regarded Jesus as their anchor, as liberating and enhancing, as Love's most perfect exponent. For them, he evoked openness rather than obscurity as well as honest dialogue and trust in being in the world. The Christ had 'come to teach his people himself' and was ever-coming.

Thus the Friends concentrated on the resurrected, cosmological Jesus in particular—the Logos, the Life and the Light/Spirit, the Jesus who cut through ecclesiastical, liturgical and doctrinal barriers like a sword. The Light/Spirit/Kingdom was already present in the saints as in the historical Jesus and waited its unveiling through convincement so that it could confront the sins of the world including its violence. As a consequence, the Second Coming was a reality in the *now* and the outcome was Kingdom and Testimony enacted through a Lamb's War. Convincement meant the Friends internalised the atonement and resurrection. In crucifying their old self they allowed the Seed to resurrect, to take them over. The result was an

---

[122] For *Immanû'el* see Nayler, 'A Testimony for Jesus Christ' in *Works*, p. xxxv; Perrot *Immanuel, the Salvation of Israel* (1658), 2.

[123] See Langford, 'Contract or Covenant', 377.

[124] Origen (185-254 CE), leading Patristic figure, neo-Platonist author of *On First Principles*.

automatic response of *agape* for the world, an enactment of the Jesus Way. The Jesus Way itself demanded unity which was utterly basic to their self-understanding as an obedient comm*unity* of the *Kingdom*. False unity, they argued, such as they found in Cromwell's proposal for a National Church, only served to entrench apostasy, injustice and violence.

Since their individual and collective mystical experience of the Kingdom could never be fully captured in words, the Friends worshipped in silence where they enriched their newly discovered state of salvation. Silence meant contrasting themselves to 'apostate' Christianity and threatened to subvert the traditional role of the parish clergy. As their 'wonder to the world', worshipful silence was the cradle of their Christ/Light- or Logos-mysticism and the genesis of their Leadings and Concerns in the world. It was the 'place' where the spiritual Jesus incarnated the holy and revolutionary Kingdom, the source and inspiration of their individual and collective Testimony, the subject of Chapter 9. Just as their understanding of the Kingdom acquired an early sophistication, so, too, did their Christology, a remarkable achievement during a time of premillennialist literalness. In confronting history their radical theology re-ordered reality—from the future (i.e. the Puritan view) to the present, from the sphere of expectation to that of realised experience through a Kingdom still to be universally established.

Chapter 9: 'Demonstration of the Spirit'

- Early Quaker Testimony -

The Friends wrote an enormous number of 'testimonies' of which ten broad categories can be identified. Some were *instructive* as in 'a testimony of what we believe'. Others were overtly *theological*: 'a testimony of the true Light'. Many were *confessional* concerning their own spiritual struggles: 'a faithful testimony of that ancient servant of the Lord'. Still others were *retrospective* concerning deceased Friends or directly *prophetic* as in 'a testimony from God'. In some cases they were *apocalyptic*: a discovery [testimony as unveiling] of divine mysteries ... veiled and hidden secretly' or *apologetic* for the Quaker faith: 'a testimony of the everlasting gospel' (i.e. in the manner of the Friends). A number were *polemical or declarative*: 'a testimony against ...' in which 'warnings' or 'declarations' were issued to the wider world or to specific authorities or groups. They also wrote testimonies concerned with *suffering* as well as *immorality and apostasy*. Finally, words of *warning and advice* were directed to fellow Friends.[1]

What lay at the heart of 'Testimony'? As in the case of 'righteousness' the Bible was their guide. It first confirmed testimony in Exodus and Numbers as the Law of God. In Psalm 25:10, it was expressed as 'covenant', as God's guarantee to his chosen people. In both senses, testimony was connected to God's kingship and sovereignty. The Synoptic Gospels mention 'testimony' eight times in different ways. In Matthew 8:4 and 10:18, for instance, it is understood as 'evidence', the necessity of the disciples with their trust in God to bear public witness as servants of the

---

[1] See Runyon in *EQW*, 567-76. For each category see for example: 1. Instructive—Burrough, *The True Faith of the Gospel of Peace* and Nayler, *Love to the Lost*; 2. Theological—Howgill, *Some of the Mysteries of God's Kingdom* and Hubberthorne, *The Light of Christ Within* (1660); 3. Confessional—Burrough, *A True Description of My Manner of Life* (1663) and Howgill, *The Inheritance of Jacob Discovered*; 4. Retrospective—Coale, *The Last Testimony of ... Richard Farnworth* (1667) and Dorothy Wilson *et al*, *A Short Collection of Some of the Letters of William Wilson* (1685); 5. Prophetic—Goodaire, *A Cry to the Just aganist Oppression* (1660) and Thomas Wastfield. *A True Test of Faithful Witness* (1657); 6. Apocalyptic—D. White, *A Call from God Out of Egypt* (1662) and Dewsbury, *The Mighty Day of the Lord is Coming* (1656); 7. Polemical/Declarative—T. Lawson, *The Lip of Truth Opened* (1656) and Mason, *Zion's Enemy Discovered* (1659); 8. Suffering—J. Audland, *The Suffering Condition* (1662) and G. Benson *et al*, *The Cry of Oppression* (1656); 9. Immorality/Apostasy—Bayly, *A Testimony against Drunkenness and Swearing* (1675) and Farnworth, *A True Testimony against the Pope's Ways* (1656, i.e. against priesthood); 10. To Friends—W. Smith, *An Epistle from the Spirit of Love* (1663) and Bishop, *An Epistle of Love*.

Lord to the truth of the new dispensation. This theme of discipleship and mission among 'strangers' as bodily testimony is developed further in Mark 6:11 and 13:9 where its meaning is extended to denote a 'sign' of the truth, being-witness-to an historical event. The early Quakers amplified testimony as witness to 'love unfeigned', that grand sweep of God's power, the Kingdom.[2]

In John's Gospel, testimony is mentioned five times, most importantly in 3:32-33 where it refers to Jesus being caught up in God's love as Truth itself. This picture of Jesus is reinforced by Paul in 1 Corinthians 2:1 and underlined as faith in 2 Thessalonians 1:10-11. For Paul, faith is always subject to suffering—the suffering servant—and is implanted in every true Christian as the Word of God to which Jesus gives witness through the cross.[3] Consequently, those who suffered for the faith were also sons of God as in the sapiential (Wisdom) tradition.[4]

Biblically or, more accurately, linguistically, 'Son of God' never presupposed a filial relationship as in its Greek translation. In Aramaic and Hebrew it was used figuratively to mean a child of God but also one who possessed spiritual authority born of suffering and, as in John's Gospel, a divine and therefore an equally authoritative entity revealing the Father (Love). In the latter sense, the term could be apocalyptic. Fox and Nayler appeared to have grasped both meanings when each claimed to be 'Son of God', an assertion they used during their investigation for blasphemy at Lancaster sessions in October, 1652.[5] Rather than genealogical descent, then, Fox and Nayler were eager to convey an intimate relationship, a belonging to and unity with God, in which they were ordained to speak authoritatively about God's purposes.

Again drawing on John, the first Friends saw themselves as divine entities just as the prophets of old were divine.[6] Nayler wrote that

> the apostles exhort the saints to wait for the appearance of Christ in themselves, and to wait for the day-star arising in their hearts, and they knew themselves to be the sons [and daughters] of God by the Spirit that he had given them.[7]

---

[2] For 'love unfeigned' see, for instance, Nayler, *The Lambs War*, 4, 6-7; also 2 Cor. 6:6.

[3] Fox and Nayler *et al, Saul's Errand*, 15.

[4] See, for example, *To All that would Know*, 6. Also Fox, Ep. 181 (1659) in *LOGF*, 68 where Wisdom is mentioned three times. And Gal. 3:26 where the Friends would have read, 'For ye are all the children of God by faith in Christ Jesus', and 4: 6-7 which in part reads: 'Wherefore thou art no more a servant [or slave], but a son; and if a son, then an heir of God through Christ'. In the Wisdom tradition the teacher in Proverbs uses 'my son' and 'father' at least twenty times each to his audience.

[5] *Journal*, 133-40; *BQ*, 107; Fox and Nayler *et al, Saul's Errand* (1653), 5-7.

[6] See Jn. 1: 1, 3: 13, 10:30.

[7] Nayler, *A Discovery of the First Wisdom*, 13.

Here, too, Nayler underlined the apostolic and prophetic tradition of the Quakers' priestly authority, that of Melchizedek's order. As servanthood is a basal element of Christian testimony, so it was for the early Friends who often described themselves as 'servants of the Lord'.[8] Both 'son' and 'daughter' of God and 'servants of the Lord' in this respect were fundamental to the Quakers' self-definition as prophets and the social consciousness they believed was a substantive aspect of the prophetic tradition, to their bearing witness to the narrative of God's love of, and desire for unity with, those who turned to the Light and who bore the 'daily cross' spiritually and materially.

During the seventeenth century the generally accepted interpretation of 'testimony' was six-fold—as an open acknowledgment or profession, especially of religious faith or experience, a bearing witness to the precepts of God and, in secular terms, as an expression or declaration of disapproval, a condemnation of error, a protestation and a test (proven by evidence) and, finally, a written certificate.[9] Do these meanings relate to early Quaker insights as these emerged from their Bible reading?

Claiming to be witnesses to the Truth as it was found in the Hebrew prophets, the first Friends pictured themselves as present at the great trial of humanity in session *now* before the throne of God.[10] They had been sent to testify to the world in word and deed, by the sacrifice of their lives if necessary.[11] The Friends considered their faith absolute in origin and content. In giving witness to such, they aimed to create a crisis of belief, a holy conflict in the court of ultimate meaning.

Importantly for this task, the first Friends did not stray outside the Gospel framework.[12] As already observed in Chapter 8, they rejected an absolute distinction between on the one hand the historical Jesus (the eyewitness testimony) and the Christ/Spirit within him (testimony *par excellence*) and, on the other, the Johannine encounter with the risen, cosmological Jesus. In this respect they bore close affinity to the early

---

[8] Parnel, *A Trial of Faith*, 8.
[9] Farnworth, *The Heart Opened by Christ*, 13. A further example of witness/testimony as 'certificate' can be found in Thomas Gouldney and Thomas Curtis *et al*, 'A Certificate of the Endeavours' in Margaret Vivers, *The Saints Testimony*, 40.
[10] See Fell *et al*, *A Declaration and Information*, 7.
[11] Burrough, letter (25/Aug/1657) to Fox and Howgill, *SW*/iii/18. See also Fox, Ep. 93 (1655) in *LOGF*, 42.
[12] Thus belying N. Smith's belief that they lacked an inherited textual framework of authority. See Smith's 'Hidden Things', 65. Boobyer maintains the first Friends were only too willing to let the Scriptures stand in critical judgment if their minds were unconditionally open to the Holy Spirit's illumination of the text. Boobyer is quoted in Janet Scott, 'Reflections in a Looking-Glass', 674-5.

Chapter 9: 'Demonstration of the Spirit'

Christian communities, and the Johannine communities in particular.[13] The Friends were aware that in bearing witness to the Light that had 'reproved' them of sin, they were referring specifically or testifying to Jesus who himself testified wholeheartedly to the Light in himself, but also to the cosmological Jesus, the Christ 'that was before Jesus was'.[14] Consequently, Fox wrote that 'to believe only of a Christ [i.e. Jesus], because the Scriptures declare of him' reduced the believer to the level of Pharisee—in this case a literalist:

> but to believe in the Light, the Life that gave forth the Scriptures is seen and Christ is believed in, and hence he [the believer] hath the witness in himself, and comes to be a child of Light.[15]

For Fox and the Friends Scripture was not of itself revelation, not *the* Word of God. Its words were written by humans, though in many respects they had been guided by the Light; revelation was contained within it. They saw the Christian Testament in particular as the voice of God's healing grace that had so profoundly influenced Jesus of Nazareth. This was the position at which the early Friend and former Leveller, John Lilburne, arrived while in a cell in Dover Castle. Lilburne realised that in his 'already attained growing up measure, having the experimental witness of God within myself' he was 'already truly and really attained, in substantial, and witnessed within me, real truth.'[16] This revelation was powerful enough for him to renounce all outward wars in the manner of James 4:1-4, a passage quoted in his largely confessional *The Resurrection of John Lilburne* (1656) and which found favour in the Fox-Hubberthorne declaration to Charles II a little over five years later. Lilburne concluded that

> Carnal weapons of any kind whatsoever, having no place, nor being of no use at all in his spiritual kingdom, for his subjects are to love their enemies . . . and therefore not in the least to draw temporal weapons against their enemies.[17]

---

[13] Ricoeur, *Essays on Biblical*, 136.
[14] Nayler, *Love to the Lost*, 29: 'the Light of Christ in the conscience is a witness.' For 'before Jesus was' see Fox and Nayler *et al*, *Several Papers*, 6; *Journal*, 98, 104; Mason, *A Check to the Lofty Linguist*, 10. And for Jesus and the Light see Jn. 14:6.
[15] Fox, *The Difference between the World's Relation* (1659) in *Doctrinals*, 166; Nayler, letter (April-May 1656) to Fox, *SW*/iii/76.
[16] John Lilburne, *The Resurrection*, 10.
[17] *Ibid.*, 12. See Hubberthorne, letter (June/July 1652) to Fox, *SW*/iv/4 and Thomas Taylor, letter (18/May/1653) to Fox, *SW*/iii/29; Fox, Ep. 32 (1653) in *LOGF*, 15 in which Fox mentions 'witness' in this context four times. For a good account of convincement see that of Thomas Wynne in Jenkins, *Protestant Dissenters in Wales*, 89.

In fact, the renunciation of violence and the extolling of the Kingdom, which he mentions eight times, is the central core of *The Resurrection*. Testimony, therefore, was primarily interiorised and everything to which it was related, including any conflict arising from it, was ultimately seen as subject to the same inner holy trial. As Lilburne himself enthusiastically, even joyfully, came to understand, physical conflicts, including war, violated the very nature of the personal-cum-corporate Testimony the movement was proclaiming.

Quaker Testimony thus demanded that the Friends rose above the standards of the world. Their work of reconciliation between Love and humanity lay in bearing witness to its struggle. The victory, or true liberty, once achieved on a personal and corporate level was displayed vocally and in writing, but also through their bodies by sacrificial suffering incurred for 'Truth's sake' and thus the expiation of sin. Through their suffering, the power and peace of God would reach others also in a state of suffering. Similarly, their imprisonments and other privations would reach out to those who were imprisoned, as well as to the prisoner within the persecutor. Their own experience of captivity meant proclaiming liberty to others from a position of equality with them. Jesus and the early Church had drawn the map by which the first Friends were guided, and, just as Jesus and the early Christians suffered for the truth, so they, too, would replicate that experience. The Christian Testament was about victory in the spiritual life by way of achieving and enhancing the Kingdom at the expense of the corrupted world. As such, it meant experiencing the revealed mystery of which Nayler wrote apocalyptically in 1653 to opponents who looked,

> for a carnal Christ like themselves, who can but be in one place, or person . . . but where Christ is revealed and known, he is . . . spiritual, not carnal, not limited to one place, but fills heaven and earth, is all, and . . . he be the Light of the world; for the God of this world hast blinded the eyes of the world . . . for he is a mystery to them, and hid from all their carnal wisdom . . . for they are not of his sheep . . . but to them only in whom he dwells he is known.[18]

The conduct or 'conversation' of the new chosen and suffering ones would be a sign of their trust in the divine Life and of God's trust in them, a public guarantee, a covenant certificated through a denial not only of deception within themselves but also, as Mary Penington put it, of the 'spirit of the world' which always sought to draw the 'camp of the Lord'

---

[18] Nayler, *A Discovery of the First Wisdom*, 20. For 'Christ is revealed and known' see Lk. 17:30; Rom. 1:17. Also Henry Clark, *A Cloud of Witnesses*, 23 and Punshon, *Testimony and Tradition*, 25.

Chapter 9: 'Demonstration of the Spirit'

from the path of righteousness and unity. It was, after all, the spirit of the Kingdom and its implicit message of unity with all people and God that spurred her to join the Quakers.[19] William Dewsbury in 1655 declared in a Northampton court that 'we witness the work of regeneration to be an extraordinary work' and compared the Friends to the first Christian witnesses.[20] In this vein also, Burrough wrote in 1659 to the Deputy Governor of Dunkirk that the Friends' witness in the world was to fight the 'Lamb's battle with his spiritual weapons' since carnal weapons were ultimately impotent. The underlying theme of Burrough's writings was always of witness, the marriage of spiritual weaponry with suffering. Echoing John 8:13-17, he continued,

> we are not ministers of man, not by man's will, neither do we stand to man's judgments, to be approved, or disapproved thereby; but to the witness and testimony of God's Spirit in every conscience we do commend ourselves ... in the simplicity of Truth, in the demonstration of the Spirit.[21]

Even above the cacophony of 1659, the year of political collapse, early Quaker socio-political concerns took second stage to their primary spiritual and priestly message, a message that also proclaimed the holistic underpinning of the cosmological nature of Jesus as the Word, and therefore its independence of time and space since 'Christ fill[ed] all places'.[22] Like Jesus, Fox's refusal of Sir Henry Vane's offer of a seat in government in 1659 was a powerful display of the Quakers' lack of interest in launching a political movement. And like Jesus, they accepted Caesar's jurisdiction so long as it was based squarely on justice, on God's design for humanity. Their devotion to the Kingdom meant they would pursue a different politics from the Judaic-type hopes of Vane. Rather than another Jerusalem temple, a secular reality, they proclaimed a faith that bespoke a loving God at work in 'thick nights of darkness' leading to a different type of politics that pronounced the Kingdom as not only containing food, drink, shelter or work but justice, peace and mercy as well (Rom. 14:17). They believed theirs was

---

[19] See Penney (ed., 1992), 42 and Mary Penington's own *Account*, 30 in which Thomas Curtis, on his initial meeting with the Peningtons, introduced Quakerism with a reference to Jesus' 'doctrine'. See also Grundy, 'Learning to be a Quaker', *passim*.
[20] Dewsbury, *A True Testimony of what was done ... at Northampton* (1655) in *Works*, 69.
[21] *GADOT*, 347 (69n). See Burrough and Fisher, 'To the Deputy Governor' in *A Visitation and Warning Proclaimed*, 6; Burrough (?), 'An Account' in *A Declaration of the Present Sufferings*, 24 and 'To the Protector and his Council' (1658) in *Works*, 581; see Nuttall, *Christian Pacifism in History*, 64.
[22] 'The Examination of James Nayler' in *Works*, 14. And Fox and Nayler *et al*, *Several Papers*, 6. Also Fell, 'An Epistle to Friends by M.F.' (1654) in *Works*, 56.

a politics of compassion which, while contravening conventional wisdom, hierarchy and various aspects of patriarchy, forged the deeper revolution of the Spirit for all time. Its acceptance, inclusiveness, love and peace were fundamental to the Lamb's War.

From our discussion so far, therefore, Testimony may be deduced as possessing five inter-linked components:

- 'The Life' and 'Perfection',
- Convincement and the quest for Truth and Unity,
- Holism and Mysticism,
- A Quaker Apocalyptic,
- Witness and Prophecy.

Their mutual inclusiveness makes it difficult to distinguish between them. This is because all aspects of their theology, including their Christology, flowed into each other in the same way as they conceived themselves to be 'one of each other' and one with God.[23] Nevertheless, despite some repetition, a clarification of their finer points is attempted. Witness and Prophecy' is reserved for greater examination in Chapter 10.

Testimony: 'The Life' and 'Perfection'

During the seventeenth century, 'life' invoked, among other meanings, a condition of power and energy. It was also, of course, a biblical expression and the early Friends invariably understood 'the Life' mainly as the 'Spirit', the 'power of God', the 'Word of Life', 'Jesus', 'Eternal Life' and the 'Life of Jesus', all of which were interchangeable with 'the Kingdom'. As with 'Kingdom', 'the Life' was vital to early Quaker theology and was used abundantly. In nine randomly chosen tracts by James Nayler, for instance, the term appears 502 times. This is typical for early Quaker works in general.[24]

The first Friends understood dwelling in 'the Life' as being attuned to God, committing themselves as a 'peculiar' people (individually and collectively) and as a royal priesthood to that ultimate happiness which bespoke freedom from sin (i.e. freedom from separation from God). 'Peculiar' underlined their distinctive mission as a nation of the Kingdom, one chosen among the multitude of other 'nations' that had forsaken God

---

[23] 'One of each other' was probably inspired by Rom. 12: 4-5.
[24] These are: *A Discovery of the First Wisdom* in *Works* (13 times); *To the Life of God in All* (1659) (43 times); *Love to the Lost* in *Works* (130 times); *How Sin is Strengthened* (9 times); *A Message from the Spirit of Truth* (1658) (15 times); *A Door Opened to the Imprisoned Seed* (101 times); *What the Possession of the Living Faith Is* (83 times); *Give Ear you Gathered-Churches* (1659) (37 times); *Milk for the Babes* (1658/9) (71 times).

Chapter 9: 'Demonstration of the Spirit'

(Calvinism for example).[25] As in John, accepting 'the Life' entailed a continuous battle to maintain the spiritual alchemy of perfection through an on-going internal and external battle with the Beast for victory.[26] For Thomas Forster, 'Life Eternal' raised the 'witness which has been slain in polluted Sodom in my heart, in measure I see that witness raised that never gives rest day nor night to that in me that worships the Beast'.[27] The End-time for the Beast could be set in train in the *now* as a sign that the inner Eden might be restored and maintained so that the Kingdom would eventuate in the fullness of time. Perfection was, therefore, an ever-expectancy, Fox and Friends being well aware that in the Sermon on the Mount Jesus urged perfection upon his disciples (Mt. 5:48).[28] The greater the purity of the earthly life, they also believed, the greater the capacity for enjoying God in the next. Knarr writes that their theology of perfection led the Friends,

> to make into absolute requirements what others saw as desirable goals and principles for believers. Others certainly taught that the believer was morally improved by conversion and sanctification, but Friends insisted that improvement must extend to perfection and the struggle against sin must end in victory over every temptation.[29]

The ultimacy that perfection implied meant seeking out and then universalising the absolute good. They insisted, for instance, 'upon a radical and wholehearted compassion for the poor rather than a piecemeal and casual application of charitable principles'.[30] But the Quakers' perfection was often misconstrued as antinomian and typical of the Ranters, something that always elicited sharp responses such as we have seen from Thomas Lawson and Margaret Fell. Two years before the Bristol incident (1656), for example, which is often seen by Quaker historians as the moment when the Friends were forced to abandon a supposedly antinomian, Ranter-like understanding of perfection[31], Nayler answered Thomas Weld and four other clerics from Newcastle-upon-Tyne that it was a 'lying slander that we say every saint is perfect; for we witness the saint's growth, and the time of pressing after perfection.' Here he cited Hebrews 10:14: 'For by one offering he hath perfected for ever them that are sanctified'. In 1655 to

---

[25] Burrough, *A Declaration to all the World of our Faith*, 2. And see Ex. 19: 3-6.
[26] Fox, 'A Word from the Lord' in *News Coming up out of the North*, 17.
[27] Thomas Forster (d. 1660), letter (7/June/1655) to Dewsbury in Cadbury, *Letters to William Dewsbury and Others*, 22. Forster may have had Ps. 52:10 in mind.
[28] See *Journal*, 367-8.
[29] Knarr, *Early Quaker Theology and Social Protest*, 93.
[30] *Ibid.*, 246.
[31] Damrosch maintains this strongly in *The Sorrows of the Quaker Jesus*, 106.

Richard Baxter he protested that, 'we affirm self-perfection is but thy lying slander or that we say we are Christ or God. But . . . we witness perfection from sin so far as we have received Christ'. If the Quakers had no sin, Nayler continued, they would have no need for prayer.[32] To the General Baptist and Leveller, Jeremiah Ives in July 1656, Nayler retorted similarly that when people received Christ completely, when Christ was in them in full measure, so they also acquired perfection, that is, automatically in that *very* moment.[33] Nayler reinforced what Fox had said in 1654 to the same effect in an epistle to the movement. The way of election (the second birth) which led to perfection, Fox wrote, involved a choice—'and so who come into the election, the Seed'[34]—though God alone possessed perfect free will as Nayler also explained in 1656:

> The spiritual will [only] . . . is free, and that is from above [since] man has not free will further than he is free born from above, [and] that will which is of God only, leads to God; . . . man's destruction is of himself, . . . in Christ I have free will, . . . for none have free will but who in the light of Christ have learned to deny their own wills.[35]

When Fox told a prison minister in Worcester in 1674 that it was 'a sad and comfortless sort of striving, to strive with a belief that we should never overcome', he attacked not only the accusation that the Quakers believed they were completely free of sin but that perfection was attained only in heaven, that is, through God alone. Here he repeated 1650s theology. People sinned, Fox was saying, and Jesus' death freed them from it. That is, his death showed the way of liberation by way of Love. The Light within meant perfection was possible if one so chose the path of reconciliation and the cross, the way of the Kingdom. To reinforce his argument he quoted Romans 8:1: 'There is no condemnation to them that are in Christ Jesus.' It

---

[32] Nayler, *A Discovery of the Man of Sin* (1654), 6; his statement, 'we witness the saint's growth' is a repetition from *A Discovery of the First Wisdom*, 14. See Thomas Weld *et al*, *The Perfect Pharisee*, 14-17. Also Nayler, 'Concerning Perfection' in *Love to the Lost*, 21-4; Rigge, *Of Perfection* (1658), 6; *Journal*, 27, 134-5, 230-1. For references to 'being made perfect' see, for instance, Fell *et al*, *False Prophets, Antichrist* (1655), 5-6.
[33] Ives, *The Quakers Quaking* answered by Nayler, *Weakness above Wickedness*, esp. 13. Nayler's tract was pub. 18/7/1656; see also Fox, *Some Principles of the Elect People of God* (1661), 23-4.
[34] Nayler, 'Concerning Free Will' in *Love to the Lost*, 50-1 and 'Concerning Good Works', 28-31; also I. Penington, *The Way of Life and Death*, 61-3 for free will. Reprobation was described by Fox later in the century as '[when people] go out of his Will . . . and follow their own wills, so their Destruction is of themselves'; see See Fox, *What Election and Reprobation Is* (1679), 23-4.
[35] Nayler, 'Concerning Free Will' in *Love to the Lost*, 50-1.

was worth striving to perfect oneself with the help of the compassionate God *because* one had been given that potential.[36]

The Quakers believed that human will had a tragic tendency to fall like Adam. However, it was not bound permanently by sin as the Calvinists maintained because Truth was always attainable.[37] The traditional idea of original sin was seen as nonsense. Unlike the Puritans, they did not deny the hallowing of matter; people were not born totally evil and nor was the flesh totally wicked as the godly William Perkins and William Prynne believed; for both, the body was 'but a loathsome mass'.[38] Quaker understanding of free will was in concert with the General Baptists, Arminians and sages like Jakob Boehme, all of whom allowed some freedom for the human will. While people were free to sin, to go 'out of the truth', and set themselves towards perdition as a consequence, in justification and sanctification lay the road to God and *the* only freedom—to obey *God's* will. 'The unrighteousness is with men', wrote Nayler in 1656, 'who reject the counsel of the Lord against themselves, and choose to abide in that which God hath cursed'. Writing of individual responsibility early in 1653 from an Appleby dungeon, he underscored a previous assertion that there was 'a discerning of things that differ, to choose the good and refute the evil'.[39] In justification lay sanctification, the way of holiness leading to perfection; for the Friends the two were synonymous. By freely submitting to the will of God, Nayler was saying, individuals let go of their own freedom joyously so they may be used for divine purposes. In so doing, they waited 'to feel its drawing, and it turns [their] face towards it, and begets a willingness to give up and follow it'.[40]

Nayler's view was in tune with the Geneva Bible, according to which a person had the freedom to rise above the old dispensation, the 'serpentine wisdom', which, post Jesus, was now the way of death, a state of reprobation symbolically personified by Cain, Ishmael and Esau.[41] For the

---

[36] *Journal*, 688; see Peat in Dandelion *et al*, *Heaven on Earth*, 110.

[37] Fox, *ibid*.

[38] Wilcox, *The Theology of the Early Friends*, 31. See William Perkins, *Of the Combat of the Flesh and Spirit* (1593), 71-96 and Prynne's poem, *The Soul's Complaint* quoted in R. Porter, *Flesh in the Age of Reason*, 39. For a good account of Quaker attitudes to sin/evil see C. Spencer, 'Early Quakers and Divine Liberation from the Universal Power of Sin' in Scully and Dandelion (eds.), *passim* but esp. 54 in which Puritan and Quaker attitudes are contrasted; also pp. 55-7 for perfection. And see Radcliffe, *What is the Point of Being a Christian?*, 108.

[39] Nayler, 'Concerning Election and Reprobation' in *Love to the Lost*, 32-4. And see T. C. Jones, *George Fox's Teaching*, 82-3, 130, 146. Also Haller, *The Elect Nation*, 73-4 and Bridenbaugh, *Vexed and Troubled Englishmen*, 277 (5n). Article 10 of the 39 Articles states that humans have no free will to win salvation.

[40] W. Smith *The New Creation*, 32.

[41] See Nayler, *A Discovery of the First Wisdom*, 7, 15, 26.

more succinct Isaac Penington, a 'free will' was a misnomer; either the will stood in the image and power of God who made it or it stood in a contrary image. In the former state the will was free to do good, in the latter it had the freedom to do evil. The will was not independent of good or evil; it could be 'bound' by, and come under the command of, either state. That which was of God led only to God. George Bishop, in *A Treatise Concerning Election and Reprobation* (1664), was confident God invited and inclined the individual towards God, and, by doing so, showed up the evil in the heart.[42] Humans, therefore, as Alan Kolp affirms, were 'not radically independent since they were limited to a choice in their dependency'.[43]

The free will debate of the 1650s became entangled with some of the main issues of the day—popery, the so-called Catholic threat, plus the spectre of religious and social anarchy supposedly forged by the hated Radicals. Many a cleric bitterly denounced the Quaker view as papist; the Friends were Rome's agents. The Quaker theology of free will *was* indeed akin to that of the Council of Trent (1545-63): a Christian was saved by his or her faith *and* good works as well as by grace. Their explanations and further clarifications, however, fell on deaf ears. And with opponents condemning their view of free will as Ranter-type antinomianism, came the charge that Quakerism was basically a license to think and do what one liked, something that was deeply offensive to the English Church's divinely-ordained authority and an attack on the social cohesion that it upheld, not to mention the benefices it carried.

The Quakers' belief, similar to the hated Arminians, that everybody was potentially of the Elect seed, explains the eagerness of the movement to despatch missions but also their loud disavowal of Calvinist predestination and its spokesmen, against whom Stephen Crisp railed loudly: 'Oh horrible! that [they] say they were ministers of Christ'.[44] More specifically, Isabel Yeamans underlined the choice implicit in choosing the Way, the Kingdom:

> Until you come to know [God's] power and Life in yourselves to save you from evil you are not come to the Substance [the Christ, Spirit]; but are still running from mountain to hill, as sheep having no shepherd, seeking living Bread in desolate places.[45]

---

[42] Bishop, *A Treatise Concerning Election and Reprobation*, 12.
[43] Kolp, 'Fox Loved the Apostle Paul', 17.
[44] Crisp, *A Word of Reproof*, 2. Farnworth's *The Brazen Serpent*, 3-13 particularly addresses predestination.
[45] Isabel Yeamans (c. 1637-1704), *An Invitation to Love* (1679), 8; her quote is also typical of the Quaker 1650s approach. And Crisp, *A Word of Reproof*, 2; see esp. 3-4.

Chapter 9: 'Demonstration of the Spirit'

Once the path of righteousness was chosen, God or Christ (as one) was then one's guide as the Light within. Like the early Christians, the first Friends believed the path guaranteed restoration in the risen Christ who was 'king, prophet and high priest'; the very life of God could be in their innocent blood as a consequence. In their silence the Friends began to feel God in their hearts and, carefully attentive to the Christ who dwelt at the centre of their being, believed God could take possession of their senses, their very existence. Their worship gave hope for perfection in which there could be no difference between their essential selves—their essence—and the risen Christ. Hence, this state of essential being was also given voice through their Christ/Logos-mystical understanding of the resurrection.[46] The resurrection was proof that Jesus, who was filled with divine Life himself, likewise filled the true believers with the fullness and wholeness of God. In *this* way they claimed to know what it was to be Christ-like in the new Life. As their frequent quoting of Paul suggests, Fox and Nayler immersed themselves, and by implication the movement, into the enveloping and encompassing security that was the macro-entity of the Spirit or spiritual Jesus who was incorruptible, immortal and glorious. They had 'come to the Substance', as Yeamans advised using that well-used Quaker expression. Their desire for communion with God probably meant a familiarity with John 15: 5: 'apart from me you can do nothing; those who dwell in me as I dwell in them, bear much fruit'.

By being alert to God in themselves in this way, they claimed to see God alive in the world around them, and the responsibility this implied was enormous. Once the path of darkness was rejected, the Life ensured a spiritual baptism into an inward Church—and here they bore similarity to the Baptists—where they could move, see, speak, hear, think and feel with the feet, eyes, voice, ears, mind and hands of God just as these were manifest in Jesus and the prophets:

---

[46] Bailey, *New Light on George Fox*, 19 and *passim*. I agree with Crawford, *Women and Religion in England*, 178 that such language should not be taken literally. However, I disagree with Bailey's theory of 'celestial inhabitation' as a way of interpreting early Quaker phraseology. Consider two typical examples: in a letter (19/Feb/1653) to Amor Stoddart (d.1670), Thomas Aldam states: 'but my rejoicings is in that Christ hath made himself manifest *in* flesh *in* you.' (my emphases). 'In' as used by Aldam had ontological significance as in Quaker thinking generally, the purpose being to contrast the corporeal, carnal flesh with the body of Christ. Aldam understands this body as being infused in Stoddart's form to be sure, but for him and, later, Penington, the body of Christ was mystical—spiritual and existential. Penington in *The Way of Life and Death*, 10 quotes Eph. 5: 30: 'We are members of his body, of his flesh, and of his bones'. See 'Extracts from the A. R. Barclay MSS.', 51-2. Also Nuttall, *The Holy Spirit*, 182 for reference to seventeenth century language-use in this context. And *TLITC*, 78.

All loving the Light [wrote Fox to Friends in 1652] you love the one thing which gathers your hearts together to the fountain of Light and Life. And walking in it you have unity with one another and 'the blood of Jesus Christ cleans you from all sin'.[47]

As already stated, the blood of Jesus was metaphorical not literal; Fox equated it to the Light of the Christ.[48]

'In the Life', therefore, meant being united as a people in their striving to be one with God, to be perfect as before the fall of Adam and Eve. They could thus be reborn individually and collectively to enjoy true life and acceptance by God. The result would be the joyous liberation of being one with Jesus' self-sacrifice for Love through which they were automatically free of sin, a liberation shared through worship, prayer, ministering to each other, inter-visitation and the settling of Meetings—in short, being in the Kingdom and, at the same time, growing it.[49]

Testimony: Convincement and the Quest for Truth and Unity

The Life was initially encountered through convincement, a 'true' baptism whose 'water' was that of the Spirit, the Word.[50] The complete convincement process meant deliverance from an inner captivity, an inner Egypt, in which birth was given to the Kingdom and its Light both of which were already within them though 'hidden' as in 'all people'. It was, as already mentioned, a Gethsemane-Golgotha-Easter experience. If the process were true, it thrust the individual into a new and unprecedented society with radical norms. This thinking, however, was not exclusive to the Friends. Inner baptism was upheld by Baptists such as William Dell, Henry Denne, John Gifford and John Bunyan, but for the Quakers it was 'a method

---

[47] Fox, Ep. 20 (1652) in *Works*, 7: 28.
[48] *Cambridge*, i., 24; Ep. 155 (1657) in *Works*, 7: 147-8. See Brinton, *Friends for 300 Years*, 42.
[49] See Ep. 14 (1652) in *LOGF*, 6; Dewsbury, letter (17/Aug/1653) to Fell, *SW*/iv/130. For reference to 'Life' and 'Power' see, for instance, Nayler, *A Discovery of the First Wisdom*, 6, 8; Dewsbury, *Christ Exalted*, 10; Howgill and Burrough, *To the Camp of the Lord*, 30; Fox, *The Woman Learning in Silence*, 2; Burrough, *A General Epistle . . . to all the Saints* (1660), 2, 7; Penington, *The Scattered Sheep Sought After*, 2, 12; Burrough, *A Discovery of Divine Mysteries*, 7, 9; W. Smith, *The New Creation*, 7.

For references to 'in the Life' see Nayler, 'Concerning Light and Life' in *Love to the Lost*, 1-3; Fox, *The Second Covenant*, 5; Howgill, *Some of the Mysteries of God's Kingdom*, 13; Fox, *An Epistle General to them who are of the Royal Priesthood*, 5 and W. Smith, *The Morning-Watch*, 3.
[50] Fox, *The Eternal, Substantial Truths of God's Kingdom*, 7.

Chapter 9: 'Demonstration of the Spirit'

of daily entering and waiting upon' God 'to issue forth in new life and reflection'.[51]

According to their tracts, convincement demanded a descent into their inmost depths to identify, confront and then drive away impulses separating them from God. During convincement '*every* act and motive was branded as the fruit of self-will [which] brought them close to despair'.[52] It was a conflicting experience with one's ego and sin, a conflict that was urgent if they were to be free of the destructive forces holding them in thrall. To paraphrase T. S. Eliot, the early Quakers strove desperately to find the Life 'they had lost in living, the wisdom they had lost in knowledge.'[53] And it allowed them, as the medieval Dominican mystic, Meister Eckhart, wrote centuries previously, to 'cherish in [themselves] the birth of God, and with it all goodness and comfort, all rapture, reality and truth'.[54] Convincement enabled the immediate forgiveness of their sins as the power of the Kingdom revealed itself in creative love. The early Quaker, Dorothy White, understood well its apocalyptic nature. Those who dared to enter its fire, she said,

> Come to hear the voice of their beloved . . . to be clothed with the righteousness of God. But first, all must know the putting off, the stripping, the purifying, the dying. And so the change is wrought by the unchangeable Word, by which all things are made anew, and a new Life is brought forth. And this is the very substance of all profession, to know the Kingdom of God revealed, and to know the Son of God to bear Rule in the heart, who is come to reign and to cast out the unclean spirits. So all must come to know the effectual working of the divine Power of Life which works in the Love, which Love destroys death, which breaks the cords thereof. And all who come to know the working of the nature of Love are brought into the nature of its Life, likeness and image.[55]

In convincement the Friends were confronted by the 'Day', that is, the pure Light/the Christ or, according to their accounts, 'God's appearance' that was so pure and powerful that anything remotely contrary to it was shown up, shattered. This was the 'wrath' of the Light which *was* 'judgment'. The impact was intensely dramatic: their whole world had utterly changed.

---

[51] See Keiser, 'From Dark Christian', 59. For Quakers and Baptists see R. Harkness, 'Early Relations of Baptists and Quakers', esp. 230-1.
[52] *EQW*, 23; Barbour's and Roberts' emphasis.
[53] See 'The Eagle soars in the summit of Heaven' in Eliot, *Collected Poems*, 161.
[54] W. Smith, *The New Creation*, 28-9. Also Blakney, *Meister Eckhart*, 103.
[55] D. White, *An Epistle of Love* (1661), 4-5.

The newly convinced were nurtured by the group and were often accompanied to a smaller gathering, usually in a private home, where they could share their struggles. These daily or weekly gatherings were full of prayer, messages of guidance, silence and tears as we saw in Richard Davies' experience of a Meeting for Worship.[56] By confronting their worries, fears and sin, they strove towards poverty of soul. This, in turn, afforded a greater awareness of the enmity they had had with God and sparked opportunities for increasing their knowledge of divine ways. Here, at this inner holy of holies and in holy awe, they were able to take possession of 'the Seed' and, in the words of Origen, learn to hear Love's language.[57] Energy would flow upwards from this act of creation to enrich their spiritual growth and, through it, their Meetings whose prayer-life and unity they sought to deepen. As the Gospel of John espoused a convergence of the children of God in the Light[58] so, too, did the first Friends continually plead for unity among the 'camp of the Lord'. To this end Joan Brooksop urged:

> Oh, my dearly beloved Friends, unto whom my Life reaches, read me in the covenant of Light, and Life, and peace, where our unity stands, in that which was before words were, and shall be when words are no more.[59]

This was because,

> Christ said unto us, live, and is become unto us a place of broad rivers, and streams of everlasting Life, flowing into our hearts, to nourish his own plant in us whom he hath called and chosen, to bear testimony for his names sake.[60]

Convincement was thus a response to the grace of the Christ, an invitation to the Life. They recognised themselves as spiritual gentiles now returning as spiritual Jews, the chosen ones, from the purity of Eden to bear witness

---

[56] Barbour and Frost, *The Quakers*, 39; Feullenbach, *The Kingdom of God*, 65; Davies, *Works*, 40.
[57] An excellent insight into convincement can be found in S. Jones, *This is Lights Appearance*.
[58] See for example Jn. 12: 36, 46.
[59] Joan (or Jone) Brooksop (d. 1680), *An Invitation of Love* (1662), 11. For a letter for unity see Fell to Francis Howgill, *Markey MS*. (c.1654/55?), 3-4; Hubberthorne, letters (1654 and 1655) to Howgill, *Markey MS*., 21-2 and 20-1 respectively; Parnel, *To Friends in Essex* in *Works*, 442; Nayler, letter (1656) to Fell, *Crosfield MS*., Item 9; Rigge, letter (1657) to Fell, *Crosfield MS*., Item 6; Bayly, letter to Friends, *Harvey MSS*. (n.d.), i., Item 2.
[60] Brooksop, *An Invitation of Love*, 7-8. Brooksop here quotes Isa. 33:21. See also Susanna Bateman, *'I matter not how I appear to man'* (1658), 2.

in thought and deed to their resurrection, something that was available to anybody.[61] Convincement's exacting Damascus road was akin to the prayer of oblation in which people are exhorted to keep nothing back. It was also an experience that often involved trembling and other dramatic 'signs' as gateways into perfection. Quaking, the power of the Lord made visible, was considered the operation of the Spirit of God which brought a 'condemnation on all high looks, and upon the lofty nature', of 'bringing down the proud flesh'.[62] Convincement, then, demanded authenticity and involved waiting, an expectation in the sense of being poised so that one may be ready to act on God's will at any time. In this prayer-act a path was prepared for an inner Pentecost whose impact would, like the broad rivers of the Life, carry the Friends through their physical existence with both service and the cross as second nature.

Convincement, therefore, involved an objectification of what was subjective, the invisible was brought into the visible and returned again to enrich the invisible and so on. At these depths it led to an internalised atonement, a testimony to the crucifixion of the old self and resurrection into the new covenant: 'so dwell in the Light, and wait upon God to have the image of God renewed, and all come to witness yourselves restored by Christ into the image of God', said Fox in 1653.[63] Convincement empowered an individual to give birth to God's Light for the whole world by being in the *now* of grace and in the grace of the *now,* certain they could fall no lower than God's outreached arms.[64] Through this living on the spiritual edge (*eschaton*), through this utterly critical 'moment'—it could last months—the individual gave witness to the way and the truth of 'the Life' where God and humanity could reconcile. As convincement was a sacramental act of 'discovery' (a revelation, an unveiling), it freed the individual from Puritan determinism while heralding the possibility of wholeness that such reconciliation implied. Once turned over to the Light, the Friends were to be fearless patterns and examples to everybody, and

---

[61] They were possibly inspired in this view by Rom. 2:13-15; Ac. 3:19; Mt 3:2.

[62] Burrough, *A Standard Lifted Up*, 34. See also Fox, 'The Word of the Lord God to all you that scorn trembling and quaking' in *A Word from the Lord, Unto all the faithless Generation,* 9-12; Fox, *To all the Nations under the Whole Heavens* (1660), 2; Fox, *A Voice of the Lord to the Heathen,* 7 for quaking as a theophany; Farnworth, *A Confession and Profession* (1659), 5-6; Nayler, 'The Examination of James Nayler' in *Works,* 14-15 where Nayler quotes 'David [Ps.19?], Dn.[10:7], Hab.[3:16]'; A. Parker, *A Call Out of Egypt*, 26. Also R. Taylor, *Quaking: A Study of the Phenomena of Quaking*, 8-9 for a good account of trembling and singing in prisons by Quakers Thomas Holme and Thomas Aldam, and the Quakers' reference to the prison singing of Paul of Tarsus. See Holme, letter (*c.* March 1654) to Fell, *SW*/i/189 for trembling and crying in Chester. And *TLITC*, 53, 144-8.

[63] Fox, Ep. 32 (1653) in *LOGF*, 15.

[64] Penn, *Some Fruits of Solitude in Reflections and Maxims* (1693), maxim 31, p. 13.

they were expected to address the Seed and its 'pearl' within those they encountered.

But quaking was not confined to shaking and trembling. Nor was it necessarily an ecstatic demonstration symbolically setting the Friends apart from the world as Reay has argued.[65] Indeed this is to misunderstand early Quaker Christianity since they were never latter day Essenes cutting themselves off in despair from the world. Rather, by expressing a spiritually all-embracing view of life, quaking affirmed their own transformation was now visible to all, a dramatic signal that the world, too, was in need of *metanoia*. So, instead of renouncing the world by means of an other-worldly flight, they were exhorted to be *in* the world (as Jesus command the apostles) for its transformation, though ever-cautious as Fox's quoting of the 'little apocalypse' of Mark 13 suggested. He was concerned that the Publishers of the Truth should not to be led astray by false prophets but be awake instead to the signs of divine intervention in the historical drama that was unfolding before them.[66] Being 'not of the world' meant paradoxically being a 'new' person of the new covenant, wholeheartedly adopting the mantle of the 'second' person (Jesus as the recapitulated Adam) *in* the world. It meant being subject to the discipline of the new covenant, enjoying its glory and being 'mightily effective' for the good old cause of God. Nayler wrote in 1653 that,

> The second man is the Lord from heaven, and he that bears his image minds heavenly things ... for he is spiritual ... for the evil eye that offends is plucked out; ... and there is an eye turned inward; which pierces into the hidden treasure which is eternal.[67]

A year earlier, he wrote that the Light demanded that Friends should 'come out of the Love of the world, and arise out of all visible things and prepare to meet the Lord ... Let Love abound in you, one towards another, without being partial'.[68]

Quaking was a visible expression of their newly found life in the Spirit, an expression which involved other elaborate forms. Like the Amsterdam Anabaptists of the previous century, some walked naked into market places

---

[65] *QER*, 35-6.
[66] Fox, *An Epistle to all People on the Earth*, 5, 7.
[67] Nayler here cites 1 Cor. 15:47; Col. 1:15 and Ps. 25:14. See also 2 Cor. 10: 4 and Nayler, *A Discovery of the First Wisdom*, 11 and esp. 8-16.
[68] Nayler, *To All Dear Brethren and Friends in Holderness*, (1653) in *Works*, 31-3. See also p. 26 for Nayler's *An Epistle to Certain Friends about Wakefield* (1653), *ibid.* for 'Take heed etc'. See Farnworth *The Pure Language of the Spirit*, *passim* for a Fox-like invocation of Hebrew Testament quaking; esp. 6-7. For walking naked see William Simpson, *Going Naked for a Sign* (1660), Bds. and *BQ*, 148.

as a sign of their innocence (purity), a sign, too, that the world was clothed in filthy garments. Others smeared themselves and/or the houses of 'apostates' with excrement to publicise the foul nature of sin.[69] Such signs, perhaps inspired by Isaiah and Revelation 11:3—'and they shall prophesy a thousand two hundred and threescore days, clothed in sackcloth'—were also an outward witness to the 'heathen', like their many and varied sufferings, as a way of publicising the *inner experience* (rather than a mere demonstration) of the Christ within, the power of Light over darkness.

Unsurprisingly, opponents like Francis Higginson misunderstood them. He believed that 'real' prayer should be undefiled by gestures that could distort authentic, or produce false, feeling. At the same time, however, he could ignore the fact that his fellow Puritans, too, had long accepted the desirability of 'crying to the Lord, wrestling with the Lord, striving with him, and giving him no rest', as arch-Calvinist John Preston wrote in 1629. Another arch-Calvinist, Thomas Goodwin, suggested in 1643 that God inspired prayer 'with a quickening heart and enlargement of affections'. Church prayer manuals assumed an intense emotional relationship with God with John Donne suggesting that 'prayer [had] the nature of violence, the nature of impudence'. The Quakers would have agreed though they were well aware that in trembling they could shake themselves free of the Puritan-type conviction that the soul was a slave to sin forever.[70] 'The Lord reigns', they may have read in Psalm 99:1, 'let the people tremble', so affirming the role of the Kingdom—that is, God's saving sovereignty of wholeness—by their outward witness to the Word and their hope for the future. Thus did the first Friends defy Higginson and other Puritans, believing that in the Life they were on a trajectory towards God away from evil. In God was found a passage for every soul into its liberty. As a loving covenant was thus created with God, 'a holy pure generation' was born, so claimed William Smith, with 'its conception in the matrix of Eternity.'[71]

---

[69] See Carroll, 'Quakers in Venice', 23. He quotes Fox, *An Answer to a Paper . . . Holland* (1658), 17; the quote is most likely Fox's but the tract was only partially written by him. Fox's knowledge of the Bible may have allowed an understanding of 2 S.15:30; Isa. 20:2-4 and Mi. 1:8 as setting a precedent for such behaviour. See the following for reference to spiritual nakedness: Aldam *et al, False Prophets*, 4; Fox, *A Warning from the Lord to the Pope*, 4; Fox, Ep. 77 (1654) in *LOGF*, 35; G. Whitehead, *The Path of the Just Cleared* (1655), 4; H. Smith, *A Warning to the Priests* (1656), 4; Bateman, *'I matter not how I appear to man'*, 2; Bayly, *A Short Discovery of the State of Man* (1659), 1; Burrough *et al, A Declaration . . . to the Present Distracted and Broken Nation of England*, 6. Also Carroll, 'Early Quakers and Going Naked', *passim* and Cressy, *Travesties and Trangressors*, chp. 11 for Elizabeth Fletcher's nakedness in Oxford in 1655.

[70] See Higginson's oft-quoted passage from *A Brief Relation of the Irreligion*, 15-16. Also *EQW*, 70-1 in both editions and Garrett, 'The Rhetoric of Supplication', 339, 344, 346.

[71] W. Smith, *The New Creation*, 48.

Convincement was at once a source of faithfulness which gave birth to spiritual confidence and humility enabling the Friends to exhibit a remarkable degree of control and calm in the face of persecution. In their willingness to die, they believed, lay the ultimate proof that the Life was truly within. Jesus, after all, had likewise given testimony through his suffering and crucifixion. Indeed, convincement was an acknowledgment that suffering might be expected. When it did befall them, the Friends often welcomed it, becoming willing slaves to the physical surroundings of the prison in which they could give glory to God in holy solitude. By doing so, they were encouraged by their reading of Acts but also by fellow Friends, themselves no strangers to the dungeon. In prisons throughout England, Europe and New England, the Quakers believed they were receiving Light into their lives, yielding to God as a sacrifice that would continue 'this side eternity'.[72] So it was that Lydia Fairman could speak of the 'daily cross' which the Friends needed to bear so that they may 'be born of God an incorruptible Seed', a Seed that was to be spread to 'all people on the earth'.[73]

This was something taken literally by many of Fairman's co-religionists, including Katharine Evans and Sarah Cheevers. During their time in Malta, described as a 'curious event' by one modern Dominican commentator, both women languished for four years in a Roman Inquisition gaol on the Vittoriosa in Valetta, enduring the pain of exile, repeated interrogation (sometimes by English friars), appalling physical conditions and the temptations of freedom should they recant.[74] Their undoubted courage and patience gave them a determination to defeat their captors. Released in 1663 and still defying the authorities, their story is an epic tale of two Quakers rising above their deprivation with their inner and outer conflicts a testimony to their beliefs.[75] Single-minded in this way as they were, few Friends would spiritually 'gad abroad' (look elsewhere) for they fervently believed that their triumph would be a life without end in the resting-place of Love.[76]

Finally, the moment of convincement signified the climatic birth of an inner apocalypse by which the separated individual came to God fully repentant (transformed), revealed in his/her purity and thus free in the prelapsarian sense (pure, Edenic). Here is a reminder indeed of the poet Rilke's cry, 'my soul, dressed in silence, rises up and stands alone before

---

[72] For 'this side eternity' see Howgill, *A Lamentation for the Scattered Tribes*, 5.
[73] Fairman, A Few Lines Given Forth, Bds. And Nayler, *A Discovery of the First Wisdom*, 5, 7.
[74] Katharine Evans (d. 1692), Sarah Cheevers (d. 1664). See Vella, *The Tribunal of the Inquisition in Malta*, 31-3 and in Cadbury, 'Friends and the Inquisition at Malta', 219-25.
[75] Wedgwood, *Velvet Studies*, 129-37.
[76] For 'gad abroad' see Howgill, *A Lamentation for the Scattered Tribes*, 6.

you'.[77] When pursued successfully, it was through righteousness—coming to terms with one's sin and giving thus justice to oneself—that the Beast within stood convicted (Jn. 8:9). This allowed people to undergo a rebirth into the new covenant thus receiving the saving grace of God's Light as the 'seeds of Abraham'. Fox and the Friends knew the Gospels intimately and, in marrying the apocalyptic in Mark and Paul (the End-times for the power of sin) to the Light in John (the triumph of Love over sin)[78], they guaranteed the ultimate destruction of Mammon for those estranged from 'the Life'.[79] In doing so they imbibed the Johannine statement, 'I in them, and you in me' (Jn. 17:23).

To summarise, acceptance of the Light heralded a state of justification (holiness/salvation) and sanctification in which God was now fully present within. Through convincement, an individual was resurrected, inwardly 'mortified' (purified) and redeemed whole (returned to the love of God) and thus turned to the joy of belonging 'to a fulfilment beyond all greedy human fears and dreams'.[80] As members of this internalised Church, they were to be walking hieroglyphs of the Kingdom, the 'mystery' or 'secret' (Rom.16:26; Col. 1:26). Convincement, then, was a public affirmation that individuals accepted responsibility for their own salvation and it was assumed they would do so within the context of a caring community under the rule of the physical, spiritual and cosmological Jesus.

Testimony: Holism and Mysticism

Evidence that the Quakers' experience of convincement, their outflow of witness and understanding of 'the Life' incorporated a mystical, prophetic and holistic outlook, rests on such works as Burrough's *A Seasonable Word of Advice* (1658) and Fox's Epistle 25 (1653). Probably inspired by Galatians 3:16, Burrough asked his fellow Quakers to consider how,

> The Word . . . reached unto you . . . and precious was his Truth . . . and the seed of the Kingdom you received with joy . . . by one word of

---

[77] For references to Adam see Fox in *Saul's Errand*, 3-4. See also Nayler's explanation of the prelapsarian state in 'Concerning the Fall of Man' in *Love to the Lost*, 1-4. Rainer Maria Rilke: 'I am, O Anxious One. Don't you hear my voice' in Mitchell (ed.), 3.

[78] Nayler, *A Discovery of the First Wisdom*, 15, 21-3.

[79] Fox, *The Woman Learning*, 2 and *Doctrinals*, 80; Howgill, *A Lamentation for the Scattered Tribes*, 15-16; Fox, *An Epistle to all People on the Earth*, 7; *Journal*, 40.

[80] O'Neil, *Long Day's Journey into Night*, 153-4. And Nayler, 'Concerning Justification' in *Love to the Lost*, 50-2. Evelyn Underhill describes mortification as 'the resolving of the turbulent whirlpools and currents of your own conflicting passions, interests, desires; the killing out of all those tendencies . . . which create the fundamental opposition between your interior and exterior life'. This applies well to convincement; see her *Practical Mysticism*, 65.

Life, which is not divided; and you were begotten to live unto him, and not unto your selves.[81]

Like Fox, he invoked the name of the spiritual Jesus, the Light/Christ, as the way to the Life, Truth and unity in God since the Word, wrote Fox,

> which was in the beginning which breaks the world to pieces . . . makes all clean which is received into the heart. And this is the word of Faith which we preach . . . Therefore . . . wait in the Light which comes from Christ that with it you may receive the Life.[82]

Insights into early Quaker holism may also be gleaned from modern commentaries on the Christian mystical experience. Underpinning their holism, their one-ness with God, early Quaker mysticism bore a close resemblance to 'a certain type of concrete, historical imitation of Christ offering immediate access to God', and to what is called a 'source experience', an intense awakening to the love of God. This experience signals a fundamental change within the human psyche in which 'the old familiar picture of the world and self [the ego] . . . is radically shattered'.

Dominican theologian Eduard Schillebeeckx argued that authentic Christian mysticism is never flight from the world but an integrating and reconciling mercy with all things. A form of prayer itself, it sees God as the explicit object for the Christian life.[83] One characteristic of Christian mysticism is the 'dark night of the soul', which today is called the *via negativa* or the apophatic way. For John of the Cross, the sixteenth century Spanish mystic, the dark night anticipated a longing for 'pure faith', the ultimate objective being union with God.[84] As a result, it offers a cathartic space in which a settling of the Spirit takes place. Though painful, it can be recuperative and culminate in a condition of being in which everything is suspended momentarily in a state of divine consciousness whereby a complete embracing of the world-within-Love occurs. Richard Roach, a minister at Hackney in seventeenth century London, confirmed that,

---

[81] Burrough, *A Seasonable Word of Advice*, Bds.
[82] Fox, Ep. 25 (1653) and see also Ep. 73 (1654) both in *LOGF*, 13, 33; Fox, *To All that would Know*, 3; Fell, *An Epistle to Friends by M.F.* (1654) in *Works*, 56-7 and *An Epistle of M. Fell to Friends . . . in Lancaster Castle* (1654) in *Works*, 59; Nayler, 'James Naylers Answer' in *Saul's Errand*, 17; Fox and Nayler et al, *Several Papers*, 10; *Journal*, 218-19. Also *FFQ*, 236, 261, esp. 236-65.
[83] Schillebeeckx, *Church*, 68-9, 72. See De Certeau, *The Mystic Fable* quoted in Howells, 'Mysticism and the Mystical', 22.
[84] See Campbell (trans.), *Poems of St. John of the Cross*, 11-13; Happold, *Mysticism*, 355-66. For an important insight into early Quaker 'dark night' experience, see Nayler, *To the Life of God in All* (1659).

mystics in all parts and of all denominations . . . have overlooked and shot beyond the particularities of their own Church or party as in an outward visible form, and kept to the interior or spiritual way; in which there may be observed as great a harmony and unity even among those of externally different denominations, as there is among those in the outward way and forms a disunity and disharmony.[85]

As understood already, early Quaker convincement was a restorative experience, a process of purging of anything that barred the individual from a deeper relationship with God. As with mystical experiences generally, it implied a consistent, forward movement guided by a visible or invisible leitmotif, 'finding the secret', that is to say, discovering and truly living a life that is real in its essential, eternal sanctity[86]—'for therein is the secrets of God revealed', wrote Nayler.[87] 'Secret' is here understood as mystery (i.e. that which God can and does reveal), a reciprocity between the human and the divine, but also the enjoyment of God's gifts as in Mark. 4:11: 'Unto you it is given to know the mystery of the Kingdom of God'. As such, 'secret' and 'mystery' are apocalyptic. Leading Friend John Whitehead wrote in 1656 that the truly convinced waited 'in Spirit to know him revealed, and his life through death made manifest, which opens the mystery that hath been hid from ages'.[88] Edward Burrough commented similarly in *A Discovery of Divine Mysteries* (1661) that 'the mystery of God . . . is veiled and hidden secretly in and under all things that have a being': that is, in Truth people are conformed to the image of Jesus, to his death and righteousness.[89] Penington's long spiritual incubation before his convincement in 1656-8, graphically reveals the spiritual impoverishment of the dark night, its despair. Upon convincement, however, he experienced in his own measure the fullness of the *real* 'Life', the Seed, he had 'waited for and sought after from [his] childhood'.[90]

By such statements the Friends referred to that inexhaustible depth of meaning which they encountered in 1 Corinthians where the transforming

---

[85] Martland, 'An Inquiry into Religion's Empty World', 469-81; for Richard Roach see Gibbons, *Gender in Mystical and Occult Thought*, 7.

[86] Waaijman, 'Toward a Phenomenological Definition Of Spirituality', 5-17.

[87] Nayler, *To All Dear Brethren . . . Yorkshire* (1652) in *Works*, 30-1. See also A. Parker, letter 13/Jan/1658) to Fox, *SW*/iii/140. And Farnworth, letter (12/Nov/1653) to Fell, *SW*/iii/51 where Farnworth describes himself in terms of a *tabula rasa* awaiting the Spirit to be revealed in him: 'as a white paper book without any line or sentence'.

[88] J. Whitehead, *A Word of Reproof from the Lord*, 6. He was quoting Col. 1:26.

[89] Burrough most likely had Rom. 8:29 in mind.

[90] Keiser, 'From Dark Christian', 44; see Burrough's similar statement in *A Discovery of Divine Mysteries*, 15; Dewsbury, *The Discovery of the Great Enmity*, 22; Penington, *The Way of Life and Death*, 89.

wisdom of God is revealed to those who hear but is rejected by the princes of this world.[91] Exploring Matthew and Mark, Fox also understood how the

> Kingdom of heaven is seen, which is as a grain of mustard seed which is within, and many have received it, and are become as little children, and them that be converted into the Kingdom, they bring forth their things new and their things old; and many are digging in the field, which is the world, which is set in their hearts seeking for the pearl, and many have found it, . . . so the pearl is within you.[92]

As with convincement, then, the dark night or the apophatic way, can be transformative: an identification with the same mystery or secret whereby one is eventually brought out of oneself in an act of self-transcendence. A new reality breaks through whose 'illumination' calls either for silence or a different set of words, and a reliance on metaphor to describe the feeling of 'the presence of the whole of reality, indeed the source of the whole'.[93] This experience is likened to "lifting of the veil of ignorance', the veil that covers the essential identity of God and [humanity]'.[94]

Where are the Quakers on the spectrum of mystical experience? They were not exclusively mystical in the way we might describe, say, John of the Cross. Nor were they completely subjective since they were concerned with the outward or daily spiritual dimension.[95] In this respect, Rufus Jones has stressed their 'moral earnestness' and 'social intensity' both of which 'saved [them] from the easy pitfalls of mystical quests', which can lead people to be 'self-centred and absorbed with the inward gaze'.[96] Fox's original religious realisation (c.1647), described on page 11 of his *Journal*, is related to elements in all mystical traditions in which there is an immediate apprehension of the presence of God. In his case, it was the Christ within to which he felt bound in a continuing unity, a Presence that could truly 'speak to his condition'. In this he bears some synergy with Puritan mystics, those whose theology lay on the margins of Puritanism such as that of John Everard and Giles Randall. They believed that an authentic religious life was found in the mystical union between the soul and God.[97]

---

[91] See 1 Cor. 2:7-8; 15:51.
[92] *Pearl*, 4; he most likely used Mt. 13:31; Mk. 4:31.
[93] Schillebeeckx, *Church*, 71-2.
[94] *Ibid*.
[95] Gwyn, 'Was George Fox a Prophet?', 28-29.
[96] See Jones' 'Introduction' in *BQ*, xlii.
[97] For Puritan mysticism see Brauer, 'Reflections on the Nature of English Puritanism', 106; for Giles Randall see R. Jones, *Spiritual Reformers*, 253-4, 260-63. To Everard and Randall may be added William Dell, William Erbery, John Saltmarsh and Sir Henry Vane Jr.

Chapter 9: 'Demonstration of the Spirit'

However, that the works of Jakob Boehme, himself steeped in the writings of Meister Eckhart, were found among Fox's library of 4,050 books, and that his (Fox's) understanding of the Inward Light resonated with the mystical experience in the *scintilla animae* of Eckhart himself, the 'Living Light' of Hildegard of Bingen and to a lesser degree with the *lumen gloriae* of Thomas Aquinas, should not lead us to assume a familiarity with such thinkers. How they might have influenced him will always be a matter of conjecture. Fox's mysticism and that of the other early Quakers bore some resemblance to the neo-Platonism of the unknown Dionysius the Areopagite (or Pseudo-Dionysius) in which God is described as life, wisdom and power. Unlike Dionysius, however, their experience of God was not entirely apophatic, nor was God a nameless and ineffable One. And yet they might have agreed with Plotinus (from whom Dionysius owed much) that God was present in the centre of the soul, and that intermediaries were unnecessary for communicating with God.

In so far as it urged unity with God, the Quakers' mystical experience shared some similarity, though it should not to be overstated, with the erotic metaphor of union with God beloved by a number of medieval mystics and by Teresa of Ávila, John of the Cross and François de Sales. Their experience of the indwelling Light could indeed be intense—it was sometimes revealed viscerally during their worship gatherings—but it was never as ecstatic and ravishing as among Eastern orthodox mystics such as Maximus the Confessor or St. Simeon the New Theologian who wrote, 'I am filled with light and glory; my face shines like that of my Beloved, and all my members glow with heavenly light'. Interestingly, however, Quaker preachers occasionally used what we today might label extravagant, quasi-mystical language to describe George Fox and Margaret Fell. Thomas Holme could address Fell as 'you daughter of Zion whose face shines like the sun at noon day . . . you are covered with rich robes, your garment is unspotted', while Richard Farnworth saw Fox as 'my heart, my life, my oneness . . . you know where I am. I cannot be hid from you. You know my secrets'.[98] Nuttall understood this highly elaborate language of praise as directed not so much to the carnal person but rather the Light in that person.[99]

Though he does not specifically talk of union, Augustine of Hippo's vision of, and contact with, God is a reminder of what occurred during early

---

[98] Thomas Holme, letter (1653) to Fell, *SW*/iii/337 and Farnworth, *SW*/iii/57. Such language was not confined to the Friends. Thomas Brightman, the milleniarian whom we met in Chp. 1, was hailed by a contemporary as 'the prophet of the century, the brightest burning light of our age'. For Brightman see Lamont, *Puritanism and Historical Controversy*, 152-3.

[99] See Nuttall's *EQL*, 85 (for Richard Farnworth, Nov. 1652, to Fox, *SW*/iii/58), 155-6 (Richard Sale, Oct. 1655, to Fox, *SW*/iv/211), 192 (for Mary Prince, July 1656, to Fox, *SW*/iv/58); Coale, letter (12/Jan/1665) to Fox, *A. R. Barclay MSS.* 1/64.

Quaker convincement and the *nearness* of God that the Friends sensed in their daily lives. Augustine saw the divine Light in a 'flash of one trembling glance' and maintained it was best worshipped in silence. And while the Friends would have agreed with Walter Hilton that 'whoever loves God dwells in Light', they were keen, unlike him, to live outside the monastery walls. And there are more connections, such as that between Fox and Bernard of Clairvaux for whom 'the condition of knowledge of, and union with, God is the possession of pure and ardent love'. For Bernard and Fox, humility and charity were vital for unity with God.

With the anonymous author of the *Theologia Germanica* (Johannes Tauler?) came the view that sin 'is nought else, but that the creature turns away from the unchangeable Good and betakes itself to the changeable', a precursor to the Quaker understanding of sin as separation. Indeed, Francis Howgill's well-known query, 'why gad abroad?'—why seek elsewhere when the Kingdom was already in the midst of us?—was also seventeenth century theological code for the dangers of separation. And with Thomas à Kempis in *Of the Imitation of Christ*, the Friends would have found a practical guide to God's Reign by following Jesus along the 'royal road of the holy cross' for union with the Spirit/Christ:

> For the Kingdom is righteousness and peace and joy in the Holy Spirit which the wicked enjoy not [i.e. not granted to them]. Christ will come unto thee and comfort thee, if thou make a fit resting place for Him within thee.[100]

The sentiments here are repeatedly found in the works of, say, William Smith and Isaac Penington as well as in Fox's epistles. Penington's pre-Quaker works suggest some familiarity with Boehme, Bernard of Clairvaux, the medieval mystic Jan van Ruusbroec, the Friends of God, Heinrich Seuse (Suso) and Johannes Tauler. Seuse's *Certain Sweet Prayer* was published in 1575 and Tauler's works frequently appeared in England in the following century. Both were readily available during the 1650s, and *The History of the Life and Death of Dr. Joh. Thauler* was published in 1660.[101] Although

---

[100] *Of the Imitation of Christ* (1596), 'Of the Inward Life of Man', Bk 2, chp. 1, p. 70.

[101] For the library of George Fox see Nickalls, 'George Fox's Library', 2-27. For Jakob Boehme (1575-1624) see Rainy (ed.), esp. 20-32 for ideas similar to early Quakerism as one can see in Francis Ellington's *Christian Information* (1664), the title taken from a Boehme tract (1647). Also for Boehme and Behmenism see *TWTUD*, 148, 176, 192, 225, 289-90: although Fox owned a copy of Boehme's works, I agree with Nuttall and also Gibbons that the early Quakers drew a clear line between themselves and Behemism. See Nuttall, *The Holy Spirit*, chp. 1; Gibbons, *Gender in Mystical and Occult Thought*, 126-9; Barbour, 'Sixty Years in Early Quaker History' in Dandelion (ed., 2004), 24; Peters, *Print Culture*, 57 (63*n*). And for a Quaker riposte to Boehme's followers see Anderdon's *Against Babylon and her Merchants in England* (1660) and *One Blow at Babel* (1662). Also S. Spencer, *Mysticism in*

Chapter 9: 'Demonstration of the Spirit'

Rufus Jones argued that early Quaker faith was 'one of the great historical results' of European mysticism, it can also be argued that the Friends had an *unwitting* affiliation with some like-minded European and British mystical thinkers *and* with reformers like John Wycliffe who was specifically admired by a number of Friends such as Burrough and Samuel Fisher.[102]

Finally, our short survey brings us to some synchronicity of thought between the Friends and the Cambridge Platonists, whose central theme was the supremacy of the Inward Light of Reason.[103] The Light of Reason, perceived to be the divine Governor, the very voice of God, illuminated the conscience. It was the final authority for an individual's religious belief and practice, an authority found in the conviction of the mind legitimated by the interior testimony of the Holy Spirit rather than by ecclesiastical dogma or Church Councils. Further, this Light was enlightened by Scripture, particularly by the Gospel of John with its Platonic Prologue. A favourite biblical text of the Cambridge Platonists was Proverbs 20: 27: 'The spirit of man is the candle of the Lord'. Following Plotinus, they believed Reason was of God, a conduit indeed for bringing people to God with whom an unmediated communication was possible, and an echo of the divine within the soul, an imprint of God within humanity. And because it was semi-divine, it led beyond the sensory. Their founder, Benjamin Whichcote, wrote of the Light

> which God set up in Man, to light him; and that which by this Light he may discover, are all the Instances of Morality; of good Affection, and Submission towards God; the Instances of Justice and Righteousness to Men, and Temperance to himself.[104]

Like the Quakers, the Cambridge Platonists cried aloud for Truth that was found in the heart rather than in notions.[105] They opposed formalism in

---

World Religion, chp. 7; see esp. 212, 231-33; Happold, *Mysticism*, 184-87, 203-05, 211-212, 228-9, 235-37, 269-271, 294-96, 299-305, 314-36.

[102] R. Jones, *Spiritual Reformers*, v-vi, 337-49.

[103] Largely associated with Emmanuel and Christ colleges, they were, for the most part, Anglican clerics. They drew on the Neoplatonic tradition and contemporary philosophical developments to promote a tolerant and inclusive understanding of Christianity. Central thinkers of the school besides Cudworth were Henry More (1614–87), John Smith (1618–52) and Benjamin Whichcote (1609–83). Close associates included Nathanael Culverwell (1618–51), George Rust (1626–70), Peter Sterry and John Worthington (1618–80). Thinkers with connections to the school included the Quaker, Anne Conway (1631–79), Joseph Glanvill (1636–80), John Norris (1657–1711), and, beyond the colleges, leading divines such as Gilbert Burnet (1643–1715), Simon Patrick (1626–1707), Edward Stillingfleet (1635–99) and John Tillotson (1630–94).

[104] Campagnac, *The Cambridge Platonists*, 10.

[105] *Ibid.*, p. xix and Fleming, *Mysticism in Christianity*, 204.

prayer and worship, promoting instead a simple approach to both. Unlike the Friends, they discounted the Fall. Sympathetic to the mysticism of the *Theologia Germanica*[106] but also to Arminianism, they could never countenance God as a tyrant with a pre-determined Elect. Nor did Hell exist. Rather, God was the Good, the Form of forms, and was always reasonable and just. For them, as with Plato, the world was a mirror of this Deity, the reflection of the Ideal. For Henry More, who, like Richard Baxter, eventually came to a more sympathetic understanding of the Quaker position, the Light of Reason was expressed in an essentially rational universe, the creation of a rational God.

To recapitulate for a moment, the indwelling Light of the Friends was not to be confused with reason or conscience, both of which were subject to human discretion. The Quakers were directed, instead, by the unchanging Light, the constant and real presence of 'Christ Jesus Through their discernment of the saving grace of the Spirit—something they 'knew experientially'—the Friends believed they possessed the panacea for the ills of the human condition. The very title of a Hubberthorne pamphlet strenuously confirmed the Quakers' house as being built upon the rock of Christ.[107] Such a foundation was reinforced with an ardent belief that, as the Light of Christ rose in victory, the more the Beast edged towards its downfall: 'Woe, . . . now is the devil raging because his time is short', said Fox, who was forever keen to 'chain' the devil.[108] The Lamb's strength was proportionate to the degree of surrender, the willingness of the individual to be open to, and vulnerable for, the love of God, the Kingdom, the 'pearl'. This vulnerability would ensure emergence into the Light from the wilderness, exile, internal slavery and/or the oppression of an inner and outer 'Egypt'.

Through a purgation of sin, this internalised, mystical experience of the indwelling Light of Christ was worked into the daily lives of the Friends so that others could see the grace of God at work in the world.[109] The reward for those convinced of the Light was theopoetically described by Penington in 1658:

---

[106] Patrides, *The Cambridge Platonists*, 17-18.
[107] See *Journal*, 11; Hubberthorne, *The Quakers House Built upon the Rock Christ* (1659).
[108] *Journal*, 179. For another understanding of the potential power of love over sin see Nayler, *How Sin is Strengthened*, 3, 7.
[109] See Fox, Ep. 45 (1653), *Works*, 7: 54-7 for an enunciation for how the Quakers may emerge into the Light from the wilderness, exile, internal slavery and/or oppression of inner 'Egypt'. But see also the personal accounts of spiritual wilderness and convincement in *inter alia*, Farnworth, *The Heart Opened by Christ*; Dewsbury, *The Discovery of the Great Enmity*; Howgill, *The Inheritance of Jacob Discovered*.

> Now as this Light is felt, loved, understood in Spirit, hearkened and cleaved to in the pure faith . . . that which cleaves to it, is drawn out of the darkness by it, into the covenant of the pure eternal Light, where God is.[110]

Penington's anagogical statement is an example of 'infused contemplation', a state in the contemplative process in which God communicates with little requirement from human effort. From then on, as 'acquired contemplatives', the early Quakers became conscious of a mysterious and loving Presence in themselves and the whole universe, and submitted everything they thought and did to the power and life of the Spirit.[111] For this reason they were typical of Christian mystics who emphasised humility, a surrendering to God so they could be interiorly apt to penetrate the divine mystery.[112] The hallmark of such spiritual experiences was involvement and concern, all the more important when one considers the Quakers' mysticism led them to turn a critical eye to events around them and fuel their determination to transform society away from the grasp of the 'devil' and 'lust' (self-interest, greed).[113]

Testimony: the Quaker Apocalypse

With such a powerful mystical impulse as their own, it was not surprising the Quakers invited conflict from their militarised society dominated as it was by doctrinal conformity and widespread chiliasm. However, while the first Friends took their place in 'the common messianic excitement and the political unrest' of the time and shared that place with chiliasts, they did so entirely in opposition to them.[114] In Launceston prison in 1656, Fox repudiated Baptist and Fifth Monarchist premillennial claims that 'this year Christ should come and reign upon earth a thousand years'. Instead, in the *Journal* we hear him say: '[a]nd they looked upon this reign to be outward, whereas he was come inwardly in the hearts of his people to reign and rule

---

[110] Penington, *Some Considerations Propounded to the Jews*, 6. Also O. Davies, *God Within: the mystical tradition in northern Europe*, 4.
[111] W. Johnson, *Arise, My Love*, 92-3.
[112] See M-D. Chenu, *Aquinas and his Role on Theology*, 43.
[113] By the mid century there already existed a long English and European tradition in which the 'devil' and self-interest were conflated. See the works of Seuse and Tauler already mentioned and Benjamin Nicholson, *Some Returns to a Letter* (1653), 1-2; Farnworth, *The Ranters Principles* (1655), 7 and Winstanley, *A New-Years Gift for the Parliament and Army* (1650), *passim* but see esp. 2, 3.
[114] Maclear, 'Quakerism and the End of the Interregnum', 19 quoted in Ingle, 'From Mysticism to Radicalism: Recent Historiography of Quaker Beginnings', 86. Ingle's helpful article offers an overview of Quaker historiography up to 1987.

there ... And thousands ... have opened to him, and he is come in'.[115] And by peaceful rather than violent means.

Throughout the decade Fox and the Friends doggedly maintained that Christ was 'before Adam was', transcendent over chronological and spatial specificity. It was the same Christ that had 'come to teach his people himself', the Christ that had always been present. The *now* factor of God's Holy Kingdom ran concurrently with the Quaker anticipation of the consummation in God of all humanity occurring when 'all people' would eventually turn to the Light. This stood in sharp contrast to the outwardly war-like Puritan view that history's consummation would occur only after the physical annihilation of the forces of evil. Therefore, with a description of millennialism *per se* as a 'dynamic force in the minds of [those] who were totally involved in the reconstruction of the world'[116], comes the need to differentiate its premillennial form from early Quaker thought.[117]

Towards the end of its most formative decade, Quaker beliefs—for example, Fox's *now* conviction, just mentioned, that 'Christ is come to teach his people himself'—had the appearance of post- but more particularly amillennialism and historicist premillennialism as discussed in Chapters 1 and 8. It will be remembered that both saw the Lamb's victory as evidenced through the Spirit. The leading Quakers knew the physical world was not about to end. It had not, after all, ended on Calvary, but the End-times were always with us as William Caton and Dorothy White assured their readers in 1662.[118] With the End-time interiorised, Francis Howgill reiterated an important element of 1650s Quaker Apocalypse and Testimony. What was true for the individual, he wrote in *One Warning more unto England* (1660), was true also for the nations. That is, the dire state the country would endure if it failed to turn to the Lord and the values

---

[115] *Journal*, 261.

[116] Tai Liu, *Discord in Zion*, 3.

[117] J. Wilson, *Pulpit in Parliament*, 32-3; Bauckham, *Tudor Apocalypse*, 210; Lamont, *Richard Baxter*, 13, 55, 137 and *Puritanism and Historical Controversy*, esp. chp. 8; Lamont, 'The Muggletonians 1652-1979', 28; Davis, *Fear, Myth and History*; Fletcher, 'New Light on Religion and the English Civil War' (rev. art.), 103-5; N. Baxter, 'Gerrard Winstanley's Experimental Knowledge of God', 199; Ingle, 'George Fox, Millenarian', esp. 261. See Mullett, *Northern History*, 225-6 in which Mullett reviews David Scott's *Quakerism in York 1650-1670*: D. Scott, as we shall see in Chps. 12 nd 13, suggests York Friends were always respectable rather than revolutionary and yet adhered to the Lamb's War. See Ball, *A Great Expectation*, 'Introduction' and 7-14, 164-77, 193-211. And Hill, *The Antichrist in Seventeenth Century England*, 143; Gura, *A Glimpse of Sion's Glory*, 126; Capp, *The Fifth Monarchy*, 19 and see both his 'Godly Rule and English Millenarianism' (rev. art.), 107 and 'The Fifth Monarchists and Popular Millenarianism' in McGregor and Reay (eds.), 165.

[118] Caton, *The Testimony of a Cloud of Witnesses* (1662), Sig. A2; D. White, *An Alarum Sounded Forth* (1662), Bds. Note their post-Restoration publication dates. See also *Journal*, 104, 107, 109.

of the Kingdom: 'Oh nation, consider and take this one warning more that you proceed not further to thy hurt, and repent [transform oneself] when it is too late'.[119] The Kingdom beckoned, he was saying, guaranteeing emancipation from the Puritan fortress of fear and sin, where the natural life of humanity belonged to an undivine order and out of which the 'many professors' did 'plead for sin' (i.e. in respect to predestination).[120] Like the free-willer Radicals of previous generations, Fox and the Friends argued that since people were made in the image of God, eternal reprobation (damnation) for a non-Elect was impossible. Substantive themes such as these, including the Light, Truth, Life and the salvation they brought—all of which were present in Fox's original religious experience (c.1647) as well as in the movement as a whole—contradicted Calvinistic determinism. They also continued to lend vitality and colour to the movement's Kingdom theology and the development of Testimony throughout the 1650s and into the next decade.

Apocalypticists are usually prophets who urgently seek to influence 'the wise among the people' by exhortation. They normally transmit their mission through dramatic language and/or activity. By such means they not only highlight aspects contrary to God but also the ways in which God's healing intervention can be expected. This allows apocalypticists to open the world to the wonder of divine transcendence while advocating further specific courses of action such as conversion and, occasionally, political agitation since apocalyptic sometimes offers veiled commentaries on current political events or policies. Apocalypticism usually combines repentance and a turning to God whose redemptive purpose is already at work within the history of the age. As Farnworth wrote in 1655: 'Repentance is a forsaking the evil . . . by turning from darkness into Light to obey grace, and walk in the Light of the Lord, and in a holy and pure conversation [behaviour]'.[121] The 'specific courses' required are of a radical order, a completed rather than a momentary transformation for the better so that a new life (the Kingdom within) is lived out in the eternal *now* with works and actions inspired by God's grace. By accepting seriously the Epistle of James, for instance, the first Friends came to the same conclusion as its author: true faith issued in practical works reflected a witness of undivided commitment, a 'way' that was carried beyond death when one's name was written in the Book of Life. As a result, the apocalyptic motif is that of repentance and judgment followed by triumph and glory.

---

[119] Howgill, *One Warning More unto England* (1660), 16 and Sig. A2, 4-6; see *Journal*, 283-4 where Fox juxtaposes convincement and salvation.
[120] *TWTUD*, 252, 72, 98, chp. 8; Howgill, *A Lamentation for the Scattered Tribes*, 1-7. See also Flew, *The Idea of Perfection in Christian Theology*, 284-6.
[121] Farnworth, *The Brazen Serpent*, 12-13.

The prophetic element within apocalyptic writings and practice is proclamatory and reveals the Word/Light and the Kingdom. It points to the knowledge of existing yet hidden truths besides those that have been newly placed into the open: in other words, a dimension of human events, ordinarily closed to human view, is now disclosed.[122] Apocalypse, therefore, is incarnational as it ushers in the new creation. With the structure of reality thus changed, the future invades the present so that, in the language of the Friends, the power and life of God provides a new space for the true Elect, those who have realised and are realising their path into God as children of Light.[123]

Hence apocalypse focuses on the 'now' in which sin, corruption, alienation and death are ever-present. It also concentrates on where the lived Kingdom anticipates a superior future which is striven after—that is, the reign of peace, equality, justice and mercy, and solidarity with humanity and creation. To those aspirations and the inmost hopes for 'God's deliverer [to be] raised up', apocalypse emerges to assist people to stand firm in faith and love (solidarity) during times of national distress.[124] In this way, the harsh realities of injustice, oppression and suffering are withstood while meaning and direction are given to their lives. Some argue that such a vision is at work today in the liberation theology movement in various 'third world' countries.[125] Consequently, apocalypse is meant to assure people that God has not abandoned them and that the promised salvation *will* come.

There is a tendency, too, for apocalypse to expand the scope of prophecy to include a universal judgment of the nations; the apparently victorious wicked will be punished and the downtrodden righteous rewarded. As a result, apocalypse is cosmological and involves a particular kind of eschatological salvation in which the cosmos itself is radically transformed. In other words, it stresses divine sovereignty over history or, more accurately, it represents *ultimate* history, its true course as well as its End—the final and redemptive nonviolent victory of God in overthrowing evil so that all earthly empires are forever replaced by the Kingdom.[126] Thus apocalypse speaks in myth and symbol, theopoetry and metaphor as if 'charged with a quantum of meaning independent of the lexical plane'.[127]

Typically, the Quaker apocalypse arose in times of crisis. We have seen how crises and conflict were essential to convincement with a saving power

---

[122] Fuller, *Naming the Antichrist*, 20-2.
[123] See *Journal*, 104; Fogelklou, *James Nayler*, 119.
[124] Cohen, *A Dislocation between the Word and the Reality*, 20.
[125] See Gutiérrez, 'Option for the Poor', *passim*; Lassalle-Klein, 'Jesus of Galilee and the Crucified People', *passim*.
[126] For the idea of sovereignty over history see Rev. 17:18.
[127] Cohen, *ibid*. For a Cambridge Platonist example of such language see de Sola Pinto, 'Peter Sterry and his Unpublished Writings', 392-3.

Chapter 9: 'Demonstration of the Spirit'

to spiritually transform individuals and, through them, 'all people'. Rising above time and place—the early Quakers were quick to address each other as 'friends in the unchangeable'[128]—their apocalypse empowered the individual to communicate publicly in word and deed, as both priest and prophet, to reveal the secrets (i.e. the revelations) of God. Like the Kingdom, it demanded that the convinced live constantly and provisionally within the 'Life', in the Spirit, and to work towards establishing its peace, justice, equity, truth and mercy on the inner level so that these 'fruits' were externalised and given widespread expression. It acted as their 'subterranean spring'[129], being often encountered in conflict on three levels:

1. as each Friend confronted the Beast within; the quest for unity with God and one another;
2. within their movement as it periodically stressed its prophetic over its priestly strain;
3. with an 'apostate' and violent society heavily influenced by premillennial thinking.

Early Quaker Christ/Logos-mysticism and holism gave a strident immediacy to their understanding of apocalypse. Their resulting prophetic eschatology was—as in the case of apocalypse in general—'inscribed in a densely spiritual, politically intuitive, and, by necessity underground code'.[130] Its undercurrent nature, however, would finally disappear as the Friends underwent their Pentecost-Paracletal moment of 1659-61, signalling the collective realisation of Kingdom and Testimony among the saints for its proclamation.

The first Friends were indeed apocalyptic in the way this book describes them. Their writings alone were enough to portray their revelatory experience which, as with the first Christians, was re-presented or re-actualised for their intended audiences who could then participate in the original experience.[131] In this way they hoped their audiences could decode the message and, with the aid of the Light, come to their own understanding of, and passage into, God. The Quakers were prophets with an understanding of hope that bespoke God's design in the ordinary realities of the world. But more than that, theirs was an apocalyptic eschatology that expressed 'a more pessimistic view of the human condition and consequently emphasise[d] that human history [could] be improved only

---

[128] See 'J.H.' (John Hutchin?), letter (post-1656) to Ann Dewsbury in Cadbury, *Letters to William Dewsbury*, 17.
[129] O'Leary quoted in van Brogt, 'Apocalyptic Thought in Christianity and Buddhism', 6.
[130] Keller, 'The Attraction of Apocalypse and the Evil of the End', 69.
[131] Aune, 'The Apocalypse of John and the Problem of Genre', 89.

when God (or God's agents) actively intervene[d]'.[132] Out of despair would come hope.

Conclusion

Ten broad categories of Testimony were isolated and discussed. For the Friends, Testimony expressed their covenant with God and propelled them to be witnesses to 'love unfeigned', God's Kingdom. At the heart of Testimony lay righteousness and it demanded a total commitment best understood as apostolic and prophetic, an act of faith as discipleship. It meant partaking in, and being advocates of, a spiritual transformation on an inner level through convincement and on the outer level as 'patterns and examples' to a 'fallen world', a transformation that was subject to the healing grace of Love for themselves and for 'all people'. Their work of reconciliation on the inner level was thus projected onto the outer world, their consequent suffering being a signal that God would reach out to others, friend and foe alike, who were also in suffering. Hence, their witness, their Testimony, could be authenticated only with spiritual weapons.

More specifically, Kingdom and Testimony, being independent of time and place, assumed that the convinced should live apocalyptically, that is to say, consistently within the 'Life', working to establish its mysteries of peace, equity, truth, mercy/compassion and justice on the inner level so that these could be lived out externally. Testimony, then, gave rise to a politics of compassion and hope both of which forged a forward-looking revolution of the Spirit, a revolution that would transform the British nations and the world.

We also saw how five highly connected ingredients comprised Testimony—'the Life' and perfection, convincement and the quest for truth and unity, holism and mysticism, the Quaker apocalypse and witness and prophecy. The ultimacy that perfection implied meant seeking out and then universalising the absolute good. As a result, their devotion to the Inward Light, the pre-Easter Jesus and to the unchanging, cosmological Christ meant surrendering their will to God; free will was in God's possession only, although humans could choose darkness over the Light.

Quaker beliefs were difficult to place definitively on the spectrum of mysticism but we concluded that the Friends were Logos-, Christ- and Kingdom-mystics with similarities with some of the well-known varieties of Christian mystic thought, particularly with the Cambridge Platonists. The Quakers' powerful, mystical, holistic and apocalyptic impulse—and their outer witness—invited conflict from the wider, militarised society. Besides expression of this conflict on the inner level, it was at times experienced

---

[132] Fuller, *Naming the Antichrist*, 20.

among themselves and externally from opponents, all of which strengthened Testimony, their 1650s experience of the Kingdom, their determination to 'walk in the narrow way.'

Chapter 10: *'Walk in the Narrow Way'*

- Witness and Prophecy -

By the 1650s, the *Book of Common Prayer* had long provided the religious and legal definition of gender roles and norms. In concert with much of the literature of the times, it denied women equality with men. Women in the seventeenth century were not normally seen as individuals in their own right. Often labelled 'ladies', 'gentlewomen', 'noblewomen', 'maids', 'spinsters', 'married women' and 'widows', their individuality was important only in so far as it contributed to a functioning and godly commonwealth. Marriage was vital to a woman's identity but it was understood principally as an indissoluble arrangement for the begetting of children and, particularly among the wealthy, of maintaining social status and prestige. Biblical texts, particularly Genesis, underpinned male dominance and solemnly advised couples to live by scriptural ordinances. Women were presumed to be less able than men in resisting Satan and were consequently placed under male protection for enlightenment and guidance for their salvation.[1] Generally, they accepted their inferiority and subjection to men. How did Quaker women fare under such a régime?

'Hearkening to Wisdom's Voice'

In bearing what Jone Brooksop called 'testimony for his names sake', the early Quakers self-identified as the children of Light in which they were to live provisionally, even to suffer and die if needs be for that same Light. They also claimed, as Edward Burrough wrote in 1659, to be

> travellers in the labour of the Gospel of Christ Jesus for the Elect seed's sake, having received the glad tidings of Life, and eternal salvation into our hearts, through the revelation of Christ in us, who is our hope and glory; and the Lord has manifested greatly his power amongst us, and revealed the riches of his grace in our souls, to our own everlasting satisfaction and peace with God; and also he has made us ministers of his grace, and of his word to many others, to the turning of many from darkness to Light, and from Satan's power to God; and of him we are

---

[1] Westerkamp, 'Puritan Patriarchy and the Problem of Revelation', 574, 577, 589.

called, and ordained by his Spirit into this his work, to preach the everlasting Gospel to the nations.[2]

The Friends emphasised 'travel' in the seventeenth century religious sense of the toiling and suffering servant on a journey into God. Elizabeth Stirredge's own travelling is a typical case in point. In her seventies she recalled how the convincement she underwent in 1655 led her 'hardness' to be taken away and her heart to be opened. Having then 'received the glad tidings of [the] Life' as a new person, she continued, God 'took me by the hand and led me by the way I knew not, and made darkness light before me'.[3] Stirredge's apocalyptic story repeats the familiar theme of prophets and mystics. Sustained by Love in her discoveries, beginning in 'that desolate place' but returning her to the pure, Edenic 'sight of God', she knew the 'Beloved' would never forsake her.[4] As a consequence she was strengthened in her resolve to testify directly to Charles II to the sufferings of her fellow Quakers confident that God 'would choose the weak and the dejected, and them that were nothing in their own eyes'.[5]

Barbara Blaugdone also emphasised the necessity of departing 'from the evil within' so that she could 'willingly [take] up the cross, and [yield] obedience unto it'. Blaugdone's short but action-packed *Account* of her public life details how, as prophet, she suffered as a mediatrix for God's love for all people.[6] However, being a herald of God was always dangerous business and it was not long before the authorities ruthlessly applied their 'sword', denying her access on one occasion to her children. Like Stirredge, she was imprisoned but suffered greater privation; she was incarcerated on six occasions and whipped. In the course of her journeys Blaugdone was also savaged by a dog, stabbed and escaped another murder attempt while aboard a vessel that later floundered on rocks. And she was also set upon by pirates and robbed. Undaunted, Blaugdone never seemed to harbour resentment. She made a point, for instance, of reconciling herself with magistrate Isaac Burgess who had originally sent her to gaol. She maintained that Burgess became sympathetic to Friends as a result.[7]

---

[2] Burrough, *A Visitation and Warning Proclaimed*, 5; Penington, *The Way of Life and Death*, 2, 14-15.
[3] Elizabeth Stirredge (1634-1706) in *Works*, 20, 22. 'Hardness of heart' was a common Quaker expression; see Fox, Ep. 16 (1652) in *Works*, 7:24.
[4] Stirredge, 38-9.
[5] *Ibid.*, 30.
[6] Barbara Blaugdone (or Blagdon, c.1609-1704), *An Account of the Travels* (1691), 6, 37. For Blaugdone see also S. Davies, *Unbridled Spirits*, 249-58 and Venn, *The Autobiographies*, 28-87.
[7] Blaugdone, *ibid.*, 6-37; see esp. 10.

As with so many of the early Quakers, Stirredge and Blaugdone believed that in dying to themselves lay the only claim to justification and sanctification, to authentication as children of Light. They did so because they were desperate to enact the Jesus experience and be faithful to the responsibilities it demanded such as having a rigorous sense of religious purpose and self-discipline.[8] Both believed they had flown into the true and sure home that was Jesus; there, they found themselves expressing a particular knowledge of God which, in their own measure, presupposed union with the divine.[9] They were typical, then, of the first Friends as a whole in their struggle to live on the plane of purity, keen like the Puritans (but in their own way) to purify the Reformation in order to restore it. At the same time they had no desire to 'cover themselves with filthy rags [but rather] everlasting righteousness'.[10] Echoing the first generation of Quakers later in the century, Ann Docwra urged that, 'the divine Virtue

> must be in our selves, [since] it is not in the power of man to put it into us, it is the gift of God in our own hearts . . . which . . . is not to be denied nor concealed; this gift is given to all mankind . . . women as men, if they do wait in faith and patience to receive it.[11]

Dorcas Dole was also concerned to inform child Friends that they should 'hearken to Wisdom's voice'.[12] Her statement was consonant with the Wisdom tradition from Proverbs, Matthew and Luke in which Wisdom was justified by the behaviour of all her children. Women Friends especially felt strengthened by their faith in Wisdom. 'Embrace Wisdom', counselled Judith Zinspenninck, 'and let her dwell in your inner chambers'.[13] No doubt they were fortified by Proverbs' portrayal of Wisdom as found boldly in public places, calling aloud in the streets.[14]

---

[8] *Ibid.*, 6-37.

[9] For a further understanding of the language-use of early Quaker women see Trevett, *Quaker Women Prophets in England and Wales*, esp. 28-31, 46-7; Tarter, *Sites of Performance*, 33-4, 61-4, 85-8, 115-16, 123-6.

[10] Nayler, 'Concerning Obedience' in *Love to the Lost*, 27-9.

[11] Ann Docwra (1624-1710), *An Epistle of Love and Good Advice* (1683), 3-4. See Barbour, 'Quaker Prophetesses and Mothers of Israel' in Frost and J. Moore (eds.), 46. Also Fox, *The Woman Learning*, 4-6 and in *Doctrinals*, 80-1.

[12] Dorcas Dole (d. 1684/5), *A Salutation and Seasonable Exhortation* (1682/3), Bds., col. 1. *Cf.* this statement and the Wisdom tradition in Pr. 10:12, 15:18.

[13] See Mt. 11:19 (= Lk. 7:35) which reads in part, 'But wisdom is justified of her children'. See also Fox, Ep. 63 (1654) in *Collection*, 60; Wells, 'Trinitarian Feminism: Elizabeth Johnson's Wisdom Christology' (rev. art.), 335 and Judith Zinspenninck, *Some Worthy Proverbs* (1663), 1, *passim*; Edward Bourne (d. 1708), *A Warning . . . unto the Inhabitants of Worcester* (1660), 4. See Henry Seuse (Suso), *Horologium Sapientiae* (1491) and his description of Christ as Eternal Wisdom, a popular devotion in the fourteenth century.

[14] See Pr.1: 21; 8:2; 9: 3, 14.

From this spiritual space where they sought the gift of God's justice/righteousness—justice *per se* was regarded as the wholesome Law of God[15]—the first Quakers ventured from their communities as a people barefoot to the world and grounded in their love of, and faith in, the Word. As a result, there could be no compromise with Mammon. 'You cannot have two kingdoms', cried Joan Vokins, also in accord with the Friends of the 1650s, 'so stoop to Christ's appearance in you, he who invites all to come and learn'.[16] As missionaries, the Friends were hardly naïve as to the reception they might receive. 'The great and proud men of the world', reassured public Friend Ambrose Rigge,

> are too big to enter the straight gate, and walk in the narrow way, the preaching of the cross of our Lord Jesus to them is foolishness, [and they cannot see the straight gate] which the apostles preached, and all the true disciples and followers of Jesus Christ took up, who were crucified to the world, and the world to them.[17]

Rigge was well aware of the Pauline text in which 'to walk' was a metaphor for the way people conducted their lives. The movement's call to the nations was laced with the conviction that the Lamb's victory, the universal establishment of the Kingdom, could be realised by everybody since there was 'that of God in everyone'.[18] Giving life to this potential fulfilled the ancient apostolic tradition found only among the new and truly royal priesthood.[19]

Quoting the Sermon on the Mount, Fox wrote that while 'the Apostles and Christ did not bid that any should kill about their words, but that they should love enemies, he had no doubt that 'all [mainline] religions [those that neglect the Kingdom] will fight about religions and worships' and so were out of,

> the power of the Lord and the Spirit that the apostles was in, and so they be all out of the royal Spirit that has the royal spiritual weapons, and out of the royal Seed which said *love enemies* which is the royal command to the royal priesthood . . . and the witnesses is rising, and the

---

[15] Fox in *Saul's Errand*, 3-4.
[16] Joan Vokins (d. 1690), *God's Mighty Power Magnified* (1691), 3. See Mt. 6: 24.
[17] Rigge, *The Spiritual Guide of Life* (1691), 4.
[18] Fox, Epistle (1656) to Quaker ministers from Launceston prison (Cornwall) in *Journal*, 263. See also Burrough, 'Concerning Governors, and Governments' in *A Standard Lifted Up*, 11-12.
[19] Farnworth, letters (8/June/1653) to Fell *et al*, *SW*/iii/46, 47: 'shine forth in brightness, and reign as kings upon the earth, a chosen generation, a royal priesthood, a peculiar people . . .'.

everlasting Gospel shall be preached again amongst them that have had the words, but have slain the life of the prophets and the apostles ...'[20]

It was a witness applied to Friend and non-Friend alike because they believed that God wished to be known in the hearts of everybody, especially the afflicted. They saw the Kingdom's enactment as an exercise in compassion, which gave hope since it offered rebirth into the Life and thus a vision of God's peace for humanity. Both their striving for authenticity in the Light and their understanding of how they were 'one of another' and with humanity were bases for their solidarity. The mutual support was also vital for countering the spiritual desolation they sometimes felt in adversity. Theologian Elizabeth Johnson has described solidarity as a type of

> Communion in which deep connection with others is forged in such a way that their sufferings and joys become part of one's own personal concern and a spur to transformative action. It entails a movement out of selfish seclusion and into relationship where people bear one another up in mutual giving and receiving. It is inseparable from a liberating praxis for the common good.[21]

Thus Sarah Blackborow called Friends to a liberating praxis in which they were to,

> Love truth and its testimony, whether its witness be to you, or against you, love it, that into my Mother's house you all may come. And into the chamber of her that conceived me.[22]

Blackborow's apocalyptic and mystical imagery was a call to cleave to the eternal. It was also a quintessential statement of the active 'doing' prayer the first Friends practised. Hers was a prophetic utterance that the Truth was God and that God gave birth to Truth and Love continually. The Friends knew to their own satisfaction that all genuine love rested on Truth and that Christian love, the love found in the Sermon on the Mount for instance, was no exception.[23] The more people separated themselves from Love/God, the more they moved into the dark world, a bereft existence without the nourishing and 'tender' love of God—the early Quakers' understanding of

---

[20] Fox, *An Epistle General to them who are of the Royal Priesthood*, 10 and 25; Fox's emphasis. He usually quoted 1 Pet. 2: 9.
[21] E. Johnson, *Friends of God and Prophets*, 7.
[22] Blackborow, *A Visit to the Spirit in Prison*, 10.
[23] See C. Davis, *A Question of Conscience*, 76.

'hell'.[24] Burrough outlined its harrowing geography, a self-imposed devastating, terrifying and all-encompassing lack of love:

> All that are out of [God] are in the state reprobate, bringing forth fruits of death and darkness, being children of wrath and disobedience, in the alienation and separation from God, in the transgression unreconciled to God, the enmity ruling in the heart, being in the fall, and not restored to God again, but ignorant of his power and wisdom, having the understanding darkened that they cannot see nor perceive the things that are eternal. And in this condition his best works are sin.[25]

Naylor, decrying the Calvinist 'notion' of humanity's innate separation from God, lamented how

> the wisdom of men [had] in their imaginations... separated that which is in one, and cannot be divided in the possession; for it is one Spirit that works all these.[26]

We have returned, therefore, to holism in the way the early Friends made explicit; there was an inter-relatedness of human with human in God ('that of God in everyone') in which, according to Douglas Steere, 'the pan-sacramental sense of the holiness of every life relationship [was]... counted with [an] inward experience of communion'.[27] The idolatrous became evident as the sacrosanct nature of life was recognised and confirmed.

Women's Speaking Justified

The early Quakers' holistic and Christ/Logos-mysticism saw nothing in the Word of what today is called ageism, gender discrimination or class bias.[28] That John's Gospel 'singled out women to show the dynamics of the life of

---

[24] Burrough, *A Declaration to all the World of our Faith*, 7; S. Fisher, *Apokryta*, 21-2.
[25] Burrough *et al*, *The Principles of Truth*, 47.
[26] Nayler, 'Concerning Justification' in *Love to the Lost*, 50-2. See J. Whitehead, *A Word of Reproof from the Lord*, 6.
[27] Steere (ed.), 18.
[28] See *TLITC*, 260 (27*n*) and her chp. 5. An interesting feature of our period is that servanthood did not necessarily signify lower rank. It was often seen as an important part of a young person's education instead and a means of social advancement. Musicians and artists, for instance, were at times regarded as servants. About two-thirds of unmarried adolescents and young adults aged between 15 and 24 worked as domestic or farm servants, usually on annual contracts. This was possibly the arrangement between the future Quaker missionaries, Dorothy and Jane Waugh, and their Quaker employers, John and Mabel Camm of Camsgill Farm in Cumbria. See *BQ*, 93, 199; E. Taylor, *The Valiant Sixty*, 22, 42.

faith ... to commit oneself to Jesus ... [to] a total loss of self in his ways' was no less true of the women of the young movement.[29] In the manner of many Leveller women, they were not content to be mere followers of the leadership like their Muggletonian counterparts or dependent on a male minister for recording and categorising their spiritual experiences like Baptist women.[30] Their determination to bring in the Kingdom was amply demonstrated between 1650 and 1665 when 250 Quaker women, including such powerful advocates as Anne Audland, Sarah Blackborow, Katharine Evans, Margaret Fell, Mary Fisher, Mary Forster, Elizabeth Hooton, Margaret Killam and Dorothy White roamed the nations bearing witness as 'prophetesses' of Light; 'the Lord God has spoken', declared White, 'and therefore I will prophesy'.[31]

According to Hugh Barbour, Quaker women wrote 220 tracts out of the 3,853 the Friends are known to have written before 1700. He also informs us that eight women other than Margaret Fell had more than five tracts published, that 48 women published one tract, 82 of the 650 early Quaker authors were women and that 26 of the 59 preachers in the new world between 1656 and 1663 were also women.[32] They were the first to evangelise London and the Calvinist strongholds of Oxford and Cambridge. Forty-five percent of the Quaker preachers arriving in the American colonies between 1656 and 1663 were women.[33]

Although many more pamphlets were written by the men, Quaker women wrote a significant number of strident and religiously passionate works, almost half of which were prophetic pronouncements aimed at powerful clerics, law makers and monarchs. They did so at a time when only a small number of women were tentatively entering the arena of public writing, still fearful of upsetting the established view that men alone inherited the right, bequeathed to them by the Reformation, to independent

---

[29] Moloney, *Women First Among the Faithful* quoted in Ricci, *Mary Magdalene and many others*, 92.
[30] Mack, 'Gender and Spirituality in Early English Quakerism 1650-1665' in Potts-Brown and Stuard (eds.), 47. Leveller women were well organised as their petition to parliament of May 1649 shows; see Marik, 'Christopher Hill: Women Turning the World Upside Down', 65.
[31] Mary Fisher (c.1623-98), Mary Forster, Elizabeth Hooton (1600-71/2), Margaret Killam (d.1672). See D. White, *A Trumpet of the Lord of Hosts* (1662), 3.
[32] Barbour, 'Quaker Prophetesses', 46. According to Gill, Rosemary Foxton has 234 women writing or signing works where multiple authorship is included but that Foxton and Barbour calculate authorship according to different criteria. See Gill, *Women in the Seventeenth Century Quaker Community*, 4-8.
[33] Mary Fisher and Elizabeth Williams evangelised Cambridge; Elizabeth Fletcher and Barbara Leavens, Oxford; for Oxford sufferings see S. Fisher in *Works*, 261 and also *Sufferings*, i., 565. Thomas Firmin (1632-97), *The First New Persecution* (1654), 5 has an account of Mary Fisher's and Elizabeth Williams' treatment at Cambridge where they were 'whipped till blood ran down their bodies'. For reference to American colonies see *QER*, 26.

Chapter 10: 'Walk in the Narrow Way'

religious thought. Remarkable for the period, nearly half of all women's published works during the 1650s was produced by the Quakers, an indication of how the sectaries provided women with opportunities for public expression like never before. Their (the sectaries) belief in the spiritual equality of the sexes was especially evident in London's Independent congregations. According to Thomas, they 'allowed all their members, women included, to debate, vote and, if not preach, then usually at least to prophesy, which often came to much the same thing'.[34]

Whether or not the seventeenth century saw 'the first critique of male domination of culture and society as a conscious movement'[35], women writers and preachers certainly took huge risks to their person and estate as with the Paul-like Bludgeoned. Or like Mary Fisher and Elizabeth Hooton who were among the signatories to the first known Quaker tract issued from a grim York Castle dungeon in 1652, a rocket aimed at hireling priests and other 'corrupt' officials.[36] For their troubles, many Quaker women were stocked, ducked, branched (iron-collared), whipped and accused of cursing and witchcraft.[37] Among many examples, the *Swarthmore MSS.* records 'two Quaker women' prison visitors seized in 1655 in Evesham (Worcestershire) and stocked with their legs higher than their bodies, something which brought loud condemnation from the Quakers, including local Friend, Humphrey Smith.[38] One hundred and twenty-two women out

---

[34] Crawford, 'Women's Published Writings', 269 and K. Thomas, 'Women and the Civil War Sects', 42-62, esp. 47 and both quoted in Peters, *Print Culture*, 125; see also Peters, 127 and her chp 5, 'Women's Speaking Justified': women and pamphleteering', 124-150. Also Ezell, *Writing Women's Literary History*, 137 and Feroli, 'Engendering the Body Politic', 2-3.

[35] Radford Reuther, 'Forward' in Garman *et al*, *Hidden in Plain Sight*, xi, xiv.

[36] See Aldam *et al*, *False Prophets*, 2-5, 8. The gaol in York Castle was one of the worst in England; see Havran, *The Catholics in Caroline England*, 109.

[37] See Underdown, *A Freedom People*, 107. For ducking and branking see R. Gardiner, *England's Grievance* (1655), 10-11; branks and ducking stools were used against women who were considered to be scolds, witches, gossips, 'hussies' or naggers. The brank resembled an iron framework helmet with a lockable collar. Within the frame an iron shaft extended into the captive's mouth, acting as a gag and pressing against the tongue making any kind of intelligible speech impossible; attempts at speaking resulted in a lacerated tongue and mouth. The ducking stool was either a seat perched on the end of a long wooden arm or a chair suspended by a chain attached perhaps to a branch of a tree. Women were tied to the seat then ducked into the local pond or river. For Quaker works against witchcraft or refutations of sorcery see James Blackley *et al*, *A Lying Wonder Discovered* (1659), 2; Howgill (and Burrough), *We the Servants and Faithful Witnesses* (1656), Bds.; Farnworth, *Witchcraft Cast Out from the Religious Seed* (1655), *passim*.

[38] See H. Smith, *Something Further Laid Open* (1656), 5 for Margaret Newby and Eliz. Courten; S. Roberts, 'The Quakers in Evesham', 73; Roberts quotes a letter (25/Nov/1655) from Margaret Newby (d. 1657, one of the two women, the other being Elizabeth Cowart) to Fell, *SW*/i/359 (and in Nuttall, *EQL*, 158). Newby probably died as a result of Evesham. Roberts leans heavily on *Sufferings*. See S. Davies, *Unbridled Spirits*, 43. And H. Smith, *The*

of a total of 360 Quakers were hurled into prison between 1654 and 1659 for interrupting church services, Friends like Katharine Evans and Sarah Cheevers in Valetta (Malta) where they had disrupted a Catholic mass. Not surprisingly, the Quaker movement and its leadership roundly condemned the physical abuse of women.[39]

The mid century was a time when many believed women were devoid of souls and considered erratic, being far too emotional. And since Eve was the first transgressor, they were also blamed for *man*kind's fall from grace. Understood as inherently unreliable, then, they were regarded as troublesome, disobedient and thus candidates always for punishment. As such, they were pushed to the margins of Church and State; to question their place in the social order was to flaunt rigid conventional boundaries, if not the very will of God. Anarchy and civilisation's collapse were sure to follow. Quaker women, or at least the prophets among them, were compelled to meet this challenge since they submitted only to the leading of God.[40] So, as their powers of prophecy and preaching were recognised within the movement, and given space to develop, the growing number of women preachers began to confront the inequalities of gender and rank among their fellow Friends and within society in general. During the 1650s and 1660s in particular, their witness, courageous as it was, served to open up the spiritual prisons inherent in what Ollie has called 'hierarchical gender relations'.[41]

Their own liberating praxis and solidarity meant actively cultivating friendships among themselves and encouraging one another to preach and leave written records of their lives.[42] It also meant going beyond the accepted view of priesthood. Mabel Brailsford maintained that, in choosing the Leviticus priesthood as opposed to the more open Melchizedekan, Puritan reformers confined themselves within the 'masculine' half of the nations.[43] As self-proclaimed priests of the order of Melchizedek, then, the Friends insisted that women and men were 'helpmeets in the restoration as

---

Sufferings, Trials, and Purgings of the Saints at Evesham (*DCFB* 1655/6), esp. Sigs. B2, B5-7. Also Nuttall, *EQL*, 68.

[39] Reay in Foxton, *'Hear the Word of the Lord'*, 8-10, 19. See Gilbert, 'The Puritan and the Quakers', 120. Also Nayler, 'To the Town of Bradford', *Caton MSS.*, ii, 35 and in *Works*, ii, 592 at: <http://www.qhpress.org/texts/nayler/letters2.html#592>. And Neelon, *James Nayler*, 111.

[40] See Trevett, *Women and Quakerism*, 41.

[41] Orlie, *Living Ethically*, 101. For no distinction between men and women as prophets see Burrough, *A Just and Lawful Trial of the Teachers* (1657); Caton, *The Moderate Enquirer Resolved* (1658) and J. Whitehead, *A Manifestation of Truth* (1662), 12-13. For the vital importance of 'prophecy' to Fox and especially in relation to prophetesses see Ross, *George Fox Speaks for Himself*, 56-8.

[42] Warburton, 'The Lord hath joined us together', 414.

[43] Brailsford, *Quaker Women*, 3.

man and woman was before the Fall', and that husbands should be 'not bitter against them . . . so ought men to love their wives as their own bodies.'[44] For Quaker women, their Melchizedekan priesthood was an added source of strength for cutting through society's understanding of femininity despite still having to overcome 'internal censors [and their need for] rewriting gender possibilities [by] stretching the boundaries for women through prophetic and corporeal' action.[45]

In rising above gender, convincement meant that all Friends, as the true Church of the Light, were brides of Christ and one in the Spirit, and to such an extent that Quaker women could consider themselves innocent of behaviour universally regarded as unfeminine. One result was fearlessness in their commitment for the gender-neutral Kingdom.[46] Anne Audland, for instance, showed no fear when she accused the male authorities of inflicting suffering on her fellow Quakers, including her fellow women Friends. How long, she demanded, would it be before the 'stiff-necked and uncircumcised in heart and ears' returned to God?: 'shall the innocent always be your mark to shoot at?'[47]

The Quaker apocalypse encouraged women to make Audland-like declarations in streets, town squares, churches, at the busiest of corners and entrances of cities.[48] The Friends strongly asserted that men *and* women were earthen vessels and that, while under the old Law (as in the first chapter of Proverbs) women were forbidden to speak in places of worship, in the new covenant of the Light they were to enjoy the freedom to do precisely that.[49] In 1648, when Fox caused a ruckus in a Leicestershire 'steeplehouse' involving 'Presbyterians, Independents, Baptists and Common-prayer-men' by defending a woman whom the priest had forbidden to speak, he was raising 'Church' and its 'head' as critical issues for public discussion. By doing so he portrayed the people as confused (like the disputing Corinthians?) and himself as a (Paul-like?) missionary with a healing message underpinned by his correct scriptural interpretation (as he saw it).[50]

Quaker assertions about the role of women were startling and deeply disturbing to the *status quo*. Fox, Farnworth, Fell, Samuel Fisher and other

---

[44] Fox, *The Woman Learning*, 2; *The Second Covenant*, 21.
[45] Tarter, *Sites of Performance*, 63. See Fell, 'An Epistle to Convinced Friends . . . 1656' in *Works*, 92.
[46] Trevett, *Women and Quakerism*, 41; K. Taylor, 'The Role of Quaker Women in the Seventeenth Century', 11, 13. For Quaker women in Wales see Jenkins, *Protestant Dissenters in Wales*, 37.
[47] Anne Audland (1627-1705), 'A Warning from the Spirit of the Lord' in Vivers, *The Saint's Testimony* (1655), 11. Audland quotes Ac. 7:51.
[48] Penington, *The Way of Life and Death*, 64.
[49] Coppe, *Some Sweet Sips*, 54.
[50] See *Journal*, 22.

Friends pressed home the argument that Paul of Tarsus said nothing against the Holy Spirit speaking *through* women. Fox, drawing attention to Acts and Revelation in *Concerning Sons and Daughters* (1661), asked, 'If all women have the testimony of Jesus, have not they then the spirit of prophecy? And if all be led by the Spirit of God are they not then from under [free of] the [Mosaic/Puritan] Law? And then may they not prophecy?'[51] As with the non-Quaker Bathsua Makin, they stressed the Spirit as being 'born of God, either in male or female . . . and the Spirit of the Lord was made manifest through the female kind'.[52] 'If Christ be in the female as well as in the male', asked Fox and Farnworth, 'is he not the same? And [then] may not the Spirit of Christ speak in the female as well as in the male?'[53] So, too, Sarah Blackborow: in recalling the sapiential (Wisdom) tradition in Proverbs 5:13, she warned that, 'Wisdom hath uttered her voice to you, but the eye and ear which is abroad, waiting upon a sound of words without you, is that which keeps you from your teacher within you'. She [Wisdom] would lead the just through narrow but direct paths to show them what the Kingdom consisted of.[54]

In 1655, Margaret Vivers, arrested in Banbury (Oxon.) and liberally quoting Exodus, Isaiah and Paul, also argued for women preachers.[55] And in the same year, against the demand that women should remain silent in church, came the more strident reply of Priscilla Cotton and Mary Cole in *To the Priests and People of England*. Both were Plymouth Quakers and their predicament in, and writing from, Exeter gaol foreshadowed that of Katharine Evans and Sarah Cheevers, also natives of the West Country who would be incarcerated in Malta five years later. The Cotton-Cole tract, typically asserting that Truth would dawn on all people, linked three features—an onslaught on the clergy for their apostasy and violence, a strong advocacy on behalf of the unschooled (including 'silly women') so that they may understand Scripture and, finally, a strained exegesis in favour of women's speaking. Their case centred on their belief that the Pauline injunction of 1 Corinthians only referred to women without possession of the Spirit.[56] They reminded the 'ignorant' clerics that in Galatians 3:28 Paul stated that all were 'both male and female in Christ

---

[51] Fox, *Concerning Sons and Daughters . . . Prophesying* (1661), 11; this tract, with an amended beginning and conclusion, is a republished version of his *The Woman Learning* of which reference should be made of p. 6. See Ac. 2:17; Rev. 10:11.
[52] Farnworth, *A Women Forbidden* (1654) 1-4; Makin, *An Essay to Revive the Ancient Education of Gentlewomen* (1673 edn.), *passim*.
[53] Fox, *The Woman Learning*, 5; *Journal*, 339.
[54] Blackborow, *A Visit to the Spirit in Prison*, 7. See also Pr. 3:19, 4:13, 8:35.
[55] Vivers, *The Saints Testimony*, 13-16.
[56] See Radford Reuther, 'Forward' in Garman *et al*, *Hidden in Plain Sight*, ibid. Also Priscilla Cotton (d. 1664) and Mary Cole, *To the Priests and People of England* (1655). And crucially 1 Cor. 14:34-35.

Chapter 10: 'Walk in the Narrow Way'

Jesus' and that 'all the Church may prophesy one by one'.[57] God, after all, was 'no respecter of persons'; that is, God had no favourites except those who chose to live continually in the Light.[58]

Paul, they said, had only forbidden women to speak with uncovered heads so they may not dishonour their true head, Christ Jesus. It was also an insult to God to speak out of turn:

> If therefore any speak in the church, whether man or woman, and nothing appear in it but the wisdom of man (1 Cor. 2:4-5, 13), and Christ, who is the true head, be not uncovered, do not fully appear, Christ the head is then dishonoured.[59]

It was imperative, they continued, for men and women still locked in the old Israel, to cover themselves with *righteousness*. The weakness (apostasy) their opponents displayed meant it was *they* who were 'women' (weaker vessels) and thus forbidden to speak. For Cotton and Cole, it has been said, gender was divorced from biology leaving them free to claim spiritual manhood.[60]

Developing their argument, Cotton and Cole continued the Quaker practice of bringing the entire 'hireling' clerical community under scrutiny. Pauline reasoning that women's 'filthiness and shame' debarred them from speaking was turned on its head. Those in the transgression were indeed shameful but this could not be applied to the persecuted (i.e. proof of sincerity) followers of the Light of Christ. This assertion was important because it forcibly underlined the Quaker belief that literal obedience to all the moral teaching of the Bible made a mockery of Scriptural authority, which itself was subordinate to the Light of Christ. Mary Forster insisted that the everlasting priest, Christ Jesus, living within all (Rom.10:8), allowed spoken ministry by any person acting in accordance with divine will.[61] Sarah Blackborow warned ministers that because Christ was now risen for all, in both male and female, it was time to make use of women's God-given talents so that everybody might share in their fruits—'one Spirit,

---

[57] See also 1 Cor.14:31.

[58] For 'no respecter of persons': Dt. 1:15-17; Ac. 10:34.

[59] Cotton and Cole, *To the Priests and People of England*, 7. For 'true head Christ Jesus':1 Cor.11:3, 5.

[60] Mack, *Visionary Women*, 155. See Higginson, *A Brief Relation of Irreligion*, 3-4 in which Higginson alleges how 'one Williamson's wife', following Cotton-Cole, claimed she was not only the Son of God but also a *man* (i.e. one who now speaks with Godly authority), and that her male accusers were women instead. Also S. Davies, *Unbridled Spirits*, 232. R. Moore in *TLITC*, 57 observes how Fell's later published *Women's Speaking Justified* (1666) omits the Cotton-Cole interpretation probably for the sake of Quaker probity.

[61] M. Forster *et al*, *These Several Papers* (1659), 7.

one Light, one Life, one Power'.[62] And, if they were indeed foolish women, replied Katharine Evans to her Catholic captors in Malta, then they were the 'Lord's fools'.[63] Both Evans and Margaret Fell confirmed that God's strength was made perfect in weakness as indeed the title of Elizabeth Stirredge's collected works, *Strength in Weakness Manifest*, declared.[64] In *Women's Speaking Justified* (1666), Fell, herself no stranger to prisons, repeated the indignation women Friends felt during the 1650s:

> the Church of Christ is a woman, and those that speak against the woman's speaking, speak against the Church of Christ and the Seed of the woman which Seed is Christ. That is to say, those that speak against the power of the Lord, and the Spirit of the Lord speaking in a woman simply by reason of her sex . . . such speak against Christ.

But for Fell and Friends the true 'Church' was also the saving Kingdom that was already present as the New Jerusalem, We should understand that she and other women Quakers were neither troubled by the word 'Kingdom' nor conceived the Kingdom itself to be subjected to gender distinction since all were one in the Light. They saw the Kingdom more in terms of what may be called a Friend-dom, something that disdained as absurd both hierarchy and male spiritual pre-eminence. The Kingdom, therefore, recognised women and men as equals in the work of the spiritual Church thereby incorporating rather than ignoring the feminine:

> And our Holy City, the New Jerusalem, is coming down from Heaven and her Light will shine through the whole earth, even as a jasper stone clear as crystal, which brings freedom and liberty and perfect redemption to her whole Seed. And this is that woman and image of the Eternal God that God has owned and does own and will own for evermore.[65]

The Friends, however, were by no means unique in favouring women preachers. Other Radicals allowed the practice. The highly controversial John Goodwin encouraged his congregation at St. Stephen's (Coleman Street, London) to look beyond theological barriers in welcoming women's

---

[62] Blackborow, *The Just and Equal Balance*, 2, 13-14.
[63] Evans and Cheevers, *A Brief History of the Voyage* (ed. 1715, originally 1662), 51.
[64] See Stirredge, *Strength in Weakness Manifest*. S. Jones in *This is Lights Appearance* also said something similar; see Jones in Garman *et al*, *Hidden in Plain Sight*, 35. The idea/title was generally fairly common, however, with anti-Quaker John Jackson publishing his *Strength in Weakness* in 1655. See Barbour, 'Quaker Prophetesses', 45 and Burrough, *A Description of the State and Condition of all Mankind*, 13 for the same theme.
[65] Fell, *Women's Speaking Justified*, 5-6, 11 and in *Works*, 331-44.

Chapter 10: 'Walk in the Narrow Way'

active participation in discussions inside and outside the church despite their husbands' opposition.[66] Abiezer Coppe the Ranter went further in assuring a female correspondent that women preachers were superior because they were in the Spirit whereas men were prone to favour formal ecclesiastical structures.[67]

And yet, for a whole movement such as the Quakers to have openly encouraged a female ministry on a large scale was of shattering significance in a society in which patriarchy and misogyny were normal fare. Michele Lisa Tarter maintains that Quaker women imbibed a new thinking which disintegrated the old duality whereby men identified with the soul and women with the body.[68] We can see that, along with their male colleagues, Quaker women gave witness to a holism which countenanced oneness with God. The effect was to lend vicarious support to those women who, from the Middle Ages onwards, began that long and patient movement that is yet to encourage men in general to share the foundations and pinnacles of religious and political life on a basis of equity. In this spirit, early Quaker Ester Biddle yearned to free humanity from this running sore, this impurity, and for God the healer to 'bathe and make [it] white'.[69]

As a man of his times, however, Fox, like Farnworth and Aldam in *An Easter-Reckoning* (1653), could not countenance full social and political equality between the sexes as his popular *The Woman Learning in Silence* (1656) confirms. While Fox urged men to treat their wives with love and dignity, he adopted the Lutheran line that wives 'should be in subjection to [their] husbands . . . loving, and meek, gentle, and lowly minded'.[70] As in Paul's day, it was impossible for men in such a patriarchal culture to shed every remnant of what today is sexism; complete equality is, after all, a more recognisable praxis for *our* times.[71] When equality found expression, say, in Hobbes' *Leviathan*, it proved daring, progressive, dangerous and thus highly controversial.[72] Indeed, for most men at the time the idea was also sheer madness. And so it was perhaps inevitable that many Quaker men became increasingly concerned that women Friends were, in their view, becoming divisive in wanting separate Meetings for instance, a move

---

[66] Coleman Street was notorious among the authorities as a hotbed of radicalism. Isaac Penington Sr., Lord Mayor of London and regicide, worshipped there. See Johns, 'Coleman Street', *passim*.
[67] Gibbons, *Gender in Mystical and Occult Thought*, 136.
[68] Tarter, *Sites of Performance*, 1.
[69] Ester (or Hester) Biddle (c.1629-96), *The Trumpet of the Lord Sounded Forth* (1662), 4.
[70] See 1 Cor. 11: 3, 8-9 and cf. Fox, *The Woman Learning*, 1-2 and *TLITC*, 199-200. The same theme is visited in *An Epistle to all People on the Earth* in *Doctrinals*, esp. 92. Also Farnworth/Aldam, *An Easter-Reckoning*, 18-19.
[71] Wills, *What Paul Meant*, 98.
[72] Fox, *Doctrinals*, 81-2 and Crook *et al*, *A Declaration from the People of God* (1659), 6; for *Leviathan* see Hayduk, *Hopeful Politics*, 283 (232n).

perceived as an affront to the spiritual authority they arrogated to themselves.[73] The men were mirroring the march of patriarchy in the early Church. In line with this backward development, Quaker women gradually retreated from the prophetic ministry, particularly during the post-Restoration years, to adopt traditional nurturing roles as 'mothers of Israel', often initiating programs as it happens for the care of the poor, the sick and fellow Quakers in prison. Evidence of this development can be traced back to the early 1650s.[74] It is difficult, therefore, to agree with those who say that Quaker women in general were challenging men for leadership during that decade.[75]

Conclusion

When the Quakers yielded to the leadings of the Spirit the outcomes attracted cruel reprisals from the authorities. Nonetheless, they were bound by their obedience to the Light of the Christ, an obedience that was mystical, prophetic and led into unity with God. The Friends were compelled to further Love's Dominion, the Kingdom. By enduring punishments and yet forgiving those who had wronged them as Jesus had done, the Friends, like Elizabeth Stirredge and Barbara Blaugdone, sought God's justice for themselves, fellow Quakers and for all humanity. Outward witness was underpinned by a conviction that the Lamb's victory would be realised in the fullness of time. Being 'one of another' and with humanity was a 'doing' prayer, and it meant that Quaker women could enjoy equality in preaching, itself a significant feature in an ecclesiastical landscape in which widespread misogyny was considered normal. As we have seen, despite misogyny's prevalence, and the tendency later in the century for Quaker men to fall victim to it, the growing numbers and influence of women preachers confronted inequalities of spiritual rank within and outside the movement. This startling assertion of human rights was deeply,

---

[73] Fox was keen on separate Meetings, a position too far for John Wilkinson and John Story who led a separation; see 'The Judgment of J.W. and J.S' in John Wilkinson, *The Memory of ... John Story* (1683), 37-9 and see also a Wilkinson-Story supporter, William Rogers, *The Christian Quaker* (1680), 63-5.

[74] See John Stubbs, letter (19/Oct/1657) to Fell, *SW*/iii/124. Stubbs writes of Fell's 'remarkable gift not given to all' of 'knowledge and wisdom and discerning . . . pity, compassion and love, to mourn with those that mourns [*sic.*] and to have fellow-feeling of another's misery'.

[75] See Hobby, 'Handmaids of the Lord and Mothers in Israel' in Corns and Loewenstein, *passim* and esp. 90. Arguments for the importance of Martha Simmonds, Nayler's disciple at Bristol, are weak. She was not a major leader or writer and the idea that she aspired to the top leadership within mid-century Quakerism is without foundation. See Crawford, *Women and Religion in England,* 168-75.

even psychically, disturbing to the *status quo*. It was given witness among Friends such as Anne Audland, Sarah Blackborow, Sarah Cheevers, Priscilla Cotton, Mary Cole, Katharine Evans, Margaret Fell, Dorothy White and many other Quaker 'prophetesses', all of whom gave special witness to gender equality. It was a witness that underlined not only the Quaker insistence that all were equal under God but that truth, justice and compassion/mercy were intertwined just as they were paramount for the work of Testimony in the world and thus for furthering the Friend-dom of God.

Chapter 11: *'Because of your much Earth'*

- Equity, Truth and Justice -

The movement's insistence that all were equal under God, that God was 'no respecter of persons', drove the Friends to perform public 'signs' for the Kingdom. Going naked, church interruptions, their publications, debates with opponents, non-payment of tithes and defiant worship meetings are some of the 'signs' we have already noted. They also refused to swear oaths and doff 'the hat'. Failure to pay hat honour was considered a gross insult by those of higher social rank to whom it was due. Worse, as a sign of insurrection or dangerous religious enthusiasm it was a prisonable offence. The Friends were quick, however, to deny their hat refusal showed contempt towards any individual or organ of State. Instead, it was a means by which they drew attention to their highly stratified society which, they believed, led people into destructive, unequal relationships and thus eventually into 'Baal', the Beast. The injustices this implied were offensive to God.

The 'hat' and other signs were more than mere defiance. They were theological statements at a time when such statements were outwardly political. Hat refusal probably derived from 1 Corinthians 11: 4 in which a Christian who prayed wearing a hat insulted Christ, the Head. Christ's glory was never to be hidden but reflected 'with uncovered face' instead. Hence, in *secular*, 'carnal' surroundings such as court rooms Quakers honoured Christ by instead refusing to remove their hats, something that also paid tribute to Christ the Light in their accusers and oppressors. Similar thinking applied to titles which were seen to 'hide' the real person, the Light within them. All in all, they were certain that deference ran contrary to the spiritual equality of all. [1]

'Equity', 'truth' and 'justice' frequently appear as a troika within their works. In 1658, for instance, Fell warned Cromwell to discharge his power in 'truth, justice and equity' for 'the health and comfort of his own soul'; otherwise, if he neglected the same, woe and misery would be his end. Burrough was adamant that such 'outward rights, not only in the inner man' be given urgent legal recognition.[2] The three themes were attributes of the Light within: they were gifts of the Spirit waiting to bloom, present in all

---

[1] Nayler, 'The Examination of James Nayler' in *Works*, 11; also Burrough (?), 'An Account' in *A Declaration of the Present Sufferings*, Sig. D; Parnel, *The Fruits of a Fast* (1655), 15.
[2] Fell, 'The Substance and Import (of certain letters and papers of M. Fox to Oliver Cromwell, whilst he was Protector, and to K. Charles II and others)' in *Works*, 17; Burrough.

Chapter 11: 'Because of your much Earth'

people and evident throughout all ages. Thus was Christian equality available to anybody who welcomed the Light. It was a mechanism for liberating such gifts and condemning barriers to their expression. Equity, truth and justice were answers, therefore, to all manner of oppression.

So it was that public Friend George Whitehead in *A Word to the said John Bewick* (1660) could accuse those who as 'in Oliver's time . . . took men's goods, and cast them into prison, and made havoc and spoil abundantly'.[3] Meanwhile his movement accused priests and lawyers of 'evil-doing'. The priests, after all, ate well at their tables while abject poverty existed only a stone's throw from their doors, and lawyers amassed wealth from 'oppression'.[4] Large fees, the Friends argued, discriminated against the common people as did the proliferation of oppressive written and unwritten laws, and the bewildering number of civil and ecclesiastical courts at local and national levels. The law, they said, should also be written in accessible language rather than Latin or Greek.[5] This was a time when magistrates frequently imposed fines without due legal process and, as today, court costs were prohibitive for the majority of people. Anyone subpoenaed was often forced to travel long distances usually incurring great expense, physical difficulties and perhaps danger to limb and property from bandits.[6]

As observers of, and suffering from, the legal system, the Friends could never conceive justice or equality ever being established if authority were out of the Life.[7] Still, there was always hope because 'Truth' gave sight to the blind as Jesus had done. It was always possible, then, for true religion to be 'declared', the 'discovery' made, the 'secret' revealed for all: '[t]he leading of the Spirit of God into all Truth, to do the Truth, and speak the Truth in all things . . . this religion is . . . to be kept unspotted in the world, from its pollution'.[8] For the Friends Truth was the same as the Light, Life, Seed, Spirit, Christ, True Reality, Right Reason and the Kingdom of God. It was absolute and unitary: 'we say [it] is one, God is one, and Christ is one and the Spirit is one', declared George Bishop, 'and we all in the Truth are one' and the Friends 'witnessed it so to be'.[9]

---

[3] G. Whitehead, *The True Ministers Living of the Gospel* (1660), 2.
[4] See Burrough, *A Message for Instruction*, 4-7. Also Fox (the Younger), *For the Parliament of England and their Army, so called* (1659/60), Bds. and in *Works*, 93-4; *Honest, Upright, Faithful, and Plain-Dealing with thee, O Army* (1659), 2, 7.
[5] Fox, *59 Particulars*, 3-4; Farnworth, *The Liberty of the Subject* (1664), 12.
[6] See Fox, *An Instruction to Judges and Lawyers*, 16-17.
[7] Howgill, *An Information and also Advice to the Army* (1659) and in *Works*; see § iv, 325-6.
[8] Burrough, *To the Rulers*, 1. See Lk. 2: 34; Jm.1:27. For a 'leading' (impulse to obey God) see Farnworth, letter (October 1653) to Fox, *SW*/iii/53. For Burrough's understanding of 'true religion' see *A Standard Lifted Up*, 7-8. And Fox, *(Here all may see, that) Justice*, passim.
[9] Bishop, *The Throne of Truth*, 29.

The overarching importance the movement attached to Truth was amply demonstrated by Fox who mentioned it 1,183 times in the *Journal* and 1,392 times in 244 of his 400 epistles. These references can be divided into two categories, 'pastoral' and 'descriptive'. The pastoral entries comprise approximately 50 imperatives such as 'have hold of the Truth in yourselves'; 'adorn', 'have esteem' and 'obey' the Truth; 'lead into the Truth'; 'be diligent' and 'valiant' in the Truth, and 'answer Truth in the oppressed'. The descriptors numbered about 30. Here Truth was, *inter alia*, 'righteous', 'judgment', 'peaceable', 'weighty', 'everlasting' and 'universal'.[10]

The power of Truth for the Quakers lay in their belief that it would lead all those who trusted in the power of the Light into a patient and confident 'waiting' on God so they may be an extension of the true Church 'that ever was'. Consequently, the Friends believed Truth would also lead to a life of faithfulness, to 'study to live quietly' (inwardly, though not passively).[11] Without Truth, 'the enabler of faith', there could be no liberty of conscience, indeed no liberty. And so it compelled them, through suffering if need be, to continue witnessing for the release of justice from the bondage of those who denied God and the Kingdom, and who were violent as a result.[12] Those 'out of Truth' persecuted the innocent people of God.[13] Truth, therefore, took away 'the occasion of all wars' and brought people

---

[10] Other representative entries are:

Pastoral (inc. advice and imperative): Worship in the Truth; Come to the Truth; Never dishonour the Truth; Speak Truth in love; Be guided by Truth; Prize the standing Truth; Spread the Truth; Live in the Truth; Live Truth; Keep habitation in the Truth; Guide into the Truth; Be prisoners for the Truth; Do not slight Truth; Let Truth flow; Preach the Truth; Discern the Truth; Receive the Truth; Love the Truth; Declare the Truth; Proclaim the Truth; Testify to the Truth; Die for the Truth; Serve Truth; Confirm people in the Truth; Witness to the Truth; Promote the Truth; Use honest, simple plain speech; Have no double standards; Open all to the Truth; Be ready to sacrifice for the Truth; Be labourers for the Truth; Have a modest, decent and comely life in the Truth; Be God's ensign in the Truth; Do Truth; Be adulterated from the Truth; Have unity in the Truth; Be shod with the Truth; Be Friends in Truth; Be baptised in the Truth; Purchase the Truth (reference to Mt. 13).

Descriptive: Truth is Christ; Truth changes not; Spirit of Truth; Power of Truth; Precious Truth; Pure Truth; Testimony of Truth; Gospel of the Truth; Seed of Truth; Truth preserves everything in its place; Simplicity of the Truth; Pure language of the Truth; Truth stands over; Truth reigns over; Government in the Truth; City of Truth; Truth in God; Truth Speaks; The world speaks evil of the Truth; Truth springs up; Christ, the Ground and Pillar of the Truth; Truth in the inward parts; Truth of the heart; Out of the Truth; Scriptures of Truth are the words of God and the words of Christ.

[11] Fox, *Doctrinals*, 211-13; Nayler, *A Letter to the King* (1660) in *Works*, 599. See 1 Thess. 4: 11-12.

[12] Anon, *To the Generals, and Captains, Officers, and Soldiers* (*DCFB* 1658/*Wing* 1660), 2-3,7.

[13] Fox, *59 Particulars*, 16. Also Fox, *Here you may see what was the True Honour* (1660), 14; Fox (the Younger), *A Visitation of Love Unto All People* (1659), 5.

'into love and true heartedness'.[14] Failure to adhere to truth, justice and equity guaranteed condemnation, the agony of a spiritual void.[15]

Just as Truth was constitutive to the new dispensation ushered in by Jesus, it was *itself* the new dispensation for their own times and for which they witnessed prophetically. And much to the anger of the Calvinists, the Quakers' Truth was universally shared rather than confined to an Elect predetermined before creation. Nor was it, as William Dell observed, the preserve of the *literati*.[16] The Friends would have agreed with Ralph Cudworth, the Cambridge Platonist, that before Truth 'all works shake and tremble . . . [it] endures and is always strong. It lives and conquers for evermore. She is Strength, Kingdom, Power and Majesty of all ages'.[17]

But the Quakers went further. In *Some Things of Great Weight* (1667), Penington described Truth as of God, beyond time and space, eternal and pure, and existing before all error. Divine Truth was eternal and unchangeable, 'the same Truth that was preached in shadows under the Law, the substance [and] . . . witnessed in the Gospel'. The Truth was always fair to every person and never failed to condemn injustice, ignorance and violence.[18] Alluding to Matthew 13, Penington, like Fox, called it the 'precious pearl of price' that must be dug up by the 'plough of God' if its 'Life' and salvation were to be enjoyed. Truth gave life to all and set them free. Crucially for Penington and the Friends, Truth was with Jesus and the followers around him, that is, before the 'apostasy' and the 'latter days from it' including the so-called Christianity of their day.[19]

Early Quaker Simplicity

Along with 'truth, justice and equity' comes the Quakers' awareness of simplicity for the religious life. In Chapter 4 we observed an important outcome when lives are led in the Truth; their capacity to speak plainly out of respect for honesty and openness, but also to 'address' the Light within each person and situation. As directness was a feature of their discourse and face-to-face interaction, particularly with those who wielded power, early Quaker letters to the authorities were normally characterised by a simple but

---

[14] Fox and Nayler *et al*, *Several Petitions Answered*, 39.
[15] Nuttall, *The Holy Spirit*, 111; Burrough, *A General Epistle . . . to All Saints*, 5.
[16] Dell, *The Way of True Peace and Unity*, 217.
[17] Cudworth, *A Sermon Preached*, 81.
[18] Penington, 'Of the Pure' in *Some Things of Great Weight* (1667), 18-20 and in *Works*, i, 470. James Nayler said the same in *Love to the Lost*, 12.
[19] Penington, *ibid*.

pointed use of the written word.[20] It was a capacity that often landed them in serious trouble.

Simplicity and sobriety were also encouraged in personal appearance, in the arrangements for, and manner of, their worship, and in the conduct and maintenance of their Meetings and daily lives. They claimed their simplicity was underscored by humility in 'the face of the Lord' so that an ever-pure state might be established within the soul. Friends and non-Friends alike were asked to be 'low' in spirit, meek in manner, giving and loving in their fellowship with one another.[21] Plain language was urged upon the authorities themselves, that their legislation should be understood by all without the imposition of difficult expressions or obfuscation. Nor, they said, should plain language be a punishable offence. Thus, in a variant of hat refusal, the Friends employed 'thee' and 'thou' (to equals) instead of the formal 'you' (in deference).[22] In 1660 William Smith summarised the Quakers' position *vis-à-vis* simplicity when he wrote:

> So the image hath been made and set up, and all these branches put forth since the days of the apostles, the Spirit of Truth being lost, and people having run in the night of apostasy, they have been like blind men groping for a way to walk in.[23]

The delusion of inner falsehood as well as inequality and injustice would lead to 'carnal' (sinful) manifestations and implications. As the Subtle One (Satan, the dark world) always sought to ensnare the unsuspecting, Smith urged those out of the Light to seek the way of peace, unity and safety in God, whose refuge and rest were available to anyone who donned the armour of God in the Lamb's War for salvation. Victory in this war meant enlisting in the ranks of a different army whose *real* good old cause was one of 'true religion' whose followers would never backslide. This 'remnant' would be joined 'to that which was in the beginning . . . from which the

---

[20] Burrough, 'For the hands of Oliver Cromwell called Protector' in *Good Counsel and Advice* (1659), 3-11. See Thomas Morford (d.1694), letter (*c*.April, 1655) to Fox, SW/iv/176 for Morford's account of a meeting with Cromwell.

[21] Fox, *The Law of God the Rule for Law-makers*, 13; Penington, *To the Army* (1659) in *Works*, i. 144; Daniel Gotherson, *An Alarm to All Priests* (1660), 12; Fox, letter (5/May/1658) to Friends, *Bristol MSS.*, ii. 71-2. For 'face of the Lord' or Christ see 2 Cor. 4: 6.

[22] Fox, *59 Particulars*, 4; Fox et al, *A Battle-Door* (1660), 19; Farnworth, *The Pure Language of the Spirit, passim*; *Journal*, 416.

[23] W. Smith, *The Morning-Watch*, 18. Also Burrough, *A Visitation of Love unto the King* (1660), 14, 29. For another commentary on the dark night of apostasy and the covenant of death see Penington, *The Way of Life and Death*, esp. 57.

apostles ravened [i.e. fled] from', that is, to the Jesus Way before the apostasy.[24]

Smith reinforced the Friends' view of themselves as prophets in the Amos tradition like John the Baptist—as unfailing rivers of justice, stern in judgment, inexorable in their demands for righteousness while breathing forth warnings and exhortations, and offering no compromise.[25] In particular, they saw themselves as a collective Jeremiah, one of their favourite prophets. They, like him, offered an authoritative reformulation of the Law as the new covenant, had preached in the temple at 'Jerusalem' (against the church as an institution), spoke the language of liberation while evoking the authority of a Moses (like Jesus in delivering the Sermon on the Mount) and had undergone trial and suffering.[26] And yet, as upholders of primitive Christianity, the Friends had a self-understanding as the recapitulated incarnation, as the true heirs of Jesus, and as the current voice of God's love, including the resurrection and hope it offered. Thus simplicity also demanded a return to Edenic purity that would be carried in the heart each day the Kingdom's 'branches [were] put forth'.

Poverty and Suffering

The Friends were born into a time when their fellow Britons were divided into strictly observed social ranks or 'degrees'—peers, landed gentry, yeomen and agricultural day labourers. The latter were described in 1577 as having 'neither voice nor authority in the commonwealth, but are to be ruled and not to rule'.[27] Everyone owed obedience to superiors who, in return, offered protection to inferiors, although the existence of a 'meaner sort' in large numbers contradicted the theory. Richard Gough's *The History of Myddle* (1701) graphically shows how even the order of seating in church reflected the social architecture. The richer sort, among who were gentry like Margaret Fell, occupied the front pews which were often elaborately carved and contained equally decorative doors and cushioned seats. The poorer folk of the village and environs, in this case the labouring poor (as opposed to the 'impotent' and 'idle'), bunched together at the back of the church near the porch.

As they travelled the length and breadth of the British nations, the Quakers came into contact with extreme wealth and the inequalities and injustices that went with it. The riches of the greater 'country or landed

---

[24] W. Smith, *ibid.*, 59.
[25] See Manson, *The Servant-Messiah*, 47 and Amos 5: 21-4.
[26] See Jackson, *Essays on Halakhah*, 54.
[27] Wrightson, *English Society*, 19. See William Harrison, *Description of England*, Part 1, chp.5; also:
<http://www.fordham.edu/halsall/mod/1577harrison-england.html#Chapter%20V>.

gentry' and the lesser 'middling and parochial gentry' had ballooned during the seventeenth century as did their numbers—from 6,000 in 1540 to 18,000 by 1640. The very wealthy—'the high and lofty ones' so called by the Quakers—were the least taxed in Europe and owned 40% of the land.[28] And because they disdained manual labour, rent rather than farming provided county magnates with the greater proportion of their income. Most landowners raised rents to match price rises and expected their struggling tenants to pay up even in times of inflation and regardless of the hardship imposed. The royalist and Catholic, Sir George Middleton of Yealand (Lancs.), who receives a black mark in Fox's *Journal*, was enraged when, after outrageously demanding up to the equivalent of thirty years' rent, his tenants reminded him that 'he was not entitled to receive fines of more than four years ancient rent'.[29] However, despite the avarice of landlords, it was the rising demand for tenancies resulting from an expanding population and increasing farming profits that carried the greater responsibility for rent increases.

Quaker itinerant preachers also saw the effects of enclosures in England, called by K. Polanyi a revolution of the rich against the poor.[30] Enclosures largely succeeded in extinguishing common rights upon which smallholders heavily relied especially in respect to grazing and fuel gathering. Common and waste areas, usually owned by the Lord of the Manor, had normally been left undeveloped as villagers freely exercised the rights of which we speak. Along with land-grabs (often carried out by force), enclosures came with a terrible price for huge numbers of people, something that was criticised by many including Puritan ministers such as John Moore from Leicestershire whom we met in Chapter 1. And with the

---

[28] While there was considerable variation in wealth and social position among the gentry, historians are at pains to emphasise difficulties in defining this rank. While the wealth of 'the richer sort' increased along with their number, it differed regionally. Based on the variation in wealth and the family lineage associated with estates, a division existed in every county between the greater 'country or landed gentry' and the lesser 'middling and parochial gentry' of which Quaker families such as the Peningtons, the Crooks', the Evans' and the Docwras may have been typical. The divisions were particularly mirrored in their incomes. In 1642 at the outbreak of the first civil war, one-third of the Yorkshire gentry earned less than £100 a year. In Stockport and district (Cheshire), local notables such as Sir George Booth (Sr.) and Sir Richard Wilbraham recorded annual incomes in excess of £1,000. In 1648, Wilbraham's son and heir, enjoyed the third largest yearly income in Cheshire—£2,500. Below these came the three most powerful families in the region, the Duckenfields, the Hollands and the Hydes who each earned between £500 to £750 p.a. With an annual income below £100 came the Hollingworths and Bretlands. At £3,000 a year, George Purefey in Fenny Drayton had a considerable annual income. See Heal and Holmes, *passim* but esp. their 'Introduction'; Blackwood, *The Lancashire Gentry*, 15; D. Hirst, *England in Conflict*, 61; Nevell, *Tameside 1066-1700*, 68 and esp. 72-3.

[29] Blackwood, *ibid.*; *Journal*, 374.

[30] K. Polanyi, *The Great Transformation*, 35.

gradual concentration of agriculture nationally into fewer and fewer hands, a resulting rise in landlessness caused nationwide anguish and resentment.

Enclosures, to be sure, helped ensure that, at a time of transition from subsistence agriculture, output could keep pace with rising urban populations. But while many a pamphlet documented the plight of the people, their grievances for the most part remained unanswered. This growing and sullen majority could only look in from the margins as the wealthy assumed ever-greater authority over 'much earth' as their 'right'. It led eventually to riots with some observers, again like Moore, willing to publicly record the deepening poverty and discontent.

The early Quakers fervently believed that England had been devastated by Satan with apostasy and injustice running riot. The stench of the carnal was everywhere, they declared, its corruption all too visible and tangible. Their sense of urgency meant God's work within the context of widespread poverty could not be postponed. Complaining frequently that the powerful were 'grinding the face of the poor', they were certain the scandal of poverty and oppression was indication enough that the poor equally deserved not only divine love but truthfulness and justice from those in authority.[31] To the Friends, keen to draw attention to the causes of injustice, the poor were fully within the compass of God and vulnerable in their helplessness. They maintained that poverty and its attendant horrors were not isolated phenomena but related to the basic spiritual estrangement that set neighbour against neighbour. In concert with many others, they believed poverty represented the reality of, and the potential for, spiritual brokenness, the separation of God and humanity, but also the potential for repentance and healing. More substantively, the poor were a reminder that the ethics of the Jesus Way found in the Sermon on the Mount and in Jesus' two commandments should never be violated.

Indeed, with the poor in mind Fox reached beyond his Quaker constituency to exhort merchants to be truthful in their business transactions. Twenty-nine of the fifty-nine proposals he sent to parliament in 1659 focussed on the need for an egalitarian society including a better system of relief for the poor. In *A Warning to all the Merchants in London*—that city 'fatted in the flesh' as he once derided it[32]—his call for an end to deceitful dealings, 'cozenings' and 'cheating' was characteristic of a format that not only saw Fox attacking hat honour and all forms of deference but embarrassing the wealthy for their 'gold chains about your

---

[31] Thomas Taylor, *Some Prison Meditations in the 7th Month* (1657), 7. For a good account of poverty and Quaker involvement see Knarr, *The Early Quaker Theology and Social Protest*, 244-58 and Elmen, 'The Theological Basis of Digger Communism', *passim* and esp. 216.
[32] Fox, *The Priests Fruits made Manifest* (1657), 5.

necks, and your costly attire [which] shall eat you up.'[33] 'These gentlemen', goaded Fox, 'are brave fellows'.[34]

His love of Revelation fed a compulsion to warn the wealthy of the seductive powers of Babylon. Though they may believe, as in Jesus' day, that riches were a sign of God's favour, in the Kingdom there were no rich or poor. And so, probably with the Letter of James in mind, he took every opportunity to remind the wealthy of their duty to 'the poor, blind, women and children, and cripples, crying and making a noise up and down your streets, a dishonour to your city'.[35] Their spiritual myopia meant they failed to understand that the destitute, too, needed the Light. As a result of their sin, the rich and powerful were to bow before the coming wrath of God which would overturn 'opinions, and all manner of sects, . . . the mountains shall melt'. The 'terrible day' of sin contrasted with the glories of the Kingdom:

> Oh you great men, and rich men of the earth, weep and howl for your misery is coming, who heaps up treasures for the last day; your gold and silver shall eat you up as the rust and the canker . . . all the loftiness of men must be laid low.[36]

The young James Parnel, in a manner worthy of the Diggers and Levellers, demanded greater economic equity by which he primarily meant substantial economic restructuring involving land redistribution.[37] Like other leading Friends, he liberally evoked the memory of Jubilee (Lev. 25:1-7; Dt. 15:1-11; Ex. 23:10-11) but especially the eighth-century Hebrew prophets Amos, Hosea, Isaiah and Micah, all of whom foreshadowed the Kingdom of God as requiring social action as well as purity and depth of worship.[38] 'Woe unto you', he blasted the wealthy,

> that are called, lords, ladies, knights, gentlemen, and gentlewomen, in respect to your persons, who are exalted in the earth, who are proud,

---

[33] Fox, *The Second Covenant*, 9. See Vann and Eversley, *Friends in Life and Death*, 16, 47.
[34] Fox, *The Fashions of the World* in *Doctrinals*, 110.
[35] Fox, *A Warning to all the Merchants in London* (1658), 2, 9 and see. Lk. 14:13; Fox, *A Warning to the Rulers of England* in Nayler, *A Lamentation*, 14; see 'Fashions of the World' in *The Priests Fruits Made Manifest*, 3-5.
[36] Fox, *To All that would Know*, 9; *The Second Covenant*, 5.
[37] Parnel, *A Shield of the Truth* (1655), 1-17 and G. Harkness, *Understanding the Kingdom of God*, chp. 4 (online).
[38] According to Exodus, Jubilee proposed that in every seventh year slaves should be liberated, debts pardoned, employers honour their workers as free people (*cf.* Dt.15: 12-15), people recognise each other as brothers and sisters, and that land should be redistributed equally. See see Lev. 25:1-7, 28: 8-16; Dt. 15:1-11: Ex. 23:10-11 and Lk. 4:19.

Chapter 11: 'Because of your much Earth'

and high, and lofty; . . . because of your gay clothing, because of your much earth, which by fraud, deceit and oppression you have gotten together.[39]

Fox, too, condemned the effects of enclosures. In 1653, thundering against the rich, he quoted Isaiah 5:8: 'you that set your nests on high, join . . . field to field till there be no place for the poor, woe is your portion'.[40] The call for land redistribution was no 'utopian prescription or eschatological hope'. Rather, it was 'a practical hedge against the inevitable concentration of wealth' that was intensifying poverty.[41] The land belonged to God and without redistributive justice there could be no serious talk of establishing the Kingdom. Of course, land redistribution also meant the eradication of tithes as we can see in Fox's *59 Particulars*.[42] For Samuel Fisher, too, land grabs and tithes were a theft from the mass of people who were the original owners of the land.[43] And in *The Condition and Portion of the People of England* (1653), Nayler who was himself a farmer pulled no punches: 'Woe unto you, you fat swine. Now is the Lord come to require his corn and his wine which he gave to feed the poor and hungry, which your lusts have devoured'.[44] He saw the parlous condition of the poor as a direct result of the 'great estates'. With the ethics of the Kingdom in mind he again roared at the 'covetous' who laid 'house to house and land to land,

> till there be no place for the poor [whom you] despise . . . and [you] exalt yourselves above them and forget that you are all made of one mould and one blood . . . what shall your riches avail you at that day [which] is at hand . . . for your kingdom must be taken from you, and given to them who will bring forth fruits.[45]

---

[39] Parnel, *The Trumpet of the Lord Blown* (1655) in *Works*, 28-30, 32, 34-7; *A Shield of the Truth*, 3, 20 and *A Warning for All People* (1660), *passim*. See also Lk. 6: 20-46, 12:15-21, 14:13, 18: 23-27; Fox, *To the High and Lofty Ones* (1655), *passim* in *Doctrinals*, 28-31; Margaret Killam and Barbara Patison, *A Warning from the Lord* (1655), 3. Also Schenk, *The Concern for Social Justice in the Puritan Revolution*, 123.
[40] Fox, *The Vials of the Wrath of God* (1654), 3. Also *AOTW*, 32.
[41] See Myers *et al*, 'Say to this Mountain', 127 for a commentary on Mk. 10: 23-31, which may have influenced the Friends in this respect.
[42] Fox, *59 Particulars*, 8, 11.
[43] S. Fisher, *To the Parliament of England*, 2-3.
[44] Nayler, *The Condition and Portion of the People of England* in *Several Papers*, 21; also in *Several Papers of Confessions* (1659), 6; perhaps Nayler had Mt.7:6 and Mk. 15:11-13 in mind when using 'fat swine'. See also Fox, 'A Word from the Lord' in *News Coming up out of the North*, 13.
[45] Nayler, *A Discovery of the First Wisdom*, 33-4.

James Harrington, the rationalist, who examined the underlying causes of poverty in his *Commonwealth of Oceana* (1656), went to the hub of the matter: 'where there is inequality of estates, there must be inequality of power, and where there is inequality of power there can be no Commonwealth'.[46]

As with Fox, Thomas Lawson's *An Appeal to the Parliament, Concerning the Poor* (1660) declared for a New Israel free of beggars. 'The work of charity', Lawson wrote in a postscript to the tract,

> doth not concern parliament men, and officers for the poor only, but all other in authority to put into practice advice expressed in *Ecclesiasticus* 40: 28-29, 'My son, lead not a beggar's life, far better it is to die than to beg.[47]

Lawson's work had a strong pastoral flavour for those threatened by the spiritual void, including oppressors. With the materially poor and their own sufferings in mind, the Sermon on the Plain maxim, 'blessed are the poor' (Lk. 6:20), became a Quaker motto for the holy, perfect life. They also referred to the insistence in the Epistle of James, itself owing much to the Sermon on the Mount, that the essence of true Christianity was an honest imitation of Jesus' love of the poor.[48]

While repeatedly acknowledging due respect for Caesar, the Quakers pointed tirelessly to the paramount nature of Love, not only in their writings but through the martyrdom of Friends like James Parnel, William Robinson, Marmaduke Stevenson, Elizabeth Fletcher and Mary Dyer, and also through their sufferings from heavy fines, the invasion of homes by mobs and soldiers, and confiscation of their household goods as with the Kentish farmer, Robert Minter. At times with considerable ferocity, they were assaulted, on their way to and from Meetings and other venues of worship.[49]

---

[46] See Hayduk, *Hopeful Politics*, 630 and Harrington, *Oceana*, 41.

[47] T. Lawson, *An Appeal to the Parliament, Concerning the Poor* (1660), 4.

[48] Adamson, *James: The Man and His Message*, 463. See Hubberthorne, *A Copy of a Paper sent to the Council of State, in the year 1659* in *Works*, 234. See *TLITC*, ch. 4, esp. 53 and *GADOT*, 360 (87n).

[49] After being humiliated and beaten by students of St. John's College (Oxford) in 1654, Elizabeth Fletcher and her companion, on the orders of the university Vice-Chancellor, John Owen, were whipped while driven from the city despite protests from the mayor. Fletcher (c.1638-58) probably died from the long-term effects of the assault. Parnel died aged 20 in 1656. In McGregor and Reay, *Radical Religion*, Reay has Parnel dying of a 'fast' but Fox suspected murder through negligence; see *Journal*, 163 and also Parnel *et al*, *The Lamb's Defence Against Lies* (1655), *passim*. Robinson (d. 1659), Stevenson (d. 1659) and Dyer (d. 1660) were hanged in Boston (MA). For Fletcher see Crump (ed.), 54. See Fell *et al*, *A Declaration and an Information* (1660), 6 and Ac. 7.60 (see Fell's margin note *p*). It is possible that Sarah Cheevers, who died in 1664, did so as a result of her incarcerations, particularly in Malta between 1659 and 1662.

Burrough claimed three Friends lost their right ears in this way. Worse, some were murdered while others were thrown into overcrowded and indescribably filthy prisons, or banished (usually by clerics) and deprived of their children like Barbara Blaugdone. Other gatherings were disturbed by musket shot while stones, mud, water and sewerage were hurled into their Meeting Houses. Sometimes their clothes were ripped or they were flung into ditches and covered in dirt. At times, their hair and faces were rubbed with excrement or rotten eggs. Smoking, swearing and drinking mobs would often play drums or sing bawdy songs in their presence. Horle adds brutalisation by 'law-enforcement officers, informers and the militia, [while] they were victimised by unethical and illegal tactics, by primitive courtroom procedure, by hectoring judges and by intimated juries'. It was, he continues, 'a bleak and despairing picture'; eighty-eight works published before 1660 either described or tabulated their various sufferings.[50]

By all accounts these privations, each considered a mini-crucifixion and a blasphemy to the Light/Christ or Jesus within them, were accepted without physical retaliation.[51] 'They held their Meetings regularly, perseveringly', an anonymous witness wrote, 'and without the least concealment, keeping the doors of their Meeting Houses purposely open that all might enter—informers, constables, or soldiers, and do whatever they choose'.[52] Even Richard Baxter had to agree and it was not uncommon at the local level for non-Quakers to express sympathy and offer material support for their persecuted neighbours. One Bedfordshire minister, for instance, was forced by local pressure to return goods seized from a Quaker for tithe refusal. Kent informs us that,

> Occasionally, impropriators had trouble laying their tithe claims against Quakers because none of the Quakers' neighbours would testify about the amount of agricultural yield that Quaker farms produced. Wiltshire and Somerset records reveal that neighbours often warned tithe-

---

[50] Horle, *The Quakers and the English Legal System*, 161, 164.
[51] Knott, *Discourses of Martyrdom*, 225-6. See Burrough, *A Declaration of the Sad* (1661), 3; Burrough *et al* (?), *A Declaration of the Present Sufferings, passim* and *A Brief Relation of the Persecutions* (1662), *passim* and esp. 2-3 for Burrough's letter to the Mayor of London. The reportage style of Quaker martyrdom and other harsh sufferings probably owed much to Foxe's *Martyrs*. Punshon, *Portrait in Grey*, 41 tells us that Foxe's work was almost certainly read by the godly in Fenny Drayton. See Dawson, 'The Apocalyptic Thinking', 75-91; Haller, *Foxe's Book of Martyrs and the Elect Nation*, 224; Olsen, 'Was John Foxe a millenarian?', 623. And Fox and Hookes, *The Arraignment of Popery* (1667), 80, 81; Coale, *The Whore Unvailed* (1665), 9. For suffering as an external attack on the Jesus within see Bishop *et al*, *The Cry of Blood*, Sig. A2.
[52] Anon., 'Attitudes of Friends under Persecution', 148-9 in which the author cites Masson, who in turn leaned heavily on Sewell's *History of the Rise, Increase and Progress* (1722 [1834]), ii., 191. See Masson, *The Life of John Milton*, vi., 587-8.

resisting Quakers of approaching constables, and accounts from the Restoration period reveal that neighbours occasionally 'borrowed' particular items or animals in order to protect them from being confiscated.[53]

The suffering they incurred was regarded as a nonviolent testimony to the holiness of life as well as a warning and a mirror to the authorities of their shameful ways. There was an apocalyptic and eschatological aspect to their suffering, too. According to Hugh Barbour and Arthur Roberts, 'the bitterness of the suffering [was] also a sign of the bitterness of Satan's plight, and thus the nearness of the End' and (I add) of the old Mosaic dispensation and a justification that the new and peaceful Israel was bursting upon the nations.[54]

Clearly, at this time, before 1660, nonviolence was more typical of the Quakers' way than some historians have supposed. The vast majority of Friends took Stephen, the first Christian martyr, as their nonviolent inspiration (bound up as they were with forgiveness), combining the example he provided with loyalty and obedience to the Word, the Kingdom. Their insights into the early Christian Way would find mention and affirmation in the Burrough, Fell and Fox-Hubberthorne declarations—the insights were *not* an outcome of the declarations or something suddenly realised as the political tide turned against the republic.[55]

Defending the movement, Fox repeatedly pleaded the case for even-handedness in the administration of justice since God was no respecter of persons. Fox was emulated by Howgill and other public Friends like Lawson who upbraided magistrates as being vagabonds themselves while condemning the way they languished in the Mosaic covenant pursuing 'covetousness and pride'.[56] Fox challenged authorities of all kinds not to prey on the people but to share their tables with widows, the fatherless,

---

[53] Kent, 'Relative Deprivation and Resource Mobilisation', 538. See D. Scott, *Quakerism in York 1650-1720*, Paper 80, p.5; Skinner, *Non-Conformity in Shropshire*, 60, 133; A. Anderson, 'A Study in the Sociology of Religious Persecution', 247-62; Reay, 'Quaker Opposition to Tithes', 98-120. See Gregg, *Oliver Cromwell*, 312 in which the 1650s Friends are described as 'basically pacifist'. And Nuttall, 'Introduction: George Fox and his Journal' in *Journal*, p. xx.
[54] *EQW*, 104.
[55] See Fell *et al*, *A Declaration and Information*, 6 (esp. note *p*), 4, 5; Fox-Hubberthorne *et al*, *A Declaration from the Harmless*, 3. Also Thomas Stubbs, *Certain Papers Given Forth* (1659), 6.
[56] Howgill, *This was the Word of the Lord* (1654) and in *Works*, 6. The letter is signed by Howgill; Nayler, 'Concerning Error, Heresy, &c.' in *Love to the Lost*, 3-5; Fox, letter (*c*.1654/55?) to Cromwell, *Markey MS*. (LRSF: MSS. Box C4/1), 229; *This for each Parliament-Man* (1656), 2; *To All that would Know*, 8. Also Hubberthorne, *A True Testimony of the Zeal*, 4-6.

Chapter 11: 'Because of your much Earth'

strangers, sons, daughters and servants.[57] 'Woe is to all now,' Fox wrote in *News Coming up out of the North*,

> who seek for the fleece and wool, and make a prey of the people . . . [and] take tithes, and mingle with the world; and them that will not give it you, you sue them at the law . . . you are them that appear beautiful outwardly to men, but are full of poison within . . . you are they who say and do not, you are those that lay heavy burdens upon the people.[58]

While the Friends were concerned to address the Light of Christ within their enemies, their condemnations and judgments were built, as we have seen, on love.[59] And while their sufferings assumed victory for the Lamb, they also carried the hope that the Light would be awakened in the consciences of their opponents and persecutors. John Higgins, writing from Newgate prison in London, described elsewhere as 'that infamous castle of misery', urged the authorities to 'sink down to God's witness' in their hearts which would bring them 'into a sense of [their] own condition'. Thus would the chains of oppression be broken.[60] *News Coming up out of the North* finishes with a typical Foxian flourish, an apocalyptic warning of the spiritual Endtime: '[h]aste, haste by speedy repentance, and put off the works of darkness to meet the Lord'. For Fox, caring passionately for the salvation of those 'out of the Life', spiritual death was the ultimate folly. What sinful (or 'carnal') earthly state, what temporary gratification—even if it should span a lifetime—could compare to the freedom and happiness that could be enjoyed for *eternity* in the love of God? Why be so foolish as to invoke the dark world?

---

[57] Fox, *That all might see who they were that had a Command* (1657), 16; *The Second Covenant*, 2-4.
[58] Fox, *News coming up out of the North*, 27, 36; *To the Pope*, 61-9; *The Law of God the Rule for Law-makers*, 16-17. Also Hubberthorne, *The Real Cause of the Nation's Bondage and Slavery* (1659) and in *Works*, 219-22. The pope in 1660 was Alexander VII (1655-67).
[59] Fox, letter (c.1654/55?) to Cromwell, *Markey MS.* (LRSF: MSS. Box C4/1), 229 and letter (n.d.) to 'professors' (i.e. usually clerics), *John Tapper MS.*, 1; *This for each Parliament-Man*, 2; *To All that would Know*, 8; Howgill, *A Lamentation for the Scattered Tribes*, 5.
[60] John Higgins, *From Newgate* (1661), 3. Along with Thomas Goodaire's account, this is one of the few reasonably detailed descriptions of Quaker prison experiences, particularly the treatment they received; see esp. 2. For 16th-17th century prisons see Havran, *The Catholics in Caroline England*, 107-109. And for a graphic account of the grim conditions of Newgate where a number of Friends perished see A. Griffiths, *The Chronicles of Newgate*, 61-124, esp. 70. The Old Bailey law courts now occupy part of the site of Newgate.

Mutual Support and Issues of Conscience

In response to the inner conflict of convincement, disputation within their movement and external threats and violence, the Friends set about defining and implementing mutual support systems, but also for those outside the Quaker fold. It is a work that needs placing in the context of their campaigns against tithing and opposition to other forms of 'tyranny and oppression' including the highly punitive legal and prison systems.[61] In the seventeenth century, any building could be designated a gaol since England was devoid of a national prison infrastructure.[62] They were generally farmed out to private contractors who invariably used them for personal gain. Whatever their configuration or location, they were usually fetid places, chronically under-resourced and constantly in a state of disrepair. It was not uncommon for up to thirty people to be squeezed into highly confined spaces. Gaolers were normally paid a pittance which they augmented by selling bedding, food, drink, candles and furniture at their discretion but at highly inflated prices.

Prisons were also notorious for their brutal disregard of human suffering. According to Beier, dress, diet and the daily routine were strictly regulated in Houses of Correction (Bridewells). In the Norwich Bridewell, inmates worked from 5 am to 8 pm in summer and 6 am to 7 or 7.30 pm in winter. Each day they were allotted half an hour to eat and 15 minutes for prayer. Prisoners were whipped for disobedience and swearing. Most provincial Houses of Correction were small, a matter of one or two rooms, and administered by a few officials only.[63] Whether in a Bridewell or a standard prison like Newgate, typical inmates included unwedded mothers and their offspring, bigamists, drunkards, gamblers, scolds, slanderers and even prisoners of war. They were frequently afflicted with malnutrition, dysentery, pneumonia or TB. Gaol fever (typhus), smallpox and plague took hundreds of lives. Even in the summer, the usually overcrowded cells could be extremely cold. For the most part, inmates existed in total darkness.[64]

As prisoners, the Friends confronted not only the physical and spiritual immediacy of their surroundings but also radically questioned the very purpose of the institutions in which they languished. Thomas Goodaire's account of his time in Oxford gaol during September 1660 is particularly harrowing. He was clamped in tight, highly restrictive irons and led into a 'stinking room', refused straw and forced to lie on the cold floor. He was

---

[61] Vann and Eversley, *Friends in Life and Death*, 47. See Burrough, *A Vindication of the People of God called Quakers* (1660), 19.
[62] In London, taverns, private houses, hulks and even Gresham College were used as temporary holding areas for the overcrowded Newgate and Fleet prisons.
[63] Beier, *The Problem of the Poor*, 35.
[64] *Ibid.*

Chapter 11: 'Because of your much Earth'

abused and molested by the gaoler's wife while her son insulted and physically assaulted other Friends who had already endured the same conditions for two years for non-payment of tithes.[65]

This was typical treatment and it led the Friends to advocate prison reform, drawing the attention of the authorities to maintain prisons as

> wholesome places, that the prisoners may not lie in their own dung, and piss, and straw like chafe, having never a house-of-office [toilet] in the prison; therefore let there be an house-of-office in all goals, and let these things be mended.[66]

Incarceration meant experiencing the stark realities of prison life 'for conscience sake', pondering the nature of their alleged criminality and dwelling on issues such as capital punishment which they considered barbaric and disproportionate for such crimes as theft.[67] Was not capital punishment a denial of the Spirit in the individual? asked Fox. Did it not diminished the executioner and sever possibilities for reconciliation between offender, victim and the State? Did it not end hope for physical and spiritual rehabilitation?[68]

While in Southwark (London) in 1653/4, Nayler was deeply offended by the sight of men hanging 'in open streets' from scaffolds 'by two, three, four or five'. He appealed to the authorities to rid the land of the 'abomination'.[69] Another Quaker, William Tomlinson, had no doubt that the injustice and cruelty of execution was indicative of how legal authority was upheld by cruelty. Like Fox, but also like Richard Overton the Leveller and Hugh Peter (Cromwell's chaplain), Tomlinson believed the law should be an instrument for amendment and true justice. Rather than their lives, wrongdoers should be deprived of goods for goods taken.[70] In *59 Particulars*, Fox demanded that parliament put an end to imprisonment,

> for not appearing by an attorney ... for not doffing his hat ... for oath refusal ... for not paying clerks wages for turning the hour-glass ... to be put to death for cattle, for money or any outward thing, let them restore and mind the Law of God.[71]

---

[65] Thomas Goodaire, *A Cry of the Just against Oppression*, 4.
[66] Fox, *59 Particulars*, 13.
[67] Leading Friend Edward Byllinge went against Fox in the case of murder. See *A Mite of Affection* (1659), 3 (prop. 7).
[68] Fox, *An Instruction to Judges and Lawyers* (DCFB/Wing 1657), 6.
[69] Nayler, *To the Parliament of the Commonwealth of England* (1654) in *Works*, 748-9.
[70] Tomlinson, *Seven Particulars* (1657), 11.
[71] Fox, *59 Particulars*, 3-4.

He exhorted Members of Parliament to remove a number of prisonable offences from the criminal register such as refusal to attend a 'steeplehouse' and public preaching,[72] and to refrain from treating public preachers as vagrants.[73] Any form of revenge was the way of the first covenant and such behaviour was now redundant since the advent of the New Israel.[74] Following Paul, the Friends saw in outward reconciliation a priestly metaphor for God's saving act in Jesus' death and resurrection.[75]

Compassion found expression in other forms of Quaker witness.[76] Practical measures in regard to themselves as victims of 'oppression' were essential components of their yearning for unity and a restored relationship with God for all humanity. The maintenance of Quaker itinerant preachers and their families, therefore, and the raising of funds from within the movement, brought into focus the need for a systematic distribution of relief and for Church government, the latter recognised as a necessity from the movement's beginnings by such leaders as William Dewsbury.[77] The early Quakers simply believed that supporting one another spiritually and materially was as natural as breathing. In response to the personal requirements of prisoners and their families, then, the Swarthmoor household of the Fells, together with other Friends in the district of Ulverston, established the Kendal Fund in 1654 'for the service of Truth' to which Friends would contribute voluntarily.[78] Towards the end of that year, Fell wrote to the movement stating her wish to help 'our dear brethren . . .

---

[72] See Skinner, *Non-Conformity in Shropshire*, 56.

[73] Fox, *ibid.*, 3-13.

[74] Goodaire, *A Cry of the Just against Oppression*, 4; Fell, *The Substance and Import*, 3rd. letter (5/July/1660) to King Charles II in *Works*, 19-20; letter (October 1660) to the King, *Spence MSS.*, 3/110.

Fell wrote four recorded letters to the King up to June, 1660: 'To King Charles II', dated late May (?), *Spence* 3/10); 'To King Charles II', n.d., *Spence* 3/98 and in *Works*, 19; 'To King Charles II', n.d., *Spence* 3/117; 'To King Charles II, Duke of York and Henry, Duke of Gloucester', dated June, *Spence* 3/99 and in *Works*, 17-18: a later version of the same is found in *Spence* 3/105 according to Glines (ed.), 284; see esp. 275-84. It is likely that elements of Letter 3/117 found their way into Fell's declaration and may have been the basis for it. Her reference to carnal weaponry in the penultimate paragraph only of her declaration, mentioned by Ingle in *QRT* 30, 2 (2001), 43, was a logical development of the tract's argument and nonviolence. The work was influential for Fox-Hubberthorne. See also *FF*, 191 and 333 (16n) and Wallace, *A Sincere and Constant Friend*, 43-7.

[75] See Kim, '2 Cor. 5:11-12 and the Origin of Paul's Concept of Reconciliation', 360.

[76] As they did with John Reeve the Muggletonian who said that true Christians 'suffer all kind of wrong from all men, and to return mercy and forgiveness'. See Reeve, *A Transcended Scriptural Treatise*, 7.

[77] Dewsbury, *This is the Word of the Living God* (1653) in *Works*, 1-4; Angell, 'The Rise of Elderism', 1.

[78] Lloyd, *Quaker Social History*, 1-3. See chp. 3 and esp. p. 40. See Mullett, *Radical Religious Movements in Early Modern Europe*, 128-32; Mullett (ed., 1978), Paper 5, 19-20; Kunze, *Margaret Fell*, 94-7; E. Taylor, *The Valiant Sixty*, 23 and *BQ*, 17-18.

Chapter 11: 'Because of your much Earth'

knowing at this time they are out of purse, . . . [and those] who are of the body ought to . . . administer freely according to their abilities, as they have received of the Lord freely'.[79]

Quaker prisoners were visited, a dangerous activity that could lead to imprisonment and/or physical infection as the little known Quaker, Henry Stokes, found for himself. Sadly, he contacted the plague while visiting his son in Newgate in 1665.[80] Danger, however, did not deter Margaret Fell's young daughters, Margaret (19) and Bridget (17) from carrying letters by Fox to York prison in July 1652, only a few weeks after his sermon on Firbank Fell.[81] The families of prisoners were also supported. Much of the relief work was organised, directed and performed by women such as Sarah Blackborow who, with the support of Fox, established the Two Weeks Women's Meeting and the Box Meeting in 1659 for this purpose. Both Meetings remained unaccountable to the men, their overall aim being women's needs and concerns.[82] From the Bull and Mouth, a former alehouse in London, the Quakers distributed food, clothing, money and, importantly, words of love and encouragement to many prisoners. This was essential work for sustaining co-religionists in their witness.[83] From all these activities grew a 'Meeting for Sufferings' which would eventually emerge as a representative body of the Friends nation-wide.

As suffering was seen as a service to the Spirit and to Jesus its embodiment, the Friends were encouraged to bear up under the pressure for Truth. Suffering was a trial of faith which would lead an individual out of the path of death into 'the Life', out of the traditions and customs of the world into the assurance of eternal purity and holiness. It was a way of participating in the passion and death of Jesus by dying to the particular shapes that sin took in their age.[84] It was an act of authentication, of restoring humanity to prelapsarian wholeness (Edenic purity and salvation). The pain, isolation, deprivation and humiliation they underwent were signs of solidarity with their community of faith and the whole of suffering humanity. George Bishop considered those Friends returning from captivity

---

[79] Fell, 'Appeal to Friends in North Lancashire and Cumberland', *Thirnbeck MSS.*, vol. 1 and quoted in *BQ*, 135-7, 317-20. See George Taylor, letter (23/Sept/1654) to Fell, *SW*/i/207 and from Thomas Lawson (Dec.? 1655) to Fell, *SW*/i/214 for Lawson's request that 10 shillings borrowed by him from one Thomas Turner may be repaid from the Fund.

[80] Thomas Salthouse, *A Brief Discovery of the Cause* (1665), 2-5. For Henry Stokes see <http://home.comcast.net/~jameslstokes/henry.htm>

[81] Aldam, letter (July, 1652) to Fox et al, *SW*/i/373.

[82] See Greaves and Zaller, *Biographical Dictionary of British Radicals*. The Box Meeting derived its name from the container holding money for poor relief.

[83] William Crouch (1628-1710), *Posthuma Christiana* (1712), 22-3. The title of this work continues, 'A brief historical account under his own hand of his convincement of, and early suffering for, the Truth.'

[84] See Orlie, *Living Ethically*, 72; Creasey, *Early Quaker Christology*, 352, 357.

a blessing to the nation, a triumphant people of God, spiritually free of Babylon. Parnel's statement to the magistracy that 'my liberty under thy bonds is a bondage to thee' was not so much the taunt of a youngster but an invitation to consider the power of the Quakers' synthesis of the Kingdom and the Cause which, as we have seen, was an expression of their understanding of 'true religion' rather than a political program only.[85] Fell urged an imprisoned Howgill and Nayler (in Appleby) to 'rejoice in that they are made worthy to suffer for the Lord's sake'.[86] Like many of his compatriots, Dewsbury's suffering was, as metaphor, an act of ministry towards those 'out of the Life'.[71]

Early Quaker suffering, then, was testimony of a most public kind. According to Bauman, 'the physical acting out of the metaphors was "intended as a means of enhancing the rhetorical power . . . [but also of seizing] the attention of onlookers"'.[87] Suffering gave surety to their purgation of sin during convincement and offered tangible 'evidence' of the Lamb's victory, of power over ignorance and confusion. Privation was also a visible testimony that something new had emerged—revelation (apocalypse)-in-action, a celebration that *God's* self-unveiling (of which they were its priestly agents) was continuous. Hence, Quaker suffering was a challenge to the Puritans' premillennial interpretation of Daniel and Revelation, a challenge to the violence of the old covenant. It was an act of self-negation so that the purity achieved would be a condition of a conscientious and righteous life, an example and pattern to the world.[88] Hence, an understanding was created of the continuity between past and present ('Christ is come') first on an individual and thence on a corporate level producing space to persist through and beyond all outward and imprisoning forms.[89]

Access to Political Authority

One of the most important acts of group support was the willingness of public Friends to approach government officials at a local and national level

---

[85] Bishop, letter to Friends, *Crosse MS*. (LSRF: Temp MSS. 553/18, n.d.), 75; Parnel, *The Fruits of a Fast*, 21.
[86] Fell, letter (1653) to Francis Howgill and James Nayler, *Spence MSS.*, iii., 27. Also Thomas Salthouse and Miles Halhead (*c.*1614-*ante* 1681), letter (9/Feb/1656) probably to Fell, *Caton MSS.*, iii., 89-91; Fox, letter to Friends, *Audland MS*. (LRSF: MS. Box P2/18., n.d.), 104.
[87] See Bauman, *Let Your Words Be Few*, 86.
[88] See 'The Argument' heading the Book of Revelation in the Geneva Bible in which the True Church suffers in order to cleanse itself as a preparation for the Providential plan for humanity. We have seen how *Martyrs* provided role models for suffering. For Friends as agents or messengers of Jesus Christ see Dewsbury, *The Discovery of the Great Enmity*, 3.
[89] See Orlie, *Living Ethically*, 72 and Nuttall, *The Holy Spirit*, 104.

Chapter 11: 'Because of your much Earth'

to mediate the freedom of Quaker prisoners. This, too, could act as metaphor. The Friends were gaoled for their righteousness but, as the righteous, they should be freed. The very act of opening the prison doors would ensure for those 'out of the Life' a measure of the Light if they chose to acknowledge the gift. Up to the end of 1659, the Friends had enjoyed relatively easy access to Cromwell, his son Richard, members of the returned Rump as well as the junta of major-generals and the Committee of Safety under General Charles Fleetwood (with Sir Henry Vane in prominent attendance). Despite an acrimonious discussion with Fox in 1658, Vane turned to the Quakers (as well as the Baptists and Fifth Monarchists) the following year. He was keen for their support as the Protectorate suddenly began to unravel—a chance at government no less! But, as already noted, Fox was no Zealot. Like Jesus, his chief interest was *God's* saving power through a reformation of values and personal transformation (repentance).[90]

Personal audiences with the powerful presented opportunities for sharing beliefs or submitting *apologia* for Quaker witness, such as the refusal to pay tithes or swear oaths. While encounters such as these were often excuses for hectoring those in power, at other times they were conducted in a civil and 'tender' manner as the meeting in 1660 between Richard Hubberthorne and Charles II illustrates. Hubberthorne gave the king an account of the sufferings certain Friends were undergoing. Requesting their freedom, he also explained the position of Quakers in regards to the Oath of Allegiance which, like all oaths, they found impossible to swear in 'conscience sake'. Swearing, we remember, implied dishonesty and a failure to be a pure witness to Truth.[91] Hubberthorne then assured Charles of the peaceful intention of the movement. In return, the king, impressed though a little amused by his diminutive guest, seemed convinced the Quakers meant no harm.

In a letter to Margaret Fell, a Friend named Walter Clement wrote of Charles' 'moderate carriage' towards Hubberthorne, mentioning the king's 'promises that no persecution shall be as for our religion'. But Clement suspected Charles of duplicity. Fell had seen the king earlier and handed him a letter also describing the sufferings of the Quakers. She pleaded for the release of Fox, recently arrested and imprisoned at Lancaster.[92] A month later she and Ann Curtis returned with the same petition with Curtis offering herself for Fox. This gesture impressed the king and it resulted in a

---

[90] Sir Henry Vane Jr., President of the Council in 1659, admired the Quakers for their moral integrity. However, he understood their 'Light' as a recipe for antinomianism which was antithetical to his struggle for a theocracy of Godly order. His 'Kingdom' was both inner and, most definitely, outer. See Parnham, 'The Nurturing of Righteousness', 7.

[91] Hubberthorne, *Something that lately passed in Discourse between the King and R. H.* (1660) and in *Works*, 268-72. Also *BQ*, 476-7. The Baptists also refused the same oath.

[92] Walter Clement, letter (10/June/1660) to Fell, *SW*/i/321; *BQ*, 490.

writ of *habeas corpus*. Fox was then brought to London for trial but soon released. There followed a brief period of sunshine in which Charles' guarantee of liberty of conscience made at Breda in Holland (1660) promised to be the order of the day. A leading Friend, Thomas Moore, was admitted to King and Council on behalf of the Quakers. He was allowed to wear his hat in the royal presence and was assured of Charles' tolerance towards the movement. The Council planned to investigate the sufferings of the Friends and issue a suitable proclamation (an insistence by Moore) reinforcing the King's Writ in the matter, something not always enforced by local magistrates.

However, a period of parliamentary vindictiveness followed especially after the Fifth Monarchist uprising of January 1661 after which the short period of toleration came to an abrupt end. Fears of Quaker involvement in the Venner escapade flew hither and thither. Arrests and persecution proceeded apace. Though most of the 4,200 incarcerated Friends were released shortly afterwards, the incident showed how Quaker activity could be distorted, a distortion already magnified in the press during the preceding decade and which now fed entrenched fears about the aims and methods of the movement.[93]

Hubberthorne had reiterated something before the king that Fox asserted in 1653. That is, the principal objective of government was 'the keeping of the peace', sustaining a level of ordered government in which civil society could then admit the free expression of the Light within everybody. Many were suffering for their conscience, Fox reminded the authorities, and the law was in transgression of God's superior Law as a consequence: 'They that fear the Lord they have mutual peace among themselves, you need not make a law for them; for the law is upon them that are without fear of God'.[94] They that dwelt in the Light, he continued, followed the way of peace, which was necessary for a wholesale purgation of the Beast and a national turning to the Light, a principle from which all else, including outward peace, would flow. Later, with the monarchy restored, keeping the peace translated itself into 'honouring the king' with the parallel idea that no harm should be levelled at anybody's person. In this belief was found the true liberty of the nation.[95] The purpose of government,

---

[93] O'Malley, 'The Press and Quakerism', 176; *BQ*, 478.

[94] Fox, 'A Warning to the Rulers of England' in Nayler, *A Lamentation*, 11.

[95] Fox, *A Word in the behalf of the King* (1660), 3; Henry Fell (*c*.1630-*c*.1674), 'O King!' in Fox *et al, For the King and his Council, These* (1660), 5-6. For "honouring the King': 1 Sam.10: 25. Prevailing at the time was the ancient idea of a 'contract' between the people and monarch. In theory at least, in return for their allegiance, the people expected the monarch's protection from enemies, probably one reason why the top echelons of the republic's government never succeeded in ridding 'monarchy' from people's minds. By the seventeenth century the 'enemy' to the moneyed classes was anyone who threatened life or

Chapter 11: 'Because of your much Earth'

Fox later maintained, was to bring people to God and to protect the innocent (those in the Light) against evildoers[96], among whom he and the Friends always included priests and lawyers.[97]

In their conscientious objection to tithe payment, too, the Friends turned for help to that other arm of republican government, the military. Like Abiezer Coppe and the anonymous and probably non-Quaker author of the *Good Old Cause Explained* (1659), they urged the soldiery to 'turn to [their] first integrity', to the Light within of which the Good Old Cause was one expression. God, after all, helped the army gain victory over the old régime. Had not the army been the hope of the nations, the defender of the Cause and its keystones of the new republican order—liberty of conscience, freedom of religious observance, and the guarantor of religious and civil rights?

In many parts of the country the parliamentary standing army, as yet a novelty for Britain, was the only effective instrument of government as in the Palestine of Jesus when the Roman army, too, was involved in civil administration.[98] The army was to be deployed fairly at all times, the Friends implored, especially with those who had given it their active support. Burrough in January 1660, despairing as he saw the country turning against the Commonwealth, asked the army plaintively: 'Is there no hope of your return to the Good Old Cause?'[99] His deceptively simple question contained a sting in its tail; the Reformation still awaited implementation, and there was always the nagging matter of a troubled conscience. Six years earlier an indignant Fox, complaining to Cromwell

---

property, even the government with its taxes, rules and regulations, restrictions and orders—in short, intruders into the private realm of people's lives. See also Lee, 'Cromwell, the king who never was', 27.

[96] Fox, *Quaker Testimony Concerning Magistracy* in *Leek MS.* (n.d.), 19; Nayler, 'Concerning Government and Magistracy' in *Love to the Lost*, 24-7; Penington, *Some Few Queries and Considerations Proposed to the Cavaliers* (*DCFB/Wing* 1660) and in *Works*, i. 288.

[97] Hubberthorne, *The Real Cause* and in *Works*, 219-22. Also *The Mittimus Answered by which Rich. Hubberthorne was sent Prisoner to Norwich Castle* (1654) in *Works*, 37. Though wary of Quaker theology, John Milton shared the Friends' distrust of hirelings. See his 1659 letter to parliament entitled *Considerations touching the likeliest means to remove hirelings out of the Church* and his championing of liberty of conscience in *A Treatise of Civil Power in Ecclesiastical Causes* in M. Hughes (ed.), 854, 840. Fox sometimes coupled lawyers and 'pharisees' (i.e. untrustworthy, tricky and exploitative people); see Mt. 12:14; Mk. 3: 6; Lk. 6:7.

[98] Stambaugh and Balsh, *The Social World of the First Christians*, 34-5, 77-8. For an informative account of Roman army administration see A. Jones, 'The Roman Civil Service', *passim* and esp. 44-7. Also M. Hirst, *Quakers in Peace and War*, 58-9.

[99] Burrough, *To the Whole English Army*, Bds.

The Early Quakers and the 'Kingdom of God'

that Quakers had been unjustly removed from the military, asked what hope there was now that the army had turned apostate.[100]

Yet Quakers were still being turned out of the military in 1659. As Reay tells us, General Monck (whom Fox despised) removed about 40 Quakers from his own army, a tiny percentage given the 40-60,000 people in 1659 accorded the title 'Quaker' by modern historians. Such action was conducted periodically. Cromwell, for instance, had ordered the removal of argumentative and insubordinate elements including Quakers in 1657, a move supported by officers such as one Major Richardson. Writing to Monck, Richardson expressed his 'fear [that] these people's principles will not allow them to fight'.[101] Monck in Scotland and Henry Cromwell in Ireland were only too eager to follow the Protector's directive with Henry complaining to Thurloe as early as 1655 that the Quakers' principles and practices,

> are not very consistent with civil government, much less with the discipline of an army. Some think them to have no design, but I am not of that opinion. Their counterfeited simplicity renders them to me the more dangerous.[102]

To Henry, the Quakers were 'our most considerable enemy', the targets of his wrath in this case being probably Howgill and Burrough, and perhaps Barbara Blaugdone later, who were touring Ireland.[103] The Quakers, however, had allies such as trooper William Morris who was prepared to defend them as peaceful supporters of the Good Old Cause to which he believed Henry Cromwell adhered.[104]

Despite such protestations, disillusionment with the military and civil authorities had long consolidated itself among the Radicals even before the Friends appeared in sizeable numbers between 1652 and 1654. Coward tells us by that date the disillusionment was 'complete', particularly in lieu of the Rump's dilatory record on constitutional reform and thus its failure to usher in the much hoped-for 'godly reformation'.[105] As the decade progressed,

---

[100] *Journal*, 176-7; Howgill, *An Information and also Advice* and in *Works*, 325.

[101] George Monck (1608-70). See the letter from Richardson to Monck (from Aberdeen, 26/March/1657) in *Thurloe*, vi., 145. See *Journal*, 319-23; Reay, 'Quakerism and Society' in McGregor and Reay, *Radical Religion*, 154.

[102] Henry Cromwell (1628-74). See Reay, *ibid*. Also Hutton, *The British Republic*, 95-8; Sansbury, *The Restoration and the Quaker Peace Testimony*, 8. And *Thurloe*, iv. 508 for Evans' letter (6/April/1655).

[103] H. Cromwell quoted in Horle, *The Quakers and the English Legal System*, 15.

[104] And army officers, too, whom he was prepared to browbeat if they showed an interest in the wayward Quakers. See William Morris, *To the Supreme Authority* (1659), 11. And Hutton, *The British Republic*, 100.

[105] Coward, *The Stuart Age*, 245-7.

Chapter 11: 'Because of your much Earth'

Quaker belief in the untrustworthiness of governments and parliaments, already profound, only deepened. Their distrust intensified during the period 1658-9.[106] They came to see the 'Transgressor' (Satan) in both Cromwell and later in his son, Richard. Writing to Oliver in 1657/8, on the day after the two men met, Burrough asked, 'Is it not your own unfaithfulness to the principle of God in you, which bears witness against the persecution of the innocent?'[107] Other Friends like Mary Howgil could not restrain themselves. Oliver, she wrote, was a 'stinking dunghill in the sight of God', an oppressor for disturbing Meetings and imprisoning Friends. By denying the Lord, Cromwell was the essence of the carnal. Though Howgil was admonished by Friends, there being 'little service for the Lord in her ministry but rather hurt', her frustration and anger were shared by many Quakers and non-Quakers.[108]

Of course, the Friends' reaction was too rigid a judgment. They had taken Cromwell at his word without understanding the changing and difficult contexts of 1650s politics, certainly not from an administrative angle. Nor did they recognise the Protector's positive achievements— government committees that were less corrupt than formerly, a greater emphasis on taxing the rich, improvements in the provision of schooling, his valiant attempts at reconciling the many competing claims of religious groups like theirs, and a measure of tolerance which helped movements such as their own to take root. The Friends' attitude to day-to-day politics was often more visceral than practical.[109]

However, many a supporter of the Good Old Cause, besides the Quakers, felt betrayed by their former battlefield companions. Not without reason, they inveighed against army corruption.[110] But anger was not confined to those who had fought. Isaac Penington, his quill aiming trenchant criticism at anybody opposed to religious and civil liberty, demanded a straight answer of the army leadership: why had so much blood

---

[106] John Colleens (Collins?), *A Word in Season to all in Authority* (1660), 6.

[107] Burrough, 'For the hands of Oliver Cromwell called Protector' (1659) and in *Works*, 556; see Hubberthorne, *A Word of Wisdom and Counsel to the Officers*, Bds. for reference to Cromwell's Dunbar promise. Reference has already been made to Nayler at Dunbar under Lambert.

[108] Mary Howgil, *A Remarkable Letter to ... Oliver Cromwell*, 1; sister or cousin of Frances Howgill? See Gill, 'Ministering Confusion', 25.

[109] Of course many reactions to Cromwell's Protectoral power by various parliamentarians and Commonwealthsmen (i.e. those attaining prominent positions in the Rump like Sir Henry Vane Jr., Sir Arthur Haselrige) were anything but visceral. See Morrill, 'Cromwell: Hero or Villain?', 34.

[110] Penington, *To the Army* in *Works*, i. 143: '. . . fear the Lord in your reasonings, and beg earnestly of him to keep the simplicity alive in you, that the fleshly wisdom get not mastery over it.'; Nayler, 'Concerning Government and Magistracy' in *Love to the Lost*, 24-7; Crook, *An Epistle of Love . . . in Present Sufferings* (1660), 17.

been spilt if such liberty had no value?[111] Liberty, whether of conscience or of another kind, could only be guaranteed by following the Law of Christ Jesus rather than recourse to physical violence.[112] Fox, too, remained steadfastly unimpressed with the political power brokers whom he and other Friends lobbied throughout the decade. While some 'returned to the Lord', others had clearly 'rejected the counsel of God' to their spiritual detriment.[113] Consequently, the authorities were urged to look beyond parliament.[114] In this way, cried Burrough, they would understand the folly of living out of the Light and see that which 'convinces [them] of sin' and 'reproves [them] in secret of violence'.[115]

Leading Quakers urged parliaments to pass only God's noble acts while members were to be good examples to the people. Penington, Howgill and Burrough were certain that failure to deliver on promises contravened the Kingdom and its Law of God. They were drawing attention to the way power within the army and parliament had concentrated itself among a few notables; a clique could never be trusted to protect the freedoms of the British peoples.[116] Once Kingdom principles were forgotten, moral and spiritual legitimacy were lost. For this reason, argued George Fox the Younger, as many people as possible should have a say in the way they were ruled. The interests of the disenfranchised poor, he continued, were ill-represented by those who made decisions on their behalf; indeed, they often acted *against* those interests. Prospective parliamentarians should be chosen for their adherence to equity and justice and, once elected, ought to seek the good in and for everyone by 'respecting no person'.[117] Such a practice would ensure 'the mind of Christ would be in them'.[118]

Universal suffrage, therefore, was essential. Tract after tract, Quaker and non-Quaker, repeated the fundamental assertion that parliaments had ceased to hear the cry of the poor[119]—more the pity, the Friends maintained, for the Good Old Cause was fought with the poor in mind. However, the Friends assured their rulers that there *was* time for restitution before evil completely engulfed the nation. It would be the wise who 'prize it' and

---

[111] Penington, *To the Parliament, the Army, and all the Well-affected* in *Works*, i., 136.
[112] See Burrough, *To the Parliament of the Common-wealth of England* (1659), 3-5.
[113] Fox, *To the King of Spain* and *Doctrinals*, 195.
[114] Penington, *ibid.*,137.
[115] Burrough (and Howgill), 'An Invitation to all the Poor Desolate Soldiers' in *The Visitation of the Rebellious Nation of Ireland* (1655), 8.
[116] Rigge, *O Ye Heads of the Nation* (1659), 3; Fox (the Younger), 'To the Army' (1659) in *Works*, 85.
[117] Fox (the Younger), *A Few Plain Words to be considered by those of the Army* (1659), 6.
[118] Fox, *To the Emperor . . . Austria*, 12. Also Dewsbury, *The Discovery of the Great Enmity*, 4.
[119] Fox, *To the Protector and the Parliament of England* (1658), 12; *To the Council of Officers of the Army*, 5; Penington, *ibid.*, 136; Burrough, *ibid.*, 2-4.

prepared for the Lord's inward coming.[120] Besides its priestly and prophetic overtones, 'prize' had eschatological meaning: here in the *now* was a time to redeem the soul and turn to the Eternal.[121] By ridding the land of oppression, the consciences of the authorities would be eased, a great prize indeed.

Clearly then, in warning 'heathens' of the dangers of the (inner) End-time, the Friends took advantage of outward political events to enhance a sense of urgency. By doing so they targeted all levels of society. Charles himself did not escape their scrutiny, becoming the focus of Quaker attention early in his reign. He was warned not to meddle in religious affairs since many a leader had fallen on *that* sword. The king was advised to honour his Declaration of Breda concerning liberty of conscience; 'he that hath the Word of the Kingdom is to minister it freely', Hubberthorne had previously suggested in a letter to the parliament in 1659.[122] As with the Commonwealth and Protectorate before him, Charles was implored not to impose heavy burdens on the poor. He was also warned against sumptuousness, reminded that just government was God-heeding government and that the fulfilment of the Law of God could only be found in 'true religion'.[123] Compassion should be a foundational instrument of governance and it would protect the king against spiritual folly; the just sword was the power of God.[124]

Repeating the second commandment of the Kingdom, they assured Charles that the inward Spirit would guide him to love his neighbour as he loved himself. That is, he should be attentive to justice for all. He was further reminded that God, formerly the army's commander-in-chief, was the true king and judge[125] and that to act for God, to put the true Kingdom into practice, would bring him a greater liberty.[126] For the early Friends the need for compassion and truth in public life was allied to the religious and political toleration they demanded for themselves. However, they

---

[120] Dewsbury, *To All Nations, Kindreds, Languages* (1660) and in *Works*, 181. See Burrough's spiritual-political warning to the Committee of Safety, *A Message to the Present Rulers of England* (1659), 12: God's cause is always greater than humanity's.

[121] See Nayler, *A Discovery of the First Wisdom*, 16. For the 'restitution of all things' see Ac. 3:21.

[122] Hubberthorne, *A Word of Wisdom and Counsel to the Officers* (1659), Bds.

[123] Nayler, 'Concerning Government and Magistracy' in *Love to the Lost*, 24-7; Burrough, *A Standard Lifted Up*, 10-11 and *To the Rulers*, 2-3.

[124] Fox, *To the Council of Officers of the Army*, 2-5, 8; *This is to all Officers and Soldiers of the Armies* (1657), 1.

[125] Burrough (and Howgill), 'An Invitation', 37; Burrough, *To the Parliament of the Common-wealth*, 1-7; Fox, *To the Council of Officers of the Army*, 2-3.

[126] See Caton, *An Epistle to King Charles II* (1660), 12, 14. And Mt. 22: 36-40 which portrays the Kingdom in essence and *cf.* Lev. 19:18; Dt. 6:5; Rom. 13: 8-10; Gal. 5: 14; Jm. 2:8; 1 Jn. 2:7.

encouraged the king to usher in a new age of religious freedom for all. The 'Jew', 'Turk', 'papist', 'heathen' (in this case the non-Christian) and other Protestants should be free to worship, maintain their own ministry and assist the poor. Only if the faith of the saints were sound would there be no need to fear strangers for they would be overcome with love rather than carnal weaponry, persecution and imprisonment.[127] In their fellowship—the rule of the saints—all people would be counted in esteem before God. Heretics and schismatics, too, would be free of restrictions since liberty of conscience was an ordinance of God to be maintained only by the Light of Christ.[128]

Addressing matters of conscience rested upon the continued strength of Quaker spiritual solidarity under persecution, and the unifying charisma of Fox and other strong personalities among the movement's leadership. Help in this matter also came from the practice of shared spiritual autobiographies, tight editorial authority over manuscripts from about 1653 onwards (many of which were collaboratively written and published) and the strategic distribution of tracts and broadsides by Fox, Farnworth, Fell, Nayler, Burrough, Aldam and others. Important additional influences included the development of their network of local and regional Meetings, the uniformity of their worship and theological coherence.[129] Together, these factors helped formulate 'a collaborative corporate conscience' which, in turn, helped the Quakers resist the State when necessary and claim an authority based on the Spirit and Jesus in seeking an alternative political and social order founded on the Kingdom.[130]

Conclusion

Friends laboured in the Light to be faithful to progressive and liberating principles, and were willing to face dire consequences as a result. 'Equity', 'truth' and 'justice' frequently appeared as a troika within Quaker tracts but the principle that all were equal under God, including its outward expression such as refusal of hat honour, precipitated angry and sometimes dangerous reactions from opponents. In the face of intensifying harassment from the various authorities, the Friends maintained that truth, itself underpinning equity and justice, was 'the enabler of faith'. It led to a

---

[127] Fox, 'To Charles late proclaimed King' in Fox *et al*, *The Copies of Several Letters* (1660), 4, 7, 9. While they should be free to worship, papists nonetheless remained the object of Fox's ire – 'filthy dreamers': see *Works*, 1: 473-5, 553.

[128] Burrough, *For the Soldiers, and All the Officers of England, Scotland and Ireland* (1654).

[129] N. Smith maintains the Friends were a disparate body instead. See his 'Exporting Enthusiasm' in Healy and Sawday, *Literature and the English Civil War*, 249. For an example of the Friends' editorial practice see Thomas Holme, letter (6/Aug/1655) to Fox, *SW*/iv/244 in which phrases are erased or altered by Fox for possible blasphemy.

[130] Orlie, *Living Ethically*, 71.

simplicity involving plain speaking and sobriety underscored by humility and patience. They warned that the delusion of inner falsehood, inequality and injustice would lead to negative, 'carnal' manifestations.

For the Friends, extreme wealth, inequalities and injustices were hateful realities. The scandal of widespread poverty was indication enough that the poor, those who were the special children of the Kingdom, equally deserved care and truth from the authorities. From time to time the Quakers' criticisms of authority and the 'high and lofty ones' propelled them onto the political plane. Their opposition to tithes implicitly questioned the unequal distribution of land that was proceeding apace in the mid century. Though charges of corruption were tempered with the acknowledgment of Caesar's lawful position, the powerful still attacked the movement. The Friends claimed that their nonviolent reaction and mutual support were testimonies to the holiness of life as well as a warning and a mirror to the authorities of their shameful ways. Their nonviolence was also bound up with forgiveness, loyalty and obedience to the Word, an understanding that would later express itself in their three declarations of 1659-61. It was an understanding that was *not* (as Hill and others have averred) an outcome of the declarations or something suddenly realised when the political tide turned against the republic in the final years of the decade. Clearly, the nonviolent Quakers believed in a functional sovereignty of God over human affairs.[131]

This chapter also addressed issues of conscience, *viz*: keeping the peace, the role of the magistrate, the purpose and conduct of government as well as issues centring on the Good Old Cause, liberty of conscience and worship, and the treatment of Friends in prisons and the military. The highlighting of such matters rested upon the continued strength of Quaker spiritual and corporate solidarity and was important in focussing the movement's attention on the Lamb's War and the realities of its own oppression.

---

[131] Schmidt, *Quaker Political Pamphlets*, 263.

Chapter 12: 'Dwell in that which Leads into Peace'

- The Sword and Quaker 'Violence' -

The Friends understood oppression and violence as the work of the Antichrist, and that their cessation would help bring the peace of the Spirit and the Kingdom to the British nations and their governors.[1] By the late 1650s however, with many considering the Good Old Cause long betrayed, it was clear to the Quakers and others that the parliamentary and military perpetrators of outrages, whether physical or administrative, were as 'rotten' as their royalist predecessors.[2] The Lord 'is come', they proclaimed, and would plead the cause of the innocent. Despite this, they continued to urge the authorities to fear God, to do good to all and violence to none for the 'terrible day of the Lord' was already present—that is, the Kingdom was *now* and should be lived as such. Salvation would be withheld from England, its governments and individuals if people failed to turn to the commonwealth of the saints, the Jesus Way. Deliverance could never be achieved by turning to sin and the carnal sword.[3] All arbitrary government was contrary to good conscience and self-defeating, therefore, particularly in matters of religion. Coercion could indeed enforce higher church attendance but would never ensure true knowledge of the Kingdom.

Drawing attention in 1658 to 'above twenty hundred' persecuted and imprisoned,[4] Fox complained bitterly about the disturbance of 'thousands of families' and the way in which the courts were used to harass the movement.[5] Prisons, fines and 'spoilings' of goods, he declared, brought needless hardship to the 'innocent'. His concern reached beyond borders. In 1660 he wrote open letters to various foreign kings, emperors and to Pope

---

[1] Fox, *To the Council of Officers of the Army*, 2; for the importance of peace for the Kingdom (as the Power of God) see Fox, Ep. 9 (1652), in *Collection*, 11.
[2] Fell, *To the General Council of Officers of the English Army*, 3; Thomas Zachary (d.1686), *A Word to the Officers of the Army* (1657), 7; Wollrich, *A Plain and Good Advice to the Parliament-Men, and Officers of the Army* (*DCFB* 1658/*Wing* 1659), Bds.; Bishop, *Mene Tekel*, 1.
[3] Burrough, *For the Soldiers*; Burrough (and Howgill), 'An Invitation' 35-7; Daniel Gotherson, *An Alarm to All Priests*, 75; Anon, *Spiritual Discoveries to the Overgrow of Popery, Root and Branch* (1657/8), 17-19.
[4] Fox, *To the Protector and the Parliament of England*, 13 in which he warns Cromwell that prisons can lead people into evil ways. Fox's and other Friends' experiences of gaol galvanised their advocacy of prison reform. Up to 20 to 30 people could be herded together, usually in fetid, confined spaces. See also Fox, *To the Council of Officers of the Army*, 3, 5; Howgill, *The Measuring Rod of the Lord* (1658), 13.
[5] See, for instance, Fox, *To Those that have been Formerly* (1660), 5.

Chapter 12: 'Dwell in that which Leads into Peace'

Alexander VII advancing Quaker beliefs while demanding the release of prisoners and an end to persecution.[6]

As with Harrington for whom 'sword' meant legal jurisdiction, the Quakers insisted that the magistracy should exercise lawful force only when absolutely necessary, that it should be tempered at all times with fairness and restraint.[7] Accordingly, Richard Hubberthorne in *The Good Old Cause Briefly Demonstrated*, published in May 1659, advocated the use of the 'civil and military sword' for 'justice sake' and opposed the propagation of religion by means of the 'material sword'. For Hubberthorne, the 'Cause' was of 'true religion' and the Kingdom but only when it became 'the work of God' which led 'from . . . acts of violence'.[8] The 'civil and military sword', being compliant with a judicious and righteous use of force, acknowledged the need of the State to physically restrain those intent on violence or other forms of 'evil-doing' in the interest of 'keeping the peace'. The injunction, possibly Pauline, on page five of the Fox-Hubberthorne declaration to 'neither turn your swords backward, upon such as the law was not made for (i.e. the righteous) but for the sinners and transgressors, to keep them down', reflected his and Fox's position.[9]

However, like Penington in *Somewhat Spoken to a Weighty Question* (1661), the declaration emphasised the power of good in eventually overcoming evil.[10] Evil was neither to be denied nor confronted by negatively applied force but rather by an honest determination never to surrender the prominence that goodness of its nature deserved. Any action against evil-doers, then, would be legitimate if judged by the purest of motives and expressed within the compass of true magistracy which originated from the loving God. In this way the peace of Jesus would come:

---

[6] Fox, 'To the King of France' (1660), 28 in *For the Emperor of China* and *Doctrinals*, 189; Fox, *To the Emperor . . . Austria* and *Doctrinals*, 181; *To the Pope*, 61-9 and *To the King of Spain* in *For the Emperor of China*. See also Evans and Cheevers, *A Brief History of the Voyage*.

[7] Fox, 'A Paper of George Fox's to Oliver Protector' (1655) in *Journal*, 220-1. See Cole, *The Quakers and Politics*, 63. This was the year in which the government newspaper, *The Public Intelligencer* (27th and 28th February 1655), described Fox as 'the great Quaker' and the Quakers in general as 'the perfect objects of humility and repentance, their aspect as demure as their habit'. See also *BQ*, 560. For Harrington's sword see *Oceana*, 7 and *Works*, 41.

[8] Hubberthorne, *The Good Old Cause*, Sig. A$^{1-2}$.

[9] Fox-Hubberthorne et al, *A Declaration from the Harmless*, 5. Emphasis is theirs. 'Neither turn your swords [judgment] backward' etc. probably derived from their understanding of Isa. 59:14 and influenced by Lm. 1:8, but also see Rom. 13:1-4 where all authority which is lawful and for the common good derives from God (cf. Mt. 22:19-22; Mk. 12:17; Jn. 19:11 and 1 Cor. 12:7). For Fox-Hubberthorne see Appendix 2.

[10] Penington, *Somewhat Spoken to a Weighty Question* (1661), *passim* and esp. 8 and in *Works* (1681), 323. See also *QFP*, §24.21. This work contains the well-known statement, 'I speak not against any magistrates or peoples defending themselves . . . but yet there is a better state . . . which . . . must begin in particulars'.

'in sincerity and truth', the declaration asserted, 'and by the Word of God, have we laboured [for our beliefs] to be made manifest... that both we and our ways might be witnessed in the hearts of all people'.[11]

For Fox, Burrough, Penington and William Smith, the Cause pointed ultimately to a 'better state' of nonviolence, to the Kingdom in which there *would* be no violence. It was confirmation that the political State had not yet 'come into the gospel life'. The leading Friends believed, as Penington would acknowledge in 1661, that those whom God had drawn out of the Fall should not be required to fight, that they should be regarded instead as 'chosen to be an example of meekness and peaceableness in the places where they live'.[12] Thinking perhaps of 1 Corinthians 3:1-4 where Paul addresses those who, like the various British authorities, had failed to die to the old Israel, the Quakers considered their detractors (including the authorities) as occupying equally undesirable space, unable to learn the folly of destructive forms of violence including warfare and its preparation. Such people were ignorant of the better state—the Kingdom in which the newly resurrected inward Jew had no need of violence. Like Paul, the Quakers would show by example, by stepping outside the circle of violence as witnesses to the truth of the Spirit/Christ.

Early twentieth century Quaker writer, Margaret Hirst, correctly interpreted the magistrate's sword—that is, Hubberthorne's 'civil and military sword'—as a metaphor for civil authority, the right implementation of justice. More precisely, her view conformed to the application of 'sword' from the late Middle English period as symbolising penal justice, the authority of a ruler and/or a magistrate in the person of the monarch or the State, and, generally, 'authority', 'jurisdiction' and the 'powers of government'.[13] The same depiction features on the cover of Hobbes' *Leviathan*, where the mythical king holds aloft the sword of civil administration in the same manner as Lady Justice over the Old Bailey law courts in London today. A broadside to the parliament in 1659, probably non-Quaker, was also clear on the matter:

> You are the rightful and natural head of our country, from whence all subordinate powers and administrations civil are derivative, without which a legal new parliament cannot be called: law and common right denies that to the sword; it is inherent only in you.[14]

---

[11] Fox-Hubberthorne *et al*, *A Declaration from the Harmless*, 5-6.
[12] Fox, Ep. 177 (1659) in *LOGF*, 66. Also Burrough, *A Visitation and Warning Proclaimed*, 5-9. See, too, W. Smith, *A Right Dividing, or a True Discerning* (1659), 3; Penington, *Somewhat Spoken*, 8 and Ambler, *The End of Words*, 38.
[13] M. Hirst, *The Quakers in Peace and War*, 58. Middle English period = c.1066-1470.
[14] Anon, *A Declaration of the Well-affected to the Good Old Cause* (1659), Bds.

Chapter 12: 'Dwell in that which Leads into Peace'

Fox's *This is to all Officers and Soldiers* (1657) also uses 'sword' to mean 'justice' and 'the Lord God':

> you are to be ruled with the sword of the Lord God ... and he that does evil, acts contrary to the just, so the sword of justice takes hold upon him.

Here Fox underlines the importance of legal authority where it conforms to the Law of God (the Kingdom). In *To the Council of Officers of the Army* (1658/9), for example, the author demands (the parentheses being his own):

> O when will your persecutions and oppressing cease in these Nations! Until then, you shall not have peace from the Lord, until the persecutors and oppressors sword be put up ... the just sword, (the power of God) which does secretly work to do service ... to destroy all hypocrites.[15]

Clearly, 'sword' here is not a physical weapon. Rather, it is a metaphor, most likely from Revelation 19:18, depicting the Light, the power or Word of God, an outpouring of divine wrath. This wrath was regarded not so much punitively but as encompassing God's merciful purpose in anticipating redemption for the wrong-doer before s/he was engulfed by the dark world.[16] As Hirst maintained, the Quakers' use of 'sword' 'should be interpreted primarily in relation to judgment and condemnation ... particularly by God', or as 'the *law in general* and its officers and other representatives', and in a way that speaks of redemption, justice, mercy/compassion.[17] This view radically contradicted that of mid seventeenth century political theorists, the authorities and dissidents like the Fifth Monarchists all for whom 'sword' represented harsh law enforcement.

Burrough's 1655 message, *An Invitation to all the Poor Desolate Soldiers in Ireland*, provides another example of the early Quakers' familiar message that 'violence [should be done] to no man':

> if you stand in the fear of the Lord, your sword will be a terror and dread to them that fear him not, but live contrary to the Light in their own consciences, which Light if you love, it is your command to march by and your rule to judge by, and weapon to fight withal.[18]

---

[15] *This is to all Officers*, 1; *To the Council of Officers of the Army*, 2. And M. Hirst, *The Quakers in Peace and War*, 58-9.
[16] See Rev. 1:16, 2:2, 19:12.
[17] Hirst, *ibid.*, chp.14 and esp. 113; my emphasis. See Childress, 'Answering That of God in Every Man', 25-7 and Fox, *This is to all Officers*, 1.
[18] Burrough, 'An Invitation' in Burrough and Howgill, *The Visitation of the Rebellious Nation*, 35-7. For a discussion of ambiguity in early Quaker writings see Oliver, *Quaker*

The individual soldier was warned that the Transgressor would tempt him to do more than indulge in what we now call restraint or police action, which the Quakers thought legitimate, but that the Light would warn him against excessive, that is, destructive use of the sword (and, if not his weapon, then his authority). Burrough, Howgill and the Friends never defined what was excessive; they hoped the individual conscience would be guided by 'that of God within' and the expectations of the Kingdom. Indeed, they were setting an absolute standard by which they hoped all would walk.

What Kind of Army?

In the absence of a properly coordinated law enforcement body, people in the mid century, including the Quakers, looked to the army. But what kind of army was it? It would be anachronistic to equate it with its present day counterparts. Gerrard Winstanley has done us great service by clearly outlining the difference between a 'ruling army' and a 'fighting army'. His *The Law of Freedom* (1652) legitimates what was already, in effect, a police function and one that had public consent. A 'ruling army', he wrote,

> is called magistracy in times of peace, keeping that land and government in peace by execution of the laws ... and all people arising to protect and assist their officers, in defence of a right ordered government, are but the body of an army.[19]

The 'ruling army' differed from a 'fighting army'

> called soldiers in the field, when the necessity of preservation by reason of a foreign invasion or inbred oppression, do move the people to arise in an army to cut and tear to pieces, either degenerate officers or rude people who seek their own interest, and not common freedom, and through treachery do endeavour to destroy the laws of the common freedom, and to enslave both the land and people of the commonwealth to their particular wills and lusts.[20]

During and after the civil wars, including the 1650s, the army had acquired a visible and permanent presence in society. Coleby's important work shows conclusively that its involvement in civil administration grew to the point where army commanders, with the agreement of Westminster,

---

Testimony, 26, 29, 40. Also Punshon, *Portrait in Grey*, 50 and Nuttall, 'The Letters of James Nayler' in Birkel and Newman (eds.), 43.
[19] Winstanley, *The Law of Freedom*, 64.
[20] *Ibid.*, 64-5.

Chapter 12: 'Dwell in that which Leads into Peace'

regularly assumed roles in local and county government as an arm of British government *per se*. While individual commanders could be oppressive, fixed garrisons were generally popular with the public especially when the soldiery performed governmental duties, including policing, in a responsible and peaceful manner as a 'ruling army'. Some historians have suggested a state of crisis in military-civilian relations but Coleby found important examples where the opposite was true, where co-operation and good-will were the norm. In Portsmouth between 1653 and 1660, for instance, only one case is recorded of a civilian abusing soldiers.[21] The Portsmouth example appears typical, it being replicated in all regions where the military were in control or enjoyed an important presence.

This may help explain why people, including the Quakers, where willing to co-operate with the ubiquitous military. It can be no surprise that in dangerous situations, such as the country repeatedly found itself during the 1650s, the hope of a socially cooperative and responsible army would have been a source of security.[22] Of course, the primary task of any military is to wage war and, if the above analysis of tracts is accepted, then the Friends drew a line beyond which there would be no accommodation with deliberate injury to people or with any preparation for such. That is to say, irrespective of the Quakers' attitudes to the 'sword', like the Baptists they could never countenance war, the wilful advantage by force of one party at the murderous expense of others.[23] Here was a nonviolent stance to which the Friends held consistently during the 1650s as a welter of written evidence suggests, a selection of which we shall consider shortly (see also Appendix 5). Further, it was a stance underpinned by a predominantly *religious* outlook, a Kingdom rather than secular-cum-political worldview as suggested principally by a Marxist school whose ideas we will also examine soon.

---

[21] Coleby, 'Military-Civilian Relations on the Solent', 952-7, 961.
[22] See Aldam's letter (19/Feb/1653) to Capt. Amor Stoddart in 'Extracts from the A. R. Barclay MSS.', 51-2. Also *TLITC*, 62. For army local government activity and policing see Coleby, *ibid.*, 952-7. And Weddle, *Walking in the Way of Peace*, 251.
[23] See Appendix 5 for an indication of the substantial number of references in Quaker tracts during the 1650s denouncing war and carnal weaponry. See also *LOGF* for Fox's Eps. 9 (1652), 3 (he quotes Mt. 26:51-53 as in Fox-Hubberthorne); 24 (1653) and 11; 55 (1653), 25-6; 123 (1656), 51; 139 (1657), 56; 131 (1658), 53-4; 158 (1658), 62 (he quotes Sermon on the Mount); 171 (1659), 65-6; 177 (1659), 66. For among the many biblical references used in their tracts in this matter see for instance: Ps. 46:9; Qo. 9:18; Ws. 6:1-4; Isa. 3:25, 65:25; Jl. 4:20-21; Zc. 9: 9-10; Mt. 21:5; Lk. 12:51-53; Jn. 18:36; Rom. 6:12-24; 2 Cor. 10:3-6; Eph. 6:11-17; Heb. 4:12; Jm. 4:1-3. The Baptists' public anti-war position derived from their Confessions of Faith of 1612 (Article 35) and 1614 (Article 85).

Violent Quakers?

While maintaining the movement's nonviolence, I wish at this point to address two important works which a number of historians, including a Marxist school, interpret as examples of early Quaker non-pacifism, indeed as revealing a marked propensity for violence since they appear to advocate war against Spain, Rome and the Ottoman Empire. The first, *To the Council of Officers of the Army*, is attributed to Fox but there is some doubt over his authorship. Hirst supposes George Fox the Younger, Burrough and perhaps other Friends, and she may be right. The work is very close in style to another letter, 'Oh! Oliver' (January, 1658) which we examine below. *To the Council* is undated but was most probably written in the second half of 1658 or early 1659.[24] The second by Burrough, 'To the English Army', was addressed to the garrison at Dunkirk and is found in *A Visitation and Warning Proclaimed* (May, 1659) co-authored with Samuel Fisher.[25]

These works challenge my understanding of Quaker language as expressed in Chapter 4 that their military, apocalyptic, theophanous and anagogical discourse went hand in hand with the use of metaphor, allegory, symbolism and rhetoric. These, including their 'plaining', confrontational language and Christ/Logos mysticism were conduits, I argued, for the deliberate creation among their many audiences of a critical awareness of the revolutionary Kingdom, the truest guide to the holy life of justice, peace and compassion in the Light. Can the two works be interpreted in the same way or must they be treated as a special case, that is to say, taken at face value? If so, how would such a reading reflect back on my argument about the nature of Quaker language?

What do the works say? In *To the Council*, 'Fox' vents his frustration at the government and army over their lack of righteousness, their moral weakness. Both are thoroughly lambasted for persecuting the movement rather than attacking the real source of trouble—popery and other 'heathenish' behaviour:

> Had you been faithful to the power of ... God ... [and] gone into the midst of Spain ... to require the blood of the innocent that there had been shed and commanded them to have offered up their inquisition to

---

[24] According to M. Hirst, Fox's authorship cannot be disproved but she, too, believes *To the Council*'s linguistic style had more in common with that of ex-soldier Fox the Younger and that other parts of the work is very similar to Burrough's writing. It is possible, Hirst continues, that the work was erroneously bound into a volume of Fox's works during the eighteenth century and assumed thereafter to have been his. See her *The Quakers in Peace and War*, 118-22. Regarding its dating, *DCFB* has 1659; see also R. Moore's *Quaker Publications 1652/3-1659: Bibliography*.

[25] Burrough, *A Visitation and Warning Proclaimed*, 28-35.

Chapter 12: 'Dwell in that which Leads into Peace'

you . . . . and knocked at Rome's gates . . . and set up a standard . . . then you should have sent for the Turk's idol, the Mahomet, and plucked up idolatry.[26]

Burrough's letter also displays an apparent violent intent in urging the army likewise 'to set up [its] standard at the gates of Rome'. It brims with Hebrew Testament imagery in which God guarantees honour and victory to those who eradicate apostates and their 'idolatrous' teaching; 'avenge the blood of the guiltless through all the dominions of the pope,' cries Burrough, so that the army may 'bind their kings with chains, and their nobles with fetters of iron [Ps.149:8]'.[27]

The immediate political context in which the works were written was a traumatic one for the Friends. There was instability at home and threats from abroad. The Good Old Cause, so important to the movement, was in mortal danger from both, but also from other forms of 'popery' such as a return to monarchy and episcopacy. The future Charles II, seen by many including the Friends as a symbol of popery, was again plotting to capture the throne with help from Spain.[28] So did 'Fox' and Burrough at this moment of national crisis accept violence as a means of defending their country and defeating hostile domestic forces? If so, I contend it signified no more than a momentary 'wobble', a sudden panic, occasioned perhaps by the realisation that the synthesis between their understanding of the Kingdom, the Cause and 'true religion' was indeed in imminent danger of dissolution.

Now, to argue that it was more than this would leave unexplained the repeated calls to nonviolence that characterised their writings up to, and very soon after, this point. That is to say, if we do accept that the two works reflected a moment of fear or panic and a loss of focus, equally we must accept that it was short lived. Hirst, who believes Burrough could not 'be cleared from a confused attempt to make the best of both worlds, to use the weapons of war while praising the gospel of peace', is convinced that his later Restoration works, notably *A Visitation of Love to the King* (May,

---

[26] *To the Council of Officers of the Army*, 2-3. For a fuller exposition of these two works and Burrough's two broadsides below, see my *GADOT*, 26-7, 90-1.

[27] Burrough, *A Visitation and Warming Proclaimed*, 29, 35. Uncited references to probably include Ex. 15: 16; Dt. 2: 25, 20: 4, 21: 9; 32: 13; 1 S. 2: 30; 1 Maccabees 7: 18; Josh. 18: 12; Lm. 4: 13; Ezk. 38: 20; Isa. 25: 12, 49: 22; Jer. 4: 6, 50: 2. 51: 12, 27. Possible Christian Testament references: Jn. 13: 28; Heb. 13: 21; 2 Cor. 5: 12; Rom. 3: 16, 12: 19; 1 Jn. 3: 16. Braithwaite, betraying his bourgeois embarrassment with the early Friends, practically ignores Burrough's military language; see *BQ*, 358-9.

[28] See Burrough's letter (Oct. 1658) to Richard Cromwell in *Good Counsel and Advice Rejected*, 64, in which he refers to this Anglo-Dutch war against Spain hoping the army is being 'faithful to God in it'. However, the phraseology is ambivalent and cannot be taken as proof of violent intent on his behalf. The war ended with the English gaining Dunkirk.

1660) and *A Vindication of the People of God called Quakers* (Dec, 1660), are proof he came to realise that he had made a mistake.[29]

If all this is true, it is difficult to understand why the Marxist school in particular refuses to acknowledge the continuity between the Quakers' renewed emphasis on nonviolence and that of the 1650s decade as a whole. Perhaps they failed to understand what lay behind the synthesis—the Kingdom and its Lamb's War with both incorporating the Friends' understanding of the Good Old Cause not merely as a political program but an expression of the 'true religion' of the 'Church of Christ' as we saw in Hubberthorne's *The Good Old Cause Briefly Demonstrated*. Here was a failure that may have derived from an ignorance of the Quakers' religious aims and discourse especially in its apocalyptic, theophanous and anagogical forms, as these were directly related to their propagation of the Kingdom. The possibility that the tracts represented a sudden panic or momentary 'wobble', although psychologically credible, in no way weakens my argument that Quaker language before and after any such 'wobble' took the above forms. Therefore I will now argue that the language of 'Fox' and Burrough in the works under discussion is indeed to be understood in this way, that they are theological and continuous with their 1650s experience of Kingdom and Testimony.

First, then, I believe they are a call for 'all people' to set up their standards (of God) at the gates of sin, the Antichrist, which separates people from God. But to do this successfully they must 'deny themselves', yield to 'the pure principle of God [within]', so that they 'come out of that which can be shaken' and enter 'into that which cannot', that is, the 'everlasting Kingdom', the 'Truth', the same Kingdom that *'cannot be obtained by an outward sword'* [my emphasis]. Only then will the 'prison-doors' be 'set open' so they can be a 'dread of all the Nations'; in other words, to all that which is sinful within them and thus foreign to God. In this way they will know that 'peace [which] is a dread to all the contrary', that which is life-giving and not death-dealing. In opening themselves to the Light of Christ, by allowing it to invade them, they will obtain the Power of God, the strength to defeat all that which oppresses, imprisons, tortures, kills or drives them into poverty not only on the inner level but also on the outer. Thus they will be able authentically to 'plead the cause of the innocent'. This Power is a source of courage. It can 'break down rocks and hills' and march on 'idolatry' and 'heathenish' conduct, but only if they have faith, not fear. The works are an invitation in a fear-ridden environment for people to come to the Substance, into the security of Love, so they may be 'over' their destructive feelings as well as the evil of the world like 'a

---

[29] Hirst, *ibid.*, 120.

Chapter 12: 'Dwell in that which Leads into Peace'

winde', like a *ruach* of the Kingdom. Then will true freedom and 'true religion' reign.[30]

The language of the works is certainly not unique: it is found throughout Quaker works generally up to that point, something for which there is abundant evidence as we can see in Appendix 5. And our anagogical explanation, which is wholly commensurate with the Friends' approach to life, God and the Jesus Way, may help explain Hirst's belief that Burrough used 'the weapons of war while [ending his paper] praising the gospel of peace'. There was no 'mistake' as she maintained since Burrough's apocalyptic and theophanous message, *because* it was typical of Quaker language, could do no other than be expressed in the anagogical language of the 'gospel of peace' (as we see at the end of his paper).

Second, given all we have demonstrated so far in this book about the Quakers' relationship to the Jesus Way and the gospel of peace, any support for violence by a 'fighting army', to use Winstanley's term, would have meant abandoning what they consistently declared to be within, present in the *now* and everlasting, but also promulgated by Jesus, the Prince of peace.[31] Such support would have meant a shift of faith of such colossal proportions as to eviscerate the truth of their convincement and with it the very meaning and purpose of their very lives as prophets of the Light, as the second priesthood of the Jesus Way. It would have meant spiritual death no less and thus separation from their 'Beloved'. Such a consuming intimacy with the Kingdom suggests that for the Friends *not* to have followed the Jesus Way (which had been in their very 'flesh and bone', remember, since convincement) would have been *inconceivable*. Were they not prepared to *die* for the Kingdom at any time? Some had already done so while others had endured much privation and humiliation in its name; in *To the Council*, 'Fox' mentions 'above' 2,000 Friends.[32] Many more would experience the same in the years after the Restoration when 243 Friends would perish, including Burrough himself. This is hardly abandoning the Kingdom or a flight from Mammon but a conscious *living* of the Jesus Way into the new and hostile politico-constitutional dispensation with *exactly the same*

---

[30] For the three forms of language of which we speak see, for example, Fox, *To the Council of the Officers of the Army*, 1 (for apocalyptic language), 1-4 and esp. 7 (for theophanous language) and 1-2 (for anagogical language); Burrough, *A Visitation and Warning Proclaimed*, 28-9 (for apocalyptic), 32 (for theophanous) and 28, 32-4 (for anagogical). The following citations may have used for the two works: Dt. 2: 25, 20:4, 32:13; Jg. 1:1; 1 S. 2:30; Ps. 103: 16, 132: 2, 149:8; Pr. 31: 9; Isa. 40: 4; 59: 19; 62: 10; Jer. 4: 6; 50: 2, 51: 27; Dn. 6: 26; Lk. 3: 5; Ac. 23: 11; Heb. 12: 27; Rev. 19:7-8, 21:1-21; 1 Maccabees 3: 25; 7:18; 2 Esdras 15:9.

[31] See Nayler, *The Lambs War*, 3.

[32] Fox, *To the Council of Officers of the Army*, 3: 'Consider that above twenty hundred have been persecuted and imprisoned within these few years for conscience sake towards the Lord.'

politics of compassion that had characterised their Testimony so far as these were based on the Sermon on the Mount. Their willingness to submit totally to the Kingdom, and thus to enjoy an ever-deeper relationship with it, also evinced any lack of dependency on a purely political understanding of their times and specifics such as the Good Old Cause. In other words, the Marxist school and others appear to have little, if any, appreciation that the Friends were motivated by their convincement into the Kingdom and its nonviolent Lamb's War, *not* by external interests, events or pressure.

Therefore, I believe we are on safe ground in maintaining that Burrough and other Friends were busy in 1659 *upholding* and *enriching* their Kingdom praxis, and that it was not surprising he and yet others were keen to engage with political and social issues, in particular equity and justice, *where these informed their hopes for spreading the Kingdom* in England and throughout the world. Further, their dogged determination to follow the Jesus Way, despite the national crises of that turbulent year, as well as their fears and disillusionment with 'carnal' politics and its main players, affirmed a theological continuity with their 1650s experience of Kingdom and Testimony, *the* peace testimony. It was a continuity amply demonstrated in the overwhelming majority of their works during the period 1657-9, concerned as these were with spiritual/theological rather than, though not in opposition to, political matters. Fox's own works during 1659, for instance, concentrated on the Light of the Christ and the Kingdom just as they had done in 1657 and 1658 (see Appendix 6). It was this same determination that propelled the movement to carry their 1650s experience of Kingdom and Testimony into the next decade and beyond. It might even be argued that any 'wobble' could have been catalytic in this new-found determination for pursuing the Lamb's War. In any case, a way was now opened for the Pentecost-type 'moment' (Oct. 1658-Jan. 1661), their collective realisation of the unconditionality to time and space of the Kingdom. Interestingly, Burrough's remark to Independent Samuel Eaton that the 'Covenant of God' (Kingdom) stood 'not upon condition but on free love and mercy' was published on the 21st May (1659).[33] We can gain insights into this momentous development through the forms of language already mentioned and which have been misunderstood.

Let us now examine the language-use of the short (400-word), 'Oh! Oliver', published in Burrough's compilation of letters, *Good Counsel and Advice* (July, 1659); we will come to the Burrough broadsides shortly:

---

[33] Burrough, *Some False Principles*, 12; for unconditionality see also Fox, *To All that would Know*, 4.

Chapter 12: 'Dwell in that which Leads into Peace'

Oh! Oliver,
 Had you been faithful and thundered down the deceit, the Hollander had been your subject and tributers; and Germany had given up to have done your will; and the Spaniard had quivered like a dry leaf, wanting the virtue of God; the king of France should have bowed under you his neck; the Pope should have withered as in winter; the Turk in all his fatness should have smoked. You should not have a-stood trifling about small things but minded the work of the Lord as he began with you at first. Sober men and true hearts took part with you. Oh! take heed and do not slight such least [*sic.*] you weaken yourself, and not disown such as the Lord has owned. Your dread is not yet all gone, nor your amazement. Arise and come out, for had you been faithful you should have crumbled Nations to dust . . . Now is your day of trial. Take heed of joining hands with the wicked against the innocent, but hear the voice of God, and that will keep you from hardness of heart. And mind the Law of God with which you may answer that of God in everyone . . .[34]

First, note the similar wording to the 'Fox' quote cited above: 'Had you been faithful . . .' bears the stamp of Fox the Younger (particularly in how it ends) and perhaps Burrough. Still, whoever wrote it, the letter adopts the opening gambit of George Bishop's own to Cromwell dated 16th July, 1656 in which the once almighty Oliver, whose zeal could have conquered all before him, is bombarded with colourful metaphors, powerful insights and searing questions, which serve to highlight his weakened if desperate position. According to Bishop, it was a position born of his failure to protect the 'innocent' and to turn towards the Light, a failure to enact the true Kingdom (or in Fox's case the 'Law of God').[35] That the tenor of Bishop's letter is replicated by all the correspondence in Burrough's *Good Counsel and Advice* means 'Oh! Oliver' should be understood in the context which the Burrough collection represents, that is to say, an approach at once pastoral and encouraging, but also authoritative if somewhat patronising, while at the same time anxious and urgent. Fox's letter, again like Bishop's, pleads the real old cause of the Kingdom. The time Oliver should prize is *now*, the time of his inner trial in which he must face himself lest he, England and the world miss the opportunity now presenting itself—to experience and give witness to the Kingdom.

As with Bishop's letter and *Good Counsel*, 'Oh! Oliver' does not advocate physical invasion. Instead, the power of God—should Cromwell 'mind it'—would guarantee supreme authority over his European

---

[34] Fox, 'Oh! Oliver' in Burrough, *Good Counsel and Advice*, 26-7.
[35] Bishop, *The Warnings of the Lord* (1660), 1-17; especially 1-2, 17.

neighbours [heathens]. The letter urges the Protector to open himself to the Light so that it may invade his soul and by implication the nation and world; in doing so, the darkness would be dispelled. 'Oh! Oliver', like Bishop's letter, a precursor to *To the Council* and *A Visitation and Warning*, helps us understand how both 1659 tracts conformed to the apocalyptic and theophanous thinking that was second nature to the Quaker imagination, indeed characteristic of their daily discourse and writing as discussed in Chapter 4. *Importantly, this thinking allowed outer events, looming large in the public imagination, to be interpreted as stark inner realities that needed urgent attention so that people could experience the reality of the Light, the Kingdom, and the salvation it freely offered.*

This also appears to be the case with the two Burrough broadsides discovered by Reay, the second of which, he avers, demonstrates the Quakers' non-pacifism.[36] These being prickly times with rumours circulating of sectarian insurrection, the London Men's Meeting declined publication for fear that the broadsides' language (perhaps the military and apocalyptic tone of the second) would be misconstrued by the authorities, unscrupulous or otherwise. I believe Rosemary Moore is correct in saying that Fox would have disapproved of the second broadside had he attended the discussion. Any hint of armed force, whether intentional or not, would have met as usual with his strong disapproval, a position that incidentally raises questions about his authorship of *To the Council*.[37] Though unpublished, however, they remain important for our purposes. The first, *To the Parliament of the Commonwealth*, is addressed primarily to the recalled Rump parliament (and also to the army). It may have been composed between 13th May and 27th June. Unambiguously peaceful, it called on the 'authority aforesaid' to establish a committee comprising Presbyterians, Independents, Baptists and Quakers to seek reconciliation among the various parties in the political chaos currently engulfing the country.[38] Reay, not concerned with this broadside, concentrates on the second, *To the Parliament and the Army (in general)*, which he says was probably written in late August.[39] It bears some affinity to the Dunkirk letter and begins with 'our Kingdom is not of this world . . . and our weapons which have defended us are not carnal but spiritual', a dramatic and theologically loaded opening which Reay ignores without explanation. Burrough then expresses disgust at how the now corrupt army had turned its back on the

---

[36] Reay, 'The Quakers and 1659: two newly discovered broadsides by Edward Burrough', 104.
[37] *TLITC*, 171.
[38] *Ibid.*, 108, 104-5.
[39] Alternatively, it may have been written during Burrough's time in Dunkirk and perhaps discarded as unsatisfactory for publication but preserved nonetheless for future reference. This broadside invites many possibilities as to its aim and timing.

Chapter 12: 'Dwell in that which Leads into Peace'

Good Old Cause and more specifically from abolishing tithes. He goes on to express bewilderment over a recent cashiering of Quakers from the army 'in which we would have been of service to you and our country'. Precisely what *kind* of 'service' Burrough does not explain. At the same time he assured the authorities that if they were to repent and establish righteousness (justice) then the Friends would be prepared to give their lives in defence of the Cause; 'oh then' he wrote quoting Revelation 12:11, 'we should rejoice, and our lives would not be dear to lay down'.

Was Burrough suggesting Quaker support for armed force: is this another example of a possible 'wobble'? Or was he saying he and the Friends were prepared to lay down their lives for the synthesis of Kingdom, Cause and 'true religion'? I raise this issue in respect to the three important aspects with which he introduced the broadside and which are quintessentially of the Jesus Way and thus nonviolent—the Kingdom, the movement's spiritual warfare against the 'powers of darkness' and the paramountcy of redemptive suffering.[40] Burrough is sure that violence itself was a sign of people's resistance to the 'truth' and 'true judgment', and he concludes his paper with reference to both.[41] Therefore, it seems Burrough remained loyal to the Jesus Way. According to Hugh Barbour and Arthur Roberts, vital to Quaker belief and life was that 'the Spirit could never move people to violence or persecution . . . because to do so would be inherently contrary to the real conquest of evil which was the heart of the Spirit's work on earth'.[42]

By way of summarising this section, I set out four insights gained from the two works, the broadsides and 'Oh! Oliver' into the thinking and language of Fox, Burrough and Friends in 1659:

1. Mindful of our discussion of Quaker language in Chapter 4, we have seen how the works contain apocalyptic phraseology, theophanous imagery and anagogic perceptiveness.[43] As we have seen, very many Quaker works published during the decade contained these three mediums. In *To All that would Know the Way to the Kingdom* (1653), for instance, Fox wrote theophanously that before God 'the mountains shall melt, and the rocks shall cleave . . . and his thunders [will] begin to utter

---

[40] *Ibid.*, 107. There might be a link between this letter and a later one (early summer, 1660) to the King by Mary Penington, whose household Burrough was a visitor in 1659-60. See R. Moore, 'The Life of Isaac Penington' in *KMOLW*, 31-2.
[41] *EQW* (ed. 1973), 355.
[42] *Ibid.*, 356.
[43] There is an apocalyptic element in anagogy; see Henri de Lubac in Quinn, 'John Donne's Principles of Bibilcal Exegesis', 322 (20*n*).

their voices that the mysteries of God may be opened'.[44] For Fox, theophany spoke of the inner coming, indeed the immediacy (or invasion) of God and his own part in the peaceful unfolding of the Kingdom; theophany, therefore, could also be apocalyptic and anagogical.[45] Crucially and typically, the two tracts and the second Burrough broadside also reveal the prophet's lament for what might have been but also *the forlorn wish of the psalmist for a mighty and righteous army to carry the holy fight to the temples of idolatry.* This is entirely consistent with Fox's and Burrough's understanding and use of the Hebrew Testament and the prophetic messages within it (e.g. Ps. 149:8).

2. We know the Friends liberally invoked the Bible's military language—warrior language—as a normal part of their daily communication: 'Kill, cut off, destroy; bathe your sword in the blood of Amalek', cried Howgill in 1654 while declaring the Lamb's War.[46] Historian Nicola Baxter advises that 'justice cannot be done to the Quakers unless their works are approached on the level of the language they employed [and that] translation of their ideas into modern secular language changes the concepts themselves'.[47] With this in mind, any claim for Fox's and Burrough's controversial language as a means for promoting physical violence is *utterly incongruent* to the Friends' constantly repeated proclamation during the 1650s of an inward Kingdom with a strong ethos of nonviolence. For instance, in an epistle concerned for 'young and raw people that might sometimes come among us', Fox wrote immediately prior to Sir George Booth's rebellion which broke out in Cheshire in August 1659, that:

> Fighters are not of Christ's Kingdom, but are without Christ's Kingdom: for his Kingdom stands in peace and righteousness, but fighters are in the lust (i.e. greediness): and all that would destroy men's lives are not of Christ's mind, who came to save men's lives. Christ's Kingdom is not of this world; it is peaceable and all that are in strife are not of his Kingdom. All that pretend to fight for the gospel

---

[44] *To All that would Know*, 5 and see *Journal*, 16, 22, 27.
[45] *Ibid.*, 22 and Bauckham, 'The Eschatological Earthquake in the Apocalypse of John', 4.
[46] Howgill in 'To the Camp of the Lord in England' in *Works*, 32.
[47] N. Baxter, 'Gerrard Winstanley's Experimental Knowledge of God', 199.

Chapter 12: 'Dwell in that which Leads into Peace'

> are deceived; for the gospel is the power of God, which was before the devil or fall of man was. And the gospel of peace was before fighting was. Therefore they that pretend fighting, and talk of fighting so, are ignorant of the gospel. All that talk of fighting for Zion are in darkness. Zion needs no such helpers.

He continues:

> They that would be wrestlers with flesh and blood, throw away Christ's doctrine; the flesh is got upon them, and they are weary of their sufferings. Such as would revenge themselves are out of Christ's doctrine. Such as being stricken on one cheek would not turn the other are out of Christ's doctrine. Such as do not love one another, nor love enemies, are out of Christ's doctrine.

And then:

> The Jews' sword outwardly, by which they cut down the heathen, was a type [that is, a figure] of the spirit of God within, which [spirit] cuts down the heathenish nature within. So live in the peaceable Kingdom of Christ Jesus... and not in the lusts from whence wars arise.[48]

3. We also saw in Chapter 4 how people raised in the 'arte of rhetorique' could go beyond otherwise acceptable language boundaries and often did so in a highly-charged socio-political, ecclesial and military environment and one grounded in fear. And we noted how there was a lower threshold of confrontational language at work when compared to our own today. The marriage of metaphor, military language and the political realities of 1659 again enabled Fox and Burrough to use *rhetoric* to dramatise their message for maximum effect; perhaps, then, they conform to Fox's similar reasoning in 'Oh! Oliver'. In addition, informed readers would have known that, logistically, an actual English invasion and occupation of France, Spain, Italy and Turkey was a fantasy'.

---

[48] Fox, Ep. (1659) to Friends, *Ellwood*, 200(2)-202(2) and written not long before Booth's rebellion (1st August).

4. During the seventeenth century as today, 'blood' was associated with the vital principle of life and used to arouse hostile feelings among soldiers of an enemy. But Fox and Burrough engaged both meanings *apocalyptically* in pleading for a convincement on a grandiose scale so that the 'Life' and Light, along with its gifts of justice and forgiveness, would be advanced and preserved for future generations. In so doing, and this seems true for the second broadside, they were calling upon all, soldier and civilian alike, to urgently expiate the bad blood of sinfulness, the real enemy who at any moment could invade their hearts. Here was something in line with Nayler's motivations in Bristol less than three years earlier. In other words, purification would lead to a resurrected people who would welcome the implications of Jesus' Second Coming which was already at hand. The goal of consummation, true freedom and wholeness for all, would be achieved only by submitting to the will of God by means of a righteous life. This was a way of hope through which union between God and humanity would come. To effect this, people needed to die to the old covenant to embrace the New; the head of the serpent within needed to be ruthlessly crushed so that the Light and Kingdom may arise among 'all people', all 'nations'.[49]

In sum, the two tracts and Burrough's broadsides were a prophetic call to all people to cut out the canker of inner and outer sin, a call made all the more explicit by the use of apocalyptic, theophanous, anagogical and military language, their love of the metaphor and an inclination always to use the 'arte of rhetorique'. Outer sin included those unsavoury influences within the Church in England and among the governing élites to which terms such as 'Babylonian bawd', 'Turk', 'Rome', 'papist/popery' and other colourful imagery were applied. There is nothing in this approach that is inconsistent with the writings of the movement during the decade.

The Marxist Interpretation of Quaker History

Our four suggestions create problems for the secular but particularly the Marxist view which, although somewhat dated, remains influential among sections of the Religious Society of Friends today. Indeed, one cannot minimise the contribution Marxist historians have made to our

---

[49] For conflation of blood, Life and Light see *Cambridge*, i., 24 and also Ep. 155 (1657) in *Works*, 7: 119-20 and Brinton, *Friends for 300 Years*, 42. Barbour also posits a theological explanation for Burrough's bloodthirsty passage in *A Visitation and Warning Proclaimed*; see Barbour's 'The Lamb's War', 151.

understanding of the turbulent times in which the early Quakers lived. However, in my view, they have failed to fully grasp the Quakers' message of the Jesus Way, their specific use of the Bible, military language and 'the arte of rhetorique': no written work of the Friends in our period was secular, nor were they political to the exclusion of their religious worldview.

But according to scholars such as Cole, Hill, Reay and Maclear, early Quakerism was a predominantly socio-political movement. They say the Friends, without a collective peace testimony during the 1650s, fell into disillusionment and experienced a failed 'millennialism' (which they do not fully explain). Defeated, they made a compromise with the new political reality and disappeared from mainstream politics into quietism.[50] During the last quarter of the twentieth century, this view took a powerful hold among Quakers. And it must be admitted that the writings of the Marxist school are impressive, if not dazzling, with narratives flowing with the easy assumption that there is, logically and rationally, no alternative to their apparently well-researched view. But a closer look reveals at least five serious flaws:

1. They approach the Quakers with ideological assumptions that are inherently opposed to objective scholarship. This has led to a number of glaring mistakes. For instance, they fail to give due weight to religious motivations, particularly at the anagogical level as we have seen. An example is their ignorance of the process by which religious Concerns are tested. Movements of a mystical kind experience a development whereby an individual's Inward Light, taken on trust in the early days of a movement, is eventually submitted to the testing of the group. Writing about the Friends of God, for instance, Rufus Jones noted:

   > Those who have had this first-hand experience, and belong to this 'upper school of the Holy Spirit', are the true teachers and guides of the rest. For this reason the Friends of God insisted, as a matter of the first importance, that all who were in the stage of 'preparation' should submit themselves entirely to the counsel and direction of some holy man of the 'Society'.[51]

---

[50] The Friends' long-standing refusal to swear oaths debarred them from public office. However, this prohibition did not prevent them after 1660 from contributing importantly to local life socially, educationally, economically *and* pursuing the Lamb's War. See Mullett, 'Conflict, Politics and Elections in Lancaster', 61-86 and esp. 63-4.

[51] R. Jones, *Studies in Mystical Religion*, 259.

This kind of internal development, with its own dynamic, is not necessarily a response to external pressures whether social or political. Hence the Marxist school understands Fox-Hubberthorne as accommodating to the Restoration as an external event only. But if that were the case, why did their school not accommodate on other issues such as the suffering of the Friends? Further, Hill's understanding of Fox-Hubberthorne as a 'peace principle' misplaces *the* peace *testimony*. It fails to comprehend the declaration's *Kingdom* worldview, its 'real intent', that it was a statement of a deeply held *religious* commitment throughout the 1650s to Kingdom and Testimony with their Christ/Logos-mystical underpinnings. 'Peace principle' therefore, gives Fox-Hubberthorne a supreme importance never intended by its authors. As observed in the Overview, the document does not deserve the authority implied in such prominence. He and his colleagues were looking for the peace testimony in the wrong place.[52]

2. Their choice of quotations is highly selective. Sometimes the Friends are quoted out of context, displaying the school's desire to see in seventeenth century radicalism an antecedent for twentieth century revolutionary ideals. In Chapter 4, for example, we noted Reay's assertion that Fox's declaration in *The Lambs Officer is Gone Forth* (1659), 'now shall the Lamb and saints have victory' (which Fox states twice on pages 13 and 14 of the tract) was an indication of Quaker non-pacifism. Instead, we have seen how the work is an apocalyptic invocation of peaceful means against all kinds of popery (including Rome), something reinforced by Fox's pointed question only four lines after the above declaration on page 14: 'Are not all your carnal weapons that you persecute withal, the whores-cup of Rome, which . . . has killed the creatures, and wrestled with flesh and blood?'[53] On the evidence of the majority of pamphlets written between 1658 and 1659 taken alone, I believe Schmidt is correct in his observation that,

---

[52] See above, Chp. 4 for Reay's misunderstanding of Fox's statement in *The Lambs Officer*, 13, 14 concerning 'victory'. And see *QER*, 101-11, esp. 101.

[53] See Fox, *ibid.* and *To the Pope*, 61-6; *Doctrinals*, 202; *QER*, 101-11, esp. 101 and Hill, 'Quakers and the English Revolution', 170, 172.

in order to identify [the] Quakers as the heirs of the revolutionary legacy of the 1640s and 1650s, it was crucial for [Marxist] scholars to advance the concept that [the] Quakers did not believe in or practice pacifism. Perhaps this was based upon an assumption that to make a revolutionary impact a group must be willing to use violence in order to make their threat and challenge to the established order credible and viable.

3. Their school relies heavily on the works of the Quakers' opponents who had turned the Friends into a fearsome, sometimes blood-thirsty, vanguard of social and political revolution. As Larry Ingle confirms, the Marxist approach is 'constructed on rumour, myth and hearsay, it cannot do justice to the Quakers' real intent'.[54]

4. They (and others) place too much emphasis on 1660 as a turning point. According to Coward, 'few historians now accept that 1660 marked such a decisive turning point towards constitutional monarchy and the secularisation of politics and society'.[55] Nor had it much significance for the Friends' faith and practice because their Kingdom arose above time, space and events. So-called *petit bourgeois* behaviour was no indication of a decline in Quaker dynamism, which was carried over the 1660 'divide' well into the century. David Scott's work on York Friends of the 1650s, for instance, describes a group who, although dominated from the beginning of the movement by a business élite, and 'socially solid and respectable rather than millenarian and revolutionary' [i.e. violent], nonetheless do not renege on the Lamb's War. His research belies Marxist claims that post-1660 Quakers were content to withdraw timorously into the shadows of English provincial life.[56]

5. One cannot speak of 'defeat' of what was an eschatological experience. By their nature, such experiences necessarily have the future in mind. In the Quakers' case, theirs was a

---

[54] Ingle, 'From Mysticism to Radicalism', 92 (43*n*).
[55] Coward, *The Stuart Age*, 281.
[56] See Mullett, *Northern History*, 225-6 for a review of Scott's *Quakerism in York 1650-1670*.

present and future vision, realised and realising, mostly 'now' but also 'not yet' (i.e. a realised eschatology). The Kingdom's universality stood in sharp contrast to the political machinations of their day as these were confined to a specific period of time. And yet the Friends were not otherworldly since they had a concrete Concern for the world as the Kingdom demanded. Their call for unity in Christ was a call for a new world order since the old one had long gone as a result of Jesus' witness, death and resurrection. In their own era they could see signs of this in the rapid demise of the Puritan republic. When Margaret Fell in *A Declaration and an Information* spoke of 'fruits being made manifest', she meant the appearance in her generation of the new covenant, the true Church as already come, a new beginning of God's historical activity as this was mediated through her movement. Again, this is not the language of defeat but of hope, a hope that was abundantly evident in the 1650s and which continued after the Restoration.[57] To adapt the words of theologian Carl Braaten, their gospel was not news about another world, but one born from the history of God in *this* world for the sake of *this* world's place and future in the Kingdom.[58]

Marxism, of course, can be seen as a secularised version of the Kingdom dynamic. Its adherents correctly recognise that as this dynamic is lost the Church becomes conservative, even a 'mystical opiate'. They were wrong, however, to see the Quakers in this way. The so-called 'defeat' of the Radicals did not apply to the Friends until roughly after the death of Fox in 1691 and particularly during the 1700s when many Friends, probably the majority, adopted pietism and fell into social isolation.[59] In all fairness to the later Friends, however, the England of the 1680s or 1690s was different from that of the 1650s. Then, the Quakers were revolutionary even though they comprehensively rejected violence, as a review of their works to 1663 in the next sub-section shows.

By way of a final comment on the Marxist influence, we saw how the Leveller-Digger revolution looked back to a golden age of pre-Norman England. The Friends looked to something deeper and everlasting. In hoping their own revolution (experienced initially on an inner level through

---

[57] Fell *et al*, *A Declaration and an Information*, 6; Howgill, *A Visitation of Love*, 5.
[58] Braaten, *The Future of God*, 138.
[59] Hill, *The Experience of Defeat, passim*. R. Moore and Ingle also ascribe to the defeat theory. See *TLITC*, chapter 13; *FF*, chapter 12 and esp. 88, 190-2.

convincement) would usher in the never-ending Kingdom, they combined an awareness of themselves as a royal priesthood with the realised eschatology just mentioned. The meaning and implications of this development is what the Marxist scholars failed to grasp. The result has been a considerable distortion of Quaker beginnings.[60] I have said their writings have more to do with twentieth century polemics and conditions: however, the Quakers they identified as precursors of the proletarian revolution they so earnestly desired for the present never existed.

Who was a 'Quaker' in 1659? Attitudes to Violence and War

Much of the Marxist argument rests on a close relationship of the Quakers with the military. While there existed a small Quaker presence in the army and navy—there were perhaps up to forty Friends expelled by George Monck in 1659—a number of important factors need our consideration.

The fluid and rapidly expanding 'membership' of the movement in those uncertain times[61] made it easy for their opponents to identify as 'Quaker' anyone holding radical or unusual views. Misidentification in the 1650s and 1660s was a common feature of life in general, and Quaker credentials were not always verifiable. With good reason, therefore, Cantor also warns against denominational labelling during a century in which hopping between sects was common; the Friends were easily mistaken for others.[62] In 1654, for instance, the early Quaker John Wilkinson, giving account of his trial at Gloucester, reported that 'the grand jury brought in a petition... that Ranters, Levellers and atheists, under the name of Quakers, made a disturbance, and petitioned some speedy course might be taken'. During his Appleby trial, magistrate Briggs may have confused James Nayler with the Leveller, John Naylier.[63] In Wiltshire, the magistracy

---

[60] Marxist treatment of the Diggers follows the same path. For Hill, Winstanley's God is immanent only. For a refutation of Hill's work in this respect see Mulligan *et al*, 'The Religion of Gerrard Winstanley', *passim*; Bradstock, 'Sowing in Hope', *passim*. Malcolm's work on attitudes of the English rural populace towards Charles I during the civil wars also exposes Marxist *a priori* comments; see 'A King in Search of Soldiers', 252. Weddle's appendix to her *Walking in the Way of Peace* (2001) offers an effective criticism of the Cole, Hill and Reay school; one wonders why it was merely appendixed. And see both my *MOP*, Chps. 2 and 5 and *GADOT* in which I critically examined their school's thinking; see esp. *GADOT*, 26, 28, 48-9, 89-90.
[61] Formal membership of a 'Religious Society of Friends' began in Great Britain in 1737.
[62] Hutton, *The British Republic*, 8. Referring to opposition to his plans for Quaker organisation, Fox complained that 'many [Quakers] are as dark as the priests'. See L. Benson, *What did George Fox Teach about Christ?*, 14-15. For further evidence of fluidity of membership see Cantor, 'Quakers in the Royal Society, 1660-1750', 176. And see *QER*, 19.
[63] See Neelon, *James Nayler*, 64 and 'The Examination of James Nayler' in *Saul's Errand*, 30. Naylier wrote one tract and co-authored another; see esp. *The Foxes Craft Discovered*

accused Sir Walter St. John, lord of the manor of Lydiard Tregoze (nr. Swindon), of being 'a rogue and a rebel, an anabaptist and a Quaker', probably for his association with non-conformists and his Cromwellian sympathies.[64] Thomas Tany (or Theauraujohn) the Ranter was mistaken for a Quaker when flailing his sword against the doors of the Commons. There were MPs who had never seen a 'Quaker'.[65] Not unreasonably they, too, confused the Friends with Ranters, Anabaptists, Levellers and, later, with Fifth Monarchists. For his part, Fox periodically lamented the paucity of spiritual awareness among the 'camp of the Lord'.[66] What status, then, may be accredited to the beliefs of any individual purporting to be a 'Quaker' given the variegated nature of spiritual development outside the movement's leadership?

Within such a movement where record keeping was habitual, where the spoken word was of central significance and accentuated by the practice of silence, together with the plethora of spies reporting directly to Secretary Thurloe, Quaker support for war or any spilling of blood would have been carefully and repeatedly recorded. The Thurloe correspondence actually confirms a faithful compliance with nonviolence. Appendix 5 confirms what may be said with confidence: *Quaker writings throughout the 1650s reveal substantial evidence of oft-repeated statements against the use of 'carnal' weaponry and insurrection.* Civil war experiences led some, such as William Dewsbury, to adopt absolute pacifism, a position that was accorded great respect within the movement by virtue of the fact that he was much loved and highly influential within it. Others came to a Dewsbury-like position through their reading of the Bible. They, like Fox, saw the logic of the Christian Testament, 'the Light that cometh from Christ the Truth', as leading only to nonviolence. So, too, some like Thomas Lurting after a long internal struggle while serving in the military.[67]

In 1651, Fox, who had refused an army commission the previous year, proclaimed, 'that which is set up by spiritual weapons is held up by spiritual

---

(1649), 7 in which the authors, of which Naylier was one, refer to the Leveller petition of 11th Sept., 1648.

[64] For Walter St. John who served in parliament in the 1650s see K. Taylor, 'Chalk, Cheese and Cloth', 173.

[65] A. Clarke, *Prelude to Restoration in Ireland*, 52-3. Clarke also mentions a Maj. Peter Wallis described invariably as a 'Quaker' and a 'Quaker sympathiser'. See also John Wilkinson, letter (25/Aug/1654) to George Taylor *et al*, *SW/i/36*; Underdown, 'The Independents Reconsidered', 64, 81 for difficulties in defining certain 'parties'; J. Davis, 'Religion and the Struggle for Freedom in the English Revolution', 511; Hutton, *The British Republic*, 95.

[66] See, for instance, the controversy over the 'Proud Quakers' led by Rice (Rhys) Jones in *Journal*, 63, 337-8 and Nayler, letter (7?/Nov/1654) to Fox describing his meeting with Rice Jones in Nottingham: 'much confusion did appear in him . . . he defended swearing'.

[67] See Fox, Ep. 139 (1657) in *LOGF*, 56.

weapons, not by carnal weapons'.[68] In 1652 in an epistle to Friends and quoting Hosea 9 he powerfully condemned physical violence including war, which he saw as murderous: failure to bring 'forth the Substance, the birth from above' meant bringing 'forth children to murder'.[69] As far back as 1653, Nayler at Appleby advanced the cause of inner and outer peace:

> For where envy and strife is, there is confusion and every evil work: but that wisdom which is from above, is first pure, then peaceable, gentle, and easy to be entreated, full of mercy and good fruits, without partiality, without hypocrisy.[70]

After experiencing the battle of Dunbar (1650), his internalisation of the Kingdom's peace was such that the idea of going to war was absurd. In the same year Thomas Lawson, as yet a priest and calming his parishioners as they were about to attack Fox, told them that 'if our worship and doctrine cannot be maintained without fear and violence, 'tis time to leave it'. Agnes Wilkinson loudly voiced her opposition to violence in 1653 as a small band of her fellow Quakers favoured army action after the fall of the Rump. 'Strip yourself naked of all your carnal weapons', she admonished them, 'for the Lord is coming to judge Men . . . and carnal weapons shall be broken'.[71] In *A Lamentation* (1653), Nayler expressed sorrow at the corruption of power into violence and 'the will of men brought forth instead of equity'.[72] His abhorrence of violence, oppression and the corruption they brought led him to grieve for England's condition. After observing, over a lengthy period, how the army and parliament had betrayed the Good Old Cause he wrote:

> all hearts are full of oppression and all hands are full of violence, their houses are filled with oppression, their streets and markets abound with it, their courts which should afford remedy against it, are wholly made up of iniquity and injustice, and the Law of God is made altogether void, and Truth is trodden under foot, and plainness is become odious to the proud, and deceit set on high; and the proud are counted happy, and the rich are exalted above the poor.[73]

---

[68] Fox, 'The Peacemaker has the Kingdom and Dominion', 6-7 in T. C. Jones, *'The Power of the Lord*, p. xxxvi. Winstanley said the same; see *New Law of Righteousness*, 43.
[69] Fox, Ep. 9 (1652) in *Collection*, 11.
[70] Nayler, *A Discovery of the First Wisdom*, 6; he quotes Jm. 3:14-17.
[71] See John Wilkinson, letter (1653) to Fell, *SW*/iv/228; *QER*, 81; *FFQ*, 270.
[72] Nayler, *A Lamentation*, 34.
[73] *Ibid.*, 3-4. See Lk. 1:51-52.

Both Nayler and Fox were adamant in 1654 that 'in dwelling in the Word, it takes away the occasion of wars, and gathers our hearts together to God, and unto one another, and brings to the beginning, before wars was.'[74] When, in the same year, and in Cromwell's presence, Fox and Thomas Aldam signed a document renouncing violence 'against any man', they did so *on behalf of the movement* and were confident of its support.[75] Edmund Peckover, a veteran of Cromwell's army of nine years, received an honourable discharge also in 1655 despite adopting a pacifist belief that war was unChristian.[76]

In the same year the government newspaper, *The Public Intelligencer* described the Quakers as 'the perfect objects of humility and repentance, their aspect as demure as their habit'.[77] Also in 1655, the former Cromwell loyalist, George Bishop, in correspondence with John Thurloe, reported that he was 'looking after a Kingdom that cannot be shaken and [was] studying peace with truth'.[78] Burrough, Lilburne, John Harwood and others again in 1655, Nayler and Hubberthorne in 1656, and Fox three years later, stipulated the 'sword' should be used 'justly' (where Christ the Light X was the ultimate Law-giver) to curb the transgressor within but fairly against 'evil-doers'.[79] 'Do violence to no man,' Burrough wrote,

> but to be terrors, and reprovers, and correctors of all violence, and of such who live in it: And it [this time the Light] will teach you not to strengthen the hands of evil-doers, but to lay your swords in justice upon every one that doth evil: And it will teach you not to make war, but to preserve peace in the earth.[80]

Harwood in *The Path of the Just Cleared* (1655) probably used Romans 13:1-7 to justify the Friends' obedience to the authorities—hardly a revolutionary attitude in the Marxist sense. According to Paul, all authority derived from God if it was lawful and for the common good; in this way

---

[74] Fox and Nayler *et al, Several Papers*, 7.

[75] *Journal*, 197. My emphasis.

[76] Penrose, 'Edmund Peckover: ex-soldier of the Commonwealth and Quaker', 88-90.

[77] Fox, 'A Paper of George Fox's to Oliver Protector' (1655) in *Journal*, 220-1. See also Cole, *The Quakers and Politics*, 63; *The Public Intelligencer* (27th and 28th February 1655); *BQ*, 560.

[78] Bishop, letter (22/May/1655) to Thurloe, *Rawlinson MS. A.* 26., fo. 29 (Bodleian Library, Oxford) and also quoted in Feola-Castelucci, *George Bishop*, 75.

[79] Burrough (and Howgill), 'An Invitation', 35-7; Nayler, 'Concerning Error, Heresy, &c.' in *Love to the Lost*, 11-13; Hubberthorne, *The Antipathy betwixt Flesh and Spirit* (1656), 4; Fox, *To the Council of Officers of the Army*, 4; Fell, *This was given to Major-General Harrison*, 5. See Lilburne, *The Resurrection,* for a clear renunciation of carnal weaponry and for *his* pacifism.

[80] Burrough (and Howgill), 'An Invitation', *ibid*.

Chapter 12: 'Dwell in that which Leads into Peace'

Christian ethics entered civil life. All the more reason, the Friends concluded, to follow the imperative of loving one's neighbour to achieve unity in the Word. But obedience to the authorities should not come at the expense of justice or nonviolent correction for the wrong-doer. The same Pauline passage would be embedded in Fox-Hubberthorne in 1661: 'in the uprightness of our hearts we may, under the power ordained of God, for the punishment of evil-doers'.[81]

In March 1655, Maj.-Gen. William Goffe complained to Thurloe that a 'Col. Jenner's lieutenant' had turned Quaker and failed to turn up for a muster. In 1656, Francis Ellington and other Friends assured the authorities the Quakers were innocent of armed insurrection:

> the seed that the Lord has brought out of the North country has grown to . . . ten thousands in all parts of England . . . yet not one of these soldiers has as much as a stick in their hands; but they have a sword in their mouths and with it they slay the nations.[82]

The Dutch ambassador reported in the same year that Quakers had mutinied in Col. Robert Phaire's regiment in Ireland.[83] Protests such as these usually took place over the taking of human life or matters related to equality. For Burrough in 1657, the Kingdom would be 'set up and advanced in the Earth' as a preliminary state 'but not by the might of man, or the arm of flesh' but by 'patient suffering under the injustice and oppression of men, . . . till they be overturned and confounded'.[84] He warned further against rebellion. Instead, God's will is best carried out by 'upright walking' and by,

---

[81] See John Harwood *et al, The Path of the Just Cleared* (1655), 10. For similar references see Aldam *et al, False Prophets*, 4, 6; Farnworth, 'A Mite given forth' in *A Message from the Lord*, 34-5; Burrough, *A Visitation and Warning Proclaimed*, 5; Burrough, *To the Parliament of the Common-wealth*, 5; Burrough *et al, A Declaration . . . to the Present Distracted and Broken Nation of England*, 8, 13; Fox (the Younger), *Honest, Upright* in *Works* (1659), 4-5. See Mt. 22: 36-40 for the Kingdom in essence.

[82] Francis Ellington *et al, A True Discovery of the Grounds of Imprisonment* (1655 [*DCFB* 1656]). Hill has Ellington as ranterish in *TWTUD*, 125. See *FFQ*, 154; Lurting, *The Fighting Sailor turn'd Peaceable Christian* (for 1650s), 11-13, 15-20; and Capp, *Cromwell's Navy*, 305, 325.

[83] See Maj.-Gen. William Goffe, letter (22/March/1655) to Thurloe, iv., 642-3 and for reference to Col. Phaire (Robert Phayre) see Ambassador William Nieupoort, letter (12/May/1655) to States-General (Holland), Thurloe, *ibid.*, 757 and A. Clarke, *Prelude to Restoration*, 52-3. Phaire, a veteran of the New Model Army and the Munster wars, was a regicide. Seemingly mercurial in spiritual affairs, he may have dabbled for a short time in Quakerism but was also described as a Baptist and Muggletonian; see Barnard, 'Crisis of Identity among Irish Protestants', 76.

[84] Burrough, 'Concerning the Kingdom of Christ' in *A Standard lifted up*, 12. See Ezk. 21:27; Zc. 4:6.

patient suffering under the cruelty and oppression of the devil's government and kingdom; more reaches to overthrow them than the rising to rebel in any way of outward offence toward them, or defence from them.'[85]

In 1658 Burrough wrote to Sir Henry Vane, reassuring the then government leader that '[y]ou've heard that we make war amongst you . . . this is not true. Our Kingdom is not of this world'.[86] Douglas Gwyn suggests that, while access to the military and its leadership had once opened up socio-political space for Quaker activity, their 'covenant of Light did not allow Friends to form determinate relations with the army' any more than it allowed them to join a coalition [later] in 1659 with Vane.[87] In 1657, in addition to disgust at judges and lawyers over their advocacy of the death penalty for theft as an attack on the poor,[88] Fox exhorted 'all people on the earth' to,

come out of the bustlings [to discover the] way of peace [for in the bustlings] there stands all the world, . . . throwing dirt one to another, where the enmity is and fighting one with another with the weapon that is carnal, and warring one against another . . . therefore all people dwell in that which leads into peace.[89]

Also in 1657 he declared 'war is error' while his eschewing of violence to teachers was unequivocal; 'the rod' was not an actual stick but the 'nurture and love of God' and the fostering of inner discipline for their spiritual welfare.[90] The Kingdom would be won by spiritual weapons only, something which David Scott tells us the business-orientated Quakers of York consistently held throughout the 1650s.[91] The Friends in New England (where they first arrived in 1656) also shunned violence, the authorities there complaining in 1657 about the Quakers' refusal of militia training.[92] In November 1657, Cromwell informed the judiciary that the peaceable Quakers should be 'pittied' the error of their conviction and spared undue harassment by the magistrates or courts.[93]

---

[85] Burrough, *ibid.*
[86] Burrough, letter to Sir Henry Vane Jr., *Ellwood MSS.*, ii. 27-8.
[87] Gwyn, *The Covenant Crucified*, 210, 212. See *Journal*, 315, 323; Morrill, 'The Stuarts' in K. Morgan (ed.), 344.
[88] Fox, *An Instruction to Judges and Lawyers*, 5-8.
[89] Fox, *An Epistle to all People on the Earth*, 1-2.
[90] For 'war is error' see *A Declaration of the Ground of Error*, 4. Also *A Warning to all Teachers of Children* (1657), 2.
[91] Fox, *ibid.*, 57. See D. Scott, *Quakerism in York*.
[92] Weddle, 'The Basis of the Early Quaker Peace Testimony' in Mullett (ed., 1991), 91.
[93] Calkins, *Prophecy and Polemic*, 43.

Chapter 12: 'Dwell in that which Leads into Peace'

Nayler re-emphasised Quaker nonviolence more specifically in *The Lamb's War* (1657/8) in which he protests that the Friends 'war not against men's persons, so their weapons are not carnal, not hurtful to any of the creation.'[94] As with Burrough two years later, the Lamb's weapons were underlined as 'righteousness and holiness to God', truth, 'love unfeigned', patience, lowliness of mind, meekness, gentleness, faithfulness—Pauline themes consistently replayed by the early Quakers throughout the decade.[95] A year later in 'Not to Strive, but Overcome by Suffering', also from prison and published at least two years before Fox-Hubberthorne, Nayler stridently advocates nonviolence and peacemaking:

And [the] seed all should know which is beloved of the Father and heir of the everlasting Kingdom, who strives not by violence but entreats; who seeks not revenge, but endures all contradictions from all against himself, to the end he may obtain mercy for all from the Father. And this is the seed of eternal peace, and the eternal peace maker.[96]

Penington, newly convinced in 1658, wrote to a near relative in February 1659 that the Friends 'love the souls of their enemies, and think no pains or hazard too much for the saving of them; being persecuted, they bless, being reviled, they entreat and pray for their persecutors'.[97] In 1658, Fox universalised the Quakers' conviction of spiritual weaponry with a condemnation of the Roman Church and its violence.[98] He strongly advocated nonviolence in *59 Particulars* and in his *Catechism for Children* (1660) which appeared some months before the Fox-Hubberthorne declaration.[99]

In 1659, in *A Visitation and Warning*, much of it written in Dunkirk, Burrough evokes Revelation 19:7-8 and 21:1-21 with their vision and yearning for the peaceable realm of God. And in his supposedly aggressive letter to the army garrison in the town, he states, '. . . and there is a Kingdom which not of this world, which cannot be obtained by an outward sword'.[100] Almost immediately upon returning from Dunkirk on the 20th or

---

[94] Nayler, *The Lambs War*, 4, 6, 7. For the relationship of apocalypse to violence and nonviolence see Charry, "'A Sharp Two-edged Sword': Pastoral Implications of Apocalypse', 163; A. Y. Collins, 'Apocalyptic Themes in Biblical Literature', 128.

[95] Nayler, *ibid*. See Burrough, *A Discovery of Some Part of the War* (1659).

[96] Nayler, Ep. 11 in *Works*, 729 (see Appendix 3).

[97] Penington, *Letters*, Letter LXXXI (pub. 1844) dated 14th, 12th Mo., 1658 (14 /Feb/1659), 223-4.

[98] Fox, *The Papist's Strength*, 3.

[99] Fox, *59 Particulars*, 16: 'where the devil [murders and persecutes] . . . the true Magistrates never did with carnal weapons'. Also Fox, *A Catechism for Children*, 98-9 and quoted in Angell, 'The Catechisms of George Fox', p. 10 of 13 pp. The precise date is unknown.

[100] Burrough, *A Visitation and Warning Proclaimed*, 33-4.

21st May, he set about emphasising peace and reconciliation to the parliament and army in the spirit of the Kingdom. His desire for a harmonious relationship between conflicting political parties is clear enough and emerges from one of the broadsides discovered by Reay.

Also in 1659, Fox petitioned parliament to 'let no man bear the sword that does violence to any man'[101] and pronounced to Friends that 'to bear and carry carnal weapons, men of peace, they cannot'. Henry Stubbe protested that his fellow Quakers could be safely compared to the nonviolent primitive Christians.[102] Another 1659 tract, possibly by early Quaker Ellis Hookes to the apprentices of London, denounced violence as a means of enacting the Good Old Cause. In the same year, Fox advised Francis Gawler, a Friend in Cardiff, that the Friends did not fight, endorsing his note with the words 'which G.F. forbad, and said it was contrary to our principles'.[103] In December 1659, James Strutt recalls how his conversion to the Gospel of peace forbad him to continue as a naval captain.[104] And as late as the 9th March 1660, General Monck made an order 'requiring the soldiers to "forbear to disturb the peaceable meetings of the Quakers, they doing nothing prejudicial to the parliament or Commonwealth of England"'.[105] In May 1660, Hubberthorne declared that 'the revelation of Jesus Christ . . . can neither be set up, nor pulled down by the [material] sword'.[106] A month later Burrough warned the London Anabaptists that evil is destroyed 'without sword or carnal weapons'.[107] And on October 20th, three months before the king received the Fox-Hubberthorne declaration, Edward Bourne, echoing Burrough, urged the persecutors of fellow Quakers in Worcester to adopt peace and nonviolence by becoming followers of the Lamb 'who makes war with the sword of his mouth'. It was a warning so important to Bourne that he took pains to place it prominently on the title page of his tract.[108]

For his part, Fox astringently witnessed against violence by a life-long public opposition to it. According to his *Journal*, he suffered physical

---

[101] Fox, *59 Particulars*, 9, 16.

[102] Henry Stubbe (1632-76), *Light Shining out of Darkness* (1659), 1-19, 88-92. See *QER*, 98; Richardson and Ridden, *Freedom and the English Revolution*, 30; Harris, *London Crowds in the Reign of Charles II*, 33; Hill, *The Experience of Defeat*, 136.

[103] Fox, correspondence (1659) in T. C. Jones, *'The Power of the Lord'*, letter 117. See Hookes (and Burrough?), *A Presentation* (1659), 2, 5. Also *BQ*, 462; Nuttall, *Christian Pacifism*, 54; Francis Gawler, letter (26/Jan/1659/60) to Fox, *SW*/iv/219.

[104] Strutt, *A Declaration to the Whole World*, 9-12.

[105] *BQ*, 471. See *SW*/iii/141 for a paper, endorsed by Fox, as 'an order by g monk'; *Cambridge*, i., 352, 461.

[106] Hubberthorne, *The Good Old Cause*, 2.

[107] Burrough, 'An Answer to . . . Anabaptists' in Hubberthorne, *An Answer to . . . Anabaptists* (1659), 24.

[108] Bourne, *A Warning . . . unto the Inhabitants of Worcester* (1660), 14.

beatings without retaliation and intervened in brawls with a view to enlightening those in the peaceful way of the Kingdom.[109] In Ulverston market in 1652, for instance, he bid a soldier who had appointed himself as his body-guard to sheath his rapier.[110] These incidences are rarely highlighted by those questioning the pacifism of Fox whose *The Secret Works of a Cruel People* (1659) should leave no doubt about his position in this respect. The tract was addressed to parliament and its position derived from the example of the primitive Church to whose experience Fox was devoted, and for which he consistently risked his life:

> Oh who would have believed that such a thirst would have risen among you, that nothing will quench but the blood of the innocent, and the blood of them that keep the command of Christ, and walks in the Doctrine of the Apostles [Kingdom]! Was there ever the like heard of in the Scriptures or New Testament . . . I am grieved that you . . . bring such a pain upon yourselves and such dishonour upon the Truth.[111]

Fox himself was neither without flaws of personality nor blind to the unsavoury realities of life, but he claimed to be dead to its sin of which violence was a too-frequent component. When beaten or imprisoned, he practiced what may be called radical forgiveness towards those who injured him. Time and again he would say he rose above his own imprisonments to free those in spiritual bondage. This Golgotha-type forgiveness, what nineteenth century Quaker Caroline Stephen called an 'undaunted persistence in blessing', was another hallmark of his nonviolence which, along with that of other early Friends, remains as judge and standard today.[112]

Peter Brock maintained that, by 1659 and probably before, there were already Quaker conscientious objectors to military service in the county militias. In 1658, a case of conscientious objection is recorded from Maryland, while German Quakers (former Mennonites) at Kriegsheim in the Palatinate refused to bear arms. Brock concluded that if opposition to military service already existed among Quakers in the New World and Europe it is likely it had become 'fairly widespread' among British Quakers

---

[109] *Journal*, 229.
[110] *Ibid.*, 128-9 and *Ellwood*, 86.
[111] Fox, *The Secret Works of a Cruel People* (1659), 17 and see 1, 16. See also Crook *et al*, *Liberty of Conscious Asserted* (1661), 5, 6 in which Crook, in regard to 'force of arms', writes that 'the primitive Christians detested that form of proceedings' while repeating King James' belief to parliament (1609) that, 'It is a pure rule in divinity that God never loves to plant his Church with violence and blood'.
[112] Stephen, *Quaker Strongholds*, 117.

still earlier.[113] I believe our survey so far verifies Brock's assertion: despite 'oppression', 'persecution' and a politically weak position, the early Friends were more confident (than historians have hitherto supposed) in insisting that authorities emulate 'the Apostle' in harming no one; 'either you or your soldiers'. Later, in 1660, Fox wrote to the king maintaining, as usual, that the Quakers witnessed 'against sin and filth, riots plots and tumultuous meetings'.[114] His assurances were no less emphatic than those to the former republican leaders. The Quakers would not seek their own defence but would strive to overcome their enemies with good.

And yet, despite their repeated protestations of nonviolence, the Friends continued to be accused of gun-running, spying and armed rebellion.[115] A Major Woods, writing to future Lord Chancellor Hyde in April 1660, had the Quakers joining Maj.-Gen. John Lambert's revolt after having 'sold their whole estates to raise money for the present design', a rumour for which there was no solid evidence.[116] Still, Bulstrode Whitelocke, the MP and diplomat, noted that in 1659 a strong consensus had the Quakers as a real threat to political stability.[117] Alternatively, diarist Thomas Rugg believed the Quakers innocent of any 'late rising' (in 1660) for 'not one of them was found in arms nor owned the cause'. Samuel Pepys agreed: the Quakers were 'clapped up without any reason'.[118]

George Fox the Younger in 1659 went further in challenging the authorities to submit evidence of Quaker insurrection and of any warlike manner: 'if we plot, prove it and we will suffer for it'. He also advised the army that it should 'feel a freedom . . . which convinces you of evil for the bearing of a carnal weapon': violence against the innocent, or excessive restraint of wrong-doers, was always unjustified.[119] As if to vindicate Fox the Younger, rumours about Quaker involvement in musters before Booth's own in August 1659 could not be proved. According to Blackwood, 'even the early [Lancashire and Cheshire] Quakers were not violent men [nor] were they social and political Radicals'.[120] This was illustrated by a bizarre

---

[113] Brock, *Pacifism to 1914: an Overview*, 17.

[114] Fox and John Stubbs (?), *For the King* (1660?), 2.

[115] Peters, *Print Culture*, 225 mentions a 'plot' concocted by the Leveller John Wildman at whose initial meetings George Bishop and Anthony Pearson were present. She relies here on Gardiner, *Commonwealth and Protectorate*, iii. 211-13 but the evidence is, as usual, sketchy.

[116] Hill, *The Experience of Defeat*, 136. See letter (20/April/1660) from Woods to Lord Chancellor Hyde in which the correspondent, referring to Lambert's muster, noted that it was the first time 'any of the considerable Quakers have joined with Lambert'. See *Clarendon*, iii, 730.

[117] Spalding (ed.), 511.

[118] Sachse (ed.), 142; Samuel Pepys (1633-1703); see Latham (ed.), 230.

[119] Fox (the Younger), *A Few Plain Words*, 1-6; Fell, *This was given to Major-General Harrison*, 7.

[120] Blackwood, *The Lancashire Gentry*, 76; *Cambridge*, i., 343, 460.

Chapter 12: 'Dwell in that which Leads into Peace'

but probably effective demonstration, perhaps a 'sign', by the Quaker, Robert Widders. Riding among the ranks of Booth's army in Cheshire, he admonished them as heathens for resorting to physical violence while reassuring them the Lord would break them to pieces with his rod of iron.[121] At the end of the 1650s the Quakers in Cheshire actively supported the well-known John Bradshaw, a leading anti-militarist.[122] In short, the 'Quaker fear' of 1659/60 was a whipped up story, a deception like the Popish Fear (1641) and the Popish Plot (1678).[123]

However, according to a local historian, P. Clarke, there may have been a 'minor category of fighting Quakers [in Westmorland in 1661] supposedly disowned by their peace-loving sect'.[124] This may help explain Howgill's concern in 1663 that some calling themselves Quakers were involved in the Kaber Rigg plot of that year. Anti-Quakers like Daniel Fleming, a Westmorland JP, were quick to seize the opportunity presented to them by this insignificant 'uprising' to publicly blame Independents and the Quakers in particular for their 'mischief': 'We have too many this part of the country joining upon that part of Lancashire where George Fox and most of his cubs are, and have been a long time kennelled'.[125] It seems that some local justices were quick to include,

> under the name of 'Quaker' every dissentient from their own religion except the papists. Westmorland was also full of Quakers who had been disowned by, or who has seceded, from the [Religious] Society of Friends for in those days of religious excitement men roamed rapidly from one religion to another.[126]

Though Richard Greaves lays emphasis on a Quaker leadership eschewing violence, incidents such as Kaber Rigg suggest the possibility of small and geographically isolated groups, either associated with the Friends or

---

[121] Anne Cleaton, letter (5/March/1655/6) to Fell, *SW*/i/380 and Bittle, *James Nayler*, 90-1.
[122] John Bradshaw, a friend of Judge Thomas Fell (1598-1658), Vice-Chancellor of the Dutchy Court of Westminster. Sanders, 'The Quakers in Cheshire during the Protectorate' quoted in Morrill, *Cheshire 1630-1660*, 227. Also A. Parker, letter (7/Aug/1660) to Fox, *SW*/iii/145 in which Parker writes, 'two more Friends have been imprisoned on the charge of going with some of Lambert's soldiers to take some men, after that [Royalist] George Booth's [Cheshire] party was routed . . . I look upon it to be better by much to be passive than active in such a case as this'.
[123] Morrill, *Cheshire 1630-1660*, 322.
[124] See also P. Clarke, 'The Sectarian 'Threat', 165.
[125] *Ibid.*, 170.
[126] Anon, *The History of Westmorland*, 220-4; *FF*, 215-16. Kunze, 'Religious Authority', 172 (5*n*) is also convinced the Friends were not involved. Kaber (or Kipper) Rigg is a moorland area in northern Yorkshire. The plot is also known as the Northern Plot or locally as the Farnley Wood Plot. See Hopper, 'The Farnley Wood Plot', *passim*.

containing convinced Quakers, joining violent uprisings.[127] By 1663, he wrote, Quaker leaders had still failed to persuade all their followers that conspiracy and fighting were wrong. However, Greaves could only mention six Friends who may have been indirectly involved with the plot. Hopper, the historian of Kaber Rigg, provides a detailed account of the muster but makes no mention of Quaker involvement. Despite the lack of evidence, then, and yet mindful of Howgill's and Fox's concern, it is reasonable to suppose that any Friend involved in such activity could not have fully understood convincement and its implications, the adherence of the movement and its leadership to the Kingdom or the meaning of the Pentecost-Paracletal experience of 1659-61 which is discussed in the next chapter.

What, then, of Quakers in the army and local militias? We know a small number of Quakers were still enlisted in the army in 1658-9, but again there is no evidence that they promoted or were the cause of injury to human life. And while, again, a small number joined the militias in England during 1659, the vast majority did not. In fact, there were probably only nine such known Friends and their precise role remains unknown.[128] Hardly a paragon of organisation, the militias, whose role was mainly administrative, had not fired a shot since the first civil war of 1642-5. Quaker involvement in military action or insurrection of any kind was therefore minimal, indeed infinitesimal, compared to the overall number of Friends who maintained the Kingdom line and its Lamb's War.

Conclusion

The Friends regarded oppression and violence as the work of the Antichrist, a work that withheld salvation from England, its governments and individuals. Persecution was also spiritually demeaning for their 'oppressors' and it separated them from God. The cessation of oppression and violence would bring the peace of the Spirit to the nations and to its rulers. The Quakers continually demanded that the magistracy should exercise lawful force only, that such force should be tempered at all times with fairness and restraint, something mentioned on page five of the Fox-Hubberthorne declaration. 'Sword' was used as a metaphor for civil authority, the right implementation of justice. Its use, they said, should conform at all times to the Kingdom, the Jesus Way.

Importantly, the army cannot be equated with today's professional forces. In various parts of the country, for example, it was heavily involved

---

[127] See his *Enemies Under His Feet*, 86; *Deliver us from Evil*, 176-77, 201 and also Greaves and Zaller, *Biographical Dictionary*, 68.
[128] Cole, *The Quakers and Politics*, 142-3. See also Barbour, 'The 'Lamb's War'', 146.

Chapter 12: 'Dwell in that which Leads into Peace'

in civil administration and policing activity. Fixed garrison commanders were at times active in local and county government. They were generally supported *because* they might have been the only effective means of civil authority, something which may help explain the interaction and co-operation, rather than any alliance, between the military and the people including Quakers. However, irrespective of police action, the Friends, like the Baptists, never countenanced war which was, of course, the army's principal *raison d'être*.

And who exactly *was* a Quaker? It was not always easy to know without a formal membership which emerged in the eighteenth century. There was much hopping between sectaries and denominations during the 1650s and we saw how 'Quaker' was often used pejoratively. Were there Friends in the military? Yes: while some had fought in the civil wars—Craig Horle mentions 'at least ninety Quaker leaders' as veterans—others were still enlisted by 1660 but in very insignificant numbers, and while some historians have claimed 'many' enlisted Friends, we await conclusive evidence.[129]

This chapter has produced a selection of oft-repeated statements during the 1650s *against* the use of 'carnal' weaponry from a large number of sources going back to the very early 1650s (see Appendix 5). These corroborate the argument that violence was consistently regarded within the movement as contrary to the new covenant and a serious backsliding on the convincement process. And yet, despite their repeated protestations of nonviolence, the Friends continued to be accused of gun-running, spying and armed rebellion. These accusations continued spasmodically up to 1660 with the Venner rising and as late as 1663 with the Kaber Rigg plot. Yet, as far as we know, not one Friend shed the blood of another person. Clearly, the timbre of the movement during the decade was nonviolent with the Friends repeatedly emphasising that the Kingdom was to be spread by spiritual weapons only, by 'love and mercy' as Burrough said.[130]

---

[129] Horle, *The Quakers and the English Legal System*, 12; Cole, 'The Quakers and the English Revolution', 39; M. Hirst, *The Quakers in War and Peace*, 527-29. See *TLITC*, 122 in which Moore writes, 'Most Quaker soldiers were finally expelled from the army because their discipline was suspect, not because they objected to fighting'. Here Moore quotes Anon, *To the Generals, and Captains, Officers*, 6 but her assertion is impossible to prove. See also *SW*/iv/237 which contains a paper entitled, *A Testimony of Some of the Soldiers that were Turned Out of the Army who Owned Themselves to be Quakers, 1657*, signed by eight men claiming to be 'officers and soldiers'. Also Fox, *To the Council of Officers of the Army*, 2; Howgill, *To all you Commanders and Officers of the Army in Scotland, especially* (1657), 3; And Cole, *ibid.*, 14 and *Cambridge*, i., 308 for Fox's claim that army officers like one Lt. Foster were convinced and how Foster was one of those later 'turned out of the army for owning truth'.

[130] Nayler, 'The Examination of James Nayler' in *Works*. And see Appendix 3.

The Marxist school as a whole not only misunderstood the Quakers' use of apocalyptic, theophanous, anagogical and military language for stressing the case for the peaceable Kingdom but, crucially, their synthesis of the Good Old Cause and the 'true religion' of the Kingdom. Our exegesis of two tracts by Fox and Burrough and the two Burrough broadsides accentuates *the continuity of theological thinking* from the early days of the movement through to 1659 and beyond the Restoration as we shall see in Chapter 13—a consistency that rose above political events and to which the movement as a whole awoke during the critical Pentecost-type 'moment'. The 'moment' will also be explored in the next chapter. The 'true' army, 'true' sword, 'true' blood, the 'true' invasion and the 'true' standard were of the Lamb with a message of peace, justice and compassion. It was a message enunciated for over seven years before the advent of the three declarations of 1659-61 and which would be a defence against the 'heathens' kingdom symbolised as it was by the various forms of popery in England, Irish popery, the Vatican, the European Catholic Powers and the Ottomans. It was a message evidenced by correspondence to parliamentarians and others in 1659, reflecting a position held throughout the 1650s that proclaimed the peaceful sovereignty of God that 'was come and coming'.[131]

---

[131] For Quaker correspondence to parliamentarians in 1659 see Schmidt, *Quaker Political Pamphlets, passim* but esp. 40-125, 263.

Chapter 13: *'Arise, Shine for Light is Come'*

- Testimony, Pentecost and the Kingdom -

The first Friends saw themselves as harbingers of an energetic and nonviolent revitalisation of the Jesus Way of the Kingdom which they were certain superseded the other imperfect variants of Christianity. And their own deep experience of rediscovering that Kingdom meant they were incapable of ignoring wider social, ecclesiastical and political events or the welfare of the people. Although profoundly disappointed over the political failure of the Good Old Cause and the reintroduction in 1660 of the monarchy, House of Lords and the Church of England, it was precisely their rediscovery on a corporate level of the Covenant of Peace that enabled the early Quakers to sustain their overall aim of offering the world the hope of a restored relationship with God.

They did so by means of a profound Pentecost-Paracletal 'moment'. Just as in Acts 15:7, where we see the original Pentecost as a Spirit-filled proclamation of the Word and the Kingdom, the Quakers' already existing Pentecostal beliefs and practice would be *more fully realised on a corporate level* during the period between Fox's illness at Reading in late summer 1659, the year of political chaos, and January 1661. The three declarations, published in this 'moment', may be understood as a tapestry of their 1650s experience of Kingdom and Testimony. They reflected the cosmological nature of their Pentecost and their witness as Paracletal for all time in a manner similar to Paul's soteriology in Romans.[1]

With their gospel of holism and inner-orientated spirituality, their devotion to the Jesus Way and their universal and cosmological vision expressed through their Lamb's War for salvation, the Quakers' response to the collapse of the republic (and thence the restored monarchy) was predominantly spiritual, as we saw in Chapter 12, with the political a secondary feature.[2] Here was a response that fired a determination to carry

---

[1] See Rom. 11: 25-36. Crudely, this is Paul's call to everybody, and especially the hardhearted, to open themselves to the Truth as preached by the remnant, the New Israel, who are unlocking the mystery of God's love and Kingdom.

[2] See Lloyd, *Quaker Social History*, 1-3, 40 and esp. chp. 3; Ingle, 'George Fox, Millenarian', 263 and *FF*, 57, 69, 73-4; R. Moore in *FFQ*, 261 draws a similar conclusion, pinpointing the differences between Barbour, Hill and Gwyn. She writes that the Quaker experience as taught by Fox should be understood holistically; if all people followed the Light this would inevitably affect the governance of the country. See also *AOTW*, 76, 73-81, 119; Sansbury, *The Restoration and the Quaker Peace Testimony*, 4. And L. Wilson, *Essays*

their understanding of the Gospel Way, indeed the Good Old Cause as it conformed to 'true religion', into the political reality of the Restoration and to suffer the consequences. Hence, while it may be legitimate to describe the early Quakers as 'the most radical of the Revolution sects', as Reay does, it is also important to stress their eagerness in continuing to act critically within the political-religious framework of British society *after* the Restoration, especially during the 1670s and 1680s when the Friends suffered severe persecution.[3] The early Quakers continued to be revolutionary because they were prepared to maintain their Kingdom focus.

Three Forms of Conflict

While the Friends adjusted themselves with considerable difficulty to their spiritually and psychologically fractured society, it is not surprising that such a stressful experience projected itself within their ranks as conflict. It did so despite their forging a 'remarkable coherence' (as Reay affirms) to their faith and practice.[4] But without conflict, Quakerism and its Testimony would never have arisen for three reasons:

1. Disillusionment with, and fear of, a life lived 'out of the Truth' was a signal for the individual to confront the Beast within. Its defeat gave power to an inner Second Coming, a saving state. This essentially was their convincement.

2. Fox's re-affirmation during 1659 of spiritual concerns over political activity within Quaker circles was designed to drive home his belief in the 'rule of the saints', a rule that made a mockery of trusting temporal events and powers. Those days were gone, he was saying, if indeed they ever really existed.[5] A new 'dawning day' had begun and was continuing to be proclaimed, a spiritual reality that was confident in its faith since Love, the Inward Light, was its foundation. Love alone would conquer all fear.[6] Better, therefore, to recognise the dawn that the death of the republic has

---

on the Quaker Vision of Gospel Order, 16 in which early Quakerism is described as a 'gestalt'. Also Kunze, *Margaret Fell* and 'Poore and in Necessity', 559-80.

[3] *QER*, 101 and esp. 101-11. See also Kirby, 'The Quakers' Efforts to Secure Civil and Religious Liberty', *passim*.

[4] *QER*, 12 but N. Smith disagrees: see his *Perfection Proclaimed*, 63. Also McDowell in Gill, 'Identities in Quaker Women's Writing 1652-60', 279 but esp. Gill's *The Women of Grub Street*, 12 and 270; Hobby, 'Come to Live a Preaching Life' in D'Monté and Pohl (eds.), 80-1.

[5] *Journal*, 357-9.

[6] See Fox and John Stubbs (?), *For the King*, 4; Fox, 'To Charles late proclaimed King', 4 in which Fox advises the King: 'be still and patient in the wisdom of the Lord, until that go over all, and to order with that.'

Chapter 13: 'Arise, Shine for Light is Come'

given and forge a constructive though not total accommodation with the new political *status quo*.

As Schmidt powerfully emphasises, the cornerstone of the Quaker pamphlets addressed to MPs and members of the army during the period of the restored Rump in 1659 was 'to proclaim and apply the central insights of Fox that had given rise to the movement' in the first place.[7] In response to the Marxist view that the Quakers' renunciation of 'carnal weaponry' was 'some sort of abandonment of radical fibre' comes David Scott's questioning of the post-1660 'decline' theory to which I have already alluded. Despite the conservative tone of York Quakerism during the 1650s, he says, its main distinguishing feature was a dogged

> but undemonstrative [and nonviolent] keeping of the faith and there is little to suggest that either the persecution of the 1660s or the meeting's increased emphasis on discipline from the 1670s stifled a spirit of radical exuberance among the city's Friends.[8]

It is reasonable to suggest, then, that the Lamb's War was carried forward by the Friends in York and its environs beyond 1660. Indeed Scott states that to see Restoration Quakerism as less interesting than 1650s Quakerism 'is to miss the point not only of Quakerism itself but of the place it occupies at the centre of our understanding of the English revolution as a whole'.[9] As asserted in Chapter 12, there was no retreat from political activity during or after 1661.[10]

Nor, as confirmed in Chapter 9, were early Quaker mysticism and holism suddenly discovered as a form of quietism after the Restoration. They had been present from the movement's beginnings and therefore could not constitute 'a doctrine of moral defeat, an escape from a too harsh reality, [or] a withdrawal from effective action on the level of everyday affairs'.[11] Such a view is amply demonstrated, among other incidences, by their continued agitation during the period 1660-80 for liberty of conscience and the eradication of tithing, campaigns that saw the imprisonment of 11,000 Quakers and the death, as we have seen, of another 243. Here was a testimony that continued well into the next century, though by then not as

---

[7] Schmidt, *Quaker Political Pamphlets*, 274.
[8] See D. Scott, *Quakerism in York*, 2, 32.
[9] Nuttall, 'George Fox as Pacifist', 8; Jonathan Scott, 'Radicalism and Restoration: The Shape of the Stuart Experience' (rev. art.), 453-67 and esp. 457. Gwyn in Dandelion *et al*, *Heaven on Earth*, 129-30; *TLITC*, 293. For Weddle see my 'Seventeenth Century Quaker Pacifism', 290-6 and for a critique of the Cole, Hill and Reay school see my *MOP*, chps. 2, 5.
[10] Reay, 'The Quakers, 1659', 195; Cole, *The Quakers and Politics*, 276, 283-4.
[11] Sabine, *The Works of Gerrard Winstanley*, 50.

vociferously.[12] All in all, the intensely religious Quakers were forging a different kind of politics, a different kind of revolution, based squarely on the values and practice of the Kingdom, on the Sermon on the Mount. The Quakers' devotion to the Kingdom was such that their readiness to be crucified for the gospel of Love may help explain their movement's different path to political involvement.

3. Conflict and suffering focussed the Friends on the welfare of others as Chapter 11 has shown. That Quaker poor relief appeared to be constructive rather than palliative suggests a greater degree of organisation than might otherwise have been the case if mere provision of charity were its driving force.[13] Helping people to help themselves involved, as today, complicated strategies as well as persistence and carefully worked out time frames. These would have inevitably encountered and/or generated problems which, in turn, may have intensified in an age of restricted communications, societal dislocation, political oppression and a culture of fear. Therefore, in their Jesus-like craving for a new religious paradigm, for a New Heaven and New Earth, it is hard to imagine a disinclination to answer the *world's* needs.[14] As a result, we reject any characterisation of the first Friends as the 'monks of the new bourgeois world' who sought isolation from the rest of society after the return of the monarchy.[15]

The Lamb's War was a battle for the right understanding of the Kingdom, indeed of Christianity itself, the most recognised and institutionalised form being underscored by premillennialism and 'apostasy'. According to the Friends, literalism was incorporated into Calvinistic fatalism while apostasy encapsulated the opinions of those 'out of the Life' who had failed to commit themselves to the salvation offered by the indwelling Light of Christ.[16] However, the Friends could not escape apostasy themselves. They were not immune from the Beast and were warned it would appear among them should they fail to keep to the Light of Christ and the Kingdom. The river of righteousness was as much the Quaker Rubicon as it was for others. In its denial, they repeatedly said, violence, war and disunity on both an internal and external plane were

---

[12] On p. 44 of 'Christian Dialogue', Freiday says nearly 500 died; it is not clear whether he means post-1660 or from 1656 when James Parnel died in Colchester.

[13] Lloyd, *Quaker Social History*, 40.

[14] Their desire for reconciliation between humanity and God contradicted Calvinism which taught that no such accommodation was possible. See Dodd, *The Parables of the Kingdom*, esp. 34. Arthur Roberts stresses a 'realising eschatology' but I here argue for both; see Roberts' review of *TLITC* in *Quaker History*, 60. And H. Smith, *The Time and Everlasting Rule from God*, 36, 70; J.G (John Gibson?), *The Ancient of Days is Come, passim*.

[15] For 'monks of the new bourgeois world' see Cole, *The Quakers and Politics*, 284.

[16] Fox, *A Word in the Behalf* (1660), 5; D. White, *A Lamentation unto this Nation* (1661), 3-5.

assured. Hence Fox's many reminders to his fellow Quakers, as far back as 1653, 1655, 1656 and indeed through the whole decade, to be watchful, to 'keep out of plots and bustling, and the arm of the flesh', to refrain from 'jangling', including any inclination towards physical conflict.[17]

Fox was well aware of the inner 'Babylon' in everybody, and his keen spiritual insight and sensitivity to others led him to perceive 'Ranterish' strains within the movement. 'The pearl in you come to know', he urged as a precaution. Apostate habits would dissipate in the camp of the Lord if the 'secret' or 'pearl'—the right apocalypse for those 'in the Life'—was revealed through the true second priesthood to the 'carnal' world.[18] Indeed, the reality of the 'pearl' being 'layen under the earth' gave potency to the hope already influencing their struggles for the Lamb's victory.[19]

Towards the end of 1659, long after the publication of *59 Particulars* in May, Fox concluded that crying up the Good Old Cause was now *passé*, a backward-looking exercise (refrain from 'jangling'). In all probability he came to believe that the political turn of events was a result of God's will or disfavour. Yet he may have had Jesus' refusal to join the Zealots in mind, an awareness that the Kingdom, being 'over all', could not be governed by human affairs or established by people without God's help.[20] Compared to the glory of the true restoration of the Jesus Way, any non-Quaker advocacy of the Good Old Cause and even a restored Stuart monarchy might have seemed petty, something else that may partly explain the Friends' speedy acceptance of the new political dispensation.

'A great travail in my spirit': Fox and Burrough, 1659

That the Quaker apocalypse and Kingdom, those disturbing undercurrents to the widespread premillennialism, should be launched into prominence between late 1659 and early 1661 as a corporate Pentecost-Paracletal experience also required the stimulus of external conflict. So it was that the

---

[17] Fox, Eps. 37 (1653) and 106 (1655) in *Works*, 7: 43-5, 108: the former is a very 'James' (the apostle)-type letter. See *Journal*, 357 and Ep. 4 (1652) in *LOGF*, 2 in which Fox, seven years before Reading, advises Friends that 'God is not the author of confusion but of peace. All jarrings, schisms and rents are out of the Spirit, for God hath tempered the body together'. In 1659 he may have been thinking of Mt. 13:20-21 as he worried about unclean spirits within the movement. See also his *(Here all may see, that) Justice*, passim. And my *MOP*, Appendix 4, for 67 early Quaker works listed under Salient Theme 1, 'Keeping to the Light of Christ'.

[18] *Pearl*, 5.

[19] *Ibid.*, 4. See Rev. 15:2 for victory ('over the Beast').

[20] This also meant keeping out of physical fighting. See M. Hirst, *The Quakers in Peace and War*, 57. Also *Journal* 356-7 for an important 1659 epistle by Fox to the movement to this effect. This epistle and another quoted on p. 358, and also found in *SW*/ii/103 and *Ellwood*, 200(2)-202(2), were forerunners to the three later declarations.

events leading up to, and including, the crisis of that intensely critical and dangerous period impacted momentously on the sensitive Quaker leadership. It did not stop there, for it carried through to the wider imagination of the Friends with their various experiences of political and social catastrophe.

In Chapter 11 mention was made of the return of the Rump on the political demise of Richard Cromwell in May 1659 and how the Radicals, including the Friends, saw a chance for reform. As they welcomed the recalled Rump and the new government under the Council of State, an upsurge in Quaker hopes gave rise to a flurry of tracts, petitions and deputations to parliament in favour of their usual demands, particularly an end to tithing and the repression they had suffered in the latter days of the Protectorate. Persecution subsequently eased and the Friends were invited to submit suitable names for service as JPs. It was at this point that Fox wrote to parliament, probably in June or July, with his list of fifty-nine recommendations.[21] The Friends hoped that out of turmoil would come peace and a major step towards the establishment of the Kingdom.

While it was too late for the unpublished broadsides mentioned in the previous chapter (events had overtaken them), elements from them subsequently found their way into three more of his publications.[22] The first, *To the Parliament . . . who are in place of Authority*, appeared on the 6th October. In it he urged parliament yet again to free the nation of 'bondage and captivity' and 'tyranny and oppression' by promulgating the principles of the Good Old Cause. The tract was anti-monarchical and a radical call for a 'just government' to be led by those who should enact it 'in all things pertaining to the Kingdom of Christ Jesus'.[23]

By November, this time in couple of published broadsides, *To the Parliament . . . at Westminster* (12th Nov) and *To the Present Assembly . . . at Westminster*, Burrough still retained some hope that the Rump would abolish tithes and usher in the Kingdom with its 'peace, truth and righteousness'. However, with political events moving rapidly it was not long before the Quakers and other Radicals realised the parliament's complete impotence in respect to their dreams. Tithes were not abolished and only a feeble declaration for religious toleration emerged. It was yet another disappointment at the hands of Mammon. As the weeks went by, the expectations expressed in *A Message to the Present Rulers of England* (1st Nov) for a government that would do justice to the Lamb were looking decidedly forlorn. Signs of Burrough's disillusionment are now much

---

[21] Fox, *59 Particulars, passim*.
[22] Burrough, *To the Parliament . . . at Westminster*, Bds.
[23] Burrough, *To the Parliament of the Common-wealth of England . . . who are in place of Authority*, 3.

clearer; the nation will be punished by God if injustice and wickedness persist, if the leaders continue fighting against the Lamb and the Kingdom.[24] Then in December the Men's Meeting endorsed what has been described within these pages as the Friends' first significant declaration of the 'moment' of Pentecost, *A Declaration . . . To the Present Distracted and Broken Nation of England*. Burrough incorporated much of his writing of the previous eight months into the tract, but his tone now reflected the change that was taking hold of the movement as a whole—a deeper awareness of their 1650s experience towards a corporate, eschatological understanding of the Kingdom.

Meanwhile, in late June a physically ill and deflated Fox had taken up residence in the Reading home of Quakers Thomas and Ann Curtis. His sickness meant a forced stay until October. The result was a rudderless movement; Fox, after all, had 'provided the main link between the centre and the regions'.[25] Information about the activities of various leading Friends who appeared to be enmeshed in the political imbroglio—Burrough (as we have seen), George Bishop, Francis Howgill, Richard Hubberthorne, Anthony Pearson, Isaac Penington, Thomas Salthouse and other lesser known Friends such as Esther Biddle—caused him some dismay.[26] Fox had attracted political Radicals to the Quaker cause, and he worried lest some were reversing the spiritual emphasis (he so repeatedly advised) in favour of the political. Evil, in other words, was likely to prevail if the movement in the new messianic age they were unfolding for humanity was persuaded to follow a 'carnal' political path. It would have been a deflection from the true faith: like Jesus, Fox entrusted all moral choices to the Reign of God.[27] The Kingdom could not be brought in by people alone.

At that moment, however, ill health meant Fox was in no position to influence affairs. Despite his pleas for unity within the movement, letters and tracts from a number of prominent Friends, particularly from the above, flew rapidly in the direction of the authorities.[28] Suspecting a collapsing interest in proposed Quaker governmental involvement and growing public opinion against it, leading Friends were also disputing support for Sir Henry Vane. Margaret Fell found herself in the middle, laying emphasis on the tribulations of the nation as a sign of inward chaos, a sign that the

---

[24] *Ibid.*, 14 and *A Message to the Present Rulers of England, passim*.
[25] *TLITC*, 170.
[26] For Biddle see Calkins, *Prophecy and Polemic*, 63-4. See also Bishop, *The Warnings of the Lord, passim* for letters during 1659 to Oliver and Richard Cromwell, parliament, the Army Council etc.
[27] See Coffey, *Grace: the Gift of the Holy Spirit*, 75-6.
[28] Sansbury, *The Restoration and the Quaker Peace Testimony*, 4; Fox, Ep.189 (15/Oct/1659) in *LOGF*, 69.

authorities should step in the way of God 'rather than those he cast out'.[29] But she, too, shared Fox's concern about the driven political activism of some Friends.

And yet both need not have worried. Though the number of Quaker pamphlets had indeed risen enormously from the previous year as Reay has said—approximately 90 were published in 1658 along with nearly 200 in 1659—those mentioning militancy and violence did so in *opposition to them*.[30] As Schmidt says, 'the authors dealt with political, economic and social matters insofar as they believed that these *created obstacles* to the proclamation and acceptance of their religious message.'[31] Schmidt's point is important because the upsurge in Quaker writings suggests a strong expectation that something profoundly spiritual was at work within the movement, an expectation expressing a theology that presaged hope rather than despair and defeat. Perhaps these were 'signs of [a] greater maturity' as Moore suggests.[32]

Fox's Reading episode is worth further examination. It has been described nebulously as his 'hour of darkness' or 'nervous breakdown'.[33] In the *Journal*, he remembered his ten-week sojourn as being 'under great sufferings and exercises and in a great travail in my spirit'. Certainly, he and the Quaker leadership had a vivid sense of grief over what might have occurred on the political level; Burrough's disappointment was palpable. And Fox well understood the movement's confusion over the next step in the drama, confusion reminiscent of the apostles before the original Pentecost. There are echoes here, too, of Paul's distress over the state of the Corinthian *ekklēsiai*, 'the gatherings in Jesus'.[34]

It is reasonable to suppose, therefore, that Fox feared a further outbreak of civil war, prolonged periods of anarchy as well as renewed persecution of the movement and perhaps even its scapegoating for any initiation of hostilities. After all, violence being normal for the times, the 1650s were marked by political and religious instability, army revolts and royalist

---

[29] For 1658 and 1659 works eschewing militancy or violence (approx. 80 and 200 respectively) see Runyon in *EQW*, 575 in both editions. And Leachman, *'From an Unruly Sect '*, 263. Also Burrough, *A Message to the Rulers of England*, 10; Fell, *To the General Council of Officers*, 7.

[30] See Anderdon, *God's Proclamation, passim*.

[31] Schmidt, *Quaker Religious Pamphlets*, viii; my emphasis.

[32] *TLITC*, 170.

[33] See *BQ*, 355; Graham, *War from a Quaker Point of View*, 38 refers to Fox's 'struggles'. Graham unnderstood 'the standard peace testimony' to have dated from Reading, but I disagree with this strict interpretation. Brayshaw sees Reading as one of Fox's 'psychic states' but these states cannot be separated from his mysticism; see *The Personality of George Fox*, 86-8. Along with Brayshaw, Gwyn in *AOTW*, 41 is nearer the truth with 'depression'. Also Hill, *The Experience of Defeat*, 10.

[34] For 'Corinthian *ekklēsia*': 1 Cor. 1:10; 3:3; 11:18.

uprisings in which some feared involvement by the 'papist' Quakers.[35] Fox mentions the chaotic political in-fighting among the country's leadership, its 'hypocrisy' and 'treachery' and, as already noted, hints that a number of Friends were betraying 'the Truth', perhaps a reference also to the few Quakers who may have accepted appointments as commissioners for the militia, including Curtis himself. Curtis was acting against Fox's wishes, and we can assume some tension in the household, which would not have aided Fox's delicate physical and spiritual state.

His illness possibly stemmed from the severe fever that stalked England during 1658 and 1659, perhaps a virulent form of influenza or pneumonia. Ergotism is another possibility or maybe a disease associated with salmonella or brucellosis, both of which were commonplace at the time. Whatever the cause, it resulted in Fox describing all such events in the darkest of terms. His language is ponderous with images of 'unclean spirits'.[36] While much else regarding Reading is unknown, the mystical Fox seemed to have experienced apophatically a 'way of affliction rather than mere depression or an "'hour of darkness'".[37] His account echoes Gethsemane, Jesus' trial before Pilate (Cromwell's acknowledgment of the Quakers' innocence) and the crucifixion mentioned twice in the more evocative text of the *Cambridge Journal* (1911).[38]

It is worth noting that in the seventeenth century 'travail' could mean physical and/or mental work associated with suffering, but also gaining knowledge in a subject through study. Fox, therefore, may have entered into a long period of biblical and prayerful reflection causing him to dwell not only on the state of the movement itself, and on the safety and welfare of his fellow Quakers, but perhaps on the all-important 'secret' inherent in his writings, sufferings, disputations and the various experiences with the authorities. He might have even composed some of his large *apologia*, The

---

[35] *Cambridge*, i., 340-1. The *Cambridge* is more explicit. Thinking possibly of Lm. 1:20, Fox continues to say that, 'strife was got uppermost in people that they were ready to sheath there swords in one another's bowels . . .'. See also Hayduk, *Hopeful Politics*, 239.

[36] *Journal*, 353-6; see 356 for the account of unclean spirits: 'the plagues of God were upon me'. See also *Cambridge*, i., 341-3 described as 'spiritual exercises at Reading' by Penney (ed., 1924), 176. For disease at this time see D. Hirst, 'Locating the 1650s' 375-6. Hirst writes: 'In 1658 the churchwardens of Dorchester [Kent] collected money to relieve "the calamity of extraordinary sicknesses in most part of the Nation"', a verdict confirmed by Brian Duppa [Bishop of Salisbury] outside London when he lamented 'this fatal autumn, no place can hold out'. The following year the parish clerk at Shrawardine [Shropshire] noted 'a time of great sickness and distresses in these parts and generally all the land over'. Zoonotic disease, i.e. from animals such as rats, was common. For ergotism in the seventeenth century see Matossian, 'Why the Quakers Quaked', *passim*.

[37] Holmer (ed.), esp. 218-21.

[38] *Cambridge*, i., 342-4, 346-8, 384.

Great Mystery, during this period.[39] As a result, it is possible his time at Reading provided much room for thought which led to a revitalising of his own Quakerism with fresh insights into the nature of the Kingdom and its promise of a New Heaven and New Earth for the movement and 'all people'.

Indeed, he may have undergone a recapitulation of the Quaker way that compelled him to declare, 'and so when I had travailed with the witness of God . . . [then] I came to have ease and the light {Power and Spirit} shone over all'.[40] He probably remembered the spiritual pain which led to his original religious enlightenment and yet, too, its joy. In 1647/8 he had had 'wonderful depths' opened to him 'beyond what can by words be declared' and he claimed to have received 'the Word of Wisdom, that opens all things', that he knew God 'but by revelation', and that he came 'to know the hidden unity in the Eternal Being'.[41] The impression gained from this account, and from the many spiritual testimonies of convincement extant from the 1650s, is of an emergence or journeying from darkness. Interestingly, 'travail' also had 'journey' as one of its stronger meanings.

It was about this time that Fox composed an epistle which again recognised the Kingdom as the pre-eminent concern of the Friends:

> All Friends everywhere . . . take heed to keep out of the powers of the earth that runs into the wars and fightings which make not for peace . . . and will not have the Kingdom . . . [And] the Just sets the one against another . . . [for] he that goes to help amongst them is from the Just in himself . . . [so] keep in the peace and the love and power of God and unity and love one another lest any go out and fall with the uncircumcised . . . [Therefore] have a Kingdom which has no end and fight for that with spiritual weapons . . . [and so] there gather men to war as many as you can and set up as many as you will with these weapons.[42]

Keeping 'out of the powers of the earth' was a plea to his fellow Friends to mind the sovereignty of God, a sovereignty that belied the slavery of the 'world', a sovereignty that upheld their freedom and which came only through the Spirit/Christ. This was a freedom from sin, passions and

---

[39] Comparison between Pilate and Cromwell has also been made by Gwyn, *The Covenant Crucified*, 171 and esp. 178 but in relation to Nayler. For *The Great Mystery* and Reading link see *EQW*, 290.
[40] *Cambridge*, i., 343; see esp. 343-7. Fox's parenthesis. See also Nickalls', 'Preface' in *Journal*, viii.
[41] *Ibid.*, 28; for 'Word of Wisdom' see 1 Cor. 12:8. See Chp. 5 for 'open'. For 'this hidden unity', Fox may have thought of Isa. 45:15.
[42] *Journal*, 358 and also in *SW*/ii/103.

Chapter 13: 'Arise, Shine for Light is Come'

pleasures, corruption, the Mosaic Law and the elemental spirits of which Paul speaks in Galatians 4:3.[43] To be free in this way guaranteed their status as sons and daughters of God, as warriors of the Word who were unfolding the Jesus Way of love, peace, justice, hope and the unity these brought.[44]

The Quaker Pentecost

After his battle with unclean spirits, again described in a typically apocalyptic manner, Fox emerged from Reading victorious as if reconvinced, but to a greater level of his being as the tenor of his writings suggest. 'The Lord is king over all the earth', he declared joyously and triumphantly in mid October in marked contrast to his recently debilitated physical and mental state, 'and Christ has all power in heaven and in the earth; and he is king of kings and Lord of lords, let him rule and reign in all your hearts by faith, and exalt him in the land, and in your assemblies'.[45]

Here was an apocalyptic message to the whole movement to enact the Kingdom in their hearts, among themselves and with all people. His undoubtedly new-found sense of urgency heralded yet another re-'discovery' of 'Jerusalem'. What he had written in 1657 when deliberating on the nature of his movement was no less true in 1659 for this particular Pentecostal *now* was also 'a time of waiting', 'a time of receiving' and

> a time of speaking; the Holy Ghost fell upon them, that they spoke the wonderful things of God (Ac.2:2-4) and these were they that were gathered together with one accord . . . and Christ commanded the assemblies that were met together, to wait for the Holy Ghost and the Power, not to depart, but to wait for the promise of the Father at Jerusalem. So the saints were not to forsake the assembling of themselves together, but to exhort one another, in as much as they saw the Day approaching (Heb. 10) . . . [And so I say] wait on the Lord, and be of good courage, and he will strengthen thy heart.[46]

Gwyn's assertion that 'the stance with which [Fox] emerged [from Reading] similarly testifies to his singular hope of a renewed Church' could equally apply to the Quaker movement.[47] The call of 'Jerusalem' or Zion was an

---

[43] Paul's elemental spirits = 'basic principles' under which it was possible to be in bondage.
[44] See the introduction to Ephesians (1:3-14) and the following: Lk. 2:29; Jn. 8: 34; Ac. 4:24; Rom. 8: 15; Gal. 4: 3, 7, 9 and 5:1; Tt. 3:3; Phm. 16; 2 Pet. 2: 1, 19; Jude 4; Rev. 6:10. See also Coffey, *Grace: the Gift of the Holy Spirit*, 211-12.
[45] Fox, Ep. 189 (15/Oct/1659) in *Works*, 7:179.
[46] Fox, *An Epistle to all People on the Earth*, 10. See also *Journal*, 367-70 for the reinvigorated Fox as an embodiment of the energy of the New Jerusalem.
[47] *AOTW*, 41.

inner climactic event whose logic signalled an outer need for gathering and again commanding the 'assemblies'. Fox's authority mirrored Paul's confident demand that the Corinthian assemblies should emulate him to secure a sure foundation.[48] And he seemed intent upon recreating Paul's concern (in Romans) for a unified vision of the whole Quaker community, the Seed of Abraham, with a divine purpose for humanity, an eschatological confirmation of God's promises to gather all peoples under the love of God, the Kingdom.[49] For the Quakers, then, renewal and re-energising were in the air, a renewal probably more easily realisable among the saints than Fox had anticipated, possibly due to the movement's 1658-9 publications (to which I have referred) which emphasised the priestly and the prophetic over outward militancy.

'And so in the Lord's power', he wrote, 'I came to London again' but this time transfigured like the hero of myth and of the sixty thousand Quaker faces, bursting to teach the lesson he had learned of the Life within him, the Life now renewed.[50] Such was his revitalised sense of purpose and depth of faith, it was as if the Spirit had returned again to these latter day disciples as the triumph of the Word. The Spirit seemed indeed to be moving in their corporate heart with the 1650s promise of the messianic age complete. The righteous were being vindicated in their new resurrection, in their heralding of the Kingdom, in their restoration of the true Israel with its guarantee of salvation. Put another way, the Second Coming as already present was now corporately vindicated, the present and future were bound together in an epiphany of Kingdom and Testimony realised collectively and for all the nations (see Amos 9). As with the post-Pentecost apostles, they were truly gathered together as at no other time in their short history. Like the Separatists of Firbank Fell, their waiting was over.[51]

Their Pentecost was giving greater depth and meaning to their 1650s experience, calling forth a new spiritual era and redefining time and place while also reversing ideas and events as did Jesus in the Sermon the Mount. It provided what modern theologians might call an *eschaton* moment. The need now was to broadcast their 'moment' to the world since they believed themselves to be very much in the world for all people. The Spirit that was in Jesus—like the Good Old Cause, he had been forsaken by the ungodly— was again forging its followers into a committed community of the

---

[48] We note here the corporate incarnation we find in Paul. See 1 Cor. 1: 1-4: 21 and esp. 4: 6 and Peat in Dandelion *et al*, *Heaven on Earth*, 239 and 63-5.
[49] See Crafton, 'Paul's Rhetorical Vision', 328.
[50] Joseph Campbell wrote, 'typically . . . the hero of myth [achieves] a world-historical macrocosmic triumph [and] brings back from his adventure the means for the regeneration of his society as a whole'. See Campbell, *The Hero with a Thousand Faces*, 20, 37-8.
[51] For 'they were truly gathered together as at no other time': Ac. 4: 6; 20:8.

Chapter 13: 'Arise, Shine for Light is Come'

Kingdom for the future of humanity: 'The Lord is king of all the earth', Fox cried triumphantly on 15th October,

> and Christ has all power in heaven and in the earth; and he is king of kings and lord of lords, let him rule and reign in all your hearts by faith, and exalt him in the land, and in your assemblies . . .'[52]

As with the author(s) of Revelation, Fox faced the twin challenges of disappointment and rallying the camp of the Lord. And yet, in the manner of the Lukan Jesus, his journey towards 'Jerusalem' gave the movement a catechesis of discipleship, the means by which they could link the stories of the previous decade into a coherent vision to secure a purposive path as sons and daughters of God, as a collective Messiah in unveiling God's justice and mercy. The leadership had already provided the theology for a tight corporate unity in anticipation of the passion of Jesus that they, too, would suffer[53]: 'there is a winter before the summer comes', Fox had again warned chillingly from Reading, again in mid October.[54]

After his visit to London ('New Jerusalem'), the Quaker Pentecost proper now unfolded with greater tempo. Between London and the end of 1660, Fox swept momentously through twenty counties, a considerable physical undertaking at the time.[55] Despite being detained in Lancaster Castle from June to October of that year, he covered England with a resurgent universal message—'keep you out of the changeable things, and there the Seed comes up'. By virtue of the efficient network of Friends' 'assemblies', this apocalyptic message of hope spread with new vigour and like wildfire throughout the whole movement as a *kerygma* of renewal.[56] The words he used at this time, with their implication of the Paracletal promise, were outwardly similar to those uttered many times before. Yet, at this moment they were, more precisely, a deeper reflection of the Light as a

---

[52] Fox, Ep. 189 (15/Oct/1659) in *LOGF*, 69-70.
[53] See Tiede, "The God Who Made the World!', 430-1. For Fox's sense of unconditionality see his 1659 epistle in the *Journal*, 358 also found in *SW*/ii/103.
[54] Fox, Ep. 189 (15/Oct/1659) in *LOGF*, 69-70. Fox, like Jesus, anticipated persecution.
[55] *Journal*, 361-93.
[56] See Fox, Ep. 181 (1659) in *LOGF*, 68. Between approximately October 1659 and 25th May 1660 (when the King landed in England), Fox twice visited London, by now the centre of the Friend's organisation and where, since *c.*1655, men Friends had held fortnightly Meetings for Business. He also visited nineteen counties: Norfolk, Suffolk, Essex, Huntingdon, Cambridge, Hampshire, Dorset, Somerset, Cornwall, Devon, Gloucester, Worcester, Leicester, Derbyshire, Nottinghamshire, Yorkshire, Lancashire, Westmorland and Cumberland. Fox also attended many Meetings including the larger General Meetings at Balby, Warmsworth, Skipton (all in Yorkshire) and Arnside in Westmorland. See *Journal*, 359-74.

living reality manifest among the saints.[57] Here was a speaking in tongues on the inner level. But also, it may be added, on the outer level because, by addressing the Jesus Way for a spiritually diverse multitude, the Friends, like Peter and the disciples in Acts 2:14-47, were re-energised into demonstrating its universality among the 'gentiles' ('all people'). And so, in *The Promise [the Kingdom] of God Proclaimed* (1660), Fox could indeed proclaim:

> the glory of the Lord is risen . . . and you will see and flow together . . . and the Lord God shall be your everlasting Light and the days of your mourning shall be ended.[58]

A little before this time, in his introduction to Fox's *The Great Mystery,* which he probably penned between August and October 1658, Edward Burrough also referred to the Paracletal nature of the Quaker movement during its foundation years, c.1647-52:

> In our diligent waiting and fear of his name, and hearkening to his word, we received often the pouring down of his spirit upon us, and the gift of God's holy eternal spirit as in the days of old, and our hearts were made glad, and our tongues loosened, and our mouths opened, and we spoke with new tongues . . . And much more might be declared hereof . . . of the several and particular operations and manifestations of the everlasting spirit that was given to us, and revealed in us.[59]

That Burrough wrote this passage probably late in 1659 (five or six months after his trip to Dunkirk) is significant and should not only be seen in the context of his writings during that year—in it he again outlines a nonviolent position—and the quickening among his fellow Friends as to their own Upper Room experience (Ac.1:12-26). Note the fusion of expectancy and the Paracletal reference as apocalyptic ('revealed in us'). Here Burrough was speaking for all Quakers as they began to look to the future with foresight. There was yet a great and glorious job to be done, he was saying in effect, a new spiritual awakening to set in motion with its special language and politics to impart to the whole world. Consequently, in an intense collective awakening to the cosmological reality of apocalypse and its Kingdom worldview, *the whole flock of God everywhere*—the 1660 title of an Ambrose Rigge pamphlet—were now able to concentrate their entire

---

[57] *Ibid.,* 357, 361-2.
[58] Fox, *The Promise of God Proclaimed* (1660), Bds., col. 1 and Swete, *The Holy Spirit in the New Testament*, 72-4.
[59] Burrough, 'Epistle to the Reader', *The Great Mystery*, unnumbered pp. 9-10; see also Burnyeat, 'An Account of John Burnyeat's Convincement' in *Works*, 11-12. And Mt. 10:26.

Chapter 13: 'Arise, Shine for Light is Come'

experience of the 1650s towards the mission and 'trial' ahead, an ordeal that would test their faith, just as *his* passion and trial had tested the faith of Jesus.[60]

As people of a new Pentecost, the Friends understood themselves collectively to be powerfully commanded by the Light to be a city set upon a hill (Mt. 5:14), the latest expression of God's promise, the unified body of a New Israel with a timeless vision and voice. Timelessness did not mean being devoid of temporal meaning for Penington wrote in February 1660:

> The ... work of reformation is begun by that power which is able to carry it on, and that which now stands in the way thereof will be overturned. And although the cause and work of reformation may justly become a reproach, yet the foundation of reformation which God has laid is glorious.[61]

They also saw themselves as a 'Light to the gentiles', crashing through the boundaries of time and space to turn the world's eyes to the Light of God, a world blinded by the Beasts, the Antichrists of ignorance, vanity, greed and war (Jn. 12:40).[62] From a period of Gethsemane, that period of disillusionment and confusion, the 'despised remnant' (another apocalyptic allusion) was now a people of resurrection, returnees from the exile of the recent catastrophes in a way similar to the Israelites' homecoming from Babylon and the disciples' Paracletal homecoming after the death of Jesus. For this reason, Dorothy White's address to the parliament during these months contained the prophet's theophanous warning that looked beyond the immediate political horizon: 'the time cometh that a day of quaking shall pass over all that have not yet known quaking'.[63] Even the heavens should take note! Here was a spiritual restoration—the true restoration, that of the Kingdom—burdening itself with the task of bringing the messianic hope of the new covenant to a higher spiritual and *political* awareness.

Pentecostal Hope: Victory not Defeat

Sensing a profound change was happening, the General Meeting at Skipton in Yorkshire on 25th April, 1660, in tones reminiscent of Isaiah 12:6 ('shout

---

[60] Rigge, *To the Whole Flock of God Everywhere* (1660), 1-2, 4.
[61] Penington, *Some Considerations Proposed ... Distracted Nation* (1659), Bds., col. 2.
[62] Munck, *The Acts of the Apostles*, 14; Pannenberg, *Theology and the Kingdom of God*, 52-4. And see Fox-Hubberthorne *et al*, *A Declaration from the Harmless*, 3. For a 'Light to the Gentiles' see Fox-Hubberthorne, *ibid.*, 5; *Pearl*, 2; H. Smith, *Idolatry Declared Against* (1658), 2.
[63] D. White, *This to be Delivered* (1659). Thomason has no day or month of publication.

aloud and sing for joy, O royal Zion'), celebrated their movement's new vision of a resurrected and future hope:

> Arise... everyone to the ministry yourselves which is the Seed, Christ; for England is as a family of prophets which must spread over all the nations, as a garden of plants and the place where the pearl is found which must enrich all nations with the heavenly treasures, out of which shall the waters of life flow and water all the thirsty ground; and out of which nations and dominions must go the spiritually weaponed and armed men to fight and conquer all nations and bring them to the nation of God, that the Lord may be known to be the living God of nations, and his Son to reign and his people [to be] one'.[64]

'His people' were 'chosen' to be the New Israel, a living spiritual Kingdom. This apocalyptic and eschatological call was a recognition of just how revitalised their spiritual warfare was in this moment of Pentecost. The General Meeting's call was probably influenced by Fox's *To All the Nations Under the Whole Heavens* but especially his *The Promise of God Proclaimed*. Both were typical of the exalted, triumphal tone and global outreach of works he published during this period. In *The Promise* we see him calling upon the whole world to 'Arise' and

> shine for Light is come... and you shall break forth on the right hand and on the left, and your seed shall inherit the gentiles and the desolate cities shall be inhabited, Isa 54 [3] mark, the gentiles shall inherit the seed, and so become heirs, and this is the covenant said the Lord God that lives for ever, my spirit that is upon thee.[65]

Now refreshed and united as never before, the Friends knew the God who had been lost to them was now found; humanity's 'dark inventions' had been conquered.[66] The future beckoned, a renewed Pentecostal-Paracletal hope could be 'sound[ed] forth' to rejoice in 'the living God for evermore'. Josiah Coale called on all who were hungry and thirsty to join the Friends in their Kingdom adventure: 'the Fountain of Life is opened', the 'Everlasting fold of Rest' beckons, the 'Everlasting Covenant of Light,

---

[64] *Second*, 351. See *Journal*, 386 for the same triumphalist language in an epistle from Lancaster a little later in 1660: '... for God hath a mighty work and hand therein. And he will yet change again until that come up which must reign; and in vain shall powers and armies withstand the Lord, for his determined work shall come to pass'. Fox seems to refer here to Jer. 25:12, 27:8; Mt. 24:6 and Lk. 21:9.

[65] See *Promise of God Proclaimed* (1660), Bds.; *To All the Nations Under the Whole Heavens*, 5.

[66] Fox, *Truths Triumph in the Eternal Power*, title pg.

Chapter 13: 'Arise, Shine for Light is Come'

Life and Peace' in which they may dwell awaits, and all because the 'Everlasting God of Jacob' has 'arisen in this day of his Power'. Thomas Taylor also saw a 'faithful God' arising whose 'appearance [was] like the sun'. William Smith witnessed a God who was 'raising his seed in his own time'. Uninhibited in praying aloud, he celebrated the everlasting Kingdom: 'O thou holy righteous Seed, thy day is come, thy day is come . . . thou glorious birth . . . everlasting glory and endless dominion for ever'.[67] There was to be no retreat for a flock that sensed the Seed arising in them collectively 'to grow and multiply [so wrote Humphry Wollrich] as the stars in the firmament, and as the sands in the seashore without number'—but only if their unity mirrored the 'first and the last, the alpha and omega, the beginning and the end'.[68] Their regenerated understanding was of the Life indestructible like that of Jesus and Melchizedek, both in whose eternal priesthood they felt immersed as a miracle in the Spirit.

As with many others in the movement, Richard Hubberthorne came to appreciate how the followers of the inward Christ now 'had ample leeway to fashion their own new world'.[69] At this point the Friends' prophetic hope was confirmed in its relationship *with* apocalypse rather than being replaced by it. In other words, their view of the Life led to an optimistic, albeit realistic, appreciation of *humanity's* direction into the new world of the Kingdom, unlike the followers, say, of Second Isaiah or even the Ranters of their own day who retreated (like the Essenes) into an *other-worldly* apocalypse. 'In the belief of the light', assured Penington, 'and in the fear placed in the heart, there springs up a hope, a living hope, in the living principle, which hath manifested itself, and begun to work'.[70]

Penington's crystallisation of their Pentecostal-Paracletal experience, the resurrected hope already mentioned, underlined that 'something' of clear significance had indeed occurred as at the first Pentecost. With a greater intensity and a refocussing of the Light, fear and confusion seemed to vanish among the Quaker leadership and a powerful sense of fellowship in the Spirit was given birth. In their reading of First Isaiah, the Friends felt themselves newly anointed like Cyrus with a hope that would sustain the true restoration of Israel, that grandiose cosmic order under the sovereignty of God.[71]

---

[67] Coale, *An Invitation of Love* (1660), 3-4; Thomas Taylor, *A Testimony for the Lord God* (1660), 1, 14; W. Smith, *A Short Testimony* (1660), 12-13.

[68] Wollrich, *The Unlimited God* (1659), 22, 12; H. Smith, *To all that want Peace with God* (1660), 13.

[69] Ingle, 'Richard Hubberthorne and History: the Crisis of 1659', 190.

[70] Penington, *The Scattered Sheep Sought After* in *Works*, i. (1995), 127.

[71] See Isa. 44:28, 45:1, 48: 9-12, 52:7-8. Braithwaite refers to the Pentecost-type nature of early Quakerism only in passing, thus missing the full implication of any such experience for 1659-61 and beyond; see *BQ*, 514.

So it was that this promissory message with its sense of ultimate, universal purpose and direction was carried by Fox to Friends from late 1659 to January 1661. It was a precursor to the three declarations: it was fully contained in them and lent insight to the movement as a whole so that the Friends may see how the promise of God's compassion and forgiving grace for all humanity was now being reaffirmed through them.[72] To this end, Fox-Hubberthorne quoted John 6:45 where the Jews (i.e. the Puritans/authorities) were offered another opportunity to accept the risen Lord now alive in the current realising of the Jesus Way. The unfolding Pentecost, and the three declarations that encapsulated it, including Burrough's introduction to *The Great Mystery*, constituted the point at which the Kingdom character of the movement broke free of chronological time into Eternity, indeed as if to rejoice in that 'intersection of time with the timeless', as the poet T. S. Eliot described the incarnation. Thus, as in Ephesians 6:18 and Revelation 1:8, Quaker perseverance and patience coalesced, with the result that the restrictions of time and space were rendered forever impotent.[73] The theologian Paul Tillich's words are true for the early Quaker Pentecost as they are for our own times. For the Friends,

> the Christ [was] not an isolated event which happened once upon a time; [it was] the power of the New Being, preparing [its] decisive manifestation in Jesus as the Christ in all preceding history and acknowledging [itself] in all subsequent history.[74]

The unconditional character of their Pentecost to time and space, and their sometimes dangerous witness for the Kingdom, suggest that the pre-Restoration Friends neither desired 'survival' nor 'self-preservation' in the secular sense that Barry Reay suggests. Nor did they reflect a philosophy of hope emphasising the present only.[75] Instead, the Pentecost gave authority to their preservation of the true Israel for all humanity in any age; 'refreshing it in time, up to God, out of time, through time', so Fox had said in *To All that would Know*.[76] Although Ball in his *A Great Expectation*

---

[72] *Journal*, 386; *LOGF*, 65-70; Fell *et al*, *A Declaration and an Information*, 7.

[73] Fox, *An Epistle to all People on the Earth*, 10-11. See also Sleeper, 'Christ's Coming and Christian Living', 133-9. And Burrough, 'Epistle to the Reader', *The Great Mystery*, unnumbered p.11 in which he writes, 'not with weapons that are carnal, but by the sword that goes out of [Jesus'] mouth (Rev. 2:16; 19:21), which shall slay the wicked, and cut them to pieces'. See Eliot, 'The Eagle soars in the summit of Heaven' in *Collected Poems*, 161.

[74] Tillich, 'Existence and the Christ' in *Systematic Theology*, ii (1957) quoted in Brinton, *Ethical Mysticism*, 30-1.

[75] *QER*, 35.

[76] *To All that would Know*, 4.

underestimates the role of the Kingdom in determining the Quakers' Lamb's War for radical social, ecclesiastical and political change, he nevertheless maintains that the eschatological factor in early Quakerism was more than the fusion of both individual inspiration and collective and physical participation in the struggle for the Kingdom:

> This might have been sufficient to produce a narrow sectarian revolution with strong political overtones. It was not sufficient to initiate the Kingdom according to Quaker understanding. The Lamb's War was to be fought on the basis of an eschatological stress distinctive to Quakerism, and the war would be won and the final victory obtained only as that distinctive emphasis was communicated by the Friends to all people everywhere.[77]

Pentecostal Hope: Concluding Reflection

The events of 1659 to early 1661 gave rise to a more profound rediscovery of the Quaker 'pearl'—the Kingdom soul and ethos of the movement—the launching of which gave life to the 'things that were [after all] eternal'. The superficiality of Mammon was thus exposed again with the mystery of the Kingdom revealing itself apocalyptically. The depth of Quaker Testimony—its mystery or secret in the mystical and holistic sense already discussed—was not something adjacent to the daily life of their community but interwoven into it like the blood they were 'dear to lay down'.[78] This Pentecost-Paracletal 'moment' was to have profound implications. Through it Fox emerged physically reinvigorated and spiritually reawakened after a debilitating illness to inspire a movement demoralised over the failure of the republic and Good Old Cause, and perhaps even fearful that an imminent rule of the Saints as an *inner* reality would prove chimerical. However, out of their despair and disappointment, the sap of their inward life allowed them to 'rise atop', though not ignore, political events to devote time and energy to the greater reality of the Kingdom.

It was largely Fox's rediscovery and it alerted the Friends to the imperative of a collective engagement with the Beast so they may self-define in the light of spiritual incompleteness, but also to an understanding that a restored relationship with God was to be striven towards *as if nothing else mattered*. By taking hold finally of the Quaker imagination, the Pentecost-Paracletal experience—the Quaker apocalypse—acted as a catharsis ushering in a transformation (*metanoia*) as an intense, yet joyous,

---

[77] Ball, *A Great Expectation*, 201.
[78] John Collins, *The Apocalyptic Imagination*, 282-3.

collective experience. Hope, inherent in the imminence of an inner Second Coming, would be the keystone to the Quaker future.

Theirs was a Pentecost quickly consolidated in the material world by the network of settled Meetings and advantaged by regular intervisitation, preacher mobility and by two important features both of which enhanced the confidence of Friends as a collective—a growing structure of mutual support and excellent contacts with high authority affording the opportunity for mediating/negotiating the freedom of individual Friends.[79]

Burrough's declaration and the presentation of its Fell and Fox-Hubberthorne equivalents to Charles II need understanding, therefore, as outward signs of the Quaker Pentecost. Together, the declarations affirmed the nonviolent experience as an always dominant factor within the movement. Politically, any such pronouncements would have been prudent in view of the rampant rumours of Quaker violence, especially as a new political and constitutional era beckoned. But much more importantly, they expressed the belief—again, always present in the movement but unappreciated by the authorities and public at large—that the Quaker message had a universal and eschatological, rather than a particular, insular or even secular application. The declarations should be seen in this light, as a finished tapestry of Kingdom and Testimony, the weaving of which had proved spiritually, and, on occasions, physically traumatic. They also confirmed that Kingdom and Testimony would continue to develop and sustain the movement through a time of increased and systematic persecution. Further, they affirmed the Friends' contemplative, Kingdom nature rather than a suddenly 'adopted' political expediency and compromise. That is to say, rather than a knee-jerk reaction of accommodation and compromise so favoured by various historians, the declarations asseverated the deeper current of Quaker thought and spirituality at work during the 1650s. Famously, Fell wrote:

> We are a people that follow after those things that make for peace, love, and unity, it is our desire that others feet may walk in the same, and do deny and bear our testimony against all strife, and wars, and contentions that come from the lusts that war in the members, that war against the soul, which we wait for and watch for in all people, and love and desire the good of all; for no other cause but love to the souls of all people, have our sufferings been, . . .[80]

---

[79] Such speed of information—as if overnight—was demonstrated in 1663 when, hearing of the death of Burrough, the Friends nationally were suddenly engulfed in grief and panic.
[80] Fell *et al*, *A Declaration and an Information*, 7.

The three declarations—together Fox Hubberthorne and Fell mention 'testimony' ten times—were the outcome of a transformation that had proceeded throughout the decade to be sure but then to erupt at its end. It was a transformation resulting in a new-found sense of corporate self-confidence that would enable the Friends to engage with the world at a spiritually mature level. The declarations were neither a renunciation of the world nor a signal of defeat. Contained in Fell and Fox-Hubberthorne, for instance, are five references from John's Gospel which suggest the declarations were *the* vital means by which the Pentecost and its Paracletal hope was expressed—1:14; 6:45; 10:12-13; 16:13 and 18:36. That is, John retained a hope based on the experience of what Jesus the man had already achieved while proclaiming the hope that the risen Jesus was currently achieving.[81]

Post-Pentecost, the Friends saw themselves as a coherent, functioning example of how the Christ had come to teach the people and would continue to do so down the ages. Committing yet again to nonviolence, they yielded (again collectively) as a royal priesthood to Christ Jesus and, through each other, to the whole of humanity and to Truth. With fear and confusion gone, the movement focussed on a new beginning. It confidently proclaimed the Word was now indeed flesh (Jn. 1:14), a visible presence in their very carnal world, an unveiled sign of God's activity. But they knew themselves to be a remnant, too, mirroring the vulnerability of the 'babe' at Bethlehem and within themselves, and thus determined to teach by example in simplicity, love and trust. And it was as 'babes', as the sons and daughters of God, as the children of Light, that the Kingdom was now fully and unconditionally revealed.[82]

Therefore, as they assimilated the cosmological implications of their Pentecost, they engaged with the world on a wholly different level, sowing the seeds of Christian love for their spiritual progeny. What the Brazilian theologian Leonardo Boff wrote of the early Christians may apply equally to the first Friends. 'The primitive Church', Boff argues,

> was prophetic; it joyfully suffered torture and . . . It did not care about survival because it believed in the Lord's promise that guaranteed it would not fail. Success or failure, survival or extinction, was not a problem for the Church: it was a problem for God.[83]

---

[81] See Burge, The *Anointed Community*, 143.
[82] Mt. 11.25, 27 would have been important influences here.
[83] Boff, *Church: Charism and Power*, 50-1; Cole, *Quakers and Politics*, 284; Reay, 'The Quakers, 1659', 195. For Quaker concern about future generations of Friends, see the dying words of Francis Howgill in John Bolton *et al*, *A Short Account of the Latter End*, 5.

After Reading, Fox was like Peter after original Pentecost, 'pouring out his spirit to all mankind' (Ac. 2:17-21; Jl. 3:1). Another opportunity was now at hand for all people to hear the Word. The gift of eternal life had been available to everyone since the Friends arose as a people, but the movement had come to believe that the Light now shone with greater luminosity. Symbolically in Fox, and through him to others, it was a living reality, its very portability expressing a cosmological dimension which he might have seen in his much read Daniel: 'the saints of the most High shall receive the Kingdom, and possess the Kingdom for ever, for ever and ever'.[84]

The early Quaker global view prevented a pursuit of an eschatological finale because their apocalypse embraced the total sweep of history into Eternity. The salvation they envisaged for those 'out of the Life'—so that they may be *of* the Life—gave meaning to their endurance and survival as a community. By discovering a new beginning, just as the nation had done in a material sense, they looked with trust, humility and patience through the prism of the three declarations to a point beyond the 'carnal' of which they were very much a critical part. Defending their cherished beliefs and supporting those in need, their political involvement *increased* after the Restoration but was fortified by the post-Pentecost, regenerated spirituality and orthopraxis of their Kingdom and Testimony. Energised by a persistent projection of their hope, they began to record their dialogue with God so that it would carry down the aeons as an eschatological continuum. The Friends thus continued to advocate their radical, Christian universalist message of the Kingdom, a message that confronted the mainline Christian denominations of their day as it continues to do so in our own times.

---

[84] See Dn. 7:18, 22, 27 and *cf.* 4:13.

Epilogue: *Finding the Common Language*

- Kingdom and Testimony and its Universality -

We have described how the Quakers' faith and practice was born of an urgent desire to follow the Jesus Way in which the Sermon of the Mount was pivotal to their individual and corporate experience of Kingdom and Testimony. Just as Jesus sought renewal for Judaism, the early Friends pursued a similar path in regard to the Christianity as it was practiced in the British nations and internationally ('all people'). In doing so, we saw how they synthesised their own understanding of the Bible (and thus the Kingdom) and the Good Old Cause, thus giving both a different religious colouring as 'true religion'. It was a unique interpretation for the times and one sharply at odds with the military-political-ecclesiastical *status quo* in their fear-ridden and dysfunctional society. Their Lamb's War sought to turn the world upside down in the same spiritual sense as the Beatitudes. Indeed, when the Friends confronted the Westmorland clerics and JPs in 1653, it was already apparent that the very essence of the Quaker experience was not social, economic or political but Christ/Logos mystical: 'our habitation is with the Lord and our country is not of this world, neither are our conditions known unto the world for who[ever] had the power of truth was never known unto the world'.[1] Their theology was an orthopraxis; though not of the world they were certainly *in* the world and working towards its salvation, that is to say, its wholeness and unity in God.

Occupying centre stage in this salvific program was the Kingdom of God itself—or what today may be called the Rule or Presence of Love or the Covenant of Love or Peace despite Fox's rare use of the terminology of love itself.[2] While the cosmological Kingdom had always enjoyed independence of time and space, it was their 1650s experience culminating in a Pentecost-Paracletal 'moment' that had corporately unearthed this 'pearl' which had been long 'layen under the earth ... since the days of the apostles'. In their claim to have rediscovered the pearl for the world, the Friends were certain they ensured its voice for any age, a voice of redemption and wholeness leading to peace, justice and compassion on an inner level and their enactment on the outer through the Lamb's War.

Our encounters with early Quaker Testimony show how it emerged from continual rounds of inner and outer conflict, the 'pearl' of conciliation constantly revealing its Kingdom character. In their rough and ready times,

---

[1] Fox and Nayler *et al*, *Several Petitions Answered*, 4.
[2] T. C. Jones, *George Fox's Teaching*, 275.

the early Friends knew from Paul that the sword of Jesus inevitably brought division and conflict but that through the 'daily cross' reconciliation and redemptive wholeness were assured.[3] Early Quaker Thomas Ellwood's description of his estrangement from his father is one of many vivid illustrations of how family relationships were sometimes rent apart as individuals turned to the Light in their consciences. Joan Vokins recalled late in the century how 'for many years' she 'could not take comfort in husband, children, house or land or any visibles for want of the marriage union with the Lamb of God'.[4] This 'sword' set apart those who wished to build what twentieth century, US Friend Thomas Kelly called the Blessed Community, the Kingdom, from those who were indifferent to, or who feared and opposed, it.[5] Through the conflict of convincement, the early Friends escaped a spiritual prison to testify to what they believed was a living, challenging, advanced and mature Christianity rediscovered, as we have said, for the whole world and for all time, a refreshing of the early Church's Kingdom-centred message. As a result, they were prepared to risk everything for the Kingdom's spread, including their lives.

Fired within the crucible of conflict and oppression, Kingdom and Testimony meant a full apprehension of patience, unity and hope, all of which involved a complete and joyous giving over to God. Fundamentally, this rested on the quality of their worship. What was true for Quaker Wilfred Allott in 1945 was also true for the first Quakers: where the sacred was brought forth in prayer and worship, people and Meetings held together.[6] William Penn noted how the first generation of Friends waited *together* at their deepest levels in the Light and, in this way, brought forward 'the divine spring'.[7] They made the claim that inner strength would come from their vulnerability, a strength found through 'weakness'. Thus the maturation of Quaker Testimony went hand-in-hand with a humility that helped the movement labour through the dark maze of persecution in the patient expectation that the British nations and all humanity would eventually turn to the Light.

We have observed how their internal 'battle', from pride to humility, was in fact *necessary* for wholeness, a battle that inevitably entailed taking up the 'daily cross'. A British Friend, Eva Pinthus, has commented that,

---

[3] For 'sword of Jesus inevitably brought division and conflict': Heb. 4:12.
[4] Ellwood, *The History of the Life of Thomas Ellwood* (1714), 75-8. See also Henry Clark, *A Cloud of Witnesses*, 16 and Vokins, *Works*, 18.
[5] Kelly, *A Testament of Devotion*, 51-61.
[6] Allott, *Worship and Social Progress*, 14; Hodgkin, *Silent Worship*, 45-6.
[7] Allott, *ibid.*

The cross, among other things, shows us Jesus meeting and in the long run overcoming evil with a love that is willing to suffer to the very end. The cross is not so much a symbol of suffering as of redemptive love.[8]

At a time of widespread literalism and premillennialism and, on occasions, extreme violence, we saw how the nonviolent Lamb's War was the early Quakers' outward means by which the Kingdom would be spread. Paradoxically, they risked life and limb by publicly acknowledging that violence was no panacea for overcoming evil and that it was the antithesis of the Jesus Way. They exhorted their fellow Friends and others outside the movement, therefore, never to resist evil with evil.[9] More crucially, they believed such violence was a resistance to Truth and an affront to the Holy Spirit's work in the world. This conviction lay at the heart of Quaker Testimony, which was unveiled as fully matured during their Pentecost-Paracletal moment from October 1659 to January 1661.

The three important declarations of the same period—Burrough, Fell and Fox-Hubberthorne—were a tapestry of the Quakers' intense fourteen-year experience. With their contents understood as independent of space and time like the Kingdom itself, the declarations were not a sign of defeat as a number of historians have maintained particularly in relation to Fox-Hubberthorne. Rather, the Pentecost, which arose from confusion and despair comparable to that experienced by the post-Calvary disciples, revitalised the 'camp of the Lord'. The result was a Lamb's War of the 1650s carried into the following three decades as the Friends continued to impart their message and confront the authorities in the hope of furthering God's Kingdom.[10]

This dynamic of inner and external challenge (where they surrendered their pride and self-will to the Inward Light of the Christ) can be expected in any authentic expression of Testimony, in any historical period as it achieves and consolidates each new level of maturation into wholeness and perfection in the Light.[11] With this in mind, Testimony may be seen as a distillation of the Kingdom in its promulgation of Jesus' two commandments and the Sermon on the Mount. From this distillation have flowed a number of insights, values and activities I have grouped into four

---

[8] Pinthus, 'Shake All the Country', *FQ*, 386-8. See also *EQW*, 158.
[9] Hubberthorne, *The Antipathy betwixt Flesh and Spirit*, 4; Penington, *Somewhat Spoken*, 7-8 and see Fox, *The Law of God*, 3; *A Word in the Behalf of the King* (1660), 8-9; letter (n.d.) to Anon., *Headley MS.* (LRSF: MS. Box Q4/5 and in Portfolio 10/53), 38. See 12(*n*) below for salient theme 24.
[10] See London Yearly Meeting (of the RSF), *Who are the Friends of the People?* (c.1795), Bds.
[11] See my *GADOT* and *MOP* for a detailed account of the growth and development of Quaker Testimony in Apartheid South Africa, 1960-94.

inter-linked categories—'Faith and Worship', 'Theology and Christology', 'Practice within the Movement' and 'Practice outside the Movement'[12]:

Faith and Worship

1. **A Particular View of Prayer.** Their prayer took a number of distinct forms (e.g. silence and waiting, recitation, poetry, petitional) but was only effective, they maintained, when the prayer was authentic in her/his desire to work 'in' the Spirit and the Holy Kingdom, and to spread them. This prayer needed a firm foundation of humility, vulnerability ('strength through weakness'), perseverance and thus patience. Its essential elements were forgiveness and compassion.[13]

2. **Silence, Waiting and Listening.** The Logos/Christ- or Kingdom-mystical Friends waited upon God in silence in immediate communication, what today may be called 'holy obedience'. Out of their silences grew abilities in listening and discerning God's voice and purpose. Silence was their vehicle of true worship. 'Wait' denoted a dwelling in God, in the Light, as well as an 'anticipation', a readiness to act immediately for the 'Lord's sake', for the Kingdom and its righteousness/justice (*dikaiosýnē*). While the practice of worshipful silence threatened 'hireling priests', it also opened up the possibility of ready (experiential) access to the Lamb without intermediaries such as an infallible Scripture (so-called by the Calvinists/Puritans), an ordained priesthood, creeds,

---

[12] See *MOP*, Appendix 4, 363-78 for 1,286 citations from 212 original sources by 44 authors (mostly leading Quakers with 30+ titles to their name), all under 26 of their most salient Kingdom themes, 1652-61:
 1. Warning to Keep to the Light/to Christ; **2.** Corrupt officials; **3.** Concerning Equity, Truth and Justice; **4.** Concerning the Poor, Tyranny and Oppression; **5.** Concerning Violence/the Peaceable Intentions of Friends; **6.** Concerning the World's Riches as Dust/The Dangers of Material Wealth; **7.** Expressions of Love and Unity among the Friends); **8.** Affirmation of an Inner Spirituality; **9.** Suffering for God (usually in prison/visiting prisoners); **10.** Concerning Tithes, Oaths and a National Church; **11.** Concerning Liberty of Conscience; **12.** The Terrible Day of the Lord/the End-time; **13.** Concerning the Army's Reneging on the Good Old Cause; **14.** Judgments about, and Interactions with, other Churches/Sects; **15.** Plain Speech, Simplicity and Humility; **16.** Face-to-face Interaction with Authority/Letters to Authority; **17.** Words of Encouragement (generally); **18.** Hat Honour Controversy; **19.** Prison Sentences and Prison Conditions; **20.** Truth attacked by Corrupt Officials (priests, JPs, politicians) and the Law; **21.** God and Caesar; **22.** Appeals of Stay of Execution/No Revenge; **23.** Concerning Silence; **24.** Resist Not Evil with Evil; **25.** Equality of Women in Worship and Ministry; **26.** Provision for Sufferers (Friends and non-Friends).
[13] See, for instance, W. Smith, *A Manifestation of Prayer*, Bds.; Nayler, 'Concerning Worship' in *Love to the Lost*, 8-11; Britten, *Silent Meeting, a Wonder to the World, passim*.

dogma or other Church teachings. In the silence, God was 'no respecter of persons' and so all Friends, as members of the true Church of the Light, were spiritually equal before God; the Light in them was the same Light though it was given to each in his/her own measure. Silence and listening were also the bases of a distinct form of community governance (without voting) and the nurturing and testing of Leadings and Concerns. Trust in waiting upon God for discerning the ways of the Kingdom (rather than by consensus) was at the heart of this process. They expected the conduct of their movement's administration to replicate the Kingdom.

3. **Obedience** to the Spirit/Christ and to the demands of the Kingdom—especially discipleship—were hallmarks of the first Friends' faith and practice, what Rob Tucker called 'revolutionary faithfulness'.[14] They resembled the disciples after Jesus' death but also the Separatists and Seekers who had waited patiently, often worshipping in silence, over a considerable period of time in hope and trust for the messenger (or 'angel' as in Revelation) to lead them kerygmatically into the New Israel.[15] It was these people who witnessed the *ruach* of Fox's prophetic call and became Finders. Obedience meant the Friends self-proclaimed as a 'peculiar people', a living Kingdom, whose life on the spiritual edge (*eschaton*) placed them on the margins of society. From this standpoint they furthered (i) an incarnational ecclesiology in which they approached people by proactively entering the public space, (ii) a messianic spirituality by engaging in the Kingdom's politics of compassion and (iii) an apostolic leadership through their itinerant royal and prophetic priesthood, and their establishing of what I have called 'eschaton communities'.[16]

4. **Confidence in God**. They exhibited a total faith in, love for and commitment to God through a Christ/Logos-mysticism with Jesus and with Scripture as a supreme, though not 'infallible', guide. Their courage (that is to say, their outpouring of faith) was founded on their confidence in God as Love, together with their knowledge and experience of the Kingdom itself. Fidelity to the unchanging Kingdom meant they could not keep the Light, their ultimate authority, under a bushel. Warning non-Friends and opponents

---

[14] Tucker, 'Revolutionary Faithfulness', *passim*.
[15] See Rev. 11:15; 14: 6.
[16] See the work of Frost and Hirsch, *The Shaping of Things to Come*, 36-107 quoted in Cronshaw, 'The Shaping of Public Theology in Emerging Churches', 2-4. For 'peculiar people' see 1 Pet. 2: 9.

alike to keep to the Light/Christ—a message especially aimed at the authorities, the 'corrupt' or 'apostates' who were 'out of the Life'—was an essential theme of their writings. They hoped such people would turn to the Light and enlist in the Lamb's War for salvation for 'all people'. Their confidence in God was also the basis of warnings sent to fellow Quakers to hold fast to the Light and Kingdom values, particularly during times of persecution.

5. **Inward Security.** They joined the spiritual army of the Lamb to further the Kingdom for inward rather than outward security, for confronting the world with spiritual confidence rather than hiding from it. This security entailed a total giving over to God regardless of the circumstances. To become a Quaker meant donning the mantle of a conflicted person who trusted completely in God—battling a self-destructive ego (the Beast), outward evil and maintaining unity within the Friends by healing rifts among them if possible. Their weapons were not the outward sword, musket or pike. Still less were they bitterness, cynicism and hatred but sometimes a justifiable anger/indignation and a determination to establish righteousness/justice. These were fed by the fruits of the Kingdom (i.e. love, peace, justice, truth, joy and mercy), all of which were kept fresh by authentic prayer and worship. They believed strongly that there was no peace and justice without compassion.

6. **Apocalyptic Hope**. Out of their disillusionment with the temporal authorities and the failure of the Good Old Cause, came their Pentecost and an apocalyptic hope that bespoke a realised and realising eschatology, that is, 'Jesus was come and coming' 'to teach his people himself'. These went beyond the confines of the premillennial thought that was widespread at the time. Though the Friends were realistic about the human potential for evil, they were confident in the ultimate victory of Kingdom and Testimony in the 'fullness of time' over the dark world, the empire of evil. Hence, their Pentecost was universal, beyond time and space. They spoke of 'eternity' as in John's Gospel, sometimes equating it (like his term, 'eternal life') with God or the unchanging and everlasting Kingdom. The meaning of their Pentecost was bequeathed to subsequent generations and therefore was relevant to any age. Importantly, they internalised the imminent end of the world found in the Books of Daniel and Revelation. The End-time, being inner, signified the desire to usher in the new covenant, the Day of the Lord, by defeating the Beast within, eradicating the inner and outer

old Mosaic dispensation within as well as the traditions and practices of Calvinism and those of the 'apostate' mainstream Church. Their patience and perseverance in the face of persecution, and the way they sometimes put their bodies on the line for 'justice sake', meant a message of hope and confidence in the Kingdom, along with encouragements to fellow Friends often emerging from grim prison cells. Thus they were faithful to the true purpose of Apocalyptic, the rediscovery of the Kingdom and its spread upon earth 'as it is [also] in heaven'.

7. **Spiritual Renewal.** Like the primitive Jesus movement, they pursued a wholesale renewal of the British nations including the English Church, but also of the wider Church and the world at large. This renewal was given sign and symbol by their individual convincement, their unity as a worshipping community, their forging of individual and corporate Testimony out of a tripartite experience of conflict and their corporate Pentecostal-Paracletal 'moment'. This 'moment' gave a maturity to their understanding of the Kingdom and its unconditionality to time and space. It was the Kingdom, their unifying principle, through which they expressed a cohesiveness and essential identity as priests and prophets of the new covenant.

Theology and Christology

1. **Concentration on the Light of Christ.** The Friends never dissociated themselves from the historical Jesus as some of their opponents maintained, although for the most part the leadership avoided propositions about his nature. Details about his life were of less concern than faith in the spiritual and cosmological Jesus, the Light. To borrow the words of Walter Wink, they saw Jesus as 'numinously activating, religiously compelling and spiritually transformative'.[17] As their anchor, the physical Jesus was Love's most perfect exponent, he who, by means of the Spirit/Christ 'which was before the world was', gave the world and humanity the Kingdom of God. He was the truest guide to discipleship. The spiritual and cosmological Jesus was indeed God, whose gift to humanity was the unchanging Light in everybody. Though given in different measure to individuals, it was the same Light in all people. The Light was primary, their absolute Rule, the source of true experience, their final authority and the Kingdom within.

---

[17] Wink, 'The Myth of the Human Jesus' in Hedrick (ed.), 103.

2. **Present and Future Kingdom.** Much of their writings confirm a belief in the Kingdom 'now', as emphasised in Luke's Gospel, and to a lesser extent 'not yet'. Not merely future, the Kingdom and the Spirit/Christ who inspired it were ever-coming. Being 'patterns and examples', letting their lives speak, constituted the trope of the present yet emerging Kingdom (i.e. a realised eschatology).

3. **Salvation or Wholeness/Perfection** or, as one might say today, maturity in the Spirit, was the divine gift for 'all people' including those without knowledge of Jesus. Salvation did not depend on the atonement as the wider Church understood it. The atonement, internalised by the Friends as their convincement experience, affirmed their unity with God by crucifying sin and ignorance; it led to the resurrection of the Inward Light out of its darkness, its inner tomb. Their theology of the Light, their re-emphasising of the Jesus Way, gave each person a guide for living in the 'Life' (Kingdom), for using their creative power to love themselves and their neighbour as they loved God. Thus, through their rediscovery of the 'pearl' came the divine offer of universal redemption. Refusal would be the individual's own responsibility and foolish since it would result in needless and devastating separation from God. However, as we have seen, separation was not be confused with an irrevocable break since God always sought a healing unity with everybody in whom God in some measure resided.[18]

4. **Repentance and Suffering**. Their call to the cross, to repentance, to a coming together with and in God was in relation to individual and national transgression, to forgiveness and the need for transformation through a spiritual baptism into the New Israel. People were to be born again into Christ the Light (to be an Edenic person) in order to spread the Kingdom and its justice, peace and mercy. Only with repentance (transformation of thoughts and habits that prevent people from entering the Kingdom) could the good news of the Kingdom and the Sermon on the Mount be known. And only with the help of God's grace could this be accomplished. Their convincement, in convicting the Beast within so that they would 'come to know the working of the nature of Love', was the initial means of forging Testimony.[19] It was often harrowing and

---

[18] For sin as separation see Nayler (with Hubberthorne), *An Account from the Children*, 52. Also Angell, 'Universalising', 53.
[19] D. White, *An Epistle of Love*, 5.

tested the authenticity of their repentance. Repentance was also linked to deliverance from spiritual exile and from injustice in the guise of material poverty, ignorance and physical affliction. It involved returning to the Life, in living its potential, in being transfigured. In their suffering they respected the suffering of others. It was also a statement to the authorities that the 'poor', the 'innocence' or 'babes' (themselves and the actual poor, the victims of injustice) should not be afflicted. For these reasons, the Kingdom was no utopian prescription but one of *topia*, potential happiness for all people. Transformation, therefore, was concerned with both the secular and religious realms since the Friends believed that there could be no difference between orthodoxy (teaching) and orthopraxis (right living).

5. **The Jesus Way Revived**. In striving to replicate the Jesus Way, in absorbing the *halakhah* of Jesus, the Friends sought to live Matthew 5-7 literally and perfectly. Their theology and practice of the Kingdom was a head-on challenge to the mainline Christianity of their day to change its ways and return to the true Way of Jesus. Their charge that the Church had been 'in apostasy since the apostles' days' highlighted its neglect of the Kingdom through its many compromises with the State and the use of violence. Importantly, they accused the Church of attenuating Jesus' two great commandments and the Sermon on the Mount, of casuistry in no longer acknowledging the need for taking them literally. The Roman Church in particular was seen to be devoid of the Kingdom. It was the grand oppressor, the Antichrist, Babylon, the perpetrator of atrocities over the centuries, the ultimate outward Church. They were certain, therefore, that the Kingdom had disappeared from the wider Church and politics where previously it had been central to the Synoptic Gospels. Interestingly, this view is being increasingly adopted by modern theologians. Crucially, the Friends believed that the more people were estranged from the Kingdom their resulting lack of compassion grew in tandem with self-absorbed religious practices. As a result, any move away from the Kingdom was a step nearer the apostasy of which the Friends consistently warned, and to perpetrating oppression and violence. It was vital, then, to strive for inner and outer peace, justice and mercy/compassion in order to deepen the reign of the Christ within. The greater the Kingdom's assimilation into the lives of people and organisations the more likely that empathy and peace with others would develop.

Fox was not merely concerned with the nature of 'Church' but much more with the Church *as the inward and outward expression of the Kingdom*, of the Jesus Way and the unity this implied with God, each other and all humanity. The Church not 'built by hands' (Ac.17:24) came immediately into existence when three or more were gathered in Jesus' name. As they were temples of the Lord, 'the real' Church of the Kingdom would be portable while at the same time free of the burden of liturgies, dogmas, creeds and a murderous tradition. The Friends were pro-tradition in the way they looked back to primitive Christianity but anti-tradition in the way they rejected the Church (e.g. 'popery', the 'Norman yoke' and the Marian atrocities). They were anxious, desperate even, to re-focus ecclesiology onto the Kingdom and keen to create a tradition of their own in which the survival and victory of their message lay *only* in the Kingdom.

Practice within/outside the Movement

1. **Love of Each Other and Neighbours.** Intervisitation was not merely a 'visit' but an essential form of worship. Introducing visiting Friends was a sacramental act with cosmological import. The introduction (or self-introduction) of a visitor to the group was not only a matter of simple identification but a recognition of 'that of God' in him/her and therefore in and among themselves as a worshipping community. All being 'one of another', inter-visitation was a sacred undertaking and a form of 'publishing'. Forging unity and solidarity through their Meetings (whether big, small or isolated), their mutual support and accountability to a Monthly, General or Yearly Meeting, were all sacramental activities typical of the Kingdom, the same Kingdom for which they were willing to surrender 'freedom' in order to serve these eschaton communities.

2. **Coherence.** Though there were differing emphases in belief, the Friends possessed a theological coherence because the nature of the Kingdom was something upon which they could all agree.[20] It is often said among modern Friends that the first Quakers opposed theologising *per se* as indulging in mere 'notions'. This is incorrect: 'Any teaching or expounding of Scriptures *out of the Life*', wrote Penington, 'shuts up the Kingdom, for the life is the Kingdom'.[21] Their theological coherence was conveyed to the movement as a whole through intervisitation, epistles and tracts, accounts of debates and sufferings, mutual help, testimonies to deceased

---

[20] See Punshon, *Letter to a Universalist*, 16.
[21] Penington, *The Jew Outward*, 13; my emphasis.

Friends and an editorial policy administered by Fox, Fell and leading Friends such as Aldam, Bishop, Burrough and Dewsbury. The Quakers generally were willing to submit their manuscripts to these Public Friends: for this reason it is more accurate to emphasise their 'editorship' rather than 'censorship' of works during the 1650s in particular. The self-styled 'Publishers of the Truth' had a gift for publicity, the distribution of their literature and for evangelising. They used publications skilfully to propagate their theology in respect to the Kingdom *vis-à-vis* the authorities, government policies and long-held societal traditions such as tithing, the 'hat' and oaths.

3. **Righteousness and True Justice**. In their quest to establish the Kingdom, the Quakers understood righteousness ethically and in terms of justice. Their convicting of sin through convincement meant achieving justice for oneself (*dikaiosýnē*) and subsequently for one's neighbour before the 'throne' of God/Love (the conscience).[22] True justice was healing, tempered with mercy and joy and was thus salvific (Rom. 14:17). In the name of equity, truth and justice, the Friends addressed not only non-Quakers, including the 'corrupt' who were intent on persecuting the children of Light, but also the central authorities (army, parliament and individuals like the Cromwells). They did so in the hope that the British nations would return to the Good Old Cause, which guaranteed, *inter alia*, liberty of conscience, and that they would grasp the utter necessity of righteousness/justice. Their understanding of equity, truth and justice—all tempered with compassion—enriched the Cause turning it into a strategy of 'true religion' in their Lamb's War for the 'Covenant of Peace', the 'synthesis' we have mentioned.[23]

4. **Equality, Inclusiveness and the Wisdom Tradition**. True justice also implied the spiritual equality of all before God whether they were men or women, old or young, rich or poor, British or foreign. Fox's catechisms for children were carefully constructed to highlight the Inward Light and Kingdom but they also displayed his respect for the young as essentially equal in the Spirit to himself. In the Quaker's faith and practice there was no Calvinist-type 'Elect', no hierarchy in Christ. The true Elect were all those of any age, social rank or gender who lived continually in the Light of Christ,

---

[22] See Jamison, 'Dikaiosyne in the Usage of Paul', 94.
[23] For 'Covenant of Peace' see Fox, Eps. 63 (1654), 67 (1654), 106 (1655), 115 (1656) and 145 (1657), *Works*, 7: 60, 62, 86, 92 and 112 respectively.

who came 'to the Substance'. The Friends were particularly concerned for the poor in spirit and body. By stressing the possibility of wholeness and perfection in the 'now', the strong affiliation to the Wisdom tradition they also found in Proverbs 1:20-21 and 9:3 and in John's Gospel—'Wisdom has uttered forth her voice to you'[24]—allowed them to integrate the prophetic and Apocalyptic, Wisdom and eschatological hope with a concern for the afflicted. This tradition and its inclusiveness was a gift to the ages.[25] Their identification with Wisdom helped formulate an understanding of themselves as children of Light and, by implication, their appreciation of Mt. 11:19 (Lk. 7:35)—'Wisdom is justified of all her children'—as indeed a gift for 'all people'.[26]

5. **'Good Works' as Social Justice,** which grew out of a demonstrably profound knowledge of the Gospels, the Pauline Letters and the Letter of James, were seen as acts of prayer that empowered the poor in spirit and body. Consequently, the Friends advocated personal salvation and social redemption, protesting over the way the Kingdom had been stymied by corruption, apostasy and oppression. They issued warnings and correspondence to lawyers and clerics whom they believed were complicit in oppressing the poor. They also confronted those equally 'out of the Life' in the government and army—those considered to be in the old dispensation of the Mosaic Law—that they may accept the Light within. Good works were the outward building blocks of solidarity with the poor for spreading the Kingdom, that same Covenant of Peace that arose from what today may be called a 'grassroots' praxis of which they were an example. Its non-hierarchical nature knew only the Christ, the Inward Light, as its teacher, a teacher whose Gospel order would subvert the structures of domination and injustice.

6. **Plain Speech, Simplicity and Humility**. Since Fox and the Quaker leadership were concerned to forge a good name for the nascent movement, they issued warnings and exhortations to the authorities emphasising the honesty and reliability of their community. In regard to the Friends themselves, these took the form of warnings and urgings to maintain righteousness, to display a courageous

---

[24] Blackborow, *A Visit to the Spirit in Prison*, 7.
[25] For the inclusivity of the Jesus movement see Schüssler Fiorenza, *In Memory of Her*, chapter 4 and esp. 118-54.
[26] See above Chp. 10 and the Wisdom writings of Sarah Blackborow, Dorcas Dole and Judith Zinspenninck.

demeanour, and to lead a simple and innocent (pure) life. To non-Quakers in general they urged honesty in both trading and interpersonal relations, and that all may help the materially poor. By doing so they would experience the Light within themselves, which may then lead to enlisting in the army of the Lamb.[27] The Friends exercised a teaching and preaching ministry.

7. **The Three Declarations** that proclaimed nonviolence were theological works, prophetic and apocalyptic, as well as a tapestry of the 1650s experience of Kingdom and Testimony—*the* peace testimony. Together, Fox-Hubberthorne and Fell mention 'testimony' ten times. *Many* examples exist of other declarations that reiterated their oft-repeated mantra against carnal weaponry (see Appendix 5). The Friends were strong advocates of a nonviolent political, social and spiritual revolution that only the Kingdom could bring. Thus they were a danger to the apparatus of government and establishment. Rather than a 'peace principle', so-called by Christopher Hill, the peace *testimony* of the 1650s was a deeply held religious commitment unto death if need be, a commitment whose objective was unity with the loving God. The declarations had eschatological import and for this reason the Quakers were not defeated in 1659-60. Their nonviolence, the logic of the Kingdom, was an announcement that the Kingdom had already begun in the present.

8. **The Lamb's War** was a quest to enact the Kingdom and its Sermon (along with the Letter of James) in particular, to deliver the Light of Christ to the world. Love was more important than principles and it was to be incarnate in practice as Jesus had preached in Mt. 5-7. The Lamb's War was a nonviolent confrontation with 'empire' as this was expressed militarily, ecclesiastically and politically by way of social status, destructive economics and cultural tradition, including the language and praxis of secular power. Like Jesus, their revolution was of the Kingdom with its 'new' politics of compassion, justice and peace; it had socio-political outcomes that, equally, could not be violent.

    To ensure the success of their revolution they often employed shock tactics—church interruptions, public nakedness, refusal of hat honour, plain speech and other biblically inspired modes of expression.[28]

---

[27] See Bennett, 'Exalted in our Nation', 388.
[28] See also *MOP*, 215-16 and *GADOT*, 145-7.

At the root of the Lamb's War lay God's year of favour or Jubilee (Lev. 25:1-7, Dt. 15:1-11: Ex. 23:10-11 and Lk. 4:19), which proposed (according to Exodus) that in every seventh year slaves should be liberated, debts pardoned, employers honour their workers as free people (*cf*: Dt.15: 12-15), people recognise each other as brothers and sisters, and that land should be redistributed equally. And from Leviticus 28:8-16, leading Friends such as Fox, Parnel and Samuel Fisher would have read of the Jubilee year (each 50th year) in which land was to be returned to people and their families.

9. **Staunch Refusal to be Second Best.** The Friends were highly articulate about their living faith and its God-filled experience. The Kingdom demanded the full headline and centre stage. And they were never content to be footnotes to current dialogue or events.

10. **Rudimentary Ecumenism.** Despite an eventual (if wary) accommodation after mid 1659 with those of different opinions and practices, they were determined never to compromise their devotion to Jesus, their worship of the Light, their knowledge and understanding of the Kingdom or their belief that only through the Christ/Spirit 'that was before Jesus was' could salvation be realistically attained. The writings of second-generation Quakers (e.g. Robert Barclay and William Penn), while retaining the essential nature of Quaker ideas, attempted to draw on the common basis with other denominations in order to promote religious toleration and an end to the persecution of Friends.

Rediscovering the Core

It is the contention of this book that the Kingdom of God or Covenant of Love (or Peace) as it has come down to us through the early Friends is worthy of our close attention, whether we are Quaker or not. The Covenant can give rise to spiritual insights, provide a valuable focus for prayer, meditation and worship, sustain Leadings and Concerns and can help forge an agreed religious language that does not descend to a uniformity of thought or a specific ideology. It can assist people to enunciate healthy absolutes while promoting inquiry and inter-denominational and inter-faith dialogue; it cannot be exclusive to any one Christian tradition. Further, the Covenant of Love could lead all present-day Friends and others into a homecoming—a qualitative unity, purpose and flourishing.

Surprising though it may seem as we look back over 350 years, there is nothing outdated about early Quaker thinking in regard to these matters. Consequently, this book affirms that present-day Friends are not so much in possession of a 'history or 'story'—both can be set aside after all—but a *continuing theology* that recognises how their origins can help influence the present and future in positive ways. Indeed, we have confirmed that most beliefs and practices of contemporary Quakers derive from the unconditional nature and values of the Kingdom orthopraxis of their religious forebears. However, the late Howard Brinton offered a word of warning: 'The preservation of the original purpose', he wrote in 1953, 'is not the same as the preservation of the visible form in which that purpose was first expressed.' To revive the 'visible ways of primitive Quakerism', he continued, would be impossible and inappropriate, and yet 'to revive that which was at the heart of the original awakening and the original witness is to meet a need as old as humanity, yet still fresh, essential and new'.[29] We grow old but the hope that the Kingdom expresses remains forever young.

To romanticise the early Quakers or their ghastly times is ill-advised. Such a course prevents us from recognising their flaws of which we may recall a few. For instance, despite the fact that conflict in the three principal forms we have described gave rise to Testimony—conflict within individuals, among the Friends and externally from hostile forces—it is clear the movement failed to escape *unnecessary* discord with individuals and agencies outside their community, discord which belied their repeated advice to place disputation into the Light and let faith in the Love of the Christ/Spirit take its course. We saw how a legitimate use of the harsh language of Jesus and Paul did not prevent an often unreasonable and even abrasive position *vis-à-vis* non-Quakers. Furthermore, some of their works express highly prejudicial opinions about the Irish, Jews, Turks and most things foreign, opinions no different from those of the wider society. There was also an element of fantasy to their thinking, such as their attempts to convert the Sultan and the Pope, or attempts to replicate Jesus' healing miracles. Their assertion that everybody was equal before God was compromised by a general acceptance by Quaker men of the entrenched gender norms of their patriarchal environment, particularly in the face of what was, by the standards of their own Quakerism, an expectation by the women of the movement for equality on all levels.

Though perfectly understandable, their complete dismissal of mainline Christianity as apostate and their vehement opposition to every manner of popery whether Catholic or Protestant, prevented a meaningful appreciation of the wider Church's positive attributes, achievements and learning along with its mystical tradition. It thus denied them the company

---

[29] Brinton, *Friends for 300 Years,* p. vii.

of authoritative allies past and present in their struggle for a new spiritual dispensation, people with accessible works of their own which, in many aspects, were little different from their own. Here we mention John Everard's *Some Gospel-treasures* (1653) and Joannes Evangelista's *The Kingdom of God in the Soul* (1657), an uncannily Quakerish work highlighting the 'divine Light', unity in God, a process similar to convincement and a powerful emphasis on the Kingdom as within and spiritual.[30] And we must not forget the Cambridge Platonists who found some commonality with Quakerism.

And yet, for the Quakers it was a simple matter: 'they who are not with us are against us' and 'they that gathereth not with [us] scattereth abroad' (*cf*: Mt.12: 30). It was yet another contradiction since their message included reconciliation and unity for 'All People on the Earth'. Creative associations with like-minded thinkers, therefore, might have ensured a better platform for their views. Henry Denne, for instance, though a 'hireling priest', lent considerable support to the Quaker worldview. As far as we know, the Friends never acknowledged him.[31] And despite their reasonable complaints towards, and anger at, the established Church in England and the Puritans, they were also unwilling to concede ground in debates or in written communications with opponents in general. Fox's perfunctory, finger-wagging 'answer' to John Owen in *The Great Mistery* is a good example of how the Friends, even with sound arguments, could dismiss a fine and subtle mind.[32]

We have also seen how a political and ecclesiastical *naïveté* appeared on a number of fronts in the Lamb's War. The Quakers were over-critical of Oliver Cromwell and the various governments of the 1650s, failing to acknowledge the good they did. It was an attitude that backfired repeatedly as they closed their minds to lessons they may have learnt from the various authorities they confronted. Their fanatical desire to eradicate lawyers and the two universities was as irrational as their blanket condemnation of the clergy, many of whom displayed a deep concern and love for the people they served. Of course, some *naïveté* is understandable when one takes into account the lack of precedence among the general polity in drafting constitutional frameworks and measures for keeping the peace. Fox's *59 Particulars*, for example, which he addressed to the Parliament, could never have shared the same intellectual stage as proposals by Winstanley, Hobbes,

---

[30] See Everard's's *Some Gospel-treasures* (1653), 798. Evangelista was a Dutch Capuchin friar from s'Hertengobosch. His work was originally published in 1639.
[31] Henry Denne (1606/7-*c*.60), *The Quaker no Papist, passim*. See the debate between Denne, Thomas Smith, author of *The Quaker Disarm'd* (1659) and *A Gagg for the Quakers* (1659), and George Whitehead in Whitehead, *A Key of Knowledge* (1660). See Hammond, 'Thomas Smith', 180-94, esp.186-93 and Punshon, *Testimony and Tradition*, 53.
[32] Fox, *The Great Mistery*, 263-4.

Harrington, Baxter and Samuel Rutherford, the author of *Lex Rex* (1644), all of which were highly detailed and sophisticated for the times. At the same time, there is no need to suppose Fox's ideas in this matter were any less totalitarian than theirs; that the early Quakers displayed a certain authoritarianism is hard to deny.[33] In this vein, the early Friends were 'assassins of fun'; their religious worldview was overly serious with many frowns and harsh words aimed at those who saw laughter, dancing, sports and music as important to their lives.

Still, for all that, the early Friends saw their earnest witness to Kingdom and Testimony as an apocalyptic, salvific, priestly and prophetic experience that revealed the Light of Christ for 'all people'. This 1650s experience, *the peace testimony*, was a call for everybody to reveal and *live* the Holy Kingdom *as* salvation. The demands of the Covenant of Love ensured public notoriety and persecution as they gave a visibility to their faith through the 'daily cross' and to the inbreaking of God's sovereignty at a time of great suffering and spiritual discord in Britain. For their part, the three declaration*s* rendered historical reality transparent to the saving (holistic) activity of God and thus reached beyond time and space.

In their conduct of the Lamb's War, the early Friends saw direct connections between their suffering and that of the ancient prophets, of Jesus himself as well as those under the heel of oppression and deprivation as a result of civil war and cruel politico-ecclesiastical indifference. In confronting the harsh conditions of their day, including governmental persecution of periodic and varying intensity, and facing internal trials of fear, despair and loneliness, it is no surprise that a major feature of early Quakerism was its compassionate identification with the poor and those they believed were separated from God; they felt it deeply in their 'bowels'. This commitment to a developing understanding of social justice was itself 'a fundamental lesson' for others. From it sprang their conviction that nothing would be changed substantively by political (and violent) revolution, and that the juggernaut of injustice and other forms of evil, and its apparent invincibility, would be defeated only by the Life and Power of their rediscovered pearl, the Kingdom. Such sin—any sin—was a death-dealing social reality they felt called upon to eradicate because it spelt disunity between the people of God and between God and humanity.

Their devotion to the Rule of Love was a vocation, then, a total commitment, the guiding yet controlling purpose of their lives. It was also the outcome of their mystical oneness with God because, as the Rule of Love was perfect, so they too could be perfect. As they fell into sin, the Light and its Reign would diminish. At the heart of their constant plea that

---

[33] Winstanley, *The Law of Freedom, passim*; Samuel Rutherford (*c.*1600-61), *Lex Rex* (1644), *passim*.

the Friends' communities should pray together and be in unity was the fear that the Kingdom would fade along with its fruits and hope. This is precisely why in epistles to Friends, Fox repeatedly urged purity, that they be 'innocent' as Adam and Eve before the Fall, and that, in the words of the Scottish poet, Edwin Muir, they should dwell in 'the green springing corner of young Eden'.[34] As a continuum of hope, their devotion to the Reign of Love was a call to subsequent generations to give birth to an 'extraordinary work' (William Dewsbury, 1655) whose conception would be in the 'matrix of Eternity' (William Smith, 1661).

Consequently, the early Quaker understanding and experience of suffering was cosmological. This *Tao*, so to speak, with its flow and 'rightness', continued as they strove to make the Kingdom constantly operative. They did so by co-working with God to deprive destructive aggression of its power, by confronting structural violence that victimised the innocent, and by seeking and following paths that freed humans to encounter the 'secret' within themselves and others. In so doing, they distinguished between, on the one hand, a confused understanding of conscience and, on the other, the Light of Christ (and its saving wholeness) which *informed* the conscience. And their faith meant having no fear. This does not mean they were always unafraid of assault, prison and torture. Instead, they were convinced that threats of violence and personal privation, the idea of an infallible Bible or Church teaching, scepticism or a relativity of value and purpose could never ultimately harm them.

The first Friends' experience and propagation of the Kingdom incorporated the acceptance of a holy burden on two accounts. First, by discerning the mysteries of God in history (Dn. 2:18), that is to say the way of Truth encountered in revealed faith and continual revelation. And second, the application of these mysteries to the world with a view to its ultimate fulfilment in God and of God in humanity.[35] We saw that continual revelation was not an invention of the Quakers but something which became inlaid into their theology and cosmology. Being immersed in the Jesus Way, they were not anti-tradition as continual revelation can suggest to some. Instead, they used tradition creatively as the Light-filled source of their innovative thought and revolutionary practice. The Light, however, was not 'new' since it had existed before creation. It was the same for Truth. Key to this understanding was an enormous confidence in their original convincement and their discernment processes. Within them, they believed, were the keys to truth, to a diminution of internal conflict and henceforth to a growth of unity among themselves and with God. This gave

---

[34] Muir, 'Transfiguration' in *Collected Poems*, 198-200.

[35] For 'discerning the mysteries of God in history': Dn. 2:18f; 'its ultimate fulfilment in God and of God in humanity': Lk. 6:20-26; Mt. 5:2-11.

witness to a faith that was, *as* the Kingdom, to be *lived* in the daily round in the struggle to ever-transform hope into Love. They knew this was one of Jesus' most essential messages.

'Their' Kingdom can be best appreciated, then, as a lived experience and radical encounter with hope. It bespeaks still an eschatological continuum entailing a witness to the reality that God, being Love, is always pregnant with self-disclosure. God needs the children of Light to enact the Rule of Love, those 'peculiar people' who marginalise themselves at the spiritual edge (*eschaton*) in every generation. This is what the first Friends did with the result that their Meetings became eschaton communities with a prophetic message for all people and for all times. And not only for Christians. They wanted to eradicate *any* separation between humanity and God. As a consequence, their most earnest desire was to bring people together as the body of Christ. Arguably, the mission of today's Religious Society of Friends remains the same. Therefore, a reading of early Quaker tracts not only confirms their urgency in enacting the values of the Kingdom and a rabid certainty in their faithfulness in this respect, but that the more spiritually sophisticated among them articulated the ancient hope of the Lamb's ultimate victory over evil by means of the authority invested in their 'apostolic' or royal priesthood. This second priesthood, wrote Fox, destroyed everything that created 'a separation from God' for it 'had the royal Law', which gave rise to the 'royal Love where no enemies can come'.[36]

It is our contention that Jesus' great Sermon is for the twenty-first century as much as it was for the people of first century Palestine and seventeenth century England, and that it requires only a slight transference out of those contexts in order to 'speak to our condition'.[37] Thus Kingdom and Testimony with their Sermon basis can powerfully inform modern, Life-enhancing visions alert to oppression, forced marginalisation, violence and warfare, and thus help heal other tragic, self-inflicted demarcations within humanity. In so doing, it sustains a prophetic call for unity rather than division. The Christ-Logos mysticism underpinning Kingdom and Testimony is likewise prophetic in preserving both the historical relevance and moral power of Jesus' witness, including the Sermon on the Mount.[38] Consequently, if known and fully appreciated by contemporary Quakers of all persuasions, the standards set down by their religious forebears through their Kingdom-Testimony orthopraxis can act as benchmarks for the conduct and aspirations of Friends and non-Friends alike. And they can open up further possibilities for priestly and prophetic witness by providing a 'sharing space' for

---

[36] Fox, *An Epistle General to them who are of the Royal Priesthood*, 9.
[37] See G. Harkness, *Christian Ethics*, 51.
[38] T. C. Jones, *George Fox's Teaching*, 272.

common action. As a result, present-day Leadings and Concerns could enjoy a solid, coherent and far-sighted theological foundation without the need to relinquish religious tradition.

The Covenant of Kingdom and Testimony, that Jesus Way in the manner of Friends, has never fostered a culture of fear, for fear never serves the pursuit of Truth.[39] As a result, the Covenant of Peace will always remain inclusive, welcoming and full of a hope that impels us to what is beyond our sight.[40] Further, such a foundation can provide mature spiritual nurture to Friends and others, and lasting qualitative support when challenging the idolatries of the 'principalities and powers' in the struggle for justice, peace and compassion. Above all else, the Covenant is the means by which Friends can flourish together and share a language of the Word, a language without contempt or domination, a language that takes advantage of the spaciousness of the Kingdom in making room for differences, though not for radical incompatibility.

Importantly, Kenneth Boulding has warned that any dissociation from its Christian [and thus Kingdom] origins would deprive Quakerism of too much of its content to make it viable. What would remain?, he asks: 'Friends sitting in solemn silence', comes his answer, 'listening to helpful little speeches, and doing a lot of imaginative good works'. While these are laudable, he continues, 'they seem hardly adequate to meet the infinitely complex needs of [humanity]'. It is wise counsel.[41]

Finally, Kingdom and Testimony provides a *unifying* and *liberating* conversation between humanity and Love/God. In fact, it has always been liberating for when religion ceases to be so it becomes authoritarian and oppressive. Invoking the words of the poet W. B. Yeats, it remains for me to say that the Light and Truth of true religion, of the Covenant of Peace, continues to dwell in Quakerism's 'deep heart's core' where God's Freedom and Love reign. It is my sincere hope and prayer that this 'pearl' will touch the souls of generations to come.

---

[39] See Radcliffe, *What is the Point of Being a Christian?*, 188-9.
[40] *Ibid.*, 88.
[41] Boulding, *The Evolutionary Potential of Quakerism*, 24.

GLOSSARY and APPENDICES

Glossary

AGREEMENT OF THE PEOPLE (Oct., 1647; Jan. and May, 1649) was a proposal of constitutional ideas composed by representatives of the army ranks (the 'Agitators'), Levellers in the army (headed by John 'Free-born' Lilburne—see 'Levellers' below) and the General Council of the New Model Army. They were presented during the Putney Debates held at the Church of St. Mary the Virgin, Putney. Among other things, the Agreement proposed: (i) biennial parliaments, (ii) freedom of conscience in religion, (iii) sovereignty of the Commons, (iv) an end to impressment for military service, (v) equality of all citizens before the law.

ANABAPTISTS claimed to be inspired directly by the Holy Spirit and 'felt the inner grace of regeneration so strongly that they set great store by baptism'. They believed baptism was a 'release from death'—it was a form of convincement—and considered infant baptism meaningless. Martyrdom was central to their witness. Their understanding and practice of the Lord's Supper meant that its participants, rather than the elements of bread and wine, were its central focus. Jesus, their guide, was present at the Supper but only in the lives of his followers. Bread represented the Gospel, the wine Jesus' suffering. They projected themselves visibly onto society at large as a redeemed community demanding (and working towards) purity in local and national life. They were generally nonviolent, supported freedom of conscience and thus voluntary church attendance. Anabaptists opposed oaths, tithing and private property. Like the Quakers, they considered all other Churches apostate for having either abandoned or failed to follow the Kingdom of God.

ANTINOMINIANISM, from two Greek words meaning 'against the law', is the doctrine that there are no moral laws that God expects Christians to obey; one may live without regard to the righteousness of God. In other words, one can use God's grace as a license to sin and then trust grace to cleanse one of sin. It extends justification by faith alone to its logical conclusion asserting that, as good works do not promote salvation, so neither do evil works hinder it. As all Christians are necessarily sanctified by their vocation and profession, they are incapable of losing their spiritual holiness (justification) or final salvation by an act of disobedience to, or even by, direct violation of the Law of God. Many antinomians in Fox's day led lives as moral as any of their opponents. They were bibliocentric and drew on the Reformed tradition. As with the Quakers, they sought to recover primitive purity and urged a holy life. Antinomian teachings were perceived as hostile to government and established authority, the polar opposite of legalism.

APOCALYPSE is the revelation of hidden things by God to a chosen prophet, apostle or people. The Book of Revelation, for instance, refers to the 'unveiling' or 'revelation' of Jesus as Messiah. Apocalyptic literature, born of crisis, is a means of addressing that crisis to a religious community. Apocalyptic religious writings are regarded as a distinct branch of literature with several characteristic features: (i) dreams (i.e. in Daniel) or visions (i.e. in Revelation), (ii) angels or messengers, (iii) the Beast, also known as the Antichrist in Christian works, (iv) the future as a major player in the drama in which the writer vividly presents a picture of coming events, especially those connected with the end of the present age (e.g. 'that which shall come to pass in the latter days', Dn. 2:28). In nearly all apocalyptic writings the eschatological element is prominent. The growth of speculation regarding the age to come and the hope for the chosen people more than anything occasions the rise, and influences the development, of apocalyptic literature. Apocalypse is also expressed through (v) fantastic imagery—often strange living creatures as in Revelation 4, and (vi) mystical symbolism or codes (e.g. horns (Dn. 7, 8); trumpets (Rev. 8); 'vials of the wrath of God' (Rev. 16); the dragon (Rev. 12: 3-17)). Modern allusions to 'end of the world' are to be compared with the 'end of the age' found in the King James Bible. The word translated as 'world' is actually the Greek word 'eon' or 'age'.

THEOPHANY refers to a visible though not necessarily material appearance of God that may include prophetic visions: natural phenomena such as earthquakes are important to this genre.

APOSTOLIC usually signifies the inherited spiritual authority conferred upon a people by the Apostles who in turn received their authority from Jesus. See **MELCHIZEDEK'S ORDER**.

JAKOB BOEHME (1575-1624) was born in Altseidenberg (nr. Görlitz) in Germany. For Boehme, the Deity was immeasurable, could not be described definitively and was 'process', that is, an eternally generating series without beginning or form. A major issue running through Boehme's work was the perennial question of how Deity could contain evil. For Boehme evil was the rebellion of self-centred activity against the passive, unyielding, mysterious power of the self-contemplating God. All humans were fundamentally one whose self-knowledge came from the one God-man, Adam-Jesus. Boehme gave expression to the balance of feminine and masculine functions in the Deity and in human nature. Redemption was the restoration to the wholeness within oneself in alignment with continuing divine purpose. Boehme's cosmic vision rejected both apocalyptic prophecy and historical and literal chiliasm. In seventeenth century England it was usually known as 'Behemism'.

The original **BOOK OF COMMON PRAYER** was the title of a number of prayer books used by the Anglican Communion. A product of the English Reformation, it was published in 1549 during the reign of Edward VI. His successor, Mary I, banned it but upon her death a compromise version (between the 1552 and 1549 editions) was published in 1559. The 1549 edition was the first prayer book to contain the forms of service for daily and Sunday worship in English, and within a single volume. It included morning and evening prayer, the Litany, Holy Communion, the orders for baptism, confirmation, marriage, 'prayers to be said with the sick', and a funeral service. It set out in full the Epistle and Gospel readings for the Sunday Communion service. Bible readings for daily prayer were specified in tabular format along with the Psalms and canticles.

BRIDEWELLS (Houses of Correction) were named and modelled after the first such institution built at Bridewell in Blackfriars (London) and chartered in 1553. They were reserved for people whom magistrates thought idle or a nuisance (although not necessarily criminal) yet redeemable. Their aim was the reform of offenders by instilling the virtues of hard work usually in the form of spinning or weaving. However, their penal aspect came to dominate. In the late sixteenth century they were situated in many areas mainly to suppress vagrancy. An Act of 1576 mandated them for all corporation towns. Prisons like Newgate were usually for the irredeemable although many were inmates of the Bridewell type.

A **CHAPEL OF EASE** is a church building other than the parish church, built within the bounds of a parish for the attendance of those who cannot reach the parish church conveniently.

ENCLOSURE or **INCLOSURE** was the process that ended traditional rights such as mowing meadows for hay or grazing livestock on common land. Once enclosed, such land use became restricted to the owner and it ceased to be common land. In England and Wales the term is also used for the process that ended the ancient system of arable farming in open fields. Under enclosure, such land was fenced (enclosed) and deeded or entitled to one or more owners. Enclosures caused a considerable amount of poverty including homelessness. Anti-enclosure riots were not an uncommon feature of the agricultural landscape during Tudor and Stuart times.

ESCHATOLOGY is the branch of theology dealing with the four last things—death, judgment, heaven and hell—and the final destiny of the soul and humankind. It is a doctrine or belief about the Second Coming or the Kingdom. It involves not only expectancy and the hope of a new situation brought about by God but the eventual consummation of all things with an awareness of its realisation already in the present. In mysticism, eschatology refers metaphorically to the end of ordinary reality and reunion with God, something that has strong resonance with the Quaker concept of salvation (wholeness, unity in God, perfection, inner Eden).

FAMILISTS or the **FAMILY OF LOVE** were followers of Hendrik Niclaes (1502?-80) whose beliefs were brought to England by Christopher Vittels, a Dutch itinerant joiner. Niclaes is said have claimed to be Deity incarnate. Familists believed that heaven and hell could be found on earth upon which men and women could recapture the innocence of Eden. Crucifixion, resurrection and final judgment were internalised states on the way to perfection. All things came by nature and only the Spirit within could understand the Scriptures. Familists were expected to hold property in common. Their ministers were lay and itinerant. Familism was by no means widespread although it was strong in the north of England. Little evidence exists that any of its communities survived after the 1620s. However, its ethics may have influenced groups like the Diggers and possibly a number of Friends.

GENERAL and **PARTICULAR BAPTISTS** grew from the work of John Smyth (1570-1611/12), a Church of England minister who developed Puritan and Separatist views while seeking biblical reform in the Church. When he failed in this task, Smyth joined a small Separatist congregation in Gainsborough (Lincs.). As Separatism grew, it became dangerous to meet openly, so the congregation split into two groups for convenience. The group led by Smyth migrated to Amsterdam in 1607 where they enjoyed religious liberty. In Amsterdam they came into contact with Dutch Mennonites, a branch of the Anabaptist family that taught religious liberty and baptism of believers only. Here Smyth and his followers formed the first Baptist congregation. After Smyth's death, Thomas Helwys (*c*.1550-*c*.1616) led the congregation back to England and established a Baptist church at Spitalfields, London. Although persecuted and stigmatised as 'Anabaptists', the Baptist faith grew steadily throughout England and Wales but eventually developed into two broad groupings:

1. 'General' Baptists believed in Arminian free will rather than Calvinist predestination as taught by the Presbyterians. They strongly emphasised personal salvation and that it was possible for someone to fall from grace or lose his/her salvation. Set prayers and recitations were regarded as a discouragement to true religion and some churches encouraged prophesying, where members said whatever they believed God had inspired them to say. By 1650, there were at least 47 General Baptist churches in and around London.

2. 'Particular' Baptists arose during the mid 1640s with stricter regulation of congregations and an acceptance of predestination. Also by 1650, Particular Baptist churches had been established in and around London.

GRINDLETONIANS followed an interior religion founded by Roger Brierly (1586-1637), rector of Grindleton near Clitheroe (mid Lancs.) which nestles under the shadow of Pendle Hill. An acquaintance of James Nayler, Brierly's ideas may have provided the seedbed for Quakerism in the area around Clitheroe and Sedbergh (Cumbria) to the north. Grindletonians gave precedence to the Spirit rather than a literal interpretation of the Bible, and they believed in the possibility of heaven on Earth. They were generally anti-clerical and preached a form of perfectionism in which a true Christian life was possible without sin (i.e. it was possible to master sin). What people did was holy; true Christians could never commit a gross sin. They denied the significance of ordination.

INDEPENDENTS, whose rise can be traced to *c*.1581, owe their existence to Robert Browne (*c*.1550-1633) of Tolethorpe (Rutlandshire), often called the father of Congregationalism. 'Brownist' was a common term for an early Separatist of the Independent variety before 1620. Independents opposed uniformity of worship and a State Church, although they were willing to accept a non-coercive and a loosely structured Church as a compromise. Like Presbyterians, they were not a homogeneous group, adhering to fixed principles even during the Protectorate. 'Independent', again like 'Presbyterian', was more applicable to individuals in respect to particular issues at certain times.

Despite a general opposition to Presbyterianism, some were themselves Presbyterian and still others were 'religious Independents' looking towards a negotiated settlement between King and Parliament. While numerically weak at Westminster, 'political Independents' (e.g. Cromwell) were well represented among army officers, though it is believed some were royalist 'in feeling'. Indeed, some were willing to accept Charles II if his powers were curtailed before the army was disbanded. Not all political Independents were committed to religious Independency (i.e. the right of each congregation to its own form of worship). Moderate Independents wanted autonomous local congregations ('Congregationalism').

PRESBYTERIANS were more conservative than Independents and stronger in Scotland where they replaced Catholicism in 1559. Scottish Presbyterianism strove to extend its ecclesiastical jurisdiction over the British nations and the 1643 treaty between the English parliament and Scotland was a means to this end (see Chronology). In general, Presbyterians wanted a reformed Church along Genevan lines. Presbyterian authority was embodied in the Westminster Assembly, a Church council appointed by the Long Parliament in 1643 to reform the English Church. From the Assembly came the *Directory for the Public Worship of God* and the *Westminster Confession*. All Presbyterian ministers were regarded as equal, with leaders elected from congregations. In practice, however, Presbyterian government was dominated by an élite and organised along lines of regional class with a General Assembly as its central decision-making body. They were not always united, sometimes splitting at a local level.

JUSTICES OF THE PEACE (JP) were officeholders of great local significance during the seventeenth century and often with wide powers of discretion. These limited the powers of central government to impose policies in the localities, and gave scope to local initiative in shaping central government policy. Normally a volunteer, a JP could be a local clergyman, Lord of the Manor (such as the Purefeys in Fenny Drayton) or landed aristocracy. He acted as a channel between the localities and decisions made by the Crown and Privy Council, and was an essential source of information for central government about local affairs. As lay judges, JPs presided over Quarter Sessions and met monthly in each Hundred to supervise its work including that of the petty constables, churchwardens and Overseers of the Poor. In this capacity, they dealt with petty crime and sent reports to the sheriffs who, in turn, forwarded more important crimes to the Assizes. Most criminal cases were tried before local juries at the Assizes and Quarter Sessions presided over by judges from London and JPs respectively. Juries tended to manipulate verdicts to shape punishments. After the interrogation of accused persons, JPs usually controlled the escalation of complaints into formal accusations, probably with an eye to the exorbitant cost of the Assizes themselves.

They also helped regularise meetings of petty sessions as well as procedures for licensing alehouses, gambling and apprenticing poor children. Under republican rule, JPs were permitted to conduct marriages, an alarming measure for some and passively resisted by many chiefly because it secularised one of life's major rites of passage. Bridge repair and highway maintenance were also important tasks for JPs.

JPs were supervised by the Privy Council together with a combination of its regional representation, lord lieutenants and Assize judges who visited the counties twice a year from London and reported back to Westminster.

LEADINGS and CONCERNS are central aspects of Quaker faith and practice. Throughout this book they are identified by an upper-case C and L. A Leading finds its source in 'holy obedience', here understood as listening to the Spirit with discernment and responding with integrity. Hence, a Leading is not only a matter of individual perception and reason, however insightful, but the result of an inner Spirit-led prompting. Quakers are urged to be open to the daily clues that might suggest a Leading towards a God-directed activity. Leadings may be brought before a Meeting for Worship for Business and/or a smaller Meeting for Clearness in which questions will be asked, practical considerations of a general nature offered and personal and (possibly) financial realities raised. A Friend with a Leading will not be offered detailed advice since the process belongs to him/her. If a Leading is not a true calling it should not be pursued. Alternatively, a Leading may be set aside for future consideration. Of course, a person may have concluded confidently and prayerfully prior to any such process that s/he was clearly 'under Concern'. Quakers believe that a true Concern will stand the test of time and any obstacles encountered. While discernment can involve a lengthy period, a Meeting might decide quickly to support a Leading considering it in 'right ordering' and thus a Concern for the Meeting itself—and possibly a Yearly Meeting (a national corporate body) should its significance allow progression to that level.

LEVELLERS were mainly active in the period 1647-9. They were Radicals, being the advanced reform party, and supported mainly by Londoners and the ranks of the New Model Army. Their demands almost wholly corresponded to the Good Old Cause: (i) almost universal male suffrage, (ii) abolition of the monarchy and House of Lords, (iii) that the Commons be the centre of power, (iv) religious toleration, (v) a redistribution of seats in populated areas and elections every 1-2 years, (vi) social reform, (vii) equality before the law, (viii) abolition of billeting, press-gangs and tithes, (ix) freedom of religious worship and organisation, (x) abolition of trading monopolies, (xi) opening up of enclosed land and (xii) security of tenure for copyholders. Levellers engaged in the Putney debates with army officers in 1647. They were led by John Lilburne (later Quaker), Richard Overton, William Walwyn, John Wildman, Edward Sexby and Thomas Rainborough. Some of their leaders were executed by Cromwell and Gen. Thomas Fairfax at Burford (Oxfordshire) in 1650.

TRUE LEVELLERS were also known as the **DIGGERS**, a utopian group led by Gerrard Winstanley who hailed from Wigan (Lancs. b.1609-c.76). Their communism was denounced by the Leveller leadership who believed in private (individual) property. Like the Quakers, they spoke of an indwelling Light/Christ and an inward Kingdom. Also like the Quakers they were nonviolent, advocated equality (and refused to pay hat honour), silent worship and righteous behaviour. They campaigned for the abolition of tithes, the disestablishment of the Church of England and agrarian reform involving a wholesale redistribution of land and common ownership. The primitivist Diggers combined economics, politics and theology into a whole world view.

For Winstanley, equality meant that all distinctions based on socio-economics fell away in God's presence. Thus all Diggers were without rank and the evil of private property—hence 'True' Levellers. They gave practical and public notice of their intention to effect Eden's return by establishing communes, first in 1649 on St. George's Hill in Weybridge (Surrey) and later, in the same year and with about fifty others, on Cobham Heath (Surrey). Other Digger communes sprung up in Buckinghamshire, Northamptonshire and Kent. The experiment was ruthlessly cut short, particularly in Surrey, by the Council of State acting on behalf of local landed interests.

LOLLARDY was a late medieval reform movement (c.1382-1430) based on the writings and teachings of John Wycliffe (c.1330-84), Oxford University theologian and biblical scholar of note. Master of Balliol College in the period c.1360-61, he retired to the benefice of Lutterworth in Leicestershire and died there after a second stroke. He emphasised the inward aspects of religion and the mystical source of grace which the Bible revealed to all of God's people. In promoting the Bible's universal availability, he considered it more important than the Church's teaching. He favoured good works, believed in the priesthood of all believers and rejected outward sacraments as insufficient for salvation. Each person was damned by his/her own guilt. Lollardy favoured equality of the sexes and included women preachers. Wycliffe also opposed tithing and saw friars and bishops as agents of the Antichrist. He also preached against wealth, ostentation and war. Between c.1382 and 1409, groups of lay preachers (*lollaert* in Dutch) travelled the English countryside in pairs preaching a newly reformed Christian doctrine based on Wycliffe's scholarly writings. The Quakers were well aware of Wycliffe's movement and held it in some esteem. There was a powerful Lollard tradition in the West Riding of Yorkshire.

MELCHIZEDEK'S ORDER. For the early Quakers, Ps.110:4 affirmed Melchizedek as representative of the priestly Davidic line through which future kings of Israel were ordained as 'rightful king'. The Friends saw themselves as seeds of Abraham, the royal priesthood of the New Israel they were busily unfolding. As inheritors and messengers through convincement of the Davidic line (of which the cosmic Jesus was the 'king, prophet, high priest' and inspiration), the Jesus Way they propounded was understood to possess spiritual dominion over the earth and was fundamental, therefore, of God's plan for humanity.

MUGGLETONIANS were founded in 1652 by the nonviolent Radical John Reeve, but on his death were led by his cousin, Lodowicke Muggleton (1609-98). Both believed they were the two witnesses spoken of in Rev. 11: 3: 'And I will give power unto my two witnesses, and they shall prophesy a thousand two hundred and threescore days, clothed in sackcloth'. As premillennialists Muggletonians anticipated a physical Second Coming. God existed in heaven (which was six miles above earth) only when Jesus was alive. He was impersonal, detached and measured between 5 and 6 feet tall. Muggleton denied predestination and believed more in a heaven on earth, that the soul was mortal and that hell existed within humanity. External religious ceremonies were unnecessary. Prayer, worship or overt acts of religious faith such as martyrdom were without purpose. Jesus was God on earth. While he walked the earth, Moses and Elijah looked after heaven but only until the resurrection.

According to <http://www.exlibris.org/nonconform/engdis/muggleton.html>,

> Muggleton preached a form of anti-trinitarianism, or early Unitarianism. The Man Jesus was the true God who had come down to Earth while the Old Testament prophets, Elijah and Moses, kept an eye on Heaven. Man was in the Third Age of the Spirit, according to the twelfth-century Joachimite tradition, or the Third Commission according to some.

Muggletonians, who never proselytised, believed they could damn and bless according to the will of God, and the apparent success of such damning (apparently resulting in the death of certain religious opponents, mainly Quaker) brought the sect great prestige. A vigorous tract war with their Quaker opponents lasted until Muggleton's death. Muggletonians found support at the grass root levels of English society and included large numbers of active women. The sect died out in the twentieth century.

PARLIAMENT in England underwent rapid change in the period, 1639-60. It was suspended during Charles' '11-year tyranny' from 1629 until recalled in 1640. Between April and May 1640, the 'Short Parliament' sat, the 'Long' Parliament having begun in November, 1640. After Cromwell's defeat of the Scots at Preston (August 1648), Col. Thomas Pride in December purged the Commons of its Presbyterian (less radical) Members. This left a 'rump' of 100 Independents, the party of Cromwell. The Rump executed Charles, declared a Commonwealth and governed with a Council of State; 41 Members of the Rump comprised the Council. In April, 1653, Cromwell dissolved the Rump (and the Long Parliament as a consequence) and, along with a military dominated Council, selected 140 'saints', mostly gentry, to a 'Nominated' Parliament on July 4th: 129 Members came from England, 5 from Scotland and 6 from Ireland. This parliament was also known as the Nominated Assembly of Saints, the Little Parliament and the 'Barebone's Parliament' after Praise-God Barebone, a nominee for the City of London.

Five months later and constantly disrupted by radical dissenters, it was asked to go by army officers whose Council then presented Cromwell with the Instrument of Government. The Instrument approximated to a written constitution. The end of the 'Barebone's' heralded a Protectorate (1654) comprising a Council of State, the Commons and Lord Protector (Cromwell). A 'Second Chamber' was added in May 1657 and the Protector was given the right to nominate his successor.

Cromwell's over-reaction to minor royalist uprisings helped to bring about the Rule of the Major-Generals (Aug. 1655). Each was responsible for one of eleven

Glossary

regions in England and Wales. They were unpopular, and the experiment was abandoned in Jan. 1657 effectively killing off military government in England. Meanwhile, Cromwell had dissolved the first Protectorate Parliament in 1655 because of its constant wrangling over the Instrument. A second Protectorate Parliament (1656-8) was called and the Humble Petition and Advice (1657) offered Cromwell the crown which he refused.

Cromwell died in 1658 and was replaced by his son, Richard. As Lord Protector, Richard ruled with a third Protectorate Parliament (Jan.-Apr. 1659). A recalled Rump signalled the end of his Protectorate and elected a Council of State nominally led by Maj.-Gen. Charles Fleetwood, but whose effective head was Sir Henry Vane Jr. The Council proved ineffective and in October 1659 ceased to sit. Another coup similar to Fleetwood-Vane and led by Maj.-Gen. John Lambert dissolved the Rump and installed a Committee of Safety, still under Fleetwood but with Vane a prominent civilian member. The move was unpopular, leaving General George Monck to demand a return to parliamentary rule (the Rump); he marched south from Scotland to secure it. The Committee of Safety dispersed in December, and after a week without a government the Rump was reinstated by three regiments of the army. Entering London on 3rd February 1660, Monck secured the readmission of Members 'purged' by Col. Pride in December, 1648. The Long Parliament thus returned but in March 1660 called 'free elections' and dissolved itself.

After Charles Stuart issued the Declaration of Breda (April, 1660) in which he expressed a willingness to settle all disputed issues with parliament, the Convention Parliament was installed (April-Sept). This parliament outlined the details of a Restoration settlement and proclaimed Charles as king on 8th May, 1660. After the Restoration, the Convention was replaced by the Cavalier Parliament which lasted until 1679.

PREDESTINATION includes the doctrine that God predestines from eternity the salvation of certain souls ('supra-lapsarianism'). 'Double predestination', as in Calvinism, is the belief that God foreordains certain souls to damnation. Predestination is posited on the basis of God's omniscience and omnipotence, and is closely related to the doctrines of divine providence and grace. A predestinarian doctrine is suggested in Paul, but it is not developed (see Rom. 8:28-30; 9: 6-29). Augustine of Hippo's interpretation of the doctrine, while individualistic, has been the basis for most subsequent versions, both Protestant and Roman Catholic. Pelagianism, in opposition to Augustine, held that by granting every individual freedom of choice, God willed the salvation of all souls equally, a view that became popular in liberal Protestant theology. The then Roman Catholic view, as stated by Aquinas, was less individualistic than Augustine's. Aquinas maintained that God willed the salvation of all souls but that a few were granted special grace that, in effect, foreordained their salvation. The damned may be said to be reprobated to hell only in the sense that God foresaw their resistance to the grace given them. The Roman Catholic Church taught that predestination was consistent with free will since God moved the soul according to its nature. Calvinism, on the other hand, rejected the role of free will and taught that grace was irresistable, and that God by an absolute election saved the souls of some and abandoned the souls of others.

In the seventeenth century, **ELECTION** generally meant the exercise of deliberate choice or preference, especially in relation to conduct. Other meanings included judicious selection and discrimination.

PRELAPSARIAN denotes the pure state of humanity before the Fall, an Edenic state.

PROPHESYINGS were meetings of clergy in the localities for prayer and sermons followed by mutual criticism and discussions about the state of the Church. They began spontaneously in various parts of the south-east of England, c.1571. Edmund Grindal (1519?-83), a Marian exile and Archbishop of Canterbury (1575-83), was shocked to see how few ministers preached regularly to their flocks. He decided to rectify the problem by encouraging prophesyings which had already been pioneered in Zürich. They quickly became popular being often attended by zealous laymen. But Queen Elizabeth believed they were a disruption and an attack on royal control of the Church. She wanted them stopped but Grindal refused and was sequestrated from his jurisdictional in 1577, though reinstated in 1582.

RANTERS were mystical anarchists notorious for swearing, drinking, bawdy songs, tobacco smoking and sexual licence. Although in many respects nihilist, they often wrote daring and sophisticated religious tracts. Ranters were said to have simultaneously held antinomian (see above) and pantheist beliefs. For Ranters, God was not only the creator of all things but was in all things, yet beyond good and evil. Sin, therefore, which was the negation of God, could not exist. The historical Jesus was less important than the eternal Christ, and they rejected an individually known life after death along with heaven and hell. Historical controversy surrounds the Ranters. Were they an organised movement with a theology? Some historians do not think so. Were they a relatively isolated group of individuals with different beliefs, 'a projection of deviance' so to speak or an 'expression of religious anxiety' by those who saw their times as cataclysmic?

THE REMONSTRANTS was the title chosen by the 43 followers of Jacobus Arminius. They met at The Hague (The Netherlands) in January, 1610 with one of their number, Jan Uytenbogaert, drawing up a remonstrance, their Five Articles, which all 43 Remonstrants ratified in July of that year. The Articles include: (i) conditional rather than absolute predestination, (ii) universal rather than limited atonement, (iii) the necessity of regeneration and transformation through the Holy Spirit, (iv) the possibility of both resistance to, and rejection of, God's grace and (v) if incorporated into Christ through true faith, the assurance of security in the fight for victory against Satan, sin, the world and one's own flesh. The remonstrance was controversial, even shocking. Inevitably, it came under review by a National Synod of Dutch divines (with foreign observers) held in the Dutch city of Dordrecht in 1618–19 (known by the English as Dort). The judgments of the Synod are known as The Canons of Dort or Canons of Dordrecht and set forth what is often referred to as the Five Points of Calvinism, commonly denoted 'TULIP': total depravity, unconditional election, limited atonement, irresistible grace, and perseverance of the saints.

SABBATARIANISM began in the seventeenth century. Puritans and others like them demanded Sunday observance in line with the fourth commandment. God our Father must be obeyed, and since He had rested on the seventh day, so, too, must His children rest. They put a stop to many Sunday occupations.

THE *SWARTHMORE MSS.* are not to be confused with pre-publication book manuscripts. Instead, they comprise six folio volumes (principally containing early Quaker letters) and are held in the Friends House Library in London. The *MSS.* provide an insight into the early Friends as people with emotions and day-to-day experiences rather than as cold spiritual warriors in print. Many aspects of the lives of Quaker preachers are recorded, including insights into the growth of the Quaker community and its organisational development, crowd reactions to preachers, feelings of fear, despondency and elation, evidence of mutual caring and support, and success in the field. The letters shed light on the early Quaker practice of travelling in pairs as a source of spiritual well-being and companionship, and how it encouraged a more efficient organisation and oversight of local Meetings. The *MSS.* also provide a picture of early Friends' sufferings including harassment by authorities and details of detention and imprisonment. Highlighted is the essential role Margaret Fell played in the nascent movement and the close bond between correspondents.

THE WESTMINSTER ASSEMBLY (1643-9) was convened by parliament to settle Church government according to the Solemn League and Covenant (1643). It consisted of 120 Puritan clergy, 30 laymen and (later) 8 Scottish commissioners. It issued the *Directory of Worship*, the Catechism, the Westminster Confession of Faith (1647, Calvinist) and a plan to establish Presbyterianism nationwide. The Confession of Faith was probably influenced by the Lutheran Formula of Concord of 1577.

The **SOLEMN LEAGUE AND COVENANT** was an alliance between the English parliament and the Scots in their struggle against Charles I. In return for the help of a Scottish army, parliament agreed to pay £30,000 a month for its upkeep and to establish Presbyterianism in England.

WITCHCRAFT was considered a gross heresy and its prosecution was probably justified by Exodus 22:18 ('Thou shalt not suffer a witch to live'). During the 1640s and 1650s, the popular mercuries (newspapers) and a host of pamphlets helped spread rumours about, and deepened fear of, witchcraft. That midwives and other healers were regarded as witches is indicative of the part magic played in popular culture. And yet, relatively few people in England—those believed to have made covenants with the Devil or who wore distinctive 'devilish' clothing—were accused of witchcraft. Rather, they were more likely to be accused of *maleficium*, the resulting activity of witchcraft (such as sorcery) that caused harm to an accuser and/or death or illness to an accuser's children, relatives or animals.

During an era when denial of witchcraft was a repudiation of the revealed Word of God, accused women often expressed a profound Christianity. This may partly explain why Matthew Hopkins, a self-appointed 'witchfinder-general' from

Essex, failed to produce evidence that witchcraft was practiced as a religion. Between 1570 and 1670, nearly 600 people (of whom approximately 480 were women) perished in England for witchcraft, healing and white magic. The figure was higher in Scotland where more than 1,500 witches met a terrible death in the 1590s alone. Papists (including Jesuits), Jews, Turks, Spaniards, pirates, foreigners and strangers were 'witches' of a different variety. A number of Quakers, including Fox, were accused of witchcraft.

YEOMEN ran farms ranging from under 10 to 88 acres. Richer 'husbandmen' were sometimes accorded the superior title of 'yeomen', though husbandmen in general were usually poorer. As with 'Puritan', 'yeoman' was difficult to define. Sir Francis Bacon described them as 'a middle people of a condition between gentlemen and cottagers or peasant'. Most yeomen were poor freeholders (particularly in the North), leaseholders or copyholders with prescribed obligations to landlords. They were regarded as hard workers, took an interest in local affairs, were usually parliamentarian in their sympathies and faithfully attended church. Most of the Quaker public preachers were yeomen or 'statesmen' as they were sometimes called in the North. The vast majority of the 70-80,000 yeomen in England and Wales could ill-afford to send their children to a grammar school or university. As a class, the yeomanry went into decline towards the end of the seventeenth century.

APPENDIX 1

Number of 'Kingdom' Entries in Works (1652-62) by Authors with over 20 Solo Works, 1652-92 (K = Kingdom; A = Alternative)

1. Early Quaker Author	2. Approx no. of Works, 1652-62	3. Works in my Possession	4. No. and % of Works with 'K'	5. No. of 'K' Entries	6. No. of works with 'A's only	7. Total no. and % of works with 'K' & 'A's	8. No. and % of works with neither 'K' nor 'A's
Bayly, W.	16	16	10 (63%)	38	3	13 (81%)	3
Bishop, G.	20	20	19 (95%)	104	1	20 (100%)	0
Burrough, E.	90	90	61 (68%)	259	20	81 (90%)	9
Crook, J.	17	17	8 (47%)	28	5	13 (76%)	4
Crisp, S.	2	2	1 (50%)	2	0	1 (50%)	1
Dewsbury, W.	14	14	9 (64%)	66	4	13 (93%)	1
Farnworth, R.	34	34	28 (82%)	85	3	31 (91%)	3
Fell, M.	13	13	7 (54%)	28	5	12 (92%)	1
Fox, G.	171	152	72 (46%)	519	72	144 (93%)	8
Fox, G (the Ygr).	32	28	16 (57%)	31	8	24 (86%)	4
Howgill, F.	38	38	23 (61%)	136	12	35 (92%)	3
Hubberthorne, R.	38	38	18 (47%)	69	14	32 (84%)	6
Mason, M.	11	11	9 (82%)	29	0	9 (82%)	2
Nayler, J.	87	84	58 (69%)	342	14	72 (86%)	12
Parnel, J.	16	16	8 (50%)	36	5	13 (81%)	3
Penington, I.	35	35	22 (63%)	148	10	32 (91%)	3
Perrot, J.	26	24	19 (79%)	75	3	22 (92%)	2
Rigge, A.	7	7	5 (71%)	12	2	7 (100%)	0
Smith, H.	45	42	19 (45%)	40	11	30 (71%)	12
Smith, W.	25	23	13 (57%)	45	7	20 (87%)	3
Taylor, T.	7	6	5 (83%)	23	0	5 (83%)	1
Whitehead, G.	22	18	10 (56%)	52	4	14 (78%)	4
Whitehead, J.	10	7	7 (100%)	20	0	7 (100%)	0
Total Authors	Total	Total	Total & %	Total	Total &%	Total & %	Total
23	776	735	447 (61%)	2187	203 (28%)	650 (88%)	85 (12%)

Principal Quaker authors were chosen, i.e. those with 20+ solo works between 1652 and 1692, the year following Fox's death. I concentrated principally on works published during 1652 and 1663. They vary in length from considerable volumes (i.e. Fox's *The Great Mystery*) to broadsides and half-page (A5) contributions. Their average length is 4 to 20pp. The works in my possession were closely examined although some 'Kingdom' references may have been missed. 'Kingdom' was counted when it referred only to the 'Kingdom of God' (of Heaven, Christ, Messiah). Not all works, of course, refer to the Kingdom. Some, for instance, emphasise such issues as the Friends' sufferings. References to the kingdom of the 'devil', 'Satan' or the 'world's kingdom' (and slight variants) were not included in the total (col. 5), although it would have been legitimate to do so since they are a contradiction to the Kingdom and would have added considerably to the total. Principal alternatives for 'Kingdom' were 'Law of God', 'doctrine of God (and Christ)', 'dominion', 'sovereignty (or dominion) of God', 'everlasting covenant' and 'power of God', where the latter referred only to the Kingdom rather than 'Gospel' or 'Christ'. Careful attention was paid to the alternatives' context. I did not duplicate works, i.e. *The Son of Perdition* which falls under either E. Burrough's name or G. Whitehead's. The important column in the table is Col. 7, indicating a considerable relationship with the Kingdom within each author. The average number of 'Kingdom' entries per work is 3 and nearly 9 out of 10 works mention 'Kingdom' or an alternative.

APPENDIX 2

1. A DECLARATION FROM THE HARMLES & INNOCENT PEOPLE OF GOD, CALLED QUAKERS, AGAINST ALL PLOTTERS, AND FIGHTERS IN THE WORLD

GEORGE FOX, RICHARD HUBBERTHORNE *et al*
(21/11th Mo., 1660 = 21st January, 1661)

For the removing of the ground of Jealousie and Suspicion from both magistrates and People in the Kingdoms, concerning Wars and Fightings. And also something in Answer to that Clause of the King's late Proclamation, which mentions the QUAKERS, to clear them from the Plot and Fighting, which therein is mentioned, and for the clearing their innocency.

OUR principle is, and our practices have always been, to seek peace, and ensue it, and to follow after **righteousness** and the knowledge of God, seeking the Good and Welfare, and doing that which tends to the peace of All. Wee know that Warres and Fightings proceed from the Lusts of men, as **James 4: 1-3**, out of which Lusts the Lord hath redeemed us. And so out

(PAGE 2) of the Occasion of war; the occasion of which War, and the war it self (wherein envious men, who are lovers of them-selves more then lovers of God, lust, kil, and desire to have mens Lives or Estates) ariseth from the Lust. All bloody Principles & Practices we (as to our own particular) do utterly deny, with all outward wars & strife, & fightings with outward Weapons, for any end, or under any pretence whatsoever. And this is our Testimony to the whole world.

And whereas it is objected;
But although you now say, *That you cannot Fight, nor take up Arms at all; yet if the Spirit do move you, then you wil change your Principle, and then you will sell your Coat, and buy a Sword, and Fight for the* **Kingdom of Christ**.

Answer; As for this, We say to you, That Christ said to Peter, Put up thy Sword in his place; though he had said before, he that had no Sword, might sell his Coat & buy one (to the fulfilling of the Law and Scripture) yet after when he had bid him put it up, he said, He that taketh the Sword, shall perish with the Sword; And further, Christ said to Peter, Thinkest thou that I cannot now pray to my Father, and he shall presently give me more then twelve Legions of Angels? And this might satisfie Peter **(Lk. 22:36)** after he had put up his Sword, when he said to him, He that took it, should perish by it, which satisfieth us **(Mt. 26: 51-53)** and in the Revelations it's said, He that kills with the Sword, shall perish with the Sword; and here is the Faith and the Patience of the Saints; and so **Christ's Kingdom** is not of this World, therefore do not his Servants Fight, as he told Pilate the Magistrate, who crucified him: And did they not look upon Christ as a raiser of Sedition? And did not he say, Forgive them? But thus it is, that we are numbered amongst Transgressors, and numbered amongst Fighters, that the Scriptures might be fulfilled.

That **Spirit of Christ**, by which we are guided, is not changeable, so as once to command us from a thing as evil, & again to move unto it; And we do certainly know, & testifie to the World, that the **Spirit of Christ** which leads us into all Truth, wil never move us to fight and war against any man with outward Weapons, neither for the **Kingdom of Christ**, nor for the Kingdoms of this World.

(PAGE 3) First, Because the **Kingdom of Christ**, God will exalt according to his promise; and cause it to grow and flourish in **righteousness**; not by might, nor by power of outward sword, but by my spirit, saith the Lord **(Zc. 4: 6)**. So those that use any Weapon to fight for Christ, or for the establishing of his **Kingdom** or **Government**, both the Spirit, Principle and Practice in that, we deny. Secondly, And as for the Kingdoms of this World, we cannot covet them; much less can we fightfor them; but we do earnestly desire and wait, That (by the **Word** of **God's Power**, and its effectual operation in the hearts of men), the Kingdoms of this World may become the **Kingdoms of the Lord**, and of his Christ, that he might Rule and Reign in men, by his Spirit and Truth; that thereby all people out of all different Judgements and Professions, might be brought into love and unity with God; and one with another; and that they might all come to witness the Prophet's words, who said, Nation shall not lift up Sword against Nation, neither shall they learn War any more **(Isa. 2:4; Mic. 4:3)**.

So we, whom the Lord hath called into the obedience of his Truth, have denyed Wars and Fightings, and cannot again any more learn it. And this is a certain Testimony unto all the World, of the truth of our hearts in this particular, That as God persuadeth every man's heart to believe, so they may receive it; For we have not (as some others) gone about cunningly with devised Fables: Nor have we ever denied in Practice, what we have profes'd in Principle, but in sincerity and truth, and by the **Word of God**, have we laboured to be made manifest unto all men, that both we and our wayes might be witnessed in the hearts of all people: And whereas all manner of Evil hath been falsely spoken of us, Wee hereby speake forth the plain Truth of our hearts, to take away the occasion of that offence, that so we being innocent, we may not suffer for other mens offences, nor be made a prey upon by the wills of men, for that of which wee were never guilty; but in the uprightnesse of our hearts we may, under the Power ordained of God, for the punishment of Evil-doers, and for the praise of them that

(PAGE 4) do well, live a peaceable and godly life, in all godliness and honesty; for although we have always suffer'd, and do now more abundantly suffer, yet we know that it's for **righteousness sake**; For our rejoicing is this, the Testimony of our Consciences, that in simplicity and godly sincerity, not with fleshly wisdome, but by the Grace of God, we have had our Conversation in the World **(2 Cor. 1: 12)**. Which for us is a Witness for the convincing of our Enemies. For this we can say to all the world, We have wronged no mans person, or possessions; we have used no force, nor violence against any man; we have been found in no Plots, nor guilty of Sedition; when we have been wronged, we have not sought to revenge our selves; we have not made resistance against Authority; but wherein we could not obey for Conscience-sake, we have suffer'd even the most of any people in the Nation; we have been counted as sheepe for the slaughter, persecuted and despised, beaten, stoned, wounded, stocked, whipped, imprisoned, haled out of Synagogues, cast into Dungeons and noisome Vaults, where many have dyed in bonds, shut up from our Friends, denied needful Sustenance for many dayes together, with other the like Cruelties;

and the cause of all this our sufferings, is not for any evil, but for things relating to the Worship of our God, and in obedience to his Requirings of us; For which Cause wee shall freely give up our Bodies a sacrifice, rather than disobey the Lord: For we know, as the Lord hath kept us innocent, so he will plead our Cause, when there is none in the Earth to plead it; So we, in obedience unto his Truth, do not love our lives unto the death, so that we may do his will; and wrong no man in our Generation, but seek the Good and peace of all mens. And he that hath commanded us, That we shall not swear at all **(Mt. 5: 34)** hath also Commanded us That we shall not kill **(Mt. 5: 21)**; So that we can neither kill men, nor swear for or against them. And this is both our Principle and Practice, and hath been from the beginning. So that if we suffer, as suspected to take up Arms, or make war against any, it is without any ground from us; for it neither is, nor ever was in our hearts since we owned the truth of God; neither shall we ever do it, because it is contrary to

(PAGE 5) the **Spirit of Christ**, his **Doctrine**, and the practice of his Apostles; even contrary to him for whom we suffer all things, and endure all things. And whereas men come against us with Clubs, Staves, Drawn Swords, Pistols cock't, and do beat, cut, and abuse us, yet we never resisted them; but to them our hair, Backs, and Cheeks have been ready; but it is not an honour, to Manhood nor Nobility, to run upon harmless people, who lift not up a hand against them, with Arms and Weapons.

Therefore in love we warn you for your souls good, not to wrong the Innocent, nor the Babes of Christ, which hee hath in his hand, which he tenders as the Apple of his Eye; neither seeke to destroy the Heritage of God; neither turn your Swords backward, upon such as the law was not made for, i.e., the Righteous; but for the Sinners and Transgressors, to keep them down. For those are not Peace-makers, neither the Lovers of Enemies; neither can

(PAGE 6) they overcome Evil with Good, who wrong them that bee Friends to You and All Men, and wish Your Good, and the good of all people on the Earth. If you oppress us as they did the children of Israel in Egypt; and if you oppress us as they did when Christ was born, and as they did the Christians in the primitive times; we can say, The Lord forgive you; and leave the Lord to deal with you, and not revenge ourselves. And if you say, as the Council said to Peter and John, You must speak no more in that Name: and if you serve us as they served the Three Children spoken of in Daniel; God is the same as ever he was, that lives for ever and ever, who hath the Innocent in his Arms.

Oh Friends! offend not the Lord and his Little Ones; neither afflict his People; but consider, and be moderate, and do not run on hastily into things; but mind, and consider **Mercy, Justice, and Judgement**; that is the way for you to prosper, and get the favour of the Lord. Our Meetings were stopped and broken up in the days of Oliver, under pretence of Plotting against him, and in the days of the Parliament and Committee of Safety, we were looked upon as Plotters to bring in KING CHARLES; and now we are called Plotters against KING CHARLES. Oh that men should lose their Reason, and go contrary to their own conscience, knowing that we have suffered all things, and have been accounted Plotters all along, though we have declared against them both by word of mouth and Printing, and are clear from any such things, though we have suffered all along because we would not take up carnal weapons to fight withal against any; and are thus made a prey upon, because we are the innocent lambs of Christ, and cannot avenge our selves. These things are left on your hearts to consider: But we are out of all those things, in the patience of the Saints; and we know, that as Christ said, He that takes the Sword, shall perish with the sword **(Mt. 26:52; Rev. 13:10)**.

> This is given forth from the People called Quakers, to
> satisfy the King and his Council; and all those that have
> any jealousie concerning Us, that all occasion of suspition
> may be taken away, and our Innocency cleared.

(PAGE 7) POSTSCRIPT

Though we are numbered with Plotters in this late Proclamation, and put in the midst of them, and numbered amongst Transgressors, and to have been given up to all rude, mercilesse men, by which our Meetings are broken up, in which we edified one another in our holy Faith, and prayed together to the Lord that lives for ever, yet he is our pleader for us in this **Day**; the Lord saith, They that feared his Name, spoke often together, as in Malachy, which were as his Jewels: And for this cause, and no evil-doing, are we cast into Holes, Dungeons, Houses of Correction, Prisons; they sparing neither old nor young, men nor women; and just sold to all Nations, and made a prey to all Nations, under pretence of being Plotters, so that all rude people run upon us to take possession; for which we say, The Lord forgive them that have thus done to us, who doth, and will enable us to suffer: And never shall we lift up hand against any man that doth thus use us: But that the Lord may have mercy upon them, that they may consider what they have done; for how is it hardly possible for them to requite us for the wrong they have done to us? Who to all Nations have sounded us abroad as Plotters, who were never found Plotters against Power or Man upon the Earth, since we knew the **Life & Power** of Jesus Christ manifested in us, who hath redeemed us from the World, all works of darkness, and Plotters that be in it; by which we know the Election, before the world began. So we say, The Lord have mercy upon our Enemies, and forgive them, for that they have done unto us.

(PAGE 8) Oh do as ye would be done by; and do unto all men as you would have them do unto you; for this is but the Law and the Prophets.

And all Plots, Insurrections, and Riotous Meetings we do deny as deeds of darknesse, knowing them to be of the Devil, the Murderer; which we in Christ, which was before they were, triumph over them: And all Wars and Fightings with Carnal Weapons, we do deny, who have the Sword of the Spirit. And all that wrong us, we leave them to the Lord; and this is to clear our Innocency from that Aspersion cast upon us, that wee are Plotters. For we are harmlesse; who soever hurts us, in so doing doth a seven-fold hurt unto himself; because we can hurt no man, but do love all men, and pray for, and desire to do good to all men, though they be Enemies to us: And out of this life, there is no true and sound Faith: But all is corrupt, destroying and perishing the soul.

This the People called QUAKERS do witness to all the world.

Notwithstanding our publication of this, is in order to no other end, but nakedly for the clearing of our innocency; yet such hath been the apparent maliciousness of such as are, in present Power in this City, that rather then our Innocency and Integrity should bee understood by the People, who through Lying Accusations are prejudiced against us; have done what in them lay, to prevent us coming forth to publike View, by a Violent and Unjust taking away the whole first Impression.

QQQQQQQQQQ

2. A DECLARATION AND AN INFORMATION FROM US THE PEOPLE OF GOD CALLED QUAKERS

MARGARET FELL *et al*
(5/4th Mo., 1660 = 5th June, 1660)

(PAGE 2) We who are the People of God called Quakers, who are hated and despised, and every where spoken against, as people not fit to live, as they were that went before us, **(1 Cor. 4: 9-13)** who were of the same **spirit, power, & Life** and were as we are, in that they were accounted as the off-scouring of all things, by that Spirit and Nature that is of the world, and so the Scripture is fulfilled, **(Gal. 4)** he that is born of the flesh persecuteth him that is born of the Spirit, We have been a suffering people, under every Power & Change, and under every profession of Religion that hath been, & borne the outward power in the Nation these 12 years, since we were a People, and being that throw the old Enemy which hath continually appeared against us, not only in the profane people of the nation, but also in the highest profession of sorts; and sects of Religion, we have suffered under, and been persecuted by them all; Even some persecuted & imprisoned till death; others their bodies bruised till death; stigmatized, bored thorow the tongue, gagged in the mouth, stockt, and whipt thorow Towns & Cities, our goods spoiled, our bodies two or three years imprisoned, with much more that might be said, which is well known to the Actors thereof;

and this done not for the wronging of any man, nor for the breach of any just Law of the Nation, nor for evil doing, nor desiring any evil, or wishing any hurt to any man, but for Conscience sake towards God, because we could not bow to their worship, and because we could not maintain a Ministry, which Ministry we could not joyn with nor own; So we look upon it to be unjust to maintain them, we receive nothing from, nor cannot trust our Souls under their Teaching, who Teach for hire, and Divine for money, which the Prophets of the Lord cryed wo against; And Christ said, a hireling was a Thief and a Robber, **(Jn. 10: 12-13)** and would fly because he was an hireling; And they are maintained by Tithes, contrary to Christ and the **Apostles Doctrine, (Heb. 7:12)** who said the Priesthood was changed that took Tithes, and the Law also that gave them, and who witnessed CHRIST JESUS to be the Everlasting Offering once for all, who saith, such an High-Priest hath become us, which is holy, harmlesse, undefiled, separate from Sinners, and made higher than the Heavens who in the dayes of his flesh, when he had offered up prayers and supplications, with strong cryes and Tears, unto him that was able to save him from death and was heard

(PAGE 3) in that he feared, though he was a Son yet learned he obedience, by the things which he suffered, **(Heb. 5: 7-9)** and being made perfect became the Author of Eternal Salvation unto all them that obey him. And for obedience to him and his commands (do we suffer), who hath said, swear not at all, **(Mt. 5: 34-35; Jm. 5:12; 2:10)** And he said Call no man Master upon earth, for ye have one Master in Heaven; and who hath said How can you believe that seek Honour one of another, and not the Honour that comes from God onely, and who hath said let your Yea be Yea, and your Nay, Nay, for whatsoever is more then this, cometh of evil;

And because we cannot respect persons, which is contrary to the **Apostles Doctrine and practice**, who hath said, **(Ac. 10:34; Mt. 22:16)** of a Truth God is no respecter of Persons, but in every Nation he that feareth God, and worketh Righteousness, is accepted of him; And the Apostle James exhorted his Brethren not to have the Faith of our Lord Jesus Christ with respect of persons, for if you respect persons you commit sin, and are convinced of the Law as Transgressors, and contrary to this **Faith and Doctrine** we are made Transgressors by the Powers of the Earth, because we cannot respect persons, and commit sin, and be made Transgressors of the Law of God: And this hath been the onely ground and cause of our sufferings, because we obeyed the Command of Christ, the Author of our Eternal Salvation, and observed the **Apostles Doctrine and practice**; and not for any other cause or end have our sufferings been, but for Conscience sake, because we cannot bow to mens wills and worships contrary to the Command of Christ Jesus our Everlasting Priest, King, and Prophet, whom, we serve with our spirits, and worship in that, which the World calls Heresie **(Ac. 24:14).**

And now because that several of you, who are most concerned in this Government, are not acquainted with our principles and practices, neither have known our Innocency and sufferings, and the Old Enemy by whom we have suffered, at this time being ready to incense and instigate, and infuse secretly into the minds of them who are strangers to us, against whom we have not transgressed, neither do we desire to give any just occasion of offence to these present Governors, who yet have not done us much wrong, in making any Law against us,

Appendix 2

that we know of; And we do believe would not, if ye did rightly understand our Innocency and Integrity, nakedness and singleneß in our carriage towards all men upon the face of the earth, and if ye would but examine and search out our carriage and behaviour towards all mens persons, Souls, and Estates, if these things were searched out and Examined

(PAGE 4) thorow the Nations, and that no prejudice were let into your minds from others words, which proceed from secret envy, malice and hatred, & not from any just ground they have against us, but, as it is, from a contrary spirit and mind, as it was in the Jews against Christ, and in all others against the Apostles, so it is the same now against us, but this we commit to the Lord who will plead our cause, and clear our Innocency, who hath said vengeance is Mine, and I will repay it; And now that they know we cannot swear, nor take an Oath, for Conscience sake, but have suffered because we could not take them; Now do the Magistrates of several Countyes of the Nation, through the suggestion of the Priests envy, which is inveterate against us, Tender us; an Oath, which they call the Oath of Allegiance, with several other Engagements, what their own wils can invent, on purpose to ensnare us, that upon the denial thereof they may cast us into prison, & have already cast several of us into prison at their own pleasure.

We do therefore declare to take of all Jealousies, Fears, and Suspitions of our Truth and Fidelity to the King, and these present Governours, that our intentions & Endeavours are and shall be Good, True, Honest, and Peaceable towards them, and that we do Love, Own, and Honour the King and these present Governours, so far as they do rule for God and his Truth, and do not impose any thing upon Peoples Consciences, but let the Gospel have its free passage through the consciences of men, which we do not know that they have (by any law) as yet imposed;. And if they grant liberty of Conscience towards God and towards Man, then we know that God will blesse them: For want of which hath been the overthrow of all that went before them: We do not desire any liberty that may justly offend any ones Conscience, but the Liberty we do desire is, that we may keep our Consciences clear and void of offence towards God and towards men, and that we may enjoy our civil Rights and Liberties of Subjects, as freeborn English men. And this we do in the presence of the Lord declare, not in flattering Titles, but in reality and truth of our hearts, and shall manifest the same; Now that we may be clear in the presence of the living God, and of all just and moderate men, that they may not have their hands in Blood and Persecution, as those have had that are gone before, and that they may not be ignorant of us, and of our principles and practice, & so receive information against us from others envy, which may be contrary to our very principles, and the truth as it is in Jesus; Therefore that we may be free from

(PAGE 5) the blood of all men, **(Ac. 20: 26)** & that they may not have a hand in Persecuting and Oppressing the Innocent, whose cause God hath pleaded and will plead, We do therefore inform the Governors of this Nation high and low; That we are a People that desire the good of all People and their peace, and desire that all may be saved, and come to the knowledge of **the Truth (1 Tm. 2:4; Ac. 13: 47; Rev. 21: 24; 1 Cor. 4: 6) the Way, and the Life,** which is Christ Jesus, **the Everlasting Covenant**, which is given for a Light to the Gentiles, and to be the

Salvation to the ends of the Earth, and all the Nations that are saved must walk in this Light of the Glorious Gospel, which hath shined in our hearts, and given us the light of the Knowledge of the **Glory of God** in the Face of Jesus Christ. And to this Light we direct Peoples minds, that every one in particular may have a Teacher and Testimony according to the **Righteousness of Faith** which speaketh on this wise, The **Word** is very nigh in the heart and in the mouth. **(Rom. 10:8)** And if every one would come to this, there would be a feeling of Gods Justice and Righteousness, and our intents to be just Innocent, and Righteous, who hath said, I will come near to Judgement, and be a swift witnesse against the Sorcerer and Adulterer, and false swearer **(Ml. 3:5)**.

Now, if every one would turn to this witnesse in their own Consciences, this would keep them from oppressing and persecuting of others without cause, for God is coming to teach his People himself, by his own light and Spirit, who hath said, it is written in your law, you shall be all taught of God, **(Jn. 6: 45)** which many of us now do witnesse; for which cause are we persecuted, the children of the Lord are taught of the Lord, and are established in Righteousnesse, and are far from Oppression **(Isa. 54:13-14)**.

The Testimony that we have born, hath been chiefly against the Priests, Teachers, and Professors of these Nations, that are out of the **Life & power**; for when it pleased the Lord to reveal his Son in us, we saw them to be absolute deceivers of the People, and betrayers of their souls, for they lead them wholly from that of God in them to the letter of the Scripture without them, and to their own Inventions, and Imaginations, and meanings which they speak, who are not taught of God themselves. For, for all their high profession, there is scarce one of them that dares say they have the infallible Spirit of God, the same as the Apostles had, that gave forth the Scripture; The Apostle saith that which may be known of God is manifested in them, for God shows it unto them. No People can retain God in their knowledge and worship him as God, but first they

(PAGE 6) must come to that of God in them; But these Teachers deny this **Doctrine**, and have manifested themselves several ways to all sober minded People, to be men not fearing God, and are not true to their Principles; for who have minded them, and seen their Carriage and Behaviour in all these Changes that have been these 8 years (which have been many, as may be further manifest,) for there have been Changes of Governments, of Parliaments, and Protectors several in these Eight years, and all these have been warned not to uphold these Priests contrary to Peoples Consciences, but that every one might have their Liberty, that they that would have them might maintain them and they that could not receive their Doctrine, might not be forced to maintain them; but this would not satisfie their Covetous Practice, but they went on in the way of Cruelty, persecuting and Oppressing the Innocent, and casting into Prison, and took treble Dammages, and spoiled their Goods, and made Havock of poor Peoples Encrease, and Fruits of their Labours; neither would the magistrates hear, but suffered them to go on in their Persecution, and upheld them by a Law to the oppressing of the Innocent, until the Lord, by his mighty Power overturned them, and broke them one after another;

and those Priests turned to every Power, and every Government, as it turned; and made Petitions, and Addresses, and Acknowledgments to every Change of

Appendix 2

Government, and Conformed to every Power, and shewed much Love and Zeal to every present Power for their own ends, though many of them were Instruments to throw others out; Yet through their Deceit and Subtilties, have kept themselves in, in all these Times, and Changes.

Now, let any honest hearted People judge, whether these be sound Principled men, that can turn, conform, and transform to every Change according to the Times? Whether these be fit men to Teach People? But their Fruits are manifest, and God doth discover them more and more, that they cannot proceed much longer; Their Folly is so much made manifest, they have used their utmost endeavours to cause Persecution to continue upon us: But the Lord hath seen it, and we commit to him, & can freely say, The Lord forgive them for what they have done to us, **(Ac. 7: 60)** But for the bearing our Testimony against them for the deceiving and betraying of poor ignorant People that are blind, and led by them that are blind into the ditch, **(Mt. 15:14)** We cannot but in pitty and love to Peoples Souls, bear our Testimony against them, Therefore have our Sufferings been because

(PAGE 7) we desire the good of all People, and the Salvation of their Souls; and this is all we desire, and Suffer for, that all might come to the knowledge of the Lord, who said, They should all know him, from the least to the greatest. **(Heb. 8:11)**.

We are a People that follow after those things that make for **Peace, Love, and Unity**, it is our desire that others feet may walk in the same, and do deny and beare our Testimony against all Strife, and Wars, and Contentions that come from the Lusts that war in the members, that warr against the Soul, which we wait for and watch for in all People, and love and desire the good of all; for no other cause but love to the Souls of all People, have our sufferings been, and therefore have we been numbered amongst the Transgressors, and been accounted as sheep for the slaughter, as our Lord and Master was, who is the Captain of our Salvation who is gone before us, who though he was a Son,

yet learned he Obedience, by the things that the suffered, who said my **Kingdom** is not of this World, if my **Kingdom** were of this world, **(Jn. 18:36)** then would my Servants fight, but my **Kingdom** is not from hence; This is he that comes to save mens lives, and not to destroy them, **(Lk. 9: 56)** and this is he that is our Lord & Master, whose Testimony we must seal with our blood, if it be required of us; And our Weapons are not Carnal but Spiritual, **(2 Cor. 10; 4)** who have given our Backs, our Cheeks, and our Hair to all professions, out of the **Life and Power**, to be smitten, who have done it to purpose, which the Lord hath overturned, who were often warned by us, under whom we have undergon cruel sufferings.

And now You are come up into the Throne to be tried, we cannot but warn you in your day to do justly, and to love Mercy **(Mic. 6:8)** whereby the violence of the wicked might be stopt, which is for your own good, and prosperity. And so we desire and also expect to have the liberty of our Consciences and just Rights, and outward Liberties, as other people of the Nation, which we have promise of from the word of a King, that we may not be made a prey upon by the profane envious People and Priests which we have borne our Testimony against their corruptions, who thirst not only after our Estates & Liberties, but our blood also, who have already begun to search our Houses, and to apprehend our Members, & cast them into Prison, there to be kept without bail or mainprize, under pretence as if we were Thieves, Murderers, or Traytors, who are Enemies to no mans Person upon the Earth, which they cannot lay to our charge, whereby they endeavour to take away our lives. Treason, Treachery, and false Dealing we do utterly deny; false dealing, surmizing,

(PAGE 8) or plotting against any Creature upon the Face of the Earth, and speak the truth in plainnesse and singlenesse of heart, and all our desire is your good, and **Peace, and Love, and Unity**, and this may thousands will seal with their blood, who are ready not only to believe, but to suffer, but only that the blood of the Innocent may not come upon your selves through false information.

QQQQQQQQQQ

3. TO THE PRESENT DISTRACTED AND BROKEN NATION OF ENGLAND, AND TO ALL HER INHABITANTS

EDWARD BURROUGH *et al*
(20/10th Mo., 1659 = 20th December, 1659)

A Presentation and Declaration from the Seed of God, and from the People called Quakers, with their Sense and Knowledge published, concerning the present Divisions and Confusions come to passe in the Land, with the Causes thereof laid down and discovered, and also good Councel and Advice held forth, how Peace and Unity may be restored, and how the present tribulations may be removed.

Oh poor distressed Nation, and full of troubles; how art thou broken and divided? how hath divisions & distractions compassed thee about, and entred into thy bowels? and how are thy inhabitants, and thy people divided even into hatred one against another? and how are they filled, as with mischiefe, one towards another? even as it were, thirsting for the blood of one another Oh! How are thy Rulers and thy Subjects, thy great men and thy poor, confounded amongst themselves? and how is the wisedom of thy wise men turned into folly; and their union into present contention? and how do they seeke the overthrow one of another; and how do they lye in waite to be avenged one against another? and how are the hearts of many filled with envy, contention, and revenge; and love, peace and unitie, are farre away; meeknesse, patience, and long suffering, which ought to be among thy people, seemes to stand afar off; And oh Nation, this is the day of thy trouble, and the begining of thy sorrows. And for as much as it hath pleased the Lord God Almighty, to bring and suffer things thus to be brought to passe, as if he would make our Nation a heape, and suffer destruction upon it, and having suffered the Rulers and great men to overturne and break down one another, and to rend and tear one another from off the Throne; pulling down others, and setting up themselves, even

(PAGE 2) thorough their ambition and vaine glory, and for corrupted ends to themselves; whereby this our Nation is brought into present confusion, and many are begotten thorough these things into fury, heart burnings, and maliciousnesse; as if men were ready to devoure each one his neighbour, and their Brother; about Government and Rule; being greatly divided and distracted in this matter; some crying up oneway of Religion, and Church, and Civil Government; and some crying up another way, being each one sort of people seeking themselves, and the prosperitie of their own interests, and to have their own desires accomplished, but few seeking the Lord, and to advance him in **truth, and righteousnesse**

And because of this, there is no establishment in the Earth, but strife, and contention, and heart-burnings in the bowels of the Nation, and great want of **true love, true unitie, and true peace**, and all the contrary doth abound among the people; because of which the Nation is subject to present misery, even to bloodshed and murthers, and liable also to greater judgments, which may also come upon it, because of these things; all which we have deeply considered, with mourning, and with breakings of heart, on the behalfe of the Nation, the Land of our Nativitie; we have seen, we have seen, the cause of thy distractions, to be the Sins of thy Rulers and People, and we have seen the effect of them, to be dolefull and miserable unto thee, except the hand of the Lord turne it backward.

And oh, How do we mourn and lament, to behold the out goings of men, and the present condition of the People and Rulers, in this the day of their trouble; alas they do not behave themselves towards the Lord that his judgments may be turned away, they do not seeke him in **truth and righteousnesse**, they do not turne unto him with all their hearts, neither do they tremble at his **Word**: But they the rather reject his **Counsell**, and despiseth his **visitation**, and they seek themselves, and exalt their own horne, and loves the honour of this world, and their hearts are hardned, and the great men seemes to be utterly insensible of what the Lord is a doing, but seekes great things for themselves, and each one rejoycing of anothers fall, and glorying in their advantages one over another; one sort being first down, and another sort comes up, boasting themselves over the fall of their Enemies, and not knowing, that their time also is but very short.

(PAGE 3) And thus is our poor Nation tossed to and fro thorough the ambition of men; who even make a prey upon the poor peoples Persons and Treasure, for their own corrupted ends; and thy Rulers hath not had respect unto the **counsell of the Lord**, but seemes to refuse the way of peace, and even adds fewell to the fire of Gods wrath, by heaping up one transgression upon another, and they receive not the instructions of the Almighty. Behold, oh Nations, great trouble is upon thee, and the men that should rule thee, and which have pretended to govern thee, they do not walk in the **way of thy peace**, neither do they bring healing to thee. These things we have considered, and thus we lament over thee, and over thy present State; Oh Nation, how art thou like an ungirded vessell, that is ready to fall one piece from another? and how art thou like a body without a head, and all thy joynts out of order? and what confusion art thou fallen into, which is thy present State, and art even as a widdow without a husband, and art left comfortlesse unto this day, and ready to devoure thy self thorough the envy that lodgeth in thy owne bowells, though thou hast had Kings over thee, and chosen the Parliaments, and set up

Protectors; and Committees and Councels have bin created in thee, to have bin as a defence upon thee, and to have borne the Sceptre of thy Government; but alas these have all left thee, and thou art now as alone, and left in trouble, and confusion, and none of all these that sitte on thy Throne, have brought salvation unto thee, but thou art left comfortlesse even as a widow unto this day, and the Staffe of thy hand hath pierced thee, and thy strength and confidence hath betrayed thee, and them whom thou hast chosen have wrought no deliverance at all in thee, even the men that thou thoughtest should have healed thee, they have made thy wound more incurable, and they in whom thou hast reposed trust, they have been deceitfull and treacherous in thee, for many have sought themselves, and who should be the greatest, and they have trifled away many precious houres in vaine contentions about Government, what it should be, and who should Govern, while as no good thing hath been effected by them, but in the meane time of their delaies, and while they have been making themselves rich with the Nations Treasure, and loved this worlds perishing honour, and vaine titles, the Nation hath starved for want of **mercy and just judgment**, and the cause of its necessity hath bin forgotten, and **mercy and truth**, and the freedome

(PAGE 4) of the people neglected, and the cause of the fatherlesse, widdow, and stranger, and the cause of the afflicted people, have they not respected; Oh Nation, the men that have sitten on thy Throne, they have left thee groaning under great oppressions, wounded with the spirit of Tyranny yet un-cast out, and thy people are yet unhealed, but the breach hath been made wider, even by that Spirit which hath possessed thy Kings, thy Parliaments, thy Protectors, thy Councils, thy Committees, who hath proved Phisitians of no valew, but have bin the increasers of thy greefe, and even because of their iniquities, and the Sin of their ambition and oppression, hath the Lord dealt thus with them, and suffered them to dash one another in pieces; and through judgment unto themselves and thee, oh Nation, are they at present ceased from thee, and thou art left alone, and without a deliverer in the Earth, full of troubles and distractions;

oh that thou wouldest now look unto the Lord, and seek him in **righteousnesse**, that he may heale thee, for there is none of all them that do pretend to Rule thee, that do rightly proceed in the way of thy deliverance, they do not apply healing balm unto thy wound, they rather add unto the cause of thy sorow, then removes it from thee, their hearts are not aright before the Lord, and how then should they prosper in their doings. All these things have we viewed, and pittied the condition of our Nation, and thus we do declare the very cause of these things that are come to passe in thee, is in that, oh Nation, thou hast sinned, thou hast sinned; and the cry of thy iniquities is come up before the Lord, even the sinns of thy Rulers, and thy People, is the Cause of Gods displeasure against thee,

and he is provoked, through their transgressions; in thee is found the blood of the innocent, in thee is found the murther of Souls, in thee is found treachery against God, and hypocrisie and dissimulation with God and men, in thee is found pride, and oppression, whoredom, and drunkenness, stealing, and murther, in thee is found the very burthen of iniquitie, and the full measure of transgression, even the transgression of Gods whole Law, deceit is found in the unsoundnesse of heart, and unconstancy in all good things, multitude of hypocriticall fastings, prayers, and

Appendix 2

services, in thee is found, even destroying sins of all sorts doth abound, and thou hast provoked the Lord God by thy abominations: Thy Rulers have bin oppressors, thy Teachers

(PAGE 5) deceivers of Soules, and thy People are froward, and perverse, against the Lord, in thee is found the men that judge for rewards, and the Priests that preach for hire, and the Prophets that divine for money; thy sins are like Israels of old, for number, and greatnesse, and thou hast lost Gods favour, and gain'd his fury, by thy own doings, and thou art the very cause of this misery, and hast brought it upon thy self, and because thou art departed from the living God by thy transgression, therefore hath he confounded thee, and turned thy wisdome into folly, and he is departed from thee, and out of thy counsells, and men are left to the counsells of their own hearts, and as it were ready to destroy one another, Ruler against Ruler, and Neighbour and Friend full of strife one against another, and this hapned unto thee as a judgment for thy iniquities, who hast also neglected a glorious **day of visitation**;

thy Rulers and Inhabitants have bin warned, and the cry of repentance hath bin sounded towards them all; by a despised people, but warning hath not bin regarded, but the **Word of the Lord** rejected by thy Rulers and People, and loe what wisdome is there in them, not so much wisdome from God as can preserve them, but it may be just with the Lord to suffer them to drink the blood one of another, even because they have sinned against God, and rejected his **counsell**, therefore is this come to passe in the Nation : for hadst thou, oh Nation, walked in the light of the Lord, it had bin better with thee, had every one obeyed the Light in his own conscience; and had every one sought the Lord, and not himself, had thy Rulers Ruled for God, and had thy people bin Ruled of God, then this day had not bin a day of trouble, but it had bin a day of joy, and sorrow and anguish had bin removed farr from thee, and blessings had filled thy habitations.

And now whereas many wise men have bin advising and consulting the peace of this our Nation, and they have given in their counsell for the removing these troubles, yet **peace and unitie** seemes to be farr away, and though they have sought peace for this Nation, yet they have not walked in the perfect way thereof, for innocency, truth, and simplicitie, have bin wanting, which God only will blesse, and by flatteries, and deceipts, and the pollicy, and wisdome of this world, have they thought to make up thy breach but it cannot be, for in the way of that proceeding will not the Lord be found in a needfull time; and his presence hath bin wanting in their counsells, and therefore the **fruit of peace** is not yet

(PAGE 6) grown up, this we have seen, and therefore thus we do declare, O Nation, the inward cause of thy distractions must be removed, even thy iniquities must be forsaken, and thy transgressions repented of; thou must forsake thy former waies and doings that are not right, thou must leave off thy hypocrisies and flatteries with God and men; thou must repent thee of thy profanenesse, and of thy profession also, thy sin and thy righteousnesse must thou put away, which are both abominations unto God, thou must cease to do evill, and learn to do well, and thou must be uncovered of thy Sheeps cloathing, thy large profession of Religion, and the multitude of thy prayers, and Sermons, and the number of thy Oblations, and

Offerings, these things have not bin pleasant unto the Lord from thee, but because hereof is he the rather provoked against thee, and thou must be stripped of thy filthy garments, and sett as in the day that thou wast borne, before thou canst be cloathed with divine righteousnes,

and O Nation, thou must be changed, not in name only, but in nature; thou must be converted, that the wrath of the Lord may be turned back from thee; every inhabitant in thee must becom a fighter against the evil in his own heart, and the plague thereof must be sought out and removed; the sin must be forsaken that judgement may cease, and every one must cease to provoke the Lord, and no longer vex his Spirit within them, and every one must love the light of Christ in his own conscience, and become a follower of it, that will lead him out of all sin, and every man must put off his transgressions and forsake himself, and lay down the enmity, and cast it out of his heart, that he hath against Persons,

and he must warr against the Enemies of his own Soule, and the Enemies of his own house must be slayne, even his own lusts, and even the evil affections of his own heart must he become an Enemie unto, and every man must deny the false Teachers and Deceivers, and must come to be taught of the Lord, every one must turne to him, and come into his **Covenant**, and hear his Word, and obey his **Voice**, and become humble and meek, and must tremble at the word of the Lord, and must become upright and innocent. And O Nation, if it were thus with thee, then shouldest thou be a happy people if thou dost thes things, then shal all thy breaches be healed, and thy sorrows be turned into joy, and the Lord shal cease to smite thee, & his anger shal be turned clean away: This is our counsel unto thee, remove thy iniquities by repentance, be converted to the Lord, and he shall heale thee, and his love shall be shed abroad;

(PAGE 7) peace, plenty and satisfactions, unity and concord shall be unto all thy inhabitants, and the Lord himself shall be thy **King**, thy Judge and thy Law-giver: he will judge thee with equity, and not with oppression; he will teach thee in the perfect way, and thou shalt not err, he will defend thee from all thy Enemies, and Tyrants shall not have power over thee; Oh Nation if thou do these things, even turn to the Lord with all thy heart, that he may walk in thee, and dwell in thee, then should thy light break out of obscurity, and the dew of mercies should fall upon thee, and it should be unto thee as a Morneing without cloudes, and thou should'st be refreshed after all thy sorrowes; the Nation should be happy, and the People blessed, and the **Government of peace, and truth** should be established, never to be confounded any more.

And thus thy iniquities being removed, the plague should cease, and the cause of destruction being taken away, no fruit thereof should appear, wherefore let men cease to hatch mischiefe one against another, and to seek vengeance one of another; and let them seek with all speed, and sincerity, to get victory over their own sins, and that vengeance may be taken upon their own transgressions; and this is our councell for the healing of our Nations breach, and for turning away of the anger of the Lord. But and if, O Nation thou continue in thy perversenesse, and in transgressions which the Lord hates, and if thou wilt not turn to him that smiteth thee, and love his Rod that corrects thee, but wilt alwaies greive the Spirit of the Lord, and will be obstinate, and stout-hearted against the Lord, and his reproofes, and if thou wilt continue in thy accustomed sins, then shall the reward thereof be upon thee, even breach upon breach, and one judgment upon another; and mercy shall be with-holden from thee, and the dew shall not fall upon thee, but thou shalt be as a barren heath; and thou shalt be given up to consume thy self, in mischiefe, and in thy heart burnings one towards another,

if thou wilt set up Rulers of thy own proud and ambitious men, and wilt not choose the Lord to Rule over thee, but reject him, and his people, then shall thy breach never be healed by the men whom thou choosest, but through them shall thy breach be more desperate, and thy wound made more incurable, and if thou wilt set up Teachers that teach for filthy lucre, and Prophets that divine for money, and Priests that preach for hire, and will not receive the **Covenant of the Lord**, and him to be thy Teacher, by his Spirit; then shalt thou Err in thy wayes,

(PAGE 8) and stumble, and fall, and never know perfect peace with God, nor one with another; but as thou lovest oppression and deceit, and walkest in transgression, so shall it be unto thee, and thou must eat the fruit of thy own doings, misery upon miseries shall be upon thee, and thou shalt not see the face of the Almighty to refresh thee; wherefore, O Nation, consider before the night comes upon thee, when no way will be found by thee to be delivered, for in the midst of thy confusions; God is a working, he hath a work to bring forth, which shall be a work of great mercy, and deliverance, or of sorrow, and of great judgment, even to the whole Land.

And as for us, we hereby declare unto thee, we are not thy Enemies, we seek not thy hurt, nor do we desire vengeance upon our Enemies, we seek not thy destruction; but we desire thy repentance, that thou mayest be healed; we have not the spirit of mischiefe, and rebellion in our hearts towards thee, neither are we for one party, or another, nor do we side with one sort, and rebell against another, neither do we joyne our selves to this sort or the other, nor do we warr against any by carnall weapons, neither shall we ever provoke the Nation against us, otherwise then by our righteous and holy walking, &we do declare that we are not for men, nor names, nor shall we joyne with this, or that sort of men, but as they act righteousnesse alone, nor any thing which yet appears, can we fully embrace or rejoyce in; for they are all corrupted in their waies, and that cursed spirit of self seeking, seemes to be the rule of, and to leaven their principall actions, and we rather yet chuse to suffer by all, as for a long time we have don already; then to lose our integrity, and innocency, by joyning to any, in their unjust waies, for we reject all places of corrupted honour, and we are yet kept free.

It is true, we are a people gathered of the Lord into one Spirit, and though a people little in account, and very low in reputation, and greatly reproached, and even a suffering people by all sorts of men, yet we are a people loved of the Lord, and his presence is among us, and his dread filleth our hearts, and though we are accounted as a cast-out people, yet are we dreadfull unto the wicked, and must be their fear, for we have chosen the Sonn of God to be our King, and he hath chosen us to be his people; and he might command thousands, and ten thousands of his Saints at this day, to fight for his cause, he might lead them forth, and bring them in, and give them victory over all

(**PAGE 9**) their Enemies, and turne his hand upon all their persecutors but yet his **Kingdome** is not of this World, neither is his warrfare with carnall weapons, neither is his victory by the murthering, and killing of mens persons, neither hath he chosen us for that end, neither can we yet beleeve that he will use of us in that way, though it be his only right to rule in Nations, and our heireship to possesse the uttermost parts of the Earth, but for the present we are given up to beare, and suffer all things for his names sake, and our present glory, and renowne therein stands, till the appointed time of our deliverance, without the Arme of flesh, or any multitude of an hoast of men; this we declare, and O Nation, though we have born thy reproaches these many yeares, and have passed under the Rod of thy wicked Rulers, and people, and have bin afflicted through their hard-heartednesse, though we never have provoked thee otherwise then by our well doing; and though persecution, imprisonments, whippings, banishments, and all hard things have bin our portion from thee, yet this hath bin for righteousnesse sake, and not for any evil doing,

and we have borne all these things in much patience, and we are not now provoked against thee, to seek thy hurt, or to work evill in thee, and though thou hast smitten us, yet would we have thee to be healed, and though thou hast sought to destroy us, yet would we have thee to repent and be saved, and we are at this day thy mourners, and are afflicted for thee in our hearts, even because thou hast provoked the Lord against thee, though we do rejoyce in the judgments which smiteth thee; yet we mourn for thee who hath deserved such wo full stripes; and also because thou refusest the way of peace, and counteth them that reprove thee even thy Enemies, and hardnest thy heart against Gods instructions; and counteth his free borne people thy bond slaves; who hath not any larg portion, nor great places of honour in this Nation, nor any thing to glory in from thee, but sufferings, afflictions, and tribulations; where is the place in this Nation, that we have not bin reproached? in what Streete have we not bin reviled; and in what Prison have we not bin unjustly imprisoned? and among what sort of people have not we bin hated? and what one of thy Judges and Rulers can cleare themselves before the Lord, from the guilt of our unjust sufferings. O Nation, our portion in thee, for these many years, hath bin thy cruell reproaches; our greatest place of honour in thee hath bin under thy cruell oppressions, and these things, and the guilt thereof

(**PAGE 10**) will God charge upon thee, and reward thee for, one time or another; yet notwithstanding all this, our present desires for thee are good, and not evil, that thou mayest be saved and not destroyed, healed and not wounded unrecoverably; and we would not add unto thy grief, by any just provocation, through any evil towards thee, neither would we work offence in thee, further then what thou takest for righteousnesse sake, and for the exercise of our pure conscience. And though there hath bin in this Nation divers and sundry overturnings of late dayes, and some have bin turned out, and others brought into place, each one sort of them crying against the evil of another, and promising to accomplish such and such good things in this Nation; yet alas, what is there effected unto this day? what freedom and true liberty to subjects more then was many years ago? what oppressions taken off from the people? what establishment in Government?

Appendix 2

Alas, not any of these things are accomplished, neither do we see a right thing propounded, and rightly prosecuted, by any party yet appearing; but the cause hardly yet appears, carried on by any among them, which can be said of it, this is of the Lord, and is perfectly right, and the Lord will prosper it, for the most of the men that have yet appeared on the Throne, they have rejected the **Word of the Lord**, and his **Councel**; and what wisdom is there in them, only the policy, and subtiltie, and wisdom of this world, wherein they build, but the Lord throws down, even before it be finished; and they consult therein, and the Lord dasheth to peeces; they set up, but he pulls down, because they want his spirit and wisdom, and his authoritie amongst them, and they are as the Potsheards of the earth, that the iron Rod must break in peeces; and this we declare, the men (yet) seem not to appear in all these Parties, which are worthie to handle the Lords Sceptre, and to be crowned with the honour of Authoritie in **his Government**; but even this partie, and the other party seems to be unworthie to rule for the Lord, for they appear to be choaked with the honour of this world, and corrupted thereby, and uncapable of receiving that anointing that men must have, that shall truly rule for God; and though many in our days that have ruled over us, have promised great things to the Nation, yet we see all hitherto have wanted power to perform, and have not bin blessed with the Presence of the Lord, so as this Nation hath bin healed and redeemed by them,

(PAGE 11) and we are utterly out of all hopes of this party, or the other party, of this man, or that man, to bring salvation unto this Nation, from all its bonds and oppressions, for we know, whatsoever men professe to do, yet they cannot performe any good thing, nor Rule for God in our Nation, till that themselves be reformed, and ruled by him, and have the Spirit of God poured upon them for such a work, and this we declare, till that a man, or men, be ruled of the Lord, they can never rightly Rule for him, nor bring deliverance and freedome to an oppressed Nation, though men may, and have promised much, yet their fruit is but little; and thou O Nation, hast long bin deceived by such men, who have flattered thee with the multitude of faire words, and promised thee deliverance; and hereby might'st thou learn wisdome, O England, never more to rest under the shadow of such men, make no more a mountain to cover thy self, rest not under the shaddow of dead Trees, that wants the vertue of God, but now look at the living God, and wait for that King of righteousnesse, and peace, whose rights alone it is to Rule, for he alone can bring salvation to thee, he alone can heale thy breaches, even Jesus Christ, whose coming is at the doore, and in the mean time O Nation, while he is absent, thou art dry, and barren, and empty, thou art tossed, and shaken, and thou art tossed, and perplexed, and cannot be rightly comforted; for men shall not be a rest unto thee, but one after another shall they be overturned,

for it is the Lord alone, and under **his Government** shall people finde perfect rest, and freedom from all oppression, for what is a King? and what is a Parliament? what is a Protector, and what is a Councell? or any other sort of men, while the presence of the Lord is not with them, and while his Spirit and Authority is wanting to them, what can any of these bring forth, none of all these whatsoever, if the Lord be not cheefe in them, and amongst them, and his **counsell** their only guide, shall be any otherwise unto this Nation, then as a broken Reed to leane upon, and no more then a shaddow which shall not save the people from the heat, nor from the storme; this we know, and this we declare, in the Name of the Lord: and we are not for Names, nor for Men, nor for Titles of Government, nor are we for this party, nor against the other, because of its name, and pretence, but we are for **Justice**, and **Mercy, and Truth**, and **Peace, and true freedom**, that these may be exalted in our Nation; and that goodnesse, righteousnesse, meeknesse, temperance, peace, and unity, with God, and one with another; that these things may abound, and be

(PAGE 12) brought forth abundantly, such a **Government** are wee seeking, and waiting for, wherein **truth, and righteousnesse, mercy, and justice**, unity and love, and all the **fruites of holynesse** may abound, and all the contrary be removed, cast out, and limmitted, and we are not for such and such Names, and Titles of Government, that promises faire, and performes nothing; but if a Council, if a Parliament, if any one Man, or a number of men whatsoever, that shall have the Spirit of the Lord poured on him, or them, and shall be annointed of the Lord for such an use, and end, to Govern this Nation, under such only shall the Nation be happy, and enjoy rest, from such men fitted of the Lord, and called by him, and under such a **Government of Truth, and righteousnesse,** shalt thou O Nation, enjoy rest from all thy Travells, and under such a Government, shall the righteous rejoyce; and the whole Land sing for joy of heart, when Tyranny, and oppression shall be cleane removed, strife, and contention, and self seeking, utterly abandoned, and when **peace, and truth**, flowes forth as a streame, and the Lord alone rules in thy Rulers, and he the principall amongst them, and under such men, and such a Government only and not under any other, shalt thou O Nation, be happy, and thy people a free people.

Wherefore, O Nation! when wilt thou begin to look to the Lord: when wilt thou begin to set up him, and not man, when wilt thou minde his **Power and Presence** in and through men, more then any men themselves; when shall it once be, O ye people of our Nation, that ye will seek after him, to be the principal and chief power among you: Oh let your eyes be turned to the Lord alone, that he may deliver you, and bring salvation and freedom, and look no more at men, but only as they are in him, guided by his Spirit; and only expect good from men, as they are guided by the Lord; and then shall you not ever any more be deceived, as long you have bin, with Kings, with Parliaments, with Councels, with Armies, nor any others; for in these have you trusted, and not in the Lord; from these have you expected great things without him; whenas alas, what shall men accomplish, or what can they bring forth, while they reject the **Counsel of the Lord**, and his Word, as hitherto they have done, and therefore hath he broke them and confounded them, yea, and he will break them and crush them under his Rod, even till they come to learn his judgments, and know him the alone Power, and give honour to him that doth whatsoever he will, and he will overthrow once

(PAGE 13) and againe, even till he comes, whose right it is to Rule, and he is at work in this his day, and because of iniquities doth he visit with tribulation, and through great tribulation, and overturneing of Men, and Powers, will he advance his own **Kingdome**, and **Government**, and the end of all these things shall bring forth his glory, and men that will not honour him by dealing righteously in their day upon Earth, they must honour him in their destruction, at their latter end, and let not men glory one over another, while some are put down, and others set up, but let them all know, they have but each sort their houre, and their end will come even as others for an **everlasting Kingdome, and Government** will God set up, that must rule over all, and this is the hope of a poor despised people, though for present hated of all, and sought to be destroyed by all, yet our soules are anchored and stay'd, even in the sure promises of our God, in this the day of the Nations trouble,

and though we are very poor, and rejected of all, and have nothing to glory in amongst any party or sort of people, but even in our reproaches, and sufferings, which we sustain from all, yet have we perfect rest in God, and satisfactions over all these distractions, we know him in whom we have beleived, and we trust in the shaddow of his wing, and we are not of a doubting heart, concerning what can come, or whomsoever doth Rule, for this we know, though all seeke after our blood, yet he can deliver us if he will, we know him that can do all things, and if he save none can destroy, if he blesse none can curse; him we know, and in him we rest, and we give our power in all things to him, and not unto mortall man, whose breath is in his nostrills, who must perish as the dung, we cannot be afraid of their horror, nor can we be drawn by their love, but we trust in his Name, and under his defence shall we be saved, we give our power to him, to be defended and preserved by him alone, and we are well contented with our sufferings, and murmurs not, our sufferings are our present Crown;

but yet woe unto that Authority which maketh us to suffer, and woe unto the men upon whom God shall charg the guilt of our oppressions, and woe unto that Spirit that is found acting against Gods annointed, behold, ye Mountaines of the Earth, behold! ye Rulers, and ye People, the Lord hath blessed his people, and every tongue that riseth up in witnesse against them shall be condemned, and every weapon that is formed against them shall be broken; this is our hope in this gloomy day, and the hope of a **Kingdome of righteousnesse**, and peace which must be set up, is our refreshment in this day of trouble, and let not our Enemies glory

(PAGE 14) over us, for though we are poor, yet shall we be made rich, and though we have no carnal weapon, yet shall we conquer, and thus have we declared our selves in much plainnesse and sinceritie to our Nation whom we love, and whose present condition we pity and lament over, and we are friends to any Appearance of good, that may come forth in truth and sinceritie, and as righteousnesse doth appear in any, we are ready to joyne with it in our prayers and desires, yea, and otherwise; even that which hath the image of our God upon it, whenever it shall appear, we shall rejoyce therein, and adde our help thereunto that it may prosper,

for the establishing of righteousnesse in the earth, our all is not dear unto us, though hitherto we have bin silent and not medling with this party or the other, but by way of reproof of the evil in all, and informing all to the good; and it cannot be charged upon us, that we have sided with one or another, for we have beheld all hitherto but of **the right way** as we have said; but we truly seek the general good of our Nation, and though we are accounted, so and so, yet we have not lost true reason nor understanding, but we well know what is wrong, and what would be right, even in way of Government, but the time appears not to be yet, when innocencie and simplicitie of heart can be embraced, for men are yet too wise in their own wisdom, and cannot receive the **Councel of the Lord** that they may prosper, and therefore are they, and must they be confounded amongst themselves; and dashed one against another, till they learn the way of **Righteousnesse and Truth**.

APPENDIX 3

James Nayler, 'Not to Strive, but Overcome by Suffering' (1658/9)

Children of God, seek a Kingdom in you, that flesh and blood strive not for, nor cannot enter therein, a Kingdom undefiled, and that fadeth not away, hid from that which feeds on earthly things, a heavenly Kingdom, bearing heavenly fruits, and where heavenly things abound; wherein the heavenly Spirit rules, guides, and brings forth fruits of itself, heavenly fruits, the fruits of grace and meekness, and of a lowly mind, the fruits of peace and gentleness, and forbearance amongst yourselves.

These are heavenly fruits, and the virtues of the tree of life, and that which the loftiness of flesh and blood looks not for, nor doth esteem, which loves the praise of men, and to be known in that which this world can see into with the outward understanding: but wait with patience to feel that quickened, which is sown in tears, and springs up with joy, out of the sight of the natural understanding, that that alone may bear you, and therein all your fruit may be found, and so come to the knowledge of the tree by its fruits; and let the life open the understanding (and not the notion, or a sight) that is the heavenly learning of Christ Jesus the righteous, full of grace and truth; but striving to get up to the knowledge of heavenly things in notion and form, before the thing itself be born and brought forth, this is the wrong way to learn Christ, and the way of the world, that veils the life; for this knowledge stands in the sensual part, to exalt and puff up the mind above the meekness and lowliness that is in the Spirit of Christ Jesus, and beguiles the soul of the simplicity in which it should feed; and so a tree may grow high and hard and strong, yet fruitless and out of the power, got above the poor, above the innocent, out of the feeling of the sufferer and man of sorrows where he is; and the end of this growth is not in the pure rest, for the higher anyone grows here, the more doth that wither and die in them, which is soft, and tender and melting, which makes one, and is the true fold for lambs, where the lions must lie down in the end, if they come to rest, and that eye put out which looks to be great among men, that comes not into the rest, but hath strife in the mind, strife in words and secret smitings, which defile the rest, and lead into the division and separation; but the little child leads into the rest, and that which is lowly gives the entrance.

So feel that which is lowly and meek to arise above self, that which stills all strife at home in your minds, and gives peace in temptation and tribulation; that's a soft and tender thing in you, that is the peace-maker, that's blest of God. And this is first felt under the world, under the strife, suffering by the strife in patience, to bring to the end of the strife and the world, and in the end of it, and all exaltation, he comes to arise over the world and the enmity, who is not of a striving nature, but lives by hope, and believes to see to the end of all things under which he suffers, and to outlive every temptation by suffering. And so by an everlasting life comes over the world, and to reign over all things that are not of that eternal nature; but not to join with the evil.

And he that in the particular is born of this, hath overcome the world in himself, and knows how to walk towards his brother in that which hath power over the world and outlives all, whereby he can suffer therein, and brings forth its own undefiled into one to rest, ever aiming in all ministrations at the Kingdom of truth, peace and holiness, which is the end of all gifts and callings amongst the brethren, and is only obtained as that arises in all which suffers by the world but is not of the world, which he that is Christ's minister comes to turn men unto.

And this seed all should know, which is beloved of the Father and heir of the everlasting Kingdom, who strives not by violence but entreats; who seeks not revenge, but endures all contradictions from all against himself, to the end he may obtain mercy for all from the Father. And this is the seed of eternal peace, and the eternal peace maker, which was foreordained of the Father and hath power to endure all things and subdue all things by overcoming.

So this seek in yourselves and all men, and in it seek one another as brethren. This is that which is perfect, and is never to be done away, neither can it be overcome of the world; wrath cannot enter it, pride cannot enter it; it strives for nothing but to live its own life, which the world strives not for; nor can any that are of it strive with it; the worldly spirit seeks not that crown, whose life is to suffer all things, to be meek, and low, and poor, and rejected; reviled, contemned of all the world, bearing the reproach of all that's above that of God in all. And little striving in the will of man is there for this Kingdom, or the cross that belongs thereto, which no exalted mind can bear nor glory in.

And this is the righteousness that exceeds the scribes and Pharisees, and professors, and that wherein they cannot enter; nor can any reign in this Kingdom, but who can bear the cross which leads to the crown, and hath a habitation in that which cannot be moved with change nor kindled with wrath. This is the heritage of the meek, and the Kingdom which only belongs to the poor in spirit and pure in heart, where the hardness of heart is broken, and melted, and self dead; many spirits desire to look into it; but few to live the life of it; it's only for the heirs who are born through sorrow, and slain with ease; to whom flesh and blood is an enemy, and with the eye that looks out lightly esteemed amongst men.

APPENDIX 4A
83 Key Words/Phrases from the Fox-Hubberthorne and Fell Declarations, including a 1650s source for each

1. **Innocent/innocence:**
J. Audland, *The Innocent Delivered out of the Snare* (1655), 6.
2. **Righteousness:**
Fox, Ep.19 (1652), *LOGF*, 9.
3. **Knowledge of God/the Lord:**
Penington, *The Way of Life and Death* (1658), 46.
4. **Seek the Good and Welfare:**
Farnworth, *A Brief Discovery of the Kingdom* (1653), 22.
5. **War (carnal):**
Harwood, *The Path of the Just Cleared* (1655), 10.
6. **Lusts:**
Rigge, *The Banner of Love* (1657), 9.
7. **Blood/bloody:**
Dewsbury, *The Discovery of Man's Return* (1654), 8.
8. **Testify/Testimony to the whole world:**
Fox (the Younger), *Honest, Upright* (1659) in *Works*, 80.
9. **Peter in Gethsemane:**
Lilburne, *The Resurrection* (1656), 4.
10. **Faith and Patience of the Saints:**
Wollrich, *The Unlimited God* (1659), 21.
11. **Not of this world (the Kingdom):**
Parnel, 'The Trumpet of the Lord' (1655) in *Works*, 36.
12. **Pilate the magistrate:**
Bishop *et al*, 'To the Reader', in *The Cry of Blood* (1656), 8.
13. **Father forgive them:**
Farnworth, *A Message from the Lord* (1653), 7.
14. **That the Scripture might be fulfilled:**
Aldam *et al*, *False Prophets* (1552), 2.
15. **The Spirit (of Christ) is unchangeable:**
D. White, *An Epistle of Love*, (1661), 2.
16. **Truth:**
Mason, *A Check to the Lofty Linguist* (1655), 15.
17. **Exalt according to his promise:**
Dewsbury, *Christ Exalted* (1656), 5.
18. **Grow and flourish in righteousness:**
Hubberthorne, *The Rebukes* (1657), 73.
19. **Zc 4: 6b:**
W. Smith, *A Right Dividing* (1659), 7.
20. **We cannot covet them:**
Fox, *To All that would Know the Way to the Kingdom* (1653/5), 9.
21. **Word:**
H. Clark, *A Cloud of Witness* (1656), 4-9.
22. **In the hearts of men:**
Crook, *A Defence of the True Church* (1659), 8.
23. **Rule and Reign:**
Parnell, *To Friends in Essex* (1655) in *Works*, 441.
24. **Love and unity:**
W. Smith, *The New Creation* (1661), 7, 8.
25. **Obedience to his Truth:**
H. Smith, *A Warning to the Priests* (1656), 8.
26. **God persuadeth every man's heart to believe:**
Blackborow, *Herein is held forth the Gift* (1659), 6.
27. **Laboured to be made manifest:**
Howgill, *This is Only to Go*, (1656), 9.
28. **Evil falsely spoken of us:**
Hubberthorne, *A True Testimony . . . University-Men* (1654) in *Works*, 43.
29. **Ordained of God:**
Fox (the Younger), *Honest, Upright* (1659 in *Works*, 77.
30. **Conversation in the World:**
Fairman, *A Few Lines Given Forth* (1659), Bds.
31. **Conscience sake:**
Howgill, *An Information and also Advice* (1659) in *Works*, 331.
32. **Sheep for the slaughter:**

W. Smith, *A Short Testimony* (1660), 3, 10.

33. **Haled out of synagogues:**
Vivers, *The Saints Testimony* (1655), 14.

34. **Freely give up our Bodies a sacrifice:**
Parnel, *To Friends in Essex* (1655) in *Works*, 444.

35. **Plead our Cause:**
W. Bayly, *The Blood of Righteous Abel* (1658), 3.

36. **We shall not swear at all:**
Byllynge (Burrough?), (1659), 1.

37. **Contrary to the Spirit of Christ, his doctrine:**
G. Benson, *The True Trial of Ministers* (1655), 5.

38. **Babes of Christ:**
M. Forster et al, *These Several Papers* (1659), 4.

39. **Apple of his eye:**
Blaugdone, *An Account of the Travels, Sufferings* (1691), 25 (for 1650s).

40. **Heritage of God:**
Howgill, *An Answer to a Paper* (1654) in *Works*, 7.

41. **Neither turn your swords backward:**
Fox, *This for each Parliament Man* (1656), 8, 9.

42. **Overcome evil with good:**
Nayler, *The Lamb's War* (1657), 7.

43. **Three children in Daniel (ch. 3):**
Dewsbury, *Christ Exalted* (1656) 5.

44. **God is the same . . . in his Arms:**
Howgill, *General Epistle to the Camp* (1655), 31.

45. **Mercy, Justice and Judgment:**
W. Bayly, *Iacob is Become a Flame* (1659?), 1.

46. **The innocent lambs of Christ (hath been slain):**
T. Taylor, *Some Prison Meditations in the 7th month* (1657), *passim*.

47. **They that feared his Name spoke often together:**
Fairman, *A Few Lines Given Forth* (1659), Bds.

48. **Election:**
Burrough, *A Declaration to the World of our Faith* (1657) in *Works*, 442-3.

49. **World: before the world began, in which there is no End:**
Crisp, *A Word of Reproof* (1658), 3.

50. **Hated and despised:**
Nayler, *A Word from the Lord . . . Professors* (1654) in *Works*, 176.

51. **Same Spirit, Power and Life:**
Hookes, *The Spirit of Christ* (1661), 5-6.

52. **The Offscouring of all things (many refs to 'despised people of God'):**
Crook et al, *A Declaration of the People of God* (1659), 2.

53. **Authority (priestly/Jesus'):**
W. Smith, *A Right Dividing* (1659), 7.

54. **Authority (outward/Govt. etc.):**
Hubberthorne, *The Mittimus Answered* (1654) in *Works*, 38.

55. **Being made perfect:**
Caton, *A Moderate Inquirer* (1659), 19-20.

56. **A hireling was a Thief and a Robber:**
Aldam et al, *False Prophets* (1652), *passim*.

57. **Author of Eternal Salvation:**
W. Smith., *The Dayspring from on High* (1659), 4.

58. **Powers of the Earth:**
Parnel, *The Trumpet* (1655) in *Works*, 28-34.

59. **Nakedness:**
Bateman, *'I matter not how I appear to man'* (1658), 2.

60. **Vengeance is mine and I will repay it:**
J. Whitehead, *The Enmity between the Two Seeds* (1655), 13.

61. **Not in flattering titles:**
Anon, *To the Generals, and Captains* (1657), 6.

62. **Blood and persecution:**
Burrough, 'To All you Generals', in *A Trumpet of the Lord* (1656) in *Works*, 8.

63. **The blood of all men:**
G. Whitehead, *The Path of the Just Cleared* (1655), 8.

64. **Whose cause God hath pleaded and will plead:**
Penington, *A Brief Account of Some Reasons*, n.d. (*DCFB* supposes 1659), Bds.

65. **All may be saved and come to a knowledge of the Truth, Way and the Life:**
W. Bayly, *A Warning from the Spirit of Truth* (1658), 16.

66. **Everlasting covenant [Promise]:**
Penington, *The Scattered Sheep Sought After* (1659) in *Works*, 104-5.

67. **Walk in this Light:**
Rofe, *The Righteousness of God* (1656), 1.

68. **Light to the Gentiles:**
Coale, *An Invitation of Love* (1660), 4.

69. **Righteousness of faith:**
Howgill, *A Lamentation of the Scattered Tribes* (1656) in *Works*, 78, 80.

70. **Will come near to [the Day of] Judgment:**
Farnworth, *A Message from the Lord* (1653), 18.

71. **Sorcerer, Adulterer [etc.].**
Farnworth, *Witchcraft Cast Out* (1655), passim.

72. **For God is coming to teach his People himself:**
Dewsbury, *Christ Exalted* (1656), 18.

73. **Life and Power:**
J. Whitehead, *A Word of Reproof* (1656), 7.

74. **Letter of the Scripture:**
Crook, *The Defence of the True Church* (1659), 5.

75. **The infallible Spirit of God:**
Fox, *Newes . . . North* (1654), 4.

76. **Overturned them:**
J.G. (John Gibson?), *The Ancient of Days is Come* (1657), 3.

77. **But their fruits are manifest:**
Howgill, *General Epistle to the Camp* (1655), 28.

78. **God doth discover them more and more:**
Crisp, *A Word of Reproof* (1658), 1.

79. **People that are blind, . . . :**
Blackborow, *Herein is Held Forth the Gift* (1659), 2.

80. **And led by them that are blind into the ditch:**
Fell et al, *False Prophets, Antichrists* (1655), 5.

81. **Salvation of/love to their souls:**
Parnel, *A Trial of Faith* (1654) in *Works*, 6.

82. **They should all know him, from the least to the greatest:**
Aldam et al, *False Prophets* (1652), 6, 7.

83. **Up to the throne to be tried:**
Wollrich, *The Unlimited God*, (1659), 12.

APPENDIX 4B

637 Selections mentioning the 83 Key Words/Phrases from 206 Works (1652-61) by 46 Authors.

1. Aldam *et al*, *False Prophets* (1652), 3.
2. Anderdon, *A Visitation in Love* (1660), 12.
3. Anon, *To the Generals, and Captains* (1657), 6.
4. J. Audland, 'Letter to Oliver Cromwell' (1658) in *Works*, 6.
5. ____ *The Innocent Delivered out of the Snare* (1655), 6.
6. Bateman, *'I matter not how I appear to man'* (1658), 2.
7. W. Bayly, *A Short Discovery* (1659), 1.
8. ____, *A Warning from the Spirit of Truth* (1656), 28-32.
9. ____, *Iacob is Become a Flame* (1659?), 1.
10. ____, *The Blood of Righteous Abel* (1658), 3.
11. G. Benson, *The True Trial of Ministers* (1655), 5.
12. Byllynge (Burrough?), *A Mite of Affection* (1659), 1.
13. Bishop, *The Cry of Blood* (1656), *passim*.
14. ____, *The Throne of Truth* (1657), 18.
15. Blackborow, *A Visit to the Spirit in Prison* (1658), 7.
16. ____, *Herein is Held Forth the Gift* (1655), 7.
17. Blaugdone, *An Account of the Travels, Sufferings,* (1691), 25 (for 1650s).
18. Burrough *et al* [?], 'An Account of some Grounds' in *A Declaration of the Present Sufferings* (1659), 24.
19. ____, 'An Answer to ... Anabaptists' in Hubberthorne, *An Answer ... Anabaptists* (1659), 24.
20. ____, 'Concerning the Gospel of Christ', *A Standard Lifted Up* (1657) in *Works*, 249.
21. ____, 'Epistle to the Reader', in Fox, *The Great Mystery* (1659), 4.
22. ____, 'For the Hand of Oliver Cromwell' (1658/9), *Good Counsel and Advice* (1659) in *Works*, 557.
23. ____, 'To All that are Moved' (1658) in *Works*, 386.
24. ____, 'To all you Jesuits', *An Alarum ... Pope's Borders* (1659) in *Works*, 533.
25. ____, 'To All you Generals', in *A Trumpet of the Lord*, (1656) in *Works*, 8.
26. ____, 'To the Parliament and Army (in general)', Reay, B., 'The Quakers and 1659: two newly discovered broadsides by Edward Burrough', *JFHS*, 108.
27. ____, 'To the Protector and his Council' (1658) in *Works*, 581.
28. ____, *A Declaration to the World of our Faith* (1657) in *Works*, 442-3.
29. ____, *A Faithful Testimony* (1659), 7.
30. ____, *The Fourth General Epistle to all the Saints* (1660) in *Works*, 659-66.
31. ____, *A Measure of the Times* (1657), 33-4.
32. ____, *A Visitation and Warning Proclaimed* (1659), 20.
33. ____, *A Warning ... Underbarrow* (1654) in *Works*, 12.
34. ____, 'An Answer to Priest Jackson' (1659) in *Satan's Design Defeated* in *Works*, 524.
35. ____, *An Invitation to all the Poor Desolate Soldiers* (1655) in *Works*, 83.
36. ____, *Concerning Government and Magistracy* (1657) in *Works*, 354.
37. ____, *Concerning the Gospel of Christ* (1657) in *Works*, 249.
38. ____, *Discovery of Divine Mysteries* (1661) in *Works*, 824.
39. ____, *For the Hands of the Protector* (1657) in *Works*, 558.

Appendix 4B

40. ____, *General Epistle to the Saints* (1658) in *Works*, 389.
41. ____, *Good Counsel and Advice* (1659) in *Works*, 580.
42. ____, letter (25/April/1654) to James Nayler, in *SW*/iv/170.
43. ____, letter (1658) to Sir Henry Vane, *Ellwood MSS.*, ii, 27-8.
44. ____, *Stablishing against Quaking* (1656) in *Works*, 153.
45. ____, *The True Faith of the Gospel of Peace* (1656) in *Works*, 141.
46. ____, *The Walls of Iericho Razed* (1654), 1.
47. ____, *The Woeful Cry of Unjust Persecutions* (1657), 2.
48. ____, *To the Camp of the Lord* (1655) in *Works*, 66.
49. ____, *To the Parliament of the Common-wealth* (1659), 4.
50. ____, *To the Present Distracted and Broken Nation of England* (1659), 4-5, 8-9.
51. ____, *To the Rulers and to Such* (1659) in *Works*, *passim*.
52. ____ Howgill, *The Visitation . . . Ireland* (1656), 3.
53. Caton, *The Moderate Inquirer* (1659), 27.
54. H. Clark, *A Cloud of Witness* (1656), 4-9.
55. Crisp, *A Word of Reproof* (1658), 1.
56. Crook, *A Declaration of the People of God* (1659), 2.
57. ____, *A Defence of the True Church* (1659), 8.
58. Dewsbury, *Christ Exalted* (1656), 5, 9, 10.
59. ____, *Discovery of the Great Enmity* (1655), 18-19.
60. ____, *The Discovery of Man's Return* (1654), 15.
61. ____, *A True Testimony* (1655), 69.
62. Ellwood, *History*, 32-33 (for 1657/8?).
63. Fairman, *A Few Lines Given Forth* (1659), Bds.
64. Farnworth, 'A Mite Given Forth' in *A Message from the Lord* (1653), 26.
65. ____, *A Brief Discovery of the Kingdom* (1653), 11.
66. ____ *A Message from the Lord* (1653), 17.
67. ____, *A Woman Forbidden* (1654), 1.
68. ____, letter (1652) to Fox in Ingle, H., *Quaker History* 79, 1 (1990), 35-8.
69. ____, *Witchcraft Cast Out* (1655), *passim*.
70. Fell, 'Epistle to Friends, 1654' in *Works*, 53.
71. ____, *A Loving Salutation to the Seed of Abraham* (1656), 14.
72. ____, *A Testimony of the Touchstone* (1656), 4.
73. ____, *An Epistle to Friends in Lancaster Castle* (1654) in *Works*, 60.
74. ____ *et al False Prophets, Antichrists* (1655), 5.
75. ____, letter (1653) to Col. West, *Works*, 40.
76. ____, *To the General Council of Officers* (1659), 1.
77. M. Forster *et al*, *These Several Papers* (1659), 4.
78. Fox, 'A Measuring Rod Concerning Liberty and Persecution', *The Pearl* (1658), 3.
79. ____, 'The Answer of GF' in *Saul's Errand* (1653), 5.
80. ____, 'To All the World' in *News Coming up out of the North* (1654), 42.
81. ____, *A Warning from the Lord* (1654), 4.
82. ____, *A Warning to all Teachers of Children* (1657), 5.
83. ____, *An Epistle to all People on the Earth* (1657), *Doctrinals*, 95.
84. ____, Ep., 16 (1652), *LOGF*, 8.
85. ____, Ep., 1 (1651), *LOGF*, 1.
86. ____, Ep., 123 (1656), *LOGF*, 51.
87. ____, Ep., 13 (1652), *LOGF*, 5 ('and none of you be sayers only, but doers of the Word').
88. ____, Ep., 131 (1658), *LOGF*, 53-4.
89. ____, Ep., 138 (1657), *LOGF*, 55.
90. ____, Ep., 139 (1657), *LOGF*, 56.

91. ____, Ep., 14 (1652), *LOGF*, 6.
92. ____, Ep., 151 (1657), *LOGF*, 59.
93. ____, Ep., 153 (1657), *LOGF*, 60.
94. ____, Ep., 155 (1657), *LOGF*, 61.
95. ____, Ep., 158 (1658), *LOGF*, 62 (quotes Sermon on the Mount).
96. ____, Ep., 171 (1659), *LOGF*, 65-6.
97. ____, Ep., 177 (1659), *LOGF*, 66.
98. ____, Ep., 19 (1652), *LOGF*, 9.
99. ____, Ep., 2 (1652), *LOGF*, 1.
100. ____, Ep., 24 (1652), *LOGF*, 12.
101. ____, Ep., 30 (1653), *LOGF*, 15.
102. ____, Ep., 33 (1653), *LOGF*, 16.
103. ____, Ep., 4 (1652), *LOGF*, 2.
104. ____, Ep., 42 (1653), *LOGF*, 18.
105. ____, Ep., 48 (1653), *LOGF*, 22 ('all wait, that ye may come to witness the covenant of life made with your souls. . .').
106. ____, Ep., 51 (1653), *LOGF*, 23.
107. ____, Ep., 53 (1653), *LOGF*, 25.
108. ____, Ep., 55 (1653), *LOGF*, 25-6.
109. ____, Ep., 6 (1652), *LOGF*, 3.
110. ____, Ep., 61 (1654), *LOGF*, 28.
111. ____, Ep., 63 (1654), *LOGF*, 29.
112. ____, Ep., 64 (1654), *LOGF*, 30.
113. ____, Ep., 68 (1659), *LOGF*, 68.
114. ____, Ep., 74 (1654), *LOGF*, 34.
115. ____, Ep., 74 (1656), *LOGF*, 34.
116. ____, Ep., 77 (1654), *LOGF*, 35.
117. ____, Ep., 79 (1654), *LOGF*, 36.
118. ____, Ep., 9 (1652), *LOGF*, 3 ('Christ is come and is coming').
119. ____, *Journal*, 65. See pp. 67, 71-2, 129 in which Fox again refuses army commission (1651).
120. ____, letter (1652) *The Peacemaker has the Kingdom*, 6-7, in T. C. Jones, '*The Power of the Lord Is Over All*', p. xxxvi.
121. ____, letter (1659) in T. C. Jones, *ibid*., letter 117.
122. ____, *News Coming up out of the North* (1654), 27.
123. ____, *The Ground of High Places*, (1657), 3.
124. ____, *The Lambs Officer* (1659), 1.
125. ____, *The Pearl* (1658), 18.
126. ____, *The Priests Fruits made Manifest* (1657), 1, 2-4.
127. ____, *The Second Covenant* (1657), 4.
128. ____, *The Secret Works of a Cruel People* (1659), 1.
129. ____, *The Vials of the Wrath of God* (1654), 4, 3.
130. ____, *The Woman Learning in Silence* (1656), *Doctrinals*, 78-9.
131. ____, *This for each Parliament Man* (1656), 1.
132. ____, *To All that would Know the Way to the Kingdom* (1653/5), *Doctrinals*, 3.
133. ____, *To the Council of Officers* (1659), 3.
134. ____, *To the High and Lofty Ones* (n.d., DCFB 1655), *Doctrinals*, 29.
135. ____, *To the Parliament* (1659), 9, 16.
136. ____, *To the Protector* (1656), 34.
137. ____, *Trumpet of the Lord Sounded* (1654), 1.
138. ____, *Who are the Parliament* (1659), 15.
139. ____, *To Thee Oliver Cromwell* (1655), 1.

140. ____ Nayler in *Several Papers* (1654), 1.
141. Fox (the Younger), G., 'Honest, Upright' (1659) in *Works*, 75.
142. ____, *A Few Plain Words* (1659) in *Works*, 89.
143. G., J. (John Gibson?), *The Ancient of Days is Come* (1657), 3.
144. Harwood, *The Path of the Just Cleared* (1655), 10.
145. Howgill, *A Lamentation of the Scattered Tribes* (1656) in *Works*, 83.
146. ____, *An Answer to a Paper* (1654) in *Works*, 7.
147. ____, *An Information and also Advice* (1659) in *Works*, 331.
148. ____, *General Epistle to the Camp* (1655), 33.
149. ____, *This is Only to Go* (1656), Sig. A.
150. ____, *This was the Word of the Lord* (1654) in *Works*, 6.
151. ____ Burrough, *Answers to Several Queries* (1654), 12, 18.
152. Hubberthorne, *A True Testimony . . . University-Men* (1654) in *Works*, 43.
153. ____, *The Antipathy betwixt Flesh and Spirit* (1656), 4 (*DCFB* 1654).
154. ____, *The Good Old Cause Briefly Demonstrated* (1659), 2.
155. ____, *The Mittimus Answered* (1654) in *Works*, 37.
156. ____, *The Rebukes of the Reviler* (1657), 73.
157. J. Lilburne, *The Resurrection* (1656), 10.
158. Lurting, *The Fighting Sailor turn'd Peaceable Christian* (1650s), 11-13, 15-20.
159. Nayler, *A Lamentation* (1653) in *Works*, 102.
160. ____, 'Concerning Christ Jesus' in *Love to the Lost* (1656) in *Works*, 57.
161. ____, 'To All Dear Brethren . . . Holderness' (1654) in *Works*, 33.
162. ____, *A Discovery of the First Wisdom* (1653) in *Works*, 106.
163. ____, *A Salutation to the Seed of God* (1655), 31.
164. ____, *A Word from the Lord . . . Professors* (1654) in *Works*, 176.
165. ____, *Salutation* (1656), 23, 27.
166. ____, *The Examination of James Nayler* (1653) in *Works*, 16.
167. ____, *The Lamb's War* (1657), 7.
168. ____, *The Power and Glory of the Lord* (1653), 5.
169. ____, *To the Parliament of the Commonwealth of England* (1654) in *Works*, 749.
170. ____, *Weakness above Wickedness* (1656), 13.
171. A. Parker, letter (1660) to Fell, *SW/i/*170.
172. Parnel, 'The Trumpet' (1655) in *Works*, 36.
173. ____, *Christ Exalted into His Throne* (1655) in *Works*, 16.
174. ____, *The Trial of Faith* (1654) in *Works*, 6.
175. ____, *The Watcher* (1655) in *Works*, 171.
176. ____, *To Friends in London* (1655) in *Works*, 436.
177. ____, *To my dear Friends . . . London* (1655) in *Works*, 434.
178. ____, *To Friends in Essex* (1655) in *Works*, 441.
179. I. Penington, *A Brief Account of some Reasons*, n.d. (*DCFB* 1659), Bds.
180. ____, *A Voice out of the Thick Darkness* (1651) 'Preface' [a pre-Q work].
181. ____, *The Axe Laid to the Root* (1659), 12-13.
182. ____, *The Scattered Sheep Sought After* (1659) in *Works*, 113.
183. ____, *The Way of Life and Death* (1658), 57.
184. Rigge, *Of Perfection*, (1657), 2.
185. ____, *The Banner of God's Love* (1657), 14.
186. ____, *To the Whole Flock of God* (1660), 1.
187. Rofe, *The Righteousness of God* (1656), 1.
188. H. Smith, *A Warning to the Priests* (1656), 4.
189. ____, *Idolatry Declared Against* (1658), 2.
190. ____, *The Fruits of Unrighteousness* (1658), 5.
191. W. Smith, *A Right Dividing* (1659), 3.

192. ___, *A Short Testimony* (1660), 3, 10.
193. ___, *The Dayspring from on High* (1659), 4.
194. ___, *The New Creation* (1661), 7.
195. ___, *The Reign of the Whore Discovered* (1659), 9.
196. M. T. and Hebden, Letter to W. Dewsbury (1657), Cadbury, H., *JFHS*, Sup, 22 (1948), 23.
197. T. Taylor, *Some Prison Meditations in the 7th Month* (1657), 16.
198. Vivers, *The Saints Testimony* (1655), 14.
199. D. White, *An Epistle of Love* (1661), 2.
200. ___, *This is to be Delivered to the Councellors*, (1659), 2.
201. G. Whitehead, *Cains Generation*, (1655), 2.
202. ___, *The Path of the Just Cleared* (1655), 3.
203. J. Whitehead, *A Reproof from the Lord* (1656), 6, 7.
204. ___, *The Enmity between the Two Seeds* (1655), 11.
205. J. Wilkinson (1653), *SW*/iv/228.
206. Wollrich, *The Unlimited God* (1660), 12.

APPENDIX 5

Quaker condemnation of war, rebellion and 'carnal' weaponry during the 1650s was abundantly evident. The following is a small representation, 1650-60:

1. I. Penington, *A Voice out of the Thick Darkness* (1650), 'Preface' (a pre-Quaker work).
2. S. Jones, *This is Light's Appearance* (1650), *passim*.
3. Fox's 1651 refusal of an army commission in *Journal*, 65 and 67, 71-2, 129.
4. Fox's 1651 horror at the 'blood' in Lichfield reminding him of a massacre 'in Diocletians time' in *Journal*, 71-2.
5. Fox, Ep. 9 (1652) in which Fox conflates peace and the Kingdom, and roundly condemns the evil of physical violence including war.
6. J. Wilkinson, letter (1653) to Fell, SW/iv/228.
7. Nayler, *The Examination of James Nayler* (1653) in *Works*, 12.
8. Nayler, *A Discovery of the First Wisdom* (1653), 5.
9. Fox laments the corruption of power into violence, 'the will of men brought forth instead of equity' in Nayler, *A Lamentation* (1654) in *Works*, 99.
10. Fox and Nayler *et al*, *Several Petitions Answered*, 26.
11. Fox and Nayler *et al*, *Several Papers* (1654), 7, 10 (p. 7: for truth and war are incompatible).
12. *Journal*, 179 for passive resistance (1654 entry).
13. Nayler, 'Concerning Error, Heresy, &c.' in *Love to the Lost*, (1654), *Works*, 298.
14. Howgill, *This was the Word of the Lord . . . to O. Cromwell* (1654), *Works*, 6.
15. Hubberthorne, *The Mittimus answered* (1654), *Works*, 38.
16. Burrough, 'An Invitation to all the Poor Desolate Soldiers' (1655), *Works*, 83, 94.
17. Fox & Aldam (1655) to Cromwell denying violence 'against any man', *Journal*, 197-8.
18. Lurting, *The Fighting Sailor turn'd Peaceable Christian* (1710), 11-13, 15-20. For incidents during the late 1640s and 1650s.
19. Harwood *et al*, *The Path of the Just Cleared* (1655), 10 (see Rom. 13: 1-7).
20. H. Clark, *A Description of the Prophets* (1655), 13.
21. Hubberthorne, *The Antipathy betwixt Flesh and Spirit* (1656), 4.
22. J. Lilburne, *The Resurrection* (1656), 10.
23. Fox, *An Epistle to all People on the Earth* (1657), *Doctrinals*, 95.
24. Fox, *A Warning to all Teachers* (1657), 2.
25. Fox, *A Declaration of the Ground of Error* (1657), 4.
26. Burrough, 'Concerning the Kingdom of Christ' in *A Standard Lifted Up* (1657), 10-11.
27. Fox, *The Papist's Strength* (1658), 3.
28. Nayler, *The Lamb's War* (1658), 4, 6, 7.
29. Burrough, letter (1658?) to Sir Henry Vane [Jr.], *Ellwood MSS.*, ii, 27-8.
30. Nayler, Ep. 11, 'Not to Strive, but Overcome by Suffering' (1658/9) in *Works*, 727-30.
31. Burrough [?], 'An Account of some Grounds' in *A Declaration of the Present Sufferings* (1659), 28.
32. Burrough, 'An Answer to . . . Anabaptists' in Hubberthorne, *An Answer to . . . Anabaptists* (1659), 24.
33. Hookes (Burrough?), *A Presentation to London* (1659), 2, 5.
34. Burrough, 'Epistle to the Reader', *The Great Mystery* (1659), 10-11.
35. Burrough *et al*, *To the Present Distracted and Broken Nation of England* (1659), *passim*.

36. Fox, letter (1659) in T. C. Jones, *The Power of the Lord Is Over All'*, letter 117.
37. Fox, *59 Particulars* (1659), 9, 16.
38. Hubberthorne, *The Good Old Cause Briefly Demonstrated* (1659), 2.
39. Strutt, *A Declaration to the Whole World* (1659), *passim* but esp. 9-12.
40. Burrough, *A General Epistle to all the Saints* (1660), 1-2.
41. A. Parker, letter (22/Aug/1660) to Fell, *SW*/i/170.

APPENDIX 6

Fox's Tracts, 1657-9: Specific References to Jesus and Christ/Light

Tract	Year	Wing Ref. No.	Historical Jesus	Typical example on page	Christ/ Light	Typical example on page
That all Might See	1657	F1931	Yes	8	Yes	19
Of Bowings	1657	F1869	Yes	26	Yes	11
Concerning Good Morrow	1657	F1766	? (Christ Jesus)	11	Yes	10
A Warning to all Teachers	1657	F1983	No	-	Yes	3
The Priests' Fruit	1657	F1883	Yes	6	Yes	4
The Ground of High Places	1657	F1834	No	-	Yes	1
To all the People ... Steeplehouses	1657	F1951	Yes	4	Yes	4
To you that are Crying	1657	F1964	Yes	1	Yes	3
The Second Covenant	1657	F1898	Yes	3	Yes	1
'Christ's Way and Judas' Way' in *The Second Covenant*	1657	F1898	? (Christ Jesus)	20	Yes	20-1
A Testimony of the True Light	1657	F1929	Yes	10	Yes	6
A Declaration of the Ground of Error	1657	F1791	Yes	8	Yes	5
To all People on the Earth	1657	F1805	Yes	2	Yes	4
This is to all Officers and Soldiers	1657	F1935	? (Christ Jesus)	5	Yes	5
Here are Several Queries	1657	F1839	Yes	15	Yes	9
The Priests and Professors Catechism	1657	F1882	Yes	6-7	Yes	4
Something Concerning Silent Meetings	1657	F1909A	Yes	Bds.	Yes	Bds.
A Catechism for Children	1657	F1756C	Yes	58	Yes	2
An Instruction to Judges	1657	F1848	Yes	15	Yes	28-9
A Few Queries for Thomas Moore	1657	F1817A	Yes	2	Yes	1
To all the Magistrates in London	1657	*Doctrinals*, p. 105	No	-	No	-
To the Protector	1658	F1961	Yes	15	Yes	8
The Law of God	1658	F1856	Yes	5	Yes	6
The Papist's Strength	1658	F1877	Yes	6	Yes	1
An Answer to a Paper ...	1658	F1742	Yes	22	Yes	23

Title	Year	Wing #	?	#	?	#
Holland						
A Reply to the Pretended	1658	F1890	Yes	11	Yes	32
The Pearl	1658	F1879	Yes	5	Yes	2
A Warning to all the Merchants	1658	F1985	No	-	Yes	4
Here is Declared the Manner	1658	F1840	Yes	5	Yes	6
'The Cause of all Error' in Penington, The Way of Life & Death	1658	P1219	Yes	95	Yes	95
John James	1658	F1853B	? (Christ Jesus)	2-3	Yes	1
Several Warnings... Baptise People	1659	Not on EEBO/Wing	N/A	-	N/A	-
59 Particulars	1659	F1958	Yes	6-7	Yes	19
To the Council of Officers	1659	F1955	No	-	Yes	3, 6
The Lamb's Officer	1659	F1855	Yes	4	Yes	5-6
An Epistle to all the Christian Magistrates	1659	G1414	Yes	4-6	Yes	14-15
An Answer to Dr. Burgess his Book	1659	F1743	Yes	4-6	Yes	4, 10
A Primer for Scholars	1659	F1884	Yes	42-3, 54	Yes	39, 42
The Serious Peoples' Reasoning	1659	F1900	No		Yes	7
An Answer to Thos. Tillam's Book	1659	F1747	Yes	5	Yes	3, 5, 12
'The Difference between the World's Relation' in The Sins of a Gain-saying	1659	R2044	No	-	Yes	12
'A Paper to New England' in Secret Works	1659	F1899	Yes	16	Yes	17
' And the Faith of Such' in M. Fell, A Paper Concerning such... Will of Man	1659	F634A	No	-	Yes	2
This is to Goe	1659	Not on EEBO/Wing	N/A	-	N/A	-
To the People of Uxbridge	1659	F1959	No	-	Yes	Bds.
Surely the Magistrates of Notts.	1659	F1923A	No	-	Yes	Bds.
All you People that... Tenderness	1659	Not on EEBO/Wing	N/A	-	N/A	-
TOTAL 47	1657 (20) 1658 (10) 1659 (16)		Y (30); N (10); possible yes (4); N/A (3)		Y (43); N (1); N/A (3)	

458

BIBLIOGRAPHY

> For references to early Quaker epistles and letters see Footnotes. Most seventeenth century works cited below carry a Wing reference number (e.g. N249) from the Donald Wing catalogue for location on *Early English Books Online (EEBO)*. Other materials are located on *Eighteenth Century Collection Online (ECCO)*.
>
> L = London; NY = New York; C = Calvert; S = Simmonds; W = Wilson; N.p. = Place of publication unknown; n.p. = publisher unknown; n.d. = date unknown.

Early Quaker Manuscripts (i.e. Collected Papers, L: LRSF)

A.R. Barclay MSS.; Abraham MSS.; Audland MS. (MS. Box P2/18); *Bristol MSS.; Caton MSS.*, vols. ii, iii.; *Crosfield MS.; Crosse MS.* (Temp MSS. 553/18); *Ellwood MSS.*, vol. *ii.*; *Harvey MSS.; John Tapper MS.; Leek MS..; Markey MS.* (MSS. Box C4/1); *Spence MSS.; Swarthmore MSS.* (8 vols.); *Thirnbeck MSS.*

Early Quaker Collections (*Works*)

Joseph Besse, *A Collection of the Sufferings of the People called Quakers* (L: Hinde, 1753: *ECMC* 5083); 2 vols.
John Burnyeat, *The Truth Exalted* (L: Northcott, 1691: B5968).
Edward Burrough: Hookes, E. (ed.), *The Memorable Works of a Son of Thunder and Consolation* (L: n.p., 1672: B5980).
John Camm (and **John Audland**), *The Memory of the Righteous Revived* (L: A. Sowle, 1689: C390).
William Crouch, *Posthuma Christiana or, a Collection of Some Papers of William Crouch* (L: J. Sowle, 1712: *ECMC* 2671).
Richard Davies, *An Account of the Convincement of . . . Richard Davies* (L: Hinde, 1765: *ECMC* 2008), 2nd.ed.
William Dewsbury, *The Faithful Testimony of that Ancient Servant of the Lord . . . William Dewsbury* (L: A. Sowle, 1689: D1267).
Margaret Fell, *A Brief Collection of Remarkable Passages and Occurrences* (L: J. Sowle, 1710: *ECMC* 1275).
Samuel Fisher, *The Testimony of Truth Exalted* (L: n.p., 1679: F1058).
George Fox, *Gospel-Truth Demonstrated in a Collection of Doctrinal Books* (*Doctrinals*. L: T. Sowle, 1706: *ECMC* 4593).
___, *The Works of George Fox* (Philadelphia, PA.: Gould/NY.: Hopper, 1831); 8 vols.
___, *A Collection of Many Select and Christian Epistles* (L: T. Sowle, 1698: F1764).
George Fox (the Younger), *A Collection of the Several Books and Writings, Given Forth* (L: W, 1662: F1996).
Roger Hebden, *A Plain Account of Certain Christian Experiences . . . of Roger Hebden* (L: T. Sowle, 1700: H1346A).
Luke Howard, *Love and Truth in Plainness Manifested* (L: Sowle, 1704: *ECMC* 5644).
Francis Howgill, *The Dawnings of the Gospel Day* (L: n.p., 1676: H3157).
Richard Hubberthorne, *A Collection of the Several Books and Writings* (L: Warwick, 1663: H3216).
Thomas Lurting, *The Fighting Sailor Turned Peaceable Christian* (L: n.p., 1710: *ECMC* 5987).

James Nayler: Whitehead, G. (ed.), *A Collection of Sundry Books, Epistles and Papers Written by James Nayler* (L: J. Sowle, 1716: ECMC 4593).
___, *Memoirs of the Life . . . James Nailer* (L: Roberts, 1719: ECMC 2786)
James Parnel, *A Collection of Several Writings Given Forth* (L: n.p., 1675: P528).
Isaac Penington, *The Works of the Long-Mournful and Sorely-Distressed Isaac Penington* (L: Clark, 1681: P1149) and also (L: Phillips, 1784: ECMC 6832); 4 vols.
Elizabeth Stirredge, *Strength in Weakness Manifest* (L: T. Sowle, 1711: ECMC 1323 and 1141).
Thomas Taylor, *Truths Innocency and Simplicity* (L: T. Sowle, 1697: T591).
Joan Vokins, *God's Mighty Power Magnified* (L: Northcott, 1691: V685).
George Whitehead: Besse, J. (ed.?), *The Christian Progress of that Ancient Servant and Minister of Jesus Christ, George Whitehead* (L: J. Sowle, 1725: ECMC 9348).
Robert Widders, *The Life and Death, Travels and Sufferings of Robert Widders* (L: n.p., 1688: L2019).

Early Quaker Primary Sources

G., J. (John Gibson?), *The Ancient of Days is Come* (L: C, 1657: G6696).
Aldam, T. et al, *A Brief Discovery of the Kingdom of the Antichrist* (N.p.: n.p., 1653: A894B or F472A)
___ et al, *False Prophets and False Teachers Described* (N.p.: n.p., 1652: A8948BA).
Anderdon, J., *A Visitation of Love* (L: W, 1660: A3084)
___, *Against Babylon and her Merchants in England* (L: W, 1660: A3078).
___, *God's Proclamation* (L: C, 1659: A3081).
___, *One Blow at Babel* (L: n.p., 1662: A3082).
Anon, *Spiritual Discoveries to the Overgrow of Popery, Root and Branch* (L: n.p., 1657/8: S4997).
___, *To the Generals, and Captains . . . of this Present Army* (N.p.: n.p., n.d. DCFB 1658/Wing 1660: T1396).
Atkinson, C. et al, *The Standard of the Lord* (L: C, 1653: A4128).
Audland, A. et al, *The Saint's Testimony Finishing through Sufferings* (L: C, 1655: S365).
Audland, J., *The Innocent Delivered out of the Snare* (L: C, 1655: A4196).
___, *The Suffering Condition* (L: n.p., 1662: A4198).
Barclay, R., *An Apology for the True Christian Divinity* (N.p.: n.p., 1678: B721).
Bateman, S., *'I matter not how I appear to man'* (L: n.p., 1658: B1097).
Bayly, W., *A Short Discovery of the State of Man* (L: Westwood, 1659: B1536).
___, *A Short Relation or Testimony* (L: Westwood, 1659: B1537).
___, *A Testimony against Drunkenness nd Swearing* (N.p.: n.p., 1675: B1539).
___, *A Warning from the Spirit of Truth* (L: n.p., 1658: B1544).
___, *Deep Calleth unto Deep* (L: n.p., 1663: B1522).
___, Epistle to Friends, *Crosse MS.* (L: LRSF, Temp. MSS. 553/18, n.d.).
___, *Jacob is Become a Flame* (N.p.: n.p., 1659?: B1530).
___, *The Blood of Righteous Abel* (L: M. W., 1659: B1519).
Benson, G., *The True Trial of Ministers* (L: C, 1655: B1903).
___ et al, *The Cry of Oppression* (L: C, 1656: B1900).
Biddle, E., *The Trumpet of the Lord Sounded Forth* (L: n.p., 1662: B2865).
Bishop, G., *A Few Words in Season* (L: W, 1660: B2993).
___, *A More Particular and Exact Relation* (L: Cotes, 1645: B3019B).
___, *A Tender Visitation of Love* (L: W, 1660: B3007).
___, *A Treatise Concerning Election and Reprobation* (L: n.p., 1664: B3011A).
___, *A Treatise Concerning the Resurrection* (N.p.: n.p., 1662: B3012).
___, *An Epistle of Love to All the Saints* (L: W, 1661: B2992).
___, *Jesus Christ, the Same Today as Yesterday* (L: C, 1655: B2995).

Bibliography

___, *Mene Tekel* (L: Brewster, 1659: B3000).
___, *The Throne of Truth* (L: C, 1657: B3008).
___, *The Warnings of the Lord* (L: Inman, 1660: B3016).
___ et al, *The Cry of Blood* (L: C, 1656: B2990).
Blackborow, S., *A Visit to the Spirit in Prison* (L: S, 1658: B3065).
___, *Herein is Held Forth the Gift* (L: S, 1659: B3063).
___, *The Just and Equal Balance Discovered* (L: M.W., 1660: B3064).
Blackley, J. et al, *A Lying Wonder Discovered* (L: S, 1659: B3075).
Blaugdone, B., *An Account of the Travels, Sufferings* (L: T.S., 1691: A410)
Bolton, J. et al, *A Short Account of the Latter End of . . . Francis Howgil* (N.p.: n.p., 1671: B3509).
Bourne, E., *A Warning . . . unto the Inhabitants of Worcester* (L: W, 1660: B3849).
Briggs, T., *An Account of the Travels . . . Thomas Briggs* (L: n.p., 1685: B4665).
Britten, W., *Concerning the Kingdoms of God and Men* (N.p.: n.p., 1660: B4824).
___, *Silent Meetings, a Wonder to the World* (L: W, 1660: B4825).
___, *The Power of God* (L: W, 1660: B4824A).
Brooksop, J., *An Invitation of Love* (L: W, 1662: B4983).
Burrough, E., *A Brief Relation of the Persecutions and Cruelties* (L: n.p., 1662: B4629).
___, *A Declaration of the Sad and Great Persecutions* (L: W, 1661: B5994).
___, *A Declaration to all the World of our Faith* (L: S, 1657: B5995).
___, *A Description of the State and Condition of all Mankind* (L: C, 1657: B5998).
___, *A Discovery of Divine Mysteries* (L: W, 1661:B5999).
___, *A Discovery of Some Part of the War . . . Kingdom of the Lamb* (L: W, 1659: B5999A).
___, *A Faithful Testimony Concerning . . . True Worship* (L: S, 1659: B6002).
___, *A General Epistle to all the Saints* (L: W, 1660: B6005).
___, *A Just and Lawful Trial of the Teachers* (L: S, 1657: B6008).
___, *A Measure of the Times* (L: S, 1657: B6012).
___, *A Message for Instruction* (L: S, 1658: B6013).
___, *A Message to the Present Rulers of England* (L: C, 1659: B6015).
___, *A Seasonable Word of Advice* (N.p.: n.p., n.d. *DCFB /Wing* 1658: B6003).
___, *A Standard Lifted Up, . . . unto all Nations* (L: C, 1657, *DCFB* 1658: B6029).
___, *A Testimony against a Great Idolatry* (L: S, 1658: B6032).
___, *A True Description of my Manner of Life* (L: W, 1663: B6045).
___, *A Vindication of the People of God called Quakers* (L: W, 1660: B6053).
___, *A Visitation of Love unto the King* (L: W, 1660: B6056)
___, *A Warning from the Lord . . . Underbarrow* (L: C, 1654: B6057).
___, *An Invitation to all the Poor Desolate Soldiers* (1655) in *Works*.
___, *Concerning Government and Magistracy* (1657) in *Works*.
___, *Concerning the Gospel of Christ* (1657) in *Works*.
___, *For the Hands of the Protector* (1657) in *Works*.
___, *For the Soldiers, and all the Officers of England, Scotland and Ireland* (N.p.: n.p., 1654: B6003).
___, *Good Counsel and Advice Rejected by Disobedient Men* (L: S, 1659: B6006).
___, *Satan's Design Defeated* (L: S, 1659: B6022).
___, *Some False Principles and Errors* (L: S, 1659: B6023A).
___, *Stablishing against Quaking* (L: C, 1656: B6028).
___, *The Everlasting Gospel of Repentance* (L: W, 1660: B6001).
___, *The Fourth General Epistle to all the Saints* (1660) in *Works*.
___, *The General Epistle to all the Saints* (L: W, 1660: B6005).
___, *The Principles of Truth* (N.p.: n.p., 1660: B6018 and P3498).
___, *The True Faith of the Gospel of Peace* (L: C, 1656: B6046).
___, *The True State of Christianity* (L: S, 1658: B6047).

___, *The Walls of Jericho Razed* (L: C, 1654: B6056A).
___, *The Woeful Cry of Unjust Persecutions* (L: C, 1657: B6058).
___, *To the Parliament of the Common-wealth of England . . . at Westminster* (L: S?, 1659: B6038 and B6038A (a copy).
___, *To the Parliament of the Common-wealth of England . . . who are in place of Authority* (N.p.: n.p., 1659: B6039).
___, *To the Rulers, and to Such as are in Authority* (L: S, 1659: B6040A).
___, *To the Whole English Army* (L: C, 1659: B6041).
___, *Truth (the Strongest of All) Witnessed Forth* (L: C, 1657: B6051).
___ **Howgill, F.**, *A Visitation of the Rebellious Nation of Ireland* (L: C, 1656: B3188).
___ **Howgill, F.**, *To the Camp of the Lord* (L: n.p., 1655/6: H3184); later rpt as *This is Only to Go amongst Friends* (L: S, 1656: H3182).
___ and **Fisher, S.**, *A Visitation and Warning Proclaimed and an Alarum Sounded in the Pope's Borders* (L: S, 1659: B6055).
___ *et al, A Declaration of the Present Sufferings of Above 104 Persons* (L: S, 1659: B5993).
___ *et al, A Declaration . . . to the Present Distracted and Broken Nation* (L: S, 1659: B5989).
Byllinge, E. (Burrough?), *A Mite of Affection* (L: C, 1659: B2902).
___, *A Word of Reproof* (L: S, 1659: B2903).
Caton, W., *An Abridgement or a Compendium . . . of Eusebius* (L: S and W, 1661: E3419) later published as *An Abridgment of Eusebius* (L: Holden, 1698: E3420).
___, *An Epistle to King Charles II* (L: S, 1660: C1513).
___, *The Moderate Enquirer Resolved* (L: Hoye, 1658: C1515).
___, *The Testimony of a Cloud of Witnesses* (N.p.: n.p., 1662: C1520).
Clark, H., *A Cloud of Witnesses* (L: C, 1656: C4452).
___, *A Description of the Prophets, Apostles, and Ministers of Christ* (L: C, 1655: C4453).
___, *A Rod Discovered* (L: Clark, 1657: C4457).
Coale, J., *An Invitation of Love* (L: S, 1660: C4754).
___, *The Last Testimony . . . Richard Farnworth* (L: n.p., 1667: F488).
___, *The Whore Unvailed* (N.p.: n.p., 1665: C4760).
Colleens (Collins?), J., *A Word in Season to all in Authority* (L: W, 1660: C5235).
Cotton, P. and **Cole, M.**, *To the Priests and People of England* (L: n.p., 1655: C6474).
Crisp, S., *A Word of Reproof to the Teachers of the World* (L: S, 1658: C6946).
Crook, J., *A Defence of the True Church* (L: S, 1659: C7202).
___, *An Epistle of Love to all that are in Present Suffering* (L: W, 1660: C7204).
___, *Tithes No Property* (L: S, 1659: C7214bA)
___ **Penington, I.**, *Truth's Principles* (L: n.p., 1662: C7217).
___ *et al, A Declaration of the People of God* (L: S, 1659: C7201).
___ *et al, Liberty of Conscience Asserted* (L: W, 1661: L1960).
Dewsbury, W., *A True Testimony of What was done . . . at Northampton* (L: C, 1655: T3123).
___, *Christ Exalted and Alone Worthy* (L: C, 1656: D1258).
___, *The Discovery of Man's Return* (L: C, 1653: D1259).
___, *The Discovery of the Great Enmity of the Serpent* (L: C, 1655: D1264).
___, *The Mighty Day of the Lord is Coming* (L: C, 1656: D1271).
___, *To All Nations, . . . with your Princes and Rulers* (L: W, 1660: D1274).
___, *The True Prophecy of the Mighty Day of the Lord* (L: C, 1654: D1279).
___, *This is the Word of the Living God* (1653) in *Works*.
Docwra, A., *An Epistle of Love and Good Advice* (L: n.p., 1683: D1778)
Dole, D., *A Salutation and Seasonable Exhortation* (L: Bringhurst, 1683: D1835).
Ellington, F., *Christian Information Concerning these Last Times* (L: n.p., 1664: E541).

Bibliography

___ *A True Discovery of the Grounds of Imprisonment* (N.p.: n.p., 1655, *DCFB* 1656: T2683).
Ellwood, T., *Journal or Historical Account of... George Fox* (L: Northcott, 1694: F1854 and *WMC* 815).
___, *The History of the Life of Thomas Ellwood* (L: T. Sowle, 1714: *ECMC* 7266 and L: Routledge and Sons, 1885).
Evans, K. and **Cheevers, S**., *A Brief History of the Voyage* (L: W, 1663: T2369A and L: T. Sowle, 1715: *ECMC* 1275).
Fairman, L., *A Few Lines Given Forth* (L: S, 1659: F257).
Farnworth, R., *A Call Out of Egypt and Babylon* (L: C, 1653: F480). See below, *An Easter-Reckoning*.
___, *A Confession and Profession of Faith in God* (L: C, 1659: F478).
___, *A Message from the Lord* (N.p.: n.p., 1653: F491A).
___, *A True Testimony against the Pope's Ways* (L: C, 1656: F509).
___, *A Voice of the First Trumpet* (N.p.: n.p., 1653: F512B).
___, *A Woman Forbidden to Speak in the Church* (L: C, 1654: F514).
___, *Light Risen out of Darkness Now in these Latter Days* (L: C, 1653: F490).
___, *The Brazen Serpent Lifted Up* (L: C, 1655: F471).
___, *The General Good to all People* (L: C, 1653: F483 [Thomason E.703 [6]]).
___, *The Heart Opened by Christ* (L: C, [1654] 1655: F485).
___, *The Liberty of the Subject* (N.p.: n.p., 1664: F489).
___, *The Pure Language of the Spirit* (L: C, 1655: F494).
___, *The Ranters Principles and Deceits* (L: C, 1655: F501).
___, *The Spiritual Man* (L: C, 1655: F505). This work also Fox's *True Judgment*.
___, *Truth Cleared of Scandals* (L: n.p., 1654: F512).
___, *Witchcraft Cast Out from the Religious Seed* (L: C, 1655: F513).
___ **Aldam, T**., *A Brief Discovery of the Kingdom* (N.p.: n.p., 1653: A894B).
___ **Aldam, T**., *An Easter-Reckoning* (N.p.: n.p., 1653: F480) in 2 edns.
___ **Nayler, J**., *A Discovery of Faith* (L: C, 1653: F479 and N270).
Fell, C. et al, *A Few Words to the People of England* (L: n.p., 1655: F840).
Fell, M., *A Call unto the Seed of Israel* (L: W, 1668: F626).
___, *A Loving Salutation to the Seed of Abraham* (L: S, 1656: F634).
___, *A Testimony of the Touch-Stone for all Professions* (L: S, 1656: F636).
___, 'Appeal to Friends in North Lancashire and Cumberland', *Thirnbeck MSS.*, vol. 1.
___, *An Epistle to Friends in Lancaster Castle* (1654) in *Works*.
___, *For Manasseth ben Israel* (L: C, 1656/7: F632).
___, *This was Given to Major-General Harrison and the Rest* (L: S, 1660: F638).
___, *To the General Council and Officers of the Army* (L: S, 1659: F638C).
___, *To the General Councel of Officers of the English Army* (L: S?, n.d. *DCFB* 1659: F638A).
___, 'The Testimony of Margaret Fox Concerning her Late Husband, George Fox' in Ellwood (1694).
___, *Womens Speaking Justified* (L: n.p., 1666: F642).
___ et al, *A Declaration and an Information* (L: S and W, 1660: F628).
___ et al, *False Prophets, Antichrist* (L: C, 1655: F631).
Firmin, T., *The First New Persecution* (L: C, 1654: F977).
Fisher, S., *ΑπόκρyπτΑ ΑπόκΑάyπτΑ. Velata Quædam Revelata* (L: W, 1661: F1047).
___, *Rusticus ad Academicos* (L: W, 1660: F1056).
___, *To the Parliament of England* (L: n.p., 1659: F1059).
Forster, M. et al, *These Several Papers was sent to the Parliament* (L: Westwood, 1659: F1605).
Fox, G., *A Catechism for Children* (L: C, 1657: F1756).

___, *A Cry of Repentance* (L: S, 1656: F1779).
___, *A Declaration Concerning Fasting and Prayer* (L: S, 1656: F1785).
___, *A Declaration of the Ground of Error* (L: C, 1657: F1791).
___, *A Declaration to the Jews* (L: White, 1661: F1792).
___, *A Distinction between the Phanatick Spirit and the Spirit of God* (L: W, 1660: F1796).
___, *A Few Plain Words . . . to the Teachers and People of the Nation* (L: W, 1660: F1817).
___, *A Primer for the Scholars and Doctors of Europe* (L: S, 1659: F1884).
___, *A Reply to the Pretended Vindication* (L: S, 1658: F1890).
___, *A Testimony of the True Light* (L: C, 1657: F1929).
___, *A Testimony of what we Believe of Christ* (N.p.: n.p., 1677: F1930).
___, *A Visitation to the Jews* (L: C, 1656: F1978).
___, *A Voice of the Lord to the Heathen* (L: S, 1656: F1979).
___, *A Warning from the Lord to the Pope* (L: C, 1656: F1981).
___, *A Warning to all Teachers of Children* (L: S, 1657: F1983).
___, *A Warning to all the Merchants in L* (L: S, 1658: F1985).
___, *A Warning to the Rulers of England* (York: Wayt, 1653).
___, *A Warning to the World* (L: C, 1655: F1987).
___, *A Word in the behalf of the King* (L: W, 1660: F1993).
___, *An Answer to a Paper which came from the Papist Lately out of Holland* (L: S, 1658: F1742).
___, *An Answer to Dr. Burgess his Book* (L: S, 1659: F1743).
___, *An Answer to the Arguments of the Jews* (L: M.W., 1661: F1745).
___, *An Answer to Thomas Tillam's Book* (L: S, 1659: F1747).
___, *An Epistle General to them who are of the Royal Priesthood*, (L: S, 1660: F1802).
___, *An Epistle to all People on the Earth* (L: C, 1657: F1805).
___, *An Instruction to Judges and Lawyers* (L: S, n.d. DCFB /Wing 1657: F1848).
___, *Christ's Light the only Antidote* (N.p.: n.p., 1662: F1761. A rpt. of *The Ground of Desperation* [N.p.: n.p., 1655?: F1833]).
___, *Concerning Good-morrow* (L: S, 1657: F1766).
___, *Concerning Sons and Daughters . . . Prophesying* (L: M.W., 1661: F1772).
___, *For the Emperor of China and his Subordinate Kings and Princes* (L: W, 1660: see Doctrinals).
___, *(Here all may see, that) Justice and Judgment is to Rule* (L: S, 1656: F1838).
___, *Here is Declared the . . . Naming of Children* (L: S, 1658: F1840).
___, *Here you may see what was the True Honour amongst the Jews* (L: W, 1660: F1841).
___, *News Coming up out of the North* (L: C, 1654: F1867).
___, *Of Bowings* (L: S, 1657: F1869).
___, *Quaker Testimony Concerning Magistracy, Leek MS.* (L: LRSF, n.d.).
___, *Some Principles of the Elect People of God* (L: W, 1661: F1907).
___, *Something Concerning Silent Meetings* (N.p.: n.p., 1657: F1909A).
___, *Something in Answer to Lodowick Muggleton's Book* (L: n.p., 1667: F1914).
___, *Something in Answer to the Old Prayer Book* (L: W, 1660: FHL, Box 28/12).
___, *Surely the Magistrates of Nottingham* (L: S, 1659: F1923A).
___, *That all Might See who they were that had a Command* (L: S, 1657: F1931).
___, *The Eternal, Substantial Truths of God's Kingdom* (L: W, 1661: F1814).
___, *The Great Mystery of the Great Whore Unfolded* (L: S, 1659: F1832).
___, *The Ground of High Places*, (L: S, 1657: F1834).
___, *The Lambs Officer is Gone Forth* (L: S, 1659: F1855).
___, *The Law of God the Rule for Law-makers* (L: C, 1658: F1856).
___, *The Line of Righteousness* (L: W, 1661: F1857).
___, *The Pearle Found in England* (L: S, 1658: F1878).
___, *The Priests Fruits Made Manifest* (L: S, 1657: F1883).

Bibliography

___, *The Promise of God Proclaimed* (L: S, 1660: F1888A).
___, *The Second Covenant* (L: S, 1657: F1898).
___, *The Secret Works of a Cruel People* (L: n.p., 1659: F1899).
___, *The Trumpet of the Lord Sounded* (L: C, 1654: F1969).
___, *The Unmasking and Discovery of Anti-Christ* (L: C, [1653] 1655: F1974).
___, *The Vials of the Wrath of God Poured Forth* (L: C, 1654: F1975).
___, *The Woman Learning in Silence* (L: S, 1656: F1991); republished as *Concerning Sons and Daughters* as above.
___, *This for each Parliament-Man* (L: S, 1656: F1933).
___, *This is to all Officers and Soldiers of the Armies* (L: S, 1657: F1935).
___, *To All that would Know the Way to the Kingdom* (N.p.: n.p., 1653: *WMC* F1942. *EEBO* has the March 1654 [F1942A] and later editions of this important work).
___, *To all the Ignorant People* (N.p.: n.p., 1653/4: F1948). A Fox work?
___, *To all the Nations under the Whole Heavens* (L: W, 1660: F1950).
___, *To the Council of Officers of the Army* (N.p.: n.p., n.d. *DCFB* 1658/59: F1955).
___, *To the High and Lofty Ones* (L: n.p., 1655: F1956A).
___, *To the Parliament of the Comon-wealth of England* [*59 Particulars*] (L: S, 1659: F1958).
___, *To the Protector and Parliament of England* (L: C, 1658: F1961).
___, *To Those that Have Been Formerly in Authority* (L: W, 1660? *DCFB* /*Wing* 1660: F1963).
___, *True Judgment* (L: C, 1654: F1967). This work is Farnworth's *The Spiritual Man*.
___, *Truth's Triumph in the Eternal Power* (L: S, 1661: F1971).
___, *What Election and Reprobation Is* (L: n.p., 1679: F1989).
___ **Fell, H.**, *For the King and his Council, These* (N.p.: n.p., 1661: F1822).
___ **Gould, A.**, *An Epistle to all the Christian Magistrates* (L: S, 1659: G1414).
___ **Hookes, E.**, *The Arraignment of Popery* (L: n.p., 1667: F1750A).
___ **Howgill, F.**, *The Papist's Strength* (L: S, 1658: F1877).
___ **Hubberthorne, R.** et al, *A Declaration from the Harmless and Innocent People of God, Called Quakers, against all Plotters and Fighters in the World* (L: W, 1660/1: F1786).
___ **Nayler, J.**, *A Word from the Lord, Unto all the Faithless Generation* (L: C, 1654: F1991A).
___ **Nayler, J.**, *Saul's Errand to Damascus* (L: C, 1653: F1894).
___ **Nayler, J.**, *Several Papers* (N.p.: n.p., 1653: F1903).
___ **Nayler, J.**, *Several Petitions Answered* (L: C, 1653: N316A).
___ **Nayler, J.**, *To Thee Oliver Cromwell* (L: C, 1655: F1962)
___ et al, *A Battle-Door for Teachers and Professors* (L: W, 1660: F1751).
___ et al, *The Copies of Several Letters* (N.p.: n.p., n.d. *DCFB* 1660: F1778).
Fox, G. (the Younger), *A Few Plain Words to be Considered by . . . the Army* (L: S, 1659: F2002).
___, *A Noble Salutation* (L: C, 1660: F2007).
___, *A Visitation of Love unto all People* (L: S, 1659: F2018).
___, *For the Parliament of England and their Army, So Called* (L: M. W., 1659/60: F2003).
___, *Honest, Upright, Faithful, and Plain-Dealing with thee, O Army* (L: S, 1659: F2005A).
Fuce, J., *The Fall of a Great Visible Idol* (L: S, 1659: F2257A).
Gargill, A., *A Brief Discovery of the . . . Popish Religion* (L: C, 1656: G258).
Goodaire, T., *A Cry of the Just Against Oppression* (L: S, 1660: G1087).
Gotherson, Daniel, *An Alarm to All Priests, Judges and Magistrates, Soldiers and all People* (L: Cottrel, 1660: G1351).
Gotherson, Dorothea, *To all that are Unregenerated* (L: W, 1661: G1352).
Greene, T., *An Alarm to the False Shepherds* (L: W, 1660: G1839).
Harwood, J., *A Description of the True Temple* (L: S, 1658: H1103).
___ et al, *The Path of the Just Cleared* (N.p.: n.p., 1655: W1944).

Hickock, R., *A Testimony Against... the Ranters* (L: S, 1659: H1918).
Higgins, J., *From Newgate, A Prisoner's Just Cause Pleaded* (L: S, 1661: H1952A).
Hollister, D., *The Harlots Vail Removed* (L: n.p., 1658).
Homwood, N., *A Word of Counsel* (N.p.: n.p., 1675: H2579).
Hookes, E. (Burrough?), *A Presentation to London* (L: n.p., 1659: H2661A).
___, *The Spirit of Christ* (L: C, 1661: H2662).
Howard, L., *A Few Plain Words of Instruction* (L: S, 1658: H2985).
___, *The Devils Bow Unstringed* (L: S, 1659: H2984A).
Howgil, M., A Remakable Letter (L: n.p., 1657: H3191).
Howgill, F., *A Lamentation for the Scattered Tribes* (L: C, 1656: H3170).
___, *A Testimony Concerning... Edward Burroughs* (L: Warwick, 1662: T809).
___, *An Answer to a Paper* (L: n.p., 1654: H3154).
___, *An Information and also Advice to the Army* (N.p.: n.p., 1659: H3167).
___, *One Warning more unto England* (L: S, 1660: H3176).
___, *Some of the Mysteries of Gods Kingdome Declared* (L: S, 1658: H3179).
___, *The Great Case of Tithes and Forced Maintenance* (N.p.: n.p., 1665: H3165).
___, *The Glory of the True Church* (L: C, 1661: H3162).
___, *The Inheritance of Jacob Discovered... Egypt* (L: C, 1656: H3168).
___, *The Invisible Things of God* (L: S, 1659: H3169).
___, *The Measuring Rod of the Lord* (L: C, 1658: H3171).
___, *The Mouth of the Pit Stopped* (L: S, 1659: H3172).
___, *The Rock of Ages* (L: G.C., 1662: H3178).
___, *This was the Word of the Lord... to Oliver Cromwell* (L: n.p., 1654: H392).
___, *To all you Commanders and Officers of the Army in Scotland, especially* (N.p.: n.p., 1657: H3183).
___ **Burrough, E.**, *Answers to Several Queries* (L: C, 1654: B5984).
___ **Burrough, E.**, *We the Servants and Faithful Witnesses* (Dublin: n.p., 1655: B6075A).
___ **Parker, A.**, *A Visitation of Love* (L: n.p., 1664: H3187).
Hubberthorne, R., *A Word of Wisdom and Counsel to the Officers and Soldiers* (N.p.: n.p., 1659: H3242).
___, *A True Separation* (N.p.: n.p., 1654: H3238).
___, *A True Testimony of Obedience to the Heavenly Call* (N.p.: n.p., 1654: H3239).
___, *A True Testimony of the Zeal of Oxford Professors and University-Men* (L: C, 1654: H3240).
___, *Something that Lately Passed in Discourse Between the King and R. H.* (L: G.C., 1660: H3234).
___, *The Antipathy Betwixt Flesh and Spirit* (L: S, [1654] 1656: H3220).
___, *The Difference of that Call of God to the Ministry* (L: S, 1659: H3223).
___, *The Good Old Cause Briefly Demonstrated* (L: S, 1659: H3223A).
___, *The Horn of the He-Goat Broken* (L: C, 1656: H3224).
___, *The Light of Christ Within* (L: S, 1660: H3227).
___, *The Mittimus Answered* (N.p.: n.p., 1654) in *Works*.
___, *The Quakers House Built upon the Rock Christ* (L: n.p., 1659: H3227A).
___, *The Real Cause of the Nation's Bondage and Slavery* (L: S, 1659: H3228).
___, *The Rebukes of a Reviler Fallen on His Own Head* (L: C, 1657: H3229).
___, *The Record of Sufferings for Tythes* (L: S, 1658: H3230).
___, *Truth and Innocence Clearing Itself* (L: C, 1657: H3241).
___ **Atkinson, C.**, *The Testimony of the Everlasting Gospel* (N.p.: n.p., 1654: H3237).
___ **Burrough, E.**, *An Answer to a Declaration Put Forth by... Anabaptists* (L: S, 1659: B5983 and H3218).
___ **Lawson, T.**, *Truth Cleared and the Deceit Made Manifest* (L: n.p., 1654: H3241).
Jones, S., *This is Lights Appearance* (N.p.: n.p., 1650: J989).

Bibliography

Keith, G., *The Benefit, Advantage and Glory of Silent Meetings* (L: n.p., 1670: K144).
Killam, M. and **Patison, B.**, *A Warning from the Lord to the Teachers* (L: C, 1655: K473).
Lawson, T., *An Appeal to the Parliament, Concerning the Poor* (L: W, 1660: L722).
___, *The Lip of Truth Opened* (L: C, 1656: L725).
Lilburne, J., *The Resurrection of John Lilburne* (L: C, 1656: L2176).
London Yearly Meeting, *Who are the Friends of the People* (N.p.: n.p., c.1795).
Mason, M., *A Check to the Lofty Linguist* (L: C, 1655: M926).
___, *The Proud Pharisee Reproved* (L: n.p., 1655: M933).
___, *Zion's Enemy Discovered* (N.p.: n.p., 1659: M933A).
Nayler, J., *A Discovery of the First Wisdom from Beneath* (L: C, 1653: N272 and N273).
___, *A Discovery of the Man of Sin* (L: C, 1654: N274).
___, *A Door Opened to the Imprisoned Seed* (L: S, [1659] 1667: N276).
___, *A Lamentation (by One of England's Prophets,) . . . this oppressed Nation* (N.p.: n.p., 1653: N292).
___, *A Public Discovery of the Open Blindness* (L: C, 1656: N305).
___, *A Salutation to the Seed of God* (L: C, 1655: N309).
___, 'A Testimony for Jesus Christ' (1658/9) in *Works*.
___, *A Vindication of Truth* (L: C, 1656: N326).
___, *An Answer to a Book called, The Quaker's Catechism* (L: n.p., 1655: N258).
___, 'An Epistle to Several Friends about Wakefield' (1653) in *Works*.
___, *Churches Gathered against Christ and his Kingdom* (L: C, 1654: N267).
___, *Deceit Brought to Daylight* (L: C, 1656: N269).
___, *Give Ear You Gathered-Churches* (N.p.: n.p., DCFB 1659: N281A).
___, *How Sin is Strengthened, and How it is Overcome* (L: S, 1657: N285).
___, *Love to the Lost* (L: C, 1656: N294).
___, *Milk for the Babes* (L: W, 1661: N299).
___, 'Not to Strive, but Overcome by Suffering' (1658/9) in *Works*.
___, *Several Papers of Confessions* (L: n.p., 1659: N316).
___, *Sin Kept Out of the Kingdom* (N.p.: n.p., 1653: N371A).
___, *The Boaster Bared* (L: C, 1655: N266).
___, *The Lamb's War against the Man of Sin* (L: S, 1657 [1658]: N291), 2nd.ed.
___, *The Power and Glory of the Lord* (L: C, 1653: N302).
___, 'To Friends in Lincoln' (8/May/1655) in *Works*.
___, *To the Life of God in All* (L: S, 1659: N321).
___, *Truth Cleared from Scandals* (N.p.: n.p., 1654: N324).
___, *Weakness above Wickedness* (L: C, 1656: N327).
___, *What the Possession of the Living Faith Is* (L: S, 1659: N328).
Hubberthorne, R., *An Account from the Children of Light* (L: S, 1660: N256).
Travers, R., *A Message from the Spirit of Truth* (L: S, 1658: N298).
Nicholson, B., *A Blast from the Lord* (L: C, 1653: N1104) and found in *Some Returns to a Letter* (L: C, 1653: N1106) which Wing lists as a separate publication.
Pain (Payne), J., *A Discovery of the Priests* (L: C, 1655: P188).
Parker, A., *A Call Out of Egypt* (L: C, 1656: P378).
Parnel, J., *A Shield of the Truth* (L: C, 1655: P533).
___, *A Trial of Faith* (L: n.p., 1654: P535).
___, *A Warning for All People* (L: S, 1660: P540).
___, *Christ Exalted into His Thone* (N.p.: n.p., 1655: P527).
___, *Goliah's Head Cut Off* (L: C, 1655: P531).
___, *The Fruits of a Fast* (L: C, 1655: P530).
___, *The Trumpet of the Lord Blown* (L: C, 1655: P539).
___, *The Watcher* (L. C, 1655: P541).
___, 'To Friends in Essex' in *Works*.

___ et al, *The Lamb's Defence Against Lies* (N.p.: n.p., 1655: L249).
Pearson, A., *The Great Case of Tithes Truly Stated* (L: C, 1657: P989).
Penington, I., *A Brief Account of Some Reasons* (N.p.: n.p., 1659/60: P 1154).
___, *A Voice out of the Thick Darkness* (L: Macock, 1650: P1217).
___, *An Echo from the Great Deep* (L: Macock, 1650: P1163).
___, *Concerning the Sum or Substance* (N.p.: n.p., n.d.: P1158).
___, *Examination of the Grounds and Causes* (L: Lloyd, 1660: P1166).
___, *Expositions with Observations* (L: Macock, 1656: P 1167).
___, *Some Considerations Proposed . . . Distracted Nation* (N.p.: n.p., 1660: P1191).
___, *Some Considerations Propounded to the Jews* (N.p.: n.p., n.d. DCFB 1660: P1192).
___, *Some Few Queries and Considerations . . . to the Cavaliers* (L: n.p., n.d. 1659? DCFB /Wing 1660: P1194).
___, *Some of the Mysteries of God's Kingdom Glanced At* (N.p.: n.p., 1663: P1197).
___, *Some Queries Concerning the Work of God in the World* (L: W, 1660: P1200).
___, *Some Things of Great Weight* (L: n.p., 1667: P1204).
___, *Somewhat Spoken to a Weighty Question* (L: S, 1661: P1206).
___, *The Axe Laid to the Root* (L: Lloyd, 1659: P1152).
___, *The Consideration of a Position* (L: W, 1660: P1161).
___, *The Flesh and Blood of Christ* (N.p.: n.p., 1675: P1168).
___, *The Jew Outward* (L: Lloyd, 1659: P1144).
___, *The New Covenant of the Gospel* (L: W, 1660: P1180).
___, *The Scattered Sheep Sought After* (L: Lloyd, 1659: P1187).
___, *To the Army* (N.p.: n.p., 1659: P1213).
___, *To the Parliament, the Army, and all the Well-affected* (L: C, 1659: P1215).
___ et al, *The Way of Life and Death Made Manifest* (L: Lloyd, 1658: P1219).
Penington, M., *Account . . . of Mary Penington* (L: Harvey and Darton, 1821).
Penn, W., *A Brief Account of the Rise . . . of the Quakers* (L: T. Sowle, 1694: P1257).
___, *Some Fruits of Solitude* (L: Northcott, 1693: P1369).
Perrot, J., *A Visitation of Love* (L: S, 1658: P1638).
___, *Battering Rams against Rome* (L: W. 1661: P1612).
___, *Discoveries of the Day-dawning* (L: S, 1661: P1615).
___, *Immanuel, the Salvation of Israel* (L: S, 1658: P1619).
___, *To the Prince of Venice* (L: W, 1661: P1633).
Rigge, A., *Of Perfection* (L: n.p., 1657: R1486).
___, *O Ye Heads of the Nation* (L: S, 1659: R1487).
___, *The Banner of God's Love* (L: C, 1657: R1475).
___, *The Spiritual Guide of Life* (L: n.p., 1691: R1491).
___, *To the Whole Flock of God Everywhere* (L: S, 1660: R1497).
Robertson, T., *A Horrible Thing Committed in this Land* (L: S, 1658: R1609).
Rofe, G., *The Righteousness of God* (L: C, 1656: R1788).
Rogers, W., *The Christian-Quaker* (L: n.p., 1680: R1850).
Salthouse, T., *A Brief Discovery of the Cause* (N.p.: n.p., 1665: S470).
___ **Collens, J.**, *The Line of True Judgment* (L: S, 1658: S474).
Sewel, W., *History of the Rise . . . of the . . . Quakers* (L: J. Sowle, 1722: ECMC 3544).
Sicklemore, J., *To all the Inhabitants of . . . Youghal* (N.p.: n.p., 1657: S3750).
Simmonds, M. et al, *O England! Thy Time is Come* (N.p.: n.p., 1656: S3793).
Simpson, W., *From One who was Moved of the Lord* (L: S, 1659: S3843).
___, *Going Naked as a Sign* (L: W, 1660: S3845).
Smith, H., *A Sad and Mournful Lamentation* (L: M.W., 1660: S4071).
___, *A Warning to the Priests* (L: n.p., 1656: S4085).
___, *Idolatry Declared Against* (L: S, 1658: S6064).
___, *The Lamb and his Day Proclaimed* (N.p.: n.p., n.d. DCFB 1660/1?: S4065).

Bibliography

___, *The First and Second Priesthood* (N.p.: n.p., n.d. *DCFB* 1657: S4058).
___, *The Sufferings . . . of the Saints at Evesham* (N.p.: n.p., n.d. *DCFB* 1655/6).
___, *Something Further Laid Open* (L: n.p., 1656: S4073).
___, *The True and Everlasting Rule from God Discovered* (L: S, 1658: S4083).
___, *To all that want Peace with God* (L: W, 1660: S4079).
___, *To the Musicioners* (L: Westwood, 1658: S4082).
Smith, W., *A Manifestation of Prayer in Formality* (N.p.: n.p., 1663: S4314).
___, *A Right Dividing, or a True Discerning* (L: S, 1659: S4325).
___, *A Short Testimony* (L: S, 1660: S4328).
___, *An Epistle from the Spirit of Love* (N.p.: n.p., 1663; S4296).
___, *The Dayspring from on High* (L: S, 1659: S4295).
___, *The Morning-Watch* (L: W, 1660: S4317).
___, *The New Creation* (L: W, 1661: S4320).
___, *The Reign of the Whore Discovered* (L: S, 1659: S204A).
Strutt, J., *A Declaration to the Whole World* (L: Strutt, 1659: S6017).
Stubbe, H., *Light Shining Out of Darkness* (N.p.: n.p., 1659: S6056).
Stubbs, T., *A Call into the Way to the Kingdom* (L: C, 1655: S6084).
___, *Certain Papers given Forth* (L: S, 1659: S6086).
Swinton, J., *A Testimony for the Lord* (N.p.: n.p., 1663?: S6287).
Taylor, T., *A Testimony for the Lord God* (L: W, 1660: T585).
___, *Some Prison Meditations in the 7th Month* (L: C, 1657: T582).
___, *To the People of England* (L: S, 1660: T583).
Tomlinson W., *A Word of Reproof to the Priests or Ministers* (York: Wayt, 1653: T1855).
___, *Seven Particulars* (L: C, 1657: T1851).
Travers, R., *For Those that Meet in Worship at the Steeplehouse* (N.p.: n.p., 1659: T2059).
___, *This is for any of that Generation* (N.p.: Westwood, 1659/60: T2064).
Vivers, M., *The Saints Testimony* (L: C, 1655: S365); see Audland, A.
Wastfield, T., *A True Testimony of Faithful Witness* (L: C, 1657: W1036).
White, D., *A Call from God out of Egypt* (L: n.p., 1662: W1746).
___, *A Lamentation unto this Nation* (L: W, 1661: W1751).
___, *A Trumpet of the Lord of Hosts* (N.p.: White, 1662: W1755).
___, *A Visitation of Heavenly Love* (L: W, 1660: W1759).
___, *An Alarum Sounded Forth* (N.p.: n.p., 1662: W1744).
___, *An Epistle of Love and of Consolation* (L: W, 1661: W1748).
___, *This to be Delivered to the Counsellors that are sitting in Council* (L: S, 1659: W1753).
Whitehead, G., *Cain's Generation* (L: C, 1655: W1898).
___, *Jacob Found in a Desert Land* (L: C, 1656: W1936).
___, *The Divinity of Christ* (L: n.p., 1669: W1925).
___, *The He-goats Horn Broken* (L: W, 1660: W1933).
___, *The Key of Knowledge* (L: W, 1660: W1939).
___, *The Light and Life of Christ Within* (L: n.p., 1668: W1941).
___, *The Path of the Just Cleared* (L: C, 1655: W1944).
___, *The Seed of Israel's Redemption* (L: S, 1659: W1955).
___ **Burrough, E.**, *The Son of Perdition Revealed* (L: S, 1661: W1962).
___ **Nayler, J.**, *The True Ministers Living of the Gospel* (L: S, 1660: W1968).
Whitehead, J., *A Manifestation of Truth* (L: n.p., 1662: W1979).
___, *A Word of Reproof from the Lord* (L: S, 1656: W1980).
___, *The Enmity between the Two Seeds* (L: n.p., 1655: W1975).
___ **Penington, I.**, *A Small Treatise* (L: W, 1661: W1981).
Whitehouse, J., *The Doctrine of Perfection Vindicated* (L: W, 1663: W1984).
Wilkinson, J., *The Memory of . . . John Story* (L: Gain, 1683: M1702).

Wilson, D. et al, *A Short Collection of some of the Letters of William Wilson* (L: Northcott, 1685: W2955).
Wollrich (or Woollrych), H., *A Plain and Good Advice to the Parliament-Men, and ... Army* (N.p.: n.p., n.d. *DCFB* 1658/*Wing* 1659: W3297).
___, *One Warning More* (L: W, 1661: W3296).
___, *The Unlimited God* (L: n.p., 1659: W3303).
Yeamans, I., *An Invitation to Love* (L: n.p., 1679: Y20).
Zachary, T., *A Word to the Officers of the Army* (L: C, 1657: Z4).
Zinspenninck, J., *Some Worthy Proverbs* (L: Warwick, 1663: Z13).

Non-Quaker Primary Sources

à Kempis, T., *Of the Imitation of Christ* (L: Short, 1596 [1658]: *STC* 23980).
Abbott, R., *The Danger of Popery* (L: Stephens and Meredith, 1625: *STC* 57).
Ames, W., *The Marrow of Sacred Divinity* (L: Griffin, 1642: A3000).
Andrewes, L., *Institutiones Piae* (L: Seile, 1630: *STC* 599).
Anon, *A Declaration of the Well-affected to the Good Old Cause* (L: J.C., 1659: D777).
___, *An Agreement of the People of England* (L: Partridge, 1649: A781).
___, *An Anti-Brekekekex-Coax-Coax, or, A Throat-hapse for the Frogs and Toads* (N.p.: n.p., 1660: A3483A).
___, *An Exact Relation of the Bloody and Barbarous Massacre at Bolton* (May 28th, 1644) (L: Meredith, 1644: E3683).
___, 'Blackletter Ballads' at: <www.lukehistory.com/ballads/worldup.html>.
___, *England's Division, and Ireland's Distraction* (L: Bates, 1642: E2961).
___, *('a dyer') Study to be Quiet: or, a Short View of the Miseries of War* (L: Alsop, 1647: S6091).
___, *The Beast Wounded* (Amsterdam: Richt Right Press, 1638: *STC* 22032).
___, *The Character of an Old English Protestant Formally Called a Puritan* (N.p.: n.p., 1670: C2013).
___, *The Declaration and Standard* (L: Laurenson, 1649: E3544).
___, *The Good Old Cause Explained, Revived and Asserted* (L: n.p., 1659: G1078).
___, *The Midwives Just Complaint* (L: T.S., 1646: M2004).
___, *The Rider of the White Horse* (L: Underhill, 1643: R1447).
___, *The True Picture of Quakerism* (L: Roberts, 1736: *ECMC* 9415).
Baker, A., *Sancta Sophia* (Douai: Patte and Fievet, 1657: B480).
Baker, R., *Theatrum Redivivum, or The Theatre Vindicated* (L: Eglesfield, 1662: B513).
Barlow, W., *The Sum and Substance of the Conference held ... at Hampton Court* (L: Law, 1605: *STC* 1457).
Baxter, R., *A Christian Directory* (L: N. S, 1673: B1219).
___, *One Sheet Against the Quakers* (L: White, 1657: B1334).
___, *The Glorious Kingdom of Christ* (L: Parkhurst, 1691: B1277).
___, *The Quaker's Catechism* (L: Underhill, 1655: B1295).
___, *The Worcester-shire Petition to Parliament Defended* (L: Tyton, 1653: B1455).
Bernard, R., *A Key of Knowledge for the Opening of ... Revelation* (L: Kyngston, 1617: *STC* 1955).
Birch, T. (ed.), *A Collection of the State Papers of John Thurloe, Esq.* (L: Gyles, 1742: *ECMC* 5279 and 5125). And at: <http://www.british-history.ac.uk/source.asp?pubid=609>.
Blome, R., *The Fanatic History or an Exact Relation and Account of the Old Anabaptists, and New Quakers* (L: Sims, 1660: B3212).
Blount, T., *Glossographia: or, A Dictionary* (L: Newcomb, 1656: B3334).
Boehme, J., *Four Tables of Divine Revelation* (L: Blunden, 1654: B3408B).

Bibliography

Bolton, R., *A Three-fold Treatise Containing the Saints Sure and Perpetual Guide* (L: Harford, 1634: *STC* 3255).
Bradshaw, W., *English Puritanism* ([1605, 1610] L: n.p., 1641: B4158).
Brierly, R..., *A Bundle of Soul-Convincing* (Glasgow: Brown, 1676: B4658A).
Brightman, T., *A Revelation of the Revelation* (Amsterdam: n.p., 1615: *STC* 3755).
Bucer, M., *A Treatise how by the Word of God* (N.p.: n.p., 1557?: *STC* 3965).
Buchanan, G., *De Jure Regni Apud Scotos* ([Edinburgh: Ross, 1579: *STC* 3974] N.p.: n.p., 1680: B5275).
Bugg, F., *Some of the Quakers Principles and Doctrines* (L: Gwillim, 1693: B9395).
Bunyan, J., *Some Gospel Truths Opened* (L: Wright, 1656: B5598).
___, *Works of that Eminent Servant of Christ, Mr. John Bunyan* (N.p.: Marshall, 1692: B5477).
Butler, S., *Hudibras* (L: n.p., 1663: B6296).
Calamy, E., *England's Looking Glass* (L: Raworth, 1642: C237).
___, (as Imprimatur), *The Soldiers Pocket Bible* (L: G.B and R.W., 1643: S4428).
Calver, E., *England's Sad Posture* (L: Alsop, 1644: C315).
Calvin, J., *The Institution of Christian Religion* (trans. T. Norton. L: Griffin, 1634: *STC* 4425).
Campanella, T., *Thomas Campanella an Italian Friar and Second Machiavelli* (L: Stephens, 1660: C400).
Campion, E., *The History of Ireland* (Dublin: Company of Stationers, 1633: *STC* 25067a).
Cannes, J., *Fiat Lux* (N.p.: n.p., 1661: C429).
Carier, B., *A Carrier to a King* (N.p.: n.p., 1614: *STC* 46255).
Carleton, G., *Tithes Examined* (L: Knight, 1606: *STC* 4644).
Cary, M., *The Little Horn's Doom and Downfall* (L: Cary, 1651: C737).
Cawdrey, D., *Vindiciae Clavium* (L: Whaley, 1645: C1640).
Church of England, *Constitutions and Canons Ecclesiastical* (L: Barker, 1640: *STC* 10080).
Cleaver, R..., *A Godly Form of Household Government* (L: Man, 1603: *STC* 5385).
Coppe, A..., *Some Sweet Sips of Some Spiritual Wine* (L: C, 1649: C6093).
Cotton, J., *The Keys of the Kingdom of Heaven* (L: Overton, 1644: C6437).
Cox, L., *The Art or Craft of Rhetoric* (N.p.: n.p., 1532: *STC* 5947).
Croese, G., *The General History of the Quakers* (L: Dunton, 1696: C6965).
Croft, H., *The Naked Truth* (N.p.: n.p., 1675: C6970).
Cromwell, O., *Letters from Ireland* (L: Field, 1649: L1778).
Cudworth, R., *A Sermon Preached . . . House of Commons* (Cambridge: Daniel, 1647: C7469).
Danson, T., *The Quakers Folly Made Manifest* (L: Allen, 1659: D215).
Deacon, J., *A Public Discovery* (L: Hirones, 1656: D487).
___, *Nayler's Blasphemies Discovered* (L: Waterson, 1657: D486).
___, *The Grand Imposter* (L: Brome, 1656: D484).
Dell, W., *Right Reformation* (L: Tyler, 1650: D928).
___, *Spiritual Sermons and Discourses* (L: C, 1651: D929).
___, *The Building and Glory* (L: C, 1647: D918A).
___, *The Way of True Peace and Unity* (L: C, 1651: D940).
Denne, H., *The Quaker no Papist* (L: Smith, 1659: D1024).
Dod, J., *Exposition of the Ten commandments* (L: Man, 1603: *STC* 6967.5).
Donne, J., *The Poetical Works of Dr. John Donne* (Edinburgh: n.p., 1779: *ECMC* 1988), vol. 3.
Douch, J., *England's Jubilee* (L: Royston, 1660: D1958A).
Dudley, F., *The Arts of Logic and Rhetoric* (N.p.: n.p., 1584: *STC* 10766).
Durham, W., *Maran-Atha, the Second Advent* (L: Maxey, 1656: D2832).

Eaton, S., *The Quakers Confuted* (L: White, 1654: E125).
Edwards, T., *Gangraena: or, a Catalogue . . . Last Four Years* (L: Smith, 1646: E228).
England and Wales (i.e. Govt.), *A Proclamation Prohibiting the Disturbing of Ministers* (L: Hills and Field, 1654: C7163).
Erbery, W., *The Bishop of London* (L: n.p., 1652: E3223).
___, *The Grand Oppressor, Or the Terror of Tithes* (L: C, 1652: E3226).
___, *The Testimony of William Erbery* (L: C, 1658: E3239; microfilm only).
Etherington, J., *A Description of the Church of Christ* (L: Fosbrooke, 1616: STC 12567).
Evangelista, J., *The Kingdom of God in the Soul* (Paris: de la Fosse, [1639] 1657: J744A).
Everard, J., *Some Gospel-Treasures Opened* (L: Harford, 1653: E3533).
Farmer, R., *Satan Inthroned in his Chair* (L: Thomas, 1657: F444).
___, *The Great Mysteries of Godliness and Ungodliness* (L: Ballard, 1655: F441).
Feake, C. (and **Kellet, J.**) *et al, A Faithful Discovery of a Treacherous Design* (L: Brewster, 1653:F568). See earlier print entitled *Discovery of the Quakers.*
Featley, D., *Ancilla Pietatis* (L: Bourne, 1626: STC 10726).
Fossett, T., *The Servants Duty* (L: Eld, 1613: STC 11200).
Foxe, J., *Acts and Monuments* (L: Company of Stationers [Basle: 1554; in English 1563] 1641: F2035).
Fuller, T., *The Church History of Britain* (L: Williams, 1655: F2416).
Gardiner, R.., *England's Grievance Discovered* (L: Ibbotson and Stent, 1655: G230).
Gifford, G., *A Brief Discourse of Certain Points* ([L: Cook, 1581: STC 118455] L: Field and Kingston, 1612: STC 118475).
Goodwin, T., *The World to Come. Or, The Kingdom of Christ Asserted* (L: n.p., 1655: G1266).
Gouge, W., *Of Domestical Duties* (1616) in *The Works of William Gouge* (L: Beale, 1627: STC 12109a), vol. 2.
Grigge, W., *The Quakers Jesus* (L: Simmons, 1658: G2023).
Grimston, H., *Mr. Grymstons Speech in Parliament* (L: n.p., 1641: G2037).
Hall, T., *Chiliastro-matrix Redivivus: A Confutation of the Millenarian* (L: Starkey, 1657: H428).
___, *The Pulpit Guarded* (L: Cottrell, 1651: H4383).
Harrington, J., *The Commonwealth of Oceana* (L: Pakeman, 1656: H809A).
___, *The Oceana of James Harrington and his Other Works* (L: n.p., 1700: H8161).
Harrison, W., *Description of England*, Part 1 at
    <http://www.fordham.edu/halsall/mod/1577harrison-england.html#Chapter%20V>.
Hartlib, S., *A Description of the Famous Kingdom of Macaria* (L: Constable, 1641: H983).
Herbert, G., *The Windows* at: <http://swc2.hccs.cc.tx.us/rowhtml/Herbert/windows.htm>.
Heywood, O., *A Narrative of the Holy Life and Happy Death . . . of John Angier* (L: Parkhurst, 1683: H1772).
Higgenson, T., *A Testimony to the True Jesus* (L: Brewster, 1656: H1950).
Higginson, F., *A Brief Relation of Irreligion of the Northern Quakers* (N.p.: H.R., 1653: H1953).
___, *A Brief Reply* (L: H.R., 1653: H1954).
Hobbes, T., *Leviathan* (L: Crooke, 1651: H2248).
Holmes, N., *Apokalypsis Anastaseos. The Resurrection-Revealed* (L: Ibbotson, 1653: H2560).
Hooker, R., *Of the Laws of Ecclesiastical Polity* (L: Windet, 1593: STC 13712) and at: <http://www.luminarium.org/renlit/hookbib.htm>.
Hyde, E., *State Papers Collected by Edward, Earl of Clarendon Commencing from the Year 1621* (Oxford: Clarendon, 1786).
Ives, J., *The Quakers Quaking* (L: Cottrel, 1656: I 1103)
Jackson, J., *A Sober Word to a Serious People* (L: Cottrel, 1651: J78A).

___, *Strength in Weakness* (L: Mayock, 1655: J78B).
Jonson, B., *The Alchemist* (L: Burre, 1612: *STC* 14755).
Knox, J., *The Copy of an Epistle* (Geneva: n.p., 1559: *STC* 15064).
Laud, W., *A Relation of the Conference* (L: Badger, 1639: *STC* 15299).
Leech, H., *A Triumph of Truth* (Douai: n.p., 1609: *STC* 15363).
Leslie, C., *The Snake in the Grass* (L: Brome, 1696: L1156).
Lilly, W., *A Collection of Ancient and Modern Prophecies* (L: Partridge, 1645: L2217).
Lupton, D., *The Quacking Mountebank, or The Jesuit Turned Quaker* (L: E.B., 1655: L3493).
Makin, B., *An Essay to Revive the Ancient Education of Gentlewomen* (L: J.D., 1673: M309).
Mather, C., *Principles of the Protestant Religion Maintained* (Boston: Pierce, 1690: A1029).
Milton, J., *Areopagitica* (L: n.p., 1644: M2092).
___, *The Ready and Easy Way* (L: Milton, 1660: M2174).
Montagu, J. (ed.), *The Works of the Most High and Mighty Prince, James* (L: Barker and Bill, 1616: *STC* 14344).
Montagu, R., *Appello Caesarem* (L: Lownes, 1625: *STC* 18030).
___, *A Gag for the New Gospel?* (L: Snodham, 1624: *STC* 18038).
Moore, J., *The Crying Sin of England* (L: Williamson, 1653: M2558).
Morris, W., *To the Supreme Authority* (L: S, 1659: M2813).
Naylier, J., *The New Made Colonel* (L: J.M., 1649: N332).
___ **and Marshall, J.**, *The Foxes Case Discovered* (N.p.: n.p., 1649: F2044A).
Norden, J., *The Surveyors Dialogue* (L: Busby, 1610: *STC* 18640b).
Northbrooke, J., *Spiritus est Vicarius Christi in Terra* (L: Byshope, 1577: *STC* 18670).
Overbury, T., *A Wife, now the Widow of Sir Thomas Overburie* (L: Lisle, 1614: *STC* 18907).
Owen, J., *A Sermon Preached to the Parliament, Octob. 13th, 1652* (Oxford: Lichfield, 1652: O 806).
___, *The Advantage of the Kingdom of Christ* (Oxford: n.p., 1651: O 711A).
___, *Vindiciae Evangelicae* (Oxford: Robinson, 1655: O 823).
Parliament, *A Proclamation Prohibiting the Disturbing of Ministers* (L: Hills and Field, 1655: C7163).
___, *London Flames Discovered* (L: Field [?], 1667: L2928).
___, *Several Proceedings* (L: Field, 1653: E2297).
Pagitt, E., *Heresiography* (L: M. Oaks, 1645: P174 and 180).
Parker, H., *A Discourse Concerning Puritans* (L: Bostock, 1641: L1876).
Perkins, W., *A Reformed Catholic* (Cambridge: Legat, 1598: *STC* 19736).
___, *Christian Oeconomie* (L: Kyngston, 1609: *STC* 19677.3).
___, *The Works of . . . William Perkins* (Cambridge: Legat, 1603: *STC* 19647).
___, *Two Treatises* [II. *Of the Combat of the Flesh*] (Cambridge: Legat, 1593: *STC* 19758).
Philips, E., *The New World of English Words* (L: Brooke, 1658: P2068).
Phillips, J., *Wit and Drollery Jovial Poems* (L: Brooke, 1661: W3132).
Prynne, W., *Anti-Arminianism* (N.p.: n.p., 1630: *STC* 20458).
___, *Histrio-Mastix, The Players Scourge* (L: Sparke, 1633: *STC* 20464).
___, *The Church of England's Old Antithesis* (L: n.p., 1629: *STC* 20457).
___, *The Perpetuity of a Regenerate Man's Estate* (L: Jones, 1626: STC 20471).
___, *The Quakers Unmasked and Clearly Detected* (L: Thomas, 1655: P4045).
Ram, R., *The Souldiers Catechism* (L: Wright, 1644: R196).
Reeve, J., *A Transcended Spiritual Treatise* (L: Reeve, 1652: R683).
Richardson, A., *The Logicians School-Master, or, A Comment on Ramus Logick* (L: Dawson, [1629: *STC* 21012] 1657: R1378).

Rogers, J., *Sagir, Sagir, or Doomsday Drawing Nigh* (L: C, 1653: R1814).
___, *The Plain Case of the Common-weal* (L: Chapman, 1658: P2643).
Rushworth, J., *Historical Collections* (L: Boulter, 1682: R2317).
Rutherford, S., *Lex Rex, The Law and the Prince* (L: Field, 1644: R2386).
Saltmarsh, J., *Sparkles of Glory* (L: C, 1647: S504).
Seldon, J., *The History of Tithes* [L: n.p., 1618: STC 22172.7).
Seuse (Suso), H., *Certain Sweet Prayers* (N.p.: Carter, 1575: STC 23443.5).
___, *Horologium Sapientiae* (L: Caxton, 1491: STC 3305).
Shadwell, T., *The Lancashire-witches and Tegue O Divelly, the Irish Priest* (L: Starkey, 1682: S2853).
Sheppard, W., *The Parson's Guide or The Law of Tithes* (L: Lee, 1654: S3204).
Sibbes, R.., *The Bruised Reed and Smoking Flax* (L: Dawlman, 1630: STC 22479).
Smith, T., *A Gag for the Quakers* (L: J. C., 1659: S4231bA).
___, *The Quaker Disarmed* (L: J.C., 1659: S4227).
Spenser, E., *The Works of that Famous English Poet, Mt. Edmond Spenser* (L: Edwin, 1679: S4965).
Spilbery, J., *Heart-Bleedings for Professors Abominations* (L: Tyton, 1649: No Wing no.).
Stalham, J., *Contradictions of the Quakers* (Edinburgh: n.p., 1655: S5184).
___, *The Reviler Rebuked* (L: Hill, 1657: S5186).
Stephen, N., *A Plain and Easy Calculation* (L: Keynson, 1656: S5450).
Sterry, P., *The Appearance of God to Man* (L: n.p., 1710: STC 2668).
Stuart, Charles (King Charles I), *Eikon Basilike* (L: n.p., 1649: E311).
Stuart, James (King James VI/I), *A Puritan Set Forth in His Lively Colours* (L: N. B., 1642: J142).
___, *Basilikon Doron* (Edinburgh: Waldegrave, 1599: STC 14353).
___, *Declaration Concerning Vorstius* (L: Barker, 1612: STC 9233).
___, *The True Laws of Free Monarchies* (Edinburgh: Waldegrave, 1598: STC 14409).
Stuart (Steward), R., *Three Sermons* (L: Bedel and Collins, 1657: S5527).
Sturgion, J., *A Plea for Toleration* (L: Smith, 1661: S6093).
Tauler, J., *A History . . . of Dr. Joh. Thauler* (L: Lloyd, 1660: H2168bA).
Taylor, J., *Lucifer's Lacky* (L: Greensmith, 1641: T477).
Temple, J., *The Irish Rebellion* (L: Gellibrand, 1646: T627).
Temple, T., *Christ's Government in and over his People* (L: Gellibrand, 1642: T634).
Tillinghast, J., *Generation-work* (L: Chapman, 1653: T1173).
Traske, J., *The Power of Preaching* (L: Butter, 1623: STC 24177).
Turner, J., *Choice Experiences* (L: Hils, 1653: T3294).
Tyndale, W., *The First Part of the Bible* (L: Day, 1551: STC 2087).
Vicars, J., *A Sight of Ye Trans-actions of these Latter Years* (L: Jenner, 1646: V327).
W., A., *A Letter from One . . . in the Army . . . to his Wife* (L: n.p., 1643: W1).
Walwyn, W., *The Vanity of the Present Churches* (L: Clows, 1649: W693A).
Warwick, P., *Memoirs of the Reign of King Charles 1* (L: Chiswell, 1701: ECMC 10062).
Webster, J., *The Judgment Set* (L: Hartford, 1654: W1210).
Weld(e), T. et al, *The Perfect Pharisee* (L: Tomlins, 1653: C5045A).
White, J., *First Century of Scandalous, Malignant Priests* (L: Miller, 1643: W1778).
Williams, R., *The Bloody Tenent yet more Bloody* (L: C, 1652: W2760).
Wilson, T. (a), *A Complete Christian Dictionary* (L: Cotes, 1655: W2943).
Wilson, T. (b), *The Arte of Rhetorique* (L: n.p. [later pub. Kingston], 1553: STC 25799).
Winstanley, G., *A New-Years Gift for the Parliament and Army* (L: C, 1650: W3050).
___, *The Fire in the Bush* (L: C, 1649/50: W3043).
___, *The Law of Freedom in a Platform* (L: C, 1652: W3040A).
___, *The Mystery of God* (L: C, 1649: W3048).
___, *The New Law of Righteousness* (L: C, 1649: W3049).

___, *The Saints Paradise* (L: C, 1648: W3051).
Yates, J., *Ibis ad Caesarem* (L: Mylbourne, 1626: STC 26083).

Journal Articles

Adams, J., 'Alexander Richardson's Puritan Theory of Discourse', *Rhetorica* 4, 3 (1986).
Amussen, S., 'Punishment, Discipline and Power... in Early Modern England', *JBS* 34, 1 (1995).
Anderson, A., 'A Study in the Sociology of Religious Persecution: The First Quakers', *JRH* 9, 3 (1977).
Angell, S., 'The Catechisms of George Fox', *Quaker Theology* 9 (Fall-Winter 2003) at: <http://www.quaker.org/quest/issue-9-angell-01.htm>.
___, 'Universalising and Spiritualising Christ's Gospel: How Early Quakers Interpreted the Epistle to the Colossians', *Quaker Studies* 11, 1 (2006).
Anon, 'Attitudes of Friends under Persecution', *JFHS* 4 (1907).
Aune, D., 'The Apocalypse of John and the Problem of Genre', *Semeia* 36 (1986).
Aylmer, G., 'Collective Mentalities in Mid Seventeenth-Century England: 1. The Puritan Outlook', *Transactions of the Royal Historical Society* (5th ser.) 36 (1986).
___, 'Collective Mentalities in Mid Seventeenth-Century England: 2. Royalist Attitudes', *Transactions of the Royal Historical Society* (5th ser.) 37 (1987).
___, 'Collective Mentalities in Mid Seventeenth-Century England: 3. Varieties of Radicalism', *Transactions of the Royal Historical Society* (5th ser.) 37 (1988).
___, 'Collective Mentalities in Mid Seventeenth-Century England: 4. Cross Currents: Neutrals, Trimmers and Others', *Transactions of the Royal Historical Society* (5th ser.) 39 (1989).
___, 'Did the Ranters Exist?', *PP* 117 (1987).
Barber, S., 'Nothing but the First Chaos': Making Sense of Ireland', *The Seventeenth Century* 14, 1 (1999).
Barbour, H., 'The Early Quaker Outlook', *Church History* 26 (1957).
Barclay, A., 'Extracts from the A. R. Barclay MSS.', *JFHS* 28 (1931).
Barnard, T., 'Crisis of Identity among Irish Protestants, 1641-1685', *PP* 127 (1990).
Bauckham, R., 'The Eschatological Earthquake in the Apocalypse of John', *Novum Testamentum* 19, Fasc. 3 (1977).
Bauman, R., 'Observations on the Place of Festival in the Worldview of Seventeenth-Century Quakers', *Western Folklore* 43, 2 (1984).
Baxter, N., 'Gerrard Winstanley's Experimental Knowledge of God', *JEH* 39, 2 (1988).
Bender, H., 'The Pacifism of the Sixteenth Century Anabaptists', *Church History* 24, 2 (1955).
Bennett, R., "Exalted in our Nation': Some Issues in Quaker Identities', *FQ* 31, 8 (1997).
Betteridge, M., 'The Bitter Notes: The Geneva Bible and Its Annotations', *Sixteenth Century Journal* 14, 1 (1983).
Bitterman, M., 'The Early Quaker Literature of Defence', *Church History* 42, 2 (1973).
Blackwood, B., 'Plebeian Catholics in the 1640s and 1650s', *Recusant History* 18 (1986-7).
Bossy, J., 'The Character of Elizabethan Catholicism', *PP* 21 (1962).
Boulton, D., 'The Quaker Military Alliance', *FQ* 31, 8 (1997).
Braaten, C., 'Modern Interpretations of Nestorius', *Church History* 32, 3 (1963).
Braddick, M., 'Small Steps Can Lead to Utopia', *History* (BBC) 10, 2 (2009).
Bradstock, A., 'Sowing in Hope: the Relevance of Theology to Gerrard Winstanley's Political Programme', *The Seventeenth Century* 6 (1991).
Brady, C., 'Spenser's Irish Crisis: Humanism and Experience in the 1590s', *PP* 111 (1986).
Brauer, J., 'Reflections on the Nature of English Puritanism', *Church History* 23, 2 (1954).
Bruhn, K., "Sinne Unfoulded': Time, Election and Disbelief among the Godly in Late Sixteenth and Early Seventeenth Century England', *Church History* 77, 3 (2008).

Buckham, J., 'The Mysticism of Jesus and Paul', *The Biblical World* 41, 5 (1913).
Burrage, C., 'The Antecedents of Quakerism', *EHR* 30, 117 (1915).
Cadbury, H., 'Friends and the Inquisition at Malta', *JFHS* 53, 3 (1974).
___, 'Marginalia: James Nayler', *JFHS* 28 (1931).
___, 'The Basis of Early Christian Antimilitarism', *J. of Biblical Literature* 37, 1-2 (1918).
Cantor, G., 'Quakers in the Royal Society, 1660-1750', *Notes and Records of the Royal Society of London* 51, 2 (1997).
Capp, B., 'Godly Rule and English Millenarianism' (rev. art.), *PP* 52 (August 1971).
Carroll, K., 'Early Quakers and Going Naked', *Quaker History* 62, 2 (1978).
___, 'Quakers in Venice, 1657-1658', *Quaker History* 92, 1 (2003).
Charry, E., '"A Sharp Two-edged Sword": Pastoral Implications of Apocalypse', *Interpretation* 53, 2 (1999).
Childress, J., '"Answering That of God in Every Man": An Interpretation of Fox's Ethics', *QRT* 15, 3 (1974).
Christianson, P., 'The Causes of the English Revolution: A Reappraisal', *JBS* 15, 2 (1976).
Clancy, T., 'Papist-Protestant-Puritan: English Religious Taxonomy 1565-1665', *Recusant History* 13, 4 (1976).
Clark, K., 'Realised Eschatology', *J. of Biblical Literature* 59, 3 (1940).
Clarke, P., 'The Sectarian "Threat" and its impact in Restoration Cumbria', *Transactions of the Cumberland and Westmorland Antiquarian and Archaeological Society* 78 (1988).
Cohen, A., 'Two Roads to the Puritan Millennium: William Erbery and Vavasor Powell', *Church History* 32, 3 (1963).
Colclough, D., '"Parrhesia: the Rhetoric of Free Speech in Early Modern England', *Rhetorica* 17, 2 (1999).
Coleby, A., 'Military-Civilian Relations on the Solent 1651-1689', *HJ* 29, 4 (1986).
Collins, A. Y., 'Apocalyptic Themes in Biblical Literature', *Interpretation* 53, 2 (1999).
Collins, J., 'The Church Settlement of Oliver Cromwell', *History* 87 (2002).
Collinson, P., 'Religion, Society, and the Historian', *JRH* 23, 2 (1999).
Cooper, T., 'Reassessing the Radicals' (rev. art.), *HJ* 50, 1 (2007).
Crafton, J., 'Paul's Rhetorical Vision and the Purpose of Romans: Towards a New Understanding', *Novum Testamentum* 32, fasc. 4 (1990).
Craven, A., 'Ministers of State: the Established Church in Lancashire during the English Revolution, 1642-60', *Northern History* 45 (2008).
Creasey, M., 'The Quaker Interpretation of the Significance of Christ', *QRT* 1 (Autumn 1959).
Cressy, D., 'Conflict, Consensus and the Willingness to Wink: the Erosion of Community in Charles I's England', *Huntington Library Quarterly* 61, 2 (1998).
Cronshaw, D., 'The Shaping of Public Theology in Emerging Churches' (paper, Australian Association of Mission Studies & Public and Contextual Theology Conference (Canberra, Oct. 4th, 2008) at:
<www.csu.edu.au/special/accc/worddocs/Papers%20&%20Publications/AAMS%20missions%20conference/Cronshaw.pdf>.
Cust, R., 'Anti-Puritanism and Urban Politics: Charles I and Great Yarmouth', *HJ* 35, 1 (1992).
___, 'Was there an Alternative to Personal Rule?: Charles I, The Privy Council and the Parliament of 1629', *History* 90, 299 (2005).
D'Angelo, M., 'Abba and 'Father': Imperial Theology and the Jesus Traditions', *J. of Biblical Literature* 111, 4 (1992).
Daly, J., 'Cosmic Harmony and Political Thinking in Early Stuart England', *Transactions of the American Philosophical Society* (New Series) 69, 7 (1979).
Daniels, C., 'Convergent Friends: the Emergence of Post-Modern Quakerism', *Quaker Studies* 14, 2 (2010).

Davis, J., 'Religion and the Struggle for Freedom in the English Revolution', *HJ* 35, 3 (1992).
De Grazia, 'M., 'The Secularisation of Language in the Seventeenth Century', *J. of the History of Ideas* 41, 2 (1980).
De Groot, J., 'Prison Writing, Writing Prison during the 1640s and 1650s', *Huntington Library Quarterly* 72, 2 (2009).
De Sola Pinto, V., 'Peter Sterry and his Unpublished Writings', *The Review of English Studies* 6, 24 (1930).
Donahue, J., 'Jesus and the Kingdom of God', *America* 197, 7 (2007).
Doud, R., 'Rahner's Christology: a Whiteheadian Critique', *The J. of Religion* 57, 2 (1977).
Durland, W., 'Was George Fox a Prophet?', *QRT* 17, 1 (1976-77).
Durston, C., 'The Fall of Cromwell's Major-Generals', *EHR* 113, 450 (1998).
Elmen, P., 'The Theological Basis of Digger Communism', *Church History* 23, 3 (1954).
Endy, M., 'Puritanism, Spiritualism and Quakerism' at: <www.quaker.org/quest/issue1-2.html>.
Erskine, J., 'Margery Kempe and Her Models: The Role of the Authorial Voice', *Mystics Quarterly* 15, 2 (1989).
Fincham, K. and Lake, P., 'The Ecclesiastical Policy of James I', *JBS* 24, 2 (1985).
Finney, G., 'Ecstasy and Music in Seventeenth-Century England', *J. of the History of Ideas* 8, 2 (1947).
Fletcher, A., 'New Light on Religion and the English Civil War' (rev. art.), *JEH* 38, 1 (1987).
Foakes-Jackson, F., 'The Kingdom of God in Acts and the 'City of God'', *Harvard Theological Review* 12, 2, (1919).
Foster, H., 'Liberal Calvinism: the Remonstrants at the Synod of Dort in 1618', *The Harvard Theological Review* 16, 1 (1923).
Freiday, D., 'Christian Dialogue in the Seventeenth Century', *QRT* 88, 28 (1997).
___, 'The Early Quakers and the Doctrine of Authority', *QRT* 15, 1 (1973).
Freyne, S., 'The Galilean Jesus and a Contemporary Christology', *Theological Studies* 70 (2009).
Frost, J., 'Review of Ingle, L., *First Among Friends*', *Church History* 64, 2 (1995).
___, 'The Dry Bones of Quaker Theology', *Church History* 39, 4 (1970).
Fursha, E., 'Key Concepts in Caspar von Schwenkfeld's Thought', *Church History* 37, 2 (1968).
Garrett, C., 'The Rhetoric of Supplication: Prayer Theory in Seventeenth-Century England', *Renaissance Quarterly* 46, 2 (1993).
George, C., 'Puritanism as History and Historiography', *PP* 41 (1968).
Gilbert, C., 'The Puritan and the Quakers: Thomas Hall and Jane Higgs', *JFHS* 57, 2 (1995).
Gill, C., 'Identities in Quaker Women's Writing 1652-60', *Women's Writings* 9, 2 (2002).
___, 'Ministering Confusion: Rebellious Quaker Women, 1650-1660', *Quaker Studies* 9, 1 (2004).
Grant, F., 'The Gospel of the Kingdom', *The Biblical World* 50, 3 (1917).
Greaves, R., 'The Role of Women in Early English Nonconformity', *Church History* 52, 3 (1983).
___, 'Traditionalism and the Seeds of Revolution', *Sixteenth Century Journal* 7, 2 (1976).
Green, I., 'Clerical Prospects and Clerical Conformity in the early Stuart Church', *PP* 90 (Feb., 1981).
Gribben, C., 'Deconstructing the Geneva Bible: the Search for a Puritan poetic', *Literature and Theology* 14, 1 (2000).
Grundy, M., 'Learning to be a Quaker: Spiritual Formation and Religious Education among Early Friends', *Quaker Studies* 11, 2 (2007).

Gucer, K., 'Not Heretofore Extant in Print': Where the Mad Ranters Are', *J. of the History of Ideas* 61, 1 (2000).
Guiton, G., 'Seventeenth Century Quaker Pacifism', *Reviews in Religion and Theology* 9, 4 (2002).
___, 'The Early Quakers and the Kingdom of God', *QRT* 113 (2010).
Guthrie, S., 'Human Suffering, Human Liberation and the Sovereignty of God', *Theology Today* 53, 1 (1996).
Gwyn, D., 'Captivity Among the Idols: the Early Quaker View of Sin and Evil', *QRT* 22, 4 (1987).
___, 'James Nayler and the Lamb's War', *Quaker Studies* 12, 2 (2008).
Gilliam, E. and Tighe, W., '"To Run with the Time": Archbishop Whitgift, the Lambeth Articles and the Politics of Theological Ambiguity in Late Elizabethan England', *The Sixteenth Century Journal* 23, 2 (1992).
Gutiérrez, G., 'Option for the Poor Arises from Faith in Christ', *Theological Studies* 70 (2009).
Haigh, C., 'Puritan Evangelism in the Reign of Elizabeth I', *EHR* 92, 362 (1977).
Hammond, P., 'Thomas Smith: a Beleaguered Humanist of the Interregnum', *Bulletin of the Inst. of Historical Research* 46, 133 (1993).
Harkness, R., 'Early Relations of Baptists and Quakers', *Church History* 2, 4 (1933).
Harlow, J., 'Preaching for Hire', *Quaker Studies* 10, 1 (2005).
Hardin, R., 'Bunyan, Mr. Ignorance and the Quakers', *Studies in Philology* 69, 4 (1972).
Haughey, J., 'Schillebeeckx's Theology', *Theology Today* 38, 2 (1981).
Hazelton, M., '"Mony Choaks": The Quaker Critique of the Seventeenth-Century Public Sphere', *Modern Philology* 98, 2 (2000).
Healey, R., 'The Jew in Seventeenth-Century Protestant Thought', *Church History* 46, 1 (1977).
Hexter, J., 'The English Aristocracy, Its Crises, and the English Revolution, 1558-1660', *JBS* 8, 1 (1968).
Hibbard, C., 'Early Stuart Catholicism', *J. of Modern History* 52, 1 (1980).
Hill, C., 'Quakers and the English Revolution', *JFHS* 56, 3 (1992).
Hincks, E., 'The Apostle Paul's Mysticism', *The Biblical World* 2, 5 (1893).
Hirst, D., 'Locating the 1650s in England's Seventeenth Century', *History* 81, 263 (1996).
Hirst, M., 'A Tract Attributed to George Fox', *JFHS* 15 (1918).
Hoare, R., 'The Balby Seekers and Richard Farnworth', *Quaker Studies* 8, 2 (2004).
Holland, S., 'George Abbot: "The Wanted Archbishop"', *Church History* 56, 2 (1987).
Hopper, A., 'The Farnley Wood Plot and the Memory of the Civil Wars in Yorkshire', *HJ* 45, 2 (2002).
Howells, E., '"Mysticism and the Mystical', *The Way* (Supplement 2001/102).
Hudson, E., 'English Protestants and the *Imitatio Christi*, 1580-1620', *The Sixteenth Century Journal* 19, 4 (1988).
Hutchins, H., 'The Fundamental Thought and Purpose of Matthew, 1', *The Biblical World* 1, 3 (1893).
Ingle, L., 'From Mysticism to Radicalism: Recent Historiography of Quaker Beginnings', *Quaker History* 76, 2 (1987).
___, 'George Fox, Millenarian', *Albion* 24, 2 (1992).
___, 'Richard Hubberthorne and History: the Crisis of 1659', *JFHS* 56, 3 (1992).
James, M., 'The Political Importance of the Tithes Controversy in the English Revolution, 1640-60', *History* (New Series) 26, 101 (June 1941-March 1942).
Jamison, L., 'Dikaiosyne in The Usage of Paul', *J. of Bible and Religion* 21, 2 (1953).
Jardin, L., 'Dialectic Teaching in Sixteenth-Century Cambridge', *Studies in the Renaissance* 21 (1974).
Johns, A., 'Coleman Street', *Huntington Library Quarterly* 71, 1 (2008).

Johnson, G., 'From Seeker to Finder: a Study in Seventeenth Century English Spiritualism before the Quakers', *Church History* 17 (1948).
Jones, A., 'The Roman Civil Service', *J. of Roman Studies* 39, Parts 1 and 2 (1949).
Jordan, W., 'Sectarian Thought and its Relation to the Development of Religious Toleration, 1640-60', *Huntington Library Quarterly* 13, 2 (1940). Part 1.
Josselin, R., 'Extracts relating to Quakers from the Diary of the Rev. Ralph Josselin (1616-83), Vicar of Earls Colne, Essex', *JFHS* 34 (1937).
Keiser, R. M., 'From Dark Christian to Fullness of Life', *The Guilford Review* 23 (1986).
Keller, C., 'The Attraction of Apocalypse and the Evil of the End', *Concilium* 1 (1998).
Kent, S., 'Relative Deprivation and Resource Mobilisation: a study of early Quakerism', *British J. of Sociology* 33, 4 (1982).
Kim, S., '2 Cor. 5:11-12 and the Origin of Paul's Concept of Reconciliation', *Novum Testamentum* 39, 4 (1997).
Kirby, E., 'The Quakers' Efforts to Secure Civil and Religious Liberty, 1660-96', *J. of Modern History* 7, 4 (1935).
Kolp, A., 'Fox Loved the Apostle Paul', *QRT* 25, 2 (1991).
Kourie, C., 'Christ-mysticism in Paul', *The Way* (Supplement 2001/102).
Kuenning, L., 'Fox's Message Was Not About A Message', *QRT* 22, 3 (1987).
Kunze, B., '"Poore and in Necessity": Margaret Fell and Quaker Female Philanthropy in Northwest England in the Late Seventeenth Century', *Albion* 4 (1989).
___, 'Religious Authority and Social Status in Seventeenth-Century England', *Church History* 57, 2 (1988).
Kyle, R., 'John Knox's Concept of Divine Providence', *Albion* 18, 3 (1986).
Lake, P., 'Calvinism and the English Church', *PP* 114 (1987).
___, 'The King (The Queen) and the Jesuit: James Stuart's 'True Law of Free Monarchies', *Transactions of the Royal Historical Society* 14 (2004), 6th series.
Langford, M., 'Contract or Covenant', *FQ* 35, 8 (2007).
Lamont, W., ''Puritanism as History and Historiography: Some Further Thoughts', *PP* 44 (1969).
___, 'The Left and Its Past: Revisiting the 1650s', *History Workshop* 23 (Spring, 1987).
___, 'The Muggletonians 1652-1979: A 'Vertical' Approach', *PP* 99 (1983).
___, 'The Rise of Arminianism Reconsidered: Comment', *PP* 107 (1985).
Lassalle-Klein, R., 'Jesus of Galilee and the Crucified People: the Contextual Theology of Jon Sobrino and Ignacio Ellacuría', *Theological Studies* 70 (2009).
Lee, C., 'Cromwell, the king who never was', *Living History* 3 (June 2003).
Levine, J., 'Matter of Fact in the English Revolution', *J. of the History of Ideas* 64, 2 (2003).
Llewellyn-Edwards, T., 'Richard Farnworth of Tickhill', *JFHS* 56, 3 (1992).
Loades, D., 'The 'Bloody' Queen', *History* (BBC) 7, 3 (2006).
Loomie, A., 'London's Spanish Chapel before and after the Civil War', *Recusant History* 18 (1986-7).
Maclear, J., 'Popular Anticlericalism in the Puritan Revolution', *J. of the History of Ideas* 17, 4 (1956).
___, 'Quakerism and the End of the Interregnum', *Church History* 19 (1950).
Malcolm, J., 'A King in Search of Soldiers', *HJ* 21, 2 (1978).
Manning, D., 'Accusations of Blasphemy in English Anti-Quaker Polemic, *c*.1660-1701', *Quaker Studies* 14, 1 (2009).
Marcus, J., 'Entering into the Kingly Power of God', *J. of Biblical Literature* 107, 4 (1988).
Marik, S., 'Christopher Hill: Women Turning the World Upside Down', *Social Scientist* 32, 3/4 (2004).
Martland, T., 'An Inquiry into Religion's Empty World', *J. of Philosophy* 90, 9 (1993).
Matar, N., 'Some Notes on George Fox and Islam', *JFHS* 8, 55 (1989).

Matossian, M., 'Why the Quakers Quaked: the Influence of Climatic Change on Quaker Health, 1647-59', *Quaker History* 96, 1 (2007).
McCullough, P., 'Lancelot Andrewes and Language' at: <www.geocities.com/magdamun/andrewesmccullough.html>.
McDowell, N., 'A Ranter Reconsidered: Abiezer Coppe [1619-72] and Civil War Stereotypes', *The Seventeenth Century* 12, 2 (1997).
McGee, J., 'Conversion and the Imitation of Christ', *JBS* 15, 2 (1976).
McGregor, J., 'Ranterism and the Development of Early Quakerism', *JRH* 9, 4 (1977).
McKim, D., 'The Functions of Ramism in William Perkins' Theology', *The Sixteenth Century Journal* 16, 4 (1985).
Metzger, B., 'The Geneva Bible of 1560' at: <www.theologytoday.ptsem.edu/oct1960/v17-3-article6.htm>.
Meyer, F., 'The Relation of the New Testament to the Mosaic System', *The Old and New Testament Student* 13, 3 (1891).
Miller, J., '"A Suffering People': English Quakers and their Neighbours c.1650-c.1700', *PP* 188 (Aug. 2005).
Miller, R., 'Christ-Centredness and Quaker Identity', *Friends Journal* 55, 7 (2009).
Moore, J. D., 'Calvin Versus the Calvinists?: The Case of John Preston', *Reformation and Renaissance Review* 6, 3 (2004).
Morrill, J., 'Cromwell: Hero or Villain?', *History* (BBC) 9, 9 (2008).
___, 'The Religious Context of the English Civil War', *Transactions of the Royal Historical Society* 34 (Fifth Series: 1984).
Mosse, G., 'Puritan Radicalism and the Enlightenment', *Church History* 29, 4 (1960).
Muessig, C., 'Preaching the Beatitudes in the late Middle Ages', *Studies in Christian Ethics* 22, 136 (2009).
Mullett, M., 'Conflict, Politics and Elections in Lancaster, 1660-1688', *Northern History* 19 (1983).
___, '"Men of Knowne Loyalty': The Politics of the Lancashire Borough of Clitheroe, 1660-1689', *Northern History* 21 (1995).
___, Review of Scott, D., *Quakerism in York 1650-1670* (1991), *Northern History* 24 (1993).
Mulligan, L. *et al*, 'The Religion of Gerrard Winstanley', *PP* 89 (1980).
Nesti, D., 'Early Quaker Ecclesiology', *QRT* 18, 1 (1978).
Newcomb, B., 'The English Puritan Clergy's Acceptance of Political Parties, 1570-1700', *JRH* 19, 1 (1995).
Newman, B., 'Henry Suso and the Medieval Devotion to Christ the Goddess', *Spiritus* 2 (2002).
Nickalls, J., 'George Fox's Library', *JFHS* 27 (1931).
Nicole, R., 'John Calvin's View of the Extent of the Atonement', *Westminster Theological Journal* 47 (1985).
Noonan, K., '"The Cruell Pressure of an Enraged, Barbarous People': Irish and English Identity in Seventeenth-Century Policy and Propaganda', *HJ* 41, 1 (1998).
Nuttall, G., 'George Fox as Pacifist', *Friends Journal* 30, 8 (1984).
___, '"Nothing Else Would Do': Early Friends and the Bible', *FQ* 22, 10 (1982).
O'Connell, P., 'Thomas Merton's Vision of the Kingdom', *Logos* 3, 4 (2000).
O'Day, G., 'Jesus as Friend in the Gospel of John', *Interpretation* 58, 2 (2004).
O'Malley, T., '"Defying the Power and Tempering the Spirit': A Review of Quaker Control over their Publications, 1672-1689', *JEH* 33, 1 (1982).
___, 'The Press and Quakerism', *JFHS* 54, 4 (1979).
Olsen, P., 'Was John Foxe a Millenarian?', *JEH* 45, 4 (1994).
Ong, W., 'Tudor Writings on Rhetoric', *Studies in the Renaissance* 15 (1968).
Palmer, V., 'Did William Penn Diverge Significantly from George Fox in his Understanding of the Quaker Message?, *Quaker Studies* 11, 1 (2006).

Parnham, D., 'The Nurturing of Righteousness: Sir Henry Vane on Freedom and Discipline', *JBS* 42, 1 (2003).
Peabody, F., 'Mysticism and Modern Life', *The Harvard Theological Review* 7, 4 (1914).
Penrose, E., 'Edmund Peckover: ex-soldier of the Commonwealth and Quaker', *JFHS* 2 (1905).
Perrin, N., 'Eschatology and Hermeneutics', *J. of Biblical Literature* 93, 1 (1974).
Pinthus, E., 'Shake All the Country in their Profession: the Relevance of George Fox's Peace Testimony for Today', *FQ* 18, 8 (1974).
Questier, M., 'Arminianism, Catholicism and Puritanism in England in the 1630s', *HJ* 49, 1 (2006).
Quinn, D., 'John Donne's Principles of Biblical Exegesis', *J. of English and Germanic Philology* 61, 2 (1962).
Reay, B., 'Quaker Opposition to Tithes 1652-1660', *PP* 86 (1980).
___, 'The Quakers and 1659: two newly discovered broadsides by Edward Burrough', *JFHS* 54, 2 (1977).
___, 'The Quakers, 1659, and the Restoration of the Monarchy', *History* 63, 208 (1978).
Roberts, A., 'Review of *TLITC*', *Quaker History* 90, 2 (2001).
___, 'The Relevancy of George Fox', *FQ* 18, 8 (1974).
___, 'The Universalism of Christ in Early Quaker Understanding', *QRT* 24, 1 (1989).
Roberts, C., 'The Kingdom of Heaven', *Harvard Theological Review* 41, 1 (1948).
Roberts, S., 'The Quakers in Evesham 1655-1660: A Study in Religion, Politics and Culture', *Midland History* 16 (1991).
Rollinson, P., 'The Civil War in Hereford' at: <www.colbirch.org.uk/pages/hereford.php>.
Schochet, G., 'Patriarchalism, Politics and Mass Attitudes in Stuart England', *HJ* 12, 3 (1969).
Schwartz, H., 'Arminianism and the English Parliament 1624-1629', *JBS* 12, 2 (1973).
Schwartz, J., 'Hobbes and the Two Kingdoms of God', *Polity* 18, 1 (1985).
Scott, H., 'The Teachings of Jesus', *The Biblical World* 1, 6 (1893).
Scott, Jonathan, 'Radicalism and Restoration: The Shape of the Stuart Experience' (rev. art.), *HJ* 31, 2 (1988).
Scott, Janet, 'Reflections in a Looking-Glass', *FQ* 22, 10 (1982).
___, 'The Meaning of Hope', *FQ* 32, 8 (2001).
Shepherd, M., 'The Epistle of James and the Gospel of Matthew', *J. of Biblical Literature* 75, 1 (1956).
Sleeper, C., 'Christ's Coming and Christian Living', *Interpretation* 53, 2 (1999).
Smith, N., 'Elegy for a Grindletonian: Poetry and Heresy in Northern England, 1615-40', *J. of Medieval and Early Modern Studies* 33, 2 (2003).
Smyth, A., 'Printed Miscellanies in England, 1640-1682: 'storehouses of wit'', *Criticism* (2000) at <www.findarticles.com/p/articles/mi_m2220/is_2_42/ai_68364661>.
Solt, L., 'Anti-Intellectualism in the Puritan Revolution', *Church History* 25, 4 (1956).
Spurr, J., ''A Special Kindness for Dead Bishops': The Church, History and Testimony in Seventeenth Century Protestantism', *Huntington Library Quarterly* 68, 1&2 (2005).
Stassen, G., 'Recovering the Way of Jesus' at <www.epcra.ch/papers/belgien/strassen.htm>.
Stevens, G., 'The Teaching of Jesus. VI. The Kingdom of God', *The Biblical World* 5, 6 (1895).
Stillman, R., 'Hobbes' *Leviathan*: Monsters, Metaphors, and Magic', *English Literary History* 62, 4 (1995).
Stone, L., 'The Bourgeois Revolution of Seventeenth Century England Revisited', *PP* 109 (1985).
Tawney, R., 'Religious Thought on Social and Economic Questions in the Sixteenth and Seventeenth Centuries', *J. of Political Economy* 31, 4 (1923). Part 1.

Taylor, K., "Chalk, Cheese and Cloth': The Settling of Quaker Communities in Seventeenth Century Wiltshire', *Quaker Studies* 10, 2 (2006).
___, 'The Role of Quaker Women in the Seventeenth Century, and the Experiences of the Wiltshire Friends', *Southern History* 23 (2003).
Tennant, P., 'Parish and People: South Warwickshire in the Civil War', *Warwickshire History* 7, 6 (1989/90).
Terrar, E., 'Gentry Royalists or Independent Diggers?: The Nature of the English Catholic Community in the Civil War Period of the 1640s', *Science and Society* 57, 3 (1993).
Thomas, K., 'Women and the Civil War Sects', *PP* 13 (1958).
Thomas, S., 'Religious Community in Revolutionary Halifax', *Northern History* 40 (2003).
Tiede, D., '"The God Who Made the World!": Preaching Luke's Gospel in an Apostolic Era', *Currents in Theology and Mission* 27, 6 (2000).
Tucker, R., 'Revolutionary Faithfulness', *QRT* 9, 2 (1967-8).
Underdown, D., 'A Reply to John Morrill', *JBS* 26, 4 (1987).
___, 'The Independents Reconsidered', *JBS* 3, 2 (1964).
Van Brogt, J., 'Apocalyptic Thought in Christianity and Buddhism', *Dialogue* 27 (2000).
Waaijman, K., 'Toward a Phenomenological Definition of Spirituality', *Studies in Spirituality* 3 (1993).
Wallace, D., 'George Gifford, Puritan Propaganda and Popular Religion in Elizabethan England', *Sixteenth Century Journal* 9, 1 (1978).
Warburton, R., '"The Lord hath joined us together, and wo be to them that should part us': Katharine Evans and Sarah Cheevers as Travelling Friends', *Texas Studies in Literature and Language* 47, 4 (2005).
Warren, M., 'The Quakers as Parrhesiasts: Frank Speech and Plain Speaking as the Fruits of Silence', *Quaker History* 98, 2 (2009).
Wells, H., 'Trinitarian Feminism: Elizabeth Johnson's Wisdom Christology' (rev. art.), *Theology Today* 52, 3 (1995).
Westerkamp, M., 'Puritan Patriarchy and the Problem of Revelation', *J. of Interdisciplinary History* 23, 3 (1993).
White, P., 'The Rise of Arminianism Reconsidered', *PP* 101 (1983).
___, 'The Rise of Arminianism Reconsidered: a Rejoinder', *PP* 115 (1987).
Wilson, D., 'The King's Good Book', *History Today* 61, 1 (2011).
Woolrych, A., 'The Cromwellian Protectorate: A Military Dictatorship?', *History* 75, 243 (1990).
___, 'The Good Old Cause and the Fall of the Protectorate', *HJ.* 13, 2 (1957).
Worden, B., 'Providence and Politics in Cromwellian England', *PP* 109 (1985).
Worden, W., 'Text and Revelation: George Fox's Use of the Bible', *QRT* 30, 3 (2001).
Zaller, R., 'Henry Parker and the Regiment of True Government', *Proceedings of the American Philosophical Society* 13, 2 (1991).

Books and Lectures

Abbott, W. (ed.), *The Writings and Speeches of Oliver Cromwell* (Oxford: Clarendon, 1988).
Acheson, R., *Radical Puritans in England 1550-1660* (L: Longman, 1990).
Adamson, J., *James: The Man and His Message* (Grand Rapids, MI.: Eerdmans, 1998).
Adair, J., *Puritans* (Stroud: Sutton Publishing, 1998).
Allott, W., *Worship and Social Progress* (Swarthmore Lecture. L: Allen and Unwin, 1945).
Ambler, R., *The End of Words: Issues in Contemporary Quaker Theology* (L: QHS, 1995).
___, *Truth of the Heart* (L: Quaker Books, 2001).
Angell, S. (ed.), *Friends Consultation on Eldering Conference Proceedings* (Richmond, IN.: Quaker Hill Conference Center, 1982).
Anon, *The History of Westmorland* at:

Bibliography

<http://archiver.rootsweb.com/th/read/Atkinson-uk/2001-09/0999634849>.
Aquinas, T., *Summa Theologica* (Westminster, MD.: Christian Classics, 1948).
Ashley, M., *England in the Seventeenth Century, 1603-1714* (Harmondsworth: Penguin, 1954).
___, *Life in Stuart England* (L: Batsford, 1964).
Aylmer, G., *Rebellion or Revolution? England 1640-1660* (Oxford: OUP, 1986).
Bailey, D., *New Light on George Fox* (San Francisco, CA.: Edwin Mellen, 1992).
Ball, B., *A Great Expectation: Eschatological Thought in English Protestantism to 1660* (Leiden: Brill, 1975).
Barbour, H., 'Sixty Years in Early Quaker History' in Dandelion (ed., 2004).
___, *The Quakers in Puritan England* (Richmond, IN.: Friends United Press, 1985).
___ Frost, J., *The Quakers* (Richmond, IN.: FUP, 1994).
___ Roberts, A. (eds.), *Early Quaker Writings* ([Grand Rapids, MI.: Eerdmans, 1973] Wallingford, PA.: Pendle Hill, 2004).
Barclay, A. (ed.), *Letters of Early Friends* (L: Harvey & Darton, 1841).
Bauckham, R., *Tudor Apocalypse* (Oxford: Sutton Courteney, 1978).
Bauman, R., *Let Your Words Be Few* (Cambridge: CUP, 1983).
Beier, A., *The Problem of the Poor in Tudor and Early Stuart England* (L: Methuen, 1983).
Bennett, M., *The Civil Wars Experienced: Britain and Ireland, 1638-1661* (L: Routledge, 2000).
Benson, L., *Catholic Quakerism* (Philadelphia, PA.: Book and Publications Committee, Philadelphia YM [RSF], 1973).
___, *What did George Fox teach about Christ?* (Reading: George Fox Fund, [1984] 1991).
Bien, P., *The Mystery of Quaker Light* (Wallingford, PA.: Pendle Hill, 2006).
Birkel, M. and Newman, J. (eds.), *The Lamb's War: Quaker Essays to Honour Hugh Barbour* (Richmond, IN.: Earlham College Press, 1992).
Bittle, W., *James Nayler 1618-1660* (York: Sessions, 1986).
Blackwood, B., *The Lancashire Gentry and the Great Rebellion 1640-1660* (Manchester: Manchester University Press, 1978).
Blakney, R., *Meister Eckhart: a modern translation* (NY.: Harper and Row, 1957).
Boff, L., *Church: Charism and Power* (NY.: Crossroad, 1988).
Booy, D., *Autobiographical Writings by Early Quaker Women* (Aldershot: Ashgate, 2004).
Borg, M., *Jesus: A New Vision* (San Francisco, CA.: HarperCollins, 1991).
Bossy, J., *The English Catholic Community* (L: Darton, Longman & Todd, 1975).
Boulding, K., *The Evolutionary Potential of Quakerism* (Wallingford, PA.: Pendle Hill and Australia Yearly Meeting, 1964).
Brailsford, M., *Quaker Women* (L: Duckworth, 1915).
Braithwaite, W., *Spiritual Guidance in Quaker Experience* (Swarthmore Lecture. L: Headley Bros., 1909).
___, *The Beginnings of Quakerism* (Cambridge: CUP, 1955).
___, *The Second Period of Quakerism* (Cambridge: CUP, [L: Macmillan, 1921] 1961).
Braaten, C., *The Future of God* (NY.: Harper and Row, 1969).
Bray, T. et al, *The Sixteen-Fifties* (Milton Keynes: Open University Press, 1981).
Brayshaw, A., *The Personality of George Fox* (L: Allenson, 1933).
___, *The Quakers* (York: Sessions, 1982).
Breay, J., *Light in the Dales* (Norwich: Canterbury, 1996).
Bridenbaugh, C., *Vexed and Troubled Englishmen, 1590-1642* (L: OUP, 1975).
Brigden, S., *New Worlds, Lost Worlds* (Harmondsworth, Allen Lane, 2001).
Brinton, H., *Friends for 300 Years* (L: George Allen and Unwin, 1953).
___, *The Ethical Mysticism in The Society of Friends* (Wallingford, PA.: Pendle Hill, 1967).
___, *The Society of Friends* (Wallingford, P.A.: Pendle Hill, 1949).
Britain Yearly Meeting, *Quaker Faith and Practice* (L: Britain Yearly Meeting, 1995).

Brock, P., *Pacifism to 1914: an Overview* (Toronto: Brock, 1994).
Brockbank, E., *Richard Hubberthorne of Yealand* (L: Friends' Book Centre, 1929).
Brook, B., *The Lives of the Puritans* (L: Black, 1813). 3 vols.
Burge, G., *The Anointed Community* (Grand Rapids, MI.: Eerdmans, 1987).
Cadbury, H., *Letters to William Dewsbury and Others* (*JFHS* Supp. 22. L: Bannisdale Press, 1948).
___, *Quakerism and Early Christianity* (Swarthmore Lecture. L: Allen and Unwin, 1957).
Caldwell, P., *The Puritan Conversion Narrative* (Cambridge: CUP, 1983).
Campagnac, E., *The Cambridge Platonists* (Oxford: Clarendon Press, 1901).
Campbell, J., *The Hero with a Thousand Faces* (Princeton, NY.: Princeton University Press, 1968).
Campbell, R. (trans.), *Poems of St. John of the Cross* (Glasgow: Collins, 1983).
Capp, B., *Cromwell's Navy* (Oxford: Clarendon, 1989).
___, *The Fifth Monarchy Men: a study in Seventeenth-Century English Millenarianism* (L: Faber and Faber, 1972).
Chenu, M-D., *Aquinas and his Role on Theology* (Collegeville, MN.: Liturgical Press, 2002).
Chilton, B. and McDonald, J., *Jesus and the Ethics of the Kingdom* (L: SPCK, 1987).
Clark, P. et al (eds.), *The English Commonwealth 1547-1640* (Leicester: Leicester University Press, 1979).
Clarke, A., *Prelude to Restoration in Ireland: the end of the Commonwealth 1659-1660* (Cambridge: CUP, 1999).
Coffey, D., *Grace: the Gift of the Holy Spirit* (Sydney: Catholic Institute of Sydney, 1979).
Cohn, N., *The Pursuit of the Millennium* (Fairlawn, NJ.: Essential Books, 1957).
Coleby, A., *Central Government and the Localities: Hampshire 1649-1689* (Cambridge: CUP, [1987] 2002).
Collins, J., *The Apocalyptic Imagination* (NY.: Crossroad, 1984).
Collinson, P., *Godly People: Essays on English Protestantism and Puritanism* (L: Hambleton, 1983).
___, *The Birthpangs of Protestant England* (L: Macmillan, 1988).
___ (ed.) *The Religion of Protestants: The Church in English Society, 1559-1625* (Oxford: Clarendon, 1982).
Conley, T., *Rhetoric in the European Tradition* (L: University of Chicago Press, 1990).
Cooper, W., *A Living Faith* (Richmond, IN.: Friends United Press, 1990).
Cope, J., 'Seventeenth-Century Quaker Style' in Fish, S. (ed.).
Corns, T. and Loewenstein, D. (eds.), *The Emergence of Quaker Writing* (L: Frank Cass, 1995).
Coughlin P., 'Counter-currents in Colonial Discourse: the political thought of Vincent and Daniel Gookin' in Ohlmeyer (ed.).
Coward, B., *The Stuart Age: England 1603-1714* (L: Longman, 1994).
___, *Oliver Cromwell* (L: Longman, 1991).
Craik, G., *Sketches of the History of Literature and Learning in England* (L: Knight, 1845).
Crawford, P., *Women and Religion in England 1500-1720* (L: Routledge, 1993).
Creasey, M., *The Christ of History and of Experience* (Shrewsbury Lecture. Shrewsbury, NJ.: Manasquan and Shrewsbury Monthly Meetings [RSF], 1967).
Cressy, D., *Travesties and Transgressors in Tudor and Stuart England* (Oxford: OUP, 2000).
Cross, C., *Church and People, 1450-1660* (L: Fontana, 1976).
Crump, C., (ed.), *The History of the Life of Thomas Ellwood* (L: Methuen, 1900).
D'Monté, R. and Pohl, N., (eds.), *Female Communities 1660-1800: Literary Visions and Cultural Realities* (Basingstoke: Macmillan, 2000).
Damrosch, L., *The Sorrows of the Quaker Jesus* (Cambridge, MA.: Harvard University Press, 1996).

Bibliography

Dandelion, P. (ed.), *The Creation of Quaker Theory* (Aldershot: Ashgate, 2004).
___ et al, *Heaven on Earth: Quakers and the Second Coming* (Birmingham: Curlew and Woodbrooke, 1998).
Davies, A., *The Quakers in English Society, 1655-1725* (Oxford: Clarendon, 2000).
Davies, O., *God Within: the mystical tradition in northern Europe* (NY.: Paulist Press, 1988).
Davies, S., *Unbridled Spirits: Women of the English Revolution* (L: The Women's Press, 1998).
Davis, C., *A Question of Conscience* (L: Hodder and Stoughton, 1967).
Davis, J., *Fear, Myth and History: The Ranters and the Historians* (Cambridge: CUP, 1986).
Dickens, A., *The English Reformation* (L: Batsford, 1989), 2nd.ed.
Dodd, C., *The Interpretation of the Fourth Gospel* (Cambridge: CUP, [1953] 1968).
___, *The Parables of the Kingdom* (NY.: Scribner's Sons, [1935, 1936] 1961).
Dolan, F., *Whores of Babylon: Catholicism, Gender and Seventeenth Century Print Culture* (Ithica, NY.: Cornell University Press, 1999).
Dunn, J. and McKnight, S. (eds.), *The Historical Jesus in Recent Research* (Winona Lake, IN.: Eisenbrauns, 2005).
Dunn, R. and Dunn, M., *The World of William Penn* (Philadelphia, PA.: University of Pennsylvania Press, 1986).
Dyck, H. (ed.), *The Pacifist Impulse in Historical Perspective* (Toronto: University of Toronto Press, 1996).
Edwards, M. (ed.), *Scarborough 966-1966* (Scarborough: Scarborough and District Archaeological Society, 1966), 2nd rpt.
Eliot, T. S., *Collected Poems 1909-1962* (L: Faber and Faber, 1990).
Evelyn, J., *The Diary of John Evelyn* (L: Macmillan, 1908).
Ezell, M., *Writing Women's Literary History* (Baltimore, MD.: The Johns Hopkins University Press, 1993).
Feullenbach, J., *The Kingdom of God* (Manila: Divine Word Publications, 1989).
Fager, C. (ed.), *Papers from the Quaker Theology Roundtable* (Wallingford, PA.: Pendle Hill, 1995).
Feola-Castelucci, M., *George Bishop* (York: Sessions, 1996).
Firth, C. and Rait, R. (eds.), *Acts and Ordinances of the Interregnum 1642-1660* (Holmes Reach, FL.: Gaunt, 1972). See 1911 version at:
<http://www.british-history.ac.uk/source.asp?pubid=606&page=19>.
Firth, K., *The Apocalyptic Tradition in Reformation Britain 1530-1645* (Oxford: OUP, 1979).
Fish, J. (ed.), *Seventeenth-Century Prose* (NY.: OUP, 1971).
Fleming, W., *Mysticism in Christianity* (L: Scott, 1913).
Flew, R., *The Idea of Perfection in Christian Theology* (NY.: Humanities Press, 1968).
Fogelklou, E., *James Nayler: the Rebel Saint* (L: Ernest Benn, 1931).
Foxton, R., *'Hear the Word of the Lord': A Critical and Bibliographical Study of Quaker Women's Writings, 1650-1700* (Melbourne: Bibliographical Society of Australia and New Zealand, 1994).
Frost, J. and Moore, J. (eds.), *Seeking the Light: Essays in Quaker History* (Wallingford, PA.: Pendle Hill, 1986).
Fuller, R., *Naming the Antichrist* (NY.: OUP, 1995).
Gardiner, S., *History of the Commonwealth and Protectorate* (NY: AMS Press, 1965); 4 vols., vol. 3.
Garman, M. et al (eds.), *Hidden in Plain Sight: Quaker Women's Writings 1650-1700* (Wallingford, PA.: Pendle Hill, 1996).
Gentiles, I. et al (eds.), *Soldiers, Writers and Statesmen of the English Revolution* (Cambridge: CUP, 1998).

Gibbons, B., *Gender in Mystical and Occult Thought* (Cambridge: CUP, 1906).
Gill, C., *The Women of Grub Street: Press, Politics and Gender in the Literary Marketplace 1678-1730* (Oxford: Clarendon, 1998).
___, *Women in the Seventeenth Century Quaker Community* (Aldershot: Ashgate, 2005).
Glines, E. (ed.), *Undaunted Zeal: The Letters of Margaret Fell* (Richmond, IN.: Friends United Press, 2003).
Goergen, D., *The Mission and Ministry of Jesus* (Wilmington, DE.: Glazier, 1986).
Gough, R., *The History of Myddle* (Firle: Caliban Books, 1979).
Graham, J., *War from a Quaker Point of View* (L: Headley Bros., 1915).
Graves, M., *Preaching the Inward Light* (Waco, TX.: Baylor University Press, 2009).
Gray, J., *The Biblical Doctrine of the Reign of God* (Edinburgh: Clark, 1979).
Greaves, R., *Enemies Under His Feet: Radicals and Nonconformists in Britain, 1664-1677* (Stanford, CA.: Stanford University Press, 1990).
___, *Deliver Us from Evil: the Radical Underground in Britain, 1660-1663* (NY: OUP, 1986).
___ Zaller, R., *Biographical Dictionary of British Radicals in the Seventeenth Century* (Brighton: Harvester Press, 1982).
Gregg, P., *King Charles 1* (Berkeley, CA.: University of California Press, 1984).
___, *Oliver Cromwell* (L: Dent, 1988).
Griffiths, A., *The Chronicles of Newgate* (L: Chapman and Hall, 1884).
Grubb, E., *The Historic and Inward Christ* (Swarthmore Lecture. L: Headley Bros., 1914).
Guiton, G., *The Growth and Development of Quaker Testimony, 1652-1661 and 1960-1994: Conflict, Non-Violence and Conciliation* (Lewiston, NY.: Edwin Mellen, 2005).
Gura, P., *A Glimpse of Sion's Glory: Puritan Radicalism in New England 1620-1660* (Middletown, CT.: Wesleyan University Press, 1984).
Gwyn, D., *Apocalypse of the Word* (Richmond, IN.: Friends United Press, 1986).
___, *Seekers Found: Atonement in Early Quaker Experience* (Wallingford, PA.: Pendle Hill, 2000).
___, *The Covenant Crucified* (Wallingford, PA.: Pendle Hill, 1995).
Hadley King, R., *George Fox and the Light Within* (Philadelphia, PA.: Friends Book Store, 1940).
Haller, W., *Foxe's Book of Martyrs and the Elect Nation* (L: Cape, 1963).
___, *The Elect Nation: the meaning and relevance of Foxe's Book of Martyrs* (NY.: Harper and Row, 1963).
Happold, F., *Mysticism* (Harmondsworth: Penguin, 1970).
Harkness, G., *Christian Ethics* (NY.: Abingdon Press, 1957).
___, *Understanding the Kingdom of God* (Nashville, TN.: Abingdon Press, 1974) and at: <www.religion-online.org/showchapter.asp?title=577&C=740>.
Harris, T., *London Crowds in the Reign of Charles II* (NY.: CUP, 1987).
Hastings, A. *et al* (eds.), *Christian Thought: A Brief History* (Oxford: OUP, 2002).
Havran, M., *The Catholics in Caroline England* (Stanford, CA.: Stanford University Press, 1962).
Heal, F. and Holmes, C., *The Gentry in England and Wales 1500-1700* (Stanford, CA.: Stanford Univeristy Press, 1994).
Healy, T. and Sawday, J., *Literature and the English Civil War* (NY.: CUP, 1990).
Hedrick, C. (ed.), *When Faith Meets Reason* (Santa Rosa, CA.: Polebridge Press, 2008).
Herrup, C., *The Common Peace* (Cambridge: CUP, 1987).
Hill, C., *Puritanism and Revolution* (NY.: Schocken, 1958).
___, *The Antichrist in Seventeenth Century England* (L: OUP, 1971).
___, *The Collected Essays of Christopher Hill* (L: Harvester Press, 1986).
___, *The English Bible and the Seventeenth-Century Revolution* (L: Allen Lane, 1993).
___, *The Experience of Defeat* (L: Faber and Faber, 1984).

Bibliography

___, *The World Turned Upside Down* (Harmondsworth: Penguin, 1975).
___ Dell, E. (eds.), *The Good Old Cause: the English Revolution of 1640-1660* (L: Lawrence and Wishart, 1949).
Hirst, D., *England in Conflict, 1603-1660* (L: Arnold, 1999).
Hirst, M., *The Quakers in Peace and War* (NY.: Garland, [1923] 1972).
Hodgkin, L., *Silent Worship* (Swarthmore Lecture. L: Allen and Unwin, 1919).
Holmer, P. (ed.), *Søren Keirkegaard: Edifying Discourses* (NY.: Harper and Bros., 1958).
Hopkins, G., *Poems* (L: OUP, 1956).
Horle, C., *The Quakers and the English Legal System 1660-1688* (Philadelphia, PA.: University of Pennsylvania Press, 1988).
Horsley, R., *Jesus and Empire* (Minneapolis, MN.: Fortress Press, 2003).
Hughes, M. (ed.), *John Milton: Complete Poems and Major Prose* (NY.: Odyssey Press, 1957).
Hughes, G., *Swearing: a Social History Language, Oaths and Profanity in English* (Oxford: Blackwell, 1991).
Hutton, R., *The British Republic 1649-1660* (L: Macmillan, 1990).
Ingle, L., *First Among Friends* (Oxford: OUP, 1994).
Ives. E. (ed.), *The English Revolution 1600-1660* (L: Arnold, 1968).
Jackson, B., *Essays on Halakhah in the New Testament* (Leiden: Brill, 2008).
Jarrett, B., *The English Dominicans* (L: Burns and Oates, 1921).
Jenkins, G., *Protestant Dissenters in Wales, 1639-1689* (Cardiff: University of Wales, 1992).
Jewell, H., *Education in Early Modern England* (L: Macmillan, 1998).
Johnson, E., *Friends of God and Prophets: A Feminist Theological Reading of the Communion of Saints* (NY.: Continuum, 1998).
Johnson, W., *Arise, My Love: Mysticism for a New Era* (NY: Maryknoll, 2000).
Jones, R., *Spiritual Reformers in the 16th and 17th Centuries* (L: Macmillan, 1914).
___, *Studies in Mystical Religion* (L: Macmillan, 1925).
Jones, T. C., *"The Power of the Lord Is Over All": The Pastoral Letter of George Fox* (Richmond, IN.: Friends United Press, 1989).
Jonson, B., *The Alchemist*, Act 3 at: <http://www.levity.com/alchemy/jn-alch2.html>.
Kähler, M., *The So-called Historical Jesus and the Historic, Biblical Christ* (trans. and ed. C. Braaten. Philadelphia, PA.: Fortress Press, 1977).
Katz, D., *God's Last Words* (L: Yale University Press, 2004).
Keeble, N., *Cambridge Companion to Writings of the English Revolution* (Cambridge: CUP, 2001).
Keiser, R. M. and Moore, R., *Knowing the Mystery of Life Within* (L: Quaker Books, 2005).
Kelly, T., *A Testament of Devotion* (NY: HarperCollins, [1941] 1992).
Kendall, R., *Calvin and English Calvinism to 1649* (Oxford: OUP, 1979).
Knott, J., *Discourses of Martyrdom in English Literature 1563-1694* (Cambridge: CUP, 1993).
Kishlansky, M., *A Monarchy Transformed: Britain 1603-1714* (Harmondsworth, Penguin, 1997).
Kolp, A., *Fresh Winds of the Spirit* (Richmond, IN.: Friends United Press, 1991).
Kunze, B., *Margaret Fell and the Rise of Quakerism* (L: Macmillan, 1994).
Lacey, P., *Leadings and Being Led* (Wallingford, PA.: Pendle Hill, 1985).
Ladd, G., *A Theology of the New Testament* (Grand Rapids, MI.: Eerdmans, 1974).
Lamont, W., *Puritanism and Historical Controversy* (L: University College Press, 1996).
___, *Richard Baxter and the Millennium* (L: Croom Helm, 1979).
Lampen, J., *Wait in the Light* (L: QHS, 1981).
Langford, M., *Quakers and Christianity* (Gloucester: George Fox Fund, 2005).
Latham, R. (ed.), *The Shorter Pepys* (L: Bell and Hyman, 1985).
Levy, L., *Blasphemy* (Chapel Hill, NC.: University of N. Carolina Press, 1993).

Liechty, D. (ed.), *Early Anabaptist Spirituality* (NY.: Paulist Press, 1994).
Lloyd, A., *Quaker Social History 1669-1738* (Westport, CT.: Greenwood, 1950).
Loades, D. (ed.), *John Foxe and the English Reformation* (Woodbridge, CT: Scolar, 1997).
Loukes, H., *Friends Face Reality* (L: Bannisdale Press, 1954).
___, *The Quaker Contribution* (L: SCM, 1965).
MacCulloch, D., *Reformation* (L: Penguin, 2003).
MacFarlane, A. (ed.), *The Diary of Ralph Josselin 1616-83* (L: OUP, 1976).
Mack, P., *Visionary Women* (Berkeley, CA.: University of California Press, 1992).
Mackey, J. (ed.), *An Introduction to Celtic Christianity* (Edinburgh: Clark, 1989).
Mair, G. (ed.), *Wilson's Arte of Rhetorique, 1560* (Oxford: OUP, 1909).
Manson, T., *The Servant-Messiah* (Cambridge: CUP, 1953).
Masson, D., *The Life of John Milton* (L: Macmillan, 1859-88).
Marshall, P. (ed.), *The Impact of the English Reformation, 1500-1640* (L: Arnold, 1997).
Massyngberde-Ford, J., *Revelation* (Garden City, NY: Doubleday, 1975).
McDowell, N., *The English Radical Imagination, 1630-1660* (Oxford: Clarendon, 2003).
McGrath, A. (ed.), *The Blackwell Encyclopaedia of Modern Christian Thought* (Oxford: Blackwell, 1997).
McGregor, J and Reay, B. (eds.), *Radical Religion in the English Revolution* (Oxford: OUP, 1984).
McNeill, J. and Battles, F. (transs. and eds.), [John Calvin] *Institutes of the Christian Religion* (Philadelphia, PA.: Westminster Press, 1960); 2 vols.
Milton, A., *Catholic and Reformed* (Cambridge: CUP, 1995).
Miner, E., (ed.), *Seventeenth Century Imagery: Essays on the Uses of Figurative Language from Donne to Farquhar* (Berkeley, CA.: University of California Press, 1971).
Mitchell, S., (ed.), *The Selected Poetry of Rainer Maria Rilke* (NY.: Vintage, 1989).
Moltmann, J., *Theology of Hope* (L: SCM Press, 1967).
Moore, R., *Notes on Lists of Seventeenth Century Publications* at: <www.qhpress.org/rmoore>.
___, *The Light In Their Consciences: the Early Quakers in Britain, 1646-1666* (University Park, PA.: Pennsylvania State University Press, 2000).
Morgan, K., (ed.), *The Oxford Popular History of Britain* (Oxford: Parragon/OUP, 1993).
Morgan, N., *Lancashire Quakers* (Halifax: Ryburn Academic Publications, 1993).
Morrill, J., *Cheshire 1630-1660: County Government and Society during the English Revolution* (L: OUP, 1974).
___ (ed.), *Revolution and Restoration* (L: Collins and Brown, 1992).
Muir, E., *Collected Poems* (L: Faber and Faber, 1963).
Mullett, M., *Catholics in Britain and Ireland, 1558-1829* (NY.: St. Martins', 1998).
___, *John Bunyan in Context* (Keele: Keele University Press, 1996).
___, *Radical Religious Movements in Early Modern Europe* (L: Allen and Unwin, 1980).
___ (ed.), *New Light on George Fox* (York: Sessions, 1991).
___ (ed.), *Early Lancaster Friends* (Lancaster: University of Lancaster Press, 1978).
Munck, J., *The Acts of the Apostles* (NY: Doubleday, 1981).
Myers, C. et al, *'Say to the Mountain': Mark's Story of Discipleship* (NY.: Maryknoll, 2000).
Naphy, W. and Roberts, P. (eds.), *Fear in Early Modern Society* (Manchester: Manchester University Press, 1997).
Neelon, D., *James Nayler: Revolutionary to Prophet* (Becket, MA.: Leadings Press, 2009).
Nevell, M., *Tameside 1066-1700* (Tameside Metropolitan Borough Council and Greater Manchester Archeological Unit, 1991).
Nickalls, J. (ed.), *The Journal of George Fox* (L: RSF, 1986).
Nolan, A., *Jesus Before Christianity* (Maryknoll, NY.: Orbis Books, [1976] 2007).

Bibliography

Nuttall, G., *Early Quaker Letters from The Swarthmore MSS, to 1660 (vols. 1, 3, 4) Calendared, Indexed and Annotated by G. F. Nuttall* (L: LRSF, 1952).
___, *Christian Pacifism in History* (Oxford: Blackwell, 1958).
___, *The Holy Spirit in Puritan Faith and Experience* (Oxford: Blackwell, 1947).
___, *To the Refreshing of the Children of Light* (Wallingford, PA.: Pendle Hill, 1959).
___ Chadwick, O. (eds.), *From Uniformity to Unity, 1662-1962* (L: SPCK, 1962).
O'Neil, E., *Long Day's Journey into Night* (New Haven: Yale University Press, 1976).
Ohlmeyer, J. (ed.), *Political Thought in Seventeenth Century Ireland* (Cambridge: CUP, 2000).
Ong, W., *Rhetoric, Romance and Technology: Studies in the Interaction of Expression and Culture* (Ithica, NY.: Cornell University Press, 1971).
Orlie, M., *Living Ethically, Acting Politically* (Ithaca, NY.: Cornell University Press, 1997).
Owens, W. (ed.), *Seventeenth-century England: A Changing Culture* (Totowa, NJ.: Barnes and Noble, 1981).
Pannenberg, W., *Theology and the Kingdom of God* (Philadelphia, PA.: Westminster Press, 1977).
Parliament, *Journal of the House of Commons* (1803).
Parry, R. (ed.), *The English Civil War and After, 1642-1658* (L: Macmillan, 1974).
Patrides, C. (ed.), *The Cambridge Platonists* (Cambridge, MA.: Harvard University Press, 1970).
Peck, L., 'Kingship, Counsel and Law in Early Stuart Britain' in Pocock and Schochet (eds.).
Penington, I., *Letters of Isaac Penington* (York: Linney, 1844: 3rd edn.).
___, *Letters of Isaac Penington* (Philadelphia, PA.: Assoc. of Friends, 1859).
Penney, N. (ed.), *Extracts from State Papers Related to Friends 1654-1672* (L: Headley Bros., 1913).
___ (ed.), *The Journal of George Fox* (Cambridge: CUP, 1911: *The Cambridge Journal*, i.e. *Spence MS.*).
___ (ed.), *The Journal of George Fox* (L: Dent, 1924: the *Short Journal*, i.e. to 1664/5).
___ (ed.), *Experiences in the Life of Mary Penington* (L: Friends Historical Society, 1992).
Pennington, J., *Heaven and Earth in the Gospel of Matthew* (Leiden: Brill, 2007).
Penny, D., *Freewill or Predestination* (Woodbridge: Royal Historical Society/Boydell Press, 1990).
Perrin, N., *The Kingdom of God in the Teaching of Jesus* (L: SCM Press, 1963).
Peters, K., *Print Culture and the Early Quakers* (Cambridge: CUP, 2005).
Peterson, E., *Reversed Thunder: The Revelation of John and the Praying Imagination* (San Francisco, CA.: Harper and Row, 1988).
Pickvance, J., *A Reader's Companion to George Fox's Journal* ([L: QHS, 1989] Kelso: Curlew, 2001).
Pocock, J. and Schochet, G. (eds.), *The Varieties of British Political Thought* (Cambridge: CUP, 1993).
Pollard, A. (ed.), *Records of the English Bible . . . 1525-1611* (L: Frowde/OUP, 1911).
Polanyi, K., *The Great Transformation: the Political and Economic Origins of our Times* (Boston, MA.: Beacon Press, 1957).
Poole, K., *Radical Religion: from Shakespeare to Milton* (Cambridge: CUP, 2000).
Porter, R., *Flesh in the Age of Reason* (L: Allen Lane, 2003).
Potts-Brown, E. and Stuard, S. (eds.), *Witnesses for Change* (New Brunswick, NJ.: Rutgers University Press, 1989).
Punshon, J., *Letter to a Universalist* (Wallingford, PA.: Pendle Hill, 1989).
___, *Portrait in Grey: a short history of the Quakers* (L: QHS, 1984).
___, *Reasons for Hope: the Faith and Future of the Friends' Church* (Richmond, IN: Friends United Press, 2001).
___, *Testimony and Tradition* (Swarthmore Lecture. L: QHS, 1990).

Questier, M., *Catholicism and Community in Early Modern England* (Cambridge: CUP, 2006).
Radcliffe, T., *What is the Point of Being a Christian?* (L: Burns and Oates, [2005] 2009).
Rainy, C., (ed.), *Jacob Boehme* (L: Black, 1911).
Rauschenbuch, W., *Christianising the Social Order* (NY.: Macmillan, 1912).
Reay, B., *The Quakers and the English Revolution* (L: Temple Smith, 1985).
Reddish, M., (ed.), *Apocalyptic Literature: A Reader* (Nashville, TN.: Abingdon, 1990).
Ricci, C., *Mary Magdalene and many others* (Minneapolis, MN.: Fortress, 1994)
Richardson, R. and Ridden, G. (eds.), *Freedom and the English Revolution* (Manchester: Manchester University Press, 1986).
Ricoeur, P., *Essays on Biblical Interpretation* (L: SPCK, 1981).
Ritschl, A., *Three Essays* (trans. P. Heffner. Philadelphia, PA.: Fortress Press, 1972).
Roberts, A., *Through Flaming Sword* (Portland, OR.: Barclay Press, 1959).
Ross, H., *George Fox Speaks for Himself* (York: Sessions, 1991).
Royle, T., *The British Civil War* (L: Palgrave Macmillan, 2004).
Russell, C., *Unrevolutionary England 1603-1642* (L: Hambleton, 1990).
___, (ed.), *The Origins of the English Civil War* (L: Macmillan, 1973).
Sabine, G., *The Works of Gerrard Winstanley* (NY.: Russel and Russel, 1965).
Sachse, W. (ed.), *The Diurnal of Thomas Rugg 1659-1661* (L: Camden 3rd ser. 91, 1961).
Sanders, E., *The Historical Figure of Jesus* (L: Allen Lane, 1993).
Schenk, W., *The Concern for Social Justice in the Puritan Revolution* (L: Macmillan, 1948).
Schillebeeckx, E., *Church* (NY.: Crossroad, 1990).
Schweitzer, A., *The Quest for the Historical Jesus* ([1906] NY: Macmillan, 1910 in English).
Scott, D., *Quakerism in York 1650-1720* (York: Borthwick Institute, 1991), Paper 80.
Scott, J., *England's Troubles* (Cambridge: CUP, 2000).
Scott-Warren, J., *Early Modern English Literature* (Cambridge: Polity, 2005).
Schüssler Fiorenza, E., *In Memory of Her* (NY.: Crossroads, 1995).
Scully, J. and Dandelion, P. (eds.), *Good and Evil: Quaker Perspectives* (Aldershot: Ashgate, 2007).
Sharman, C., *No More But My Love: letters of George Fox, Quaker* (L: QHS, 1980).
Sharpe, K., *Remapping Early Modern England* (Cambridge: CUP, 2000).
___ Lake, P. (eds.), *Culture and Politics in Early Stuart England* (Stanford, CA.: Stanford University Press, 1993).
___ Zwicker, S. (eds.), *Politics of Discourse: The Literature and History of Seventeenth-Century England* (Berkeley, CA.: University of California Press, 1987).
___ Zwicker, S. (eds.), *Refiguring Revolutions* (Berkeley, CA.: University of California Press, 1998).
Smith D., *Constitutional Royalism and the Search for a Settlement, c.1640-1649* (Cambridge: CUP, 1994).
Smith, J., *A Descriptive Catalogue of Friends' Books* (L: Smith, 1867); 2 vols.
___, *Bibliotheca Anti-Quakeriana* (NY.: Krause Reprint, 1968).
Smith, N., *Perfection Proclaimed* (Oxford: Clarendon, 1989).
Sobrino, J., *Christology at the Crossroads* (L: SCM Press, 1978).
Solt, L., *Saints in Arms: Puritanism and Democracy in Cromwell's Army* (Stanford, CA.: Stanford University Press, 1959).
Spaeth, D., *The Church in an Age of Danger: Parsons and Parishioners 1660-1740* (Cambridge: CUP, 2000).
Spalding, R. (ed.), *The Dairy Of Bulstrode Whitelocke, 1605-1675* (Oxford: OUP, 1990).
Spencer, S., *Mysticism in World Religions* (Harmondsworth: Penguin, 1963).
Spufford, M., *Contrasting Communities: English Villagers in the Sixteenth and Seventeenth Centuries* (L: CUP, 1974).

Bibliography

Spurr, J., *English Puritanism 1603-1689* (NY.: St. Martin's, 1998).
Stambaugh, J. and Balch, D., *The Social World of the First Christians* (L: SPCK, 1986).
Stassen, G., *Just Peacemaking: Transforming Initiatives for Justice and Peace* (L: Westminster John Knox, 1992).
Steere, D. (ed.), *Quaker Spirituality: selected writings* (NY.: Paulist Press, 1984).
Stephen, C., *Quaker Strongholds* (L: Hicks, 1891).
Suso, H., *Little Book of Wisdom and Little Book of Truth* (L: Faber and Faber, 1953).
Swete, H., *The Holy Spirit in the New Testament* (L: Macmillan, 1921).
Tai Liu, *Discord in Zion: The Puritan Divines and the Puritan Revolution 1640-1660* (The Hague: Martinus Nijhoff, 1973).
Talbot, N., *Myths and Stories, Lies and Truth* (Backhouse Lecture. Newcastle, NSW: Australia YM [RSF], 1999).
Tangye, R., *The Two Protectors: Oliver and Richard Cromwell* (L: Partridge, 1899).
Taylor, E., *The Valiant Sixty* (L: Bannisdale Press, 1951).
The Geneva Bible (L: University of Wisconsin Press, 1969).
Thomas, K., *Religion and the Decline of Magic* (Harmondsworth: Penguin, 1973).
___, *Man and the Natural World* (L: Allen Lane, 1983).
Thomason, T., *Catalogue of the Pamphlets . . . Collected by Thomas Thomason 1640-1661* (Nendeln, Liechtenstein: Kraus Reprint, 1969).
___, *The Thomason Tracts 1640-1661: An Index to the Microfilm Edition* (Ann Arbor, MI.: University Microfilms International, 1981).
Tholuck, F., *Commentary on the Sermon on the Mount* (trans. R. Brown. Philadelphia, PA.: Smith, English & Co., 1860).
Toon, P., *Puritans, the Millennium and the Future of Israel* (Cambridge: Clark, 1970).
Trevett, C., *Quaker Women Prophets in England and Wales 1650-1700* (Lewiston, NY.: Edwin Mellen, 2000).
___, *Women and Quakerism* (York: Sessions, 1995).
Tyacke, N., *Aspects of English Protestantism c.1530-1700* (Manchester: Manchester University Press, 2001).
Twigger, R., *Inflation: the Value of the Pound, 1750-1998* (L: House of Commons, 1999).
Underdown, D., *A Freedom People* (Oxford: Clarendon, 1996).
___, *Revel, Riot, and Rebellion* (Oxford: Clarendon, 1985).
Underhill, E., *Practical Mysticism* (L: Dent, 1919).
Underwood, T., *Primitivism, Radicalism, and the Lamb's War* (NY.: OUP, 1997).
Vann, R. and Eversley, D., *Friends in Life and Death* (Cambridge: CUP, 1992).
Vella, A., *The Tribunal of the Inquisition in Malta* (Valetta: University of Malta Press, 1973), Historical Studies Paper 1.
Viviano, B., *The Kingdom of God in History* (Wilmington, DE.: Glazier, 1988).
Wallace, T., *A Sincere and Constant Friend* (Richmond, IN.: Friends United Press, 1992).
Ward, K., *Holding Fast to God: a Reply to Don Cupitt* (L: SPCK, 1983).
Warmington, A., *Civil War, Interregnum and Restoration in Gloucestershire 1640-1672* (Woodbridge: Boydell Press, 1997).
Weddle, M., *Walking in the Way of Peace* (Oxford: OUP, 2001).
Wedgwood, C., *Velvet Studies* (L: Cape, 1946).
Weiss, J., *Jesus' Proclamation of the Kingdom of God* (transs. & eds. R. Hiers and D. Holland. Philadelphia, PA.: The Fortress Press, [1892] 1971).
Wilks, M. (ed.), *Prophecy and Eschatology* (Oxford: Blackwell, 1994).
Wilson, F., *Seventeenth Century Prose* (Cambridge: CUP, 1960).
Wilson, J., *Pulpit in Parliament: Puritanism during the English Civil Wars 1640-1648* (Princeton, NJ.: Princeton University Press, 1969).
Wilson, L., *Essays on the Quaker Vision of Gospel Order* (Burnsville, NC.: Celo Valley, 1993).

Williams, R., *Anglican Identities* (L: Longman, Darton and Todd, 2004).
Wills, G., *What Paul Meant* (L: Penguin, 2007).
Wood, A., *The Politics of Social Conflict: The Peak Country, 1570-1770* (Cambridge: CUP, 1999).
Woodman, R., *The Apocalyptic Vision in the Poetry of Shelley* (Toronto: Toronto University Press, 1964).
Woolrych, A., *Commonwealth to Protectorate* (Oxford: Clarendon, 1982).
Wrightson, K., *English Society 1580-1680* (L: Hutchinson, 1982).

Theses and Dissertations

Barbour, H., *The Early Quaker Outlook upon 'the World' and Society, 1647-1662* (Ph.D., Yale University, 1952).
Bershadsky, E., *John Selden's 'Historie of Tithes' and its Contexts and Ramifications* (Ph.D., Johns Hopkins University, 1994).
Boswell, C., *Plotting Popular Politics in Interregnum England* (Ph.D., Brown University, 2008).
Calkins, S., *Prophecy and Polemic: Quaker Women and English Political Culture 1650-1700* (Ph.D., Purdue University, 2001).
Chakravarty, P., *Like Parchment in the Fire: Literature and Radicalism, 1640-60* (Ph.D., State University of NY, 2004).
Cohen, S., *'A Dislocation between the Word and the Reality': Quaker Insight into Thought, Language, Identity and Truth within a Philosophical Framework* (M. Phil., Birmingham University [UK], 2002).
Cole, W., *The Quakers and Politics 1652-1660* (Ph.D., Cambridge University, 1955).
Creasey, M., *Early Quaker Christology* (Ph.D., Leeds University, 1956).
Danner, D., *The Theology of the Geneva Bible of 1560* (Ph.D., Iowa University, 1969).
Darling, J., *The Grindletonians* (Ph.D., Columbia University, NY., 1986).
Dobbs, J., *Authority and the Early Quakers* (D. Phil., Oxford University, 1995).
Feroli, T., *Engendering the Body Politic: Women Prophets and the English Revolution 1625-67* (Ph.D., Cornell University, 1994).
Figueroa-Villarreal, V., *Gustavo Gutiérrez's Understanding of the Kingdom of God in the Light of the Second Vatican Council* (Ph.D., Andrews University, Michigan, 1999).
Forde, H., *Debyshire Quakers, 1650-1761* (Ph.D., Leicester University, 1977).
Gallagher, P., *Citizens of Heaven, Residents of the Earth: the Politics of the Sermon on the Mount* (Ph.D., McMaster University, 2005).
Guiton, G., *Ministrations of Peace: the Historical-Spiritual Underpinnings of Contemporary Quaker Approaches to Conflict* (Ph.D., Monash University, Melbourne, 1999).
Halvorsen, M., *'The Day of Small Things': The Quaker Understanding of Conversion and the Inner Light* (Ph.D., Washington University, 2001).
Hayduk, U., *Hopeful Politics: Three Interregnum Utopias* (Ph.D., Sydney University, 2005).
Houlahan, M., *Writing the Apocalypse, 1649-60* (Ph.D., Toronto University, 1989).
Ion, R., *The Theology of the Early Friends* (M.A., Oxford University, 1947).
Jones, T. C., *George Fox's Teaching on Redemption and Salvation* (Ph.D., Yale University, 1955).
Knarr, G., *Watchmen of England: Early Quaker Theology and Social Protest* (Ph.D., Queen's University, Ontario, 1998).
Kuenning, L., *The Bunyan-Burrough Debate of 1656-57* (Ph.D., Westminster Theological Seminary, 2000).
Leachman, C., *From an 'Unruly Sect' to a Society of Friends: The Development of Quakerism in England c.1650-1689* (Ph.D., London University, 1997).

Bibliography

Leslie, S., *'A Friendly Debate': Religious and Political Discourse in Restoration England 1668-1674* (Ph.D., La Trobe University, Melbourne, 1993).
Marvin, J., *The Conversion Experience of Two Radicals: John Lilburne and Gerrard Winstanley* (M.A., Queen's University, Ontario, 1997).
Moore, R., *Faith of the First Quakers* (Ph.D., Birmingham University [UK], 1994).
Nelson, B., *Play, Ritual Inversion and Folly among the Ranters in the English Revolution* (Ph.D., Wisconsin University, Madison, 1985).
O'Brien, K., *Female Verbal Crime in North-West England, c.1590-1675, with Special Reference to Cursing* (Ph.D. Western Sydney University, 2000).
Oliver, P., *Quaker Testimony and the Lamb's War* (Ph.D., Melbourne University, 1977).
Porter, V., *The Use of the Sermon on the Mount in the Epistle of James* (Ph.D., Dallas Theological Seminary, 2003).
Sansbury, R., *The Restoration and the Quaker Peace Testimony: Principle in Politics* (M.A., Northumbria University, 1993).
Schmidt, D., *'Till Christ Jesus Be Exalted': Quaker Political Pamphlets During the Restoration of the Rump Parliament* (Ph.D., University of California, Santa Barbara, 1998).
Skinner, R., *Non-Conformity in Shropshire 1662-1815: A Study in the Rise and Progress of Baptist, Congregational, Presbyterian, Quaker and Methodist Societies* (Ph.D., London University, 1967).
Tarter, M., *Sites of Performance: Theorising the History of Sexuality in the Lives and Writings of Quaker Women 1650-1800* (Ph.D., Colorado University, Boulder, 1993).
Taylor, R., *Quaking: A Study of the Phenomena of Quaking, Trembling and Shaking in Early Quakerism* (M.A., University of Wales, 1992).
Underwood, T., *The Controversy between the Baptists and the Quakers in England, 1650-1689: A Theological Elucidation* (Ph.D., London University, 1965).
Venn, J., *The Autobiographies of Barbara Blaugdone, Elizabeth White, Mary Rich and Mary Penington* (Ph.D., Western Ontario University, 1998).
Walia, M., *Tearing Down Antichrist or Setting up Satan?: Radical Religion and its Critics in England, 1640-60* (Ph.D., University of California, Riverside, 2001).
Watkins, O., *Spiritual Autobiography 1642-1660* (M.A., London University, 1952).
Wilcox, C., *The Theology of the Early Friends and its Implication for the Ministry of Women in Seventeenth Century English Quakerism* (Ph.D., London University, 1991).

INDEX
(* = early Quaker)

1

1650s experience (*the* Peace Testimony), 18-20, 28, 172, 180, 190, 197, 289, 342, 344, 369, 375, 380, 391, 403, 407

A

A Declaration and an Information (by Fell *et al*), 19, 181, 186, 196-7, 354, 388 and Appendices 2, 4A
A Declaration... Broken Nation (by Burrough *et al*), 19, 181, 186, 191-3, 246, 375, 388 and Appendices 2, 4A
A Declaration of the Harmless People (by Fox, Hubberthorne *et al*), 19, 24, 181, 186, 189-90, 192-8, 259, 318, 335, 352, 359, 361-2, 366, 386, 388-9, 393, 403 and Appendices 2, 4A
A Visitation and Warning Proclaimed (by Burrough, S. Fisher), 340, 346, 361
Abbot (Archbishop George), 33, 53, 82
Acts and Monuments ('Book of Martyrs'), 17, 41, 64, 75-7, 93
see Foxe (John)
Agreement of the People, 411
America (North and South), 32, 53, 296
Ames (William), 8, 13, 46, 87
Anabaptists, 139, 145, 205, 272, 356, 362, 411, 414
Andrewes (Bishop Lancelot), 33, 37, 80-3, 86
Antichrist, 41-2, 53, 67, 71, 76, 82, 85, 87-8, 162, 164, 167, 210, 225, 334, 342, 366, 383, 399, 412, 417
Antinomian/ism, 210, 238, 263, 266, 411, 420
Apocalyptic, 18, 21-2, 26, 28, 38-9, 42-3, 76, 88, 111, 119, 121, 126, 128, 151, 153-4, 166, 171, 173, 177, 190, 192, 201, 205, 212, 226, 231, 240, 249, 254, 256-7, 260, 262, 269, 272, 274-5, 277, 283-8, 291, 294, 299, 318-19, 324, 340, 342-3, 346-8, 350, 352, 368, 373, 379, 381-5, 387, 390, 396-7, 402-3, 407, 412

Apostasy, 3, 10, 22, 53, 74, 126-7, 136-7, 139, 142-4, 146-8, 153, 159, 173, 179-81, 192, 196, 199, 215, 217, 221, 244, 250, 255-6, 273, 287, 300-1, 309-11, 313, 328, 341, 372-3, 396-7, 399, 402, 405, 411
Apostles' Days, 1, 22, 136-7, 142-4, 149, 175, 179, 196, 230, 293, 310, 363, 391, 399
Appleby (Cumbria), 7, 167-9, 230, 238, 265, 324, 355, 357
Arminian, 13-14, 17, 33, 37, 47, 53, 77, 81-9, 91, 94, 215, 247, 249, 265-6, 282, 414, 420
Arminius (Jacobus), 13, 81-3, 85, 420
Army, 26-7, 58, 72, 92, 99-100, 102-3, 105, 107-8, 111, 118, 129, 135, 137, 159, 167, 190, 204, 327-31, 338-41, 343, 346-8, 355-62, 364-8, 371, 375-6, 394, 401-2, 411, 415-19, 421
and Winstanley, 338-9, 343
New Model Army, 72, 107, 141, 359, 411, 416
Northern Army, 222
Quaker alliance with, 27, 367 *see* Coleby
Artisan, 39, 50-1
see Richardson (Alexander)
Atrocities, 32, 105-6, 109, 399-400
Audland (Anne)*, 296, 299, 305
Audland (John)*, 141, 218

B

Bancroft (Archbishop Richard), 46-7
Baptist/s, 45, 67, 82, 90, 118, 130, 139, 143, 152, 209, 218, 264-5, 267-8, 283, 296, 299, 311, 325, 339, 346, 367, 414
Barrett (William), 80, 85
Baxter (Richard), 82, 100, 209-11, 214, 217, 264, 282, 317, 406
Bayly (William)*, 152-3, 162, 227-8, 423
Beast, 5, 45, 71, 73, 116, 125, 131, 136, 144, 157, 223, 226-7, 250, 263, 275, 282, 287, 306, 326, 370, 372, 383, 387, 396, 398, 412
Bellarmine (Cardinal Roberto), 67, 87,

215
Bernard (Richard), 43-4, 222

Bishop (George)*, 100, 103-4, 153, 162-3, 237, 266, 307, 323, 345-6, 358, 375, 401, 423
Bishop's Bible, 38-9
Blackborow (Sarah)*, 154, 156, 158, 294, 296, 300-1, 305, 323
Blaugdone (Barbara)*, 291-2, 304, 317, 328
Blome (Richard), 207
Boehme (Jakob), 210, 265, 279-80, 412
Boff (Leonardo), 389
Bolton (Battle of), 105
Book of Common Prayer, 35, 57, 60, 65, 77, 80, 85, 90, 93, 97, 240, 290, 299, 412
Borg (Marcus), 200
Boulding (Kenneth), 410
Bridewell, 52, 320, 413
  see House of Correction, Prisons
Brierly (Roger), 139, 414
  see Grindletonians
Brinton (Howard), 25, 405
Bristol, 69, 133, 208, 218-23, 225, 227, 239, 244, 263, 350
Bunyan (John), 133, 208, 211, 233, 236, 248-9, 251, 268
Burrough (Edward)*, 6, 18, 24-6, 107, 114, 119-22, 125, 133, 152-3, 163-6, 176, 181, 189-97, 200, 217, 219, 226, 232-4, 236, 246-7, 249, 261, 275, 277, 281, 290, 295, 306, 317-18, 327-30, 332, 336-8, 340-50, 358-62, 367-8, 373-6, 382, 386, 388, 393, 401, 423-4, 434

C

Calvert (Giles), 214
Calvin (Jean)/Calvinism, 8, 13-14, 24, 33, 38-9, 46, 53, 60, 66, 68, 71, 77, 79-91, 94, 115, 130, 146-8, 150, 156, 175, 187, 212, 222, 242, 247-8, 263, 265-6, 273, 285, 295-6, 309, 372, 394, 397, 401, 414, 419-21
Cambridge Platonism, 182, 227, 279, 281, 288, 309, 406
Carier (Benjamin), 84, 86, 89
Carnal/Outward Weapons, 26, 159, 163, 192, 195, 259, 261, 322, 332, 334, 339, 346, 352, 356-7, 360-2, 364, 367, 371, 386, 403, 425-6, 428-9, 433, 439-40, 443 **and Appendices 2, 5**
Catholicism, 13, 17, 39, 46, 53, 66-75, 77, 82, 84, 86-9, 91, 93, 97, 175, 178, 204, 209-10, 217, 248-9, 266, 298, 302, 312, 368, 405, 415, 419
Cheevers (Sarah)*, 274, 298, 300, 305, 316
Children of Light, 29, 76, 138, 143, 155, 176, 179, 206, 219, 249, 286, 290, 292, 389, 401-2, 409
Chiliasm, 16, 41, 45, 217, 283, 412
  see Millennialism
Christ/Spirit, 238, 258, 404-5
Christology, 6, 15-16, 82, 117, 127, 226-8, 231, 236, 238, 248-9, 254-5, 262, 394, 397
Christian Testament, 16, 151, 187, 196, 230, 259-60, 356
Church of England, 26, 46, 48, 84-7, 93, 148, 206, 369, 414, 417
  Anglican, 65, 74, 86, 412
  Episcopalian, 37, 57, 60, 69-70, 97, 184, 208, 212, 225
Civil War/s, 17-18, 26, 31-2, 35-6, 44-5, 48, 59, 63, 65, 67, 69, 73-4, 78, 90-1, 94, 96, 101-2, 104, 106, 108, 138, 192, 338, 356, 366-7, 376, 407
Clarendon (Lord, formerly Sir Edward Hyde), 97, 204, 364
Cleaver (Robert), 36
Clubmen, 104
Coale (Josiah)*, 232, 384
Cole (Alan), 351, 355, 371
  see Marxist, Hill (Christopher), Reay (Barry)
Cole (Mary)*, 300-1, 305
Coleby (Andrew), 27, 338-9
Commonwealth, 7-9, 14, 24, 36, 44, 49, 53-5, 59-60, 67, 70, 93, 101-2, 146, 192, 196, 206, 213-14, 290, 311, 316, 327, 331, 334, 338, 346, 362, 418
  see Protectorate
Community, 3, 6, 12, 44, 48, 59-61, 65, 74, 89, 108, 119, 128, 139, 142, 149, 151, 178, 185, 204, 216, 227-9, 244, 254-5, 259, 275, 293, 301, 323, 380, 387, 390, 392, 395, 397, 400, 402, 405, 407, 409, 411-12, 414, 416-17, 421
Compassion, 3, 8-10, 12, 20, 29, 53, 103, 118, 125, 128, 150, 157, 160, 179, 186-7, 195, 200, 203, 227, 236, 242, 244, 262-3, 265, 288, 294, 304-5,

322, 331, 337, 340, 344, 368, 386, 391, 394-6, 399, 401, 403, 407, 410 *see* **Mercy**
Concern (as spiritual/religious), 29, 128, 255, 351, 354, 395, 404, 409, 416
Congregationalism, 77, 183, 414-15 *see* **Indeppendents**
Conscience, 10, 16, 18, 37, 39, 48-9, 51, 62, 66, 93, 99, 129-30, 134, 150, 154, 170, 174, 185-6, 191, 197, 203-4, 208-9, 211, 242-3, 248, 261, 281-2, 308, 319-21, 324-7, 330-4, 337-8, 363, 371, 392, 401, 408, 411, 426-8, 430-3, 437-8, 440
  Light in their Conscience, 209, 337, 392
Continuing Theology (Quaker 'history' as), 27, 405
Convincement, 5, 26, 124, 130, 134, 136, 150, 154, 165, 167, 169, 170, 178, 190, 192, 195, 203, 220-1, 224, 228, 230-1, 236, 240, 242-3, 247-8, 250, 254, 259, 262, 268-71, 274-5, 277-8, 280, 282, 286-8, 291, 299, 320, 324, 330, 343-4, 350, 355, 361, 364, 366-7, 370, 378-9, 392, 397-8, 401, 406, 408, 411, 417, 430
Cosmological, 14, 20, 34, 44, 53, 190-1, 197, 223, 227, 230-1, 234-5, 240-1, 247, 254, 258-9, 261, 275, 286, 288, 369, 382, 389-91, 397, 400, 408
Cotton (Priscilla)*, 300-1, 305
Council of Trent, 80, 266
Court/s, 68, 88, 100, 131, 169, 187, 213, 217, 261, 306-7, 317, 319, 334, 336-7, 360 *see* **Justice of the Peace**
  Church courts, 48, 78, 92, 100, 307 *see* **Star Chamber**
Creasey (Maurice), 227-8
Crisp (Stephen)*, 37, 122, 266, 423
Cromwell (Henry), 328
Cromwell (Oliver), 17, 35, 44, 57-9, 70-4, 93, 101, 107-8, 132, 159-60, 204-5, 209, 222, 244, 255, 306, 321, 325, 327-9, 345, 356, 358, 360, 377, 401, 406, 415-16, 418-19
Cromwell (Richard), 69, 107, 325, 329, 374
Crook (John)*, 76, 198, 227, 312, 363, 423
Cross, 11, 15, 47, 49, 78, 133, 149, 151, 166, 174, 180-1, 202, 228, 244, 257-8, 264, 271, 274, 280, 291, 293, 392-3, 398, 407, 446
Crucifixion, 5, 38, 149, 159, 173, 178, 209, 220, 248, 250, 254, 268, 271, 274, 284, 293, 317, 363, 372, 377, 393, 398, 413, 426
  Atonement, 5, 8, 13, 15, 178, 220, 246, 248, 254, 271, 398, 420
  Universal/Limited Atonement, 13, 79-80
Curtis (Ann)*, 325, 375
Curtis (Thomas)*, 375, 377

D

Daniel (Book of), 42-5, 138, 153, 186, 324, 390, 396, 412, 428
Danson (Thomas), 1, 123, 215, 248-9
Dark World, 157, 243-4, 310, 319, 337, 396
Daughter/s of God, 12, 168, 189, 229, 240, 257-8, 379, 381, 389
  see **Son/s of God**
Day of the Lord, 4-6, 54, 150-1, 153-5, 161-2, 166, 171, 176-7, 194, 201, 221, 269, 334, 370, 379, 385, 396
  Day of Judgment, 246-7
  Day of Visitation, 194, 437
  Terrible Day of the Lord, 314, 334, 394
Declaration of Breda (Netherlands), 326, 331, 419
Declaration of Sports, 62
Dell (William), 118, 143, 148, 176, 213-14, 268, 278, 309
Devil, 14, 43, 55, 58, 67, 72, 101, 106, 116, 125, 164, 282-3, 349, 360, 421, 424, 429
  see **Satan**
Dewsbury (William)*, 154, 165-7, 193, 209, 223, 261, 322, 324, 356, 401, 408, 423
Diggers (True Levellers), 99, 111, 117, 132, 135, 139, 314, 354-5, 414, 416-17
  see **Winstanley (Gerrard)**
Dikaiosynē, 130, 160, 188, 394, 401
Discern/ment, 42, 98, 126, 168, 174, 176, 178, 207, 265, 282, 304, 394-5, 408, 416
  see **Leadings, Concerns**
Docwra (Ann)*, 292, 312
Dole (Dorcas)*, 292, 402
Dominicans, 20, 69-70, 73, 80, 146, 269, 274, 276

Dordrecht (or Dort, Synod of), 82-3, 420
Double predestination, 14, 39, 41, 80, 419
  see Predestination, Eschatology
Dunbar (Battle of), 132, 329, 357
Dunkirk, 261, 340-1, 346, 361, 382

E

Earls Colne (Essex), 35, 215
Eckhart von Hochheim (Meister), 145, 269, 279
  see Mystic/ism
Eden/ic, 5, 112-13, 126, 140, 159, 161, 174, 210, 248, 263, 270, 274, 291, 311, 323, 398, 408, 413, 417, 420
  see Preslapsarian, Perfection
Edgehill (Battle of), 93, 103-4
Elect/ion 13-14, 16, 34, 38, 42, 47, 51-4, 60, 79, 87-8, 90, 96, 108, 130, 146, 149, 162, 165, 216, 222, 264, 266, 282, 285-6, 290, 309, 401, 420, 428
  see Predestination
Elizabethan Settlement, 75, 77, 79, 81-2, 89
  see Book of Common Prayer, Great Chain of Being
Empire, 5, 45, 53, 127, 157, 199, 235, 286, 340, 396, 403
Enclosures, 32, 65, 91, 312-13, 315, 413
End/End-time, 4-5, 22, 41-4, 54, 121, 138, 142, 149, 153-4, 162, 165-6, 178, 184-5, 212, 221, 225, 235-6, 263, 275, 284, 286, 318-19, 331, 385, 396, 412-13
  see Apocalyptic, Eschatology
English College (Douai in Spanish Netherlands), 74
Episcopacy, 26, 78, 81-2, 88, 90, 93, 97, 108, 138, 341
Epistle (or Letter) of James, 12, 37, 112, 118-19, 128, 130, 160, 177, 184-5, 188, 241, 259, 285, 314, 316, 402-3, 425, 430
Equality, 12, 112, 129, 177, 212, 260, 286, 290, 297, 303-7, 310, 316, 333, 359, 401, 405, 411, 416-17
  Equity, 9-10, 27, 129, 160, 187, 246, 287-8, 303, 306-7, 309, 314, 330, 332, 344, 357, 401, 438
Eschatology, 20, 22, 29, 150-1, 191, 221, 231, 235, 245, 286-7, 315, 318, 331, 353-5, 372, 375, 380, 384, 387-8, 390, 396, 398, 402-3, 409, 412-13

  see Second Coming
Eschaton, 190, 271, 380, 395, 400, 409
Evans (Katharine)*, 274, 296, 298, 300, 302, 305
Everard (John), 77, 213, 278, 406

F

Fairfax (Gen. Lord Thomas), 58, 105, 131, 416
Fairman (Lydia)*, 241-2, 274
Family of Love/Familists, 139, 413
Farmer (Ralph), 69, 208
Farnworth (Richard)*, 112, 184, 206, 215, 217, 223, 226, 279, 285, 299-300, 303, 332, 423
Fell (Margaret)*, 19, 24, 120, 124, 147, 154, 162, 166, 170, 172, 188-9, 191, 193-7, 203, 211, 227, 250, 263, 279, 296, 299, 302, 305-6, 311, 318, 322-5, 332, 354, 375, 388-9, 393, 401, 403, 421, 423, 429
Fifth Monarchy, 19, 36, 41, 45, 100, 214-15, 218, 283, 325-6, 337, 356
  see Cary (Mary), Venner (Thomas)
Firbank Fell (nr. Sedbergh, Cumbria), 1, 138, 149, 213-14, 235, 323, 380
Fisher (Mary)*, 296-7
Fisher (Samuel)*, 1-2, 114, 120, 123, 126, 183-4, 215, 232, 243, 248, 281, 299, 315, 340, 404
Forgiveness, 35, 142, 161-3, 197, 224, 227, 240, 244, 248, 269, 318, 333, 350, 363, 394, 398, 426-8, 433
Fosset (Thomas), 36
Fox (George)*, 3-4, 7-11, 13, 19, 21-2, 24, 26, 31, 35, 40, 55, 64, 75-6, 92, 112, 114, 117, 120-1, 124-7, 129-30, 133-4, 136-8, 140-5, 147-51, 153-4, 157-64, 173-4, 176-8, 181-2, 187, 189-90, 192-200, 204, 211, 213-14, 216, 219, 221-4, 227, 229-34, 236, 239, 244-5, 249, 253, 257, 259, 261, 263-4, 267-8, 271-2, 275-6, 278-80, 282-5, 293, 299-300, 303, 308-9, 312-16, 318-19, 321, 323, 325-8, 330, 332, 334-7, 340-50, 352, 354, 356-66, 368-71, 373-82, 384, 386-91, 393, 395, 399, 401-4, 406-9, 411, 422-3, 425
  To All that would Know the Way to the Kingdom (by Fox), 1, 127, 144, 158, 161, 347, 386
Fox (George, the Younger)*, 129, 340,

364, 423
Foxe (John), 17, 41, 64, 75-6, 93
see *Acts and Monuments*
France, 9, 17, 53, 74-5, 80, 100, 115, 204, 345, 349
Free will, 13, 80-2, 131, 207, 264-6, 285, 288, 414, 419

G

Gaol (Jail), 168, 205, 223, 233, 274, 291, 300, 320-1, 325, 344
Geneva Bible, 35, 38-40, 46, 64, 75, 82, 93, 122, 222, 265, 415
  Geneva (Swiss city), 8, 52, 60, 82, 415
Gentry, 39, 44, 48, 58-9, 73-4, 77, 84, 98, 134, 204, 212, 225, 311-12, 418
Geree (John), 48-9, 51
Good Old Cause, 18, 20, 26-7, 95, 98-101, 108-9, 129-30, 137, 164, 179, 192, 197, 272, 310, 324, 327-30, 333-6, 341-2, 344, 347, 357, 362, 368-70, 373-4, 380, 387, 391, 396, 401, 416
  see **Synthesis, True Religion**
Good Works, 9, 38, 52, 80-1, 184, 229, 266, 402, 410-11, 417
  see **Epistle of James**
Gospel of John, 14-15, 112, 119, 128, 140, 145-6, 149, 151, 172, 199, 223, 226, 230, 236, 238, 241, 257-9, 261, 263, 267, 270, 275, 281, 295, 383, 386, 389, 396, 402, 427, 430, 432-3
Gospel of Luke, 23, 156, 169, 187, 199, 239, 292, 316, 381, 398, 402, 425, 433
Gospel of Mark, 153, 187, 257, 272, 275, 277-8
Gospel of Matthew, 1-2, 11, 21, 24, 112, 116, 119, 128, 130, 148, 151, 153, 159, 177, 186-8, 199-200, 228, 256, 263, 278, 292, 309, 383, 399, 406, 425, 427-8, 430, 433
Great Chain of Being, 29, 35-6, 49-50
  see **Book of Common Prayer, Elizabethan Settlement**
Grindletonians, 139, 414
  see **Brierly (Roger)**
Grubb (Edward), 228, 231, 238

H

Harkness (Georgia), 24, 145

Harrington (James), 101, 210, 316, 335, 406
Hat Honour, 130-1, 185, 203, 306, 313, 332, 394, 401, 403, 417
Healing, 3, 5, 11, 142, 149, 161, 169, 172, 176, 185, 196, 227, 244, 259, 285, 288, 299, 313, 396, 398, 401, 405, 422, 435-6, 438
Hebrew Testament (i.e. Hebrew Bible), 35, 40, 47, 53-4, 146, 151, 186, 196, 200, 241, 341, 348
Higgenson (Thomas), 198
Higginson (Francis), 7, 208, 273, 301
Hill (Christopher), 47, 184, 333, 351-2, 355, 371, 403
  see **Marxist, Reay (Barry), Cole (Alan)**
Hobbes (Thomas), 101, 115, 210, 303, 336, 406
  see **Leviathan**
Holism, 23, 25, 245, 261-2, 275-6, 287-8, 295, 303, 369, 371, 387, 407
Holland, 13, 40, 53, 71, 74, 80, 82, 326, 345, 420
  Dutch, 53, 69, 81-2, 341, 359, 406. 413-14, 417, 420
Homelessness, 32, 108, 413
Hooker (Richard), 33, 80-2, 87, 89, 96
Hookes (Ellis)*, 76, 362
Howgil (Mary)*, 329 154
Howgill (Francis)*, 4, 6, 120, 122, 136, 141, 145, 149, 154-6, 181, 193, 219, 236, 242, 280, 284, 318, 324, 328, 330, 338, 348, 365-6, 375, 423
House of Commons, 48, 78, 84, 91-2, 95-8, 148, 356, 411, 416, 418
House of Correction, 52
  see **Bridewell, Prisons**
House of Lords, 93, 95, 97, 100, 369, 416
Hubberthorne (Richard)*, 19, 24, 45, 58, 100, 129, 132, 182, 189-90, 192-98, 205, 223, 259, 282, 318, 325-6, 331, 335-6, 342, 352, 358-9, 361-2, 366, 375, 385-6, 388-9, 393, 403, 423, 425

I

Independents, 45, 69, 77, 99, 131, 134, 139, 148, 176, 205, 212, 215-16, 225, 235, 297. 299, 344, 346, 365, 414-15, 418
  see **Congregationalism**
Inquisition, 69-70, 75, 86, 274, 340

Index

Instrument of Government, 135, 418-19
Interruptions (of church services), 203, 205, 215-18, 225, 298, 306, 403
Ireland, 32, 71-3, 93, 102, 122, 193, 204, 212, 328, 337, 359, 418
Irish, 17, 69, 71-3, 98, 103, 368, 405

J

Jerusalem, 2, 54, 144, 158, 175, 187, 201, 219, 222, 226-7, 230, 232, 234, 237, 246, 251, 261, 302, 311, 379, 381
see Zion
Jesuits, 17, 28, 67, 69-70, 72-4, 80, 89, 209, 225, 422
Jesus Way/The Way, 2-5, 8, 10, 12, 16, 19-20, 26, 28-9, 112-13, 127, 129, 131, 136, 140, 142-4, 149, 152-3, 158, 161, 165, 168, 170, 173-7, 179-80, 191, 194-5, 197, 201, 203, 228-9, 235-6, 238, 240, 245, 254-5, 264-7, 271, 276, 289-90, 293, 310-11, 313, 318, 326, 334-5, 343-4, 347, 350-1, 360, 363, 366, 369-70, 373, 376, 379, 382, 386, 391, 393, 398-400, 402, 408, 410, 417, 431, 435, 438, 440, 443-4
Jews, 2, 8, 19-21, 31, 44, 54, 72, 92, 123-4, 126, 151, 159-60, 172, 231, 270, 332, 336, 349, 386, 391, 405, 422, 431
   Judaic, 5, 53, 63, 231, 261
   Aramaic, 257
Johnson (Elizabeth), 294
Jones (Rufus), 25, 137-8, 210, 224, 278, 281, 351
Jones (Sarah)*, 140-1, 151, 217, 235, 270
Jonson (Ben), 46, 57
Josselin (Ralph), 35, 125, 134, 204-7, 215
Justice, 3, 6, 8-13, 18, 27-9, 98, 100, 118, 128-9, 146-7, 150, 154-7, 160-4, 167, 169, 179, 181, 186-9, 191, 194-5, 198, 203, 221, 228, 235, 242, 244, 247, 261, 275, 281, 286-8, 293, 304-9, 311, 313, 315, 318, 321, 330-2, 335-7, 340, 344, 347-8, 350, 353, 358-9, 365-6, 368, 374, 379, 381, 391, 394, 396-9, 401-3, 407, 410, 428, 432, 442
   Injustice, 5, 23, 52, 164, 169-70, 186, 193, 200, 244, 247, 255, 286, 306, 309-11, 313, 321, 333, 357, 359, 375, 399, 402, 407
Justice of the Peace (JP), 7, 10, 58, 65, 135, 141, 216, 365, 374, 391, 415-16

K

Kaber Rigg (or Northern) Plot, 365-7
Keith (George)*, 251, 253
King Charles I, 17, 45, 48, 59, 62, 67, 69-71, 77, 83-7, 90-8, 101-2, 107, 108, 355, 418, 421
King Charles II, 8, 59, 69, 197, 204, 259, 291, 325-6, 331, 341, 388, 415, 419, 428
King James VI/I, 17, 35, 37, 39, 46, 50, 62, 66, 68, 70, 76, 78-80-4, 87, 89-90, 95-6, 98, 363
King James Bible, 35, 40, 61, 64, 118, 138, 193, 206, 222, 412

L

Lamb's War, 18-19, 29, 45, 100, 128, 166, 170, 177, 179, 181, 185, 189, 191, 198-9, 201-3, 215, 216, 220-1, 224, 226, 228, 231, 236, 253-4, 262, 310, 333, 342, 344, 348, 353, 361, 366, 369, 371-2, 387, 391, 393, 396, 401, 403-4, 406-7
Lambert (Gen. John), 222, 329, 364-5, 419
Lancashire, 61-2, 68-9, 112, 132, 312, 364-5, 414, 416
Lancaster (Lancs.), 7, 216, 239, 257, 325, 381, 384
Laud (Archbishop William), 40, 71, 79, 81, 83-4, 86-94, 98, 134-5
Lawyers (Quaker attitude to), 191, 307, 327, 360, 402, 406
Leading (as spiritual/religious), 29, 169, 174, 230, 255, 298, 304, 307, 395, 404, 409, 416
Leicestershire, 31, 35, 43, 103, 134, 299, 312, 417
Leiden (Netherlands), 13, 81, 83
Levellers, 72, 99, 111, 117, 132-3, 135, 259, 264, 296, 314, 321, 354-6, 364, 411, 416-17
Leviathan, 101, 113, 303, 336
Life (the), 25-6, 113, 120, 123-4, 126, 136, 142, 149, 152-3, 156-7, 161, 168-9, 172-3, 176, 181, 184, 188,

499

191, 201, 228-30, 236, 238, 241, 243, 247, 253-4, 259, 262-3, 267-71, 273-6, 288, 291, 294, 307, 319, 323-5, 372-3, 380, 385, 390, 396, 399-400, 402, 407, 428, 431-3, 445-6
Lilburne (John)*, 99, 133, 259-60, 358, 411, 416
Literalism, 10-11, 16, 34, 38, 41, 43-4, 54, 87, 126, 138, 148, 156-7, 173, 183-5, 216, 234, 255, 259, 267-8, 274, 301, 372, 393, 412, 414
   Bibliolatry, 37, 55, 183-4, 232
Lollards, 31, 131, 139, 417
   see Wycliffe (John)
Luther (Martin), 13, 38, 89, 147, 175, 183
   Lutheran/ism, 210, 303, 421
Lutterworth (Leic.), 31, 417

M

Magistrates/Magistracy, 8, 27, 52, 54, 68, 96, 124, 135, 192, 197-8, 204-5, 208, 215, 217-18, 239, 291, 307, 318, 324, 326, 333, 335-6, 338, 355, 360-1, 366, 413, 425-6, 431-2
Mammon, 8, 49, 157, 235, 275, 293, 343, 374, 387
Marginalia (in Geneva Bible), 39-40
Marian exiles, 82, 420
Martyr/dom, 64, 69, 75, 88, 115, 199, 219, 221, 316-18, 411, 418
Marxist (interpretation of Quaker history), 20, 26, 47, 339-40, 342, 344, 350-5, 358, 368, 371
Mason (Martin)*, 182, 423
Melchizedek (Order of), 10, 145, 188, 258, 298-9, 385, 412, 417
   First ('Levitical') Priesthood, 9, 131, 298
   Second Priesthood, 9, 26, 163, 228, 343, 373, 409
Mercy, 2-3, 23, 53, 76, 129, 147, 150, 161-4, 172, 176, 187-9, 194, 198, 222, 227, 244, 247, 261, 276, 286-8, 305, 322, 337, 344, 357, 361, 367, 381, 396, 398-9, 401, 428, 433, 436, 439, 442, 446
   see Compassion
Metaphor, 5, 37, 43, 111, 115-16, 121-2, 126-8, 130, 143, 145, 154, 159, 179, 206, 220, 229, 237, 244, 246, 251, 268, 278-9, 286, 293, 322, 324-5, 336-7, 340, 345, 349-50, 366, 413

Allegorical interpretation, 43, 111-12, 127, 209, 224, 340
Anagogical language, 18, 26, 112, 121, 283, 340, 342-3, 347-8, 350-1, 368
Military language, 122, 341, 348-51, 368
Millennialism, 16, 19, 20, 38, 41-5, 52, 101, 130, 166, 198, 206, 208, 222, 225, 247, 255, 283-4, 287, 324, 351, 353, 372-3, 393, 396, 418
   Amillennialism, 41-3, 208, 247, 284
   Postmillennialism, 41-2
   Premillennialism, 16, 20, 38, 41-5, 52, 101, 130, 166, 198, 206, 222, 225, 247, 255, 283-4, 287, 324, 372-3, 393, 396, 418
Milton (John), 73, 99, 101, 120, 327
Monarch/y, 15, 39, 48-50, 59-60, 81, 90, 93, 95-7, 99, 101-2, 108, 135, 296, 326, 336, 341, 353, 369, 372-4, 416
   Court (royal), 17, 39, 70, 74, 83-4, 87, 93, 96, 98, 101, 108
Monck (Gen. George), 108, 192, 328, 355, 362, 419
Montagu (Bishop Richard), 83-6
More (Henry), 281-2
   see Cambridge Platonists
Muggleton (Ludowick), 233, 239, 417-18,
   Muggletonians, 296, 322, 359, 417-18
Mutual support (between the Friends), 24-5, 294, 320, 326, 333, 388, 400, 421
Mystic/ism (inc. Christ/Logos- and Kingdom-mysticism), 4, 9-10, 15, 23-5, 55, 89, 111-12, 117, 119, 121, 127, 139, 145, 154, 165, 168, 178, 182, 208, 210, 221-2, 228, 231, 235-6, 240-1, 252-3, 255, 262, 267, 269, 275-83, 287-8, 291, 294-5, 304, 340, 351-2, 354, 371, 376-7, 387, 391, 394-5, 405, 407, 409, 412-13, 417, 420

N

Naseby (Battle of), 58, 98, 103-4
Nayler (James)*, 1, 7-8, 10, 14, 18, 92, 114, 116, 120-1, 123, 128, 134, 153, 166-70, 182, 185, 191, 193, 198-9, 201, 208, 219-25, 227, 230, 234-5,

238-40, 243-5, 257-8, 260, 262-5, 267, 272, 277, 304, 315, 321, 324, 332, 350, 355, 357-8, 361, 414, 423, 445-6

Naylier (John, Leveller), 355-6

Neglect of the Kingdom, 1, 20, 22-4, 143, 146, 142-3, 159, 179, 196, 293, 330, 345, 399, 437
see **Apostasy, Apostles' Days**

Newgate Prison, 319-20, 323, 413

New Covenant, 7-8, 10, 29, 153, 155, 158, 162-3, 168, 171-2, 175, 190, 195, 235, 240, 242, 245, 271-2, 275, 299, 311, 354, 367, 383, 396-7

New Israel, (and Calvinist new Israel) 10, 12, 21, 29, 53, 72, 87, 96, 125, 130, 144, 146, 153, 178, 189, 221, 226, 231, 240, 254, 316, 322, 369, 383-4, 395, 398, 417
  True Israel, 5, 126, 159, 187, 380, 386
  New Jerusalem, 251, 302, 381
  see Zion

Nicholson (Benjamin)*, 34, 156, 163, 283

Norden (John), 61-3

O

Oaths, 5, 9, 130-1, 143, 163, 185, 197-8, 203, 209, 306, 321, 325, 351, 401, 411, 431
  Oath of Abjuration, 209
  Oath of Allegiance, 67, 198, 325, 431

Obedience/Disobedience, 5, 9, 25, 50, 60, 98, 116, 124, 143, 150, 163, 165-8, 173-4, 177, 218, 228, 243, 248-9, 252, 291, 295, 301, 304, 311, 318, 320, 333, 358-9, 394-5, 411, 416, 426-7, 430, 433
  Disciple/ship, 6, 9, 28, 122, 172-4, 185, 187-8, 201, 237, 254, 256-7, 272, 288, 292-3, 360, 380-1, 395, 397
  Dwell in/Indwelling, 126, 140, 160-1, 165, 171, 175, 210, 228, 238, 244-5, 253, 260, 262, 267, 271, 279-80, 282, 292, 334, 358-9, 360, 372, 385, 394, 408, 416, 438
  Faithful/ness, 9, 12, 21, 28, 73, 123, 156, 221, 252, 256, 274, 308, 329, 332, 340, 345, 356, 361, 395, 397, 409
  Listening/Waiting, 25, 89, 137-8, 140, 143, 149, 154, 156, 172, 174, 211, 242, 251-3, 257, 265, 269, 271, 276-7, 292, 308, 379, 382, 388, 392, 394-5, 416, 426, 433, 441-2, 445

Old Covenant, 5, 131, 173, 179, 324, 350
  Old Israel, 53, 157, 168, 188, 221, 301, 336

Orthopraxis, 19, 146, 152, 189, 191, 224, 390-1, 399, 405, 409

Over all, 121, 163, 165, 175-6, 179-80, 373, 378-9, 383-4, 439, 443, 445

Owen (John), 1, 148, 150, 184, 215, 316, 406

P

Pagitt (Ephraim, and *Heresiography*), 138, 205, 211

Panzani (Gregorio), 86

Papists, 17, 39, 50, 65-6, 68, 71, 74, 81, 88, 91, 98-9, 124, 142, 144, 184, 204-5, 208, 266, 332, 350, 365, 377, 422
  see **Catholicism, Popery**

Paracletal, 19, 27, 190, 197, 287, 366, 369, 373, 381-5, 387, 389, 391, 393, 397
  see **Pentecost/al**

Parliament/ary, 10, 18, 27, 36, 44, 51, 55, 58-9, 67, 69-70, 73-4, 78, 84-6, 88, 91-100, 103-9, 129, 131-2, 134-5, 190-2, 196, 204, 207, 218, 215, 253, 313, 316, 321-2, 325-31, 334, 336, 346, 357, 362-3, 368, 371, 374, 383, 401, 406, 411, 415, 418-19, 421-2, 428, 432, 435-6, 441-2

Parnel (James)*, 162, 216, 314, 316, 324, 372, 404, 423

Paul (of Tarsus), 20, 38-9, 112-13, 119, 122-3, 125, 128, 130, 145-6, 149-50, 176, 184, 188, 192, 195, 219, 227, 231, 237, 239, 245, 257, 267, 275, 297, 299-301, 303, 322, 336, 358, 369, 376, 379-80, 392, 405, 419
  Pauline, 1, 112, 116, 130, 146, 157, 160, 185, 231, 236, 239, 247, 293, 300-1, 335, 359, 361, 402

Peace, 3-12, 17-19, 21, 28-9, 47, 74, 76, 106, 113, 118, 125, 128-30, 140-2, 147, 150-1, 154-61, 164-5, 167-8, 170, 172-3, 176-7, 179, 186-8, 190-2, 194-8, 202, 205, 208-9, 214, 220-2, 227-8, 235, 242, 247, 249, 260-2, 270, 280, 284, 286-8, 290, 294, 308, 310, 318, 325-6, 328, 333-44, 346,

348-9, 351-2, 357-8, 360-3, 365-6, 368-9, 374, 378-9, 385, 388, 391, 396, 398-9, 401-4, 406-7, 410, 425-7, 431, 433-5, 437-43, 445-6
Pearson (Anthony)*, 136, 145, 218, 223, 238, 364, 375
Pendle Hill (Lancs.), 69, 414
Penington (Isaac)*, 74, 114, 120, 126, 154, 171-5, 184, 193, 227-9, 240, 246, 254, 266-7, 277, 280, 282-3, 309, 312, 329-30, 335-6, 361, 375, 383, 385, 400, 423
Penington (Mary)*, 37, 260, 347
Penn (William)*, 138, 143, 181, 253, 392, 404
Pentecost/al (and inc. Quaker Pentecost), 18-20, 27, 174, 190, 197, 271, 287, 344, 366, 368-9, 373, 375-6, 379-81, 383-91, 393, 396-7
  see **Paracletal**
Pentecostal-type 'moment' (Oct. 1658 to 1661), 18-20, 27, 190, 197, 287, 344, 368-9, 375, 380-1, 384, 387, 391, 393, 397
  see **Paracletal, Pentecost/al, Reading**
Perfection (as spiritual maturity), 5, 14-15, 25, 49, 140, 149-50, 163, 167, 172-3, 178, 186-7, 195, 201, 207, 211-12, 222, 229, 239, 254, 262-5, 267-8, 271, 288, 302, 316, 393, 397-8, 399, 402, 407, 413, 430, 437-9, 441, 443, 446
Perkins (William), 8, 13, 46, 49, 87, 89, 115, 265
Perrot (John)*, 4, 72, 423
Plague (bubonic), 32, 35, 44, 103, 320, 323
  Plague (spiritual), 124, 377, 438
Plain language, 111-14, 128, 191, 197, 249, 308-10, 333, 340, 357, 402-3, 426, 434, 443
Police action (inc. by army), 27, 107, 197, 338-9, 367
Popery, 16-17, 26, 49, 51, 53, 64, 66-7, 69, 71, 76, 93-4, 99-100, 126, 137, 179, 208-9, 212, 217, 225, 266, 340-1, 350, 352, 368, 400, 405
Poverty, 11-12, 29, 31-2, 35, 52, 61, 63, 73, 76, 96, 104, 106, 128, 131, 133, 135, 156, 161, 163, 169-72, 203, 209, 239, 263, 270, 304, 307, 311-16, 330-3, 342, 357, 360, 399, 402, 407, 413, 415, 432, 435, 445

Prayer, 33, 36-7, 47, 49, 63-4, 79, 81, 92, 140, 147, 162, 173, 228, 230, 240, 249-50, 252-3, 264, 268, 270-1, 273, 276, 282, 294, 304, 320, 377, 392, 394, 396, 402, 404, 410, 413-14, 416, 418, 420, 430, 436-7, 443
Predestination, 13-14, 17, 33, 39, 41, 77, 80-2, 85, 94, 146, 204, 222, 266, 285, 414, 418-20
  see **Double predestination, Elect/ion**
Prelapsarian, 274-5, 323, 420
  see **Eden/ic**
Presbyterian, 40-1, 53, 57, 69, 72, 77-8, 81, 83, 90, 93, 99, 122, 137, 139, 183, 205, 209, 212, 214, 225, 299, 346, 414-15, 418, 421
Presence (divine), 3, 10-11, 16, 27, 29, 34, 36, 126, 149-50, 160-3, 169, 171, 175, 191, 194, 211, 222, 227-8, 244-6, 253, 278, 282-3, 391, 417, 431, 437, 439, 441-2
Prison, 7, 59, 70, 75, 100, 105, 133, 149, 162, 164, 167-8, 205, 215-16, 219-20, 237, 244, 260, 264, 271, 274, 283, 291, 297-8, 300, 302, 304, 306-7, 317, 319-26, 329, 332-5, 342, 361, 363, 371, 397, 408, 413, 421, 427-9, 431-2, 434, 440
  see **Appleby, House of Correction, Newgate**
Prophet/ic, 3-4, 9-10, 12, 15, 22-3, 25, 28, 42, 44, 46, 52, 54, 76, 113, 117, 119, 122, 124, 128, 138-9, 142, 149, 151-2, 155, 158, 161, 166, 168, 177-8, 190-1, 195, 200-1, 206, 225-6, 228-30, 239-40, 250, 254, 256-8, 262, 267, 272-3, 275, 285-8, 291, 294, 296-301, 304-5, 309, 311, 314, 331, 343, 348, 350, 380, 383-5, 389, 395, 397, 402-3, 407, 409, 412, 417-18, 426, 429-30, 437, 439
Protector/ate, 58-9, 67, 69-70, 74, 93, 102, 107, 191, 213, 325, 328-9, 331, 346, 374, 415, 418-19, 432, 436, 441
  see **Commonwealth**
Providence, 33-5, 54, 150, 419
Prynne (William), 58, 73, 85-6, 90, 97, 99, 208, 265
Pym (John, Speaker of the Commons), 86, 91
Puritan/ism, 7, 9, 13-17, 24, 29, 31, 34-44, 46-58, 60-4, 66-7, 69-72, 76-9, 81-94, 97-9, 101, 106, 108, 122, 125, 133, 135, 138, 144, 148, 156, 158,

177, 179, 182, 184-6, 189, 192, 196, 199-200, 206-8, 213, 217, 221-2, 225, 230, 243, 246, 248, 255, 265, 271, 273, 278, 284-5, 292, 298, 300, 312, 324, 354, 386, 394, 406, 414, 421-2

Q

Quaking, 185, 207-8, 252, 271-2, 383
  Shaking/Trembling, 173, 207, 271-3, 280, 342, 358, 435, 438
Queen Elizabeth 1, 38-40, 46, 50, 61-2, 67-8, 75, 77, 88, 95, 138, 218, 420
Queen Henrietta-Maria, 17, 69-70, 97
Queen Mary 1, 17, 75, 217, 412

R

Radicals, 31, 39, 42, 60, 76-8, 82, 85, 97, 99-101, 107, 109, 131, 135-6, 148, 205-6, 211-14, 218, 224, 255, 266, 285, 302, 328, 352, 354-5, 364, 370, 374-5, 416-18
Ranters, 119, 132, 210-11, 215, 218-19, 225, 243, 249, 263, 266, 303, 355-6, 373, 385, 420
Reading (Berks.), 158, 190, 219, 369, 373, 375-9, 381, 390
Reay (Barry), 126, 272, 316, 328, 346, 351-2, 355, 362, 370-1, 376, 386
  see Marxist, Hill (Christopher), Cole (Alan)
Reconciliation, 3, 11-12, 18, 60, 142, 147, 149, 173, 188, 219, 221, 224, 227-8, 244, 260, 264, 271, 276, 288, 295, 321-2, 346, 362, 372, 392, 406
Recusant, 61, 63, 65, 68-70, 88, 138
Remnant, 5, 12, 54, 154, 188, 195, 244, 310, 369, 383, 389
Restoration (of 1660), 15, 20, 102, 135, 166, 197-8, 304, 318, 341, 343, 352, 354, 368, 370-1, 386, 390, 419
  Spiritual Restoration, 5, 140, 159, 166, 178, 181, 196, 267, 298, 373, 380, 383, 385, 412
Resurrection, 4, 25, 149, 155, 160-1, 173, 176, 178, 188, 192, 227-8, 236-7, 246, 248, 250, 254, 259-60, 267, 271, 275, 311, 322, 336, 350, 354, 380, 383-5, 398, 413, 418
Revelation, 11, 43, 126, 128, 137-8, 149, 165, 181, 192, 221, 227-8, 259, 271, 287, 290, 324, 362, 378, 408, 412

Revelation (Book of), 34, 38, 42-4, 76, 116, 119, 121, 126-7, 138, 143-4, 178, 187, 199, 220-2, 226, 230, 273, 300, 314, 324, 337, 347, 361, 381, 386, 395-6, 412, 425
Revolution (inner and outer), 2, 6, 9, 11, 19, 21, 39, 46-7, 60, 77, 84-6, 102, 117-18, 120, 125, 128-9, 142-4, 169-70, 178, 189, 205, 223, 235, 255, 262, 284, 288, 312, 340, 352-5, 358, 370-2, 387, 395, 403, 407-8
Rhetoric, 50, 111-17, 121, 123-4, 128, 151, 237, 324, 340, 349-51
  Peter Ramus, 115
  Omar Talons, 114-15
  Thomas Wilson's *Arte of Rhetorique*, 113, 123, 349-51
  see Richardson (Alexander)
Richardson (Alexander), 50-1, 115
  see Artisan
Rigge (Ambrose)*, 138, 214, 293, 382, 423
Righteous/ness, 3, 6, 8, 12, 21, 25, 27, 42, 52-3, 129-30, 140, 142, 147, 154, 156, 158, 160-3, 166-9, 173, 178-9, 181-2, 185-9, 192, 194, 197-8, 220, 227-8, 246, 256, 261, 265, 267, 269, 275, 277, 280-1, 286, 288, 292-3, 301, 308, 311, 324-5, 335, 340, 347-8, 350, 361, 372, 374, 380, 385, 394, 396, 401-2, 411, 417, 425-7, 430, 432, 435-46
Rome, 16-17, 20, 26, 53, 57, 66-71, 76, 82, 84, 86-7, 89, 93, 124, 145, 266, 340-1, 350, 352
  Romish, 66-7, 69, 86, 93, 208
Royalist, 17, 51, 56, 71, 74, 97, 99, 104-5, 107-8, 116, 134, 204, 312, 334, 365, 376, 415, 418
  Loyalist, 71, 97
Rude language/behaviour, 112, 116, 122-4, 128, 206, 338, 428

S

Saltmarsh (John), 77, 131, 139, 143, 148, 278
Salvation, 3, 6, 12-15, 19, 24, 37-8, 42, 45, 51, 53, 79-82, 92, 98-9, 128, 141, 159, 162-3, 172, 178-9, 181-2, 184, 187-8, 191, 198, 202, 214, 216, 220, 227, 230-1, 233-4, 236, 243, 250, 255, 275, 285-6, 290, 309-10, 319, 323, 334, 346, 366, 369, 372, 380,

390-1, 396, 398, 402, 404, 407, 411, 413-14, 417, 419, 430, 432-3, 436, 441-2
Salvific, 8, 391, 401, 407
Satan, 5, 13, 34, 153, 157-8, 179, 195, 207-8, 211-12, 217, 220, 290, 310, 313, 318, 329, 420, 424
Schillebeeckx (Eduard), 276
Scotland/Scottish, 71-2, 78, 90-2, 98, 102-3, 108, 115, 122, 183, 192, 328, 408, 415, 418-19, 421-2
Scripture/s, 10-11, 13-15, 34, 38, 43-4, 47, 54-5, 64-5, 79-80, 82, 96, 112, 114, 119-21, 125-6, 128, 138, 140, 142, 146-7, 156, 168, 172-3, 175, 182-5, 189, 198, 200, 205-7, 209, 224, 232-3, 236-7, 246, 249, 254, 258-9, 281, 290, 299-301, 363, 394-5, 400, 413, 425-6, 429, 432
Scriptural politics, 38, 119, 236-7, 249
Second Coming, 10, 16, 25, 41-2, 44, 149-50, 173, 225, 229, 236, 245-9, 253-4, 350, 354-6, 370, 372, 380, 388, 396, 398, 413, 418
see **Eschatology**
Sedbergh (Cumbria), 141, 154, 414
Seekers, 42, 138-40, 395
Separation, 5-6, 24, 116, 124, 127, 141, 157, 160, 164-7, 170, 178, 199, 201, 220, 223, 229, 238, 243, 247-8, 262, 269, 274, 280, 294-5, 313, 343-3, 366, 398, 407, 409, 445
see **Sin**
Separatists, 19, 36, 42, 138, 141-2, 149, 182, 380, 395, 414
Sermon on the Mount, 2, 10-12, 16, 18-20, 24, 28, 112, 130, 143, 145-8, 156, 171, 177-8, 186-7, 189-90, 201, 242, 263, 293-4, 311, 313, 316, 339, 344, 372, 380, 391, 393, 398-9, 403, 409
 Beatitudes, 2, 128, 146, 156, 172, 316, 391
 Sermon on the Plain, 157, 316
Silence, 9, 16, 25-6, 139, 150, 207, 225, 228, 249-53, 255-6, 267, 270, 274, 278, 280, 303, 356, 394-5, 410
Simmonds (Martha)*, 6, 214, 219-20, 304
see **Bristol, Ranters**
Simplicity, 9, 112, 138, 155, 261, 282, 309-11, 328-9, 332-3, 389, 402-3, 426, 445
Sin, 3, 5, 9, 13-14, 24, 31, 34-5, 42, 49, 51, 53, 59, 79, 92, 106, 116, 124, 130,

133, 137, 141, 144, 149-50, 157-8, 162-3, 165, 168-9, 171, 175-6, 182, 185, 187, 192, 197, 207, 217, 222, 228, 231, 233, 242-3, 247-8, 254, 259-60, 262-5, 268-70, 273, 275, 280, 282, 285-6, 295, 310, 314, 319, 323-4, 330, 334-5, 342, 350, 363-4, 378, 398, 401, 407, 411, 414, 420, 427, 430, 435-9
see **Separation**
Skipton (Yorks., General meeting at), 381, 383-4
Smith (Humphery)*, 4, 55-6, 154, 162-3, 213-14, 239, 297, 423
Smith (William)*, 5, 193, 240, 273, 280, 310-11, 336, 385, 408, 423
Solemn League and Covenant, 421
Son/s of God, 12, 129, 189, 229, 239-40, 257-8, 269, 301, 379, 381, 389
Spain, 17, 26, 53, 70-1, 74-5, 83, 204, 276, 340-1, 345, 349, 422
Spiritual Weapons, 112, 126-7, 227, 261, 288, 293, 356, 360-1, 367, 378
Star Chamber, 89-90, 92
Stassen (Glen), 11, 20, 24, 144
see **Apostasy, Neglect of the Kingdom**
Stephens (Nathaniel), 43
Stirredge (Elizabeth)*, 291-2, 302, 304
Suffering, 3, 5, 12, 24, 26, 31, 42, 56, 58-9, 75-6, 82, 96, 101-3, 105, 136, 150-1, 161, 163-5, 167, 170, 174, 180, 187-90, 196, 198, 200-1, 203, 218-20, 227, 232, 235, 237, 256-7, 260-1, 273-4, 286, 288, 290-1, 294, 296, 299, 307-8, 311, 316-20, 322-6, 347, 349, 352, 359-62, 364, 370, 372, 374, 376-7, 381, 388-9, 393-4, 398-400, 407-8, 411, 421, 424, 426-34, 436-7, 439-40, 443, 445-6
Swarthmoor Hall (nr. Ulverston, Lancs.), 40, 203, 224, 322
Sword, 9, 25-7, 54, 57, 60, 71, 106, 112, 119, 124, 127, 153, 167-9, 175-6, 179, 195, 197, 206, 226, 241, 244, 250, 254, 291, 331, 334-39, 342, 348-9, 356, 358-9, 361-2, 366, 368, 377, 386, 392, 396, 425-9
Synthesis, (of Kingdom, Good Old Cause and 'True Religion'), 18, 26, 109, 129, 324, 341-2, 347, 368, 391, 401
see **Good Old Cause, True Religion**

Index

T

Taylor (Thomas)*, 55-6, 385, 423
Testimony/Testimonies, 18-20, 28-9, 56, 120, 140-1, 158, 161, 164, 172, 180, 182, 185, 190, 197, 199, 202-3, 221, 223-5, 233, 236, 238, 243, 253-8, 260-2, 268, 270-1, 274-5, 281, 283-5, 287-90, 294, 300, 305, 318, 324, 333, 342, 344, 351-2, 369-71, 376, 378, 380, 387-93, 396-8, 400, 403, 405, 407, 409-10, 425-6, 432-3
'That of God in Everyone', 113, 178, 293, 295, 338, 345, 400, 432, 446
Theophany, 18, 26, 111, 120, 123-4, 153, 165, 201, 271, 340, 342-3, 346-8, 350, 368, 383, 412
Thirty-Nine Articles, 77, 85
  see Book of Common Prayer, Elizabethan Settlement
Three Declarations, 18, 170, 181, 186, 189-90, 192, 194, 202, 333, 368-9, 386, 389-90, 403, 407
  see 'A' for Declarations and also Appendix 2
Thurloe (John), 70, 121, 204, 209, 328, 356, 358-9
Tithes, 5, 9, 64, 76, 100, 117, 129-38, 141, 144-5, 163, 179, 185, 197, 203, 206, 212, 215, 232, 306, 315, 317, 319-21, 325, 327, 333, 347, 371, 374, 401, 411, 416-17, 430
To the Council of Officers of the Army (by Fox?), 337, 340-1, 343, 346
Transformation, 5-6, 11, 22, 24-5, 114, 143, 145, 159, 161, 170, 176, 191, 193, 199, 227, 239, 251, 253, 272, 274, 277-8, 283, 285-7, 294, 325, 389, 397-9, 409, 420, 433
True Religion, 18, 26, 53, 99, 109, 129, 200, 307, 310, 324, 331, 335, 341-3, 347, 368, 370, 391, 401, 410, 414
  see Good Old Cause, Synthesis
Truth, 3, 6-7, 9, 11-12, 25, 27, 29, 43, 47-8, 54, 64, 76, 99, 106, 112-13, 116, 118-21, 128, 130, 132, 136, 138, 147, 149, 153, 160-1, 163-4, 168-9, 171, 174-5, 177, 182-4, 191, 194-5, 197-8, 209-10, 212, 215, 222, 225, 228-30, 238, 241-2, 244, 247, 249, 257-62, 265, 268-9, 271-2, 275-7, 281, 285-8, 294, 300, 305-10, 313, 322-3, 325, 331-3, 336, 342-3, 347, 356-8, 361, 363, 367, 369-70, 374, 377, 389, 391, 393-4, 396, 401, 408, 410, 426-7, 430-1, 434-8, 442-6
Publishers of the Truth, 11, 120, 212, 225, 272, 401
Turkey/Ottomans, 26, 71, 124, 332, 340-1, 345, 349-50, 368, 405, 422
Tyndale (William), 35, 40

U

United States, 102
Unity (inc. disunity), 3-6, 12, 15-16, 20, 25-6, 29, 40, 43, 53-4, 87, 127-8, 137, 142 147, 155-6, 159, 161, 164, 167-8, 174, 177-9, 187-8, 192-4, 196-7, 199, 206, 211-12, 219, 221, 223-9, 235-6, 238-41, 243-5, 247-9, 251-2, 254-5, 257-8, 261-2, 268, 270, 276-80, 287-8, 304, 307-8, 310, 322, 354, 359, 372, 375, 378-9, 381, 384-5, 388, 391-2, 396-8, 400, 403-4, 406-9, 413, 426, 433-5, 438, 442
Universalism (Christian), 6, 13, 28, 45, 150, 153, 177-8, 207, 232-3, 241, 245, 255, 263, 293, 308-9, 354, 369, 381-2, 386, 388, 390, 396, 398
University, 1, 13, 38, 80-1, 84, 114, 148, 316, 417, 422
  Cambridge, 45, 80, 88, 111, 114, 134, 146, 182, 281, 288, 296, 309, 406
  Oxford, 1, 17, 40, 45, 84, 111, 134, 148, 296, 316, 417

V

Vane (Sir Henry), 99, 101, 261, 278, 325, 329, 360, 375, 419
Vatican, 67, 69, 76, 81, 87, 91, 209, 368
Venner (Thomas, Fifth Monarchist), 19-20, 198, 214, 218, 326, 367
Viviano (Benedict), 20-1, 24, 146
  see Apostasy, Neglect of the Kingdom

W

Westminster, 40, 99, 107, 131, 213, 338, 374, 415-16
  Whitehall, 44, 69, 119
Westminster Assembly, 93, 415, 421
Westminster Confession of Faith, 183, 415, 421

Westmorland, 7, 9-10, 24, 75, 139, 141, 216, 365, 391
Whichcote (Benjamin), 281
see **Cambridge Platonists**
White (Dorothy)*, 1, 269, 284, 296, 305, 383
Whitehead (George)*, 119, 150, 211, 227, 234, 236-7, 246, 307, 423-4
Whitehead (John)*, 11, 152-3, 193, 277, 423
Whitelocke (Bulstrode), 58, 364
Whitgift (Archbishop John), 87-8, 132
Wholeness, 3, 12, 29, 128, 141, 149-50, 161-2, 177-9, 186, 190, 227, 245, 267, 271, 273, 323, 350, 391-3, 398, 402, 408, 412-13
Winstanley (Gerrard), 99-101, 131, 139, 143, 213-14, 338, 343, 355, 406, 416-17
see **Diggers**
Witch/craft, 34, 69, 297, 421-2
Witness, 1, 3-5, 11-12, 25-6, 28-9, 130, 136, 142-3, 156, 168, 176, 179, 184-5, 200, 202, 209, 221-3, 227-31, 237, 239, 245, 250, 253, 256-64, 270-1, 273, 275, 285, 288, 290, 293-4, 296, 298, 303-5, 307-9, 317, 319, 322-3, 325, 329, 336, 345, 354, 362, 364, 369, 378, 385-6, 395, 405, 407-9, 411, 417, 426, 429-30, 432, 443
Wobble, 341-2, 344, 347
Wollrich (Woolrych, Humphry)*, 227, 385
Wycliffe (John), 31, 131, 281, 417
see **Lollards**

Y

Yeoman/ry, 39, 140-1, 311, 422

Z

Zion, 54, 152-3, 162, 175, 187, 204, 214, 279, 349, 379, 384

www.ingramcontent.com/pod-product-compliance
Lightning Source LLC
Chambersburg PA
CBHW021912180426

43198CB00034B/127